This book may be ke...

DAYS

...rged for each day

READINGS IN EUROPEAN HISTORY SINCE 1814

By JONATHAN F. SCOTT
Assistant Professor of History

AND

ALEXANDER BALTZLY
Associate Professor of History, Assistant Dean,
Washington Square College, New York University

NEW YORK
F. S. CROFTS & CO.
MCMXXXIV

1934

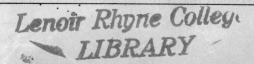

First Printing, September 1930
Second Printing, January 1931
Third Printing, October 1934

TO OUR STUDENTS
PAST AND PRESENT
IN THE
WASHINGTON SQUARE COLLEGE

PREFACE

THE primary purpose of the compilers of this volume is to stimulate the interest of students in the reading and study of history. Certain selections, such as " Lighter Aspects of the Congress of Vienna " and " Louis Philippe at the Hôtel de Ville," have been included simply because they are well written and because they recall something of the atmosphere of the times about which they were written. Other selections, such as " Agriculture in France in the First Half of the Nineteenth Century " and " Alexander as Analyzed a Century Later," are reprinted because they bring out facts or points of view which the compilers believe to be significant but which are little emphasized in textbooks. Little use has been made of documentary material for the period from 1814 to 1870 but certain documents are so essential to an understanding of the history of Europe since 1870 that the compilers are of the opinion that the inclusion of some of the most important of these will be of distinct value to students.

In accord with the prevailing trend in the study of history emphasis has been placed on social and economic developments.

The compilers take pleasure in acknowledging their indebtedness to a number of persons who have been kind enough to aid them in their work. Mrs. Miriam Hespelt and Mr. Lyman R. Bradley, of the German Department of Washington Square College, have made a translation, the high quality of which speaks for itself, from Sombart's " Deutsche Volkswirtschaft im Neunzehnten Jahrhundert." Dean Charles Hoeing, of the University of Rochester, has given the compilers valuable aid in connection with one of the selections on Fascism. Miss Margaret S. Scott, of the Brearley School, has rendered great assistance in some of the translations. Useful information and suggestions have been given by Dr. H. M. Lydenburg, Assistant Director of the New York Public Library, Professor Robert Binkley, of Smith College, Mr. A. F. Guidi, Director of the Bulletin of the Fascisti League of North America, Mr. Robert Ergang and Mr. Ross Hoffman, of the History Department of Washington Square College, and Mr. Louis Schucman, undergraduate in that institution. Miss Margaret Walker, Secretary of the History Department of Washington Square College, has helped greatly with the correspondence necessary in the preparation of this work. To all of these, as well as to the authors and publishers who have permitted them to reprint the material incorporated in this volume, the compilers extend their sincere thanks.

vii

CONTENTS

CHAPTER I

THE CONGRESS OF VIENNA (1814–1815) AND THE
PROBLEM OF EUROPEAN PEACE

CHAPTER II

REACTION AND REPRESSION (1815–1830)

CONTENTS

CHAPTER III

THE INDUSTRIAL AND AGRICULTURAL REVOLUTION IN THE BRITISH ISLES TO 1848

CONTENTS

CONTENTS

CONTENTS

PAGE

CONTENTS

CHAPTER VII

PROBLEMS OF DEMOCRACY AND NATIONALISM
(1849–1871)

CHAPTER VIII

RUSSIA (1825–1881)

CONTENTS

CHAPTER IX

INTERNAL DEVELOPMENTS ON THE CONTINENT
(1871–1914)

CHAPTER X

THE NEAR EASTERN QUESTION (1814–1914)

CONTENTS

CHAPTER XI

SOCIAL FACTORS AND TENDENCIES (1814–1914)

CONTENTS

CHAPTER XII

THE NEW IMPERIALISM

CHAPTER XIII

INTERNATIONAL RELATIONS (1871–1914)

CONTENTS

PAGE

CHAPTER XIV

THE WORLD WAR AND THE PEACE SETTLEMENT

CHAPTER XV

REVOLUTIONS AND THE NEW STATES SINCE 1914

CHAPTER XVI

THE NEW ERA

CONTENTS

READINGS
IN
EUROPEAN HISTORY
SINCE 1814

CHAPTER I

THE CONGRESS OF VIENNA (1814–1815) AND THE PROBLEM OF EUROPEAN PEACE

In September, 1814, a brilliant congress of rulers and diplomats assembled at Vienna for the reconstruction of Europe. Napoleon had been conquered and exiled to the island of Elba. Europe breathed a heart-felt sigh of relief. It seemed as though a new era of peace was dawning after the long nightmare of the revolutionary and Napoleonic wars. And on the whole hope was justified. Napoleon, it is true, while the Congress was still in session, did make a dramatic escape from Elba and for the "Hundred Days" frightened Europe once more. But he was definitively defeated at Waterloo and sent to St. Helena for the rest of his days. And by the time the Congress broke up in June, 1815, it had, for all its faults, laid the foundations of a peace which was disturbed by no major European war for some forty years.

The relief from the strain of warfare was reflected in the gaiety of the Congress of Vienna. The months rolled by in a long succession of dinners, balls, and other entertainments. This lighter side of the Congress is well depicted in an account of the Count de la Garde, which has been incorporated in the Memoirs of the Prince de Ligne. The Prince, a charming old gentleman of Belgian birth, had agreed to act as "guide and instructor" to the Count at the Congress. He died while the Congress was still in session — gay, witty, and courteous to the last.

1. LIGHTER ASPECTS OF THE CONGRESS OF VIENNA [1]

THE Congress of Vienna bore the character of a great solemnity for the celebration of the tranquillity of Europe. It was a Festival of Peace, intended to restore the political equilibrium which the struggle of armies had so long interrupted. The nations of Europe, convoked in the persons of their sovereigns, and negotiating together by means of their most enlightened ministers, was a unique spectacle, fitly concluding the extraordinary events that had led to it.

The Congress was already under way on my arrival in Vienna about the

---

[1] *The Memoirs of the Prince de Ligne.* Translated by Katharine P. Wormeley. 2 vols., London, Heinemann, 1899, vol. II, pp. 261–266, quoting from *Fêtes et Souvenirs du Congrès de Vienne,* by the Count de la Garde.

middle of October, 1814. It was then supposed that it would speedily be dissolved; but, pleasure or business, I cannot say which, ruled otherwise. Months went by and the sessions continued. Sovereigns met and discussed their national interests like brothers amicably settling, as Catherine the Great was wont to say, the affairs of their "little households"; and the Abbé de Saint-Pierre's philosophical dream of a universal peace seemed about to be realized. It is Dr. Johnson, I think, who says in reference to the great wall of China, that the grandson of the man who has seen it will have reason to be proud of that circumstance. So I, for my part, am proud of having been at the Congress of Vienna, although I bore no part in it, and had not the honour of previously knowing all the illustrious persons who formed that most memorable assembly.

When I first went to Vienna in 1807 the Prince de Ligne received me and presented me at Court and in society. The revolution in the Low Countries had deprived him of his property, a loss he bore with philosophic fortitude. The Emperor Francis II made him the commander of his own regiment of Trabans (halberdiers) and a field-marshal in 1808; and he always presided at the council of the Order of Maria Theresa. During the last twenty years of his life he devoted himself wholly to literary pursuits, and published his Works in thirty-four volumes, some of which have attained considerable celebrity; especially those in which he describes the events in which he took part, and the distinguished individuals whom he knew personally.

The day after my arrival I went to pay my respects to the prince, who readily agreed to be my guide and instructor whenever circumstances threw me in his way. "You have come," he said, "just at the right moment. If you like fêtes and balls you will have enough of them; the Congress *ne marche pas, il danse.* [The Congress dances, but does not advance.] There is, literally, a royal mob here. Everybody is crying out: 'Peace! justice! balance of power! indemnity!' As for me, I am looker-on. All the indemnity I shall ask for is a new hat; I have worn mine out in taking it off to sovereigns whom I meet at the corner of every street. However, in spite of 'Robinson Crusoe' [his nickname for Napoleon, who was then at Elba] general peace will really be concluded by this Congress of all the nations of Europe, who are now exclaiming, '*Cedant arma togae.*'"

Later the Count de la Garde went with the Prince de Ligne to a festival at the palace of the Emperor. The Count writes of this festival as follows:

At nine o'clock we reached the Burg, the Imperial palace where the Ridottos were held. The ballroom, which was brilliantly lighted, is surrounded by a gallery leading to the supper-rooms. In it were seated groups of elegant women; some in dominoes, some in fancy costumes; bands of music, stationed in different parts of the hall, played waltzes and polonaises alternately. In the adjoining rooms some of the company were performing solemn minuets with German gravity, which added a comical element to the scene. Vienna, as the prince observed, was now presenting an epitome of Europe, and the Ridotto was an epitome of Vienna. Impossible to imagine anything more remarkable than this assemblage, masked and unmasked, amid which the rulers of mankind were walking about and mingling with the crowd without the slightest distinction.

" Take notice," said the prince, " of that graceful, martial figure walking with Eugene de Beauharnais; that is the Emperor Alexander. And that tall, dignified man with the lively Neapolitan on his arm is the King of Prussia; the lady, who is making him laugh, may be an empress or a grisette. And there, in that Venetian suit, the stiffness of which scarcely conceals his affability, is our own emperor, the representative of the most paternal despotism that ever existed. Here is Maximilian, King of Bavaria, in whose frank countenance you can read the expression of his good heart. Those two young men over there are the Prince-Royal of Bavaria and his brother Charles. The latter has the head of an Antinous; but the other, Louis, whose tastes are all for literature and the fine arts, promises to give Bavaria, one of these days, a noble reign. Do you see that pale little man with an aquiline nose, near to the King of Bavaria? That is the King of Denmark, whose cheerful humour and lively repartees enliven the royal parties — they call him the *Lustig* [merry joker] of the Sovereign Brigade. Judging by his simple manners and the perfect happiness of his little kingdom, you would never suppose him to be the greatest autocrat in Europe. But he is, for all that. In Copenhagen the royal carriage is preceded by an equerry armed with a carbine, and the king as he drives along can, if he pleases, order any of his subjects to be shot. That colossal figure leaning against the column, whose bulk is not lessened by the folds of his ample domino, is the King of Würtemburg, and next him is his son, the Prince-Royal, whose affection for the Grand-Duchess of Oldenburg has brought him to the Congress, rather than the settlement of public business that will soon be his own. All this crowd of persons who are buzzing around us are either reigning princes, archdukes, or great dignitaries from various countries. With the exception of a few Englishmen (easily distinguished by the richness of their clothes), I do not see any one without a title to his name. And now I think, having sufficiently introduced you, you can work your own way. Come to me, if you get into any trouble; I am always here to pilot you."

In these souvenirs I note down only my personal recollections; it is no part of my plan to record political events; however important and interesting they may be, history has made them too well known to need further detail.

Dominique de Pradt (1759–1837), prominent in his day as ecclesiastic, politician, and writer on political subjects, had a checkered career. A member of the French nobility, ordained priest, elected deputy to the Estates-General in 1789, he became a stout opponent of the course the Revolution was taking and left France in 1791 as an émigré. But he returned under Bonaparte, who, anxious to secure support from the old nobility, granted him many favors. Among other things Napoleon had him appointed Bishop of Poitiers and then Archbishop of Malines. The Emperor also entrusted him with delicate diplomatic missions.

He lost Napoleon's favor, however, and had to retire to Malines. Reciprocating the Emperor's resentment he intrigued with Talleyrand and others to bring about the restoration of the Bourbon line of kings. But after the Bourbons had been restored he was none too popular and had to resign his archbishopric. So he retired to his estates in Auvergne where he lived the life of a great lord and attracted public attention by his writings.

The following extract from his work on the Congress of Vienna reveals clearly his feeling against Napoleon as well as his sympathy for those concepts which he believed would dominate the new age, such as liberalism, nationality, public opinion, and representative government.

2. THE *ABBÉ DE PRADT* LOOKS AT HIS WORLD AFTER *NAPOLEON'S* DOWNFALL [1]

The New State of Nations

" It is not the coalition which has dethroned me: liberal ideas ha⸱ effected it," said Napoleon, on his departure for Elba.[2] Princes! peopl⸱ hear! The destiny of all of you is included in this sentence.

Behold him acknowledging, that, for having outraged the civiliz⸱ feelings of his age, he, who of all men had it in his power to triumph o⸱ them, if this frightful privilege were given to any one among us, had l⸱ his throne.

Believe his words, because they are those of a man who never ⸱ equalled in sagacity; because they are those of a man who was never ⸱ passed in self-love; who was merely led to the confession by the convic⸱ of the irremediable consequence of his error. " I have sinned against lib⸱ ideas, and I die." Behold the will, the *amende honorable* of the greatest ⸱ rior, of the most powerful monarch, that ever appeared on the vast theatr⸱

---

[1] Dominique de Pradt, *The Congress of Vienna*. Translated from the French. ⸱ Samuel Leigh and Bossange and Masson, 1816, pp. 16–29 (condensed).

[2] At the same time he said, " I cannot re-establish myself, I have offended the pe⸱

the world. He overturned, he subdued everything, people and sovereigns; but, destitute of liberal ideas, he perished.

.   .   .   .

The revolution only gave despots to France. Civilization has destroyed despotism in Europe. But, above all, it has brought constitutions to light, and occasioned the want of them to be universally felt. The revolution gave twenty years of war to Europe. It has pressed the deceiving delusions accompanying it farther than they ought to have been carried. Civilization, in conferring honour on generous warriors, brought war into disrepute. For the future it has rendered impracticable the character which hitherto has been the most seducing, the most alluring, to man; that of conqueror, is for the future rendered unattainable. It has banished it to Tartary. Barbarism burned Moscow — civilization preserved Paris. The revolution banished commerce, to place it under the yoke of power and war. Civilization, spreading its wings, has dismissed its gaolers and opened its prison. The revolution paid no regard to religion. Civilization has fully confirmed the feeling which convinces us of the want of a mild and tolerant religion; the protectress of order, in its social and domestic state. Civilization has served as a safeguard for the world in the terrible career that it has run.

.   .   .   .

Nationality, truth, publicity! Behold the three flags under which the world for the future is to march. Misfortune will attend those who will not enlist under them.

The people have acquired a knowledge of their rights and dignity. They know that they are the principle and object of society, and of its exertions; that they do not exist for a few individuals, but that individuals exist for them.

.   .   .   .

Hence, every thing should comport with the happiness of nations. But how is this to be effected? By them or by others? Will nations resemble indolent proprietors, who commit the charge of their affairs to other hands? Because they have done so hitherto, will they do so always?

Therefore the necessity of a government which will permit nations to interfere in their own affairs and take an immediate cognizance of them; that in due time they should determine the forms arising from the varieties that distinguish different people. That this interference should exist is indispensable.

What are its guarantees? Truth and publicity. To claim them is to ask for that which cannot be refused; that which inevitably exists in all polished countries. Otherwise, after all that has passed, is it possible for men to be deceived? Deceive them! For how long? To hide even for a moment! for with the multitude of eyes that are open to public events, how is it to be expected that the mystery of today will not be exposed in the public squares tomorrow? Daylight has burst into all cabinets. Their proceedings are read through walls, through the most secret dispatches; and the wings lent them by their couriers add but to their publicity. Europe is covered with a population of readers, of writers, of men accustomed, some to manage affairs, others to provide and become instrumental to the increase and care of their fortune. Society is a species of tribune that does not remain empty, and who can flatter themselves with changing men possessed of so many means of knowing and understanding every thing? If they cannot be deceived, still less can anything be concealed. That which is not published in one country is sure to be so in another; and while there is a parliament in England, there will be a tribune for all Europe.

. . . .

It may be calculated that there are in France four millions of men who, by education, profession, and fortune, can pay attention to public affairs. It is proper to deduct from this number one hundred thousand persons, whose personal feelings render them willing to afford confidence to the authority that speaks. All the rest are on the alert. And, nevertheless, this population represents the manly and active part of the nation, and that which influences its motives. It fills almost all the inferior ranks of public administration. It serves it with eyes and with hands. It directs the interests of all the citizens, and by means of commerce it provides for their wants. This class is more numerous in the states of the North, among whom the first classes have less social consistence than in France. These are the classes that, in foreign countries as well as in France, have sapped the power of Napoleon; in France, by separating the people from him; in Germany, by raising them against him.

Therefore the relations of governments with the people are changed. Nations are become more enlightened, and consequently stronger than the governments. Hitherto it has been directly the reverse. Then the light came only from above; now it flows in on all sides.

. . . .

Hence, it is evident that there has arisen in every country a new power, called opinion, from the empire of which nothing can be taken, at the tribunal of which governments themselves incessantly appeal; for there is not one of their acts which is not a request, or rather an appeal to this power that conducts itself mildly to those willing to make their submission to it, but which, like a torrent, swallows those who would act otherwise. It is this opinion which, introducing into Europe one change, confirms those already existing, and opens a road for others. This is manifestly its work. On all sides constitutions are established, or are promised. On all sides, in dividing the nearly-equal distances of the social contract, respect is yielded to it, and its turn is come to reign. Thus is realised that which General Buonaparte said to the Directory in 1798, on his return from Campo Formio: " The era of representative government is arrived." Therefore, nations are in possession of the exercise of rights, of which, for one hundred years, they had not an idea. What a progress made by one step!

．　．　．　．　．　．　．　．　．　．　．　．　．

The natural course of things will lead to the British constitution. One or two examples liberally made, will introduce many others. Besides, how will it be possible to prevent men, sooner or later, from becoming possessed of it? . . . It is true, that to the titles of glory already possessed by Great Britain, she adds another, that of legislatrix of the universe; peaceable and beneficent laws; a sceptre more honourable than that which she wields over the ocean. This uniformity of legislation will establish very powerful bonds of union among men. It will render wars less frequent and more mild. The more wars become national, they will be the more rare and less cruel, and widely different from the ancient wars, between people who had no communication with each other. There are very few causes of war among nations! When the ministers of a people shall have to propose the payment of the expenses of a war of which they cannot justify the motives, their conduct will be more closely canvassed. By an astonishing effect, the more the popular influence is increased, the higher will the power of the sovereign be elevated; the more deeply will its foundations be placed, and the more widely will its branches extend.

．　．　．　．　．　．　．　．　．　．　．　．

The disrepute into which liberal ideas have fallen does not prevent us yielding them our homage. If much error has existed under their sanction, they have, on the other hand, admitted of a sober and correct application; for there is not a liberal idea known that has not been duly acted upon within the last twenty-five years.

Reason and justice, these two inseparable sisters, require that we should not confound liberal ideas with the blunders of those who adopt them. The material is one thing, the workman another.

Those who at their ease ridicule liberal ideas, should think of their personal interests, and reflect, that it may so happen that they will not be permitted to laugh at them. In such a case it is prudent not to commence it.

Napoleon's success in conquering a large part of Europe was facilitated by the fact that east of France lay a number of weak states, the Austrian

Netherlands, little Holland, Switzerland, a disunited Germany, a disunited Italy.

In the following selection the Abbé de Pradt shows how the powers allied against France attempted in the peace settlements that followed Napoleon's fall to strengthen some of these states and thus guard against a repetition of French conquests.

He holds, however, that the Congress of Vienna, in safeguarding Germany from the danger of attack from France, neglected to take precautions to protect Germany from the menace of Russian invasion.

3. THE ABBÉ DE PRADT COMMENTS ON THE MEASURES TAKEN BY THE ALLIES IN 1814 AND 1815 TO SAFE-GUARD EUROPE AGAINST FRANCE[1]

The first part of this plan is evidently marked in the precaution they have taken to place, at the gates of France, apparently as sentinels:

First, the King of the Low Countries.

Second, the King of Prussia; who, by his possessions behind the Meuse and the Rhine, and by those which, with a view to these precautions, have been given him on the Moselle, supports it in the first line.

Third, the German Empire, guardian of the fortress of Luxembourg.

Fourth, Austria, by the cession of Mentz, and of parts of the departments of the Saar and Mount Tonnerre, which formerly belonged to France, and which extend the territories ceded to divers princes, called to occupy them from many parts of Germany.

The intention of confining France within strong and more efficient barriers than those in which, by the ancient order of Europe, she was kept, is particularly marked in the near approach of Austria; for, by this arrangement, the rule is violated that the two states appear to have made at the treaty of Campo Formio, of keeping at as great a distance as possible from one another, in order to prevent those quarrels that their contiguity had so often produced. Except it has been done with this intention, we cannot see why Austria, so magnificently treated in Italy and in Illyria, should have been allowed to acquire so great a territory, and at so great a distance from the body of the monarchy, and with which these stray provinces can have no connexion. But it is evident that it was intended to place the keys of Mentz in powerful hands, and to load France with the weight of all Germany, joined to that of the kingdom of the Low Countries and of Great Britain, who will never separate itself from the latter state, more peculiarly its work,

[1] Dominique de Pradt, *The Congress of Vienna*. Translated from the French. London, Samuel Leigh and Bossange and Masson, 1816, pp. 72–74.

and who will always be ready to protect it against France, as a father would defend his child. France, surrounded as she will be by all the military powers of Germany, will, at no very distant period, find herself enclosed; and she, who hitherto has been so vain of her triple rampart, will, for the future, have to witness the circumstance of being as firmly enclosed by her fortresses, as heretofore she has experienced that which has enabled her to make so powerful an offensive and defensive use of them. By this arrangement France loses all political importance on the Continent. Twice has she been taught, and by severe experience, that this renowned rampart of fortresses, in the actual state and number of the European armies, availed her nothing: it is to be observed that it is on the weakest part of France that the forces of Germany will always press: for it is on the higher Meuse and the Sambre, which is the most feeble part, and through which an approach can be most easily made to the capital. This more clearly demonstrates the intention thus indicated.

Lord Castlereagh declared, in the parliament of Great Britain, that the scheme for bringing France and Prussia so nearly into contact, by the establishment of the latter between the Meuse and the Rhine, was to be dated from the time of Mr. Pitt, and that it was an idea of that illustrious minister. Whatever may be the respect due to the opinions of that celebrated man, it is impossible not to recognize a spirit in this plan truly anti-Gallican, but still not less anti-European. One danger is often resorted to from the fear of another.

Occupied as Mr. Pitt had been, for so many years, by a contest with France, whose power he saw increased and strengthened by the very game that would have ruined so many other states, he devoted his attention to the discovery of means proper to raise a barrier against France: and he lost sight of Russia, of whom he then endeavoured to make an use in his efforts to restrain his enemy. Therefore he laboured to divide that which was, and which, for the general benefit of Europe, should have continued to be united. This minister well knew, that to be neighbouring and hostile to each other, was, with states, synonymous: and, in this view of things, he perceived no better method of substituting jealousy, for the friendship that had so long united Prussia and France, than making them border one on the other.

This was a political idea of no very high character; it embraced but a short period, while those of a more correct nature embrace space and time. In his own time Mr. Pitt was unable to see his ideas realized; and perhaps it is at this moment, when it has been fully accomplished, that it would have been to him a source of regret: for the intellectual light of a character, so superior as was that of Mr. Pitt, may reappear after a short eclipse, and replace him in that situation whence his pressing political wants had sometimes driven him.

But, in providing so well for the preservation of Germany from new invasions on the part of France, the Congress has forgotten that nothing whatever has been done in its behalf against those irruptions with which Russia, in her turn, may menace her. Look beyond the Vistula, and here we shall find that she touches on Germany. The defence of the latter is weakened by the parcelling out of Saxony, which in its actual condition is only fit to be engaged in interminable quarrels with Prussia.

The Russian fleets are able to threaten the German states of the Baltic, on which the French marine can never land. In this state of things there are many dangers; and, unfortunately, nothing has been done to counteract them.

CHAPTER II

REACTION AND REPRESSION (1815–1830)

SECTION I. THE RESTORATION IN FRANCE

When it became practically a certainty in Talleyrand's mind that Napoleon's power was coming to an end he engaged in an intrigue (in which, as has been pointed out, the Abbé de Pradt shared) to bring about the restoration of the Bourbon line of kings.

In the following extract from his Memoirs Talleyrand shows why he believed the restoration of the House of Bourbon was essential to the welfare of France and of Europe. He tells, also, how he took the question up with the Tsar Alexander in the spring of 1814 after the Allies had entered Paris; how Alexander was persuaded to consent to the step; and how the French Senate decreed the restoration. But he expresses the opinion that in the last analysis the restoration of Louis XVIII to the throne of his ancestors was due rather to circumstances inherent in the situation than to the efforts of himself and others who had worked to bring it about.

4. PRINCE TALLEYRAND DISCUSSES REASONS FOR THE RESTORATION OF THE BOURBONS TO THE THRONE OF FRANCE IN 1814[1]

FRANCE, in the midst of the horror of an invasion, wished to be free and respected. This was equivalent to wishing for the return of the House of Bourbon in the order prescribed by legitimacy. Europe, still anxious, in the midst of France, wished her to disarm, and to resume her former limits, so that peace should no longer need to be constantly guarded. She required for that guarantees: this was also to wish for the return of the House of Bourbon.

Thus the requirements of France and of Europe once recognized, everything would concur to render the restoration of the Bourbons easy, for the reconciliation could thus be sincere.

The House of Bourbon alone could veil, in the eyes of the French nation, so jealous of her military glory, the impression of the reverses which had just befallen her flag.

[1] *The Memoirs of the Prince de Talleyrand.* Edited by the Duc de Broglie and translated by R. L. de Beaufort. 5 vols., Putnam, 1891, vol. 2, pp. 117–118; 122–124.

The House of Bourbon, alone, could in a moment, and without danger to Europe, dismiss the foreign armies that covered her soil.

The House of Bourbon alone could nobly aid France to again take possession of the secure frontiers indicated by policy and by nature. With the House of Bourbon, France would cease to be gigantic, but would become great. Relieved from the weight of her conquests, the House of Bourbon alone, could replace her in the lofty position that she should occupy in the social system. It alone could avert that vengeance that twenty years of violence had heaped up against her.

Every road was open to the Bourbons to reach a throne founded on a free constitution. After having tried all manner of organizations, and submitted to the most arbitrary of them, France could find rest only in a constitutional monarchy. The monarchy with the Bourbons, offered complete legitimacy, for even the most innovating minds; for it combined family legitimacy to that given by institutions, and it was that that France desired.

. . . .

The Emperor Alexander, the King of Prussia, and Prince von Schwarzenberg entered Paris on the 31st of March (1814) at the head of their troops, and after having reviewed them in the Champs-Élysées, the Czar Alexander came directly to my hotel, in the rue St. Floretin where he had been preceded in the morning by Count Nesselrode. It had been arranged that the Czar Alexander should reside at the Élysée Palace, but, on some one's advice, I do not know whose, he preferred to stay at my house.

The first point touched upon between the Czar Alexander and myself could naturally only concern the choice of government to be adopted by France. I laid stress on the reasons that I mentioned above, and I no longer hesitated to declare to him that the House of Bourbon was recalled by those who dreamed of the old monarchy with the principles and virtues of Louis XII., as well as by those who desired a new monarchy with a free constitution, and the latter fully proved it, since the wish expressed by the only body that could speak in the name of the nation, was proclaimed all over France, and found an echo in every heart.

That was the peremptory reply that I made to one of the questions that the Czar of Russia addressed me: " How can I find out that France desires the House of Bourbon? "

" By a decision, sire, that I shall take upon myself to have adopted by the senate, and of which your Majesty will immediately see the effect."

" You are sure of it? "

" I will answer for it."

I convened the senate on April 2, and, in the evening at seven o'clock, I carried to the Czar the memorable decision that I had had signed individually by all those who composed the senate. It was that which pronounced the overthrow of Napoleon, and the restoration of the Bourbons with constitutional guarantees.

The Czar Alexander was amazed, I must say, when he saw among the names of the senators who asked for the return of the House of Bourbon, the names of several of the very men who had voted for the death of Louis XVI.

The decree of the senate being rendered, the House of Bourbon could consider itself as seated almost peacefully, not on the throne of Louis XIV, but on a solid throne resting on really monarchical and constitutional foundations, which should render it not only steady but even unassailable.

I know that all I have just said may displease a great many, for I destroy, I believe, the importance of all those little efforts that a number of persons faithfully devoted to the Bourbons, boast of having made to lead to their restoration. But I speak my mind, and my opinion is, that no one has caused the restoration, nor I, nor others. Though I was able to say to the Czar Alexander, whose confidence I had had during many years, " Neither you, sire, nor the allied powers, nor I, whom you believe to possess some influence, not one of us, could give a king to France. France is conquered — and by your arms, and yet even today, you have not that power. To *force* a king upon France, would require both intrigue and force; one or the other alone would not be sufficient. In order to establish a durable state of things, and one which could be accepted without protest, one must act upon a principle. With a principle we are strong. We shall experience no resistance; opposition will, at any rate, vanish soon; and there is only one principle. Louis XVIII is a principle: he is the legitimate King of France."

SECTION II. THE HOLY ALLIANCE

Before the rulers of Austria and Prussia left Paris in 1815 they were asked to sign a curious document which had been prepared by the Emperor Alexander. It provided that the signatory sovereigns should agree to be guided, both in the government of their respective countries and in their international relations, by " the sublime truths taught by the eternal religion of God our Saviour."

Though the sovereigns of Austria and Prussia signed this document they never took it seriously. In popular estimation, however, the " Holy Alliance " of Austria, Russia, and Prussia became synonymous with that system of absolutism and repression of liberal ideas which prevailed in Europe for many years. In reality that system ought with more justice to have been associated with the Quadruple Alliance concluded the same year by the three Powers above-mentioned and England.

In his Memoirs Prince Clemens Metternich, who became head of the Austrian Ministry in 1809 and who was for many years the central figure in European politics, discusses the impression that the project of the "Holy Alliance" made on the Emperor of Austria and the King of Prussia.

5. THE EMPEROR ALEXANDER'S PLAN FOR A "HOLY ALLIANCE" [1]

During the negotiations of the second Peace of Paris, the Emperor Alexander desired me to come to him, that he might impart to me that he was occupied with a great undertaking, about which he wished especially to consult the Emperor Francis. "There are things," said the Emperor, "which feelings must decide, and feelings are under the influence of personal position and situation. These have a commanding influence on individuals. If it was a matter of business, I should ask you for your advice, but the present matter is of such a kind that not the ministers but only the monarchs are capable of deciding it. Tell the Emperor Francis that I wish to speak to him on a subject on which I can explain myself only to him. It will then be in his power to take counsel of you, my dear Prince."

After a lapse of some days, I was summoned by the Emperor Francis, who told me that early on that day he had called upon the Emperor Alexander in consequence of a request from him for a personal interview on a most important subject. "You will learn," said his Majesty, "what the subject is from this document, which he committed to my careful consideration. You know I do not like to express myself on a subject which I have not thoroughly examined. I have therefore taken this paper, which is written in the Emperor Alexander's own hand, and reserved to myself the power of expressing an opinion upon it. Read and examine it, and tell me your opinion of the document, which does not please me at all; it has indeed excited the most grave reflections in my mind."

No very severe examination was required on my part to see that the paper was nothing more than a philanthropic aspiration clothed in a religious garb, which supplied no material for a treaty between the monarchs, and which contained many phrases that might even have given occasion to religious misconstructions.

On the projected treaty, therefore, my views coincided with those of the Emperor Francis; and as the Emperor Alexander had told the Emperor Francis that the document was to be shown to the King of Prussia, his

[1] *Memoirs of Prince Metternich.* Translated by Mrs. Alexander Napier. New York, Scribner, 1880, vol. I, pp. 259–262.

Majesty ordered me to go to the King and ask his opinion of it. I found the King also agreed with the Emperor Francis, except that he hesitated to reject the views of the Russian monarch entirely. However, we came to an agreement as to the impossibility of executing the document without some absolutely necessary changes in the text. Even to this the Emperor Francis did not quite agree.

In consequence of this, I was charged by both monarchs to go to the Emperor Alexander as their common representative. In a conversation of several hours, I succeeded, not without great difficulty, in persuading the author of the necessity of changing several sentences and omitting some passages entirely.

I gave his Majesty, my Imperial master, an account of the objections which I had made without reserve about this, at any rate, useless scheme, and of my prediction of the malicious interpretation which I felt certain it would not escape.

The Emperor Francis, although he did not approve the project even when modified, agreed to sign it, for reasons which I for my part could not oppose.

This is the history of the " Holy Alliance," which even in the partial feeling of its originator had no other object than that of a moral demon-stration, whilst in the eyes of the other persons concerned the document had no such meaning, and therefore does not deserve the interpretation which was afterwards put on it by party spirit.

The most unanswerable proof of the correctness of this statement exists in the circumstance that never afterwards did it happen that the " Holy Alliance " was made mention of between the cabinets, nor indeed could it have been mentioned. Only the parties hostile to the monarchs used it as a weapon for the calumniation of the purest intentions of their opponents.

The " Holy Alliance " was not an institution to keep down the rights of the people, to promote absolutism or any other tyranny. It was only the overflow of the pietistic feeling of the Emperor Alexander, and the applica-tion of Christian principles to politics.

SECTION III. GERMAN LIBERALISM AND THE METTERNICH SYSTEM

Liberal ideas, despite the enthusiastic predictions of the Abbé de Pradt, had a hard time of it for many years after Napoleon's fall especially in Germany. German liberals had hoped that the Congress of Vienna would further German unity by providing for a firmly knit confederation of the German states. Instead the Congress had established a loosely knit confedera-tion under Austrian influence. German liberals had hoped, too, that the

Congress would order the individual German rulers to grant their subjects written constitutions providing for representative legislatures. Here again they had been disappointed. The Grand Duke of Weimar, it is true, did grant his subjects a liberal constitution. And later his example was followed by a few other rulers. But in general reaction was the order of the day.

The indignation of the liberals at this reaction found vent in agitation in the universities. And the climax of this agitation was reached in the famous Wartburg Festival of October, 1817.

The hopes that animated the students at the Wartburg Festival are brought out by the German historian Treitschke in a document of the times which he quotes.

6. THE POLITICAL PLATFORM OF A YOUNG GERMAN LIBERAL IN 1817[1]

The innocent patriotic hopes with which the students were animated at the time of the Wartburg festival find faithful expression in an Instruction which Franz Hegewisch of Kiel gave, on the way to the Wartburg, to Justus Olshausen, a student from Kiel who subsequently became a distinguished orientalist and who was for many years referendary for the Prussian universities. At this time, Hegewisch was thirty-four years of age, a skilful and discerning physician. His principles recall the well-known " Confession of Faith " of the philosopher Fries, but are far more judicious and thoughtful, and are characterised by profounder political insight. None the less, they demonstrate how nebulous and inflated were the dreams amid which the age still moved.

Fundamental Principles of October 18th

Opportunities are fugitive, life is full of difficulty; enthusiasm is transient; consequently it is desirable that good resolutions should be adopted in good time, and should be made generally known as common decisions.

We young men, assembled at the Wartburg from numerous regions of Germany (here append the principal rivers and mountains, but give no political designations), after thorough discussion, have arrived at unanimous convictions, and have come to the following conclusions.

1. Germany is, and shall remain, ONE. We cannot accept the belief that Germany is composed of thirty-eight islands. We Germans are brothers; we desire to be friends. If Germans fight against Germans on the battlefield,

[1] Treitschke's *History of Germany in the Nineteenth Century*. Translated by Eden and Cedar Paul. New York, McBride, Nast and Company, 1917, vol. 3, pp. 611–612; 613–618 (condensed). (Published in England by Jarrold & Sons, Ltd., and George Allen & Unwin, Ltd., London.)

brothers slay brothers. Whoever leads German warriors against German warriors is guilty of fratricide.

We mutually pledge one another never to oppose one another with arms in the field; we promise never to fight against our German brothers; and we solemnly declare that, everywhere and to the utmost of our power, we will diffuse and reinforce the teaching that it is accursed fratricide for German warriors to combat German warriors.

.   .   .   .

3. The doctrine that Germany is split up into North Germany and South Germany, is false and erroneous; it is the doctrine of a malicious enemy. We mutually pledge one another to fight against this doctrine. . . .

4. We young men who are members of the holy uncircumscribed and circumscribed Germanic Federation which the august princes and the free towns of Germany have combined to form, hereby declare our conviction of the truth of the following proposition and of the following corollary: If any portion of German land, west or east, south or north, be attacked, then Germany is attacked, and the war must be a war of all Germans. We recognise that if the Oder and the Rhine are not safe, there can be no safety for the Elbe and the Danube.

.   .   .   .

6. As far as in us lies, we shall honour the kings and princes and sovereign lords of the monarchical states, as those to whom honour is due, as those who desire and cannot but desire what is best for their land, as those from whom no injustice can issue. We declare our belief that if, despite this, injustice should be done in the name of the prince, the blame therefore attaches to the supreme officials, who must be placed under duress and punished in accordance with the measure of the wrong done.

7. We render homage to the just and noble grand duke of Weimar. May the praise of all those young men who have not yet mislearned to love the good and the beautiful, and to hate the hateful, serve to him as preliminary indications of the praise which posterity, freed from all dread of the existing enemies of the good, will bestow upon him. Inspired by a profound knowledge and esteem for the German people, without constraint, without reluctance, without ignoble reserves and timidities, he, before all others, has redeemed the pledge given in Vienna, in days of danger, by the German princes, and has introduced an improved constitution into his own land, a constitution which contains so much that is exemplary for all German lands. We, contemporaries, shall daily echo the saying: " God bless Bucher and Weimar! "

.   .   .   .

9. We will obey the law that has been sanctioned and put in force by the head of the state after it has been examined and discussed by the elected

representatives of the people; in the provisional state of affairs in which legislation is enforced without the collaboration of the representatives of the people, we will abstain from all punishable disobedience.

.   .   .   .

11. We express our conviction of the truth of that principle established in the early days of Germany that TAXES ARE NOT BURDENS BUT GIFTS; and we are equally convinced of the truth that popular approval of the taxes can be accorded solely by ELECTED representatives of the people, and for one year only. We declare our conviction of the accuracy of the following deduction: What each individual possesses is his own exclusive property; protection of the right of individual property is the principal purpose for which the state exists; that purpose is annulled if the supreme ruler of the state is entitled to impose taxes arbitrarily; consequently, the supreme head of the state cannot rightfully, as an arbitrary exercise of power, demand from any citizen any part of that citizen's property. How can a man call that his own of which another may demand a part, when, as often as, and as much as, he will?

12. We recognise that the owners of great estates are entitled to a quite peculiar vote and influence in the discussion of the affairs of the country, this special vote and influence being provided, either in accordance with the example of the Weimar constitution, or else in a special senate, wherein, however, there should not be deputies of all the great landlords.

13. We loudly voice our detestation of the bonds of hereditary servitude which are still maintained upon German soil under the appearance of law. We are convinced that no blessings can ever come to this country so long as such a stigma continues to exist.

.   .   .   .

16. We admit ourselves unable to understand why it is that in many parts of Germany the taxes are still just as high as were the taxes paid to foreign conquerors in the days of our bondage.

17. We pledge ourselves that should any of us at any future date enter official service, not one of us will accept any kind of office which subserves the purposes of a secret police, nor any post in the gendarmerie, nor any post in an extraordinary and illegal judicial committee, nor any office connected with the censorship of printed books; nor will any one of us ever lend his hand to the breaking of the seals of a stranger's letter (the case of war excepted).

.   .   .   .

19. We declare that we will none of us make use of the titles " *edelgeboren*," " *hochedelgeboren*," and " *wohlgeboren*"; we further declare that

we will never apply the names " mamselle " and " madame " to any woman of unblemished reputation.

. . . .

23. We wish to favour a peaceful mode of life, and to ensure that disputes shall be settled as far as possible by arbitration. We recognise that serious disputes about trifling causes, and trifling disputes about serious ills, are alike inglorious. We give assurance that we will never belong to any kind of secret society, and that we will never tolerate the institution of a secret society at a higher educational institution.

. . . .

26. We declare our conviction that many of the horrors of the French Revolution were the fault of the Jacobins, but that many other of these faults, perhaps as many, were the fault of those who did their utmost to prevent the political changes and reforms demanded by the time. We further declare our opinion and conviction that a very large part of the injustice and evil in the world arises from the long-suffering and the slothful weakness of those who endure injustice without making use of the lawful means which are available for their protection.

In the following selection J. R. Legge reproduces in translation a contemporary account of the Wartburg Festival. In a brief passage which will serve here as an introduction to the account itself Legge tells of its origin and authorship.

7. *THE WARTBURG FESTIVAL OF 1817*[1]

On 19th October 1817, at the Wartburg, the scene of Luther's encounter with the devil, was held a great students' festival, to celebrate jointly the Reformation and the battle of Leipzig. The account of the proceedings which is here given was published by a Jena professor, Lorenz Oken as he called himself, thus mitigating the crudeness of his original name, Ockenfuss. He edited a paper called Isis, in which, among encyclopaedic matter of scientific interest, he inserted political items which might not otherwise see the light of day. The number containing this account of the Wartburg proceedings was confiscated by the authorities and destroyed, and copies became of extreme rarity. Indeed, the grandson of Brockhaus, the publisher of the sheet, states in his life of his grandfather that he had never been able to set eyes on a copy. Facsimiles, however, will be found in Hans Blum's jubilee edition of his history of the German Revolution and many other illustrated commentaries on the period.

[1] J. G. Legge, *Rhyme and Revolution in Germany*. London, Constable and Company, 1918, pp. 21–25.

The Students' Festival on the Wartburg

Assured of the permission of His Royal Highness, our Grand Duke, the authorities and citizens of Eisenach took all necessary measures to make cheap, comfortable and agreeable the visit of the students who thronged to the sacred festival. They were quartered in the town for three days, the 17th, 18th and 19th October; the Hall of the Knights in Wartburg was bedecked with wreaths, and provided with tables and benches to seat seven hundred to eight hundred men. Such was the total number present at the midday meal on the day of victory, the rest of us included. Representatives had come from Berlin, Erlangen, Giessen, Göttingen, Halle, Heidelberg, Jena, Kiel, Leipzig, Marburg, Rostock, Tübingen, and Würzburg.

On the 19th at 9 A.M. the students, who had assembled in the market-place, marched to the castle, banners and a band at their head. We accompanied them. Of the professors who had this festival at heart, who saw in it the germ of some great and fruitful tree, and had come designedly to judge, from the proceedings, the students' conduct, and events that passed, what might be expected of its blossoming, there were four of us, Fries, Kieser, Schweitzer, and myself. We were shown to a place opposite the speakers. When general silence was obtained a student delivered a speech on very much the following lines: He spoke of the aim of this assembly of educated young men from all circles and all races of the German Fatherland; of the thwarted life of the past; of the rebound, and the ideal that now possessed the German people; of hopes that had failed and been deceived; of the vocation of the student and the legitimate expectations which the fatherland founded upon it; of the destitution and even persecution to which a youth devoting himself to science had to submit; finally, how they must themselves take thought to introduce among them order, rule, and custom, in a word, student-form, must earnestly and together take thought for the ways and means of facing worthily the duties of their calling, to divert in their direction the regard, at once comforting and encouraging, of grown up people who unfortunately could attain to nothing more themselves, and to be to them in days to come what they would that young men should be. The audience, and we men among them, were moved to tears, tears of shame that we had not so acted, of pain in that we were cause of such distress, of joy over this intellectual message, so beautiful, so pure, so clear, joy too for that we had so brought up our sons that they should one day win the victory where we in our folly had failed.

By one and another further encouraging speeches were delivered, and then the company made for the courtyard of the Castle until the tables were spread. There they formed themselves into groups large and small, some moving about, others standing still. . . .

In one of the groups a speech of the following tenor was delivered: Dear friends, you must not let this moment of emotion and exaltation pass in smoke. It will not return. Now or never must you be united. You must not let the matter rest at mere emotion, you must not allow any one to depart from the Wartburg without taking some real possession with him. . . . What is the situation now? What have we gained? Are our relations different from what they were before?

Are the 'nations' dissolved? Are we members of a greater society? Does each of us only represent the Students' Union of his individual university, or do we together form branches of a universal German Students' Union? Have we pledged ourselves thereto? Have we laws and regulations determining our pledge? . . .

Therefore must you give the students a handsel. Only a few laws, but if you want them in words — all students are one; they all belong to one single nation, the German; they all follow the same precepts and customs. . . . The university man, come he whence he may, can find occupation and a position in Austria, Prussia, Bavaria, Hanover, Saxony, in Swabia, Franconia, Thuringia, Hesse, Mecklenberg, Holstein, on the Rhine, in Switzerland. He speaks no more the speech of his village, of his town; he is not one who understands only this or that trade which ties him to a particular workshop or to the soil; he is a universal man! It is a shame not to have advanced oneself further by study than to be a Thuringian, a Hessian, a Franconian, a Swabian, a Rhinelander! — If the university man is by nature no provincialist, so it is unnatural to try and force him to be one by means of an artificial institution.

. . . You should only be by your precious institution that which you are as students, universal. . . . But universality does not extend over the whole world. You . . . can and will (and the German people, including its princes, will) be nothing other than educated Germans, who are like one to the other, and whose business everywhere is free. For that very reason you must give yourselves no name which conflicts with this universality. Let your name be what you are alone and exclusively, namely, the Students' Union or the League of Youth. Thereto you all belong, and no one else. But be on your guard, against wearing a badge and so sinking to party distinctions, proof that you do not realise that the status of the educated class reproduces in itself the whole state, and therefore destroys its being by breaking up into parties. Also beware of the vain thought that it is on you that Germany's being, and continuance and honour depend. Germany depends only on itself, on Germany as a whole. . . . Your duty is indeed to act firstly as parts of the head; but the head is powerless when the limbs and the entrails refuse their office. Now you stand for Youth, which has no other proper business than so to maintain itself that it grows in beauty, educates itself, does not wear itself out in dissipation, and therefore concentrates itself on the goal, and bothers itself about nothing else save in so far as it keeps clear in sight the goal which man should pursue. Yours is not to discuss what should or should not happen in the State; what alone is seemly for you to consider is, what your business shall one day be in the State, and how you can prepare yourselves to be fit for it . . . Ponder on that! Do not depart as you came! Make certain firm resolutions, and take them home with you. A written word has marvellous power! . . . To meet again, but not for three years!

Then trumpets gave the signal for dinner. 'Twas a merry meal. Wine warmed the feelings and the good resolutions that beamed from every countenance. Some toasts were proposed which did not seem to us in the spirit of the feast; therefore we kept our good wishes in our hearts.

After dinner, about 3 P.M., the procession made its way downhill and shoulder to shoulder with the Landsturm, like friends, into the city church, where the sermon aroused general emotion. Then followed a display of gymnastic exercises in the market-place, after which darkness fell. Thus every moment was passed in praiseworthy activity.

At 7 the students, some six hundred of them, each with a torch, marched up the hill to the triumphal bonfire where the Landsturm were already assembled. On the hill-top songs were sung, and another speech delivered by a student.

Afterwards trial by fire was held over the following articles, which were first displayed high in the air on a pitch-fork to the assembled multitude, and then with curses hurled into the flames. The articles burnt (indicated in the paper by vignettes) were these: a bag-wig, a guardsman's stays, a corporal's cane. . . .

At 12 there was a move to bed.

Next day the students again assembled during the forenoon at the Wartburg, and there was much discussion anent the student-form of the future, especially as regards a limit to duelling. The students from Giessen who had hitherto been split up by nationalities into hostile camps threw themselves into each other's arms and made friends. Thus did a sacred moment of freedom, when only the voice of youth was heard in counsel, accomplish what the Court of Darmstadt with all its soldiers, the whole Senate with all its laws and periwigs, could not bring about — had rather fanned the flame more fiercely! If courts and senates do not know how to handle students, there is real need that they should learn how in their policy of intimidation (there is a more expressive word, emasculation) they should conduct themselves. Force is always, as a remedy, the wrong end of the stick, and governance by soldiers will never more be endured.

Thereafter a number took their departure, but many remained for supper. Thus did the students of Germany celebrate the Festival of the Wartburg!

Many of those who manage the affairs of Germany, and still more, those who mismanage them, might well take the conclave on the Wartburg as an example.

There was no more powerful enemy of those liberal ideas whose triumph progressive Germans hoped to see realized in Germany than the uncompromising Metternich. Metternich fought "French ideas" wherever he could in Europe, but especially in the Austrian dominions and throughout the German states, where the voice of Austria was dominant.

Metternich believed his responsibility for the preservation of the stability of Europe to be a heavy one. But perhaps he bore this responsibility the better in that, as the following extracts from his Memoirs show, he did not suffer from excessive modesty.

8. METTERNICH'S OPINION OF HIMSELF[1]

September 4. . . . You can have no idea of the effect produced by my appearance at the Diet. An affair which perhaps would never have ended has

[1] *Letters of Metternich to his Wife, September 4 and September 18, 1818. Memoirs of Prince Metternich.* 3 vols., New York, Scribner, 1880–1881, vol. 3, pp. 127, 128.

been concluded in three or four days. I am more and more convinced that affairs of importance can only be properly conducted by oneself. Everything done second hand is vexatious and troublesome, and makes no progress. I have become a species of moral power in Germany, and perhaps even in Europe — a power which will leave a void when it disappears: and nevertheless it will disappear, like all belonging to poor frail human nature. I hope Heaven will yet give me time to do some good; that is my dearest wish.

September 11. . . . My visit here has been crowned with great success. I arrived at Frankfurt like the Messiah to save sinners. The Diet wears a new aspect since I have taken a part in it, and everything which seemed so impossible is concluded. I do not believe that twelve days ever bore more fruit at an equally important period. All that the intriguers were aiming to take to Aix-la-Chapelle, to interrupt the progress of affairs, is no longer in their power. In a word, I have a conviction that I have served the cause better at this moment, which does not appear to offer immense advantages, than on twenty other more brilliant occasions. This will, however, be none the less useful.

In the following letter Metternich shows why he felt it necessary that freedom of speech should be repressed in the universities. Students as such and professors as such he did not take very seriously. What he did fear was that the rising generation of students, impregnated with revolutionary ideas in the universities, would menace his beloved status quo *after they got out into the world.*

The question of the menace of the universities, as well as the "evil" of the press, to which Metternich refers briefly in the following extract, were taken up at a meeting of some of the ministers of the German Governments at Carlsbad. The results of their discussions were incorporated in the repressive Carlsbad Decrees pushed through the German Diet by Metternich in 1819.

9. THE "METTERNICH SYSTEM" IN GERMANY
METTERNICH'S FEARS [1]

I thank you for your very interesting account of the 3rd instant. I entirely share the views of Adam Muller, and in sharing them I find myself strengthened in the course I have taken. That the students' folly declines or turns to some other side than that of politics does not surprise me. This is in the nature of things. The student, taken in himself, is a child, and the

---

[1] A Letter from Metternich to Gentz, June 17, 1819. *Memoirs of Prince Metternich* (Mrs. Napier, translator). 3 vols., New York, Scribner, 1880-1881, vol. 3, pp. 286-288.

Burschenshaft is an unpractical puppet-show. Then, I have never — and of this you are a witness — spoken of the students, but all my aim has been directed at the professors. Now, the professors, singly or united, are most unsuited to be conspirators. People only conspire profitably against things, not against theories. The last, indeed, may grow to power, but this can never be the case if they leave the sphere of theology. Where they are political, they must be supported by deed, and the deed is the overthrow of existing institutions, and the *ôtez-vous de là que je m'y mette*. [Make room for me, you.]

This is what learned men and professors cannot manage, and the class of lawyers is better suited to carry it on. I know hardly one learned man who knows the value of property; while, on the contrary, the lawyer class is always rummaging about in the property of others. Besides, the professors are, nearly without exception, given up to theory; while no people are more practical than the lawyers.

Consequently, I have never feared that the revolution would be engendered by the universities; but that at them a whole generation of revolutionaries must be formed, unless the evil is restrained, seems to me certain. I hope that the most mischievous symptoms of the evil at the universities may be met, and that perhaps from its own peculiar sources, for the measures of the Government will contribute to this less than the weariness of the students, the weakness of the professors, and the different direction which the studies may take. But this feeling will never restrain me from taking steps from above; and, indeed, what seem to me the only possible measures are taken.

If we are together I can give you many satisfactory explanations of the course of the business, which at a distance I could not communicate to you without an enormous correspondence, and even then must remain futile and imperfect.

The greatest and consequently the most urgent evil now is the press. The measures referring to it which I intend to bring forward at the Carlsbad Congress I will tell you all the more gladly as I wish you to give me your opinion on my ideas without reserve, and put yourself in a position to help me effectually in Carlsbad, where the business must begin without delay.

SECTION IV. ITALIAN LIBERALISM

Giuseppe Mazzini has been called the Prophet of Italian Unity. In dark days when the idea of uniting Italy seemed to most men but a deceptive mirage, Mazzini was filled with faith that it could be made a reality. And that faith he succeeded in imparting to others. His chief concrete achievement was the founding and development of the society of Young Italy which was primarily an association for implanting in the young men of the land a living, moving faith in the cause of Italian liberty and unity.

Though leadership in the actual unification of Italy passed into other hands, Mazzini more than any other one man paved the way for it.

In the selection that follows Mazzini tells how the idea of devoting himself to the cause of Italy first took possession of his soul.

10. THE IDEA OF ITALIAN LIBERTY IS PLANTED IN THE MIND OF MAZZINI [1]

One Sunday in April 1821, while I was yet a boy, I was walking in the Strada Nuova of Genoa with my mother, and an old friend of our family named Andrea Gambini. The Piedmontese insurrection had just been crushed; partly by Austria, partly through treachery, and partly through the weakness of leaders.

The revolutionists, seeking safety by sea, had flocked to Genoa, and, finding themselves distressed for means, they went about seeking help to enable them to cross into Spain, where the revolution was yet triumphant. The greater number of them were crowded in S. Pier d'Arena, waiting a chance to embark; but not a few had contrived to enter the city one by one, and I used to search them out from amongst our own people, detecting them either by their general appearance, by some peculiarity of dress, by their warlike air, or by the signs of a deep and silent sorrow on their faces.

The population were singularly moved. Some of the boldest had proposed to the leaders of the insurrection — Santarosa and Ansaldi, I think — to concentrate themselves in, and take possession of the city, and organize a new resistance; but Genoa was found to be deprived of all means of successful defence; the fortresses were without artillery, and the leaders rejected the proposition, telling them *to preserve themselves for a better fate.*

Presently we were stopped and addressed by a tall black-bearded man, with a severe and energetic countenance, and a fiery glance that I have never since forgotten. He held out a white handkerchief towards us, merely saying, *For the refugees of Italy.* My mother and friend dropped some money into the handkerchief, and he turned from us to put the same request to others. I afterwards learned his name. He was one Rini, a captain in the National Guard, which had been instituted at the commencement of the movement. He accompanied those for whom he had thus constituted himself collector, and, I believe, died — as so many of ours have perished — for the cause of liberty in Spain.

[1] *Life and Writings of Joseph Mazzini.* 6 vols., London; Smith, Elder and Company, 1864–1870, vol. 1, pp. 1–4.

That day was the first in which a confused idea presented itself to my mind — I will not say of country or of liberty — but an idea that we Italians *could* and therefore *ought* to struggle for the liberty of our country. I had already been unconsciously educated in the worship of equality by the democratic principles of my parents, whose bearing toward high or low was ever the same. Whatever the position of the individual, they simply regarded the *man* and sought only the honest man. And my own natural aspirations towards liberty were fostered by constantly hearing my father and the friend already mentioned speak of the recent republican era in France; by the study of the works of Livy and Tacitus, which my Latin master had given me to translate; and by certain old French newspapers, which I discovered half-hidden behind my father's medical books. Amongst these last were some numbers of the *Chronique du Mois,* a Girondist publication belonging to the first period of the French Revolution.

But the idea of an existing wrong in my own country, against which it was a duty to struggle, and the thought that I too must bear my part in that struggle, flashed before my mind on that day for the first time, never again to leave me. The remembrance of those refugees, many of whom became my friends in after life, pursued me wherever I went by day, and mingled with my dreams by night. I would have given I know not what to follow them. I began collecting names and facts, and studied, as best I might, the records of that heroic struggle, seeking to fathom the causes of its failure.

They had been betrayed and abandoned by those who had sworn to concentrate every effort in the movement; the new king (Carlo Felice) had invoked the aid of Austria; part of the Piedmontese troops had even preceded the Austrians at Novara; and the leaders had allowed themselves to be overwhelmed at the first encounter, without making an effort to resist. All the details I succeeded in collecting led me to think that they *might* have conquered, if all of them had done their duty; — then why not renew the attempt?

This idea ever took stronger possession of my soul, and my spirit was crushed by the impossibility I then felt of even conceiving by what means to reduce it to action. Upon the benches of the University (in those days there existed a course of *Belles Lettres,* preparatory to the courses of law and medicine, to which even the very young were admitted), in the midst of the noisy tumultuous life of the students around me, I was sombre and absorbed, and appeared like one suddenly grown old. I childishly determined to dress always in black, fancying myself in mourning for my country. *Jacopo Ortis* happened to fall into my hands at this time, and the reading of it became a passion with me. I learned it by heart. Matters went so far that my poor mother became terrified lest I should commit suicide.

SECTION V. THE MONROE DOCTRINE

It has often been assumed that at and around the time the Monroe Doc-
trine was formulated Austria, Russia, Prussia, and France were seriously
planning intervention to recover for Spain her revolted colonies. In a scholarly
study of the Monroe Doctrine in its early years Professor Dexter Perkins
shows how little ground there is for such an assumption.

In the following passage Professor Perkins discusses the attitude of each
of these four Powers in 1824, as it appears from their deliberations on the
subject of intervention.

II. THE MONROE DOCTRINE AND THE QUESTION OF EUROPEAN INTERVENTION IN LATIN-AMERICA IN 1824[1]

Perhaps the most interesting aspect of these deliberations is the raising of the question of intervention in 1824. In 1823, prior to the message, as we have already seen, there was no coherent plan for dealing with the new states, certainly no plan of reconquest; one might even say, no discussion of reconquest. But the case is different in the period following the President's declaration. Despite the defiant language of Monroe and the aloofness of Canning, the Russian statesmen, throughout the year 1824, seem to have nourished the hope that Spain might be assisted, perhaps directly assisted, in the reëstablishment of her authority over her revolted subjects in the New World, and that she ought more than ever to be encouraged in a policy of reconquest of her former dominions. . . .

The possibility of actual armed intervention was certainly discussed at the court of the Tsar. Lebzeltern tells us that the Russian government nourished the hope that a series of allied conferences would lead to "furnishing the King of Spain with the material aid to pacify and reconquer his colonies," and La Ferronnays described Alexander as "more than ever disposed to sacrifice every other interest to the maintenance of his theories."

Why (said Nesselrode, laughingly, to the French Minister) should not the allies give some aid to Spain? What could England say, or rather what could she do, if an army composed of Spaniards, Frenchmen, Russians, Prussians, and Austrians, embarked upon ships lent and paid for by all the allies of the King of Spain, and sailed for America to reinstate him in his rights?

"This idea, extraordinary as it is," commented La Ferronnays, "is amongst those which may seduce the Emperor, and which he would be

[1] Dexter Perkins, *The Monroe Doctrine 1823–1826.* Harvard University Press, 1927. *Harvard Historical Studies,* vol. XXIX, pp. 227–235 (condensed).

very much inclined to follow up." Through the summer of 1824, this mood seems to have continued. . . .

But the Russian autocrat, though he thus considered the possibility of intervention, was hampered by the distinctly frigid attitude of his Continental allies. Russia could not act in the colonial question alone; and France, Austria, and Prussia all took a very different view of the matter from Alexander's. No one of the other powers can be said to have been at all enthusiastic about the giving of any actual aid to Spain.

The policy of France, in the winter and spring of 1824, certainly did not look toward intervention. . . . The French government would take absolutely no action in behalf of Ferdinand.

It must not be imagined, however, that the reason for this caution is to be found, in any important measure, in the message of President Monroe. Fundamental, in the first instance, was the interest of French commerce, that interest which was recognized by the sending out of agents to the New World, and by Villèle's conversations with the agents of the new states in Paris. "France," wrote Tatischev, "has subordinated the considerations of policy which we follow to the counsels of mercantile cupidity." The viewpoint herein expressed was the common explanation of the trend of French policy. . . .

With regard to Austria and Prussia, much the same things are to be said that have just been noted in the case of France. The policy of both the German courts was essentially conservative. Metternich . . . had never believed at all in the possibility of active intervention, and had not even been a very warm advocate of a congress on colonial affairs. His views in 1824 were precisely the same as his views in 1823. He set them forth at great length in a masterly memorandum of February 7, 1824, addressed to St. Petersburg and Berlin. Once again he emphasized the division of the colonies into three classes, the enormous areas of the New World in which the struggle had virtually ceased, the necessity of Spain's coming forward with proposals of a concrete character, her own impotence to accomplish anything by force, and the remote possibility of the assistance of the allied powers. The Continental powers, he declared, could never act without the coöperation of one or another of the great maritime states. England would certainly undertake no such coöperation. France, even supposing her ready to spend hundreds of millions in an enterprise whose success and advantages would be alike doubtful, had bound herself to a contrary course of action. In taking up arms in the cause of Spain, she would run the risk of a quarrel with Great Britain and the United States, both of which governments had taken so definite a stand against intervention. Under such circumstances, the action of the powers must inevitably be limited to measure of conciliation. The Prussian Foreign Minister, Count Bernstorff, took the same view. The colonial question, he wrote to Schöler, his ambassador at St. Petersburg, must be judged by what was practicable, not by what was desirable. The Continental powers are without the means of applying the force of which they dispose, and the measure of their means of action must be the measure of their obligation. Any other course would compromise their dignity, and risk the enfeeblement of sound principles by carrying these principles to an extreme. Austria, Prussia, and Russia may sway the Continent, but not the destinies of the New World. France, it is true, has naval power, but a naval force just beginning to come into its own again. She ought not to be asked to make further sacrifices in a gigantic enterprise which is beset with terrible obstacles. Her commercial interest leads her to desire peace with Great Britain. In the face of the opposition of England and the United States, no forcible intervention in the provinces of South America could be adjudged to be practicable.

In the winter of 1824, then, both the Austrian and Prussian courts were urging a moderate course upon the Tsar Alexander. They drew an argument in favor of their viewpoint from the language of President Monroe. But they did not shape their policy differently on account of the presidential declaration, but merely reiterated their already clearly expressed opposition to the armed reconquest of the colonies. . . .

All things considered, there was little actual danger of the reconquest of the colonies by the allied powers in 1824. The project was, no doubt, discussed; but having regard to all the facts of the situation, it is difficult to see how it could ever have come very near fulfilment. Only Russia had any enthusiasm whatever for such a line of action; and even Russia never made any concrete proposals for direct action on the part of the Continental powers either to Spain or to any of her associates of the Holy Alliance.

SECTION VI. REACTION IN RUSSIA

The Tsar Alexander I, tutored by La Harpe, a Swiss follower of Rousseau, inaugurated his reign in 1801 with an interest in liberal reforms. Surrounded by a group of intelligent young noblemen of liberal tendencies — Novosiltsev, Strogonov, Czartoryski — he approached such problems as peasant emancipation and government administration, and the whole atmosphere at St. Petersburg promised a new era of greater freedom and true enlightenment. War interrupted and Alexander grew older, yet even during the middle period of the reign, with the assistance of Mikhail Speranskii, the tsar retained a desire for progressive changes. When Napoleon was overthrown Prince Adam Czartoryski, himself a Pole, urged on Alexander a constitution for that part of the old kingdom of Poland which had been Prussian since

1795 and, for a few years of the Napoleonic epoch, the Grand Duchy of War-saw, and which the Treaty of Vienna now gave to Russia. The constitution established for this new kingdom of Poland, of which Alexander was king, has been hailed as the most liberal Europe then knew. How genuinely liberal it was may be gauged from the following extracts.

12. THE POLISH CONSTITUTION OF 1815 [1]

Art. I. The kingdom of Poland is joined in perpetuity to the Russian Empire.

IX. The Sovereign alone shall have the right to decide whether the kingdom of Poland shall take part in the wars of Russia, as well as in the treaties of peace or of commerce that that power may conclude.

XI. The Roman Catholic religion, professed by the majority of the inhabitants of the kingdom of Poland, shall receive the most careful attention from the government, without in any way diminishing the liberty of other sects, all of which, without exception, shall be allowed to worship freely and publicly, and shall enjoy the protection of the government. Whatever distinction there may be between Christian sects, there shall be no distinction in the enjoyment of civil and political rights.

XXVIII. All administrative, judicial, and military public business, without any exception, shall be conducted in the Polish language.

XXIX. Public offices, civil and military, may be occupied only by Poles. The positions of presidents of courts of first instance, presidents of palatinal commissions and of courts of appeal, members of palatinal councils, the offices of nuncios and deputies to the Diet, and those of senators, may be given only to landowners.

XXXI. The Polish nation shall have in perpetuity a national representative body (the Diet): it shall consist of the King and two houses. The first shall be the Senate; the second, the Chamber of Nuncios and Deputies of the Communes.

XXXIII. Any foreigner who shall have acquired property, become naturalized, and shall have learned the Polish language, shall be eligible to hold public office, after five years residence, if his conduct be irreproachable.

XXXIV. Nevertheless, the King may at his pleasure, or upon request of the Council of State, admit foreigners distinguished for their abilities to any public office except those designated in Article XC.

XXXV. The government is inherent in the person of the King. He exercises in all their fullness the functions of the executive power. All executive or administrative authority can emanate only from him.

[1] Leonhard Chodzko, Comte d'Angeberg, *Recueil de traités concernant la Pologne.* Paris, 1862, pp. 707 ff. (extracts in translation).

XL. The right to declare war and to conclude all treaties and conventions whatsoever is reserved to the King.

LXIII. The Council of State, presided over by the King, or his lieutenant, is composed of the ministers, Councillors of State, *maîtres des requêtes,* together with such persons as it shall please the King to summon specially to attend.

LXV. The Council of State includes the Administrative Council and the General Assembly.

LXVI. The Administrative Council shall be composed of the lieutenant, the principal ministers of the five governmental departments, and other persons especially summoned by the King.

LXVII. The members of the Administrative Council shall have the right to express their opinions. The opinion of the lieutenant alone shall be decisive. . . .

LXXIII. The General Assembly of the Council of State shall be composed of all the members designated in Article LXIII. . . . Its functions are:

1. To discuss and draw up all projected laws and regulations for the general administration of the country;

2. To order the trial of any administrative officers appointed by the King for breach of trust in the exercise of their duties, except all those who are under the jurisdiction of the National Supreme Court;

3. To decide in cases of conflict of jurisdiction;

4. To examine annually the accounts rendered by each of the principal administrative departments;

5. To consider abuses or anything that may derogate from the Constitutional Charter, and to draw up a general report thereon, which it shall address to the Sovereign, who shall decide what instructions are to be sent to the Senate or to the Diet.

LXXVI. The execution of the laws shall be entrusted to the various departments of public administration herinafter named, viz:

1. The Ministry of Sects and of Public Instruction;

2. The Ministry of Justice, chosen from among the members of the Supreme Court;

3. The Ministry of the Interior and of Police;

4. The Ministry of War;

5. The Ministry of Finance and of the Treasury.

A minister shall be nominated to preside over each of these ministries.

LXXVII. A minister shall be created Secretary of State, who shall be in constant attendance on the person of the King.

LXXVIII. There shall be a Court of Accounts charged with the final revision of accounts and the discharge of responsible officers. It shall be responsible to the King alone.

LXXXVII. The Diet shall meet every two years at Warsaw at a time stated in the summons issued by the King. The session shall last for thirty days. The King alone may prorogue, adjourn, or dissolve it.

LXXXIX. A member of the Diet, so long as he shall be a member, may not be arrested nor judged by a criminal court, save by vote of the Chamber to which he belongs.

XC. The Diet shall decide on all projects of civil, criminal, or administrative laws that are sent to it by the King or the Council of State. It shall act on all plans which the King may send it relating to proposed changes or modifications of the functions of offices or of constitutional powers such as those of the Diet, Council of State, the judicial organization, or the governmental departments.

XCI. The Diet shall decide, in accordance with the message of the Sovereign, on the increase or reduction of taxes, contributions, or public levies of any kind; on any changes which these may necessitate; on the best and the most equitable distribution; on the framing of the budget, both as to receipts and as to expenditures; on the regulation of the monetary system; on the raising of recruits; as well as on any other matters referred to it by the Sovereign.

XCII. The Diet shall decide further on any matters referred to it by the King in consequence of the general report which the Assembly of the Council of State is charged by Article LXXIII to render. Finally, the Diet, after having decided all these matters, shall give attention to communications, requests, representations, or claims made to it by the nuncios and by the deputies of the communes to promote the welfare and interests of their constituents. It shall transmit them to the Council of State, which shall submit them to the Sovereign. When they shall have been sent back to the Diet through the medium of the Council of State, it shall decide on such laws as are proposed in consequence of these claims.

XCIV. The Diet can concern itself only with the matters included in these functions or in the act of convocation.

XCV. The two chambers shall hold public sessions. They may, however, resolve themselves into a committee of the whole at the desire of one tenth of those members present.

XCVII. It rests with the King whether proposed laws shall be sent first to the Senate or to the Chamber of Nuncios. Proposed financial laws are an exception; they must go first to the Chamber of Nuncios.

CI. Members of the Council of State have the right to sit in the two chambers and to speak when government measures are being discussed.

They have the right to vote only in case they are themselves senators, nuncios or deputies.

CII. Propositions shall be decided by majority vote. Votes shall be given orally. A proposed law, thus adopted in one chamber by a majority vote, shall go to the other chamber, which shall discuss it and decide on it in the same manner. In case of a tie, the proposition shall be considered carried.

CIII. A proposed law passed by one chamber may not be modified by the other; it must be adopted or rejected as it stands.

CV. If the King give his assent, the proposition shall become a law. . . . If the King refuse his assent, the proposition shall be dropped.

CVIII. The Senate is composed of: Princes of the blood imperial and royal; Bishops, palatines, castellans.

CXVIII. The Chamber of Nuncios is composed of:

1. One hundred nuncios nominated by the districts, or assemblies of the nobility, one nuncio to a district;

2. Sixty seven deputies of the communes.

A marshal chosen from among its members and nominated by the King shall preside over the Chamber.

CXX. Landowners of the nobility in each district, meeting in the Dietine, shall choose one nuncio, two members of the Council of the Palatinate, and shall draw up a list of candidates for offices in the government departments.

CXXVI. The Dietines shall meet only when the King shall summon them, fixing the day, the length of the session, and the business to be decided.

CXXX. A communal assembly shall be held in each district of the commune; it shall elect a deputy to the Diet and a member of the Council of the Palatinate, and shall draw up a list of candidates for offices in the governmental departments.

CXXXI. To the communal assemblies shall be admitted:

1. All non-noble citizen-proprietors paying taxes on landed property;

2. All manufacturers and foremen; all merchants owning a business or shop valued at ten thousand Polish florins;

3. All curés and vicars;

4. Professors, instructors and other persons in charge of public instruction;

5. Every artist distinguished for his talent, his knowledge, or for services rendered to commerce or to the arts.

CLIX. The penalty of confiscation is abolished and shall never, in any case, be reëstablished.

CLXV. . . .

Given in our royal castle of Warsaw, the 15/27 November, 1815.

Alexander.

Attested a true copy.

The members of the Provisional Government:

Lanskoi,
Adam, prince Czartoryski,
Nicolas Novossiltzoff,
Thomas Warwrzecki,
Xavier, prince Druçki-Lubeçki,
Joseph Calessante Szaniawski, Secretary.

Alexander visited the capital of the new Polish kingdom in 1818, and was received with enthusiasm. His view of the experiment that was being undertaken and of the possibility of its extension to the larger empire is expressed in the speech that he made before the Diet and assembled notables.

13. ALEXANDER'S SPEECH AT WARSAW IN 1818 [1]

Representatives of the realm of Poland.

Your hopes and my vows are being fulfilled. The people whom you are called to represent are at last enjoying a national life, guaranteed by institutions which time has ripened and sanctioned.

Only by your most sincerely forgetting the past could your regeneration be brought about: it was irrevocably decided in my mind from the moment when I could count on the means of realizing it.

Jealous of the glory of my fatherland, I have been ambitious of adding a new glory to it.

Russia, in fact, in rendering you good for evil, in accordance with Christian morality, after a disastrous war, has extended its hand to you as to a brother, and among all the advantages which victory gave her she has preferred one alone, the honor of lifting up and restoring a valiant and estimable nation.

The organization which was in full force in your country has made possible the immediate establishment of that which I have given you in putting in practice the principles of those liberal institutions which have never ceased to be the object of my solicitude and whose salutary influence over all the countries which Providence has confided to my care, I hope, with the aid of God, to extend.

You have thus presented me the opportunity of showing to my fatherland what for a long time I have been preparing for it, and what it will obtain when the elements necessary to so important a work will have been developed.

Poles, now that you have abandoned the deadly prejudices which have

1 Leonhard Chodzko, Comte d'Angeberg, *Recueil de traités concernant la Pologne.* Paris, 1862, pp. 734 ff. (Translation.)

brought down on you so many evils, it is for you to consolidate your rebirth.

It is indissolubly bound up with the destinies of Russia. All your efforts must be directed to make this salutary and protective union firmer. Your restoration is defined by solemn treaties; it is sanctioned by the Constitutional Charter. The inviolability of these engagements of foreign powers and of this fundamental law assures Poland from this time on an honorable rank among the nations of Europe; all the more precious in that she has sought it vainly for a long period in the midst of the cruelest ordeals. . . .

Despite my efforts, perhaps all the evils under which you have groaned are not yet repaired. That is in the nature of things: progress is slow in the making, and perfection remains inaccessible to human frailty.

Representatives of the realm of Poland! Rise to the stature of your destiny. You are called to give a great example to Europe, whose gaze is fixed on you.

Prove to your contemporaries that the liberal institutions, whose ever-sacred principles men seek to confuse with the subversive doctrines which in our own day have threatened the social system with a frightful catastrophe, are not a dangerous illusion but, instead, when accepted in good faith, and especially when directed with a purity of purpose toward a conservative goal and one useful to humanity, they are perfectly allied to order and in a common harmony bring about the true prosperity of nations. . . .

Guided solely by love of your fatherland, purify your thoughts, see that they are independent of all selfish or group interests; declare them simply and uprightly, without yielding to the seductions that usually attend the exercise of free speech. . . .

It is in this way that your assembly will obtain the support of the country and that general esteem that such a gathering should command, when the representatives of a free nation do not pervert the august dignity that they are invested with.

First officials of the State, senators, nuncios, deputies, I have spoken my mind to you, I have pointed out to you your duty.

The outcome of your labors in this first assembly will enable me to gauge what the fatherland has reason to expect in the future from your devotion to it, as well as your sentiments toward me, and, whether, faithful to my resolves, I may carry what I already have done for you even further.

Let us give thanks to Him who alone has the power to enlighten sovereigns, to bring people together in harmony, and to bestow upon them the gifts of love and peace.

Let us pray Him to bless us and make our undertaking prosper.

The Polish Constitution and the tsar's Warsaw address were regarded with apprehension by both conservatives and anti-Polish Russian patriots.

Between Alexander and the Poles the seeds of distrust were soon sown and disillusionment followed on both sides. Meanwhile, in Russia a régime of reaction destroyed all hope of a constitutional development such as the tsar had earlier desired and for which Novosiltsev had actually drafted plans. The reaction took the form of strict censorship, a closer supervision of the universities, and the establishment of the military colonies, sponsored by Count Arakcheyev. Here is a contradiction in Alexander that has long aroused curiosity. The three following extracts give as many solutions. The first is by Prince Metternich, the reactionary and cynical first minister of Austria, who knew Alexander well and had great influence over him after 1815.

14. METTERNICH'S OPINION OF ALEXANDER'S CAREER[1]

Alexander, who had a rare opportunity when he succeeded his father on the throne, was unfortunately the child of the age. Rushing from cult to cult and from religion to religion, he stirred everything up but built nothing. Everything in him was superficial, nothing was firmly grounded. Going too far in all things and ever inclined to prefer the wrong method to the right, he left his empire at the end of a reign of twenty-five years in just the condition to which the Emperor Joseph carried his in nine. Joseph, at least, was an administrator and that the Russian monarch never was.

Chateaubriand, the great French writer, a conservative and a mystic, was also a contemporary of Alexander.

15. ANOTHER CONTEMPORARY VIEW OF ALEXANDER I[2]

Whatever noble qualities this prince may have had, in the last analysis he proved disastrous to his empire; he placed it too closely in contact with Europe and the West; he sowed in it seeds of civilization which in the end he wished to keep from coming up. Tugged in opposite directions, the people did not know what was asked of them, or what they themselves desired — ideas or a brute existence, passive or legal obedience, progress or stagnation. Alexander, a good Tatar, holding his people back in barbarism, or Alexander, the enlightened prince, leading them by degrees to the light, either alone might have served his country better. He was too strong a man to play the despot, too weak to establish liberty; his hesitation, instead of

[1] Prince Metternich, *Mémoires.* Paris, 1880–1881, 4 vols., IV, 276. (Translation.)
[2] René, vicomte de Chateaubriand, *Œuvres Complètes.* Paris, 1857–1858, 20 vols., XIX, 95. (Translation.)

creating a national emancipation, gave birth to individual independence, which, in its turn, produced not liberators but only assassins.

Exactly a century after Alexander's death the Polish historian, Kasimierz Waliszewski, published his great work on the man and his reign.

16. ALEXANDER AS ANALYZED A CENTURY LATER [1]

The mystery with which the deeds and movements of the " sphynx " have been surrounded was caused by that very care for appearances to which this grandson of Catherine, that fallacious but otherwise genial creator of prestige, devoted his greatest and most unremitting efforts. Unwilling to confess even to himself the true object of his ambition, which was to make, no matter how nor at how great a cost, a showing of greatness or heroism, of power or virtue, he invariably disguised both his ideas and his sentiments, and acted, as a rule, contrary to his natural inclinations.

A determined pacifist in theory, he was at war during the greater part of his reign, and even when he did put the sword in its sheath, he spent the greater part of his time and resources on armaments. He condemned severely the spirit of conquest, yet to the patrimony he inherited from his predecessors he added immense territories, weakening his empire in proportion as he increased its size. Burdening its future with the most serious complications, placing a large part of its frontier in contact with the irritating and menacing problem of unassimilated nationalities, he tied up its destiny more closely with those of a militarized Prussia and a Germany about to be prussianized.

Intrigued by reforms and a partisan of progress in every sense, after having daringly led his nation of untutored slaves in its path, he brutally forced it to retrace its steps, because the glory of being the Solon of a Russia civilized by his teaching flattered him less than the honor of becoming the gendarme of a Europe put in leading strings.

As a friend of enlightenment he began by multiplying schools and giving countenance to liberty of thought and of the press; then, all at once, to the approbation of La Harpe or Parrot or Nikolai Murovev he preferred that of Metternich and Photius, and lent himself to the stupidest schemes of obscurantism.

One will recognize another reason for this tacking about, namely, that the workman lacked the courage that his work called for and so, finding the pains inseparable from childbirth unpleasant, frightened by the difficulties

---

[1] Kasimierz Waliszewski, *Le règne d'Alexandre I.* Paris, E. Plon Nourrit et C^(ie)., 1925, 3 vols., III, pp. 380–385. (Translation.)

that attend any climb to a higher standard of civilization, he generally stopped half way. . . .

His intelligence was lively but limited, his training very inadequate, and his capacity for government decidedly mediocre. A few happy qualities of mind, joined to the capability of feeling now and then generous impulses, or of being lifted above himself by outside agencies — currents of popular enthusiasm or favorable circumstances — , at times permitted him to realize this lofty dream. But these moments were cut short and their fruit spoiled by faults, whether inherent or due to his intellectual and moral temperament — incoherent thinking and weakness of will, a vulgar vanity and a deep-seated egoism.

One qualification that was essential, if he were to carry out the rôle which he assumed, was lacking to him: unlike his grandmother, who was much more a German than he was, or his wife, who was much less intelligent, he never succeeded in developing that almost physical attachment to his adopted fatherland that they were conscious of feeling. He never saw in the millions of human beings subject to his laws anything but a force put at his disposition that he might use it in the working out of his schemes or to satisfy his whims.

. . . .

Taught in several schools radically opposed to each other, the pupil of La Harpe and Arakcheyev was equally inspired by both, and not successively, as most of his biographers have agreed, but simultaneously. True, like all men in the course of a long and checkered career, going through phases and passing milestones, he developed different points of view. One would not find it easy, however, to fix points of precise demarcation. Even between 1801 and 1812, in what is commonly known as his " period of wavering," he did not actually waver between Speranskii and Arakcheyev. He began by putting one to the test and holding the other in reserve, and later he brought them together into his confidence and into his government, just as he did at the same time with the cold Czartoryski and the ebullient Dolgoruki, no matter what differences of opinion and animosities he may have discovered in them, just as later he did with the dismal Nesselrode and enthusiastic Capo d'Istria, however great the abyss that separated them must have appeared, and all without being disconcerted or inconvenienced by it.

The creation of the Holy Alliance was certainly a decisive moment in his moral development. Nevertheless, the ultra-liberal address at Warsaw followed this event by three years, yet without any indication that he was going in the opposite direction, for it was made at the very time when he was encouraging the reactionary propaganda of Sturdza and Kotzebue.

The draft of a Russian Constitution, prepared in collaboration with

Novosiltsev, dates from 1820; the last renewal of the promises made to the Poles in regard to the increase of their territorial and political autonomy, from 1825, as does the assurance given to Karamzin, on the eve of the departure for Taganrog, that the tsar was not renouncing his plan of establishing a régime of legality in his realm. Nevertheless, in Russia and Poland alike, arbitrary rule and oppression were at that very time steadily increasing. . . . The organ of coördination was lacking in the mental equipment that nature and education gave him. . . . He put the most jarring contrasts side by side, even in his intimate life and in the very depths of his mind and his soul — not only his mystical transports and his sensual ardor in the jumbled relations with Mme. de Krüdener and with Maria Antonovna, but also in his familiar contact with a man like Arakcheyev, whose physical and moral grossness clashed so sharply with the refined tastes that were natural to Alexander.

Nor is it true that after 1815, won to the cause of reaction, he hid his liberal inclinations away, as Sorel puts it, in a " secret smithy." Of his own will he repeated them in the most public fashion in the Warsaw address, and that was in 1818.

Paul's son, and heir to a power the smallest fraction of which he never seriously thought of abandoning, he ingenuously imagined that he could grant a constitution to his empire without diminishing his own omnipotence. He could not see the impossibility of joining together these two principles — liberty and autocracy — and he even thought he was reconciling the paradox at Warsaw.

Catherine's grandson, he did not forget that she could call herself a republican and take d'Alembert into her confidence and be intimate with Diderot, without giving up her intention of disposing of all men and all things in her empire as arbitrarily as she did the furniture in her apartments, and he always remained, in words at least, the man whose coming to the throne had seemed to announce for Russia a new era of emancipation and of intellectual and moral improvement. The spirit of the age lent charm to such an attitude, and to be charming was always one of the overmastering preoccupations of this sovereign. But he insisted even more on being obeyed.

He accommodated to his personal ambitions and whims, not only his own life, but also that of his people, whose rise to a higher form of civilization he delayed, with one hand driving them to a premature *rapprochement* with the West, with the other placing on them a burden that exceeded their strength. People and sovereign alike, the one uncovering unsuspected reserves of energy, the other exploiting them to the extreme limit, appeared for a time to have triumphed in the ordeal, in exhibiting the proud assurance of a destiny the outlines of which dazzled the entire world. But it was to be only a flash in the pan. Quickly tiring with the excessive effort, the empire, " a colossus with feet of clay," sank under the weight of its organic diseases, which already were causing it to slide down the fatal slope where, since then, it has met with the worst of catastrophes, and, deprived of this source of energy, the emperor, but now acclaimed by the Europe that he had bound with flowers to his triumphal chariot, became what he had been before this apotheosis: a deceptive " gesticulator."

Groups of young officers who had been in Europe projected constitutional reforms for Russia which at first were discussed openly, but later, when the tsar showed disfavor to them, were matured in secret societies. Two societies were most important: a Northern " Union of Welfare," of which Rylaev, and Mikhail and Nikita Muravev were the leading spirits, and a Southern " Union of Salvation," under Pavel Pestel's guidance. Once in accord, these two groups separated because of fundamental differences. On Alexander's sudden death in December, 1825, they were led into a premature attempt to secure control, but were put down by the new tsar, Nikolai I, and five of the leaders were executed. The Decembrists, as they were called, became the heroes and first martyrs of the Russian revolutionary movement.

17. THE IDEAS OF THE DECEMBRISTS [1]

The most complete projects are those of Nikita Muravev and Pestel. The former seems, at first view, decidedly American; the constitution of the United States furnished him most of his articles on the power of the monarch. According to Muravev, the National Assembly is to have the right of declaring war; its laws, adopted by a two thirds vote, are to be in force even against the veto of the sovereign; by the same majority it is to name the judges of the Supreme Court, army commanders, etc., just as in America; the head of the executive power is to be no more than the president of a federated republic. On the other hand, Muravev has taken from the Spanish constitution of 1821 its first article: " The Spanish people, free and independent, can not be the property of any individual or family " and even its Article II: " The people are the source of power." But one must not forget that, if America is popular in Russia, it is because French newspapers and books represent it as the classic land of liberty; Bielayev recalls justly that Malte-Brun's atlas depicted it in the form of a beautiful girl with her hand stretched out toward Boston. As to the Spaniards, where had they drawn their inspiration if not from our Constitution of 1791 and the Declaration of the Rights of Man? From this last, moreover, Muravev has borrowed his

1 Émile Haumant, *La culture Française en Russie*. 1700–1900. Paris, Hachette, 1913, pp. 330 ff. (Translation.)

proclamation of the liberty of religions " on condition that they do not contravene the laws of nature and morality," and that of the citizen to the free expression of his opinions, provided he answers for them before a jury. From it he has taken his provisions in regard to the civil list, the deliberations of the legislative assembly, the naturalization of foreigners, the right to vote, etc; he follows it even in its omissions, as, for instance, when it is a question of the domicile of voters. In short, there is nothing in his system foreign to the French, save a vague tinge of federalism and a few provisions like that which makes a citizen's right to hold office depend on his wealth. And these are the very provisions, Pestel assures us, that made Muravev's scheme unpopular with the members of the secret societies.

The other project, Pestel's own, bears the French stamp still more clearly — not that Pastel was unaware of other sources. " There were shelves running along the whole length of his apartment," his comrade Lorère states, " filled with books, especially books on politics and economics, describing all possible constitutions. I do not know what this man had not read, no matter what language it was written in." But it was French books that he had read the most, and particularly those of the *idéologues* of the beginning of the nineteenth century and the philosophers of the end of the eighteenth. " Destutt de Tracy influenced me greatly," he said; for the rest, what one finds in these dockets of extracts is from Rousseau, d'Holbach, Diderot and Voltaire, etc. The non-French are scarcely represented save by Bentham and Beccaria, and by them in French translation. It is evident that when he thinks politically he thinks in our language, and as it were, with our brain. He has the absolute attitude of our theorists. Like them " he believed in the truth of his opinions as in mathematical truth." Like them, too, he takes no account of the data of experience and states, in accordance with Destutt de Tracy, that an hereditary throne engenders despotism, in spite of the fact that both of them knew the history of England. Like them, finally, and often more than they, he is radical and logical. They hesitate at times, do not always hold to the use of force, deprecate the use of the death penalty, while Pestel would keep it, and it is evident that he would not stick at using it in political cases, for his liberalism is all on the surface; at bottom he is a Jacobin.

At first he accepted monarchy but later, adhering to Destutt de Tracy, he replaced it with a Directory very much like that of the Year III. The federal system of Muravev, too, was not always distasteful to him, but it is enough for Destutt to claim that in Europe a republic must be strong, to cause Pestel to wish a Russian Republic, one and indivisible. Its inhabitants must form one single people: minorities are to be russified, by force if need be; Finland shall lose her autonomy, and that will be a good thing since that very autonomy is based on class distinctions. As for Poland, she shall become the " Vistula Republic " on condition that she contract with

Russia an alliance similar to that the Cisalpine Republic entered into with France.

The legislative power is to be exercised by two houses, somewhat analogous to the Councils of the Ancients and the Five Hundred, their members elected also indirectly. Religions are to be free, and the Jews emancipated. . . . Finally we come to the organization of the judiciary which, based on the institution of the jury, he gets from Benjamin Constant, Lolme, and Destutt de Tracy, except for one rather odd provision that comes from the *Esprit des Lois:* the tentative decision that expresses doubt and permits a retrial.

Much more than other authors of Russian constitutions, he shows a preoccupation with social questions. "It seemed to me," he stated in his deposition before the Commission of Inquiry, "that the chief tendency of our time was the struggle against aristocracies of every kind, founded as much on wealth as on hereditary privileges." He seeks to limit the field of this struggle by abolishing primogeniture and decreeing the equal division of inheritances. But would it not be better to squeeze property inequalities even more tightly? Pestel, who shares the admiration of Montesquieu for the laws of Lycurgus and Plato and for the collectivist institutions of the Jesuits in Paraguay, does not dare frankly to imitate them, but he admits, none the less, the citizen's right to the land without which he could not live. Every district is to be divided equally among its inhabitants, and what land can not be so divided is to be rented for no more than one year. He arrives at the end, then, very close to the manner of thinking of the *borodachi* themselves, the bearded folk, in whom, just a little earlier, Viazemskii recognized the only really revolutionary force in Russia.

. . . Certainly the Decembrists were wrong in wishing to "transplant France in Russia," where nothing was ready for such a transformation. For that matter, they understood this themselves, but like the revolutionists of all times, they counted on a miracle. . . . The Decembrists might have been more effective, had they been more practical and prudent. But prudence would have been inertia, which, after all, is worse than temerity; the catastrophe was probable enough, but the cause of reform was to grow in stature through the prestige of its martyrs.

SECTION VII. THE REVOLUTION OF 1830

If the Bourbon line of kings had clearly seemed to meet the needs of France in 1814, it quite as clearly failed to meet those needs in 1830. The policy of compromise between the absolutism of the Old Régime and the democratic principles of the French Revolution, on which policy Louis

XVIII *had embarked and which for some time after Napoleon's fall the*
majority of Frenchmen seemed to desire, had been rejected with disdain by
Charles X, who became king in 1824. But Charles's own stubborn, reactionary
policy, culminating in the autocratic "July Ordinances," simply led to his
own downfall in the Revolution of 1830.

After Charles's fall it became a crucial question what the new form of
government for France should be. Some of the leaders wanted a republic.
Others, like the rising young journalist, Thiers, looked to constitutional
monarchy as the best solution. In the following suggestive passage Professor
Guérard emphasizes the influence of English precedent as a factor tending
toward the second solution.

18. THE FRENCH REVOLUTION OF 1830. "A CASE OF HISTORICAL PLAGIARISM"[1]

To what extent the Duke of Orleans had carried his intrigues before
the Revolution; to what extent Thiers and other Liberals were committed
to his cause, is not yet fully known. But one point is certain: the influence
of English precedent; the memories of the Revolution of 1688 were potent
in the minds of these Parliamentarians, great students and admirers of the
British Constitution. The parallelism between the histories of the two nations, at an interval of a century and a half, was indeed striking. In both
a legitimate king was beheaded[2] and a military leader rose to supreme
power;[3] in both the old line was restored and a first king, good-natured
and sceptical, managed to die peacefully on the throne;[4] in both the bigotry
of a second king[5] determined a crisis, which led to the setting aside of an
incorrigible race.[6] All this seemed to call for the last term of the evolution:
the substitution of a new branch of the royal family, whose power would
be indubitably of constitutional origin.[7] This was a case of deliberate historical
plagiarism.

As in every French revolution (1792, 1848, 1870), whilst the moderates

[1] A. L. Guérard, *French Civilization in the Nineteenth Century*. New York, The Century
Company, 1914, pp. 101–102.
[2] In England Charles I; in France Louis XVI. (Editor's note.)
[3] In England Cromwell; in France Napoleon. (Editor's note.)
[4] In England Charles II; in France Louis XVIII. (Editor's note.)
[5] In England James II; in France Charles X. (Editor's note.)
[6] In England the Stuarts were set aside as a result of the Revolution of 1688. In France
the Bourbons were now set aside as a result of the Revolution of 1830. (Editor's Note.)
[7] In choosing William of Orange (William III of England) as king in place of the
rejected Stuart line and in compelling him to accept important constitutional limitations on
his power, the English Parliament brought to an end divine-right monarchy in England and
took a most significant step in the development of constitutional government. The question
arose in 1830, then, whether France would take a similar step. (Editor's note.)

were trying to minimize the consequences of the change, the radicals were setting up a Provisional Government of their own at the Paris City Hall. The Duke of Orleans took a bold and diplomatic step, and went to that stronghold of republicanism, to receive, as it were, the investiture of the populace. Thanks to the protection of Lafayette, who stood on a balcony with him and recommended him as " the best of Republics," the Duke, Lieutenant-General of the Kingdom since the abdication of Charles X, became constitutional King of the French, with a revised Charter and the tricolour flag.[1]

The ceremony at the hôtel de Ville on July 31,1830, when Louis Philippe was acclaimed King of France, is described in a recently translated book by Alexandre Dumas (1802–1870), the famous French novelist, author of The Three Musketeers *and* The Count of Monte Cristo. *Dumas, a staunch republican, who had taken part in the street fighting during the Revolution, was an eye-witness of the ceremony.*

19. LOUIS PHILIPPE AT THE HÔTEL DE VILLE [2]

A deputation from the Chamber was sent to the duc d'Orléans, in the first place to congratulate him and, secondly, to bring him to the hôtel de Ville. He had already got the Chamber of Peers and the Chamber of Deputies on his side. He had now only to win over the hôtel de Ville — that is to say the fortress where the great popular goddess, Revolution, had taken refuge at every outbreak for the last nine hundred years.

Revolution was there again now, and when the power came to the duc d'Orléans he was obliged to go to her to have it consecrated.

They set out: the duc d'Orléans on horseback, uneasy at the bottom of his heart, but outwardly calm. M. Laffitte followed him, and, as he could not walk on account of a sprained leg, and could not go in a carriage on account of the unpaved streets, he was carried in a sedan-chair by Savoyards. All went well from the Palais-Royal to the river-side. They were in the quarter of the middle classes, and the middle classes cheered their chosen leader. But the Pont-Neuf once passed, they were in the people's domains, and here marks of enthusiasm gradually gave way to an icy silence. At the place de Grève they found a state of open revolution, and seeing men with bare arms, the straw of the late encampment still littering the ground, and traces of fighting, elsewhere obliterated but here carefully preserved, one could not have surmised that all was over in another quarter and that the

---

[1] Thus divine-right monarchy came to an end in France and the parallel with English historical evolution in the seventeenth century was completed. (Editor's note.)

[2] Alexandre Dumas, *The Last King or the New France,* Now First Translated. Edited by R. S. Garnett, 2 vols., London, Stanley Paul and Company, 1915, vol. I, pp. 316–319.

people had resigned in favor of the Chamber of Peers, the Chamber of Deputies, and the Palais-Royal. No; the people, gloomy, uneasy, and watchful, seemed to have taken refuge at the hôtel de Ville.

The duc d'Orléans dismounted. The sombre vault of the hôtel de Ville yawned before him like the mouth of an abyss. He went up the steps, looking very pale, and disappeared with his slender following into its gloomy recess. It was a small mouthful for the stormy monster that devoured him.

M. de la Fayette was awaiting his royal visitor at the top.

Chance made me a spectator of the duke's reception. I had just come from Soissons, where, by General la Fayette's order, I had gone to collect six thousand pounds of powder.

The situation was a grave one. This step that the duc d'Orléans had taken in going to seek the people's sanction in the people's palace was a rupture, entire and lasting, with the monarchy of divine right. It was the consummation of fifteen years of scheming; it was the consecration of revolt in the person of a prince of the blood. All the same, the details of the reception were mean considering the significance of the event. It was characteristic of la Fayette to fritter away the grandeur and solemnity of circumstances and lay weight on details.

The declaration was read to the Chamber. When the reader came to these words, " A jury for offences of the press," the man who was to make the famous laws of September leant over to la Fayette and said:

" That is a useless clause, my dear general, for, as I hope, there will be no more offences of the press."

When the reading was finished, he placed his hand on his heart and answered:

" As a Frenchman I grieve for the evil done to the country and for the blood that has been spilt; as a prince I am happy to contribute to the happiness of the nation."

At this moment a man in the uniform of a general pressed through the crowd and faced the prince. It was General Dubourg, who was to help on the revolution in so powerful a fashion, a man never heard of before and never to be mentioned after it.

" You have made a sacred promise, Monseigneur," said the general to the prince. " See that you keep it; for " — and he pointed to the square filled with excited people — " for if you forget it, the people now gathered in the place de Grève will know how to recall it to you."

The prince started, flushed, and said in a voice of emotion:

" Monsieur, you do not know me. I am an honest man, and when I have a duty to fulfill I am not to be won by prayers or moved by threats."

Then, turning to la Fayette, the prince said a few words in a tone that could only be heard by those standing near. But almost at the same instant and as if to make a diversion the scene took on some grandeur. La Fayette drew him towards the window, put a tricolour flag in his hand and showed him to the populace in the sacred shadow of the national colours.

The crowd broke out into cheers. The same scene had been enacted under almost the same circumstances forty years before, with Louis XVI. Only this revolution, free from excesses, was to have neither its Flesselles, its Foulon, nor its Berthier; and whereas the earlier one had led Louis XVI in a short four years from public applause to the scaffold, the later one was to take eighteen years to conduct Louis Philippe from triumph to exile.

The spirit of revolution, manifested in France in 1830 in the overthrow of Charles X and the accession of Louis Philippe to power, quickly spread to Italy, the Netherlands, Poland, and elsewhere. The Italian Revolution was soon put down by Austrian troops, the Polish by Russian forces. In the Netherlands, however, the revolutionary movement was crowned with success. Belgium, which had been united with Holland by the Congress of Vienna to form the Kingdom of the Netherlands, succeeded in breaking away from this irksome union and in establishing her independence.

In his History of Ten Years, 1830–1840 *first published in French in 1841, Louis Blanc, socialist, journalist, historian, and political leader, discusses with fervor and insight some of the causes of the revolutions in Italy, the Netherlands, and Poland.*

20. GENERAL CAUSES OF THE REVOLUTIONS OF 1830 IN ITALY, BELGIUM, AND POLAND[1]

Italy palpitated under the sway of Austria, of which her princes were little more than the prefects; a sway the more abhorred, for that it was exercised by means of diplomacy. Deprived of the right of freely traversing their native land, and of that of publishing their opinions — assailed in their personal liberty — tracked by spies, even to their household circles — exposed to the grief of beholding, upon the least movement, the abhorred uniforms of the Austrian garrisons glistening from Rome to Ancona, from Turin to Naples — the Italians were watching with swelling impatience for the moment to shake off their chains. Those chains were however, much heavier for the enlightened men of the nation than for the rest of its inhabitants, whose physical condition was not in reality very unfortunate. But in Italy there are no distinctions of class, properly speaking, except in Piedmont, where society is constituted upon a regularly graduated scale. The Italian middle

[1] Louis Blanc, *The History of Ten Years, 1830–1840.* 2 vols., London, Chapman and Hall, 1844, vol. I, pp. 260–263.

order felt consequently that it could easily carry along with it in its train that people from which it was separated by no barrier, and of which it formed the *élite*. It is certain that the love of Italian independence existed everywhere, even among the lowest of the populace, if not in the shape of opinion, yet at least in that of instinct and sentiment. There were even countries (sic) of Italy, la Romagna for instance, where that sentiment prevailed among the people in a very intense degree. At Genoa every one still remembered the day when the Austrians, having endeavoured to force the inhabitants to help in carrying away a mortar, a child cried out *la rompo* (I will break it); a cry that roused the people, and caused the expulsion of a multitude of strangers from the city, after three days of heroic conflict. The independence of Italy was, therefore, a thought that brooded in every heart. And again, those who were naturally called to place themselves at the head of the movement looked for the achievement of independence only to the triumph of unity. In fact, though Italy was yet parted into fragments, and the memory of the federative struggles of the middle ages was perhaps not quite extinct there, Palermo and Naples were the only two cities between which there subsisted a deep spirit of enmity: Genoa herself, though remembering how flourishing she had once been, and though bending but with indignation under the yoke of Turin, even Genoa did not carry her jealousy so far as not to throw open her gates with alacrity to the Piedmontese emigrants after the insurrection of 1821, give them welcome, furnish them with money, and save them. These were to the Italian patriots sufficient motives for hope. Only let France lend them her aid, let her hinder the Austrians from crossing the Alps, and Italy was free. Rome would then readily open her gates to the insurrection advancing from Bologna; the pope, stripped of his temporal power, would preserve his spiritual authority intact; Italy, in fine, would be politically constituted after inscribing on her banners the magic word *Unity*. Such were the projects of the Italian patriots. As to the leader they would adopt, they could not have much difficulty as to their choice, seeing that in their eyes the question of nationality was the most important, and the one to be first of all determined. This it is that explains the relations which had been established between Menotti and the Duke of Modena, an artful, cruel prince, inclined to despotism, but of vigorous will, and capable of plunging into a conspiracy, if it were to result in making him king of Italy.

Belgium was scarcely less agitated than Italy, though its situation was different. In a physical point of view it had never been more prosperous than since its union with Holland. The Dutch colonies afforded important and necessary outlets for its productions. The monarch who ruled it was, moreover, a man of sound head, and unquestionably one of the most remarkable men in Europe. Deeply versed in economic science, with a taste, because with a genius for speculation, William had given the Holland-Belgic trade a very vivid, if not a very moral impetus. Some of the richest merchants of his kingdom were his partners, others his debtors; and he it was who had founded, in some sort at his own risk, the GENERAL SOCIETY of Brussels. But William was a thorough Dutchman at heart. He remembered but too well that Belgium had been united in 1815 to Holland, only as an *accession of territory*. Hence, offensive preferences, and a revolting partiality in the distribution of public employments, an exceedingly formidable grievance, since it armed against Holland the most stirring and the most enlightened portion of the Belgian population. Add to this, that the two people did not speak the same language, did not profess the same religion, had not the same habits and manners; that four millions of Belgians sent no greater number of representatives to the States-general, than two millions of Dutch; that William had insisted on introducing the use of one common language into the public documents and the proceedings of the law courts; and that, in fine, he had by the establishment of the philosophic college of Louvain, aroused against him the jealous and unforgiving power of the Belgian clergy. The alliance between the liberals and the clergy was a natural result of this state of things; that alliance was as strict as possible in 1830, and it was daily becoming more menacing to the court of the Hague. Such, however, was the physical prosperity of the Belgians, that their irritation did not prompt them to wish for the violent overthrow of the dynasty: an administrative separation would have satisfied them. Many would have even been contented with the dismissal of Van Maanen, the minister of justice, the too faithful instrument of his master's unjust desires. But it would have been far otherwise if, in breaking off its connexion with Holland, Belgium could have placed itself in a situation that would have afforded it the advantage it derived from its union with the latter country. France had but to stretch out her arms to Belgium, to conclude with it the compact of a faithful and honourable fraternity.

The situation of Poland, like that of Belgium, contained within it numerous germs of revolution. The froward warlike nobility of Poland, had submitted with fierce resentment to the treaties of 1815, and had more than once endeavored to cast off their yoke. Major Lukasinski, the instigator of a conspiracy which was discovered, had died in a dungeon; but the memory of that glorious conspirator lived in the heart of every true Pole, and his name was an object of heroic veneration among the young. A conspiracy was on the point of breaking out in Warsaw, upon the coronation of Nicolas; it failed only through the timidity of some members of the diet. In vain had Prince Lubecki, the emperor's minister, given a prodigious impulse to Polish trade; in vain had the grand duke Constantine succeeded in organizing a superb and disciplined army, Poland was bent on being independent, and impatiently endured the fierce tyranny of the grand duke, a prince of strange character, who resembled as much by his good qualities as by his defects, one of those chiefs of barbarians who overthrew the Roman empire. It cannot be said that the revolution which seemed in preparation, had not to contend with rude obstacles. Brutalized by the hereditary serfdom, which, though it had ceased since Napoleon's time to exist *de jure,* still existed *de facto,* the Polish peasants knew little of the pride of independence, for their hearts had never beaten for liberty. And as for the nobles, those alone of them ardently longed for an unknown future, whose privileges were reduced to a mere name, and who vegetated in penury; for among the nobles who possessed along with the authority of high title that of fortune likewise, hatred of the stranger's yoke was combated by the fear of anarchy. Moreover, by the side of that noblesse, whose patriotism was timid, though sincere, there was the watchful Polish aristocracy; that is to say, that class of felon nobles who had accepted from Russia the titles of dukes, counts, barons, and princes, — titles formally discountenanced by the original constitution, and the usages of the country. In spite of all this a revolution in Poland was a thing easy to foresee, and events like those of July could not but render it inevitable.

CHAPTER III

THE INDUSTRIAL AND AGRICULTURAL REVOLUTION IN THE BRITISH ISLES TO 1848

SECTION I. A GENERAL SUMMARY

British history in the first half of the nineteenth century is essentially the history of the social effects of a revolution in agriculture and industry and of the efforts to cope with conditions that were at once novel, undreamed-of, and menacing. By no effort could the past be called back, and there were many reasons why it should not be; nevertheless, the present was almost unendurable. Although the revolution was under way in both agriculture and industry before the middle of the eighteenth century, and its effects had long been felt by 1814, it was only after the conclusion of peace with France in that year that Englishmen opened their eyes to the transformation that had taken place in their life. The excerpt that follows gives a brief account of what this revolution was.

21. THE REVOLUTION IN AGRICULTURE AND INDUSTRY[1]

THE close alliance of landowners and business men during the earlier eighteenth century was based on a close community of interest. The great industry of England, up to the days of the Industrial Revolution, was the woollen industry. As the industry expanded the demand for raw wool, of course, steadily increased. But wool was a product of British agriculture — for in those days the import of wool from abroad was quite small. A brisk demand for wool was an assurance of profit to the landowner; for the grazier, getting a good price for his wool, could afford to pay a good rent for land. The landowners' Parliament was therefore always ready to give legislative protection to the woollen industry, as long as it assured a good market for the products of the land. The merchants and clothiers, on their side, had no desire to upset the political control of the landowners, as long as they were given this protection, and as long as the English aristocracy maintained an open door to the successful man of business. This open door, in contrast with the closed aristocracy of France, was the secret of the British

---

[1] G. D. H. Cole, *A Short History of the British Working Class Movement, 1789–1925.* 3 vols., London, George Allen & Unwin and The Labour Publishing Co., 1925–1927, vol. I, pp. 27–39. By permission of The Macmillan Company, New York.

oligarchical system. Not till the new industrial employers came knocking in throngs at the gates of political power did "Reform" become practical politics. And then, where France had a Revolution, England had only a moderate measure of Parliamentary Reform.

In the eighteenth century, the growth of the woollen industry, and the general expansion of trade and wealth due to trade, steadily made land dearer and more profitable to its owners. The desire of merchants to buy land, and with it a share in social prestige and political power, also helped to enhance the value of landed property. The demand for cereals and meat grew, even faster than the demand for wool, with the rise in the standard of comfort which accompanied the economic expansion.

Thus was set on foot a powerful movement towards the concentration of land ownership and the exploitation of land as a source of profit. The Enclosure Movement, which reached its greatest intensity in the latter part of the eighteenth century, was already making rapid strides in its earlier years. At first, farms were thrown together and waste lands enclosed in order to provide more profitable units for stock-rearing or arable cultivation. Then the ancient system of land-holding in the villages was attacked, as putting fatal obstacles in the way of progressive farming.

The land of England up to this time was still largely, though not everywhere, cultivated under the old system of the common fields. Each owner or customary tenant had his holdings in scattered strips here and there in the fields common to the village. Each had his pasture rights both on the fields and on the uncultivated commons. In addition, many villagers, who had no land holding of their own, or only a tiny holding attached to a cottage, exercised rights of common, recognised, or half-recognised, by law and custom, over the waste lands.

This system, standing firmly in the way of scientific agriculture, was now attacked and overthrown. A high return for the application of capital to the land, either in the form of drainage or clearance, or of stocking with extensive herds or flocks, could be got only when holdings could be concentrated and enclosed. Enclosure of the open fields became the necessary completion of capitalist agriculture and of the high rents which the capitalist farmer could afford to pay. Hence the swift extension of the Enclosure Movement during the eighteenth century. Between 1700 and 1760 we have records of over 200 Enclosure Acts and over 300,000 acres enclosed; between 1761 and 1800 of 2,000 Acts and over 2,000,000 acres enclosed; and in the first fifty years of the nineteenth century of 2,000,000 more acres and nearly 2,000 more Enclosure Acts.

The story of the fearful hardships caused to the poor by this Agricultural Revolution has been often told. Its effect was a wholesale dispossession of the rural population; for, among the peasantry, even those who were granted some land in compensation for their lost rights were, in very many cases, given it under conditions which they could not fulfill. The land had to be fenced, and often drained; and the peasant, lacking the capital to do this, had often to sell his share to the larger owners for an old song. Moreover, many, who had held no land in the old village, but only common rights attached to a cottage, lost their means of life without any compensation at all. The cow, or the pig, or the geese, could no longer be left to pick up their keep on the common; for the common, as well as the open fields, had passed into unrestricted private ownership and enclosure.

The mass of the peasantry therefore, even when they remained in the villages, were reduced to the status of wage-labourers. Moreover, two other factors contributed to press down their status still further. The new agricultural methods, based on larger holdings, required far less labour to the acre than the old. This was true pre-eminently of sheep-farming; but it applied, in less degree, to arable farming as well. The Enclosure Movement thus produced at once a large surplus of agricultural workers, and this contributed to the depression of agricultural wages and accentuated the loss caused by the disappearance of auxiliary sources of income, such as rights of common.

The second factor, of no less fundamental importance, arose, not directly out of the Enclosures, but out of the parallel revolution in industry. The expansion of the woollen industry in the earlier eighteenth century had led to a great advance of what is usually called the "domestic system." Spinning and weaving were chiefly carried on, not in factories or workshops owned by a capitalist employer, but in the homes of the peasants, or in small workshops attached to them, throughout the wool-producing districts. The system differed from place to place, and Capitalism had developed further in the Western Counties than in Yorkshire, or the Midlands, or the East. But, generally speaking, the function of the capitalist in the woollen industry remained that of merchanting and trading rather than the direct control or oversight of production. The capitalist clothier bought the yarn from the spinner and sold it to the weaver, from whom again he bought the woven stuff. Sometimes, and increasingly, he bought the raw wool and sold it to the spinner; and, in the West Country, he often retained ownership of the material throughout, giving it out, in turn, to spinner and weaver to convert into yarn or stuff at a piece-work price. But, save in the finishing processes, such as bleaching and dyeing, which required abundant water and a larger application of capital in order to secure the best return, and were, therefore, more and more brought direct under capitalist control, the productive workers remained, for the most part, isolated and semi-independent producers, working under their own control in their own homes. Until power-driven machinery came to be applied, there was no economic advantage in concentrating production under a single roof. It suited the capitalist better to remain a trader, and to leave the control of the productive processes in the hands of the producers themselves.

Under this system a great cottage industry grew up over the greater part of the country. Spinning and weaving were then often combined with small-scale agriculture by the same household. All members of the family worked at the various processes, and combined their industrial occupations with work on the land. When the one was slack they turned to the other, thus minimizing the effect both of seasonal variations and of the ups and downs of trade. The peasant and the industrial worker were not two distinct classes, but largely one and the same. The purely urban workers, skilled craftsmen or operatives in the few factory trades, were an insignificant minority of the whole population. London was the only really big city. Gregory King, in his estimate of the occupations of the people at the end of the seventeenth century, puts the total number of artisans, including their wives and children, at only 240,000, out of a population of 5,674,000, or 4.2 per cent.

As trade and production expanded during the eighteenth century, the class of town workers, of course, expanded too. But the bulk of the increase went to swell the ranks of the domestic producers, and to add to the amount of their industrial earnings. Expanding production, under the old system, meant a rise in the standard of life for the domestic producers.

The twin revolutions in industry and agriculture destroyed the basis of the growing prosperity. The peasant, depending partly on his industrial earnings and partly on his income from the land, found the latter either greatly reduced or wholly taken away by the Enclosure Movement. At the same time, or rather beginning later, but then proceeding with rapid parallel strides, came the Industrial Revolution. Power-driven machinery began to compete with handicraft, reducing the cost of production with extraordinary speed. Cotton, a cheaper substitute, to which the new machines were first extensively applied, began to oust wool from its predominant position. The peasant worker could not stand up to the machine. His earnings dwindled fast; he was thrust more and more into the position of a residuary producer, and given only what work was left to do when the machines were fully employed. The burden of trade fluctuations fell even more heavily upon him; and he could no longer turn to agriculture as an alternative occupation — for there, too, his services were no longer needed. The agricultural workers migrated, perforce, in their thousands to the new industrial districts, to seek work in the hated factories. But there remained behind in the countryside enough to scramble helplessly for jobs, and bring down still further the standard of real wages in agriculture.

The long war with France between 1793 and 1815 greatly accentuated the evils attending this double economic revolution. It led to a huge rise in prices, to which wages were slow to readjust themselves. It dislocated markets, and caused extreme fluctuations in the demand for industrial labour. It hugely stimulated agricultural production, and left behind it in the countryside an inevitable aftermath of depression and readjustment. Above all, it put into the hearts of the rich a panic fear of the poor. Fearful that the English people might follow the revolutionary example of the French, the richer classes became callous to the sufferings of the poor, and far less inclined to remedy even the most glaring abuses of the new economic order than to treat the cries of suffering as dangerous signs of popular disaffection. Thus the hardships of the economic revolution were made far worse by the political troubles of the time. Patriotism became a cloak for exploitation of unprecedented severity; anti-Jacobinism was used to cover a multitude of sins.

.   .   .   .

In the light of the preceding section, what is called the " Industrial Revolution " appears as the culmination of a long process of economic development. We are apt to think of it as the almost personal achievement of a group of brilliant scientists, inventors, and business men, who, after long ages of groping, suddenly found the means of harnessing and developing the forces of Nature so as to produce wealth in abundance thitherto unimagined. Genius doubtless played its part; but, if the analysis given in the foregoing chapter is right, the inventors and exploiters of the new machines were themselves rather products than producers of the new conditions. The inventor might invent in vain until the world was ready for his invention. Or, rather, it would be true to say that, in the realm of applied chemistry and applied mechanics, which made the greatest contributions to the transformation of industry, the inventor seldom invents at all save under the stimulus of a strong demand for his invention. Many of the principles on which the new inventions were based were known to learned men for centuries before the Industrial Revolution; but they were not applied to industry because the incentive to apply them was lacking. When conditions were ripe — when wide new markets were being opened up and a supply of wage-labour being made available — the great technical inventions came about as a matter of course.

This view of the Industrial Revolution is borne out by the fact that there is hardly a single invention of this period that can be confidently attributed to a single author. Watt did not invent the steam-engine or Stephenson the locomotive: they both improved on previous models and made them more suitable for industrial use. Almost every one of the great textile inventions is of disputed authorship; it is to this day very doubtful whether Richard Arkwright, the most famous innovator in the cotton trade, ever really invented anything at all. Most of the discoveries were made, not by great geniuses working from first principles, but by ordinary people experimenting on the basis of their predecessors' work. Inventions were so many and so great because the rapidly expanding markets and prospects of profitable production set many minds to work on the problem of increasing the output of commodities, and making labour more productive.

Only a very few outstanding instances need be given in order to make this point plain. In domestic industry on a family basis, children could spin but could not weave. The family supply of yarn tended to outrun the capacity of the weaver to make it into cloth. There was need for a speedier process of weaving. Kay's flying shuttle (1733) not merely met the need, but caused the weaver to outrun the supply of yarn. Inventive minds turned to the problem of spinning; and the new machines of Hargreaves and Arkwright again reversed the position. The evolution of the power-loom, and further improvements in the spinning processes, at last established equilibrium early in the nineteenth century.

Again, the demand for coal caused a need for deeper mine-workings. The engines of Newcomen and Watt were the response. But more coal could not be hauled over the bad roads or taken by the inadequate waterways. New roads, canals, finally locomotives, met the need. It is true that each of these inventions had results far transcending the immediate want it was designed to meet; but the mother of each invention was economic necessity. The Industrial Revolution is not explained by the great inventions. The inventions have themselves to be explained by the economic situation.

This is not the place for any technical account of the inventions or of the new productive methods to which they gave rise. It is enough here to point out briefly their effect on the situation of the workers. This was threefold. In the first place they greatly increased the productivity of labour, so that vastly greater markets were required to afford employment to the same number of persons. They did not necessarily cause unemployment, save on their first introduction; but they made the maintenance of employment depend on the ability to secure an ever-widening market.

In the second place, they largely undermined the position of the skilled workers, much of whose work could now be done by machines operated by unskilled women or children. They thus called into employment a large competing supply of labour which, having less power of resistance or a lower standard of life, was used both to beat down wages and to extend the hours of labour to an inhuman length. Children were worked, in many cases, as much as sixteen hours a day, and twelve hours became the lowest standard recognized under the new system.

Thirdly, the machine revolutionised the actual methods of production. Power-driven machinery cannot be operated economically by scattered workers. Water power, and much more, steam power, demand the concentration of labour in factories. Moreover, power and machinery first made "overheads" an important element in the cost of production. The cost of power must be spread over the greatest possible quantity of labour; the machine, which costs money, must earn its keep by being kept fully in use. Therefore the workers are not only congregated in factories, but also speeded up, and worked hard and long, in order that the machines and the power may achieve their maximum utility. The productivity of labour is increased not only in proportion to the greater efficiency of the machine, but also in proportion to the greater incentive to use it to the full. In Marx's phrase, not only the productivity, but also the intensity, of labour grows greater.

The power to produce vastly more goods thus becomes, under the conditions of the Industrial Revolution, a means, not to the lightening of labour, but to a great increase in its severity. The price of the goods made by machinery certainly fell very fast; but the cost of living did not fall, both because agricultural production could not be increased in anything like the same measure as factory production, and because, after the outbreak of the war with France in 1793, war demands and inflation caused a rapid rise of prices, especially for foodstuffs. Wages, meanwhile, wholly failed to keep pace with the change in the purchasing power of money.

Despite these adverse conditions of the new factory system, the workers might have made better headway and maintained better their standard of life had not the supply of labour increased by leaps and bounds. During the eighteenth century there was, according to all authorities, a great increase in the rate of growth of population. The first census was not taken until 1801, and no accurate figures exist for earlier times. But, though estimates differ, they agree on this point. Between 1500 and 1600, and again between 1600 and 1700, the growth of population did not exceed a million in the century. Between 1700 and 1800 the increase was nearer three millions, and between 1801 and 1831 another five millions were added. These figures, moreover, are for England and Wales alone. Thus, to the greater productivity of the individual worker, to the greatest intensity of labour, and to the increased industrial employment of women and young children, was added a most powerful fresh factor — the immensely rapid increase of population.

Why did this happen? A full discussion would take us very far into abstruse and technical questions. Everywhere, throughout the world, the coming of the industrial age has been accompanied by a sensationally rapid growth of population. In the later nineteenth century this is mainly attributable to the increasing expectation of life resulting from better sanitary provision, increasing medical knowledge, and the rise in the standard of living. But these explanations do not apply to the period of the Industrial

Revolution, when, despite heavy mortality and appalling sanitary conditions in the factory towns, the proportionate rate of increase was greater than it is today. Between 1760 and 1830 the population approximately doubled.

In the early and mid eighteenth century, doubtless one factor making for increased population was a rising standard of life, due to the rising prosperity of the country. As the wool industry and agriculture both expanded, the position of the domestic worker improved, and population expanded, probably both because the size of families increased and because the chances of survival became better. But the far more rapid growth of population during the period of the Industrial Revolution was due to a quite different set of causes. It coincided with a marked fall in the standard of life, and probably with a worsening of the conditions governing mortality.

Why, under these apparently adverse conditions, did population increase with unprecedented rapidity? An explanation is often given purely in terms of conscious motive. The Industrial Revolution created a great new demand for child labour in the textile factories. Often the children could find work, at exceedingly low wages, when the father could find none. There was thus, in the factory districts, an economic motive for increasing the size of the family. Moreover, in the country, from 1795 onwards, Poor Law relief was being given on the "Speenhamland" system, under which inadequate wages were made up to a bare living standard according to the size of the family. More children meant increased poor relief. The agricultural labourers also had thus an economic motive for increased fertility.

Both these causes doubtless counted; but it is very doubtful whether, taken together, they were the most powerful factors in stimulating the growth of population. Through the greater part of human history, population has been kept in check mainly by custom, and has remained relatively stable. But throughout the world the past 150 years have brought a great increase. In countries which have developed "great industry," the change from agricultural to industrial methods has been commonly accompanied by a big growth of population, even where the economic motives just described have not been at work, or have been far less powerful. It is at least plausible to put forward as the reason for this growth, not so much any conscious adaptation of the size of the family to economic opportunities, as the withdrawal or destruction of institutions and customs tending to limitation.

The peasants, during the Industrial Revolution, were torn from the land, and driven to live in the noisome factory towns. Even where they remained in the country the old life of the village was destroyed and the old customs were broken up. The result was a breakdown of the largely unconscious checks on population which had existed under the old system. Men married sooner, and there was no custom or idea of a customary standard to restrain the indefinite multiplication of the people.

Thus, despite starvation wages and evil sanitary conditions, population grew faster and faster, piling up in the new towns and industrial districts as economic pressure drove the labourers out of the villages. The geographical distribution, as well as the number of the people, was radically altered. In 1700 the areas of greatest population were in the west and the south Midlands. As the century advanced, population shifted northwards into Lancashire and Yorkshire and the coalfields of the north-east coast. Towns such as Manchester grew by leaps and bounds. In 1770 Manchester and Salford, with their suburbs, had, perhaps, a population of 40,000. In 1801 this had risen to nearly 95,000; and in 1831 to nearly 238,000. Glasgow, Birmingham, and other great manufacturing centers underwent a similarly swift expansion.

It was this sudden leap forward in the growth of population that caused Malthus, as early as 1798, to frame his famous theory, which, in a vulgarised form, dominated orthodox economic thinking for a whole generation. Malthus saw, in the unrestricted growth of the people, the danger of a pressure on the means of subsistence which would make impossible any rise in the standard of life beyond the barest subsistence level, and might easily pull up the whole social system by the roots. Whether it was true or false, his teaching produced disastrous results on the attitude of the rich towards the poor. Every child born in a workman's household came to appear as part of the universal menace — as an unwelcome fresh mouth to be fed. Instead of inquiring into the causes of the growth of population, and so devising fundamental remedies, statesmen and economists tried rather to prevent the poor from breeding by forcible deterrents. The new Poor Law of 1834, with its withdrawal of outdoor relief to the able-bodied, and its segregation of the sexes in the workhouse, was the embodiment of that popular " Malthusianism " which became the scientific cloak for the rich man's fear of his poor neighbour.

However rapidly population may increase, or change its location, these processes are bound to take some time. From the standpoint of the supply of labour the Industrial Revolution falls into two phases. During the earlier phase, extending to about 1800, there is a surplus of workers, owing to enclosures, in the country, but often a shortage in the factory districts. Migration has not yet taken place on a sufficient scale. This is the period during which occurs one of the worst, and most often described, abuses of the Revolution — the employment of " parish apprentices " in the factories, virtually as bond-slaves of the factory owner. The " parish apprentice " is a child who has fallen, owing to the destitution of its parents, into the hands of the Poor Law authorities. These, eager to rid themselves of the burden of the child's maintenance, virtually sell it, under indentures for a period of years, to the factory owner, who is experiencing a shortage of labour for the running of the new machines. The owner works the child what hours he pleases, and makes for its upbringing and education only what provision he pleases. The Poor Law, having got rid of the burden, washes its hands of the whole affair. Doubtless a few masters, like David Dale at New Lanark, treated these unfortunate children fairly well according to the low standards of the time. But most employers did not, justifying excessive hours and evil conditions on plea of the intensity of trade competition. This was the situation which Sir Robert Peel the elder, himself a big factory owner, meant his Health and Morals of Apprentices Act, passed in 1801, to do something to ameliorate.

But by 1801 the system of " parish apprentices " was already beginning to die a natural death. The Industrial Revolution, in consequence of the growth and migration of the people, had entered on its second phase, and the supply of labour had already caught up the needs even of the swiftly expanding industries. It no longer paid to employ " parish apprentices " when cheap child labour could be had for the asking in the factory districts. The serious decline in the position of the adult workers set in at this point. There was a scramble for jobs, and adults were increasingly displaced by their own children. Naturally, the standard of living fell.

These highly adverse conditions were made much worse by the commercial uncertainties due to war. From 1793 to 1815, with only a brief interval in 1801 and 1802, Great Britain was engaged in its struggle with France. This did not prevent trade from expanding, and it even helped greatly the growth of the industries directly ministering to war requirements. But it caused great uncertainty and fluctuation in the textile industries, especially during its latter years, when, first, the war of blockade between Great Britain and Napoleon, waged by means of the Berlin Decrees and the Orders in Council (1806-7), seriously dislocated British trade with Europe, and then the war between Great Britain and America (1812-1814) affected both markets for finished goods and the supply of materials for the cotton factories of the north. The long war caused great destruction of wealth and great fluctuation of employment; and, by draining away money for the prosecution of the war and the enrichment of those who made fortunes out of contracting and stock-jobbing, forced down the working-class standard of living to the lowest possible point.

The period of the Napoleonic wars, and of the economic crises which succeeded it, is the blackest chapter in the whole history of the British working class. Driven from the land by enclosures, made redundant or exposed to the competition of child-labour by the new machines, exposed to relentless persecution because of the fears engendered in the mind of the governing classes, both by their misery and by the " awful portent " of the

Revolution in France, and enwalled in the hideous, stinking purlieus of the new factory towns, the workers underwent a long agony, from which they emerged at length, exhausted and docile, into the Victorian era. In this age of misery, and as the child of this misery, the British Labour Movement was born.

SECTION II. ENCLOSURE

The beginnings of the Enclosure Movement are to be found in the third quarter of the fourteenth century, shortly after the Black Death had initiated a labor problem in England. In the fourteenth, and again in the sixteenth century, enclosure had consisted chiefly in the fencing off of agricultural lands that were made into sheep runs. When enclosure was carried on in the eighteenth century it was on a much greater scale, and one of the reasons for it was the desire for, and urgency of, large-scale and more productive farming. Arthur Young (1741–1820) journeyed all over England and examined agricultural conditions and possibilities, which he described not only in his four famous surveys of England but also in several of the reports he contributed to the work of the Board of Agriculture.

22. ARTHUR YOUNG'S DEFENCE OF ENCLOSURE[1]

Hampton Poyle enclosed in 1796–7; saw a very great improvement in the tract that had been *lot* meadows.

Burford was enclosed twelve years ago. It has not since produced so much corn; but infinitely more mutton and beef.

Fringford has been improved greatly in rent and produce since the enclosure, at least trebled in both. Stoke Lyne the same: no dairies in either. Mr. Bullock has enclosed Edgcot, 1100 acres, the rent of it will be trebled, and will all be pastured. Stratton Ardley was 500 *l.* a year and now it is 2500 *l.*; much of it will be under dairies. One estate there was offered for 3000 *l.*, it is now 800 *l.* per annum: great tracts have been laid down for cows.

Alvescot has been enclosed eight years, and very greatly improved, though the farmers are not the best to be found. A farm of 100 *l.* a year while open, is now 300 *l.* a year, and cheap. The vicarage was from 150 *l.* to 200 *l.*; now above 600 *l.* a year. There were 600 acres of waste, most of which was pared and burnt. One farmer has taken corn incessantly, and found the bad effects. The land now recovered: the produce of the parish is certainly trebled.

Wotton has been enclosed about 37 years, and Mr. Sotham has not the least doubt of its having yielded full four times the produce in that time

---

[1] *View of the Agriculture of Oxfordshire*, drawn up for The Board of Agriculture by the Secretary of the Board. London, 1809, pp. 91–101 (much condensed).

that it did in a like period before; and the rent is five times as much as it was in the open state.

Enclosures all around Chipping Norton, have, in the opinion and information of Mr. Dawkins, unquestionably added greatly to the food of mankind; and the country has been in consequence of them much improved.

Mr. Edmonds remarks, that enclosures have doubled rents, and they are paid with more ease; and beyond all doubt the produce of food for man is very greatly increased by them; in some cases that of pasturage more than corn; but it is very observable, that grass produce is higher in price than corn.

At Barton, the land was lett for scarcely any thing, and the farmers generally as poor as could be; enclosed, it lett at 20s. an acre, and the farmers in easy circumstances, and doing well; and in all of them farmers in general very much benefitted; nor have farms been more enlarged in consequence; they have been as much added to in open as in enclosed. But it is a great error to suppose very small farms beneficial; they are far from it, either to the community or to the occupier.

It may now be fair to enumerate some of the *advantages* arising from enclosures.

The first of these, is getting rid of the restrictions of the former course of husbandry, and appropriating each of the various sorts of land to that use to which it is best adapted.

2. The prevention of the loss of time, both as to labourers and cattle, in travelling to many dispersed pieces of land from one end of a parish to another; and also in fetching the horses from distant commons before they go to work.

3. There is a much better chance of escaping the distempers to which cattle of all kinds are liable from being mixed with those infected, particularly the scab in sheep. This circumstance, in common fields, must operate as a discouragement to the improvement of stock; and it is a further disadvantage, that the occupier is limited both in regard to *number* and *kind* of stock, instead of adopting such a number and kind as are most suitable and proper.

4. The farmer has a better superintendance of his labourers, when within the bounds of an enclosed farm, than in an open field.

5. The great benefit which arises from draining lands, which cannot so well, if at all, be done on single acres and half acres, and would effectually prevent the rot amongst sheep, so very common in open field land.

Lastly, the preventing of constant quarrels, which happen as well from the trespasses of cattle as by ploughing away from each other's land.

SECTION III. CRITICISM OF THE NEW ECONOMIC SYSTEM

The one-sidedness of the Industrial Revolution and the nature of some of the problems resulting from it are brought out by Mr. and Mrs. Hammond.

23. THE CONCENTRATION ON PRODUCTION[1]

When capital was applied to production on a large scale, it gained its profits by producing in bulk; producing, that is, for mass consumption. Energy and brains were now devoted to satisfying, not the luxurious taste of the classes that were served by the commerce of mediæval Europe, but the needs of the poor consumer.

Man's faculty for creation and self-expression develops when he can diminish the demand that the satisfaction of elementary needs for food and shelter makes upon his intelligence and his strength. Hence this vast improvement in the means for the provision of those needs marked a definite and startling advance in human history. Man, in this sense, became freer than he had ever been; his *jus in naturam,* as Spinoza put it, was infinitely greater. This aspect of the new system struck many contemporary observers as its most important aspect; they were fond of showing that the poor of their time were better off in respect of the conditions of life than the rich of other times; the cottager than the noble.

It was natural for the age that witnessed the first triumphs of the new system to worship production for profit. This great addition to the wealth of the world seemed to follow automatically when men were left to acquire at their pleasure. Swift success is a dazzling spectacle, and the new industrial system provided a new miracle every day. A visitor to a mill in Bolton or Preston watching the inventions of Crompton, Hargreaves, Arkwright and Watt, stood before a power that was conquering the world as no Caesar or Napoleon had ever conquered it. To the generation that saw on the one hand the small farmer carrying the wool he had woven on his hand-loom at home to Leeds or Halifax on the back of his horse, and on the other the great mills at Blackburn or Rochdale sending out thousands of bales of cotton to be transported by rail and ship to the other ends of the earth, it looked as if progress that had dawdled through so many centuries was, now that men had learnt its simple secret, to follow a rapid and unbroken course; as if the society that surrendered itself to the control of private profit released a force that would regenerate the world. Any people into whose hands this power had fallen would probably have been plunged into the state described by Boulton as " steam-mill mad," just as any people that had first grasped the

[1] J. L. Hammond and Barbara Hammond, *The Rise of Modern Industry,* 3rd Edition. London, Methuen, 1927, pp. 210–222 (condensed). New York, Harcourt Brace and Company.

new wealth of America in the fifteenth century would have been as frantic as the Spaniards for gold and silver.

The English people, from the whole tone and cast of its thought and politics, was specially liable to be swept off its balance by this revolution. The positive enthusiasms of the time were for science and progress: for material development and individual liberty. The restraints of custom, tradition and religion had never been so frail over the classes that held power. In the Middle Ages the Church had laid a controlling or checking hand on manners: the Guilds had hampered individual enterprise by a corporate discipline. But the Church of the eighteenth century was merely part of the civil order, without standards, authority or conscience of its own; the Guilds were dead, and their successors stood not for corporate spirit, but for property and nothing else. Thus neither Church nor Guild survived to offer any obstacle to the view that headlong wealth was the sovereign good for society and for the individual, for cities and for men.

This view was powerfully encouraged by the philosophy of confidence which the eighteenth century had substituted for a religion of awe. Mediæval religion had watched man's instincts with anxious eyes, as instincts needing to be disciplined, coerced, held fast by Pope and priest; the Puritans, though they gave him different masters, were not less suspicious of the natural man. The new philosophy, on the other hand, regarded man's instincts as the best guide to conduct, and taught that left to himself man so acted as to serve rather than injure the society to which he belonged. Capital was a magical power; man was a benevolent creature. Thus so far as an age lives by a system of belief, this age drew its wisdom from a philosophy that found nothing but good in the new force to which it had submitted.

The state of politics was also congenial to this impulse. Neither Conservative nor Radical offered any distracting or competing motive, for while they disagreed about political and administrative reform, they did not disagree about the advantages of a system under which acquisition and profit-making were unimpeded. If it was the manufacturers who promoted the new system in industry, the landowners were equally active in promoting it on their estates. The most important force in making the English an industrial people was the destruction of the village. Nations that kept the peasant could never be completely absorbed in the new industrial system, and it was the landowner, often of course the new landowner, who had come from the world of finance and industry, who pushed the English peasant out. . . .

This new power . . . descended on a society in which the intellectual and political atmosphere inclined the age to give it a free rein. Restraint of every kind on the acquisition and the use of wealth was discredited; the doctrine that the man who seeks his private gain finds the public good was accepted like a discovery of Newton's; progress was regarded as constant, and it was believed that the Industrial Revolution was making the problems of life not more but less complex. For the ascendancy of the mathematical sciences had encouraged abstractions dangerous from their simplicity. The economist dismissed moral and religious impulses, finding in selfishness the driving power of industrial enterprise. The world seemed to be organized in such a way that the capitalist's desire for profit was really the best guarantee that the consumer and the workman would benefit by his activities. . . .

The effect of this concentration is seen in the towns of the age. They were left, like everything else, to the mercy and direction of the spirit of profit. Town planning was not an unknown art; at different times in the world's history it had served the purpose of defence, of religion, of display, of commerce. Rulers with their eyes on the needs of war had planned towns like Stockholm; others, thinking of their personal glory, had planned great reconstructions in Paris or Rome. The English town of this period, which looked like the product of a tired age that had lost its stride, was really the product of an age full of energy, that had no care for order, space or plan. Public beauty seemed to have been banished by the new science. . . . All that belongs to the new life of the nation bears a character as unmistakable as the character given to a mediaeval town by its handsome buildings. The chimneys of Lancashire represented energy, initiative, ambition: qualities that had given to Manchester the grasp of a larger and richer world than that from which Tyre or Venice, Antwerp or Amsterdam had drawn their lavish wealth. The random and squalid buildings of the new Manchester where 200,000 people lived without a single public garden, were not less eloquent; they spoke for the discredit into which man's life outside this system of production had fallen, the poverty that had stricken the social consciousness of the race.

Mankind did not admire wealth for the first time; but the rich merchant of Bruges, Genoa or Norwich, like the rich Pope or the rich noble of the Middle Ages, or the rich Senator of the Roman Empire, had regarded the beauty and culture of his town as a sign of his own importance and success. Vespasian, frugal as he was, did not hesitate to begin the restoration of the Capitol, though he had inherited a debt of over three hundred million pounds. The private citizen who gave Bordeaux an acqueduct costing £160,000, or the benefactor who spent £80,000 on the walls of Marseilles, the soldier who provided free baths for slave girls at Suessa Senonum, the civic dignitaries who gave temples and theatres, these typical figures of the early Roman Empire would have been astonished to learn that in the districts of South Wales, where men had risen in a few years to such wealth as would have rivalled the wealth of Atticus or Herodes, the poorer classes had to go a mile for water, waiting in a queue a great part of the night; that the chief town of this rich district had neither public lighting nor drainage.

Yet the Industrial Revolution which had given these men their fortunes had made it much easier to supply the needs of the towns that sprang up beside their great establishments. One of the products of that revolution was gas lighting; the Soho Works were lighted with gas in 1802 to celebrate the Peace of Amiens. Great factories at Manchester and Leeds soon followed the example of Boulton and Watt. Another product was the cheap water-pipe. At the end of the American War English ironmasters were exporting water-pipes to Paris and New York. The Romans had no cheap water-pipes made by the help of mechanical power, but they could supply their towns with clean water, whereas the people of Merthyr Tydfil, their streets echoing by day and night with the clamour of forge and furnace, had to drink whatever the river brought them. Augustus' Rome, with its undeveloped mechanical arts, would not have looked more primitive to the Lancashire of Arkwright or Crompton than nineteenth-century Manchester, with its random and formless streets, would have looked to the Rome of Vitruvius, the architect of the first century B.C. who set the classical tradition, to whom the task of deciding where a town should place its temples, its circus, its forum, its amphitheatre, and how it should organize its water supply and its drainage seemed the most urgent of the tasks of a civilized society. . . .

An original and interesting writer, discussing the significance of different types of architecture, remarked that " only what can be got out of life can be put into art." Thus he traced definition and the sense of ideas in Greek art, energy and passion in Gothic art, the recovery of the balance and order of intellectual composure in the art of the Renaissance. The town of the industrial age, without beauty or method, marked the spirit of this age just as truly as St. Paul's Cathedral marked the spirit of the Renaissance, or the cathedral of Durham the spirit of the Crusades. It expressed a concentration in which religion, beauty, leisure, the life of the spirit, or the life of the senses, were all held to be rivals to the stern life of selfish duty. The purpose of man's life was not to fight or to pray, to contemplate or to create, to enjoy or to become, but to make profits, profits for himself, if a master, profits for another, if a servant. This was man's duty, and it was the duty of society to put no obstacle in his way. The Greek view of life, as the expression and exercise of many faculties, has been threatened by the asceticism of the seeker after salvation, and by the asceticism of the seeker after profits; of the cotton spinner, who lived and worked like a slave, and ruled like a slave driver, it was as true as it was of St. Simon Stylites on his pillar that he sacrificed the whole to the part of a man's life. The rage for production had swept England, as the rage for piety had swept the age of the monachists. And production had taken a form that was intensely isolating; the successful man kept his secrets, tried to find his neighbours' secrets, strove for personal gain, took personal risks, made his way by personal initiative and personal enterprise.

This concentration led to the complete neglect of the most urgent of the tasks of the age.

Thomas Carlyle wrote Past and Present *in 1843 in an effort to point out the pass England had been brought to and to demonstrate the futility of the panaceas that men were offering her in her distress. Only by a return to first principles — by a spiritual change — could the issue be met. In this passage Carlyle, not as an economist but as a prophet, is describing the results of the era of great production of wealth. In particular, he refers to the Poor Law Act of 1834, which, for the most part, abolished outdoor relief and instituted a standardized system of poor-houses.*

24. THE CURSE OF MIDAS [1]

The condititon of England, on which many pamphlets are now in the course of publication, and many thoughts unpublished are going on in every reflective head, is justly regarded as one of the most ominous, and withal one of the strangest, ever seen in this world. England is full of wealth, of multifarious produce, supply for human want in every kind; yet England is dying of inanition. With unabated bounty the land of England blooms and grows; waving with yellow harvests; thick-studded with workshops, industrial implements, with fifteen millions of workers, understood to be the strongest, the cunningest and the willingest our Earth ever had; these men are here; the work they have done, the fruit they have realized is here, abundant, exuberant on every hand of us: and behold, some baleful fiat as of Enchantment has gone forth, saying, " Touch it not, ye workers, ye master-workers, ye master-idlers; none of you can touch it, no man of you shall be the better for it; this is enchanted fruit! " On the poor workers such fiat falls first, in its rudest shape; but on the rich master-workers too it falls; neither can the rich master-idlers, nor any richest or highest man escape, but all are like to be brought low with it, and made " poor " enough, in the money sense or a far fataller one.

Of these successful skilful workers some two millions, it is now counted, sit in Workhouses, Poor-law Prisons; or have " out-door relief " flung over the wall to them, — the workhouse Bastille being filled to bursting, and the

---

1 Thomas Carlyle, *Past and Present*. First published, 1843. Edition of 1918, Oxford, Clarendon Press, pp. 1–2, 5–6.

strong Poor-law broken asunder by a stronger. They sit there, these many months now; their hope of deliverance as yet small. In workhouses, pleasantly so named, because work cannot be done in them. Twelve hundred thousand workers in England alone; their cunning right-hand lamed, lying idle in their sorrowful bosom; their hopes, outlooks, share of this fair world, shut in by narrow walls. They sit there, pent up, as in a kind of horrid enchantment; glad to be imprisoned and enchanted, that they may not perish starved. The picturesque Tourist, in a sunny autumn day, through this bounteous realm of England, descries the Union Workhouse on his path. " Passing by the Workhouse of St. Ives in Huntingdonshire, on a bright day last autumn," says the picturesque Tourist, " I saw sitting on wooden benches, in front of their Bastille and within their ring-wall and its railings, some half-hundred or more of these men. Tall, robust figures, young mostly or of middle age; of honest countenance, many of them thoughtful and even intelligent-looking men. They sat there, near by one another; but in a kind of torpor, especially in a silence, which was very striking. In silence: for, alas, what word was to be said? An Earth all lying round, crying, Come and till me, come and reap me; — yet we here sit enchanted! In the eyes and brows of these men hung the gloomiest expression, not of anger, but of grief and shame and manifold inarticulate distress and weariness; they returned my glance with a glance that seemed to say, ' Do not look at us. We sit enchanted here, we know not why. The Sun shines and the Earth calls; and, by the governing Powers and Impotences of this England, we are forbidden to obey. It is impossible, they tell us! ' There was something that reminded me of Dante's Hell in the look of all this; and I rode swiftly away. . . ."

To whom, then, is this wealth of England wealth? Who is it that it blesses; makes happier, wiser, beautifuller, in any way better? Who has got hold of it, to make it fetch and carry for him, like a true servant, not like a false mock-servant; to do him any real service whatsoever? As yet no one. We have more riches than any Nation ever had before; we have less good of them than any Nation ever had before. Our successful industry is hitherto unsuccessful; a strange success, if we stop here! In the midst of plethoric plenty, the people perish; with gold walls, and full barns, no man feels himself safe or satisfied. Workers, Master Workers, Unworkers, all men, come to a pause; stand fixed, and cannot farther. Fatal paralysis spreading inwards, from the extremities, in St. Ives workhouses, in Stockport cellars, through all limbs, as if toward the heart itself. Have we actually got enchanted, then; accursed by some god?

Midas longed for gold, and insulted the Olympians. He got gold, so that whatsoever he touched became gold, — and he, with his long ears, was little the better for it. Midas had misjudged the celestial music-tones; Midas had insulted Apollo and the gods; the gods gave him his wish, and a pair of long ears, which also were a good appendage to it. What a truth in these old Fables!

Shelley's sonnet, written very near the close of George III's long reign, represents the protest of, perhaps, the poet most sensitive to the ills of England.

25. ENGLAND IN 1819[1]

SONNET: ENGLAND IN 1819

An old, mad, blind, despised, and dying king, —
Princes, the dregs of their dull race, who flow
Through public scorn, — mud from a muddy spring, —
Rulers who neither see, nor feel, nor know,
But leech-like to their fainting country cling,
Till they drop, blind in blood, without a blow, —
A people starved and stabbed in the untilled field, —
An army, which liberticide and prey
Makes as a two-edged sword to all who wield
Golden and sanguine laws which tempt and slay;
Religion Christless, Godless — a book sealed;
A Senate, — Time's worst statute unrepealed, —
Are graves, from which a glorious Phantom may
Burst, to illumine our tempestuous day.

SECTION IV. THE CRIMINAL CODE

Up to his death in 1818 Sir Samuel Romilly made it his work, in Parliament and out, to modify the English criminal law by reducing the number of capital offences. In 1819 it is stated that there were 223 such offences, many of them petty and a large proportion of them eighteenth century additions. Romilly was successful in removing pocket-picking and a few other felonies from the list, but a real revision of the law was made only after his death, Sir James Mackintosh taking his place at the head of the movement. Selections from several of Romilly's speeches reveal some of the evils attending this archaic system.

26. EVILS OF THE BRITISH CRIMINAL LAW[2]

" I have always considered it a very great defect in the Criminal Code of this Country, that Capital Punishments should be so frequent; that they

---

[1] Percy B. Shelley, *Poetical Works.* London, Macmillan, 1890, p. 524.
[2] *The Speeches of Sir Samuel Romilly in the House of Commons.* 2 vols.. London, 1820, vol. I, pp. 38–42, 106, 108, 122–125.

have been appointed, I cannot say inflicted, for so many crimes. For no principle seems to me more clear than this, that it is the certainty, much more than the severity of punishments, which renders them efficacious. This has been acknowledged, I believe, ever since the publication of the works of the Marquis Beccaria. The impression, however, which was made in this Country by his writings, has hitherto proved unavailing; for it has not produced a single alteration in our Criminal Law; although in many other states of Europe various amendments have taken place. Indeed, if we were to take the very reverse of the principle to which I have alluded, it would be a faithful description of the English law, in its enactments and administration. It is notorious how few of those, who are condemned, actually suffer punishment. From returns which are to be found in the Secretary of State's office, it appears, that in the year 1805, there were 350 persons who received sentence of death, of whom only 68 were executed, not quite a fifth part of the number. In the year 1806, 325 received sentence of death, of whom 57 were executed; and in 1807, the number was 343, of whom there were executed 63. If we deduct from this number all those who received sentence of death for crimes which are never, or very rarely pardoned, it will, perhaps, be found, that out of 20 persons condemned to die, not more than one suffers death.

" The question, therefore, is, Whether the execution of the Law is to be the rule or the exception to be observed in the administration of justice; whether a code shall continue to exist in *theory,* which has been lately described (in language which one would rather have expected to hear from the lips of a Satirist, than from a seat of Judgment) ' as almost abrogated in *practice* by the astuteness of Judges, the humanity of Juries, and the mercy of the Crown.' I am far from being disposed either to censure or regret ‧this relaxation of the Law; I am only inquiring whether Statutes so dispensed with can be deemed any longer essential to the well-being of the State.

" Such is the general view which I have taken of the subject. But my more immediate purpose is to call the attention of the House to one class only of these severe Statutes, which have, from a change of circumstances, acquired a rigour not originally intended by their framers; Statutes, in which the capital part of the charge depends, not on the mode or season in which the offence has been committed, but on the value of the property stolen; such as the Act of Elizabeth, which punishes with death the stealing privately from the person of another to the value of twelve pence; that of William and Mary, which makes privately stealing in a shop, to the amount of five shillings, a capital Felony; and other Statutes of the same nature. So great an alteration has taken place in the value of money since those Statutes passed, that it is astonishing that the letter of the Law should have been suffered to remain unaltered to the present day, the offences, in the mean time, having become altogether so different. Perhaps there is no case which renders more striking the truth of Lord Bacon's observation, that *Time is the greatest of all innovators;* for, in proportion as every thing that contributes to the support, the comfort, and the luxuries of life has grown dearer, LIFE itself has become cheaper and of less account.

" There are many mischievous consequences, resulting from such a state of things, which do not strike the mind at first, but which become more evident, on reflection. Such Laws cannot be executed. Juries are placed in the painful situation of violating one of two duties; they are reduced to the alternative of violating their oaths, or what they are sometimes mistakenly induced to think more binding on them — the dictates of humanity. Often, against the plainest evidence, Juries have reduced the property stolen to less than half of its lowest value, in order to dispense with the capital part of the punishment. And this is now considered (as Blackstone has somewhere expressed it) ' A PIOUS PERJURY ' — words, which I regret, should ever have been put together; since nothing has a more immoral tendency than for men to familiarize themselves with the disregard of their judicial oaths! The law ought not to remain so; — it causes offenders to be acquitted against the clearest evidence; and thus, by a necessary consequence, defeats its own ends, and becomes the abettor of its own violation."

. . . .

Sir Samuel Romilly moved (on February 9, 1810) for leave to bring in Bills to repeal the Acts, 10 and 11 William III.; 12 Ann; and 24 Geo. II. (which makes the crimes of stealing privately in a Shop, goods of the value of *five* shillings; or in a Dwelling-house, or on board a Vessel in a navigable River, property of the value of *forty* shillings, capital Felonies); and spoke to the following effect:

. . . " There is probably no other country in the world in which so many and so great a variety of human actions are punishable with loss of life as in England. These sanguinary Statutes, however, are not carried into execution. For some time past the sentence of death has not been executed on more than a sixth part of the persons on whom it has been pronounced, even taking into the calculation crimes the most atrocious and the most dangerous to society, — murders, rapes, burning of houses, coining, forgeries, and attempts to commit murder.

. . . .

" The same benevolence and humanity, understood in a more confined or a more enlarged sense, will determine one Judge to pardon and another to punish. It has often happened, it necessarily must have happened, that the very same circumstance which is considered by one Judge as matter of extenuation, is deemed by another a high aggravation of the crime. The former good character of the delinquent, his having come into a country in which he was a stranger to commit the offence, the frequency or the novelty of the crime, are all circumstances which have been upon some occasions considered by different Judges in those opposite lights: and it is not merely the particular circumstances attending the crime, it is the crime itself, which different Judges sometimes consider in quite different points of view.

"Not a great many years ago, upon the Norfolk Circuit, a larceny was committed by two men in a poultry-yard, but only one of them was apprehended; the other having escaped into a distant part of the country had eluded all pursuit. At the next Assizes the apprehended thief was tried and convicted; but Lord Loughborough, before whom he was tried, thinking the offence a very slight one, sentenced him only to a few months' imprisonment. The news of this sentence having reached the accomplice in his retreat, he immediately returned, and surrendered himself to take his trial at the next Assizes. The next Assizes came; but, unfortunately for the prisoner, it was a different Judge who presided; and still more unfortunately, Mr. Justice Gould, who happened to be the Judge, though of a very mild and indulgent disposition, had observed, or thought he had observed, that men who set out with stealing fowls, generally ended by committing the most atrocious crimes; and building a sort of system upon this observation, had made it a rule to punish this offence with very great severity; and he accordingly, to the astonishment of this unhappy man, sentenced him to be transported. While one was taking his departure for Botany Bay, the term of the other's imprisonment had expired; and what must have been the notions which that little Public, who witnessed and compared these two examples, formed of our system of Criminal Jurisprudence?"

SECTION V. THE BEGINNING OF POLITICAL REFORM

As far back as the seventeen-seventies Burke, Dunning, Fox, and others had sought to effect two revisions of the electoral system. One was a more equitable redistribution of seats that would give adequate representation to newly developed centres of population and remove the obvious misrepresentation entailed by pocket and rotten boroughs. The second was to extend the franchise to the now strong and insistent commercial middle class. These efforts had failed then, but the return of the Whigs to power in 1830 gave Grey and Russell, backed by radical pressure that indicated a more powerful and consolidated public opinion than England had known before, their opportunity. The bill Russell presented in 1831 was fought bitterly, and at one stage revolution was barely averted, but in 1832 William IV's threat to create new peers forced a reluctant House of Lords to accept the change.

27. RUSSELL BRINGS IN THE REFORM BILL[1]

It is due to the question, that I should state shortly the chief points of the general argument on which the reformers rest their claim. Looking at the question, then, as a question of right, the ancient Statutes of Edward 1st contain the germ and vital principle of our political constitution. The 25th of Edward 1st, ch. 6, declares, in the name of the King, that " for no business from henceforth we should take such manner of aids, tasks, nor prizes, but by the common assent of the realm, and for the common profit thereof, saving the ancient aids and prizes due and accustomed." The 34th Edward 1st, commonly called the Statute de Tallagio Concedendo, provides, " that no tallage or aid shall be taken or levied, by us or our heirs, in our realm, without the good will and assent of archbishops, bishops, earls, barons, knights, burgesses, and other freemen of the land." Although some historical doubts have been thrown upon the authenticity of this statute, its validity in point of law is asserted in the Petition of Rights, was allowed by the Judges in the case of Hampden, and is, in fact, the foundation of the Constitution, as it has existed since the days of the Stuarts. To revert again, for a moment, to ancient times; the consent of the commonalty of the land, thus declared necessary for the grant of any aid or tax, was collected from their Representatives consisting of two knights from each county, from each city two citizens, and from every borough two burgesses. . . .

Let us now look at the question as one of reason. Allow me to imagine, for a moment, a stranger from some distant country, who should arrive in England to examine our institutions. All the information he had collected would have told him that this country was singular for the degree which it had attained in wealth, in science, and in civilization. He would have learned, that in no country have the arts of life been carried further, no where the inventions of mechanical skill been rendered more conducive to the comfort and prosperity of mankind. He would have made himself acquainted with its fame in history, and above all, he would have been told, that the proudest boast of this celebrated country was its political freedom. If, in addition to this, he had heard that once in six years this country, so wise, so renowned, so free, chose its Representatives to sit in the great Council, where all the ministerial affairs were discussed and determined; he would not be a little curious to see the process by which so important and solemn an operation was effected. What then would be his surprise, if he were taken by his

---

[1] Hansard's *Parliamentary Debates.* March 1, 1831. 3rd Series, vol. 2, pp. 1062-1072, 1082 (condensed).

guide, whom he had asked to conduct him to one of the places of election, to a green mound and told, that this green mound sent two Members to Parliament — or, to be taken to a stone wall, with three niches in it, and told that these three niches sent two Members to Parliament — or, if he were shown a green park, with many signs of flourishing vegetable life, but none of human habitation, and told that this green park sent two Members to Parliament? But his surprise would increase to astonishment if he were carried into the North of England, where he would see large flourishing towns, full of trade and activity, containing vast magazines of wealth and manufactures, and were told that these places had no Representatives in the Assembly which was said to represent the people. Suppose him, after all, for I will not disguise any part of the case, suppose him to ask for a specimen of popular election, and to be carried, for that purpose, to Liverpool; his surprise would be turned into disgust at the gross venality and corruption which he would find to pervade the electors. After seeing all this, would he not wonder that a nation which had made such progress in every kind of knowledge, and which valued itself for its freedom, should permit so absurd and defective a system of representation any longer to prevail? . . .

We propose that every borough which in that year had less than 2,000 inhabitants, shall altogether lose the right of sending Members to Parliament. The effect will be, utterly to disfranchise sixty boroughs. But we do not stop here. As the hon. member for Boroughbridge (Sir C. Wetherell) would say, we go plus ultra. We find that there are forty-seven boroughs, of only 4,000 inhabitants, and these we shall deprive of the right of sending more than one Member to Parliament. We likewise intend that Weymouth, which at present sends four Members, shall, in future, only elect two. The abolition of sixty boroughs will occasion 119 vacancies, to which are to be added forty-seven for the boroughs allowed to send only one Member, and two of which Weymouth will be deprived, making in the whole 168 vacancies. Such is the extent to which Ministers propose to go in the way of disfranchisement. But, as I have already said, we do not mean to allow that the remaining boroughs should be in the hands of select corporations — that is to say, in the possession of a small number of persons, to the exclusion of the great body of the inhabitants, who have property and interest in the place represented. . . . we therefore propose that the right of voting shall be given to householders paying rates for, or occupying a house of, the yearly value of 10 *l.* and upwards. Whether he be the proprietor, or whether he only rent the house, the person rated will have the franchise upon certain conditions hereafter to be named. . . . I shall now proceed to the manner in which we propose to extend the franchise in counties. The Bill I wish to introduce will give all copyholders to the value of 10 *l.* a year . . . a right to vote for the return of Knights of the Shire. Sir R. Peel asked, across the Table, the amount of rent which was necessary? The right will depend upon a lease for twenty-one years, where the annual rent is not less than fifty pounds. . . . We propose, however, to fill up a certain number of the vacancies, but not the whole of them. We intend that seven large towns shall send two Members each, and that twenty other towns shall send one Member each. Some of the towns which are to send two Members each, are the following: Manchester and Salford, Birmingham & Aston, Leeds, Greenwich, Deptford, & Woolwich, Wolverhampton, Bilston, and Sedgeley, Sheffield, Sunderland and the Wearmouths. . . . Next we propose an addition to the Members for the larger counties—a species of Reform always recommended, and which, I believe, Lord Chatham was almost the first to advocate. Those counties contain a variety of interests, and form an admirable constituency; in some, as in Staffordshire, there is a large manufacturing population, better represented in this way than perhaps in any other; and as County Members have unquestionably the most excellent class of constituents, they form of themselves a most valuable class of Representatives. The Bill I shall beg leave to introduce will give two additional Members to each of twenty-seven counties, where the inhabitants exceed 150,000. . . . I now come to the result.

The number of Members now belonging to this House is	658
The number to be disfranchised	168
Number remaining	490
Additional Members for Scotland	5
Additional Members for Ireland	3
Additional Members for Wales	1
Additional Members for the metropolis	8
New Members for large towns in England	34
Additional Members for counties in England	55
Total additional Members	106
Members of the House not to be disfranchised	490
Total	596

The popular excitement over the Reform Bill was greatest when in 1831 the House of Lords rejected it after it had passed the Commons a second time and after a General Election had shown that the electors' intention was to give the Whigs a mandate to pass it. Rev. Sydney Smith (1771–1845) was famous alike as a clergyman, a politician, a man of letters, and a wit.

28. RESISTING THE TIDE[1]

I feel most deeply the event which has taken place, because, by putting the two Houses of Parliament in collision with each other, it will impede the

1 Sydney Smith, " Speech at Taunton," Oct. 12, 1831. *Works.* London, 1869, pp. 664–665.

public business, and diminish the public prosperity. I feel it as a churchman, because I cannot but blush to see so many dignitaries of the Church arrayed against the wishes and happiness of the people. I feel it more than all, because I believe it will sow the seeds of deadly hatred between the aristocracy and the great mass of the people. The loss of the bill I do not feel, and for the best of all possible reasons — because I have not the slightest idea that it *is* lost. I have no more doubt, before the expiration of the winter, that this bill will pass, than I have that the annual tax bills will pass, and greater certainty than this no man can have, for Franklin tells us, there are but two things certain in this world — death and taxes. As for the possibility of the House of Lords preventing ere long a reform of Parliament, I hold it to be the most absurd notion that ever entered into human imagination. I do not mean to be disrespectful, but the attempt of the Lords to stop the progress of reform, reminds me very forcibly of the great storm of Sidmouth, and of the conduct of the excellent Mrs. Partington on that occasion. In the winter of 1824, there set in a great flood upon that town — the tide rose to an incredible height — the waves rushed in upon the houses, and every thing was threatened with destruction. In the midst of this sublime and terrible storm, Dame Partington, who lived upon the beach, was seen at the door of her house with mop and pattens, trundling her mop, squeezing out the sea-water, and vigorously pushing away the Atlantic Ocean. The Atlantic was roused. Mrs. Partington's spirit was up; but I need not tell you that the contest was unequal. The Atlantic Ocean beat Mrs. Partington. She was excellent at a slop, or a puddle, but she should not have meddled with a tempest. Gentlemen, be at your ease — be quiet and steady. You will beat Mrs. Partington.

They tell you, gentlemen, in the debates by which we have been lately occupied, that the bill is not justified by experience. I do not think this true; but if it were true, nations are sometimes compelled to act without experience for their guide, and to trust to their own sagacity for the anticipation of consequences. The instances where this country has been compelled thus to act have been so eminently successful, that I see no cause for fear, even if we were acting in the manner imputed to us by our enemies. What precedents and what experience were there at the Reformation, when the country, with one unanimous effort, pushed out the Pope, and his grasping and ambitious clergy? — What experience, when at the Revolution we drove away our ancient race of kings, and chose another family, more congenial to our free principles? — And yet to those two events, contrary to experience, and unguided by precedents, we owe all our domestic happiness, and civil and religious freedom — and having got rid of corrupt priests and despotic kings, by our sense and our courage, are we now to be intimidated by the awful danger of extinguishing Boroughmongers, and shaking from our necks the ignominious yoke which their baseness has imposed upon it? Go on, they say, as you have done for these hundred years last past. I answer it is impossible: five hundred people now write and read, where one hundred wrote and read fifty years ago. The iniquities and enormities of the borough system are now known to the meanest of the people. You have a different sort of men to deal with — you must change because the beings whom you govern are changed. After all, and to be short, I must say that it has always appeared to me to be the most absolute nonsense that we cannot be a great, or a rich and happy nation, without suffering ourselves to be bought and sold every five years like a pack of negro slaves. I hope I am not a very rash man, but I would launch boldly into this experiment without any fear of consequences, and I believe there is not a man here present who would not cheerfully embark with me. As to the enemies of the bill, who pretend to be reformers, I know them, I believe, better than you do, and I earnestly caution you against them. You will have no more reform than they are compelled to grant — you will have no reform at all, if they can avoid it — you will be hurried into a war to turn your attention from reform.

SECTION VI. THE LIFE OF THE INDUSTRIAL WORKER

In 1832 Michael Sadler secured a parliamentary investigation of conditions in the textile factories and he sat as chairman on the committee. The evidence printed here is taken from the large body published in the committee's report and is representative rather than exceptional. It will be observed that the questions are frequently leading; this reflects Sadler's knowledge of the sort of information that the committee were to hear and his purpose of bringing it out. This report stands out as one of three great reports on the life of the industrial class — the two others being that of the Ashley Commission on the mines and Chadwick's report on sanitary problems. The immediate effect of the investigation and the report was the passage of the Act of 1833 limiting hours of employment for women and children in textile work.

29. EVIDENCE GIVEN BEFORE THE SADLER COMMITTEE[1]

Joshua Drake, called in; and Examined.

You say you would prefer moderate labour and lower wages; are you pretty comfortable upon your present wages? — I have no wages, but two days a week at present; but when I am working at some jobs we can make a little, and at others we do very poorly.

[1] *Parliamentary Papers.* 1831–1832, vol. XV, pp. 44, 95–97, 115, 195, 197, 339, 341–342.

When a child gets 3s. a week, does that go much towards its subsistence? — No, it will not keep it as it should do.

When they got 6s. or 7s. when they were pieceners, if they reduced the hours of labour, would they not get less? — They would get a halfpenny a day less, but I would rather have less wages and less work.

Do you receive any parish assistance? — No.

Why do you allow your children to go to work at those places where they are ill-treated or over-worked? — Necessity compels a man that has children to let them work.

Then you would not allow your children to go to those factories under the present system, if it was not from necessity? — No.

Supposing there was a law passed to limit the hours of labour to eight hours a day, or something of that sort, of course you are aware that a manufacturer could not afford to pay them the same wages? — No, I do not suppose that they would, but at the same time I would rather have it, and I believe that it would bring me into employ: and if I lost 5d. a day from my children's work, and I got half-a-crown myself, it would be better.

How would it get you into employ? — By finding more employment at the machines, and work being more regularly spread abroad, and divided amongst the people at large. One man is now regularly turned off into the street, whilst another man is running day and night.

You mean to say, that if the manufacturers were to limit the hours of labour, they would employ more people? — Yes.

Mr. Matthew Crabtree, called in; and Examined.

What age are you? — Twenty-two.

What is your occupation? — A blanket manufacturer.

Have you ever been employed in a factory? — Yes.

At what age did you first go to work in one? — Eight.

How long did you continue in that occupation? — Four years.

Will you state the hours of labour at the period when you first went to the factory, in ordinary times? — From 6 in the morning to 8 at night.

Fourteen hours? — Yes.

With what intervals for refreshment and rest? — An hour at noon.

When trade was brisk what were your hours? — From 5 in the morning to 9 in the evening.

Sixteen hours? — Yes.

With what intervals at dinner? — An hour.

How far did you live from the mill? — About two miles.

Was there any time allowed for you to get your breakfast in the mill? — No.

Did you take it before you left your home? — Generally.

During those long hours of labour could you be punctual; how did you awake? — I seldom did awake spontaneously; I was most generally awoke or lifted out of bed, sometimes asleep, by my parents.

Were you always in time? — No.

What was the consequence if you had been too late? — I was most commonly beaten.

Severely? — Very severely, I thought.

In those mills is chastisement towards the latter part of the day going on perpetually? — Perpetually.

So that you can hardly be in a mill without hearing constant crying? — Never an hour, I believe.

Do you think that if the overlooker were naturally a humane person it would be still found necessary for him to beat the children, in order to keep up their attention and vigilance at the termination of those extraordinary days of labour? — Yes; the machine turns off a regular quantity of cardings, and of course they must keep as regularly to their work the whole of the day; they must keep with the machine, and therefore however humane the slubber may be, as he must keep up with the machine or be found fault with, he spurs the children to keep up also by various means but that which he commonly resorts to is to strap them when they become drowsy.

At the time when you were beaten for not keeping up with your work, were you anxious to have done it if you possibly could? — Yes; the dread of being beaten if we could not keep up with our work was a sufficient impulse to keep us to it if we could.

When you got home at night after this labour, did you feel much fatigued? — Very much so.

Had you any time to be with your parents, and to receive instruction from them? — No.

What did you do? — All that we did when we got home was to get the little bit of supper that was provided for us and go to bed immediately. If the supper had not been ready directly, we should have gone to sleep while it was preparing.

Did you not, as a child, feel it a very grievous hardship to be roused so soon in the morning? — I did.

Were the rest of the children similarly circumstanced? — Yes, all of them; but they were not all of them so far from their work as I was.

And if you had been too late you were under the apprehension of being cruelly beaten? — I generally was beaten when I happened to be too late; and when I got up in the morning the apprehension of that was so great, that I used to run, and cry all the way as I went to the mill.

Mr. John Hall, called in; and Examined.

Will you describe to the Committee the position in which the children stand to piece in a worsted mill, as it may serve to explain the number and severity of those cases of distortion which occur? — At the top of the spindle there is a fly goes across, and the child takes hold of the fly by the ball of his left hand, and he throws the left shoulder up and the right knee inward; he has the thread to get with the right hand, and he has to stoop his head down to see what he is doing; they throw the right knee inward in that way, and all the children I have seen, that bend in the right knee. I knew a family, the whole of whom were bent outwards as a family complaint, and one of those boys was sent to a worsted-mill, and first he became straight in his right knee, and then he became crooked in it the other way.

Elizabeth Bentley, called in; and Examined.

What age are you? — Twenty-three.

Where do you live? — At Leeds.

What time did you begin to work at a factory? — When I was six years old.

At whose factory did you work? — Mr. Busk's.

What kind of mill is it? — Flax-mill.

What was your business in that mill? — I was a little doffer.

What were your hours of labour in that mill? — From 5 in the morning till 9 at night, when they were thronged.

For how long a time together have you worked that excessive length of time? — For about half a year.

What were your usual hours of labour when you were not so thronged? — From 6 in the morning till 7 at night.

What time was allowed for your meals? — Forty minutes at noon.

Had you any time to get your breakfast or drinking? — No, we got it as we could.

And when your work was bad, you had hardly any time to eat it at all? — No; we were obliged to leave it or take it home, and when we did not take it, the overlooker took it, and gave it to his pigs.

Do you consider doffing a laborious employment? — Yes.

Explain what it is you had to do? — When the frames are full, they have to stop the frames, and take the flyers off, and take the full bobbins off, and carry them to the roller; and then put empty ones on, and set the frame going again.

Does that keep you constantly on your feet? — Yes, there are so many frames, and they run so quick.

Your labour is very excessive? — Yes; you have not time for any thing.

Suppose you flagged a little, or were too late, what would they do? — Strap us.

Are they in the habit of strapping those who are last in doffing? — Yes.

Constantly? — Yes.

Girls as well as boys? — Yes.

Have you ever been strapped? — Yes.

Severely? — Yes.

Could you eat your food well in that factory? — No, indeed I had not much to eat, and the little I had I could not eat it, my appetite was so poor, and being covered with dust; and it was no use to take it home, I could not eat it, and the overlooker took it, and gave it to the pigs.

You are speaking of the breakfast? — Yes.

How far had you to go for dinner? — We could not go home to dinner.

Where did you dine? — In the mill.

Did you live far from the mill? — Yes, two miles.

Had you a clock? — No, we had not.

Supposing you had not been in time enough in the morning at these mills, what would have been the consequence? — We should have been quartered.

What do you mean by that? — If we were a quarter of an hour too late, they would take off half an hour; we only got a penny an hour, and they would take a halfpenny more.

The fine was much more considerable than the loss of time? — Yes.

Were you also beaten for being too late? — No, I was never beaten myself, I have seen the boys beaten for being too late.

Were you generally there in time? — Yes; my mother has been up at 4 o'clock in the morning, and at 2 o'clock in the morning; the colliers used to go to their work about 3 or 4 o'clock, and when she heard them stirring she has got up out of her warm bed, and gone out and asked them the time; and I have sometimes been at Hunslet Car at 2 o'clock in the morning, when it was streaming down with rain, and we have had to stay till the mill was opened.

Peter Smart, called in; and Examined.

You say you were locked up night and day? — Yes.

Do the children ever attempt to run away? — Very often.

Were they pursued and brought back again? — Yes, the overseer pursued them, and brought them back.

Did you ever attempt to run away? — Yes, I ran away twice.

And you were brought back? — Yes; and I was sent up to the master's loft, and thrashed with a whip for running away.

Were you bound to this man? — Yes, for six years.

By whom were you bound? — My mother got 15s. for the six years.

Do you know whether the children were, in point of fact, compelled to stop during the whole time for which they were engaged? — Yes, they were.

By law? — I cannot say by law; but they were compelled by the master; I never saw any law used there but the law of their own hands.

To what mill did you next go? — To Mr. Webster's, at Battus Den, within eleven miles of Dundee.

In what situation did you act there? — I acted as an overseer.

At 17 years of age? — Yes.

Did you inflict the same punishment that you yourself had experienced? — I went as an overseer; not as a slave, but as a slave-driver.

What were the hours of labour in that mill? — My master told me that I had to produce a certain quantity of yarn; the hours were at that time fourteen; I said that I was not able to produce the quantity of yarn that was required; I told him if he took the timepiece out of the mill I would produce that quantity, and after that time I found no difficulty in producing the quantity.

How long have you worked per day in order to produce the quantity your master required? — I have wrought nineteen hours.

Was this a water-mill? — Yes, water and steam both.

To what time have you worked? — I have seen the mill going till it was past 12 o'clock on the Saturday night.

So that the mill was still working on the Sabbath morning? — Yes.

Were the workmen paid by the piece, or by the day? — No, all had stated wages.

Did not that almost compel you to use great severity to the hands then under you? — Yes; I was compelled often to beat them, in order to get them to attend to their work, from their being over-wrought.

Were not the children exceedingly fatigued at that time? — Yes, exceedingly fatigued.

Were the children bound in the same way in that mill? — No; they were bound from one year's end to another, for twelve months.

Did you keep the hands locked up in the same way in that mill? — Yes, we locked up the mill; but we did not lock the bothy.

Did you find that the children were unable to pursue their labour properly to that extent? — Yes; they have been brought to that condition, that I have gone and fetched up the doctor to them, to see what was the matter with them, and to know whether they were able to rise or not able to rise; they were not at all able to rise; we have had great difficulty in getting them up.

When that was the case, how long have they been in bed, generally speaking? — Perhaps not above four or five hours in their beds.

William Cobbett (1763–1835), after a long career as a publicist, entered the Reformed Parliament in 1833 and at once took part in the debate on the bill Lord Althorpe had introduced as a result of the Sadler Committee's report.

30. MR. COBBETT'S DISCOVERY [1]

Mr. Cobbett said, a new discovery had been made in the House that night, which would doubtless excite great astonishment in many parts; at all events it would in Lancashire. It had formerly been said that the Navy was the great support of England; at another time that our maritime commerce was the great bulwark of the country; at another time that our colonies; and it had even been whispered that the Bank was; but now it was admitted, that our great stay and bulwark was to be found in three hundred thousand little girls, or rather in one eighth of that number. Yes; for it was asserted, that if these little girls worked two hours less per day, our manufacturing superiority would depart from us.

The physical deterioration of the manufacturing class in England is still noticeable more than a century after the height of the Industrial Revolution. A medical observer's description of what the work did to the worker follows.

31. THE PHYSICAL DETERIORATION OF THE TEXTILE WORKERS [2]

Any man who has stood at twelve o'clock at the single narrow door-way, which serves as the place of exit for the hands employed in the great cotton-mills, must acknowledge, that an uglier set of men and women, of boys and girls, taking them in the mass, it would be impossible to congregate in a smaller compass. Their complexion is sallow and pallid — with a peculiar flatness of feature, caused by the want of a proper quantity of adipose substance to cushion out the cheeks. Their stature low — the average height of four hundred men, measured at different times, and different places, being five feet six inches. Their limbs slender, and playing badly and ungracefully. A very general bowing of the legs. Great numbers of girls and women walking lamely or awkwardly, with raised chests and spinal flexures. Nearly all have flat feet, accompanied with a down-tread, differing very widely from the elasticity of action in the foot and ankle, attendant upon perfect formation. Hair thin and straight — many of the men having but

[1] Hansard's *Parliamentary Debates.* 3rd Series, vol. XIX. July 18, 1833, p. 912.
[2] P. Gaskell, *The Manufacturing Population of England.* London, 1833, pp. 161–162, 202–203.

little beard, and that in patches of a few hairs, much resembling its growth among the red men of America. A spiritless and dejected air, a sprawling and wide action of the legs, and an appearance, taken as a whole, giving the world but "little assurance of a man," or if so, "most sadly cheated of his fair proportions. . . ."

Factory labour is a species of work, in some respects singularly unfitted for children. Cooped up in a heated atmosphere, debarred the necessary exercise, remaining in one position for a series of hours, one set or system of muscles alone called into activity, it cannot be wondered at — that its effects are injurious to the physical growth of a child. Where the bony system is still imperfect, the vertical position it is compelled to retain, influences its direction; the spinal column bends beneath the weight of the head, bulges out laterally, or is dragged forward by the weight of the parts composing the chest, the pelvis yields beneath the opposing pressure downwards, and the resistance given by the thigh-bones; its capacity is lessened, sometimes more and sometimes less; the legs curve, and the whole body loses height, in consequence of this general yielding and bending of its parts.

John Fielden, although himself a Lancashire factory owner, was one of the staunchest fighters for protective legislation for the cotton worker. His difficulties are such as today in the Southern states of the United States are commonly urged by manufacturers.

32. A COTTON MANUFACTURER ON HOURS OF LABOR [1]

Here, then, is the "curse" of our factory-system: as improvements in machinery have gone on, the "avarice of masters" has prompted many to exact more labour from their hands than they were fitted by nature to perform, and those who have wished for the hours of labour to be less for all ages than the legislature would even yet sanction, have had no alternative but to conform more or less to the prevailing practice, or abandon the trade altogether. This has been the case with regard to myself and my partners. We have never worked more than *seventy-one* hours a week before Sir JOHN HOBHOUSE'S Act was passed. We then came down to *sixty-nine;* and, since Lord ALTHORP'S Act was passed, in 1833, we have reduced the time of adults to *sixty-seven and a half hours* a week, and that of children under thirteen years of age to *forty-eight* hours in the week, though to do this latter, has, I must admit, subjected us to much inconvenience, but the elder hands to more, inasmuch as the relief given to the child is in some measure imposed on the adult. But the overworking does not apply to children only; the adults are also overworked. The increased speed given to machinery

[1] John Fielden, M.P., *The Curse of the Factory System.* London, 1836, pp. 34–35.

within the last thirty years, has, in very many instances, doubled the labour of both.

Sending boys up chimneys to clean them was a common practice, and a dangerous and cruel one. Lord Ashley became the chief advocate of the use of chimney-sweeping machinery and of legislation to require its use. Even earlier, however, such a law had been proposed, but it met with strong opposition. In a debate on this subject in the House of Lords in 1819 the Earl of Lauderdale well represented a large body of conservative opinion.

33. OPPOSITION TO THE CHIMNEY SWEEPERS' REGULATION BILL [1]

Their lordships had lately heard complaints of the encouragement given to machinery, in preference to manual industry. Now, though he differed most completely from those who cherished the prejudice he alluded to — though he was convinced that the introduction of machinery had not only had the effect of enriching the proprietor, but also of enabling the workman to live better and cheaper than he otherwise could have done — yet there certainly was some difference to be drawn between their encouraging and enforcing the adoption of machinery, and especially when those persons who best understood its application in the way of trade were against its introduction at all. . . . If their lordships were determined to adopt such a course, they must introduce a code of moral legislation unknown to their ancestors, and quite unsuited to their habits and laws. The better way, in his judgment, would be to leave reforms of this kind entirely to the moral feeling of, perhaps, the most moral people, on the whole face of the earth.

When Sadler was defeated for reëlection in 1833 by Macaulay, his successor as leader in the campaign for shorter hours was Lord Ashley, later Earl of Shaftesbury, whose achievements in this field exceeded any other man's. More than a generation later the old Earl of Shaftesbury, speaking for a bill to relieve conditions of textile workers in India, commented on the great gains brought about by similar legislation in England.

34. THE BENEFIT OF THE FACTORY LEGISLATION [2]

The other is the old, the often-repeated, and as often-refuted, argument that the work is light. Light! Why, no doubt, much of it is light, if measured by the endurance of some three or four minutes. But what say you, my

[1] Hansard's *Parliamentary Debates*. March 8, 1819. New Series, vol. 39, p. 901.
[2] Hansard's *Parliamentary Debates*. Apr. 4, 1879. 3rd Series, vol. CCXLV, pp. 355–356.

Lords, to a continuity of toil, in a standing posture, in a poisonous atmosphere, during 13 hours, with 15 minutes of rest? Why, the stoutest man in England, were he made, in such a condition of things, to do nothing during the whole of that time but be erect on his feet and stick pins in a pincushion, would sink under the burden. What say you, then, of children — children of the tenderest years? Why, they become stunted, crippled, deformed, useless. I speak what I know — I state what I have seen. When I visited Bradford, in Yorkshire, in 1838, being desirous to see the condition of the children — for I knew that they were employed at very early ages in the worsted business. . . . I asked for a collection of cripples and deformities. In a short time more than 80 were gathered in a large courtyard. They were mere samples of the entire mass. I assert without exaggeration that no power of language could describe the varieties, and I may say, the cruelties, in all these degradations of the human form. They stood or squatted before me in all the shapes of the letters of the alphabet. This was the effect of prolonged toil on the tender frames of children at early ages. When I visited Bradford, under the limitation of hours some years afterwards, I called for a similar exhibition of cripples; but, God be praised! there was not one to be found in that vast city. Yet the work of these poor sufferers had been light, if measured by minutes, but terrific when measured by hours.

The second of the three great reports embodies the results of the investigation into the conditions of labor in the mines made by Lord Ashley's Mines Commission of 1842. The Mines Act of 1842 that resulted prohibited the employment in the mines of all women and of boys under thirteen.

35. TESTIMONY GATHERED BY ASHLEY'S MINES COMMISSION [1]

No. 116. — Sarah Gooder, aged 8 years.

I'm a trapper in the Gawber pit. It does not tire me, but I have to trap without a light and I'm scared. I go at four and sometimes half past three in the morning, and come out at five and half past. I never go to sleep. Sometimes I sing when I've light, but not in the dark; I dare not sing then. I don't like being in the pit. I am very sleepy when I go sometimes in the morning. I go to Sunday-schools and read Reading made Easy. She knows her letters and can read little words. They teach me to pray. She repeated the Lord's Prayer, not very perfectly, and ran on with the following addition: — "God bless my father and mother, and sister and brother, uncles and aunts and cousins, and everybody else, and God bless me and make me a

---

[1] *Parliamentary Papers.* 1842, vols. XV–XVII, Appendix I, pp. 252, 258, 439, 461; Appendix II, pp. 107, 122, 205.

good servant. Amen." I have heard tell of Jesus many a time. I don't know why he came on earth, I'm sure, and I don't know why he died, but he had stones for his head to rest on. I would like to be at school far better than in the pit.

No. 137. — *Thomas Wilson, Esq., of the Banks, Silkstone, owner of three collieries.*

. . . The employment of females of any age in and about the mines is most objectionable, and I should rejoice to see it put an end to; but in the present feeling of the colliers, no individual would succeed in stopping it in a neighbourhood where it prevailed, because the men would immediately go to those pits where their daughters would be employed. The only way effectually to put an end to this and other evils in the present colliery system is to elevate the minds of the men; and the only means to attain this is to combine sound moral and religious training and industrial habits with a system of intellectual culture much more perfect than can at present be obtained by them.

I object on general principles to government interference in the conduct of any trade, and I am satisfied that in mines it would be productive of the greatest injury and injustice. The art of mining is not so perfectly understood as to admit of the way in which a colliery shall be conducted being dictated by any person, however experienced, with such certainty as would warrant an interference with the management of private business. I should also most decidedly object to placing collieries under the present provisions of the Factory Act with respect to the education of children employed therein. First, because, if it is contended that coal-owners, as employers of children, are bound to attend to their education, this obligation extends equally to all other employers, and therefore it is unjust to single out one class only; secondly, because, if the legislature asserts a right to interfere to secure education, it is bound to make that interference general; and thirdly, because the mining population is in this neighbourhood so intermixed with other classes, and is in such small bodies in any one place, that it would be impossible to provide separate schools for them.

No. 14. — *Isabella Read, 12 years old, coal-bearer.*

Works on mother's account, as father has been dead two years. Mother bides at home, she is troubled with bad breath, and is sair weak in her body from early labour. I am wrought with sister and brother, it is very sore work; cannot say how many rakes or journeys I make from pit's bottom to wall face and back, thinks about 30 or 25 on the average; the distance varies from 100 to 250 fathom.

I carry about 1 cwt. and a quarter on my back; have to stoop much and creep through water, which is frequently up to the calves of my legs. When first down fell frequently asleep while waiting for coal from heat and fatigue.

I do not like the work, nor do the lassies, but they are made to like it. When the weather is warm there is difficulty in breathing, and frequently the lights go out.

No. 134. — *Isabel Wilson, 38 years old, coal putter.*

When women have children thick (fast) they are compelled to take them down early, I have been married 19 years and have had 10 bairns; seven are in life. When on Sir John's work was a carrier of coals, which caused me to miscarry five times from the strains, and was gai ill after each. Putting is no so oppressive; last child was born on Saturday morning, and I was at work on the Friday night.

Once met with an accident; a coal brake my cheek-bone, which kept me idle some weeks.

I have wrought below 30 years, and so has the guid man; he is getting touched in the breath now.

None of the children read, as the work is no regular. I did read once, but no able to attend to it now; when I go below lassie 10 years of age keeps house and makes the broth or stir-about.

Nine sleep in two bedsteads; there did not appear to be any beds, and the whole of the other furniture consisted of two chairs, three stools, a table, a kail-ot and a few broken basins and cups. Upon asking if the furniture was all they had, the guid wife said, furniture was of no use, as it was so troublesome to flit with.

No. 26. — *Patience Kershaw, aged 17. May 15.*

My father has been dead about a year; my mother is living and has ten children, five lads and five lasses; the oldest is about thirty, the youngest is four; three lasses go to mill; all the lads are colliers, two getters and three hurriers; one lives at home and does nothing; mother does nought but look after home.

All my sisters have been hurriers, but three went to the mill. Alice went because her legs swelled from hurrying in cold water when she was hot. I never went to day-school; I go to Sunday-school, but I cannot read or write; I go to pit at five o'clock in the morning and come out at five in the evening; I get my breakfast of porridge and milk first; I take my dinner with me, a cake, and eat it as I go; I do not stop or rest any time for the purpose; I get nothing else until I get home, and then have potatoes and meat, not every day meat. I hurry in the clothes I have now got on, trousers and ragged jacket; the bald place upon my head is made by thrusting the corves; my legs have never swelled, but sisters' did when they went to mill;

I hurry the corves a mile and more under ground and back; they weigh 300 cwt.; I hurry 11 a-day; I wear a belt and chain at the workings to get the corves out; the getters that I work for are naked except their caps; they pull off all their clothes; I see them at work when I go up; sometimes they beat me, if I am not quick enough, with their hands; they strike me upon my back; the boys take liberties with me sometimes they pull me about; I am the only girl in the pit; there are about 20 boys and 15 men; all the men are naked; I would rather work in mill than in coal-pit.

This girl is an ignorant, filthy, ragged, and deplorable-looking object, and such an one as the uncivilized natives of the prairies would be shocked to look upon.

No. 72. — Mary Barrett, aged 14. June 15.

I have worked down in pit five years; father is working in next pit; I have 12 brothers and sisters — all of them but one live at home; they weave, and wind, and hurry, and one is a counter, one of them can read, none of the rest can, or write; they never went to day-school, but three of them go to Sunday-school; I hurry for my brother John, and come down at seven o'clock about; I go up at six, sometimes seven; I do not like working in pit, but I am obliged to get a living; I work always without stockings, or shoes, or trousers; I wear nothing but my chemise; I have to go up to the headings with the men; they are all naked there; I am got well used to that, and don't care now much about it; I was afraid at first, and did not like it; they never behave rudely to me; I cannot read or write.

No. 7. — Benjamin Miller, Underlooker at Mr. Woolley's, near Staley Bridge, April 14, 1841.

How do you account for women being used so frequently as drawers in the coal-pits? — One reason is, that a girl of 20 will work for 2s. a-day or less, and a man of that age would want 3s. 6d.: It makes little difference to the coal-master, he pays the same whoever does the work; some would say he got his coal cheaper, but I am not of that opinion, the only difference is that the collier can spend 1s. to 1s. 6d. more at the alehouse, and very often the woman helps him to spend it.

Do women ever become coal-getters? — Not one woman in a hundred ever becomes a coal-getter, and that is one of the reasons the men prefer them.

Edwin Chadwick (1803–1890) had taken an active part in the reform of the Poor Law and in factory legislation before he became secretary to a commission investigating sanitary conditions and means of improving them. The Commission's report, of which the summary is given below, is the third of the great reports of this epoch.

36. *CHADWICK'S REPORT ON SANITARY CONDITIONS*[1]

After as careful an examination of the evidence collected as I have been enabled to make, I beg leave to recapitulate the chief conclusions which that evidence appears to me to establish.

First, as to the extent and operation of the evils which are the subject of the inquiry: —

That the various forms of epidemic, endemic, and other disease caused, or aggravated, or propagated chiefly amongst the labouring classes by atmospheric impurities produced by decomposing animal and vegetable substances, by damp and filth, and close and overcrowded dwellings prevail amongst the population in every part of the kingdom, whether dwelling in separate houses, in rural villages, in small towns, in the larger towns — as they have been found to prevail in the lowest districts of the metropolis.

That such disease, wherever its attacks are frequent, is always found in connexion with the physical circumstances above specified, and that where those circumstances are removed by drainage, proper cleansing, better ventilation, and other means of diminishing atmospheric impurity, the frequency and intensity of such disease is abated; and where the removal of the noxious agencies appears to be complete, such disease almost entirely disappears.

That high prosperity in respect to employment and wages, and various and abundant food, have afforded to the labouring classes no exemptions from attacks of epidemic disease, which have been as frequent and as fatal in periods of commercial and manufacturing prosperity as in any others.

That the formation of all habits of cleanliness is obstructed by defective supplies of water.

That the annual loss of life from filth and bad ventilation are greater than the loss from death or wounds in any wars in which the country has been engaged in modern times.

That of the 43,000 cases of widowhood, and 112,000 cases of destitute orphanage relieved from the poor's rates in England and Wales alone, it appears that the greatest proportion of deaths of the heads of families occurred from the above specified and other removable causes; that their ages were under 45 years; that is to say, 13 years below the natural probabilities of life as shown by the experience of the whole population of Sweden.

That the public loss from the premature deaths of the heads of families is greater than can be represented by any enumeration of the pecuniary burdens consequent upon their sickness and death.

[1] *Report . . . from the Poor Law Commissioners on an Inquiry into the Sanitary Condition of the Labouring Population of Great Britain.* London, 1842, pp. 369–372.

That, measuring the loss of working ability amongst large classes by the instances of gain, even from incomplete arrangements for the removal of noxious influences from places of work or from abodes, that this loss cannot be less than eight or ten years.

That the ravages of epidemics and other diseases do not diminish but tend to increase the pressure of population.

That in the districts where the mortality is the greatest the births are not only sufficient to replace the numbers removed by death, but to add to the population.

That the younger population, bred up under noxious physical agencies, is inferior in physical organization and general health to a population preserved from the presence of such agencies.

That the population so exposed is less susceptible of moral influences, and the effects of education are more transient than with a healthy population.

That these adverse circumstances tend to produce an adult population short-lived, improvident, reckless, and intemperate, and with habitual avidity for sensual gratifications.

That these habits lead to the abandonment of all the conveniences and decencies of life, and especially lead to the overcrowding of their homes, which is destructive to the morality as well as the health of large classes of both sexes.

That defective town cleansing fosters habits of the most abject degradation and tends to the demoralization of large numbers of human beings, who subsist by means of what they find amidst the noxious filth accumulated in neglected streets and bye-places.

That the expenses of local public works are in general unequally and unfairly assessed, oppressively and uneconomically collected, by separate collections, wastefully expended in separate and inefficient operations by unskilled and practically irresponsible officers.

That the existing law for the protection of the public health and the constititional machinery for reclaiming its execution, such as the Courts Leet, have fallen into desuetude, and are in the state indicated by the prevalence of the evils they were intended to prevent.

Secondly, As to the means by which the present sanitary condition of the labouring classes may be improved: —

The primary and most important measures, and at the same time the most practicable, and within the recognized province of public administration, are drainage, the removal of all refuse of habitations, streets, and roads, and the improvement of the supplies of water.

That the chief obstacles to the immediate removal of decomposing refuse of towns and habitations have been the expense and annoyance of the hand labour and cartage requisite for the purpose.

That this expense may be reduced to one-twentieth or to one-thirtieth, or rendered inconsiderable, by the use of water and self-acting means of removal by improved and cheaper sewers and drains.

That refuse when thus held in suspension in water may be most cheaply and innoxiously conveyed to any distance out of towns, and also in the best form for productive use, and that the loss and injury by the pollution of natural streams may be avoided.

That for all these purposes, as well as for domestic use, better supplies of water are absolutely necessary.

That for successful and economical drainage the adoption of geological areas as the basis of operations is requisite.

That appropriate scientific arrangements for public drainage would afford important facilities for private land-drainage, which is important for the health as well as sustenance of the labouring classes.

That the expense of public drainage, of supplies of water laid on in houses, and of means of improved cleansing would be a pecuniary gain, by diminishing the existing charges attendant on sickness and premature mortality.

That for the protection of the labouring classes and of the ratepayers against inefficiency and waste in all new structural arrangements for the protection of the public health, and to ensure public confidence that the expenditure will be beneficial, securities should be taken that all new local public works are devised and conducted by responsible officers qualified by the possession of the science and skill of civil engineers.

That the oppressiveness and injustice of levies for the whole immediate outlay on such works upon persons who have only short interests in the benefits may be avoided by care in spreading the expense over periods coincident with the benefits.

That by appropriate arrangements, 10 or 15 per cent. on the ordinary outlay for drainage might be saved, which on an estimate of the expense of the necessary structural alterations of one-third only of the existing tenements would be a saving of one million and a half sterling, besides the reduction of the future expenses of management.

That for the prevention of the disease occasioned by defective ventilation and other causes of impurity in places of work and other places where large numbers are assembled, and for the general promotion of the means necessary to prevent disease, that it would be good economy to appoint a district medical officer independent of private practice, and with the securities of special qualifications and responsibilities to initiate sanitary measures and reclaim the execution of the law.

That by the combinations of all these arrangements, it is probable that the full ensurable period of life indicated by the Swedish tables; that is, an increase of 13 years at least, may be extended to the whole of the labouring classes.

That the attainment of these and the other collateral advantages of reducing existing charges and expenditure are within the power of the legislature, and are dependent mainly on the securities taken for the application of practical science, skill, and economy in the direction of local public works.

And that the removal of noxious physical circumstances, and the promotion of civic, household, and personal cleanliness, are necessary to the improvement of the moral condition of the population; for that sound morality and refinement in manners and health are not long found co-existent with filthy habits amongst any class of the communtiy.

SECTION VII. THE REPEAL OF THE CORN LAWS

The Corn Laws placed import duties on wheat in order to protect the English landowner. First passed in 1815, they were modified in various ways, with sliding scales that raised the duty when prices were low and diminished the duties when prices rose. The movement to repeal the Corn Laws was sponsored by a group of Liberals, many of whom, as manufacturers, desired to reduce food prices since that would increase the purchasing power of the wages they paid. Richard Cobden and John Bright did much to found the Anti-Corn Law League, which directed the propaganda, but it was Charles Villiers (1802–1898) who led the parliamentary battle for repeal. Finally Sir Robert Peel was convinced of the necessity of abolishing the Corn Laws and they were repealed in 1846.

37. VILLIERS'S ARGUMENT FOR CORN LAW REPEAL[1]

The ground on which the defence of the Corn Laws was first rested was certainly not without some plausibility before it was tested by experience: namely, that it was dangerous for this country to be dependent on other countries for its supply of food, and that, consequently, our landowners ought to be protected from foreign competition. This was the plea originally set forth for the enactment of the Corn Laws: a plea that at the time all thinking men derided, and that has since become contemptible by the practical demonstration of its utter worthlessness. It assumed that we might safely depend upon foreigners for the means of revenue, for the material of our manufactures, and, hence, for the employment of millions of our people whereby they get bread, but that it would be nothing short of imperilling our future safety to depend upon them for the bread itself.

[1] Speech in House of Commons. June 22, 1844. *The Free Trade Speeches of the Right Hon. Charles Pelham Villiers, M.P.* London, 1884, pp. 371–373, 378–381 (much condensed).

Returns laid before this House during the last twenty years prove that the expectation of being independent of supplies of food from abroad, if ever honestly entertained, has been completely disappointed. Since the Laws were passed we have been largely and constantly dependent on other countries for supplies of corn; this dependence is annually increasing; and during the last five years we have fallen short in our home supply to an amount equal to 17,000,000 quarters. Moreover, the corn that we have imported has not been grown for our market, but for the consumption of other people, and consequently it has been obtained under peculiar disadvantage to us. During the thirteen years of the duration of the Corn Law passed in 1828 no less than 30,000,000 quarters of grain actually necessary for the consumption of the people of this country were imported from foreign countries. . . .

When the only profit or gain connected with the Laws has been traced to the owners of the land, the proprietors in Parliament have repudiated the charge; they have denied that they had any interest in the Laws, and declared the single object of such Laws to be the interest of the occupier and the labourer, whose existence and well-being, as they assert, depend on their continuance. . . . Everybody is now familiar with the fact that the distress of no other class had been more prominently and more frequently obtruded upon the public than that of the farmers. In fact, it is now a matter of notoriety that they have derived no benefit whatever from the Corn Laws. Duped and deceived by them, many a farmer hampered with debt, now finds himself pledged to a rent higher than he could ever afford to pay, and openly and bitterly complains that he holds his land under circumstances the most disadvantageous for its proper cultivation. . . .

The same has occurred with regard to all the exemptions that have been procured for the farmer in the payment of taxes; there is not a landlord in the House who does not know that they only contribute to swell the rent given for the land. The members of this House dare not call a single farmer before them and ask him whether what they have done in his behalf, as they say, has been at all to his benefit. It is the evidence of one of the most competent among agriculturists that whatever relief has been procured for the farmer through Parliament has been for the advantage of landowners alone.

The assertion that these Laws are for the benefit of the labourer is equally absurd and unfounded. No one would now be bold enough to say that it is for the advantage of the labourer that the price of food should be kept up; and that high prices ensure high wages. There is a volume in this House, produced by the labours of a Commission of the Crown, that effectually disproves that assertion. In the face of that volume, never again can the advantage of the labourer be made the excuse of the Corn Laws. The evidence taken by the Commission is an authority that cannot be disputed; and it proves that no one could be lower in the scale of civilization than the agricultural labourer. Country gentlemen may now study it by the light of incendiary fires in their own neighbourhoods. Scarcely a day passes that the papers are not full of accounts of what are called the crimes of the labouring classes. . . .

Another argument to show the necessity of great caution in any change is drawn from the numerical importance of the agricultural classes in the scale of society. An analysis of the late Census recently published gives us information on this matter. It appears from these calculations that the agricultural classes about which so much has been written, and which are said to constitute seven-ninths of the whole population of the country, are only 7 per cent., and a little more, of our population. With what show of right or justice, then, can any one claim to exclude the whole mass of the people of this country from their natural right to buy their food as abundantly and as cheaply as possible, out of regard to the supposed exclusive interests of such a fraction of the community? No right can be allowed to any portion of the public to impose taxes or restrictions on the rest; and I contend that those who would continue the Corn Laws are bound to prove that they are the means of giving the most abundant supply of food to the people at the cheapest possible rate. . . .

If they care to know what would follow from Free Trade, let them ascertain what follows a good harvest: whether wages fall; whether the Home Trade is bad; whether labour is displaced. And if they wish to know what would be the effect of restricting the supply of food to the growth of this island, let them consider what they expect would follow from confining the supply of this town or the county in which it stands to the growth of its spare soil. Apply the system of the Sliding Scale to London, and attempt to make the squares, or Grosvenor Square alone, supply corn for the whole town; and what would be the effect? If the people increased and the food did not increase in proportion, would not the price of food rise and competition for food increase? Would not wages be reduced and the people be compelled to work harder for less money and less food? And would it not be said of those who refused to admit corn from without for the purpose of keeping up the rents of the square, that they were guilty of the grossest selfishness and the grossest injustice? And what is the difference, whether the principle is applied to a single town or to a whole kingdom?

The population of the country is increasing rapidly; the produce of our own soil, it is notorious, is not keeping pace with that increase; and yet we refuse to admit an adequate supply from other countries. Let in food from abroad, and customers enough would be found for it, otherwise it would not come in.

The battle over Corn Law Repeal was fought all over England. The following is from the report of a speech made in a rural district where the object was to point out inconsistencies in the repealers' arguments.

38. A DEFENCE OF THE CORN LAWS [1]

Mr. Hume, a well-known repealer, says, " If the manufacturer pays a higher price for a given quantity of labour, he is at once met by the competition of those who can get it done at a less price; *and why* at a less? *Because* the men he employs can purchase the necessaries of life at a *lower rate.* If the English *manufacturer is obliged to pay his men at a rate sufficient to meet the price of corn,* (say at 55s. the quarter) he is met by the foreign manufacturer, who pays only at a price corresponding to 35s. per quarter.

. . . .

" It was the object of the corn-laws not to insure certainty of price, but to protect the farmer against the competition of foreign producers; that, although they could not prevent fluctuation and home risk, yet they could and would protect him against foreigners, until the price rose to the sum mentioned in the acts; and thereby, in the words of the Act of Charles II, ' give encouragement for the laying out of cost and labour on land, then lying, in a manner, waste.' But this agricultural distress being admitted, let us ask our opponents what remedy they would propose? You have heard the laboured details of Mr. Moore and Mr. Bright upon agricultural distress. They say that they are the friends of you, the tenant farmers, and finding you were ill, have visited this county, with a view to relieve you. They say your pulsation is bad, accompanied with much nervous debility, — they find your markets low, and they tell you your prospect is worse, — and what do these doctors prescribe? Like Dr. Sangrado, in ' Gil Blas,' — more bleeding! " (Hear, hear, and laughter.)

Mr. MOORE — We want to bleed the landlords of their rents!

Mr. DAY — No, no; Mr. Cobden told the landlords that he wished them to have their rents and that they would get as *good rents without the corn-law as with it!*

Mr. MOORE — Where is your authority? (*Uproar*)

Mr. DAY — Mr. Cobden's speech in the House of Commons on the 15th May last, printed by the league, p. 4. I have it here if you want it. Let us test these friends of the tenant-farmers. Mr. Cobden tells landlords, that, in case of a free trade, they are to have the same rents. Mr. Bright and Mr. Moore assure the labourers that they also are to have *the same wages.* The League

[1] *The Speech of Mr. George Game Day, at Huntingdon, June 17, 1843.* 8th Ed. London, 1843, pp. 14, 32–33.

states . . . that it does not signify to you, the tenant-farmers *what the nominal price of your produce is;* and then these friends of yours propose to open the ports, and have a free trade; and you, *with rent and labour the same,* and no matter what the price of your produce is, are to compete with foreigners! So these dear friends advise you! They call you independent, and propose to keep you so, by letting in the best wheat from Dantzic, free from duty, and the freight of which at this hour, including everything, is not more than 3s. 3d. a quarter.

SECTION VIII. EDUCATION

Elementary education had long been left in the hands of two rival societies representing respectively the Church of England and the Dissenters. Mutual jealousy did much to impede the spread of popular education. The State's first appropriation was made in 1833, and in 1839 more extensive proposals were made and among them there appeared the idea of schools unconnected with a religious body. In the course of the debate in the House of Lords two bishops expressed their views on the education of the masses.

39. TWO BISHOPS OPPOSE AN EDUCATION BILL[1]

Bishop of Exeter.

Speaking as they now were, mainly of the education of the poorer classes of her Majesty's subjects, he must say that he saw very little need of secular education that ought not to be combined with religion. He did not ask, (God forbid that he should) that the poor man should not be permitted to make all the acquirements in science which it should please God to enable him to make; but looking to the poor as a class, they could not expect that those who were consigned by Providence to the laborious occupations of life, should be able largely to cultivate their intellect. If they could concentrate their views upon one great subject — above all, if they could make the Bible the corner-stone of all their learning — if they could learn history, in order to illustrate the Bible — if they could learn the various sciences to the extent to which acquaintance with them is ordinarily carried by persons of that class, in order to illustrate the Bible — he believed a larger portion of secular education would be acquired by them, than if they were cast upon the sciences, without anything scriptural and sacred whereupon to found their studies; that, in short, by making the Bible the foundation of all, and applying secular science to illustrate it, they would learn a larger amount of

[1] Hansard's *Parliamentary Debates.* July 5, 1839. 3rd Series, vol. 48, pp. 1276; 1295–1303 (condensed).

science, than if trained in those schools where nothing but science was taught. *Bishop of London*.

. . . Their avowed object is, to induce, if possible, the Government of this country to interpose its authority for the purpose of separating religious and secular education; to withdraw the superintendance of it from the Church; to subvert our national system; and to substitute for it one exclusively secular. It is openly declared by one of the chief advocates of their plans, that the absolute and entire exclusion of the Bible from the secular school, is a sine qua non to the establishment of any National system of Education.

. . . There is another Society, formed of the professed enemies of the Church, calling itself " The Society for promoting Religious Equality," which has lately passed certain resolutions, and this is one of them:

" That to compel any one to contribute to the support of religious rites of which he disapproves, or to the ministers of a church from which he conscientiously dissents, is manifestly unjust, and at variance with the spirit and principles of Christianity: that State establishments, by which any particular Church, or sect, is selected as the object of political favour and patronage, and its clergy are invested with exclusive rights and secular preeminence, involve a violation of equity towards other denominations, and are the occasion of inevitable social discord."

All this is very well; it is a plain declaration of hostility to the Church, which is no more than was to be expected from persons who are at enmity with all religious establishments.

. . . Now, when we proceed to inquire a little more particularly into the grounds of this charge, we find, that the badness of our education consists principally in this, that we devote too much time, as they think, to religious instruction, to the study and explanation of the Bible, and too little to the objects of instructing the children of the poor in those branches of secular knowledge, and those mechanical arts, which may be useful to them in afterlife. My Lords, we are content to bear this imputation. We acknowledge that we hold the great object of education to be, the training up of immortal beings, admitted by baptism into a special relation to their Maker, to a meetness for fulfilling the duties of that relation. We hold it to be more beneficial to them, and more incumbent upon us, to give them a knowledge of God and of themselves, of their duties and their destiny; to form their habits of thought and action by the rules of truth, and holiness, and charity, than to imbue them very deeply (and yet we would imbue them as deeply as a due attention to the more important object may permit) with that Secular knowledge which they will be sure to acquire for themselves, if they find it to be serviceable in promoting their advancement in life, and securing to them the world's advantages; a knowledge which, if not sanctified and guided, in its use and application, by the restraints and motives of Christianity, may be, nay, rather, my Lords, will be a curse to them rather than a blessing. Yes, my Lords, I use the words deliberately and advisedly, a curse rather than a blessing. For let me not be told, that the acquisition of knowledge, of whatever kind, cannot under any circumstances be otherwise than beneficial to man as a reasonable being, If, my Lords, we bear in mind that man is not only a reasonable being, but that he is therefore a moral and accountable agent, we shall see, that a broad ground is laid for restricting and qualifying that position. That the acquisition of knowledge, commonly so called; that knowledge, which sharpens the wit of man, exercises his faculties, and stores his memory, while it leaves untouched the conscience and the heart, that this does not of necessity benefit the person who acquires it, we learn by the testimony of fact. That education, unsanctified by religion, is evil in its tendencies, and injurious in its results, is the conclusion of sound reason, confirmed by experience. What, my Lords, is the state of the case in France at the present moment? What are the fruits of that system, which takes present utility, and not religious duty, for its mainspring and regulating principle? Do we see anything there, which should encourage us to give that prominence and value to mere secular education, which are given it by the supporters of the Central Society? Many of your Lordships are probably acquainted with the Educational Statistics of M. Guerry, and with the extraordinary results of his very careful and minute inquiries; results which may well shake, if they do not overthrow, the confidence of those who look upon education, as they understand the term, as the grand panacea, of all the evils moral and political, by which the country is afflicted. His words are these:

"While crimes against the person are most frequent in Corsica, the provinces of the South-East, and Alsace, where the people are well instructed, there are the fewest of those crimes in Berri, Limousin, and Brittany, where the people are the most ignorant. And as for crimes against property, it is almost invariably those departments that are best informed which are the most criminal — a fact, which, if the tables be not altogether wrong, must show this to be certain, that if instruction do not increase crime, which may be a matter of dispute, there is no reason to believe that it diminishes it."

It is strange, that the writer, who is an acute and sagacious person, should wholly overlook the cause of this surprising anomaly. It is at least strange that any Christian should overlook it. The cause is neither more nor less than this, that the education, of which he speaks, is a purely secular education, wholly untinctured with religion.

. . . A good education, my Lords, that is, a religious education, administered by the teachers of religion, is by far the cheapest, as well as the most effective measure of police which any Government can adopt.

The sending out of inspectors revealed the thinness of educational pro-
visions existing in England near the middle of the century.

40. ELEMENTARY SCHOOLS IN ENGLAND IN 1845 [1]

General Summary

In the preceding report of the inspection of 176 schools in the midland districts, I have stated as the result of that inspection —

That 1 in 39 of the population for whose benefit the schools were provided avail themselves of them.

That the school-rooms are a little more than one-half full.

That by the system adopted in these schools the intervention of the master in the instruction of any individual child is only occasional and incidental.

That the children are actually under the instruction of other children whose average age does not exceed 11 years. . . .

That, little independent exercise of intelligence in the process of instruction being to be expected from such youthful teachers, to adapt it to their use, it is rendered to the utmost practicable degree mechanical.

That out of the 11,782 children contained in the schools inspected in the midland district, the knowledge of 5805 does not extend beyond the letters of the alphabet and monosyllables, and that 2026 only can read the Scriptures with ease and correctness being 1 in every 5, or, more nearly, 5 in 27.

That, on a probable calculation, out of every 100 children who leave these schools annually, 75 are unable to read the Word of God with ease and correctness, and 24 of these know only the letters of the alphabet and monosyllables; that 50 of them have received no instruction whatever in penmanship and 80 have not advanced in arithmetic as far as the compound rules.

That the employment of the Holy Scriptures in teaching children to read, either in the use of the sacred volume itself or under the form of extracts, is almost universal.

That there is exceedingly needed a system of elementary schoolbooks, and particularly of Readers, adapted to the purposes of elementary education; but that such books would not be generally used in national schools unless they could be supplied at a cost greatly less than that at which such books are now sold.

That in teaching children to read very little attention is paid to their instruction in the subject matter of that which is read. . . .

[1] From report of Rev. Henry Moseley, Midlands Inspector of Education. *Accounts and Papers.* 1845, vol. 35, pp. 251, 252.

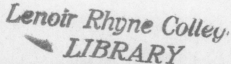

That the labouring classes appreciate a really good education, and are prepared to make sacrifices to obtain it for their children.

SECTION IX. EARLY TRADE UNIONISM

Through the initiative of William Wilberforce an act was passed in 1799 prohibiting any combination of workers for the purpose of securing better wages. A single magistrate could convict. In 1800 the law was amended to require the concurrence of two magistrates, but the trade union was illegal until 1824 when, after hearings before a committee of Parliament, the Combination Acts were repealed. Francis Place (1771–1854), a retired journeyman tailor, was the man whose efforts secured this result; Joseph Hume was the member of the House of Commons who assisted him. In 1825, however, William Huskisson was able to secure a new committee and its hearings are described below. An act of 1825 legalized trade unions but denied them the right to strike.

41. THE TRADE UNIONS' STRUGGLE FOR EXISTENCE[1]

Mr. Huskisson and Mr. Peel had concerted the whole matter. They had adopted the suggestions of the shipbuilders and shipowners, and had consented to prepare a bill on the basis of their suggestions. They had looked too lightly at the matter, or they would not have undertaken it; they undervalued the enemy they had to encounter, and thought to walk over the field without a battle. It was to be a Committee more of form than of business, and was to sit but a very few days. Mr. Huskisson named his Committee from amongst those whom he knew to be inimical to the men, and such as were sure to follow his and Mr. Peel's views. Mr. Hume could not, however, be excluded; there would have been a demand in the House that he should be placed on the Committee; and it was therefore advisable to put him on at once. In any other case the old Committee would have been revived, but that Committee had acted fairly, had made its purpose generally known, had examined every one who offered to be examined with care and the utmost impartiality. It was not therefore calculated for a special purpose, and the usual mode was impudently departed from. Neither Mr. Hume nor I expected we should be able to beat such a Committee as we did.

. . . .

The Committee soon found that it was not quite so easy to proceed in the way proposed as they had anticipated. They were not a little surprised

[1] Ms. Papers of Francis Place. Quoted in Graham Wallas, *Life of Francis Place*. 3rd Ed., N. Y., Alfred A. Knopf, 1919, pp. 226–227, 230–234, 239–240.

at finding the passage to the committee-room blocked up by men demanding to be examined, and still more so at finding that some of them sent in offers to rebut the evidence which had been given on the preceding day. Every accusation was denied almost as regularly as it was made, and evidence to the contrary was offered, not only by notes to the chairman, but by letters to individual members, and this was constantly repeated.

In the Committee of 1824 every case was made as public as possible. In this Committee great pains were taken that nothing which passed in the Committee should be known, but they were all pains to no purpose. I knew everything that passed, and always had the men ready to reply. Mr. Hume, with unexampled courage and perseverance, supported the claims of the men to be heard. Petitions to be heard were sent to the House and referred to the Committee; they who petitioned attended at the committee-room and demanded a hearing. The members could hardly get to their room or from it, so completely was the passage blocked by the men, and so well had they been instructed not readily to make way for the members. This produced considerable effect on the members of the Committee, and attracted the attention of a great many members of the House, who in consequence were apprised of the course the Committee had chosen to adopt.

Mr. Hume insisted upon it, that his bill had produced great and extensive good, and he offered the proofs by the mouths of many witnesses who were anxiously waiting outside the committee-room to be examined, they having come from various parts of the United Kingdom for the very purpose of being examined. The Committee found themselves in a dilemma, and at length consented to examine some men. This was a consequence of their fears. The injustice they contemplated was so very gross they could not encounter the exposure with which they were threatened as well in the public papers as in the House. It was this, and no love of justice, which at length operated on them. Still they did not give up their intention, but endeavoured to limit the examination to those only who were accused by name, and to this they adhered so pertinaciously as to exclude a large number of those they ought to have examined. They wholly excluded the deputies from Birmingham, Sheffield, and several other places, who were in London, and so fully satisfied was I of the impossibility of inducing them to examine others that I prevented many places sending deputies.

The working people of Dublin and Glasgow were accused of serious crimes. These accusations were recorded by the Committee, and intended to be laid before the House. Still the Committee would hear none of the persons whom it was desirable should have been sent from these places to rebut the accusations. Men's names were used as having in Glasgow abetted murder; and yet, notwithstanding the very men who had been so named wrote to Mr. Hume and to the chairman of the Committee requesting to be examined, the Committee persisted in refusing to hear them. The men said, "We are men of good character, have done no wrong to any one, are at work in the same shops and factories in which we have worked for years, and have nothing objected to us by our employers; we demand the opportunity to clear ourselves from the imputation." But no, the Committee would not hear them; it would record the accusation, add the weight of its authority to it, and leave the accused without a defence. Mr. Huskisson was base enough to call the men thus accused, and thus refused a hearing, "acquitted felons"; and yet they were unacquitted, for they had been accused only before the Committee, who had not condescended to do either them or themselves the justice of trying them at the bar of the Committee.

Notwithstanding this, no one was refused a hearing who came with a complaint against the workmen; no one was refused payment for his time and travelling expenses who gave evidence against the men, while many of the men who had been weeks in attendance, and were at length forced on the notice of the Committee and were examined by them, were refused any remuneration whatsoever. It was attempted to avoid payment by a mean shuffle. It was said the men were not summoned by the Committee, but it was shown that some of those who had received the highest rate of pay, and were men of property who did not need to be reimbursed, were not summoned; and a direct refusal to give anything to the men was the consequence. Some, however, were paid.

My time was wholly occupied from the day Mr. Huskisson made his speech till some time after the passing of the Act. I examined a vast number of persons; made digests and briefs for Mr. Hume; wrote petitions to the House and to the Committee; many letters to Mr. Wallace, the chairman; and many to other persons, all as the agent of the men, and for their adoption. No one thing that could be done was omitted, every possible advantage was taken of even the most minute circumstance, and it was by these and Mr. Hume's extraordinary exertions that the intentions of Mr. Huskisson and Mr. Peel were at length so completely defeated, and the bill called Mr. Wallace's bill was passed.

The Committee as it proceeded became exceedingly indignant. Its anger when it discovered that I obtained correct accounts of its proceedings was violent and absurd. It could not bear that I should be thus informed; that their measures should be anticipated in letters and petitions; and that, in spite of all their exertions and the advantages they possessed, they should every day be losing ground. They threatened to punish me for my temerity. I was to be sent for, to be questioned, to be reported to the House, to be committed to Newgate, for daring to interfere and tampering with their witnesses.

These were the notions these wise men entertained of justice. The masters might consult when and where they pleased; give what instructions they pleased; have the ears of members of the Committee, and go in and out of the committee-room while the Committee was sitting as often as they pleased. But the workmen were to have no one to assist them; no one was to instruct them, notwithstanding they were the party who most needed instruction. They, such as the Committee chose, were to go before a body of their superiors — great squires and members of Parliament — be cross-questioned, bullied, and intimidated, and no one was either to advise or assist them. So they concluded; so I resolved that it should not be. It happened, however, that every one of the men who entered the committee-room in awe of the great men, came out of it with feelings of contempt for those who had treated them, as they invariably did, with contumely and insult, and while they did so, as invariably exposed their ignorance and their malice to the observation of the men; and this, too, to such an extent as to take away all respect and put the men at perfect ease while under an examination which many had previously looked to with considerable dread.

. . . .

The laws against combinations were inimical to the working people in many respects. They induced them to break and disregard the laws. They made them suspect the intentions of every man who tendered his services. They made them hate their employers with a rancour which nothing else could have produced. And they made them hate those of their own class who refused to join them, to such an extent as cordially to seek to do them mischief. The amendment on the repeal of the laws was immediate, and has been increasing ever since. The people have come better together, have now (1829) incomparably more confidence in the good intentions of others to serve them than they ever had before, and are much better disposed to serve themselves. None but good results can follow. It is true the old leaven has not yet worn out. Power-looms have been broken since the repeal of the Combination Laws, and now the Spitalfields weavers, in their state of misery, have destroyed a good deal of silk in the looms. Still the extent of the mischief has been comparatively small as compared with former times, and a few years will probably put an end to everything of the kind.

The tumults caused by combinations of workmen on account of wages have generally ceased. There are now none of those outrageous proceedings which were formerly perpetual ; and although it is very probable that there will be occasional ebullitions, it is not at all likely that the conduct so very generally pursued up to the repeal of the Combination Laws will ever again be resumed.

The system of " iron laws " laid down by the " classical " economists was generally accepted in the first half of the nineteenth century in England.

Laisser faire provided opponents of trade unions with such arguments as the following.

42. A CRITICISM OF TRADE UNIONS[1]

Could the working classes be instructed in the laws, which regulate their wages, combinations from that moment would cease to exist. They would learn that wages are not dependent on the will of those who pay them, and that they can only be altered by changing the proportion between the number of labourers and the funds set apart for their maintenance. They would then see, that they might as well attempt to turn the sun from its course, as to extract from their employers the same wages as at present, and to give a third less of their labour in return. Could they be taught something of the nature and constitution of society, they would see that those, who are above them in station, whom they not unfrequently imagine to be their enemies, would be inattentive to their own interests, did they wish for aught but the prosperity and advancement of the labouring population.

SECTION X. THE CHARTIST MOVEMENT

Many who sought social and economic reform were persuaded that no great step could be taken until political changes were secured. William Lovett, a Cornish carpenter, drafted the Charter that is given below, in 1838. The agitation continued for nine years and, although Fergus O'Connor, in his Northern Star *advocated more revolutionary methods, the Chartists in general maintained a peaceful attitude. The huge petition for the Charter, already once voted down by Parliament, was presented in 1848, but the reforms were rejected until in the second half of the century most of them were accepted with little opposition.*

43. AIMS OF THE CHARTISTS[2]

In 1780, the electors of Westminster, in public meeting, appointed a committee, out of which a sub-committee was appointed to take into consideration the election of members of parliament. Charles James Fox, the leader of the Whigs, and Thomas Brand Hollis, Esq., were the chairmen of these committees. In their report to the electors they recommended — 1. Annual Parliaments, 2. Universal Suffrage, 3. Equal Voting Districts, 4. No Property Qualification, 5. Voting by Ballot, 6. Payment of Members.

The "Society of Friends of the People," was established in 1792, by Chas. Grey, Esq., (now Earl Grey,) the Hon. Thos. Erskine, Mr. (after-

---

[1] *Character, Object, and Effects of Trade Unions.* London, 1834, pp. 105–106.
[2] *The People's Charter . . . . and a Brief Sketch of its Origin.* London, 1848, pp. 7–25 *passim.*

wards Sir James) Mackintosh, several noblemen and members of the House of Commons. In 1795, they resolved to publish a Declaration, in which the right of voting should be so moderate *that there should be no condition in life in which it might not be acquired by labour, by industry, or talents.*

These are the doings of the Whigs of former times, persons whose speeches *on every other subject* our modern Whigs quote with ancestoral reverence, as texts from holy writ. Like every other irresponsible body, they have, however, degenerated. The only remedy for the evil, is to render Whig, Tory, and Radical legislators alike responsible to the people; and to instruct the people in a knowledge of their rights and duties.

We could wish it to be engraven on the memory of every Reformer, " that the people *must be free* in proportion as they Will it," — not by foolishly lending themselves to bigotry or party to become the instruments of the conceited, or selfishly ambitious, as they have too often done — nor by *violently* overthrowing the empire of title, the folly of privilege, or the dominion of wealth; for the experience of the past has clearly written for our guidance, that a change of men is not always a reformation in principle; and when a knowledge of their rights and duties shall have taught the people that their own vices and ignorance are the chief instruments by which they are bowed to the dust, titles, privileges, and wealth will lose their potency to enslave them. . . .

Among the suggestions which we received for improving this Charter, is one for embracing women among the possession of the franchise. Against this reasonable proposition we have no just argument to adduce, but only to express our fears of entertaining it, lest the false estimate man entertains of this half of the human family may cause his ignorance and prejudice to be enlisted to retard the progress of his own freedom.

．　．　．　．　．　．　．　．　．　．　．　．

THE PEOPLE'S CHARTER;
Being the Outline of an Act
To Provide for the

Just Representation of the People of Great Britain and Ireland
IN THE COMMONS' HOUSE OF PARLIAMENT,
Embracing the Principles of

UNIVERSAL SUFFRAGE, NO PROPERTY QUALIFICATION, ANNUAL PARLIAMENTS, EQUAL REPRESENTATION, PAYMENT OF MEMBERS, AND VOTE BY BALLOT.

Prepared by a Committee of Twelve Persons, Six Members of Parliament and Six Members of the London Working Men's Association, and addressed to the People of the United Kingdom.

WHEREAS, to insure, in as far as it is possible by human forethought and wisdom, the just government of the people, it is necessary to subject those who have the power of making the laws to a wholesome and strict responsibility to those whose duty it is to obey them when made.

And whereas, this responsibility is best enforced through the instrumentality of a body which emanates directly from, and is itself immediately subject to, the whole people, and which completely represents their feelings and their interests;

And, whereas, as the Commons' House of Parliament now exercises, in the name, and on the supposed behalf of the people, the power of making the laws, it ought, in order to fulfill with wisdom and with honesty the great duties imposed on it, to be made the most faithful and accurate representation of the people's wishes, feelings, and interests;

Be it therefore enacted, That from and after the passing of this Act, every male inhabitant of these realms be entitled to vote for the election of a Member of Parliament; subject, however, to the following conditions: —

1. That he be a native of these realms, or a foreigner who has lived in this country upwards of two years, and been naturalized.

2. That he be twenty-one years of age.

3. That he be not proved insane when the lists of voters are revised.

4. That he be not *undergoing the sentence of the law at the time when called upon to exercise the electoral right.*

5. That his electoral rights be not suspended for bribery at elections, or for personation, or for forgery of election certificates, according to the penalties of this Act.

ELECTORAL DISTRICTS.

Be it enacted, I. That for the purpose of obtaining an equal representation of the people in the Commons' House of Parliament, the united kingdom be divided into three hundred electoral districts. 300

II. That each such district contain, as nearly as may be, an equal number of inhabitants. . . .

V. That each electoral district return one representative to sit in the Commons' House of Parliament.

. . . .

ARRANGEMENT FOR NOMINATIONS.

XI. That no other qualification shall be required than the choice of electors, according to the provisions of this Act, providing that no persons, (excepting the Cabinet Ministers), be eligible to serve in the Commons' House of Parliament, who are in the receipt of any emolument derivable from any place or places held under government, or of retired allowances arising therefrom.

. . . .

ARRANGEMENTS FOR ELECTIONS.

XIII. That when any voter's certificate is examined by the registration clerk and found to be correct, he shall be allowed to pass on to the next barrier, where a balloting ball shall be given him by the person appointed for that purpose; he shall then pass on to the balloting box, and with all due despatch, shall put the balloting ball into the aperture opposite the name of the candidate he wishes to vote for, after which he shall without delay, leave the room by the door assigned for the purpose.

. . . .

DURATION OF PARLIAMENT.

Be it enacted, I. That the Members of the House of Commons chosen as aforesaid, shall meet on the first Monday in June in each year, and continue their sittings from time to time as they may deem it convenient, till the first Monday in June following, when the next new Parliament *shall* be chosen; they shall be eligible to be re-elected.

. . . .

PAYMENT OF MEMBERS.

Be it enacted, I. That every member of the House of Commons be entitled, at the close of the session, to a writ of expenses on the Treasury, for his legislative duties in the public service; and shall be paid   per annum.

SECTION XI. CATHOLIC EMANCIPATION AND IRELAND

Until 1829 the questions of Irish rights and Catholic Emancipation were practically one inasmuch as the seventeenth-century laws denying to Catholics a part in the political life of the kingdom bore most heavily on the Irish, a huge majority of whom were of the Roman communion. The Corporation Act of 1661 forbade the election of non-Anglicans to borough or city corporations, while the Test Act of 1673 made ineligible to office any who held to the Catholic doctrine of Transubstantiation. Sydney Smith, together with Lord Holland and Lord John Russell, struggled long for the repeal of these acts, but the greatest credit for Catholic Emancipation must be given to Daniel O'Connell, the Irish leader, whose propaganda inspired the Duke of Wellington and his ministers with lively apprehension and brought them to yield. In the first of the two following excerpts Smith touches on the legal and social disabilities of the Irish; in the second he is making a direct argument for the repeal of the prohibitory acts.

44. CATHOLIC DISABILITIES IN IRELAND [1]

The great misfortune of Ireland is, that the mass of the people have been given up for a century to a handful of Protestants, by whom they have been treated as *Helots,* and subjected to every species of persecution and disgrace. The sufferings of the Catholics have been so loudly chanted in the very streets, that it is almost needless to remind our readers that, during the reigns of Geo. I and Geo. II., the Irish Roman Catholics were disabled from holding any civil or military office, from voting at elections, from admission into corporations, from practising law or physic. . . . A Papist was disabled from purchasing freehold lands — and even from holding long leases — and any person might take his Catholic neighbour's house by paying £5 for it. . . . No Papist could purchase a freehold, or lease for more than thirty years — or inherit from an intestate Protestant — nor from an intestate Catholic — nor dwell in Limerick or Galway — nor hold an advowson, nor buy an annuity for life. £50 was given for discovering a popish Archbishop — £30 for a popish Clergyman — and 10s. for a Schoolmaster. No one was allowed to be trustee for Catholics; no Catholic was allowed to take more than two apprentices; no Papist to be solicitor, sheriff, or to serve on Grand Juries. Horses of Papists might be seized for the militia; for which militia Papists were to pay double, and to find Protestant substitutes. Papists were prohibited from being present at vestries, or from being high or petty constables; and, when resident in towns, they were compelled to find Protestant watchmen. Barristers and solicitors, marrying Catholics, were exposed to the penalties of Catholics. Persons plundered by privateers during a war with any popish prince, were reimbursed by a levy on the Catholic inhabitants where they lived. All popish priests celebrating marriages contrary to 12 Geo. I. cap. 3. were to be *hanged!*

The greater part of these incapacities are removed, though many of a very serious and oppressive nature still remain. But the grand misfortune is, that the spirit which these oppressive Laws engendered remains. The Protestant still looks upon the Catholic as a degraded being. The Catholic does not yet consider himself upon an equality with his former tyrant and taskmaster. That religious hatred which required all the prohibiting vigilance of the law for its restraint, has found in the law its strongest support; and the spirit which the law first exasperated and embittered, continues to act long after the original *stimulus* is withdrawn. . . .

[1] Sydney Smith, in *The Edinburgh Review.* 1820. *Works of the Rev. Sydney Smith.* London, 1869, pp. 345–346 (condensed).

The common admission now is, that the Catholics are to the Protestants in Ireland as about 4 to 1 — of which Protestants, not more than *one half* belong to the Church of Ireland. This, then, is one of the most striking features in the state of Ireland. That the great mass of the population is completely subjugated and overawed by a handful of comparatively recent settlers, — in whom all the power and patronage of the country is vested, — who have been reluctantly compelled to desist from still greater abuses of authority, — and who look with trembling apprehension to the increasing liberality of the Parliament and the country towards these unfortunate persons whom they have always looked upon as their property and their prey.

45. *ARGUMENT FOR CATHOLIC EMANCIPATION* [1]

I beg leave, Sir, before I proceed on this subject, to state what I mean by Catholic emancipation. I mean eligibility of Catholics to all civil offices, with the usual exceptions introduced into all bills — jealous safeguards for the preservation of the Protestant Church, and for the regulation of the intercourse with Rome — and, lastly, provision for the Catholic clergy.

I object, Sir, to the law as it stands at present, because it is impolitic, and because it is unjust. . . . Is not the present state of Ireland a premium upon early invasion? Does it not hold out the most alluring invitation to your enemies to begin? And if the flag of any hostile power in Europe is unfurled in that unhappy country, is there one Irish peasant who will not hasten to join it? . . .

But what right have you to continue these rules, Sir, these laws of exclusion? What necessity can you show for it? Is the reigning monarch a concealed Catholic? — Is his successor an open one? — Is there a disputed succession? — Is there a Catholic pretender? If some of these circumstances are said to have justified the introduction, and others the continuation, of these measures, why does not the disappearance of all these circumstances justify the repeal of the restrictions? . . .

We preach to our congregations, Sir, that a tree is known by its fruits. By the fruits it produces I will judge your system. What has it done for Ireland? New Zealand is emerging — Otaheite is emerging — Ireland is not emerging — she is still veiled in darkness — her children, safe under no law, live in the very shadow of death. Has your system of exclusion made Ireland rich? Has it made Ireland loyal? Has it made Ireland free? Has it made Ireland happy? How is the wealth of Ireland proved? Is it by the naked, idle, suffering savages, who are slumbering on the mud floor of their cabins?

[1] Speech at a clerical meeting at Beverley, April 11, 1825. *Works of Rev. Sydney Smith.* London, 1869, pp. 649–650, 654–655 (condensed).

In what does the loyalty of Ireland consist? Is it in the eagerness with which they would range themselves under the hostile banner of any invader, for your destruction and for your distress? Is it liberty when men breathe and move among the bayonets of English soldiers? Is their happiness and their history any thing but such a tissue of murders, burnings, hanging, famine, and disease, as never existed before in the annals of the world? This is the system, which, I am sure, with very different intentions, and different views of its effects, you are met this day to uphold. These are the dreadful consequences, which those laws your petition prays may be continued, have produced upon Ireland. From the principles of that system, from the cruelty of those laws, I turn, and turn with the homage of my whole heart, to that memorable proclamation which the Head of our church — the present monarch of these realms — has lately made to his hereditary dominions of Hanover — *That no man should be subjected to civil incapacities on account of religious opinions.* . . .

Of the Catholic Emancipation Bill, I shall say, that it will be the foundation stone of a lasting religious peace; that it will give to Ireland not all that it wants, but what it most wants, and without which no other boon will be of any avail.

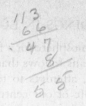

CHAPTER IV

THE INDUSTRIAL AND AGRICULTURAL
REVOLUTION ON THE CONTINENT

In the following extract the noted German economist, Professor Werner Sombart, presents a theory of the principles underlying modern technological progress.

46. THE PRINCIPLES OF MODERN ECONOMIC TECHNOLOGY [1]

WE are now about to enter upon a theme as fascinating as it is difficult; we shall discuss the technical achievements of the 19th century, or, more specifically, the development of economic technology in that century and its significance for German economic life. For, though we may not go so far as some writers — especially those representing the technical sciences — who simply identify technical and economic development, we must recognize the fact that the economic revolution which took place during the past century owes its existence in great part to technical changes. We need be no blind worshippers of technical progress, we may be very well aware that technology has little or nothing to do with inner culture or human happiness, we may know that the human race can sink back into barbarism for all its great technical achievements and the individuals of which it is composed be more miserable than ever; yet we must admire the wonderful things which the mind of man has accomplished in the field of technology during this century. It is without a parallel in human history. Never before has man in so short a time so far extended his mastery over nature. Never, so far as we know, have the foundations of technical achievement been so completely overthrown in so few generations. Anyone who wishes to understand any of the phenomena of social life in Europe in the 19th century — no matter what phenomenon it may be — must devote himself to the study of the thousands upon thousands of inventions upon which the structure of our modern technology rests.

It is no longer necessary to indulge in long winded arguments to prove this, — it is common knowledge among the cultured classes. But although

[1] Professor Werner Sombart, *Die Deutsche Volkswirtschaft im neunzehnten Jahrhundert.* Dritte, durchgesehene und auf die Gegenwart weitergefuhrte Auflage. Volksausgabe. Berlin, Georg Bondi, 1913. pp. 134–149. Translation by Miriam Hespelt and Lyman R. Bradley of the German Department of Washington Square College, New York University.

the right atmosphere for a fair evaluation of technology has thus been created, it by no means follows that such an evaluation has been made. Anyone who, like myself, attempts to tell in a few words what transformations in the economic life of our century have been brought about by technology finds himself in quite an embarrassing position. The simplest way for him to treat the subject would be to sketch briefly the technical achievements in every field. But obviously he cannot do this without copying off a *Book of Inventions* which in its most condensed form fills 729 closely printed pages as large as those of an encyclopedia — whereas scarcely a twentieth part of that space is available for his entire work. Then, again, one might think that he could find a way out of the difficulty by a process of selection, i.e. by presenting to his readers only the most important inventions and innovations. That is the usual method and the one employed in almost all the hundred and one " Outlines " which the close of the century has called forth. Yet I consider this method positively dangerous. One is apt to spend too much time on single points, to overestimate the importance of individual discoveries, and to vitiate thereby one's conclusions as to the general effect of technology. A realization of the *essential interdependence of all inventions and discoveries, both small and great,* is of the utmost importance and such a realization is impossible if I discuss, for example, the introduction of steam, or the invention of the spinning jenny, or the use of electricity, or the railroad, as isolated phenomena, apart from all the many other technical innovations. Quite aside from the fact that any such selection must necessarily be arbitrary. Moreover, these inventions which strike the popular fancy most strongly are not always the " most important " — if we care to use that term. It seems to me, for example, that Mandsley's discovery of the modern method of working iron by machinery is just as important as the invention of the spinning jenny; the use of commercial fertilizers I think more epoch-making than the use of steam power; to the innovations of Cort, Bessemer, and Thomas I should ascribe at least as much practical importance as to those of Fulton and Stephenson; Runge's discovery is perhaps of fundamentally greater importance than the inventions of Reis and Bell. And so on . . . and so on. . . . The only thing that we may safely say is this: that no one of these numerous inventions would have the same significance for practical life which it now enjoys if it had not been accompanied by other inventions and discoveries. With this recognition of the fundamental interdependence of all the phenomena of modern technology we find ourselves again at the point from which we started out. And we are once more in the dilemma of feeling obliged to enumerate them all, and yet unable to do so.

We may find a way out of our difficulty if we can discover the *distinguishing principle which underlies all the technical achievements of recent times* and if we can deduce from this principle the reasons for the triumph of modern technology. With this postulation of the problem I am going a step further than in my earlier discussion of the subject in my *Capitalism,* I am attempting to remove the last bit of casuistry which still clung to my earlier treatment of the theme, and I believe that I am now able to offer for the first time an unimpeachable *theory of the principles of modern technology.* And as we delve more deeply into the subject, the explanation, as we might expect, becomes much more simple.

The first principle upon which modern technology is based is *formal* in nature. It is founded upon the *application of the natural sciences to technology* and the consequent *transformation of empirical experience into rational knowledge.* All earlier technical knowledge — whatever marvelous results it may have obtained — had been empirical, i.e., founded upon personal experience, personally handed down from master to master, from generation to generation. Art, it was believed, was a wonderful secret which mortals had received from the gods and which they, in turn, passed on as a precious heritage to their children. Whatever Nature in her inscrutable ways offered man to help him in his work he gratefully accepted. It never occurred to the people of earlier civilizations to try to penetrate her mysteries. They knew the processes they had to employ to spin their wool, to build their bridges, to smelt their iron ore, — and with that they were content. Any chance experience which led them more quickly and more surely to their goal was looked upon as a special dispensation of Providence. They accepted it, cherished it, and passed it on to their descendents, as one hands down a treasure which has been presented to him during his lifetime. All education, therefore, consisted in learning the rules; that is, in acquiring information concerning the processes to be employed to obtain a definite result, — to reach a definite technical goal.

Into this semi-darkness of pious effort there now falls the glaring light of natural science. The challenging "I know" takes the place of the modestly proud "I can." I know why wooden piers do not rot when they stand in water; I know why water follows the piston of a pump; I know why iron disintegrates when I expose it to the air; I know why plants grow better when I fertilize the fields. I know! I know! That is the motto of modern life which has fundamentally altered all technical procedure. Things are accomplished now-a-days not because some master has particular ability, but because everyone engaged in an undertaking knows the laws underlying the technical procedure, the correct application of which guarantees success. What was formerly worked out according to rules is now accomplished according to laws, whose discovery and application are the real problems of rational procedure. Technology now becomes unconditionally dependent upon the theoretical natural sciences and their progress alone determines the limits of its capabilities. We can therefore mark the different stages in the development of modern technology by the great epoch-making discoveries in the field of the natural sciences. The first milepost is the definitive formulation of the laws of mechanics by Newton; the second marker I would place in the 1780's when Lavoisier discovered the theory of combustion; the third great event which determined the development of technology falls in the year 1828 — Wöhler's synthesis of urea; while the latest and most fruitful period of modern technology was ushered in by Robert Mayer's formulation of the law of the conservation of energy in 1841. Why these particular discoveries were of such great significance for the development of technology, the following discussion will clearly show.

For the present I wish only to emphasize the fact once more that the natural sciences did not begin to influence technology much before the last decades of the 18th century, and that it is really only in the 19th century that scientific methods invaded technical practice. This is especially true of Germany, and that is the only country with which we are here concerned.

The invention of the steam engine, which is unquestionably the child of scientific thought, falls, to be sure, entirely within the 18th century. But we must not forget that although the idea of the steam engine, born of the modern scientific spirit, did indeed develop in the 18th century, its practical realization was still restricted by the limitations of the older, empirical technology until well into the 19th century. At the beginning of the 19th century machine construction was still carried on by means of chisel, hammer, and very simple drills; the carpenter still had more to do with it than the machinist, for iron was still obtained in the traditional Old-Franconian way and was not available in any great quantities. So we may rightly say that the era of the steam engine does not begin until the 19th century, — at least not in Germany. But what is true of the steam engine and its construction is no less true of all machinery. It cannot be regarded as having profoundly influenced technology as long as it was constructed in a purely empirical spirit, which was still the case everywhere at the beginning of the 19th century.

The same spirit, however, at that time dominated all other branches of technology. In the iron industry the introduction of the puddling process (at the end of the 1780's) had, of course, marked an important step forward. But the whole process was purely empirical. No one as yet had any scientifically accurate knowledge of what took place in the smelting furnace or the puddling furnace. Huntsmann and Friedrich Krupp, the inventors of cast steel, were pure empiricists who knew nothing of the chemical composition of their product.

Farmers, to be sure, who farmed according to Thaer's method, called themselves rational farmers. But they were so, if at all, only in the economic sense. The technic of agricultural production was still entirely empirical.

Thaer's so-called humus theory by which he tried to explain fertility did not rest upon any scientific basis and was immediately discarded when Liebig established scientifically the laws of plant growth. And so it was in every field.

But what is there, then, about a process founded upon natural science that gives it the power to revolutionize technology? We shall most quickly find an answer to this question if we first make clear to ourselves upon what it is that this wholly new *principle of modern natural sciences* rests. For, of course, we shall more quickly find the key to the results which science brings about, if we understand the spirit which dominates it.

The goal of modern science, it is fair to say, is that complete *replacement of quality by quantity* which finds its ultimate and perfect expression in a mathematical formula. Kant has taught us that we have no right to speak of our knowledge of natural law until we can represent any natural process by a mathematical formula. The end and aim of this is, if I may so express it, to take the soul out of Nature. Where formerly one assumed living beings, living processes: —

> In these hills once dwelt the dryads
> Nymphs made every tree their home,
> From the urns of lovely naiads
> Poured the water's silver foam;
> Life abundant flowed through all creation
> What escapes man's senses felt and grew . . .

there is now supposed to exist — for so the stern logic of modern scientific thought demands — an interplay of inanimate bodies. It is fascinating to observe how knowledge, as it advances, argues away the souls of things, how the progress of science, to speak in modern parlance, can be traced by the gradual suppression of vitalistic beliefs. Galileo still ascribed the phenomenon of water following the piston to a *horror vacui* in nature, i.e. to an anthropomorphic dread of empty space which he believed to be inherent in all matter.[1] Then (1643) Toricelli invented the barometer and the weight of the air could be demonstrated. The phlogiston of Stahl's theory of combustion, which dwells in all matter and escapes from it in the flame — what is that but a kind of fire-soul tucked secretly away in the material world? Lavoisier's theory of combustion, in the final analysis, did nothing more than substitute a concept of quantity, expressed in a mathematical formula, for an imaginative statement of quality. And the great significance of Lavoisier's contribution to modern scientific thought is that he applied the mathematical formula, the statement of quantity, which formerly had been thought to control only the outer movements of bodies, to the inner life of the bodies as well, i.e., to the interrelation of their constituent parts. In the

[1] Expressed in the old saying: "Nature abhors a vacuum." (Editor's note.)

exhibition of the history of chemistry at the World's Fair in Paris in 1900 there were displayed some clumsy old-fashioned scales — Lavoisier's scales. They have become in a very real sense the symbol of the modern spirit.

And as in the cases which we have mentioned, so in thousands of others, the progress of scientific thought has taken the soul out of natural processes. I will mention just one more striking example of this: the overthrow of the theory of vital energy, the *vis vivendi,* by the synthesis of organic bodies (dating from 1828) whereby the psyche was finally driven out of its last hiding place — organic matter; (finally, that is to say, as far as the natural sciences of the 19th century are concerned, for we are interested only in them at present).

But all these observations have no meaning for us unless they teach us what effect this transformation in the natural sciences has had upon technology. It will be easier for us to estimate this if we try to realize the change that has been wrought through the influence of the sciences, i.e., of the modern " exact " sciences, in our whole conception of the world, — our cosmology. Our ancestors, quite naturally, from their belief in nature as animate arrived at the belief in a living God, the creator of heaven and earth. This God was nothing other than a great artist, a perfect artisan, who had created the world by virtue of his own highly personal, empirical knowledge. He makes man in his own image. And his soul lives on in his work. He creates with all the intense interest of the artisan who finds in the perfection of his handiwork his best reward. And God saw that it was good. Indeed, in the Jewish legend of the creation the true artisan nature of the creator is so plainly evident that God actually finishes his work in six week-days, the normal working time of the artisan.

In nature as our chemists and physicists conceive it, there is no longer room for an artisan-God.

> Heedless even of her Maker's honor,
> Like the dead beat of the pendulum,
> A slave, the chains of Gravity upon her
> Moves Nature, Godless, dumb. . . .

The creator has been separated from his work. He may still perhaps be thought of as the great Organizer who brings the elements together. But these, by their own " strength " form the combinations which produce the world of bodies. The creation of the world, if we may so put it, has become a rationally ordered process, which takes place according to laws that may be expressed mathematically, — laws to which the creative agent is itself subject and which must be obeyed with careful precision in order to obtain a desired result.

From the above considerations we must now be able to understand how modern science has revolutionized technology: the teachings of science have taught man to look upon technical processes as the spontaneous interplay of inanimate bodies, rather than as the emanation of a living, working personality (the artisan). In this way scientific knowledge has set technology free from the limitations imposed upon it by its dependence on organic life, — in this instance, on man. But this work of emancipation — for such it really is — does not end here. We have seen that the crowning achievement of the natural sciences in the 19th century was the removal of the soul from organic matter. This means, when transferred to practice, i.e., to technology, an emancipation from animal and plant organisms as necessary intermediaries in the production and manipulation of goods: a phenomenon of which we already have some empirical knowledge. Its enormous significance for the organization and production of economic goods I wish to discuss in more detail. But first I should like to sum up these general remarks concerning the spirit and the meaning of modern technical development by saying that from the preceding arguments we are justified in claiming as the *fundamental principle of modern technology,* to which all the epoch-making accomplishments in the technical field during the 19th century are (as I shall show later) to be attributed, the *tendency toward the practical emancipation from the limitations of the organic* — human beings, animals, or plants. Or we may express it thus: just as modern scientific theory rests upon the removal of the soul from Nature, so all the practical phenomena characteristic of modern times are to be traced back to a removal of the soul from technology.

Emancipation from the limitations of the organic: this means, in other words, the supplanting of nature by art, of living nature by inanimate nature, of quality by quantity. Such a transformation has been taking place in all the elements of technology: power, materials, and methods of procedure have all alike fallen victim to it.

To be sure, even before the 19th century men made use of water and wind as motive power, as well as of animal and human organisms. But aside from the fact that the former were of much less importance than the organic sources of power, they were, like them, subject to time and space. The whims of the water-fairies and the wind-God alone determined when and how men could use wind and water power. Only since steam and electricity have been applied to technology has man been master of a source of power in inanimate nature of which he could dispose at will. The transition to steam and electricity as motive power is, therefore, peculiarly an act of emancipation which can be plainly traced back to the modern scientific point of view.

And if mechanical *power* is predominant in modern times, so is also inorganic *material:* iron, commercial fertilizers, aniline dyes, etc.

But most important of all is this: *modern methods of procedure,* modern industrial processes, also breathe out the same spirit. They, too, are striving to be free from the limitations of the organic world. This tendency is very clearly evident in the *chemical trades* which have been built up upon the principle of the artificial synthesis of essential materials. The products of the forest's secret growth, of the plant's blossom, and of the animal's organism, are now created at will in the retort or muffle of the chemist: perfumes and flavors, colors and fabrics, fertilizers and illuminating materials.

And just as chemical procedure tends to produce raw materials without the aid of animal or plant organisms, so mechanical procedure tends, in principle, to produce goods without the coöperation of men. The economic principle of the machine, which I discussed in detail in my *Capitalism,* is based upon the substitution of human labor. The machine is a contrivance designed to do any kind of work which, without it, man would have to perform. The ideal of a perfect machine is an automatically operating mechanism which man has only to tend.

Of course, the machine is by no means exclusively a product of the 19th century. It is as old as humanity itself. Nevertheless, we are justified in calling the *principle* of the machine a *principle of modern technology* — for two reasons. First, because never before, to our knowledge, has the application of mechanical procedure to every field of industry been consciously striven for, as it is to-day. Formerly the machine was something fortuitous which one accepted without much thought, like any other tool. Now man wants the machine. The technician thinks in terms of the machine. The spirit of the machine dominates all technology except in the fields preëmpted by chemistry. The spirit of the age is so essentially concerned with the technology of the machine that we now consciously use machines to produce other machines. This production of machines by machines, which began in the 19th century (as I shall show more clearly later) is our second reason for claiming the principle of the machine as the outstanding characteristic of the technology of the 19th century.

In order to measure accurately the practical results of this new technology it is necessary to distinguish between (1) those due to the use of the scientific method as such and (2) those which the transition from the organic to the inorganic in technical procedure has brought in its train.

Of the effect of scientific *method* upon the great accomplishments of modern science, the following should be said:

In the first place, it has wrought a complete transformation in what I should like to call the *manner of acquiring technical knowledge.* This has become objectified by the adoption of rational procedure. Formerly, as we have seen, every artistic procedure was shut up in the personality of the "Master." It lived with him, it died with him. Only that which an apprentice had learned by observing him and listening to him survived after his death, — to take root once more in a personality and, perhaps, perish with it. Rational procedure, on the other hand, is independent, objective. It is knowledge made comprehensible and accessible to everyone. And once it has been set down in the written word, it has become the imperishable property of all future generations. So in a twofold sense it is freed from the fortuitousness of the purely personal: the possibility of its loss is done away with, and it no longer requires a certain individual, subject to time and space, to direct any given process. As long as industry — even modern capitalistic industry — was still in the empirical stage, it could branch out into other countries only by transplanting thither men who carried the secrets of their craft with them. The invitations to the Humiliate monks from many cities in the middle ages, the summoning of the Flemish weavers to England, the importation of Italian silk spinners and weavers to France, and the whole immigration policy of the Hohenzollerns bear witness to the fact that formerly industrial art was bound up in the artist. Then for a time it was bound up in the products: then a country would forbid the exportation of certain machines — as England did, for example, at the beginning of the last century. To-day a nation can send her young engineers and technicians to the German universities and acquire, in embryo, all the wisdom taught there to be used in any way desired. And if the practice and preservation of the technical arts have been set free by rational procedure from the haphazardness of the individual, so, to a much greater extent, has been the spread of technical knowledge. For the tentative gropings which, as we have seen, are characteristic of all empiricism, rational procedure substitutes planned, methodical research based upon knowledge of the principles of earlier methods of procedure. Experiment takes the place of hit-and-miss trying. The discoverer becomes an *inventor,* and invention itself ceases to be the dilettante pastime of an intelligent clergyman or an ingenious barber and becomes the professional occupation of scholarly experts. It is easy to see that the tempo of invention must now increase in rapidity to a degree unknown and unattainable to empiricism.

But science has not only removed the element of chance from the preservation and spread of technical knowledge. The elements of chance are disappearing more and more from execution! Technique becomes surer, more easily controllable, more exact. Of course! For now that we understand the relation between the different processes of production we can prevent and avoid harmful factors and fill in whatever gaps may occur. Entire industries have for the first time reached their full development, since chemistry and, more recently, bacteriology have provided them with the means of stabilizing production by eliminating all previously uncontrollable disturbing factors. Consider, for example, the brewing industry. Numerous measuring tools of all sorts and sizes, peculiar methods of control, exact indicators, registering apparatus, chemical tests, auxiliary physical apparatus as, for example, polarization instruments, spectroscopes, manometers, dynamometers, etc., are at the disposal of the industry to-day to help it obtain security in the manufacture of its product.

This last remark leads us to the other problem: the *importance of the new materialistic principle of modern technology in practice.* For, clearly in the perfection of measuring and weighing methods which we have just discussed we find an expression of that tendency which we have defined as the characteristic tendency of modern technology — the tendency toward emancipation from the organic, — in this case, from man himself. Former generations depended entirely upon the human faculties of feeling, tasting, smelling, and seeing, in order to measure conditions of mass or heat. Now instead of this casual subjective standard we may obtain exact, objective measurements of weight, length, warmth, thickness, and durability by scientifically constructed measuring and weighing apparatus. This emancipation has a twofold aspect: industry is set free not only from its dependence upon the chance natural gifts of certain personalities with especially fine tongues, especially sensitive nerves, clear eyes, and keen ears, but also from the natural vicissitudes of execution which are inevitable as long as living beings with warm blood in their veins are performing these functions.

And here we reach the point wherein the *essential significance of all perfected machinery* lies: it is able to carry out any undertaking with an exactness of which man is incapable. The finest tool, the most delicate graver or chisel can never do more than assist manual skill. The industrial machine, on the other hand, knows no such limitation. It does not heed the coördination of hand and eye upon which the refinement of manual skill depends. It can cut more delicately, it can repeat a process more surely and more regularly than the human hand could ever do. It actually supplants perfectly the work of the artisan.

And if this instance shows us how mechanical technology has set the industrial process free from the qualitative limitations of the organic, in other instances we may observe how modern technology breaks down the limitations of quantitative performance imposed by organic nature. The *essential significance of the use of mechanical force* is that it makes possible to concentrate any desired amount of energy at any one point, whereas human and animal organisms could never dispose of more than a limited amount of power, which could not be increased even by the collaboration of several organisms without difficulty. Of course, the industrial process had to be first taken over by industrial machines before a highly developed power like that of compressed steam, for example, could be put to any practical use. The spinning jenny must first have taken the spinning process out of the hands of human beings and transferred it to a system of inanimate bodies before a power could be applied which would drive three thousand spindles at once. The emancipatory effect of steam as motive power — as compared with wind or water — has already been discussed.

Moreover a great *emancipation from time and space* takes place when we renounce the assistance of organic matter. Space is essential to all plant growth, but it becomes unnecessary when materials are produced from mineral or other inorganic substances which take the place of the wood that spreads out over the forest or the animal who requires a piece of ground for the production of its food. Let us consider the following figures: there were in the German empire on December 2, 1907, 4,345,047 horses. In Prussia in 1907, 4,377,115 hectares, that is over one sixth of the entire acreage, were sown to oats. The locomotives of Germany represent more than 12 million horsepower. If that many living horses had to be fed, the amount of land sown to oats would have to be tripled (to say nothing of the consumption of hay), that is, almost one half of the arable land, which is now put to other uses, would have to be given over to the maintenance of horses. And then where would the wood grow to take the place of the iron we use to-day? All the forests of the earth would have to be cut down and even then there would not be enough to satisfy the demand. Quite aside from the fact that the enormous increase in the economic cost of materials would prohibit their use long before they were physically exhausted. In our present economic order, if science had not partially emancipated us, ground rents would rise so high that any such economic development as we have experienced during the 19th century would be quite unthinkable.

But modern technology has also acted as an emancipating agent with regard to *time*. In the first place, as we have already shown, it has broken through the limitations which confine the animal or the human organism and attained greater speed in the production and transportation of goods. But it saves time in another way, — by making unnecessary the natural period of growth of plant or animal, that is, again, by replacing plant or animal organisms by inorganic substances. Let us use once more the striking example of iron. A beam or a mast of iron or steel can be produced in a few weeks, whereas a tree would require decades to achieve the necessary girth. The horses which are hitched to the street-car have to be cared for for at least three or four years, whereas the electric car is ready in as many months.

Finally, however, — and this is perhaps the most important practical result of modern scientific procedure — *the basis of technical knowledge as a whole is broadened* to an extent hitherto undreamed-of. Modern technology, we know, treats the process of production as detached, as it were, from the executive organism, man. It is therefore able to separate the process into its elements without consideration of the creating hand, with a view only to the necessary sequence of cause and effect between the individual processes. The principle of the division of labor can now be applied consistently for the first time. And science by inventing clever mechanical devices provides for the exact carrying out of these separate functions into which the productive process has been divided, although they no longer correspond to the natural activity of the human organism. Instead of dividing the productive process in a way adapted to the limitations and needs of living persons, it is now divided in such a way as to obtain mechanically the desired results, as Reuleaux has said. Now we can see why it is that machinery has developed so rapidly in our century. It is because of a change in the point of view of the inventor of the machine. The machine no longer tries to imitate hand labor, or to imitate nature, but deals with its own problems in its own way, — which is sometimes quite different from the ways of nature. And once the limitations due to the peculiarities of the human organism have been removed, unlimited fields are opened up to industry. This is the supreme service which science has rendered technology. Production now becomes a synthesis of such materials and such power as are desirable for human purposes. The re-creation of the world has begun. This very science which thrust man down from the throne of power where he had sat so long, which exposed him in all his impotence, has at the same time shown him the way in which he can once more conquer the world (though, to be sure, only the world of outward phenomena).

And if in the following pages I undertake to trace this process, of which we understand only the essential principles, this penetration of science into all the fields of modern technology and the accompanying emancipation from the limitations of the organic, as it actually appears in some especially important phases of economic life, we must not lose sight of our larger problem — the significance of technical inventions for *German* economic life in the 19th century. We shall, therefore, not discuss the many inventions and discoveries which through the coöperation of all civilized nations have contributed to modern technology, but shall confine ourselves to a discussion of the decisive moments in the development or application of technological achievements in Germany. In which connection we shall pay special attention to the part which German inventors have played in the discoveries of modern times in so far as this has influenced economic conditions in Germany to any marked degree.

The spectacular economic development of Germany between the Franco-Prussian War and the Great War, especially after the accession of William II to the throne of Germany in 1888, amazed the world and alarmed the other European Powers. But this amazing progress was itself largely the outcome of a remarkable economic advance earlier in the century, usually insufficiently emphasized by historians.

In the following selection Professor Lichtenberger discusses some of the factors in this earlier advance. He shows how the idea of a " competency " — the theory that a man should have only just enough income to maintain himself and those dependent on him reasonably well in the class to which he belonged — yielded to the idea of " free enterprise," — the theory that every man should have the opportunity to acquire as much wealth as he could under free competitive conditions. He shows how, largely under the influence of the theory of " free enterprise," many of the old obstacles to individual initiative were gradually removed and the era of unrestricted competition inaugurated. Finally he traces briefly the principal phases of the economic development of Germany during approximately the first half-century of that era.

47. *THE DEVELOPMENT OF CAPITALISTIC ENTERPRISE IN GERMANY* [1]

The great fact which dominates the economic and social history of Germany, as well as that of the whole of Europe, during the nineteenth century, is the growth of capitalism, or, to use a term more generally favoured by German political economists, the system of " enterprise " (*Unternehmung*).

Former ages never felt to the same extent as the nineteenth century that greed for unlimited gain which is characteristic of the modern speculator of every category. In the pre-capitalistic era, each individual, from the lowest to the highest in the social scale, aimed only at earning enough to ensure him the means of sustenance (*Nahrung*) and a mode of life in keeping with the customs of his class. This was the ideal of the country gentleman, of the Junker,[2] who, as a rule, did not aim at the intensive cultivation of his property which would make it yield the absolute maximum of production, but only asked from his lands sufficient maintenance for his rank, the right of living like a lord on his estate for part of the year, of hunting in the autumn, paying a visit to the capital of the kingdom or province during the bad season, and providing a dowry for his daughters and supplementing the income of a son in the army. The ideal of the artisan and of the " master " was a similar one. He expected his trade to support him, together with his family and the journeymen and apprentices, who lived under his roof and

[1] Henri Lichtenberger, *Germany and its Evolution in Modern Times.* Translated from the French by A. M. Ludovici. New York, Henry Holt and Company, 1913, pp. 3–12.

[2] The landed proprietor, whose class is the dominating one in Prussia. It is from this class that all officers and higher officials are drawn. — Tr. Constable & Company, London.

formed part of his household. He never dreamt of extending his output indefinitely, but only aspired to the life of a self-supporting producer, who faithfully satisfied the ordinary demands of a very limited number of clients, whom no man had the right to lure away from him. And, like the craftsman, the tradesman had no other object than that of earning a livelihood by disposing of his goods among a more or less restricted circle of customers with whose tastes and traditional needs he was familiar.

Under these conditions, the general tendency of the age was to protect the position which a man had won, or inherited, against the results of unrestricted competition and the encroachments of neighbours, who were either too greedy or too enterprising. The landed proprietor was bound not to allow his lands to lie fallow, or to reduce the number of his tenures or the sum total of the peasant families for whom he provided a livelihood on his estate; he was even liable to help them in time of difficulty. In return, he was certain of always having at his disposal, through the institution of serfdom and forced labour, the service which was necessary for the cultivation of his property. In a similar way, the artisans were protected by their guilds, which, although they were fast dying out, still existed in rough outline at the beginning of the nineteenth century. These guilds had the effect of creating, in every town, a sort of monopoly, based either upon law or upon usage, in favour of the "masters" of the various trades, and of limiting the competition between the masters themselves in such a way as to prevent the appropriation of raw material and labour by a few individuals and to hinder the diversion of custom.

This idea of a "competency" gradually gave way to that of "free enterprise." From the end of the eighteenth century protestations resounded on every side against the barriers which barred the path to private initiative. The old organization of the rural community, which, by the partition of an estate and the inextricable mingling of the allotments, made all the inhabitants of a village dependent upon each other and forced them to cultivate their land according to a traditional plan laid down by the elders of the place for use throughout the entire area of cultivation, was set aside. The people rebelled against the feudal system of a landed aristocracy, which placed the peasant in a position of absolute subjection to his lord and denied him the opportunity of ever winning economic independence. They complained of the countless obstacles placed by the guilds in the way of the natural growth of industry and commerce; but, above all, they protested against the tutelary administration of the enlightened despotism, which, in the eighteenth century, reserved for itself all initiative in economic matters and regulated, down to the smallest detail the life and productive powers of the nation. The physiocrats in France and Adam Smith in Engand, proclaimed the blessing of *laisser-faire,* and a similar spirit inspired William of

Humboldt, in his celebrated pamphlet on the " Limits of State Interference " (1795), to raise an energetic protest against a bureaucratic system which made man into a machine, cast officials in the moulds of slavery, and stifled all independent action in the masses.

At the beginning of the nineteenth century, after the annihilation of Prussia at Jena, these ideas tended to gain the upper hand among the patriots, who set themselves the task of raising their native land from the dust. In their opinion, the weakness of Prussia relative to the French Empire was due to the fact that, whilst in France the Revolution had roused the whole nation to take a share in public life, enlightened despotism and the feudal system had crushed out every trace of spontaneity in Prussia. They accordingly set themselves the task of awakening the national conscience, of breathing life into the sluggish mass which constituted the Prussian State, and of transforming it into an organism in which every limb was alive and coöperated freely in the work of the whole system. They persuaded the king to carry out from above the Revolution which the French people accomplished from below.

It was imperative for the nation to be set free from feudal and administrative tutelage. Absolute rule, which was incapable, on its own resources, of making good the evils caused by the war, or of providing any effective relief for the various grievances of private individuals, abdicated its economic prerogatives and decided to " suppress every obstacle which had hitherto been able to prevent any individual from attaining that degree of prosperity to which his powers entitled him to raise himself." In every department of the administration, Stein endeavoured to introduce the principle of autonomy. Stein, and afterwards Hardenberg, attempted to raise the condition of the rural population by abolishing serfdom, allowing the redemption of forced labour, setting the tenant free from his lord's estate, and the peasant from the village community, and by favouring the formation of a class of independent peasantry who possessed their own land. In the towns they enfranchised the Third Estate by proclaiming the freedom of industry and commerce, destroying the guild system, and granting parochial self-government on a liberal scale. In spite of the resistance of the feudal party, which suceeded for many years in preventing this agrarian reform from being carried into execution, and, in the final liquidation of the feudal system, managed to secure enormous material advantages, the old order crumbled away after a hopeless defeat. *The State renounced the right of directing the economic life of the nation.* On a large number of cardinal points it left a clear field for private initiative, and unchained the spirit of enterprise, whose ambition had till then been thwarted by the feudal system and the guilds. The era of unrestricted competition was inaugurated. A new class of speculators now sprang into existence and grew rapidly, at first among the landed proprietors, and afterwards among the industrial and trading classes as well. They were men in whom the spirit of enterprise had become incarnate, and who were actuated only by the desire to develop their economic power indefinitely. It is this class which from that moment took the lead in the economic movement; and in a very short time unrestricted competition, by utilising for its own ends the marvellous progress in science and technical processes, which we have just sketched, succeeded in overturning and transforming with incredible rapidity the manner of life of the whole nation.

Let us trace the principal phases of its revolution during the course of the nineteenth century.

At the beginning of the century, Germany was a rather poor agricultural country, but little developed from the economic point of view. It is estimated that the Empire itself had at that time a population only of about 25 millions, of whom three-quarters, at least, lived in the country, and two-thirds were engaged in agricultural pursuits. There was very little industry and commerce. Means of communication were few and bad: Prussia in 1816 possessed only 523 miles of high-roads, and they were execrable; the post was slow, inconvenient, and costly. Moreover, the Treaties of Vienna sanctioned the political and economic partition of Germany. As soon as peace was declared, thirty-eight lines of customs frontiers paralysed all internal commerce, and, to use List's well-known description, produced " much the same result as if one decided to bind up the various members of the human body in order to prevent the blood from circulating from one to the other." Every industrial impulse was, consequently, for the time being, impossible. Moreover, the economic life of the nation was still somewhat primitive. The line of demarcation between agricultural and industrial pursuits remained very indistinct. The peasant still fashioned a large number of the utensils, clothes, and articles of all kinds which he required; and, conversely, many artisans and journeymen had, in addition to their trade, a little corner of ground which they cultivated themselves. Agriculture alone had been developed, and was even in a prosperous condition. Important demands for agricultural products arose in England owing to the growth of industry and the increase of urban centres; while Holland and the Scandinavian countries also became importers of corn. Now Germany at that time happened to be in a position to export part of her agricultural products, and was consequently able to sell a fairly large quantity of them, especially corn, abroad. This favourable state of things gave the landowners the opportunity of improving their methods of culture; agricultural processes were perfected under the able guidance of Thaer, and the price of land went up. At that moment, for various reasons, a number of important towns sprang into existence in the north of Germany, in consequence of which the spirit of enterprise awoke, and we find the growth of fairly active speculation in agricultural land.

Throughout the first half of the century this state of things changed very little, but it is possible to trace the birth of circumstances which a little later on were to bring about the economic awakening of Germany. The first factor was population, which, in consequence of the agricultural prosperity, increased by leaps and bounds; between 1816 and 1845 the number of inhabitants rose from 25 millions to 34 1/2 — that is to say, an increase of 38.7 per cent. — the highest that was ever reached during the century. Secondly, the establishment of the *Zollverein* during the thirties had the result of creating in Germany a territory of 8,253 square miles which was free from all internal customs and contained a population of at least 25 million inhabitants. The rhythm of exchange began to grow more rapid and the means of communication more frequent. New roads were made, and under the energetic sway of Nagler, the Postmaster-General, the postal service became quicker and more reliable. In 1835 the first railway line in Germany was built between Nuremberg and Fürth, and at the end of ten years — in 1845 — there was a network of 2,131 kilometres of railroad. At the same time, the first and still feeble indications of the new spirit of enterprise made their appearance in the domain of industry. The great mining industry gradually freed itself from the old forms which fettered its flight, and every day saw the growth of its own importance. In connection with certain branches of the textile industry, and especially in the spinning and weaving of cotton, factories grew more numerous and tended to monopolise the entire production. But, generally speaking, the period between 1820 and 1850 did not produce any decisive economic progress. About 1820, agriculture even underwent a crisis which lasted nearly ten years, and made itself felt by a depression in land values and numerous bankruptcies. German industry also found great difficulty in struggling against the crushing competition of England, which, in default of sufficiently high protective tariffs, inundated Germany with cheap goods. Thus the country went through a period of difficulty and discomfort, and complaints were everywhere rife about want of money and hard times.

But directly after the great crisis of 1848 everything changed. As the scale of commerce for several years turned in favour of Germany, money began once more to flow in and accumulate there. The price of agricultural products, and consequently the value of land, showed a steady rise. The triumph of reactionary principles, moreover, seemed to herald a period of internal peace. The whole country, sick of political struggles and the fruitless agitations they involved, flung itself from that moment with redoubled energy upon the conquest of material prosperity and wealth. The spirit of enterprise and the love of speculation were not confined, as they had been at the beginning of the century, to a small fraction of the public, but invaded the lowest layers of the nation, and once for all took possession of the business world. During the twenty years which separated the crisis of 1848-49 from the Franco-German War, modern capitalistic Germany was formed. We now find a great increase in credit banks, such as the *Bank für Handel and Industrie zu Darmstadt* (founded in 1853) and other similar institutions whose business consisted in collecting the financial means necessary for the organisation of great industrial speculations or means of transport, and of thus stimulating to the highest possible pitch the spirit of enterprise which gave them birth and which kept them alive. Joint-stock companies, which, in a sense, make speculation democratic and associate the most modest resources with great capitalistic enterprises, sprang from the earth on every side and multiplied with extraordinary rapidity. It is estimated that in Germany, between 1853 and 1857, the issue of shares in new banks alone amounted to 200 million thalers, and railway shares to 140 million thalers, whilst a similar increase was shown in issues of a different nature, such as railway or industrial bonds, shares in insurance companies, mining ventures, steam navigation, machinery, sugar refineries, cotton mills, etc. The years inaugurating the second half of the century formed the first lap in the marvellous economic development which was to place Germany at the head of the industrial nations of Europe. It was during this period that the network of great railways joining the principal towns of Germany to each other and the outlying districts to the centre was built. At the same time, mining and weaving industries assumed a definitely modern complexion, whilst in the domain of agriculture, scientific processes of cultivation were every day more widely employed.

If the development of German agriculture in the nineteenth century is less striking than the progress of German industry during the same period, it nevertheless represents a startling advance over anything that had taken place in the domain of German agriculture during previous centuries.

The following extract from Professor Lichtenberger's book touches on a few features of this agricultural development.

48. THE DEVELOPMENT OF GERMAN AGRICULTURE IN THE NINETEENTH CENTURY [1]

The effect which the rise of the spirit of enterprise had upon the development of German agriculture is far less striking than that produced in the domain of industry during the same lapse of time. It has even been pointed out that, superficially, Germany, judging from the distribution of agrarian property, changed very little during the last century. About 1800 there existed,

[1] Henri Lichtenberger, *Germany and its Evolution in Modern Times.* Translated from the French by A. M. Ludovici. New York, Henry Holt and Company, 1913, pp. 28-31. Constable & Company, London.

and still exist to this day, districts where large estates predominated (the country east of the Elbe), others where there were large numbers of peasant proprietors (Schleswig, Hanover, Westphalia, Brunswick), and yet others where moderate-sized and small estates were the rule (the region south-west of the valley of the Rhine). Moreover, the most varied types of undertakings subsisted peacefully side by side, without any particular one showing signs of definitely gaining the upper hand in the near future. But it was none the less certain that German agriculture had undergone a series of fundamental internal transformations, of which I will endeavor to trace the principal features.

In the first place, agricultural products had increased enormously. This result was due chiefly to the fact that the surface of the ground had been more fully utilized since the development of husbandry, which had considerably reduced pasture and fallow land. It is estimated that the ground occupied by fields and gardens was a quarter, perhaps even a third, as much again as it was during the previous century. This, however, was due principally to the perfection reached in technical processes. Scientific knowledge about the conditions necessary for the growth of vegetable produce, and especially the great discoveries of Liebig in the domain of agricultural chemistry, had the result of substituting rational methods for the old rules-of-thumb. The old plan of triennial distribution gave way to that of rotation of crops, which in its turn was supplanted by the system of intensive cultivation through the aid of chemical manures. The old primitive instruments used by the peasants in the Middle Ages were gradually replaced by complicated agricultural machines of all kinds — steam ploughs and engines for sowing, weeding, and threshing — whose numbers multiplied particularly rapidly after about 1880. The culture of paying crops was developed at the expense of those which were less remunerative. Side by side with agricultural concerns, factories sprang up, where the products of the soil underwent a transformation into industrial commodities: the beet-root grower, for instance, became a sugar-refiner as well, the potato planter a distiller. The methods of afforestation and the rearing of cattle were gradually brought to perfection, and the results obtained became every day more fruitful. The output per acre continued to increase. The number of head of cattle of all kinds grew to considerable proportions, the stock was improved, and the average weight of the animals went up. In short, it is estimated that the sum-total of agricultural production has increased at least two, if not threefold, during the last hundred years. As, moreover, the number of rural labourers has not multiplied in similar proportions, it seems evident that, owing to the progress made in technical processes, the productivity of agricultural labour has increased enormously during the last century. It is not possible, however, yet to decide to what extent it has done so, or whether at the present time this capacity for production is tending to increase or diminish, and whether, therefore, the working of the law of the gradual exhaustion of the soil is making itself felt in Germany or not.

But if, both in agriculture and industry, we find that progress has been based upon the employment of more rational technical processes, their respective modes of development are nevertheless exceedingly different. Whilst in industry, as we have pointed out, capital became concentrated in ever more colossal enterprises, this law did not make its action felt in the domain of agriculture, where we do not find that large enterprises tend to expand indefinitely. On the contrary, they seldom reach more than modest dimensions, and cultivated properties of over 2,500 acres are the rarest exceptions. Neither do we observe that small or moderate-sized concerns are fatally inferior to the large ones. Not only do the former survive, but a diminution — very slight, it is true — in large properties may even be discerned. Moreover, we do not see in agricultural enterprises that tendency towards specialisation which is so characteristic of industry. On the contrary, it would seem that to-day a greater variety of produce is obtained by any one concern than was the case a hundred years ago. It is impossible to hold the theory that the capitalist who works a large estate can produce more cheaply than the ordinary cultivator, and that wholesale production is consequently an economic necessity in agriculture. It is, therefore, incorrect to say that just as small industries are stifled by large ones, the peasant, finding it impossible to struggle against the competition of great landed proprietors, is hastening to irretrievable disaster.

In his masterly study of the Economic Development of France and Germany 1815–1914, *Dr. J. H. Clapham quotes Gustav Schmoller as pointing out that " from 1500 to 1850 the great social question of the day in Europe was the peasant question." Before the French Revolution the peasant in France and a number of other countries was often a discontented " radical," though he looked to bourgeois leadership to voice and cure his grievances. The French Revolution, however, paved the way for a solution of the peasant problem in France and, to a certain extent, elsewhere. Today the French peasantry is conservative. Its major wrongs have been righted. But the question of the urban proletariat has replaced the peasant question.*

The following extract from Dr. Clapham's book gives some of the reasons why the condition of the French peasant slowly improved after the Revolution. But the theory often advanced that the peasantry profited greatly from the purchase of land which had been confiscated by the Government during the Revolution, Dr. Clapham is strongly inclined to reject.

49. AGRICULTURE IN FRANCE IN THE FIRST HALF OF THE NINETEENTH CENTURY [1]

I. The Static Condition of French Agriculture before 1850

A French scholar writing, just after the middle of the nineteenth century, about the medieval agriculture of a progressive French province, called his readers' attention to "the stationary state in which our agriculture has remained during nearly eight centuries. Almost all the methods which we shall describe," he said, "are practised by our cultivators to-day; so that a thirteenth century peasant would visit many of our farms without much astonishment." [2] If six centuries did so little to change the fundamentals of rural life, it is not to be expected that even the years of revolution and war from 1789 to 1815 would accomplish very much. True, a great deal of land changed hands. The determination of the men of 1789 to abolish feudalism had widespread and definite results. This abolition cleared the field for the operation of new forces, as the nineteenth century ran its course. But since the Revolution was concerned more with legal and proprietary relationships than with the material foundations on which those relationships rest; and since, even, on the legal side, it was more destructive than creative; what was changed sometimes seems curiously small compared with what endured from the past.

Soil, climate, the course of ancient settlements, and the force of tradition among a peasantry mostly ignorant and generally ill-governed, had settled the conditions of rural life. No economic force had come into play, before 1815, strong enough to transform them. France had never undergone a change comparable with that inclosure movement which was in course of completion at this very time in England. There were, before the Revolution, inclosed districts; even whole provinces in which inclosed fields predominated; but to the amazement of the English traveller, accustomed to connect inclosure with improvement, in France that connection was not found. "The marvellous folly," wrote Arthur Young, "is that, in nine-tenths of the inclosures of France, the system of management is precisely the same as in the open fields." That was in 1794; but it would have been almost as true forty or fifty years later. The fact, which the Englishman did not realize, was that inclosed fields in France were generally not the recent work of improving landlords, but were inherited, with the system of management, from a remote past.

[1] J. H. Clapham, *The Economic Development of France and Germany 1815–1914.* Cambridge, University Press, 1921, pp. 6–28 (condensed).

[2] Léopold Delisle, *La classe agricole . . . en Normandie au moyen âge*, p. xl.

II. Effects of Revolutionary Legislation on (a) Free Use of Land and (b) Commons and Common Rights

Stress has been laid so far on those permanent aspects of French Agriculture which the Revolution hardly touched, because it was more concerned with the legal and proprietary relationships than with the economic foundations upon which those relationships rest. But in two important ways at least the revolutionary settlement had affected those foundations and had influenced agriculture itself, as distinguished from rights over agricultural land and agricultural persons. In the first place formal permission had been given to everyone to cultivate as he pleased. The government of the old *régime* had for centuries been anxious about the food problem, about the supply of the capital, the great towns, and the infertile districts in years of bad harvest. Everything possible had been done to keep up the production of grain in every province. As late as 1747, for example, an edict appeared forbidding the increase of vineyards without official permission; and the edict was not allowed to remain a dead letter. Since the traditional rotations of crops — the two-course rotation of the south and the three-course rotation of the north — had grain supplies primarily in view, for they went back to early times when transport was imperfect and each locality was necessarily self-sufficing, government influence had generally been thrown into the scales in their favour. Any variation in cropping which seemed to threaten the local supplies of cereals had been discouraged. Government regulated not only the rotation of crops but almost everything connected with grain, from sowing to market. It was not to be hoarded or wasted; its price was carefully supervised. But the revolutionary politicans were opposed to all this; and accordingly a law of Sept. 28, 1791 had set every proprietor free to cultivate as he pleased, to store up his crops if he wished, and to sell them as he liked. In the first generation he generally went on cultivating as his father had declared unto him; but at least a window had been opened through which the breath of change might blow.

Secondly, the legislation of the Revolution had taken direct notice of commons and common rights. The problems of commons and common rights varied greatly with the various geographical and agricultural regions of France. The most universal and the most essential type of common was the common woodland. In the Alpine zone and in all the highlands there were also very extensive common pastures, generally of good quality. Great stretches of barren heathy common, not all of good quality, were particularly numerous in the west, from the Biscay *landes* to Brittany and the Channel coast; and similar common waste was to be found in many other provinces. It was in the open-field belt of the north, as already suggested, that the problem of common was acute. In this belt, besides rights over woodland

and waste, there had always existed those rights of grazing over the stubble of the open fields, in fact over all land in the commune not inclosed or sown, which in most northern countries, and particularly in England, had proved a serious obstacle to agricultural improvement. Outside the open field belt, these rights were naturally not found in inclosed districts; nor were they at all general in districts, such as the far south, where many of the arable fields lay open. One reason for this was that the southern cultivator had learnt to provide fodder from irrigated meadows. Another was that, for climatic reasons, he had never thought of keeping a heavy stock of cattle.

Under the feudal maxim of *nulle terre sans seigneur*,[1] pre-revolutionary law had generally assumed that all commons belonged to the lord and that all rights over them were enjoyed by his grace; though even in the seventeenth century there were legists who argued, with an eye on Roman Law, that the rights had been there before the lord. The prevalent doctrine was so essentially feudal that the men of 1789 were bound to attack it. Force was given to their attack by the teaching of agricultural reformers that commons and common rights were obstacles to improvement, and by the fact that in the model agriculture of Flanders they had died out centuries earlier. Moreover the wretched condition of many commons had popularized the policy of division and cultivation, both among large landowners and among peasants. As a result considerable stretches of land had been won from the waste for tillage between 1766 and 1789.

From the first the revolutionary assemblies took the view that commons belonged to the commune and that common rights were not grounded in the lord's grace. In 1792 a further step was taken. By a law of Aug. 14 in that year the division of all commons, except common woodlands, was made obligatory. But this was far too drastic and encroached too much on the communal self-government, which was one of the earliest products of the Revolution, to be successful. Within a year division was made optional. Results naturally varied. But in the north considerable areas of common were cut up among the peasants or sold, not always wisely, by the communal authorities between 1792 and 1795. In the metropolitan area commons almost vanished. A law of 1795 held up the work of division, and in 1803 the government of the consulate stopped it altogether, at the same time confirming the divisions, and sales which had already been made. The partition of communal forests remained illegal throughout, though the communes were empowered to revise the rights of user and, if necessary, to levy a toll which was to go towards the maintenance of the woodlands and the general expense of the commune.

About one-tenth of France remained in common ownership in 1815; but the figure does not in any way indicate the position in the true agricultural

[1] No land without its lord. (Editor's note.)

districts. Most of the French commons consisted in the woods and mountain pastures of the Alps, the Pyrenees, the Vosges, and the Jura. There were
whole departments in the north-west where commons were almost unknown.

With the legislative attack on commons there naturally went an attack
on the much more harmful common grazing rights over arable land. But
these rights were difficult to deal with. It is true that the peasant's newly
acquired freedom to till his land as he pleased struck a blow at them in
principle. Under the old open-field routine, when everyone grew the same
crops, the stubbles were thrown open to the beasts on a given day; but if
variations in the course of cropping were introduced this was no longer
possible. For these reasons *vaine pâture* gradually died out during the nineteenth century. But in the early years with which this chapter deals, when
the old rotations and the old customs had been little altered, it still survived
widely though complaints of its harmful working were constant. It was, for
example, in full vigour so near Paris as the arrondissement of Rambouillet
in 1812, " although," as was officially reported, " there was no good cultivator who would not vote for the abolition of a right, which is as injurious
to the rotation of crops and the abolition of fallows as to the prosperity of
sheep rearing." " Often," the reporter went on to explain, " two and even
three shepherds arrive almost at the same moment in a field recently reaped
to feed their flocks. Each hustles his sheep with his dogs to get there first;
and, in the end, the two latest arrived have tired their flocks to no purpose,
for they have to go elsewhere." [1]

III. Changes in Land Ownership Resulting from the Revolution

In approaching the way in which land had changed hands between 1789
and 1815, it must be clearly stated that the question has as yet been imperfectly examined. Probably the materials for a thorough examination do
not exist. Note, at the outset, that there was nothing comparable with that
sharing up of large stretches of noble or church land among the peasantry
which has been witnessed in contemporary Russia. Neither the French
nobility nor the French ecclesiastics did much cultivation of their estates
in the eighteenth century; therefore there was not much land to share. The
great nobles had gone to town and let out their estates to middlemen. The
middlemen did not cultivate, but sublet to cultivators of all sorts. As a rule
the greater estates were not compact stretches of territory. They were rather
bundles of rights over a great number of scattered holdings. These holdings,
being already occupied by peasants or farmers, could not be cut up. A great
lord might quite well have no land in hand at all; though he drew a large
income from rents and *cens* [2] and other dues. Like Arthur Young's friend in

---

[1] *Le Statistique Agricole de 1814*, pp. 507–8.
[2] Feudal dues paid in the form of money. (Editor's note.)

Provence, if his *cens* vanished a large part of his estate went with it. Even if the estate happened to be continuous the situation was not different; there were *censiers, métayers,*[1] or farmers already on it. The landlord who had anything in the nature of an English home-farm was the exception. If he did keep a farm in hand, the chances were all against his cultivating it himself. In Normandy, Arthur Young was shocked to find *métayers* " where they should least of all be looked for, on the farms which gentlemen keep in their own hands." " The consequence is," he added, " that every gentleman's farm must be precisely the worst cultivated in the neighborhood "; for he had a low opinion of *métayage*. The fact was that, all over France, the smaller resident gentry were generally lords of *métayers;* and since *metayage* was not touched by legislation, and the smaller gentry weathered the revolutionary storm rather better than the great, many of them remained lords of *métayers* in 1815.

What happened was that very extensive estates, the property of royal princes, emigrant nobles, and above all of the Church, became national property and were put up to sale or exchanged for the notorious *assignats,* the paper money issued on the security of the confiscated Church land. In so far as these estates had consisted merely in rights to receive *cens,* or other feudal payments, they melted away, so to speak, in the hands of the state. But there remained a great deal of farmed land and land let on a sharetenancy, with woodlands and wastes which had been definitely in private ownership and so did not pass to the communes. The problem which has never been solved statistically is — what shares of these lands came, firstly, into the hands of the peasantry, secondly, into those of a new class of landlords or, thirdly, came back at the Restoration to the original owners or their representatives? The available evidence suggests that the second and third shares were very much greater than the first.

At the Restoration there were still large stocks of confiscated emigrants' estates, which had never been sold or granted away by Napoleon. These were restored, although the demand of the returned emigrants that their old properties should be re-established in their entirety could never be granted. But it was open to them to buy. Moreover agents acting on their behalf had occasionally bought for them in their absence. Exiles who had made their peace with Napoleon had enjoyed earlier opportunities of recovering part of their lost lands. What with repurchase and regrant, it is believed that by 1820 the old nobility had made good something like a half of its losses.

For the Church lands and the lay lands which were sold away from their original owners, the problem is both more complex and more obscure; but the

---

[1] The *métayer* was a tenant who held land on condition of sharing his crops with his landlord. The landlord's share was usually a half, but it might be as low as a third or as high as two-thirds. (Editor's note.)

probability is that no great part of them went to the peasantry, certainly not to the smaller peasantry. The gamblers in *assignats* and land speculators of 1790–9 were no doubt drawn from all classes; but the majority were bourgeois — merchants, officials, parliamentary deputies, lawyers, and those people skilled in the handling of estates who had acted as middlemen for the nobility and the Church. In the metropolitan area land was bought freely by the *bourgeoisie,* in the strictest sense of the term. Where considerable purchases by cultivators are met with, the purchasers are inevitably fairly substantial persons; and such persons, as has been seen, were rare. Some of the large farmers on ecclesiastical land took the opportunity to become owners, when their land came on the market; but the most that the small man could hope for was the addition of another fragment to his holding, if he found himself in a position to overbid the moneyed man from outside. If he were exceptionally lucky or exceptionally able he probably became a little landlord himself for there were always hard pressed cultivators ready to relieve the smallest landlord of the burden of personal labour.

. . . .

All things considered, this fresh influx of bourgeois landowners is the most significant outcome of the revolutionary land settlement.

IV. *Agricultural Improvement*

No doubt the hope of agricultural reformers in the revolutionary and Napoleonic age, that France would shortly make a considerable net addition to her supplies of foodstuffs, was in part realised during the following generation. An agriculture so skilful as that of Flanders, or that of the plain of Nîmes, added to its output merely by carrying forward and perfecting old tried methods, assimilating easily any new crop or new rotation which was appropriate to local conditions. The growth of industrial towns in the north gave the Flemish farmer still more of that manure with which he had always fed his land generously. His root crops fattened his beasts and his beasts fattened his land in profitable rotation. The farmers of the adjacent departments, now at length copying his methods, made even more progress than he, for they started from a far lower level. The steady decline of the fallow, in the north and to a less degree elsewhere, with the improvements in the strains of cattle and sheep, added directly and indirectly to the net supply of foodstuffs. Whatever the drawbacks incidental to the local disappearance and the general curtailment of commons, and such drawbacks it must be remembered were far less than in contemporary England, owing to the non-existence of a landless class in France and the fact that the decline in common land did not create such a class — whatever these drawbacks may have been, many hundreds of thousands of acres were added to the cultivated area of France between 1789 and 1848. And by the latter date the potato alone had made an appreciable addition to the national food supplies.

There is no doubt too that the average yield of the staple crops, like the average weight of the cattle and sheep, had increased as the result of an agriculture, which, taking the country as a whole and allowing for backward provinces, was perceptibly more varied and more rational. What that increase was it is not safe to guess. Estimates have been made; but the starting point is much too uncertain, and the point of arrival not nearly certain enough, to warrant their quotation. Even with a full modern statistical apparatus, average yields per acre are awkward things to get at, in a country of reticent peasants whose holdings are much divided and scattered.

Each successive decade in the nineteenth century saw a rather more rapid rate of change in agriculture. This acceleration was due in part to the cumulative results of the removal of legal or customary hindrances to the free exercise of initiative, as a result of the Revolution. In part to the increase of technical knowledge; first among those whom the peasants imitated; then among the peasants themselves, as their opportunities for education improved. In part perhaps to the increased vitality of a people lifted from a state of real misery into one of relative comfort. But in the main, there can be little doubt, to improvements in the means of communication. From 1800 to 1836 the improvement was mainly in high roads and canals. After the law of 1836, which encouraged the building of by-roads, their influence was added. Then — and far more important — came the railways of the forties.

The astonishing economic development of France, Germany, and England between the Franco-Prussian War and the Great War is clearly illustrated by the following figures. In the case of Germany and England per capita gains were partly offset by great increases in population. In France, however, the increase of population was much less.

It should be noted that in these tables of figures money values are given in terms of the currency of each country at pre-War valuations: for France, francs; for Germany, marks; for Great Britain, pounds.

50. *STATISTICS ILLUSTRATING THE ECONOMIC DEVELOP-*
MENT OF FRANCE, GERMANY, AND GREAT BRITAIN
1867–1909 [1]

I. France.

Population

1871	36,190,000
1908	39,252,000

Imports (value in francs)

1871	3,567,000,000
1907	6,223,000,000

Exports (value in francs)

1871	2,873,000,000
1907	5,596,000,000

Iron Ore Production (Metric tons. The metric ton is 2240 pounds)

1871	1,852,272
1907	10,008,500

Coal Production including Lignite (tons)

1871	13,258,920
1908	36,874,000

Merchant Marine (Net tonnage)

	Sailing Vessels	Steam Vessels	Total
1872	911,613	177,462	1,089,075
1907	662,828	739,819	1,402,647

Revenues (in francs)

1871	2,014,000,000
1907	3,968,000,000

Estimated Consumption of Coffee, Sugar and Wine

	Coffee (kilograms)	Sugar (kilograms)	Wine (hectoliters)
1871	40,000,000	284,000,000	56,000,000
1907	101,000,000	581,000,000	53,000,000

[1] 61st Congress. 2d Session. *Senate Documents, No. 578.* " Statistics for Great Britain, Germany, and France, 1867–1909."

II. *Germany*
Population

1871	40,997,000
1908	63,017,000

Imports

Total Value (in marks)	Per Capita Value (in marks)
1872 3,464,600,000	84.67
1908 8,077,093,000	127.69

Exports

Total Value (in marks)	Per Capita Value (in marks)
1872 2,492,200,000	60.91
1908 6,481,453,000	102.47

Production of Iron in the German Customs Union
(Quantity in Metric tons)

	Pig Iron	All Products Derived from Iron Ores
1871	1,492,000	1,564,000
1907	12,804,000	12,875,000

Production of Coal in the German Customs Union
(Quantity in Metric tons)

	Coal	Lignite	Total
1871	29,373,000	8,483,000	37,856,000
1907	143,186,000	62,547,000	205,733,000

Development of the Merchant Marine
(Net tonnage)

	Sailing Vessels	Steam Vessels
1871	900,361	81,994
1908	433,749	2,256,793

Revenues of the Government (in marks)

1872	1,524,548,200
1908	2,494,945,100

Per Capita Consumption in Kilograms of Certain Foreign Commodities
within the Customs Union, 1871–1907

	Coffee	Cocoa	Rice	Tropical Fruits	Tea
1871–1875 (yearly average)	2.27	.05	1.55	0.57	0.02
1907	3.02	.52	2.51	2.96	0.06

Per Capita Consumption of Beer, Tobacco, and Sugar

	Beer (liters)	Tobacco (kilos)	Sugar (kilos)
1871		1.8	4.9
1874	93	1.6	5.8
1906	118	1.5	16.8

III. Great Britain
Population, United Kingdom

1871	31,555,694
1908	44,546,803

Imports

Total value (in pounds sterling)		Per capita value		
1871	£331,015,480	£10	10s	1d
1908	£592,953,487	£13	6s	3d

Exports

Total value of British, foreign and colonial produce exported		Per capita value		
1871	£283,574,700	£19	10s	1d
1908	£456,727,521	£23	11s	3d

Iron Production

	Pig Iron (tons)	Steel Ingots (tons)	Manufactures of Steel and Iron Exported (tons)
1871			1,971,949
1875	6,365,462	723,605	1,487,869
1907	9,923,000	6,522,748	3,208,288

Coal Production (tons)

1873	128,680,131
1908	261,528,795

Merchant Marine (Net tonnage)

	Sailing Vessels	Steam Vessels	Total
1871	4,374,511	1,319,612	5,694,123
1908	1,402,781	10,138,613	11,541,394

Imperial Revenues

	Gross	Per Capita		
1870–1871	£69,945,220	£2	4s	5d
1907–1908	£146,541,737	£3	5s	10d

Per Capita Consumption of Tea and Sugar

	Tea Pounds	Sugar Pounds	
		Raw	Refined
1871	3.92	41.51	5.29
1907	6.21	37.80	49.94

CHAPTER V

DEVELOPMENTS ON THE CONTINENT
(1830–1849)

SECTION I. FRANCE

With his usual keen insight the celebrated author of Democracy in America, *Alexis de Tocqueville, attempts in his* Recollections *to analyze the causes of the Revolution of 1848. The Revolution, of which he was an eye-witness, filled him with gloom; for this new upheaval made him fear that France, instead of working toward a balanced liberty, " the passion of his life," was declining into a condition of intermittent anarchy. Filled as he was with these forebodings the exuberant optimism of his friend Ampère, with whom he had hoped to share his fears, as he admits in his* Recollections, *naturally irritated him.*

51. THE FRENCH REVOLUTION OF FEBRUARY, 1848 [1]

AND so the Monarchy of July was fallen, fallen without a struggle, and before rather than beneath the blows of the victors, who were as astonished at their triumph as were the vanquished at their defeat. I have often, since the Revolution of February, heard M. Guizot and even M. Molé and M. Thiers [2] declare that this event should only be attributed to a surprise and regarded as a mere accident, a bold and lucky stroke and nothing more. I have always felt tempted to answer them in the words which Molière's Misanthrope uses to Oronte:

Pour en juger ainsi, vous avez vos raisons; [3] for these three men had conducted the affairs of France, under the guidance of King Louis-Philippe, during eighteen years, and it was difficult for them to admit that it was the King's bad government which had prepared the catastrophe which hurled him from the Throne.

As for me, I have not the same motives for forming an opinion, and I could hardly persuade myself to be of theirs. I am not prepared to say that accidents played no part in the Revolution of February: on the contrary, they played a great one; but they were not the only thing.

---

[1] Alexis de Tocqueville. *Recollections.* Translated by Alexander Teixeira de Mattos. New York, Macmillan, 1896, pp. 79–89.

[2] Former ministers of Louis Philippe. (Editor's note.)

[3] You have your own reasons for reaching this conclusion. (Editor's note.)

I have come across men of letters, who have written history without taking part in public affairs, and politicians, who have only concerned themselves with producing events without thinking of describing them. I have observed that the first are always inclined to find general causes, whereas the others, living in the midst of disconnected daily facts, are prone to imagine that everything is attributable to particular incidents, and that the wires which they pull are the same that move the world. It is to be presumed that both are equally deceived.

For my part, I detest these absolute systems, which represent all the events of history as depending upon great first causes linked by the chain of fatality, and which, as it were, suppress men from the history of the human race. They seem narrow, to my mind, under their pretence of broadness, and false beneath their air of mathematical exactness. I believe (*pace* the writers who have invented these sublime theories in order to feed their vanity and facilitate their work) that many important historical facts can only be explained by accidental circumstances, and that many others remain totally inexplicable. Moreover, chance, or rather that tangle of secondary causes which we call chance, for want of the knowledge how to unravel it, plays a great part in all that happens on the world's stage; although I firmly believe that chance does nothing that has not been prepared beforehand. Antecedent facts, the nature of institutions, the cast of minds and the state of morals are the materials of which are composed those impromptus which astonish and alarm us.

The Revolution of February, in common with all other great events of this class, sprang from general causes, impregnated, if I am permitted the expression, by accidents; and it would be as superficial a judgment to ascribe it necessarily to the former or exclusively to the latter.

The industrial revolution which, during the past thirty years, had turned Paris into the principal manufacturing city of France and attracted within its walls an entire new population of workmen (to whom the works of the fortifications had added another population of labourers at present deprived of work) tended more and more to inflame this multitude. Add to this the democratic disease of envy, which was silently permeating it; the economical and political theories which were beginning to make their way and which strove to prove that human misery was the work of laws and not of Providence, and that poverty could be suppressed by changing the conditions of society; the contempt into which the governing class, and especially the men who led it, had fallen, a contempt so general and so profound that it paralyzed the resistance even of those who were most interested in maintaining the power that was being overthrown; the centralization which reduced the whole revolutionary movement to the overmastering of Paris and the seizing of the machinery of government; and lastly, the mobility of all things, institutions, ideas, men and customs, in a fluctuating state of society which had, in less than sixty years, undergone the shock of seven great revolutions, without numbering a multitude of smaller, secondary upheavals. These were the general causes without which the Revolution of February would have been impossible. The principal accidents which led to it were the passions of the dynastic Opposition, which brought about a riot in proposing a reform; the suppression of this riot, first over-violent, and then abandoned; the sudden disappearance of the old Ministry, unexpectedly snapping the threads of power, which the new ministers, in their confusion, were unable either to seize upon or to reunite; the mistakes and disorder of mind of these ministers, so powerless to re-establish that which they had been strong enough to overthrow; the vacillation of the generals; the absence of the only Princes who possessed either personal energy or popularity; and above all, the senile imbecility of King Louis-Philippe, his weakness, which no one could have foreseen, and which still remains almost incredible, after the event has proved it.

I have sometimes asked myself what could have produced this sudden and unprecedented depression in the King's mind. Louis-Philippe had spent his life in the midst of revolutions, and certainly lacked neither experience, courage, nor readiness of mind, although these qualities all failed him so completely on that day. In my opinion, his weakness was due to his excessive surprise; he was overwhelmed with consternation before he had grasped the meaning of things. The Revolution of February was *unforeseen* by all, but by him more than any other; he had been prepared for it by no warning from the outside, for since many years his mind had withdrawn into that sort of haughty solitude into which in the end the intellect almost always settles down on princes who have long lived happily, and who, mistaking luck for genius, refuse to listen to anything, because they think that there is nothing left for them to learn from anybody. Besides, Louis-Philippe had been deceived, as I have already said that his ministers were, by the misleading light cast by antecedent facts upon present times. One might draw a strange picture of all the errors which have thus been begotten, one by the other, without resembling each other. We see Charles I. driven to tyranny and violence at the sight of the progress which the spirit of opposition had made in England during the gentle reign of his father; Louis XVI. determined to suffer everything because Charles I. had perished by refusing to endure anything; Charles X. provoking the Revolution, because he had with his own eyes beheld the weakness of Louis XVI.; and lastly, Louis-Philippe, who had more perspicacity than any of them, imagining that, in order to remain on the Throne, all he had to do was to observe the letter of the law while violating its spirit, and that, provided he himself kept within the bounds of the Charter, the nation would never exceed them. To warp the spirit of the

Constitution without changing the letter; to set the vices of the country in opposition to each other; gently to drown revolutionary passion in the love of material enjoyment: such was the idea of his whole life. Little by little, it had become, not his leading, but his sole idea. He had wrapped himself in it, he had lived in it; and when he suddenly saw that it was a false idea, he became like a man who is awakened in the night by an earthquake, and who, feeling his house crumbling in the darkness, and the very ground seeming to yawn beneath his feet, remains distracted amid this unforeseen and universal ruin.

I am arguing very much at my ease to-day concerning the causes that brought about the events of the 24th of February, (1848); but on the afternoon of that day I had many other things in my head: I was thinking of the events themselves, and sought less for what had produced them than for what was to follow.

I returned slowly home. I explained in a few words to Madame de Tocqueville what I had seen, and sat down in a corner to think. I cannot remember ever feeling my soul so full of sadness. It was the second revolution I had seen accomplish itself, before my eyes, within seventeen years!

On the 30th of July 1830, at daybreak, I had met the carriages of King Charles X. on the outer boulevards of Versailles, with damaged escutcheons, proceeding at a foot pace, in Indian file, like a funeral, and I was unable to restrain my tears at the sight. This time my impressions were of another kind, but even keener. Both revolutions had afflicted me; but how much more bitter were the impressions caused by the last! I had until the end felt a remnant of hereditary affection for Charles X.; but that King fell for having violated rights that were dear to me, and I had every hope that my country's freedom would be revived rather than extinguished by his fall. But now this freedom seemed dead; the Princes who were fleeing were nothing to me, but I felt that the cause I had at heart was lost.

I had spent the best days of my youth amid a society which seemed to increase in greatness and prosperity as it increased in liberty; I had conceived the idea of a balanced, regulated liberty, held in check by religion, custom and law; the attractions of this liberty had touched me; it had become the passion of my life; I felt that I could never be consoled for its loss, and that I must renounce all hope of its recovery.

I had gained too much experience of mankind to be able to content myself with empty words; I knew that, if one great revolution is able to establish liberty in a country, a number of succeeding revolutions make all regular liberty impossible for very many years.

I could not yet know what would issue from this last revolution, but I was already convinced that it could give birth to nothing that would satisfy me; and I foresaw that, whatever might be the lot reserved for our posterity, our own fate was to drag on our lives miserably amid alternate reactions of licence and oppression.

I began to pass in review the history of our last sixty years, and I smiled bitterly when I thought of the illusions formed at the conclusion of each period in this long revolution; the theories on which these illusions had been fed; the sapient dreams of our historians, and all the ingenious and deceptive systems by the aid of which it had been endeavoured to explain a present which was still incorrectly seen, and a future which was not seen at all.

The Constitutional Monarchy had succeeded the Ancien Régime; the Republic, the Monarchy; the Empire, the Republic; the Restoration, the Empire; and then came the Monarchy of July. After each of these successive changes it was said that the French Revolution, having accomplished what was presumptuously called its work, was finished; this had been said and it had been believed. Alas! I myself had hoped it under the Restoration, and again after the fall of the Government of the Restoration; and here is the French Revolution beginning over again, for it is still the same one. As we go on, its end seems farther off and shrouded in greater darkness. Shall we ever — as we are assured by other prophets, perhaps as delusive as their predecessors — shall we ever attain a more complete and more far-reaching social transformation than our fathers foresaw and desired, and than we ourselves are able to foresee; or are we not destined simply to end in a condition of intermittent anarchy, the well-known chronic and incurable complaint of old races? As for me, I am unable to say; I do not know when this long voyage will be ended; I am weary of seeing the shore in each successive mirage, and I often ask myself whether the *terra firma* we are seeking does really exist, and whether we are not doomed to rove upon the seas forever.

I spent the rest of the day with Ampère, who was my colleague at the Institute, and one of my best friends. He came to discover what had become of me in the affray, and to ask himself to dinner. I wished at first to relieve myself by making him share my vexation; but I soon perceived that his impression was not the same as mine, and that he looked differently upon the revolution which was in progress. Ampère was a man of intelligence and, better still, a man full of heart, gentle in manner, and reliable. His good-nature caused him to be liked; and he was popular because of his versatile, witty, amusing, good-humoured conversation, in which he made many remarks that were at once entertaining and agreeable to hear but too shallow to remember. Unfortunately, he was inclined to carry the *esprit* of the salons into literature and the *esprit* of literature into politics. What I call literary *esprit* in politics consists in seeking for what is novel and ingenious rather than for what is true; in preferring the showy to the useful; in showing one's self very sensible to the playing and elocution of the actors, without regard to the results of the play; and, lastly, in judging by impressions rather than reasons. I need not say that this eccentricity exists among others besides Academicians. To tell the truth, the whole nation is a little inclined that way, and the French Public very often takes a man-of-letters' view of politics. Ampère held the fallen Government in great contempt, and its last actions had irritated him greatly. Moreover, he had witnessed many instances of courage, disinterestedness, and even generosity among the insurgents; and he had been bitten by the popular excitement.

I saw that he not only did not enter into my view, but that he was disposed to take quite an opposite one. Seeing this, I was suddenly impelled to turn against Ampère all the feelings of indignation, grief and anger that had been accumulating in my heart since the morning; and I spoke to him with a violence of language which I have often since recalled with a certain shame, and which none but a friendship so sincere as his could have excused. I remember saying to him, *inter alia:*

" You understand nothing of what is happening; you are judging like a poet or a Paris cockney. You call this the triumph of liberty, when it is its final defeat. I tell you that the people which you so artlessly admire has just succeeded in proving that it is unfit and unworthy to live a life of freedom. Show me what experience has taught it! Where are the new virtues it has gained, the old vices it has laid aside? No, I tell you, it is always the same, as impatient, as thoughtless, as contemptuous of law and order, as easily led and as cowardly in the presence of danger as its fathers were before it. Time has altered it in no way, and has left it as frivolous in serious matters as it used to be in trifles."

After much vociferation we both ended by appealing to the future, that enlightened and upright judge who always, alas! arrives too late.

The French Revolution of February, 1848, was followed in June by a far more bloody uprising. The Provisional Government's half-hearted attempt to put into effect Louis Blanc's idea of " National Workshops," supplying work to all who wished it, had attracted great numbers of men. The heavy expense attendant on the employment of these men having led the Government to close the workshops, the closing was the signal for the social revolution of the " June Days," which the Government finally repressed with the greatest severity. The revolt left an enduring hatred between the capitalist class and the urban proletariat.

In the following selection de Tocqueville comments on the causes and character of the " June Days."

52. "*THE JUNE DAYS,*" *1848*[1]

I come at last to the insurrection of June, the most extensive and the most singular that has occurred in our history, and perhaps in any other: the most extensive, because, during four days, more than a hundred thousand men were engaged in it; the most singular, because the insurgents fought without a war-cry, without leaders, without flags, and yet with a marvellous harmony and an amount of military experience that astonished the oldest officers.

What distinguished it also, among all the events of this kind which have succeeded one another in France for sixty years, is that it did not aim at changing the form of government, but at altering the order of society. It was not, strictly speaking, a political struggle, in the sense which until then we had given to the word, but a combat of class against class, a sort of Servile War. It represented the facts of the Revolution of February in the same manner as the theories of Socialism represented its ideas; or rather it issued naturally from these ideas, as a son does from his mother. We behold in it nothing more than a blind and rude, but powerful, effort on the part of the workmen to escape from the necessities of their condition, which had been depicted to them as one of unlawful oppression, and to open up by main force a road towards that imaginary comfort with which they had been deluded. It was this mixture of greed and false theory which first gave birth to the insurrection and then made it so formidable. These poor people had been told that the wealth of the rich was in some way the produce of a theft practised upon themselves. They had been assured that the inequality of fortunes was as opposed to morality and the welfare of society as it was to nature. Prompted by their needs and their passions, many had believed this obscure and erroneous notion of right, which, mingled with brute force, imparted to the latter an energy, a tenacity and a power which it would never have possessed unaided.

It must also be observed that this formidable insurrection was not the enterprise of a certain number of conspirators, but the revolt of one whole section of the population against another. Women took part in it as well as men. While the latter fought, the former prepared and carried ammunition; and when at last the time had come to surrender, the women were the last to yield. These women went to battle with, as it were, a housewifely ardour: they looked to victory for the comfort of their husbands and the education of their children. They took pleasure in this war as they might have taken pleasure in a lottery.

As to the strategic science displayed by this multitude, the warlike nature

[1] Alexis de Tocqueville. *Recollections.* Translated by Alexander Teixeira de Mattos. New York, Macmillan, 1896, pp. 187–189.

of the French, their long experience of insurrections, and particularly the military education which the majority of the men of the people in turn receive, suffice to explain it. Half of the Paris workmen have served in our armies, and they are always glad to take up arms again. Generally speaking, old soldiers abound in our riots. On the 24th of February, when Lamoricière was surrounded by his foes, he twice owed his life to insurgents who had fought under him in Africa, men in whom the recollection of their military life had been stronger than the fury of civil war.

As we know, it was the closing of the national workshops that occasioned the rising. Dreading to disband this formidable soldiery at one stroke, the Government had tried to disperse it by sending part of the workmen into the country. They refused to leave. On the 22nd of June, they marched through Paris in troops, singing in cadence, in a monotonous chant, " We won't be sent away, we won't be sent away. . . ." Their delegates waited upon the members of the Committee of the Executive Power with a series of arrogant demands, and on meeting with a refusal, withdrew with the announcement that next day they would have recourse to arms. Everything, indeed, tended to show that the long-expected crisis had come.

SECTION II. GERMANY

One of the most important influences leading to the prosperity and unification of Germany was the German " Zollverein " or Customs Union. With its establishment the numerous tariffs which obstructed trade and good relations among the German states were abolished for all the states that entered the union.

In the following selection an Englishman, John Bowring, reports on the Zollverein to Lord Palmerston.

53. THE ZOLLVEREIN [1]

My Lord,

In compliance with the instructions which I had the honour to receive from your Lordship, dated Foreign Office, July 14, 1839, I proceed to report on the progress, present state, and future prospects of the Russian Commercial League.

No doubt this great Union which is known in Germany by the name of the *Zoll Verein* or *Zoll Verbände* (Toll Association or Alliance), derived its first and strongest influence from a desire to get rid of those barriers to intercommunication which the separate fiscal legislation of the various states

---

[1] Report on the Prussian Commercial Union, addressed to The Right Hon. Lord Viscount Palmerston, Her Majesty's Secretary of State for Foreign Affairs, by John Bowring. *British Parliamentary Papers.* Session 16 January–11 August 1840, vol. XXI. *Reports from Commissioners,* 1840, vol. VI, pp. 381–389 (condensed).

of Germany raised among a people whom natural and national feelings, as well as common interests, would otherwise have connected more intimately and permanently together.

The Zoll Verein represents, in Germany, the operation of the same opinions and tendencies which have already effected so many changes in the commercial legislation of other countries. In the United Kingdom the Custom-house laws which separated Scotland and Ireland from England have been superseded by a general system applicable to the whole. In France the local barriers and the local tariffs have given way to a general and uniform system of taxation. Even before the Commercial League associated so many states in a common union, several less extensive combinations had prepared the way for a more diffusive intercourse. Between the states which do not form part of the Prussian League — as, for example, between Hanover and Brunswick and Oldenburgh the same tariffs have been adopted, and the payment of duties in one of the states is sufficient to secure free sale or transit in the other.

The Commercial League is, in fact, the substantial representative of a sentiment widely, if not universally, spread in Germany — that of national unity. It has done wonders in breaking down petty and local prejudices, and has become a foundation on which future legislation, representing the common interests of the German people, may undoubtedly be hereafter raised. If well directed in its future operation, the Zoll Verein will represent the fusion of German interests in one great alliance. The peril to its beneficial results will grow out of the efforts which will be made, and which are already made, to give by protections and prohibitions an undue weight to the smaller and sinister interests of the Verein. But if its tariffs be so moderate and so judicious as to allow full play to the interests of the consumers in the field of competition — if there should be no forcing of capital into regions of unproductiveness or of less productiveness — if the claims of manufacturers to sacrifices in their favour from the community at large be rejected — if the great agricultural interests of Germany recover that portion of attention from the *commercial* union to which they are justly entitled — if the importance of foreign trade and navigation be duly estimated — the Zoll Verein will have the happiest influence on the general prosperity. And that the League has been much strengthened by the experience of its benefits — that its popularity is extending — that its further spreading may be confidently anticipated — appears to be indubitable. In fact the Zoll Verein has brought the sentiment of German nationality out of the regions of hope and fancy into those of positive and material interests; and representing as it does the popular feeling of Germany, it may become, under enlightened guidance, an instrument not only for promoting the peace and prosperity of the states that compose it, but of extending their friendly relations through the world.

Considerations both of morality and economy were not wanting to recommend the Commercial Union to the German people. Not only were the numerous barriers and various legislation of the German states great impediments to trade, but they created a considerable amount of contraband traffic, and caused the country to swarm with petty smugglers who lived upon the profits which the varieties of the tariffs placed within their reach. The custom-house administration was costly, and generally inefficient, from the extent of frontier to be guarded; so that the establishment of one large, instead of a variety of small circles, has led at the same time to a great diminution of cost and a great increase of efficiency, while it has removed from all the interior of Germany that demoralising influence which the presence of multitudes of illicit traders and smugglers always brings with it.

The Zoll Verein was not, as it has been often asserted to be, a union formed in hostility to the commercial interests of other states — it was not intended prematurely to create a manufacturing population in rivalry with or opposition to the manufacturing aptitudes of Great Britain — it was by no means the purpose of its founders to misdirect capital to unprofitable employment, to sacrifice agriculture to trade, or to encourage less the field than the factory. The Zoll Verein was the substantial expression and effect of a general desire among a great nation, split into many small states, but still of common origin, similar manners, speaking the same language, educated in the same spirit, to communicate, to trade, to travel, without the annoyance and impediments which the separate fiscal regulations of every one of their governments threw in the way. If, in the natural progress of things, the tariffs of the Zoll Verein have become hostile to the importation of foreign, and especially of British, produce, it is because *our* laws have prevented the greater extension of commercial relations with Germany. We have rejected the payments they have offered — we have forced them to manufacture what they were unable to buy — and we have put in their hands the means of manufacturing cheaply by refusing to take the surplus of their agricultural produce, the non-exportation of which has kept their markets so low that small wages have been sufficient to give great comforts to their labourers.

There can be no doubt that the hostile tariffs of other nations, and especially the corn and timber laws of Great Britain, served greatly to strengthen the arguments in favour of the Commercial Union. It was felt necessary to extend the home market while foreign markets were closed, or only partially and irregularly opened, to the leading articles of German production.

" We should not have complained," says a distinguished German writer, in 1835, " that all our markets were overflowing with English manufacturers — that Germany received in cotton goods alone more than the hundred millions of British subjects in the East Indies — had not England, while she was inundating us with *her* productions, insisted on closing her markets to *ours*. Mr. Robinson's resolutions in 1815 had, in fact, excluded our corn from the ports of Great Britain: she told us we were to buy, but not to sell. We were not willing to adopt reprisals; we vainly hoped that a sense of her own interest would lead to reciprocity. But we were disappointed, and we were compelled to take care of ourselves."

Thus, while on the one hand the Zoll Verein was advocated as a measure of self-defence against the hostile legislation of foreign nations, it should not be forgotten that, as respects the confederated states, it represented the principles of unrestricted intercommunication.

As between more than 26 millions of Germans it was the establishment of *free trade;* restrictions, duties, prohibitions, custom-houses, there are none, as far as regards the various states that comprise the Commercial Union. Whatever impediments the tariffs create to commercial communication with foreign lands, the League has thrown down every barrier which stood in the way of trading intercourse between the different branches of the great German family which the League represents. And as the conception of the League was popular and national, so it cannot be denied that its workings have been *on the whole* favourable to the prosperity and to the happiness of the German community.

. . . .

Long before the Zoll Verein came into operation the same spirit which led to its formation had been exhibited in various parts of Germany, leading to sundry local and even national reforms in the commercial policy of the German states.

Some steps had been taken in Prussia, during the years 1816 and 1817, by sundry ordinances to introduce " a general and simple system of custom-house legislation," and on the 26th May, 1818, a new tariff was published, which is in fact the ground-work of the existing arrangements. Before this period a different fiscal system prevailed in different parts of the Prussian kingdom. The imposts in Brandenburg amounted to 69 groschen — 7s. 4d. per individual; in Silesia they were only 22 groschen — 2s. 3d. The new law allowed the unrestricted circulation of all foreign products which had once passed the frontier, and the free transit of all home productions. The intention of this tariff of 1818 was to establish 10 per cent as the maximum of protection; and had the intention of the Prussians been carried into effect there would have been no grounds for complaint.

In speaking of the Prussian tariff to the House of Commons, on the 7th May, 1827, Mr. Huskisson stated " that the duties on the internal consumption of British goods are what we should consider very low upon most articles, fluctuating from 5 to 10 per cent — upon no one article exceeding

15 per cent;" but this was undoubtedly an incorrect view of things, for it will appear, on the investigation of the matter, that the duties on many articles of British manufacture vary from 20 to 100 per cent upon the value; and though no doubt the duty (being levied on the weight) has much increased in ad valorem amount since 1827, it was even then from 20 to 60 per cent on the various low-priced manufactures; nor was Mr. Huskisson warranted in saying that "in the whole Prussian tariff there is not a single prohibition," inasmuch as imports of salt and playing cards are wholly prohibited except for government account.

The most important step by which evidence was given of the tendency of the different states of Germany to amalgamate their interests and to establish, instead of many tariffs, one single system, was the union of Bavaria, Würtemberg, Hohenzollern-Sigmaringen and Hohenzollern-Hechingen, in the commercial league of 28th July, 1824. Baden, the two Hesses, and Saxony were afterwards invited to join the league. The government of Prussia, alive to the state of public opinion, had entered by various treaties, from 1819 to 1830, into a commercial league with Grand Ducal Hesse, Lippe Detmold, and some smaller states, and in December, 1826, the *enclaves* (such portions of the territory as are surrounded by another state) of Mecklenburg-Schwerin, Ripen-Hesseland, Schoenberg, Anhalt-Kothen, Anhalt-Dessau, Hesse-Homburg, and other states, joined the Prussian Union; while in 1831, Saxony, Electoral Hesse, Saxe Weimar, Saxe Meiningen, Saxe Coburg, Saxe Altenburg, and others united themselves to the Bavaro-Würtemberg league. Each of these two great branches naturally sought to extend its influence, and each prepared the way for a fusion of the whole in one great association. .

On the 22nd March, 1833, a treaty was concluded between Prussia, Bavaria, Würtemberg, Electoral and Ducal Hesse; on the 30th March of the same year Saxony joined the association; on the 11th of May, Anhalt and Ducal Saxony united themselves. The ratifications were exchanged on the 11th of May. This treaty is the basis of the Zoll Verein, or Commercial League. . . .

. . . .

The objects proposed by the Zoll Verein were the removal of all restrictions to communication and transit, the abolition of all internal custom-houses, the establishment of a common tariff and system of collection, and the repartition of the receipts on all imports and exports according to the population among all the members of the League. . . . The intention of the tariff is to admit raw materials without any, or on merely a nominal, duty.

. . . .

The Zoll Verein, by directing capital to internal, in preference to external, trade, has already had a great influence in improving the roads, the canals, the means of travelling, the transport of letters — in a word, in giving additional impulse to inland communications of every sort. The isolation of the several German states, with separate fiscal interests, and often hostile legislation, prevented those facilities from being given to intercourse which are alike the evidence and the means of civilisation. On every side beneficial changes are taking place. Railways are being constructed in many parts of the German territory — steam-boats are crowding the German ports and coasting along the German shores — everything is transported with greater cheapness and rapidity.

On the surface the liberal movement in Germany made little concrete progress between the passage of the Carlsbad Decrees in 1819 and the outbreak of the Revolution of 1848. As a result of the revolutionary movements of 1830, it is true, a few moderately liberal constitutions were granted by rulers of some of the lesser German states. But soon thereafter new decrees passed by the German Diet under the influence of Metternich repressed liberalism more sternly than ever.

Underneath the surface, however, the desire for liberty and unity was spreading. And when the news of Louis Philippe's fall crossed the Rhine there broke out the most serious revolution that Germany had ever known, the most serious she was destined to know until the fall of the German Empire in 1918.

Carl Schurz, who in 1848 was an ardent young revolutionist and who later emigrated to the United States and became a major-general and, under President Hayes, Secretary of the Interior, describes in his Reminiscences *some of the stirring scenes of the Revolution of 1848 in Germany.*

54. PHASES OF THE GERMAN REVOLUTION OF 1848 [1]

One morning, toward the end of February, 1848, I sat quietly in my attic-chamber, working hard at my tragedy of " Ulrich von Hutten," when suddenly a friend rushed breathlessly into the room, exclaiming: " What, you sitting here! Do you not know what has happened? "

" No; what? "

" The French have driven away Louis Philippe and proclaimed the republic."

I threw down my pen — and that was the end of " Ulrich von Hutten." I never touched the manuscript again. We tore down the stairs, into the street, to the market-square, the accustomed meeting-place for all the student

[1] *The Reminiscences of Carl Schurz.* 3 vols., New York, Doubleday, Doran & Co., Inc., 1919 vol. I, pp. III–113; 115–123.

societies after their midday dinner. Although it was still forenoon, the market was already crowded with young men talking excitedly. There was no shouting, no noise, only agitated conversation. What did we want there? This probably no one knew. But since the French had driven away Louis Philippe and proclaimed the republic, something of course must happen here, too. Some of the students had brought their rapiers along, as if it were necessary at once to make an attack or to defend themselves. We were dominated by a vague feeling as if a great outbreak of elemental forces had begun, as if an earthquake was impending of which we had felt the first shock, and we instinctively crowded together. Thus we wandered about in numerous bands — to the " Kneipe," where our restlessness, however, would not suffer us long to stay; then to other pleasure resorts, where we fell into conversation with all manner of strangers, to find in them the same confused, astonished and expectant state of mind; then back to the market-square, to see what might be going on there; then again somewhere else, without aim and end, until finally late in the night fatigue compelled us to find the way home.

The next morning there were the usual lectures to be attended. But how profitless! The voice of the professor sounded like a monotonous drone coming from far away. What he had to say did not seem to concern us. The pen that should have taken notes remained idle. At last we closed our notebooks with a sigh and went away, impelled by a feeling that now we had something more important to do — to devote ourselves to the affairs of the fatherland. And this we did by seeking again as quickly as possible the company of our friends, in order to discuss what had happened and what was to come. In these conversations, excited as they were, certain ideas and catch-words worked themselves to the surface, which expressed more or less the feelings of the people. Now had arrived in Germany the day for the establishment of " German Unity," and the founding of a great, powerful national German Empire. First in line the convocation of a national parliament. Then the demands for civil rights and liberties, free speech, free press, the right of free assembly, equality before the law, a freely elected representation of the people with legislative power, responsibility of ministers, self-government of the communes, the right of the people to carry arms, the formation of a civic guard with elective officers and so on — in short, that which was called a " constitutional form of government on a broad democratic basis." Republican ideas were at first only sparingly expressed. But the word democracy was soon on all tongues, and many, too, thought it a matter of course that if the princes should try to withhold from the people the rights and liberties demanded, force would take the place of mere petition. Of course the regeneration of the country must, if possible, be accomplished by peaceable means. A few days after the outbreak of this commotion I reached my nineteenth birthday. I remember to have been so entirely absorbed by what was happening that I could hardly turn my thoughts to anything else. Like many of my friends, I was dominated by the feeling that at last the great opportunity had arrived for giving to the German people the liberty which was their birthright and to the German fatherland its unity and greatness, and that it was now the first duty of every German to do and to sacrifice everything for this sacred object. We were profoundly, solemnly in earnest.

. . . .

Great news came from Vienna. There the students of the university were the first to assail the Emperor of Austria with the cry for liberty and citizens' rights. Blood flowed in the streets, and the downfall of Prince Metternich was the result. The students organized themselves as the armed guard of liberty. In the great cities of Prussia there was a mighty commotion. Not only Cologne, Coblenz and Trier, but also Breslau, Königsberg and Frankfurt-on-the-Oder, sent deputations to Berlin to entreat the king. In the Prussian capital the masses surged upon the streets, and everybody looked for events of great import.

While such tidings rushed in upon us from all sides like a roaring hurricane, we in the little university town of Bonn were also busy preparing addresses to the sovereign, to circulate them for signature and to send them to Berlin. On the 18th of March we too had our mass demonstration. A great multitude gathered for a solemn procession through the streets of the town. The most respectable citizens, not a few professors and a great number of students and people of all grades marched in close ranks. At the head of the procession Professor Kinkel bore the tricolor, black, red and gold, which so long had been prohibited as the revolutionary flag. Arrived in the market-square he mounted the steps of the city hall and spoke to the assembled throng. He spoke with wonderful eloquence, his voice ringing out in its most powerful tones as he depicted a resurrection of German unity and greatness and new liberties and rights of the German people, which now must be conceded by the princes or won by force by the people. And when at last he waved the black, red and gold banner, and predicted to a free German nation a magnificent future, enthusiasm without bounds broke forth. People clapped their hands; they shouted, they embraced one another, they shed tears. In a moment the city was covered with black, red and gold flags, and not only the Burschenschaft, but almost everybody wore a black-red-gold cockade on his hat. While on that 18th of March we were parading through the streets suddenly sinister rumors flew from mouth to mouth. It had been reported that the king of Prussia, after long hesitation, had finally concluded, like the other German princes, to concede the demands that were pouring upon him from all sides. But now a whispered report flew around that the soldiery had suddenly fired upon the people and that a bloody struggle was raging in the streets of Berlin.

Enthusiastic elation was followed by a short time of anxious expectancy. At last came the report of the awful events that had taken place in the capital.

The king of Prussia, Frederick William IV., at first received the petitions rushing in upon him with sullen silence. He had so recently, and then so emphatically, even so defiantly, proclaimed his inflexible determination never to consent to any constitutional limitation of the kingly power that the thought of yielding to popular pressure anything that he fancied should be only a free emanation of the royal will was to him well-nigh inconceivable. But the situation became more threatening from day to day. Not only the language of the deputations arriving from various parts of the kingdom constantly grew more and more impetuous and peremptory, but the people of Berlin began to hold mass meetings counting by thousands and to greet with thundering acclamations the political watchwords uttered by popular orators. The municipal authorities, too, were swept into the current and begged for royal concessions. At last the king saw the necessity of yielding something. On the 14th of March he gave a "gracious" answer to an address presented by the city council, but that answer was still too evasive and indefinite to satisfy public opinion. Meanwhile bloody collisions occurred between the police, supported by military detachments and the multitude thronging the public squares and streets, in which it happened that a merchant and a university student were killed. The bitterness of feeling caused by these events was somewhat assuaged by a rumor that the king had resolved upon further and more important concessions, which would be publicly announced on the 18th. He had indeed concluded to issue an edict opening a prospect of steps to be taken in favor of national unity and abolishing the censorship of the press.

On the afternoon of the fateful 18th of March an immense concourse of people assembled in the open square in front of the royal palace, hoping to hear the authoritative announcement that popular demands had been granted. The king appeared on the balcony and was received with enthusiastic cheers. He attempted to speak, but could not be heard. In the belief, however, that he had granted all that was asked for, the people were ready for a jubilee. Then a cry arose for the removal of the bodies of troops surrounding the palace and appearing to separate the king from his people. It seemed to be expected that this, too, would be granted, for an effort was made to open a passage for the soldiers through the dense crowd. A roll of drums was heard. This was regarded as a signal for the departure of the soldiery; but, instead of the troops withdrawing, heavy bodies of infantry and cavalry appeared and pressed upon the multitude for the evident purpose of clearing the square. Then two shots rang from the infantry line and the whole scene suddenly and frightfully changed. Frantic cries arose: " We are betrayed! We are betrayed! " In an instant the mass of people who but a moment before had joyously acclaimed the king, dispersed in the adjoining streets with the angry shout, " To arms, to arms! " In all directions the thoroughfares were soon blocked with barricades. The paving stones seemed to leap from the ground and to form themselves into bulwarks surmounted by black-red-gold flags, and manned by citizens, university students, tradesmen, artists, laborers, professional men — hastily armed with all sorts of weapons, from rifles and shotguns down to pikes, axes and hammers. There was no preparation, no plan, no system, in the uprising; everybody seemed to follow a common instinct. Then the troops were ordered to the assault. When after a fierce fight they had taken one barricade, they were at short distances confronted by another and another. Behind the barricades women were busy bringing food and drink for the fighters and caring for the wounded. During the whole night the city resounded with the roar of cannon and the rattle of musketry.

The king seemed at first sternly determined to put down the insurrection at any cost; but as the street battle proceeded he became painfully conscious of its terrible character. Reports arrived in rapid succession. Now he would give an order to stop the fight and then an order to go on. Shortly after midnight he wrote with his own hand an address to " My dear Berliners." He began by saying that the firing of the two shots which had caused the excitement had been a mere accident, that a band of miscreants, mostly foreigners, had taken advantage of this misunderstanding to goad many of his good subjects into this fratricidal fight. Then he promised to withdraw the troops as soon as the insurgents would remove the barricades, and he implored them " to listen to the fatherly voice of their king, to which the grievously suffering queen joined her affectionate and tearful prayers." But the address failed to produce the desired effect. It was accompanied with the roar of cannon and the rattle of musketry, and the fighting citizens rather resented being called " a band of miscreants."

At last, on the afternoon of Sunday, the 19th of March, when one of the high commanders of the troops, General Möllendorf, had been captured by the citizens, the withdrawal of the troops was resolved upon. Peace was concluded on the understanding that the army should leave Berlin, that there should be freedom of the press, and that Prussia should have a constitution on a broad democratic basis. After the soldiery had marched off an incident occurred which in dramatic force and significance has never been surpassed in the history of revolutions. From all parts of the city solemn and silent processions moved toward the royal palace. They escorted the bodies of those of the people who had been killed in the battle; the corpses of the slain were carried aloft on litters, their gaping wounds uncovered, their heads wreathed with laurel branches and immortelles. So the processions marched into the inner palace court, where the litters were placed in rows in ghastly parade, and around them the multitude of men with pallid faces, begrimed with blood and powder smoke, many of them still carrying the weapons with which they had fought during the night; and among them women and children bewailing their dead. Then the king was loudly called for. He appeared in an open gallery, pale and dejected, by his side the weeping queen. " Hats off! " the multitude shouted, and the king took off his hat to the dead below. Then a deep voice among the crowd intoned the old hymn, " Jesus, meine Zuversicht " — " Jesus, my Refuge," in which all present joined. The chorus finished, the king silently withdrew and the procession moved away in grim solemnity.

This was a terrible humiliation to the crown, but at the same time a pointed answer to the king's address in which the fighters had been denounced as a band of miscreants, or as the seduced victims of such a band. Had there really been among them such miscreants, or persons answering our present conception of anarchists, Frederick William IV. would hardly have survived that terrible moment when he stood before them, alone and defenseless, and they fresh from the battlefield with guns in their hands. But at that moment their cry was not " Death to the king " nor " Down with royalty " but " Jesus, my Refuge! "

Nor was the history of those fateful days tainted by any act of heinous crime; indeed, two private houses were sacked, the owners of which had been caught betraying the fighting citizens to the soldiery. But while the insurgents were in complete control of large portions of the city during the whole night, there was not a single case of theft or of wanton destruction. Property was absolutely safe.

The " Prince of Prussia," oldest brother of the childless king and presumptive heir to the throne — the same prince who as Kaiser William I. was in the course of events to become the most popular monarch of his time — was reported to have given the order to fire on the people, and the general wrath turned upon him. By the order of the king, the prince left Berlin under cover of night and hurried to England. Excited crowds gathered in front of his palace on the street " Unter den Linden." There was no military guard to protect the building. A university student put upon its front the inscription " National property," and it was not attacked. Immediately after the street disturbances had ceased the shops were open again as in ordinary times.

Arms were distributed among the people from the government armories. The king declared, " I have become convinced that the peace and the safety of the city cannot be better maintained than by the citizens themselves."

On the 21st of March Frederick William IV. appeared again among the people, on horseback, a black-red-gold scarf around his arm, a black-red-gold flag at his own request carried before him, a huge tricolor hoisted at the same moment on the royal palace. The king spoke freely to the citizens. He would " place himself at the head of a movement for a united Germany; in that united Germany Prussia would be merged." He swore that he wanted nothing but a " constitutional and united Germany." At the university building he turned to the assembled students, saying, " I thank you for the glorious spirit you have shown in these days. I am proud that Germany possesses such sons." It was understood that a new and responsible ministry had been appointed, composed of members of the liberal opposition; that a constituent assembly to be elected by the Prussian people should be convoked to frame a constitution for the kingdom of Prussia; and a national parliament to be elected by the people of all the German states, to meet at Frankfurt for the purpose of uniting all Germany under a new constitutional government. The people of Berlin were in ecstasy.

" The heroes fallen in the glorious struggle for social and political liberty," as the proclamation of the municipal assembly called them, were carried for burial to the Friedrichshain cemetery, accompanied by two hundred thousand citizens, who took the coffins past the royal palace, where the king again stood with uncovered head.

Such were the great tidings the country received from Berlin. The cause of liberty and national union seemed to have achieved a decisive and irreversible victory. The kings and princes themselves, foremost the King of Prussia, had solemnly promised to serve it. The jubilation of the people was without bounds.

Since the French-German war of 1870 and the establishment of the present German Empire it has been the fashion in Germany to scoff at the year 1848, dubbing it the " crazy year," and to ridicule the " thoughtlessness " with which at that time great political programmes were made, comprehensive demands formulated, and far-reaching movements set on foot, to be followed by cruel disappointments and catastrophes. But did the German people of 1848 deserve such ridicule? True, the men of those times did not know how to deal with the existing conditions, nor to carry to the desired end the movement so victoriously and hopefully begun. It is equally true that the popular movement was disjointed and now in retrospect appears in certain lights fantastic. But what reasonable person can wonder at this? The people, although highly developed in science, philosophy, literature and art, had always lived under a severe guardianship in all political matters. They had never been out of leading strings. They had observed only from afar how the other nations exercised their right to govern themselves, and managed their active participation in the functions of the state, and those foreign nations the Germans had learned to admire and perhaps to envy. They had studied the theory of free institutions in books and had watched their workings in current newspaper reports. They had longed for the possession of like institutions and earnestly striven for their introduction in their own country. But with all this observing, learning, and longing, and striving, the larger part of the German people had been excluded by the prevailing rigid paternalism from practical experience in the exercise of political self-government. They had not been permitted to learn the practical meaning of political liberty. They had never received or known the teachings which spring from the feeling of responsibility in free political action. The affairs of government lay outside of the customs and habits of their lives. Free institutions were to them mere abstract conceptions, about which the educated and the seriously thinking men indulged in politico-philosophical speculations, while to the uneducated and the superficial they only furnished political catchwords, in the use of which the general discontent with existing conditions found vent.

Hope of uniting Germany along liberal lines took concrete form in 1848 in the calling of the Frankfort Parliament. Summoned by a self-constituted group of leaders meeting at Heidelberg, and elected by manhood suffrage, this Parliament offered the imperial crown of a united Germany to the King of Prussia. He refused; and the Frankfort Parliament frittered away its energies in futile discussion until it finally dissolved.

In his Reminiscences *Carl Schurz discusses the causes of the failure of this Parliament.*

55. THE FAILURE OF THE FRANKFORT PARLIAMENT [1]

Of the larger parliamentary bodies that had issued from the revolution of March, only the national parliament in Frankfurt was still in existence. That existence it had owed to the longing of the German people, or rather peoples, for national unity, and it was its natural and universally understood mission to weld them under a common constitution of national government into one great nation. Immediately after the revolution of March, 1848, the different German governments, and with them also Austria, because of her German possessions, had recognized this object as a legitimate one, and it was with their co-operation that in May the elections for the national parliament had taken place. The large majority of that body, in fact, the German people in general, regarded the Frankfurt parliament as the specific representative of the sovereignty of the German nation. It was

[1] *The Reminiscences of Carl Schurz.* 3 vols., New York, Doubleday, Doran & Co., Inc., vol. 1, pp. 160–162.

to be expected that the princes and those of their adherents, who may be designated as court parties, would submit to this conception of the powers of the parliament only so long, and only so far, as they found themselves forced to do so. But few of the princes, if any, were sufficiently liberal to accept a limitation of their princely prerogatives with equanimity. Every gain of the people in the matter of political power they felt to be their own loss. They were also opposed to the institution of a strong national government for the reason that this would be conditioned upon the surrender to the national authority of many of the sovereignty-rights of the different states. It was not only a national republic that individual German sovereigns feared, but they also dreaded a national Kaiser who would be apt to reduce them to the condition of mere vassals. The German princes, with the exception of the one who could hope himself to occupy the imperial throne, were therefore the natural adversaries of German unity, embodied in a strong national government. There may have been some men of national sentiment among them capable of overcoming this reluctance, but certainly there were very few. Austria desired a united Germany only if it could hope to occupy in some form the position of the leading power.

Face to face with the princes and their parties stood the national parliament in Frankfurt, that child of the revolution which might then have almost been called the orphan of the revolution. It had at its immediate disposal no administrative machinery, no army, no treasury, only its moral authority; all the rest was in the hands of the different German state governments. The only power of the national parliament consisted in the will of the people; and this power was sufficient for the fulfillment of its mission so long as the will of the people proved itself strong enough, even through revolutionary action in case of necessity, to counteract the adverse interests of the princes. The Parliament would have been sure of success in creating a constitutional German Empire, if it had performed that task quickly and elected and put into office its Kaiser while the revolutionary prestige of the people was still unbroken — that is to say, in the first two or three months after the revolution of March. No German prince would then have declined the imperial crown with a constitution ever so democratic, and not one of them would have dared to refuse the sacrifice of any of his sovereignty-rights to the national power.

But that Parliament was laboring under an over-abundance of learning and virtue and under a want of that political experience and sagacity which recognizes that the better is often the enemy of good, and that the true statesman will be careful not to imperil that which is essential by excessive insistence upon things which are of comparatively little consequence. The world has probably never seen a political assembly that contained a larger number of noble, learned, conscientious and patriotic men, and it will be difficult to find a book of the same character richer in profound knowledge and in models of lofty eloquence than its stenographic reports. But it did not possess the genius that promptly discerns opportunity and with quick resolution takes fortune by the forelock; it was not mindful of the fact that in times of great commotion the history of the world does not wait for the theoretical thinker. And thus it failed.

SECTION III. ITALY

In the following extract Michael Honan, who was a correspondent of the London Times *in Italy at the time of the Revolution of 1848, discusses the situation in the northern part of Italy on the eve of the Revolution. He takes the view that the people of that region were materially quite well off, that discontent with Austrian rule centered chiefly in the cities and that it was primarily political rather than economic, though Austrian taxation was a source of grievance.*

56. *NORTHERN ITALY ON THE EVE OF THE REVOLUTION OF 1848*[1]

At this period, the long-concealed detestation of Austria was openly avowed at Milan, and in all the great cities of the Lombardo-Venetian kingdom. The nobility, middle classes, and populace, joined unanimously in the same sentiment, in all the great towns, and all waited only for a favourable opportunity to shake off a hated yoke.

On the contrary, the rural population were either indifferent, or attached to Austrian dominion, for under the system that then prevailed the occupier of the land paid no direct taxes whatever, and whenever he had cause of complaint it was against his landlord, and not against the government that he groaned.

All contributions were collected every six months from the proprietor, whilst the peasant shared with him half the produce, in some cases two-thirds, the latter finding oxen and the instruments of husbandry, and being provided with a home, and out-buildings necessary to secure the crop, by the indulgent master.

By this arrangement the peasantry enjoyed perfect independence, and the only person who suffered was the owner of the soil; as, in adverse seasons, he had to pay the *prediale,* or produce tax, on a valuation made in a former year, so that it more than once happened, that his half or his third,

---

[1] Michael B. Honan, *The Personal Adventures of 'Our Own Correspondent' in Italy.* 2 vols., London, Chapman and Hall, 1852, vol. I, pp. 67–73.

as the case might be, did not equal in amount the impost above quoted, and he literally got nothing, the occupier and the government absorbing the whole sum.

The peasant was further indulged by being permitted to strip from the mulberry trees such leaves as were necessary for the maintenance of as many silk-worms as he could rear on his own premises. These arrangements, they say, tended to encourage habits of idleness in the rural population, and checked everything like improvement in the cultivation of the land; but this, at the same time rendered the people happy and contented, and who could complain, when before the owner touched a ducat, he who tilled the soil and his family were fed?

Moreover, I know not where improvement was required, as the bounty of Providence and the system of irrigation, which was in force even in the Mantuan shepherd's time, have rendered the Lombardo-Venetian king-dom one of the most productive that Europe presents. The waters of the northern Alps flow in streams of fertility to the Mincio, the Adige and the Po, not omitting the Olio and the Adda, so that whilst a sub-drainage is everlastingly going on by the inclination of the land to the valley of the Po, surface irrigation is abundantly provided for.

In addition to these inducements for the peasantry to remain quiet, the Austrian government took care to occupy with its troops only the principal towns, and to leave the villages and the country free from the eye-sore of the Tedeschi uniform.

How often have I asked the farmer: — "When did you last see the soldiery in these parts?" and how invariably did I receive this answer — "Why, sir, before these late movements we rarely saw a white coat.[1] Al-most seven years ago a detachment passed in this neighbourhood. It was only on the high road between Milan and Venice, Mantua or Brescia, that the Austrian military were frequently seen, and as far as we are concerned, we only knew of their existence by hearsay."

To this I may add, that the practice used by the Austrian tax-collectors towards the proprietors of the soil resembled, in a minor degree, the odious tithe system which prevailed some thirty years ago in Ireland. Good seasons and bad seasons made no difference to the unpitying agent, and the forced levy on the proprietor's torn property was inflicted at a period of the year when his banking account was at the lowest ebb.

Notwithstanding these annoyances and drawbacks, the position of the Lombard proprietors in general was to be envied. Nearly all were wealthy, and the palaces, not only in Milan, but in every other large town, and the luxury in all displayed, convinced you, that so far as material prosperity was concerned, the gentry had nothing to complain of.

[1] The white coat was a distinctive part of the Austrian uniform. (Editor's note.)

The revenues of some leading men were immense, and many of the principal nobility might compare their incomes to those of our great families, and I have seen nothing in the shape of luxurious display, not even in the Champs Elysées at Paris, which might be said so closely to rival Hyde Park in the season, as the Corso Orientale, at Milan, and the promenade of the Boulevards or Bastions connected with it.

This amazing prosperity and superfluity of wealth became, however, the main spring of the public discontent, as the nobility were carefully excluded from office or influence, and they were merely allowed like sheep to graze and get fat in the rich pastures of their native land, provided that politics were excluded from their ordinary conversation, and that they patiently bore what was called the paternal dominion of the Austrian bayonet.

What rendered their position still more tormenting was, that the government indulged them with a kind of constitution, under the name of provincial and central *congregations,* but which bodies dare not say a word in the shape of remonstrance; and it was only about the time I am now alluding to, that the central *congregations,* after an existence of thirty years, took courage to make a formal complaint.

A viceroy was established at Milan, but his power, except for the suppressing of riot, was nominal, as he could do nothing without reference to Vienna, and even a license for establishing commodious street-carriages could not be obtained, because the Home-office in the capital had other matters to attend to.

Then again the enormous sums transmitted to the central government were a natural and fertile source of complaint, and of daily vexation. During the French occupation of the same territory, a sum not exceeding twenty-nine millions of zwanzigers, or about one million sterling, was annually remitted to Paris, but for some years past, no less than eighty millions, or nearly three millions of our money, found their way to Vienna.

These millions were composed of the sums which remained in the collector's hands, after the expenses of local administration were paid, so that the public burthen consisting of the direct tax of the *prediale,* and the indirect contributions levied on salt, oil, tobacco, sugar, coffee and stamped paper, amounted, it was said, to one hundred and fifty millions of zwanzigers, or five millions sterling.

Another sore grievance was the nomination of Austrians to every public employment of any consideration, and of natives to those only where hard work was to be done for a small remuneration. No less, I was assured, than thirty-six thousand Austrian *employés* were settled in the Lombardo-Venetian kingdom, so that you may imagine how indignant a gentleman, who ought to have influence at home, felt, when he saw a German [1] bayonet

[1] *i.e., Austrian.* (Editor's note.)

at his door, a German civil authority without whose leave he could not visit any foreign land, at the head of every department, and a German upstart in each branch of the public service.

Add to all this, that the German and Italian natures are as oil and vinegar to each other. The very language of the one grates on the musical ear of the other, and under any circumstances whatever, I have made up my mind that a good social understanding cannot prevail. It may be true, that *au fond* the German is a more moral and solid character than the Milanese, but that superiority confers no advantage on the former, as the latter only hates the Tedeschi the more, because of his good name.

I must say, even for my own part, that however much I respected German superiority, I thought it a cruel dispensation for the gay-hearted Italian to be made subject to a power so *antipatico* to him, and it is only the bad use which the Italian made of his transient gleam of liberty, that reconciles me now to the presence of a foreign force.

Though the Lombards were, to use a common phrase, " fools for their pains " in undertaking a task so far beyond their moral and physical force, in 1848, yet never was there a revolution more justifiable in every sense, and even now I cannot help feeling a deep sympathy for them. If man is merely to be a stall-fed animal, for whom brute comforts are alone required, then the Italians ought to have remained passive slaves. But the spirit of independence exists, thank God, in every soil, and in my opinion, each nation has a natural right to govern itself after its own manner. I admit that Lombardo-Veneto can never be so prosperous, or so materially happy, as under Austrian rule, and that the great majority of the inhabitants are of the same mind; but liberty is the birthright of us all, and I hope one day to see that part of the peninsula free and independent.

I am sorry to add this object cannot be accomplished for many, many years, as the people at present are incapable of understanding what national liberty means. A cordial union no longer exists between the upper and lower classes, and if a successful blow be struck, republicanism or socialism will win the day.

I should not omit to state, when speaking of the condition of the landlord and peasant, that the conscription for the Austrian army to which his sons are annually exposed, was the only grievance of which he had to talk. But in the memory of man that grievance existed, and it seemed to the ignorant the natural condition of society. The burthen of the indirect contribution was not understood, save in the item of *carta bollata,* or stamped paper, of which the too frequent use was a general complaint.

SECTION IV. AUSTRIA–HUNGARY

The revolutionary storm of 1848, sweeping on to Vienna, caused the fall of Metternich and the abdication of the Emperor Ferdinand. Revolts broke out in Hungary, Bohemia, and Austria's Italian possessions. It seemed for a short time as though the ramshackle empire of the Hapsburgs might be going to pieces.

By the end of 1849, however, the revolutionary movements in the Austrian dominions had everywhere been suppressed. Concessions made by the Government under pressure were withdrawn. Once more reaction and repression took the saddle.

But one important result, too often neglected by students of history, remained. The feudal dues and services both in Austria and in Hungary had been abolished.

Some of the far-reaching effects of this abolition on the position of the peasants and the system of land-holding are brought out in the two following extracts from a report made to Parliament by Geoffrey Drage, a well-known authority on Austro-Hungarian affairs.

57. THE INFLUENCE OF THE REVOLUTION OF 1848 ON THE AUSTRIAN PEASANTRY AND AGRICULTURE [1]

The abolition of the feudal burdens upon land which Mr. Fyffe has described as "almost the sole gain that Austria derived from the struggle of 1848," practically transformed the small peasant farmers into independent proprietors. The immediate effect of the cessation of compulsory villein service (*Frohne*) was to hasten the transition from a system of home production (*Naturalwirthschaft*), regulated by custom, to the modern system of competitive production based upon money exchanges (*Geldwirthschaft*). The great proprietors, unprovided with the capital necessary to enable them to hire farm hands to supply the place of the labourers of whose traditional services they had been deprived, found themselves obliged to divide their demesne lands into small holdings, which were leased out to their former feudal dependents (*Unterthänige Bauern*). In this way the conversion of home farms worked by a bailiff into leaseholds let out for a money-rent to tenant farmers, which had begun even before 1848, became very general in Austria, though opinions are still divided as to which of the two methods

[1] Great Britain. *Parliamentary Papers.* The Royal Commission on Labour. *Foreign Reports,* vol. XI (1893–1894). Austria-Hungary and the Balkan States (Report of Geoffrey Drage), p. 72.

of cultivation is really the more successful and economical. Large manorial estates or *latifundia* are chiefly found in Bohemia, which has been called "the stronghold of the feudal aristocracy," and in Galicia, Moravia, and Lower Austria. They are very rare in Carinthia and Salzburg, and in Dalmatia, where the large properties are chiefly in the hands of the merchant or capitalist class, they are practically unknown.

58. THE INFLUENCE OF THE REVOLUTION OF 1848 ON THE HUNGARIAN PEASANTRY AND AGRICULTURE[1]

It is partly, says Dr. Hirsch,[2] the conservative tendency of the large landowners, partly the dread of reform shown by the peasantry which has hitherto prevented progress in agricultural matters in Hungary. The history of Hungary affords only a single instance of an uprising of discontented peasantry against the nobles; this was in 1514 and the consequences were a strong repression and imposition of heavier burdens. Free migration was prohibited and the peasants became and, according to Dr. Hirsch, remained serfs (*leibeigene*) until 1848 when the right of life and death (*jus gladii*) of the nobles over them was finally abolished; this account should be taken together with that of Mr. Patterson who shows, as will be seen presently, that whatever the theoretical claims of the nobles may have been, the peasantry had acquired certain rights over the land through various causes, but particularly through the Government claims on the land and jealousy towards the nobles. The great changes of 1848, which were perhaps most striking in political life, were certainly also remarkable and extended in the agricultural sphere, but the final abolition of privilege in acquisition and free disposition of landed property must not be considered as wholly sudden or violent. The very privilege of the nobles in exemption from taxation gave the government a special interest in the tax-paying classes or peasants settled on "non-noble" land. Noble land was not necessarily occupied by nobles; they often let it out in allotments to peasant tenants called *contractualists* or *curialists* to distinguish them from older tenants called *jobbagyiones,* or, after the survey of Maria Theresa in 1767–73 (*Urbarium*) urbarialists. Both classes of tenants had certain rights and it would be a mistake to consider the dues paid by the latter to the noble landlord as simply feudal dues. The forced labour (*robot*) and payments in money and kind were determined by "immemorial custom," and although, while the contractualist paid only a capitation tax, the urbarialist had to pay both a capitation and a land-tax, yet the latter gained through the anxiety of the Government to keep up the

---

[1] Great Britain. *Parliamentary Papers.* The Royal Commission on Labour. *Foreign Reports,* vol. XI, (1893–1894). Austria-Hungary and the Balkan States. (Report by Geoffrey Drage), pp. 173–174.

[2] *Ungarn's Grundbesitz Verhältnisse,* pp. 46 ff.

number of taxpayers and the area of taxable land. The government " regarded with extreme suspicion the conduct of the lord towards his peasantry. He was not allowed to evict them except for certain definite reasons set down in the law. These copyholds were hereditary and should the copyholding family die out or be evicted, the lord was not allowed to occupy the holding but was obliged to give it to another non-noble tenant." These holdings of *sessions* were fixed as to extent in given districts although they were larger in some districts than in others. The *sessio,* as it was called, varied, according to Mr. Patterson, from 16 to 40 *joch* (one joch=¼ acre) of arable land and from six to 22 *tagewerke* of meadow, or according to Dr. Hirsch, is 58 Hungarian joch. A peasant might, under certain conditions carefully regulated, hold from a quarter up to four sessions. If a landlord could not find a tenant for a vacant quarter of a session, he sometimes obtained permission from the authorities to break it up into smaller allotments assigned to cottagers (*zsellerek*) of which there are many at the present time in Hungary.

In 1848 these 'copyhold' farms were transformed by the Hungarian liberals into freehold estates, but even before this date many landlords had enabled their tenants " to buy their freedom at a moderate price," thus preparing the public mind for general measures of emancipation. The position of the *contractualists* was different from that of the urbarialists, and it was mainly due to the troubled times that followed the Reform Bill of 1848, that a confusion arose between the two forms of tenure, a confusion which tended to operate to the advantage of the peasant holder and disadvantage of the landlord. Mr. Patterson affirmed in 1869 that while there would be no doubt as to the permanent advantage to the country at large of the emancipation of the peasant lands, there could be " as little doubt that the class of noble landlords suffered severely, as the great majority of them were perfectly unprepared for the change. In the slovenly system of agriculture which was fostered in both lord and peasant by the institution of *robot* or forced labour, which formed the greater portion of the rent of these copyhold farms, the lord had not only no experience of what paying regular wages meant, but he had not even draught cattle or agricultural implements." The Government bonds bearing interest, which were given him in compensation for his losses, were thrown in large masses on the money market and sold considerably below their value. The pecuniary losses which followed through the war of Independence, subsequent defeat and enforced military service still further crippled the Hungarian landlords.[1]

Out of these circumstances, thus briefly sketched, arose a serious agricultural crisis during which the chief difficulties to be fought were those which met the large and middle-sized properties whilst the peasants suffered

[1] *The Magyars, Their Country and Institutions,* vol. 1, pp. 318–26.

comparatively little owing to their increased control of their holdings which they worked with the assistance of their families. On the other hand the large proprietors (*Latifundienbesitzer*) were able to command the credit which enabled them to tide over the period. This was not so with the smaller or middle class proprietors; suddenly bereft of the sole means known to them of cultivating their lands and unable to resort to local credit, a system which was practically unknown in Hungary, and which indeed is even now far from being satisfactorily developed; destitute of technical knowledge and hitherto more occupied with local politics than rural economy; engaged in a struggle with the absolutism of the Austrian Government, a large number of them soon found themselves face to face with ruin. Exact statistics are lacking during the first part of this period for the relative position of the various properties, but there is no doubt that from this time a process of transfer set in, which is not yet concluded, whereby the largest and the smallest holdings have increased at the expense of the middle class holdings."

CHAPTER VI

THE BRITISH ISLES (1848-1914)

SECTION I. THE EXTENSION OF THE FRANCHISE

The Reform Bill of 1832 made a breach in the walls of electoral privilege but it increased the franchise only slightly in numbers. The Liberal Party was inclined to go further after a few years but so long as Lord Palmerston lived nothing was done. He died in 1865 and in the following year the Chancellor of the Exchequer, William E. Gladstone, himself a former Tory, proposed to extend the franchise to seven pound borough householders and to lodgers whose annual rental amounted to £10. Gladstone's speech on this occasion marked his definite entry into the Liberal Party and leadership. The bill was defeated by a combination of Liberals with the Conservatives.

59. REASONS FOR EXTENDING THE FRANCHISE[1]

THE right hon. gentleman asked, " Do you think the franchise is good in itself, or do you wish to improve the institutions of the country? " Sir, I find here no dilemma. My answer is, we want to do both. The extension of the franchise within safe and proper limits is good. It will array more persons in support of the institutions of the country, and that is another good. The composition and the working of this House is admirable, and its performances have long since placed it at the head of all the legislative assemblies of the world. It does not follow, however, that it cannot be improved. . . . I think that the influence of separate classes is too strong, and that the influence of the public interest properly so called, as distinguished from the interest of sets, groups, and classes of men, is too weak. I fully admit I am not perhaps altogether an impartial judge; I speak much from my own experience during a lengthened period as Chancellor of the Exchequer, and as in a special degree and sense the guardian of the public purse. Undoubtedly, if there be a weak point in the composition of the House this is the department in which it would most readily and most clearly show itself. I believe that the composition of the House might be greatly improved; and that the increased representation of the working classes would supply us more largely with that description of Members whom we want, who would look not to the interests of classes, but to the public interest. . . .

[1] W. E. Gladstone in House of Commons, April 27, 1866. In A. T. Bassett: *Gladstone's Speeches*. London, 1916, pp. 371-376 (condensed).

My hon. friend says we know nothing about the labouring classes. Is not one single word a sufficient reply? That word is Lancashire; Lancashire, associated with the sufferings of the last four years, so painful and bitter in themselves to contemplate, but so nobly and gloriously borne. The qualities then exhibited were the qualities not of select men here and there among a depraved multitude, but of the mass of a working community. The sufferings were sufferings of the mass. The heroism was heroism of the mass. For my own part, I cannot believe that the men who exhibited those qualities were only a sample of the people of England, and that the rest would have wholly failed in exhibiting the same great qualities had occasion arisen. I cannot see what argument could be found for some wise and temperate experiment of the extension of civil rights among such people, if the experience of the past few years does not sufficiently afford it.

And now, Sir, let us for a moment consider the enormous and silent changes which have been going forward among the labouring population. May I use the words to hon. and right hon. gentlemen once used by exhortation by Sir Robert Peel to his opponents, " elevate your vision " ? Let us try and raise our views above the fears, the suspicions, the jealousies, the reproaches, and the recriminations of this place and this occasion. Let us look onward to the time of our children and of our children's children. Let us know what preparation it behooves us should be made for that coming time. Is there or is there not, I ask, a steady movement of the labouring classes, and is or is not that movement a movement onwards and upwards? I do not say that it falls beneath the eye, for, like all great processes, it is unobservable in detail, but as solid and undeniable as it is resistless in its essential character.

Benjamin Disraeli succeeded Gladstone in the Exchequer and at once, vying with the Liberals for popular favor, and acutely aware of the possibilities democracy offers to aristocratic manipulation, brought in a bill substantially the same as Gladstone's. It was passed, largely with the help of Liberal votes, and despite the bitter opposition of Lord Cranbourne, later Lord Salisbury, who objected to it as bad statesmanship and dishonest politics.

60. *A CONSERVATIVE DENUNCIATION OF DISRAELI'S FRANCHISE BILL* [1]

After all, our theory of Government is not that a certain number of Statesmen should place themselves in office and do whatever the House of Commons bids them. Our theory of Government is, that on each side

---

[1] Lord Cranbourne in House of Lords, July 15, 1867. Hansard's *Parliamentary Debates,* 3rd Series, vol. 188, pp. 1538, 1539.

of the House, there should be men supporting definite opinions, and that what they have supported in opposition they should adhere to in office; and that every one should know, from the fact of their being in office, that those particular opinions will be supported. If you reverse that, and declare that, no matter what a man has supported in opposition, the moment he gets into office it shall be open to him to reverse and repudiate it all, you practically destroy the whole basis on which our form of Government rests, and you make the House of Commons a mere scrambling place for office. You practically banish all honourable men from the political arena, and you will find, in the long run, that the time will come when your Statesmen will become nothing but political adventurers; and that professions of opinion will be looked upon only as so many political manoeuvres for the purpose of attaining office. . . . It is only because of that mutual trust in each other by which we ought to be animated . . . that we are enabled to carry on this party Government which has led this country to so high a pitch of greatness. I entreat hon. Gentlemen opposite not to believe that my feelings on this subject are dictated simply by my hostility to this particular measure, though I object to it most strongly, as the House is aware. But even if I took a contrary view, if I deemed it most advantageous, I still should deeply regret to find that the House of Commons has applauded a policy of legerdemain; and I should, above all things, regret that this great gift to the people — if gift you think it — should have been purchased at the cost of a political betrayal which has no parallel in our Parliamentary annals, which strikes at the root of all that mutual confidence which is the very soul of our party Government, and on which only the strength and freedom of our representative institutions can be sustained.

The peculiar position of the House of Lords, with its permanent Conservative majority, had often caused Liberals to wish to modify its powers. It was the Budget of 1909 that brought about the curbing of the Upper House's power and the Parliament Act was the result of a bitter and intricate political struggle. A General Election followed the rejection by the Lords of the Budget presented by the Liberal Government, headed by Herbert Asquith; and this election, held early in 1910, returned a sufficient Government majority, provided the Irish Nationalists, led by John Redmond, could be counted on. The Irish, to get the Liberals' promise to bring in a Home Rule for Ireland Bill, assented to the Budget. Since the Lords were certain to throw out any Home Rule Bill, Asquith was obliged to take the bull by the horns and, after a second General Election, late in 1910, had confirmed the decision of the earlier one, he introduced the Parliament Act. The new king, George V, promised, in the event of the House of Lords again using their veto power, to create enough new peers to establish a Liberal majority in the House of Lords, and this threat, as in 1832, gave victory to the Commons majority. The last of the three following extracts, taken from a Conservative journal, pictures the unwillingness of the Conservatives to accept defeat.

61. ASQUITH INTRODUCES THE PARLIAMENT ACT [1]

Under an unwritten Constitution such as ours — which has developed not so much by statute as by usage — there must, in time, be a growing divergence between legal powers and constitutional practice. A familiar illustration — perhaps the most familiar — is that of the Veto of the Crown. No Bill can now, any more than in the days of Queen Elizabeth, become an Act of Parliament and acquire the force of law unless it has received the express Assent of the Crown. Yet, whereas, as we know, Queen Elizabeth sometimes refused her Assent to half of the proposed legislation of the Session, no English Sovereign has attempted to exercise the Veto since the days of Queen Anne. No minister would advise it. Its revival is an imaginary danger. This is a point on which, by universal consent, there is no necessity to bring the letter of the law into harmony with what has become the unbroken and inveterate usage. But there is, and has been for more than two centuries, a similar divergence developing more slowly, but not less clearly, between the legal powers of the two Houses of Parliament in regard to finance and their actual constitutional exercise. I need not go into past history. It is sufficient to say that until the year 1909 the House of Lords had for fifty years not attempted to interfere in any way with the financial provision of the year. It was a sudden assertion as a living and active power of a legal right that had passed into practical desuetude that was the immediate occasion of the acute stage into which the constitutional question has now passed. Further, Mr. Speaker, in regard to their right of control over policy, over administration and over legislation, the legal relation of the two Houses, which have theoretically co-ordinate and co-equal powers, ceased to bear any resemblance to the actual fact. The House of Lords has long since ceased to have any real control over policy or administration. They debate such matters, and we read their Debates with interest and with profit, but their decisions are academic conclusions and have no direct influence, and can have no direct influence, on the fortunes of the Government of the day. . . . If the precedent of 1909 had been allowed to stand there would, in this respect also, have been a revolution in constitutional practice. If that precedent had been allowed to stand unquestioned the Lords could

[1] *Parliamentary Debates.* 5th Series. Commons. Feb. 21, 1911, vol. 21, pp. 1743–1746 (condensed).

always, they did then, by destroying the finance of the year, compel the Government of the day either to resign office or to appeal by dissolution to the electorate. That power, certainly for two generations, the Lords have never exercised, or even claimed the power of saying by whose hands and upon what lines the general administration of the country should be conducted. . . . Let me pass from that to the domain of legislation. Even there the legal theory of a co-ordinate authority between the two Houses has for a long time past been tacitly, if not explicitly, abandoned. It is admitted that the House of Lords must at some undefined time yield to the will of the electorate. Till, I think, in January, 1910, it was widely contended — we do not hear that contention put forward to-day — that the present House of Lords were by instinctive divination or by acquired tact possessed of, and exhibited, exactly those special faculties by which an ideal Second Chamber under a democratic system of Government would secure that the decision of the elected representatives of the people should never transcend, should never fall short of, but should always be brought into conformity with the deliberate will of the electorate who sent them here. What was and what is the Second Chamber in regard to which I said only a year ago this felicitous, this almost miraculous adaptation of means to ends was confidently asserted? It is an Assembly admittedly which is neither elected by the people nor dissoluble by the Crown. It consists of about 600 Members — and if we deem for the purpose as ostensibly non-partisan the occupants of the Episcopal Bench — it is no exaggeration to say that of the remainder, some 570 or 580, normally 500 at least belong to the Conservative or Unionist party. That is the body, hereditary in origin except so far as its composition is tempered by the sporadic action of the Minister of the day, irresponsible in the exercise of its powers, overwhelmingly partisan in its actual composition — that is the body to which the letter of the law entrusts the right to revise and delay, and, if it will, reject the considered and deliberate decision of the representatives of the people. People talk of the policy and even the necessity in the interests of democracy itself of what is called the bi-cameral Constitution. Could the most ingenious and malignant adversary of the system have devised a better reductio ad absurdum of the principle of the Second Chamber? On paper, as everyone now admits, it is an indefensible paradox, which could only be reconciled with the actual working of Democratic Government by an almost supernatural endowment of insight and self-abnegation. No country, no democratic country, and least of all our own, can safely rest its fortunes on the hazard of a perpetual recurrence of special providences. . . .

And so we have found it. For what in practice . . . is our so-called Two-Chamber system? We who support the policy of the Bill that I am going to ask the House to read a first time are constantly reproached with the intention of substituting for legislation by two chambers the uncontrolled domination of one. Yes, but what are the facts? I will only go back for fifteen years. I might carry the retrospect a great deal further if time and opportunity allowed. Take the ten years, 1895–to–1905. The constitutional question, as we now know it, was then dormant. Why was it dormant? Because we lived under the unchecked rule of a single chamber. There followed the four years, 1906–1909. I am stating what is now one of the commonplaces, and the admitted commonplaces, of political controversy when I say that during those years, with the exception of a few instances when in Lord Lansdowne's felicitous and memorable phrase the conflict would not have been on favourable ground to the Second Chamber, the House of Lords resolutely opposed, and successfully defeated, the principal controversial measures passed by the largest majorities in the whole annals of the House of Commons. The climax was reached in the autumn of 1909, when the House of Lords rejected the finance of the year.

62. THE PARLIAMENT ACT, 1911 [1]

An Act to make provision with respect to the powers of the House of Lords in relation to those of the House of Commons, and to limit the duration of Parliament. (18th August 1911.)

Whereas it is expedient that provision should be made for regulating the relations between the two Houses of Parliament:

And whereas it is intended to substitute for the House of Lords as it at present exists a Second Chamber constituted on a popular instead of hereditary basis, but such substitution cannot be immediately brought into operation:

And whereas provision will require hereafter to be made by Parliament in a measure effecting such substitution for limiting and defining the powers of the new Second Chamber, but it is expedient to make such provision as in this Act appears for restricting the existing powers of the House of Lords:

Be it therefore enacted by the King's most Excellent Majesty, by and with the advice and consent of the Lords Spiritual and Temporal, and Commons, in this present Parliament assembled, and by the authority of the same, as follows:

1. Power of House of Lords as to Money Bills

(1) If a Money Bill, having been passed by the House of Commons, and sent up to the House of Lords at least one month before the end of the session, is not passed by the House of Lords without amendment within one month after it is so sent up to that House, the Bill shall, unless the House

[1] 1 and 2 George 5, ch. 13 (extracts).

of Commons direct to the contrary, be presented to His Majesty and become an Act of Parliament on the Royal Assent being signified, notwithstanding that the House of Lords have not consented to the Bill.

(2) A Money Bill means a Public Bill which in the opinion of the Speaker of the House of Commons contains only provisions dealing with all or any of the following subjects, namely, the imposition, repeal, remission, alteration, or regulation of taxation; the imposition for the payment of debt or other financial purposes of charges on the Consolidated Fund, or on money provided by Parliament, or the variation or repeal of any such charges; supply; the appropriation, receipt, custody, issue or audit of accounts of public money; the raising or guarantee of any loan or the repayment thereof; or subordinate matters incidental to those subjects or any of them. In this subsection the expressions "taxation," "public money," and "loan" respectively do not include any taxation, money, or loan raised by local authorities or bodies for local purposes. . . .

2. *Restriction of Powers of House of Lords as to Bills other than Money Bills*

(1) If any Public Bill (other than a Money Bill or a Bill containing any provision to extend the maximum duration of Parliament beyond five years) is passed by the House of Commons in three successive sessions (whether of the same Parliament or not), and, having been sent up to the House of Lords at least one month before the end of the session, is rejected by the House of Lords in each of those sessions, that Bill shall, on its rejection for the third time by the House of Lords, unless the House of Commons direct to the contrary, be presented to His Majesty and become an Act of Parliament on the Royal Assent being signified thereto, notwithstanding that the House of Lords have not consented to the Bill: Provided that this provision shall not take effect unless two years have elapsed between the date of the second reading in the first of those sessions of the Bill in the House of Commons and the date on which it passes the House of Commons in the third of those sessions.

(2) When a Bill is presented to His Majesty for assent in pursuance of the provisions of this section, there shall be endorsed on the Bill the certificate of the Speaker of the House of Commons signed by him that the provisions of this section have been duly complied with.

(3) A Bill shall be deemed to be rejected by the House of Lords if it is not passed by the House of Lords either without amendment or with such amendments only as may be agreed to by both Houses. . . .

7. *Duration of Parliament*

Five years shall be substituted for seven years as the time fixed for the maximum duration of Parliament under the Septennial Act, 1715.

63. THE "DIE HARDS" IN THE HOUSE OF COMMONS [1]

To exaggerate the intensity of the passion displayed in the House of Commons yesterday would not be possible. In sustained fury the scene that took place exceeded the historic disturbance in Committee when the Home Rule Bill was under discussion in 1893. . . . For the first time, probably in our Parliamentary history and certainly for the first time within living memory, a hearing has been refused by an incensed Opposition to the Leader of the House. . . .

At an early stage of the proceedings it was evident that the atmosphere was dangerously charged with explosive matter. . . . Soon after 3 o'clock the keenest eye would have found difficulty in discovering a vacant seat in the Chamber. In fact the throng became so large that many members were forced to be content with such accommodation as the gangways provided. . . . Before long all the Ministers of the Crown were on the Treasury Bench. Facing them sat the leaders of the Unionists, waiting anxiously for the moment when the head of the Government would rise to vindicate the advice which had been given to the King. . . .

The loud and prolonged cheering of the Nationalist members marked the entrance of Mr. J. Redmond, whose face beamed with pleasure at his reception. . . . The Prime Minister came in immediately afterwards, and at once the Chamber rang with acclamations. All the Ministerialists and the Nationalists rose in their places and cheered again and again. . . . Amid these shouts of jubilation were mingled a long roll of angry murmurs. The Opposition were expressing their resentment. . . . Comparative quiet was restored, only to be broken, however, a minute or two later when Mr. Balfour came in from behind the Chair. His party rose as one man and cheered to the echo. . . .

When the question was put that the Lords' Amendments to the Parliament Bill be considered and Mr. Asquith rose to make his statement . . . the majority of the Unionists appeared to be quite unable to keep their passion under. Cries of "Traitor" were raised, and the Speaker appealed in vain that the Prime Minister should be treated with courtesy. . . . Lord H. Cecil, who was white with anger, rose, but in the din that continued, the point he wished to make was lost. All this time the Prime Minister was standing at the table, a sheaf of notes before him. He waited patiently to begin, but every time he opened his lips to speak he was interrupted with cries of "Divide" and "Traitor." Members rose excitedly, protesting against the interruption, and the Speaker several times sought . . . to obtain a hearing for Mr. Asquith. The response was a cry of "No." Lord H. Cecil, who

[1] The *Times*. London, July 25, 1911.

took a prominent part in the demonstration against the right hon. gentle-man, and many other Unionists kept up their opposition. Besides crying " Divide," they shouted sarcastically for Mr. Redmond, " the new leader." . . .

Mr. Asquith, who, though disconcerted, faced his opponents tranquilly, tried again to speak. They would not hear him.

The Speaker made further appeals. With great gravity of tone he pointed out to the Opposition that it was far more important for them than for the Government that the right of free discussion should be maintained. Then Mr. Asquith made another attempt but at every other word he was inter-rupted . . . and there were shouts of " give it up." He shook his head defiantly, and proceeded, but every statement he made was a signal for fresh outbursts. . . . At last his patience becoming exhausted he resolved not to persevere. Amid frantic excitement he flung down his notes. " I am not going," he said, " to degrade myself by addressing an Opposition which is obviously determined not to listen to me. A situation has been created which admits only of one Constitutional course, and unless the House of Lords will consent to restore the Bill to its original form, with, if they like, reasonable amendments consistent with its principles and purpose, we shall be compelled to invoke the prerogative of the Crown." These sentences were spoken amid an almost deafening din, but the right hon. gentleman man-aged to make them heard. When he resumed his seat everybody on the front Ministerial bench stood up and cheered, as did the whole of the party. . . .

When the Leader of the Opposition rose many people expected that, in retaliation for the treatment which the Prime Minister had received, the Min-isterialists would refuse to hear him. The expectation was falsified, for the supporters of the Government repressed any inclination they might have had to act like their opponents, and any member of the party who threatened to interrupt was at once hushed to silence. . . .

SECTION II. THE PROGRESS OF TRADE UNIONISM

Since 1825 trade unions, although legalized, had been viewed with dis-favor by every Government and, finally, the courts, holding that they were combinations in restraint of trade and therefore illegal, refused to entertain suits by which they sought to prosecute dishonest officials who had embezzled union funds. The Gurney Act of 1868 enabled unions to prosecute but not to recover and the unions pressed for definite recognition of their legal status. Gladstone's first Government, now that many laboring men possessed the vote, gave the unions this status in 1871. An amendment in 1876 more clearly defined trade unions.

64. *TRADE UNION ACT OF 1871*[1]

2. Trade Union not Criminal

The purposes of any trade union shall not, by reason merely that they are in restraint of trade, be deemed to be unlawful so as to render any member of such trade union liable to criminal prosecution for conspiracy or otherwise.

3. Trade Union not Unlawful for Civil Purposes

The purposes of any trade union shall not, by reason merely that they are in restraint of trade, be unlawful so as to render void or voidable any agreement or trust.

4. Trade Union Contracts

Nothing in this Act shall enable any court to entertain any legal proceeding instituted with the object of directly enforcing or recovering damages for the breach of any of the following agreements, namely,

1. Any agreement between members of a trade union as such, concerning the conditions on which any members for the time being of such trade union shall or shall not sell their goods, transact business, employ or be employed:

2. Any agreement for the payment by any person of any subscription or penalty to a trade union:

3. Any agreement for the application of the funds of a trade union —

   (a) To provide benefits to members; or

   (b) To furnish contributions to any employer or workman not a member of such trade union, in consideration of such employer or workman acting in conformity with the rules or resolutions of such trade union; or

   (c) To discharge any fine imposed upon any person by sentence of a court of justice; or,

4. Any agreement made between one trade union and another; or,

5. Any bond to secure the performance of any of the above-mentioned agreements.

But nothing in this section shall be deemed to constitute any of the above-mentioned agreements unlawful.

6. Registry of Trade Unions

Any seven or more members of a trade union may by subscribing their names to the rules of the union, and otherwise complying with the provisions of this Act with respect to registry, register such trade union under this Act,

[1] 34 and 35 Victoria, ch. 31 (extracts).

provided that if any one of the purposes of such trade union be unlawful such registration shall be void.

9. *Actions by or against Trustees*

The trustees of any trade union registered under this Act, or any other officer of such trade union who may be authorized so to do by the rules thereof, are hereby empowered to bring or defend, or cause to be brought or defended, any action, suit, prosecution, or complaint in any court of law or equity, touching or concerning the property, right, or claim to property of the trade union: and shall and may, in all cases concerning the real or personal property of such trade union, sue and be sued, plead and be impleaded, in any court of law or equity, in their proper names, without other description than the title of their office; and no such action, suit, prosecution or complaint shall be discontinued or shall abate by the death or removal from office of such persons or any of them, but the same shall and may be proceeded in by their successor or successors as if such death, resignation, or removal had not taken place; and such successors shall pay or receive the like costs as if the action, suit, prosecution, or complaint had been commenced in their names for the benefit of or to be reimbursed from the funds of such trade union, and the summons to be issued to such trustee or other officer may be served by leaving the same at the registered office of the trade union.

65. *TRADE UNION AMENDMENT ACT, 1876*[1]

16. *Definition of "Trade Union"*

The term "trade union" means any combination, whether temporary or permanent, for regulating the relations between workmen and masters, or between workmen and workmen, or between masters and masters, or for imposing restrictive conditions on the conduct of any trade or business, whether such combination would or would not, if the principal Act had not been passed, have been deemed to have been an unlawful combination by reason of some one or more of its purposes being in restraint of trade.

The Trade Union Act of 1871 was accompanied by the Criminal Law Amendment Act, which, by its rigorous penalizing of all strike activities, more than overbalanced the benefits gained by obtaining a definite legal status. The trade union, as in 1825, could exist as a friendly society but could not fight. The phrases of the act such as " molestation," " obstruction," and " intimidation," which, together with all picketing, became criminal, were

[1] 39 and 40 Victoria, ch. 22 (extract).

susceptible of much legal stretching. Employers immediately took advantage of the new law and in their efforts they were regularly assisted by the courts. Prosecutions were numerous and penalties harsh. Frederic Harrison, best known as a Positivist philosopher, frequently aided the unions in their legal battles.

66. A CRITICISM OF THE CRIMINAL LAW AMENDMENT ACT[1]

Politicians are not wont to be satisfied with a Statute, which lawyers may approve, if its administration in practice results in a permanent scandal. Now, what is the operation of this Act, as we read its doings in the files of local newspapers? Ostensibly and in terms, it is an ordinary part of the criminal law. In reality we find it a legal instrument which one party in a trade dispute uses to cripple the other, the party using it being in possession of the whole judicial power, and indirectly able to dispose of the police. The Act is rarely put in force, except during a hard-fought trade dispute. Then what occurs is this: — The charge ceases to be an ordinary matter of police law; it assumes the character of a party manoeuvre. The most trumpery cases are preferred, and often abandoned after the charge has had its intimidating effect. The local police busy themselves with manufacturing cases, and unseemly altercations ensue as to the party interest of the sitting magistrates. In the excited opinion of the district, every prisoner sentenced, and even every prisoner arrested, becomes a victim; every official witness is accused of perjury; and every magistrate of prejudice. Now, even supposing the Act to be just in its language, does it in practice give any guarantees for order . . . that will outweigh the hatred it scatters on the common administration of justice? I have not so bad an opinion of the working classes as a body as to think that all this animosity could possibly be awakened by an Act which was honestly employed to put down outrage. I believe they have only too much ground for their belief that the Act in its actual working is little but a class instrument, and is constantly resulting in scandalous abuses of criminal law.

I turn to some of the decided cases. Not long after the Act was passed, the struggle of the engineers for the nine hours began in the North. The dispute was singularly clear of anything like real outrage, but a number of cases were brought before the magistrates which were anything but creditable to our judicial system. I give one as a specimen. A man singly addresses a workman in the highway, receives a curt reply, and walks off. A policeman is watching them; without hearing the words that pass, he comes up to the workman addressed, asks him what the man had said to him, and then

1 Frederic Harrison; "The Criminal Law Amendment Act." Reprinted from the *Times*, London, June 2, 1873, pp. 3–4, 5–6.

goes off and arrests the man. The man, for spoken words which the policeman had extracted by questioning the other, is arrested, bail is refused, and he is imprisoned for five days. . . .

In one case before me, the employer, the real prosecutor, sends off the nominal prosecutor, a lad who asserted that he had been roughly addressed, and keeps him for a week at an hotel at the seaside. Of course it was said, to keep him out of harm's way; and of course it was replied, virtually to bribe him. In all these cases there is this objectionable feature. The person alleged to be injured or threatened is never the real prosecutor, who is some powerful employer or association of employers. The lawyers in the case in the most natural way inform the Court that they are instructed by Messrs. —— to prosecute; that this eminent firm must ask for a heavy penalty, as their works have been inconvenienced by the strike, and that Messrs. —— will be satisfied with a month's imprisonment, etc. All the while the "prosecutor," the man supposed to be injured, is no more considered than if he were an unimportant witness. If they can get him to give some colour to the case, that is enough. The whole thing is arranged between the eminent firm of Messrs. ——, their neighbours on the Bench, and the efficient officer at the head of the constabulary. It will hardly be wondered at if after this the entire district believes that the case is trumped up, that the policemen give evidence with more zeal than care, that the prosecutor is a tool, and the Bench prejudiced. Where the crime consists in stealing property, or injuring the person, a Bench of Justices may safely be trusted to decide reasonably; but they will often decide unreasonably where the crime is the speaking of words or the offering a passer-by a handbill.

This is a real, not an imaginary case. In "Turk's case" the prisoner was charged by his employer with "molesting" him by distributing, to workmen passing by in the street, handbills which quietly requested workmen not to interfere with the strike. There was no evidence of the slightest annoyance to the employer who did not even see the man with the handbills, and no evidence of any sort of "coercion," other than the attempt peaceably to persuade workmen to work for him only on certain terms. A metropolitan police magistrate, however, held that the employer had been "molested" within the Act, and he ordered the prisoner to be imprisoned for two months. The case was appealed, and no one appeared to prosecute, and the man was subsequently bailed. But for three days he had endured the life of a common prisoner, and the end of the employer was obtained. In another case (afterwards reversed) a man was arrested and sentenced to two months' imprisonment for asking a fellow workman to pay a fine due to the club, and this a bench of magistrates considered was "besetting" the man within the Act. Nor is it singular that these constructions are put on the Statute, for the clause in question consists of what is practically a single sentence of no less than forty lines in the Queen's printer's copy, and it employs several ambiguous words such as "coerce" and "beset" which are unexplained and are new in law.

The Disraeli Government, not without reluctance, under the pressure of the trade unions, passed in 1875 two acts that remedied the situation in which the legislation of 1871 had placed the unions. The Employers and Workmen Act, replacing the Master and Servant Act of 1867, was an improvement not only in name but in fact as well, for by it labor contracts, like any other contract, were made civil engagements, with the two parties equal before the law. The Criminal Law Amendment Act was repealed and its place taken by the Conspiracy and Protection of Property Act, which legalized picketing and left criminal acts to be dealt with by the ordinary criminal law.

67. CONSPIRACY AND PROTECTION OF PROPERTY ACT, 1875[1]

3. Conspiracy, and Protection of Property

An agreement or combination by two or more persons to do or procure to be done any act in contemplation or furtherance of a trade dispute between employers and workmen shall not be indictable as a conspiracy if such act committed by one person would not be punishable as a crime.

Nothing in this section shall exempt from punishment any persons guilty of a conspiracy for which a punishment is awarded by any Act of Parliament.

Nothing in this section shall affect the law relating to riot, unlawful assembly, breach of the peace, or sedition, or any offence against the State or the Sovereign.

A crime for the purposes of this section means an offence punishable on indictment, or an offence which is punishable on summary conviction, and for the commission of which the offender is liable under the statute making the offence punishable to be imprisoned either absolutely or at the discretion of the court as an alternative for some other punishment.

Where a person is convicted of any such agreement or combination as aforesaid to do or procure to be done an act which is punishable only on summary conviction, and is sentenced to imprisonment, the imprisonment shall not exceed three months, or such longer time, if any, as may have been prescribed by the statute for the punishment of the said act when committed by one person.

[1] 38 and 39 Victoria, ch. 86 (extract).

The legislation of 1875 safeguarded trade unions until, in 1901, by the decision of the courts in the Taff Vale Case, their position was again jeopardized. The Taff Vale Railway Company sued the Amalgamated Society of Railway Servants for damages done in a strike. Hitherto it had been understood that a union, not being a corporation, could not be so sued. This decision, affirmed by the House of Lords, brought into existence the Labour Party, which grew rapidly and became so strong as to wield power in the counsels of the Liberal Government that came into power in 1905. The Trade Disputes Act of 1906 gave the unions the protection they demanded.

68. TRADE DISPUTES ACT, 1906[1]

1. Amendment of Former Act

The following paragraph shall be added as a new paragraph after the first paragraph of section three of the Conspiracy and Protection of Property Act, 1875:

" An act done in pursuance of an agreement or combination by two or more persons shall, if done in contemplation or furtherance of a trade dispute, not be actionable unless the act, if done without any such agreement or combination, would be actionable."

2. Peaceful Picketing

1. It shall be lawful for one or more persons, acting on their own behalf or on behalf of a trade union or of an individual employer or firm in contemplation or furtherance of a trade dispute, to attend at or near a house or place where a person resides or works or carries on business or happens to be, if they so attend merely for the purpose of peacefully obtaining or communicating information, or of peacefully persuading any person to work or abstain from working.

2. Section seven of the Conspiracy and Protection of Property Act, 1875, is hereby repealed from " attending at or near " to the end of the section.

3. Removal of Liability for Interfering with Another Person's Business

An act done by a person in contemplation or furtherance of a trade dispute shall not be actionable on the ground only that it induces some other person to break a contract of employment or that it is an interference with the trade, business, or employment of some other person, or with the right of some other person to dispose of his capital or his labour as he wills.

[1] 6 Edw. 7, ch. 47.

4. *Prohibition of Actions of Tort against Trade Unions*

1. An action against a trade union, whether of workmen or masters, or against any members or officials thereof on behalf of themselves and all other members of the trade union in respect of any tortious act alleged to have been committed by or on behalf of the trade union, shall not be entertained by any court.

2. Nothing in this section shall affect the liability of the trustees of a trade union to be sued in the events provided for by the Trade Union Act, 1871, section nine, except in respect of any tortious act committed by or on behalf of the union in contemplation or in furtherance of a trade dispute.

5. *Short Title and Construction*

1. This Act may be cited as the Trade Disputes Act, 1906, and the Trade Union Acts, 1871 and 1876, and this Act may be cited together as the Trade Union Acts, 1871 to 1906.

2. In this Act the expression " trade union " has the same meaning as in the Trade Union Acts, 1871 and 1876, and shall include any combination as therein defined, notwithstanding that such combination may be the branch of a trade union.

3. In this Act and in the Conspiracy and Protection of Property Act, 1875, the expression " trade dispute " means any dispute between employers and workmen, or between workmen and workmen, which is connected with the employment or non-employment, or the terms of the employment, or with the conditions of labour, of any person, and the expression " workmen " means all persons employed in trade or industry, whether or not in the employment of the employer with whom a trade dispute arises; and, in section three of the last-mentioned Act, the words " between employers and workmen " shall be repealed.

The most authoritative historians of trade unionism present in the following passage the difficulties placed in the way of the unions by the Osborne Judgment in 1909. For several years the Labour Party was hampered by lack of funds consequent on this decision. In 1911 the chief practical difficulty was met by an act granting salaries to members of Parliament. An act of 1913 went further and permitted a trade union, with slight restrictions, to engage in political activity.

69. THE OSBORNE JUDGMENT[1]

The result of the dramatic victory of the Trade Disputes Act, and of the activity of the Labour members in the House of Commons, was considerably to increase the influence of the Labour Party in the country, where preparations were made for contesting any number of constituencies irrespective of the convenience of the Liberal and Conservative parties. The railway companies, in particular, found the presence in Parliament of the secretary of the railwaymen's principal Trade Union very inconvenient. Within a couple of years of the passing of the Trade Disputes Act, on July 22, 1908, one of the members of the Amalgamated Society of Railway Servants took legal proceedings to restrain it from spending any of its funds on political objects, contending that this was beyond the powers of a Trade Union. Such a contention found no support among eminent lawyers, several of whom had formally advised that Trade Unions were undoubtedly entitled to undertake political activities if their rules authorised such action and a majority of their members desired it. W. V. Osborne, the dissentient member of the Amalgamated Society of Railway Servants, took a different view; and, liberally financed from capitalist sources, carried his case right up to the highest tribunal. As a result, in December 1909, as in 1825, 1867–71, and 1901–6, every Trade Union in the land found its position and status once more gravely impugned. In what became widely known as the Osborne Judgment, the House of Lords, acting in its judicial capacity as the highest Court of Appeal, practically tore up what had, since 1871, been universally understood to be the legal constitution of a Trade Union.

The decision of the judges in the Osborne case throws so much light, not only on the status of Trade Unionism in English law, but also on the animus and prejudice which the Trade Disputes Act and the Labour Party had excited, that we think it worth treating at some length. Formally this judgment decided only that W. V. Osborne, a member of the Walthamstow Branch of the Amalgamated Society of Railway Servants, was entitled to restrain that Trade Union from making a levy on its members (and from using any of its funds) for the purpose of supporting the Labour Party, or maintaining Members of Parliament. But in the course of that decision a majority of the Law Lords, therein following all three judges of the Court of Appeal, laid it down as law (and thereby made it law until Parliament should otherwise determine), (a) that although Parliament has always avoided any express incorporation of Trade Unions, these were all now to be deemed to be corporate bodies, formed under statute, and not unincorporated

[1] Sidney and Beatrice Webb, *History of Trade Unionism*. New York, Longmans, Green & Co., 1920 Edition, pp. 608–611.

groups of individual persons; (b) that it follows, by an undoubted principle of English law, that a body corporate, created under statute, cannot lawfully do anything outside the purposes for which the statute has incorporated it; (c) that as the purposes for which Trade Unions are incorporated have to be found somewhere authoritatively given, the definition which Parliament incidentally enacted in the Trade Union Act of 1876 must be taken to enumerate, accurately and exhaustively, all the purposes which any group of persons falling within that definition can, as a corporate body, lawfully pursue; and (d) that the payment of the salaries and election expenses of Members of Parliament, and indeed, any political action whatsoever, not being mentioned as one of these purposes and not being considered by the judges incidental to them, could not lawfully be undertaken by any Trade Union, even if it was formed, from the outset, with this purpose duly expressed in its original rules, and even if all its members agreed to it, and continued to desire that their organization should carry it out.

This momentous judgment destroyed, at a blow, the peculiar legal status which Frederic Harrison had devised for Trade Unionism in 1868, and which Parliament thought that it had enacted in 1871–76. The statutes of 1871 and 1876, which had always been supposed to have enlarged the freedom of Trade Unions, were now held to have deprived these bodies of powers that they had formerly enjoyed. It was not, as will be seen, a question of protecting a dissentient minority. Whether the members were unanimous, or whether they were nearly evenly divided, did not affect the legal position. Trade Unions found themselves suddenly forbidden to do anything, even if all their members desired it, which could not be brought within the terms of a clause in the Act of 1876, which Parliament (as Lord James of Hereford emphatically declared) never meant to be taken in that sense. "What is not within the ambit of that statute," said Lord Halsbury, "is, I think, *prohibited* both to a corporation and a combination." This was the new limitation put on Trade Unions. All their educational work was prohibited; all their participation in municipal administration was forbidden; all their association for common purposes in Trades Councils and the Trades Union Congress became illegal. The judges stopped the most characteristic, and as was supposed, the most constitutional of the three customary ways that Trade Unions pursued of enforcing their Common Rules, namely, the Method of Legal Enactment; grave doubt was thrown on the legality of some of the developments of their second way, the Method of Mutual Insurance; whilst the way that the House of Lords expressly prescribed was exactly that which used to give rise to so much controversy, namely, the Method of Collective Bargaining, with its concomitant of the Strike.

SECTION III. THE RECOGNITION OF SOCIAL PROBLEMS

Social conditions in the last quarter of the nineteenth century were by no means as bad as they had been fifty years earlier, yet problems of social adjustment and organization still cried out for solution. The Fabian Society was formed in 1884 by a group of men and women who sought answers to these social questions. Among the Fabians a large number became expert in one phase or other of economic, social or political study and their influence on socialism and on the Labour Party is important. The most consistent service was rendered by Sidney Webb, G. B. Shaw, Graham Wallas, and Beatrice Webb. The following is one of the earliest and liveliest statements of Fabian purposes.

70. *A FABIAN SOCIETY MANIFESTO* [1]

The FABIANS are associated for spreading the following opinions held by them and discussing their practical consequences.

That under existing circumstances wealth cannot be enjoyed without dishonour or foregone without misery.

That it is the duty of each member of the State to provide for his or her wants by his or her own Labour.

That a life interest in the Land and Capital of the nation is the birthright of every individual born within its confines and that access to this birthright should not depend upon the will of any private person other than the person seeking it.

That the most striking result of our present system of farming out the national Land and Capital to private persons has been the division of Society into hostile classes, with large appetites and no dinners at one extreme and large dinners and no appetites at the other.

That the practice of entrusting the Land of the nation to private persons in the hope that they will make the best of it has been discredited by the consistency with which they have made the worst of it; and that Nationalisation of the Land in some form is a public duty.

That the pretensions of Capitalism to encourage Invention and to distribute its benefits in the fairest way attainable, have been discredited by the experience of the nineteenth century.

That, under the existing system of leaving the National Industry to organise itself Competition has the effect of rendering adulteration, dishonest dealing and inhumanity compulsory.

[1] Fabian Tract No. 2. *A Manifesto* (by G. B. Shaw). London, 1884.

That since Competition amongst producers admittedly secures to the public the most satisfactory products, the State should compete with all its might in every department of production.

That such restraints upon Free Competition as the penalties for infringing the Postal monopoly, and the withdrawal of workhouse and prison labour from the markets, should be abolished.

That no branch of Industry should be carried on at a profit by the central administration.

That the Public Revenue should be levied by a direct Tax; and that the central administration should have no legal power to hold back for the replenishment of the Public Treasury any portion of the proceeds of Industries administered by them.

That the State should compete with private individuals — especially with parents — in providing happy homes for children, so that every child may have a refuge from the tyranny or neglect of its natural custodians.

That Men no longer need special political privileges to protect them against Women, and that the sexes should henceforth enjoy equal political rights.

That no individual should enjoy any Privilege in consideration of services rendered to the State by his or her parents or other relations.

That the State should secure a liberal education and an equal share in the National Industry to each of its units.

That the established Government has no more right to call itself the State than the smoke of London has to call itself the weather.

That we had rather face a Civil War than such another century of suffering as the present one has been.

Even earlier, in 1878, William Booth, approaching the social evils of the day from an entirely different angle, had founded the Salvation Army. His work spread to all parts of the world. Booth possessed a talent for both organization and dramatization. H. M. Stanley's In Darkest Africa *had recently aroused the greatest interest, and Booth adapted its title to call attention to a problem nearer home.*

71. THE SALVATION ARMY'S WORK WITH THE "SUBMERGED TENTH"[1]

What, then, is Darkest England? For whom do we claim that " urgency " which gives their case priority over that of all other sections of their countrymen and countrywomen?

[1] General William Booth, *In Darkest England*. New York, Funk & Wagnalls Co., 1890, pp. 18–20 (condensed) 43–44, p. ii of preface.

I claim it for the Lost, for the Outcast, for the Disinherited of the World.

These, it may be said, are but phrases. Who are the Lost? I reply, not in a religious but in a social sense, the lost are those who have gone under, who have lost their foothold in Society, those to whom the prayer to our Heavenly Father, " Give us day by day our daily bread," is either unfulfilled, or only fulfilled by the Devil's agency: by the earnings of vice, the proceeds of crime, or the contribution enforced by the threat of the law.

But I will be more precise. The denizens in Darkest England, for whom I appeal, are (1) those who, having no capital or income of their own, would in a month be dead from sheer starvation were they exclusively dependent upon the money earned by their own work; and (2) those who by their utmost exertions are unable to attain the regulation allowance of food which the law prescribes as indispensable even for the worst criminals in our gaols.

I sorrowfully admit that it would be Utopian in our present social arrangements to dream of attaining for every honest Englishman a gaol standard of all the necessaries of life. Some time, perhaps, we may venture to hope that every honest worker on English soil will always be as warmly clad, as healthily housed, and as regularly fed as our criminal convicts — but that is not yet. . . .

What, then, is the standard toward which we may venture to aim with some prospect of realisation in our time? It is a very humble one, but if realised it would solve the worst problems of modern Society.

It is the standard of the London Cab Horse.

When in the streets of London a Cab Horse, weary or careless or stupid, trips and falls and lies stretched out in the midst of the traffic, there is no question of debating how he came to stumble before we try to get him on his legs again. The Cab Horse is a very real illustration of poor broken-down humanity; he usually falls down because of overwork and underfeeding. If you put him on his feet without altering his conditions, it would only be to give him another dose of agony; but first of all you'll have to pick him up again. It may have been through overwork or underfeeding, or it may have been all his own fault that he has broken his knees and smashed the shafts, but that does not matter. If not for his own sake, then merely in order to prevent an obstruction of the traffic, all attention is concentrated upon the question of how we are to get him on his legs again. The load is taken off, the harness is unbuckled, or if need be, cut, and everything is done to help him up. Then he is put in the shafts again and once more restored to his regular round of work. That is the first point. The second is that every Cab Horse in London has three things; a shelter for the night, food for its stomach, and work allotted to it by which it can earn its corn.

These are the two points of the Cab Horse's Charter. When he is down he is helped up, and while he lives he has food, shelter, and work. That, although a humble standard, is at present absolutely unattainable by millions — literally by millions — of our fellow-men and women in this country. Can the Cab Horse Charter be gained for human beings? I answer, yes.

. . . .

The moment that we take in hand this work we shall be compelled to turn our attention seriously to the question whether prevention is not better than cure. It is easier and cheaper, and in every way better, to prevent the loss of home than to have to re-create that home. It is better to keep a man out of the mire than to let him fall in first and then risk the chance of plucking him out. Any scheme, therefore, that attempts to deal with the reclamation of the lost must tend to develop into an endless variety of ameliorative measures, of some of which I shall have somewhat to say hereafter. I only mention the subject here in order that no one may say I am blind to the necessity of going further and adopting wider plans of operation than those which I put forward in this book. The renovation of our Social System is a work so vast that no one of us, nor all of us put together, can define all the measures that will have to be taken before we attain even the Cab-Horse Ideal of existence for our children and children's children. All that we can do is to attack, in a serious, practical spirit the worst and most pressing evils, knowing that if we do our duty we obey the voice of God. He is the Captain of our Salvation. If we but follow where He leads we shall not want for marching orders, nor need we imagine that He will narrow the field of operations.

. . . .

And yet all the way through my career I have keenly felt the remedial measures usually enunciated in Christian programmes and ordinarily employed by Christian philanthropy to be lamentably inadequate for any effectual dealing with the despairing miseries of these outcast classes. The rescued are appallingly few — a ghastly minority compared with the multitudes who struggle and sink in the open-mouthed abyss. Alike, therefore, my humanity and my Christianity, if I may speak of them in any way as separate one from the other, have cried out for some more comprehensive method of reaching and saving the perishing crowds.

Samuel and Henrietta Barnett began their married life by establishing themselves in the poor parish of St. Jude's in the heart of the crowded East End of London, where what commenced as clerical duty developed into something new and different. Enlisting the help of university men such as Arnold Toynbee, fresh from Oxford, full of imagination and the generosity of youth, they founded in 1885 the first university settlement, the idea of which Canon Barnett explains below. Toynbee Hall became a center for those men and women who wished to learn how to make headway against the diseases of society. Programs for social improvement were worked out in contact with actual conditions; constant discussion, surveys and experiments made them know their material and what could be done with it. The settlement idea spread even beyond England, and in the United States, Hull House in Chicago and Henry Street in New York are but the most famous of a large number of centers in which social reforms are prepared for by careful and accurate study of actual conditions.

72. THE SETTLEMENT IDEA [1]

Members of the Universities may for a few years settle in industrial centres, and in natural intercourse come into contact with their neighbours. There is nothing like contact for giving or getting understanding. There is no lecture and no book so effective as life. Culture spreads by contact. University men who are known as neighbours, who are met in the streets, in the clubs, and on committees, who can be visited in their own rooms, amid their own books and pictures, commend what the University stands for as it cannot otherwise be commended. On the other hand workmen who are casually and frequently met, whose idle words become familiar, whose homes are known, reveal the workman mind as it is not revealed by clever essayists or by orators of their own class. The friendship of one man of knowledge and one man of industry may go but a small way to bring together the Universities and the working classes, but it is such friendship which prepares the way for the understanding which underlies co-operation. If misunderstanding is war, understanding is peace. The men who settle may either take rooms by themselves, or they may associate themselves in a Settlement. There is something to be said for each plan. The advantage of Settlement is that a body of University men living together keep up the distinctive characteristics of their training, they better resist the tendency to put on the universal drab, and they bring a variety into their neighbourhood. They are helped, too, by the companionship of their fellows, to take larger views of what is wanted, their enthusiasm for progress is kept alive and at the same time well pruned by friendly and severe criticism.

But whether men live in lodgings or in Settlements, there is one necessary condition besides that of social interest if they are to be successful in uniting knowledge and industry in social reform. They must live their own life. There must be no affectation of asceticism, and no consciousness of superiority.

[1] Samuel A. Barnett, "Twenty-One Years of University Settlements." 1905. Published in *Practicable Socialism*. New Series. London, Longmans, Green & Co., 1915, pp. 126–130 (condensed).

they must show forth the taste, the mind and the faith that is in them. They have not come as "missioners," they have come to settle, that is to learn as much as to teach, to receive as much as to give. . . .

Twenty years ago primary education was much as it had been left by Mr. Lowe. Some University men living in a Settlement soon became conscious of the loss involved in the system, they talked with neighbours who by themselves were unconscious of the loss till inspired, and inspiring they formed an Education Reform League. There were committees, meetings, and public addresses. The league was a small affair, and seems to be little among the forces of the time. But every one of its proposals have been carried out. Some of its members in high official positions have wielded with effect the principles which were elaborated in the forge at which they and working men sweated together. Others of its members on local authorities or as citizens have never forgotten the inner meaning of education as they learnt it from their University friends.

Another instance may be offered. The relief of the poor is a subject on which the employing and the employed classes naturally incline to take different views. They suspect one another's remedies. The working men hate both the charity of the rich and the strict administration of the economist, while they themselves talk a somewhat impracticable socialism. University men who assist in such relief, are naturally suspected as members of the employing class. A few men, however, who as residents had become known in other relations, and were recognized as human, induced some workmen to take part in administering relief. Together they faced actual problems, together they made mistakes, together they felt sympathy with sorrow, and saw the break-down of their carefully designed action. The process went on for years, the personnel of the body of fellow-workers has changed, but there has been a gradual approach from the different points of view. The University men have more acutely realized some of the causes of distress, the need of preserving and holding up self-respect, the pressure of the industrial system, and the claim of sufferers from this system to some compensation. They have learnt through their hearts. The workmen, on the other hand, have realized the failure of mere relief to do permanent good, the importance of thought in every case, and the kindness of severity. The result of this co-operation may be traced in the fact that workmen, economists and socialists have been found advocating the same principle of relief. . . .

There is one other instance which is also of interest. Local Government is the corner-stone in the English Constitution. The people in their own neighbourhoods learn what self-government means, as their own Councils and Boards make them happy or unhappy. The government in industrial neighbourhoods is often bad, sometimes because the members are self-seekers, more often because they are ignorant or vainglorious. How can it be otherwise? If the industrial neighbourhood is self-contained, as for example, in East London, it has few inhabitants with the necessary leisure for study or for frequent attendance at the meetings. If it is part of a larger government — as in county boroughs — it is unknown to the majority of the community. The consequence is that the neighbourhoods wanting most light and most water and most space have the least, and that bodies whose chief concern should be health and education waste their time and their rates arranging their contracts so as to support local labour. In a word, industrial neighbourhoods suffer for want of a voice to express their needs and for the want of the knowledge which can distinguish man from man, recognize the relative importance of spending and saving, and encourage mutual self-respect.

University men may and in some measure have met this want. They, by residence, have learnt the wants, and their voice has helped to bring about the more equal treatment which industrial districts are now receiving. They have often, for instance, been instrumental in getting the Libraries' Act adopted. They have as members of local bodies learnt much and taught something.

Charles Booth, a middle-aged business man, brought up in the school of laissez-faire, having read much about poverty and slum conditions, decided to make a survey of the East End of London. In this work he was assisted by a group of investigators that included Beatrice Potter, the future Mrs. Webb. The most detailed results were published, together with charts in many colors showing the degree of poverty in each street. In the passage given here Booth indicates the method employed. The results were such as to convince him and most of his readers of the necessity of concerted action on the part of society and of the abandonment of the complete individualism that had been accepted during the previous century.

73. THE FIRST LARGE SOCIAL SURVEY MADE IN ENGLAND SINCE DOMESDAY [1]

The inquiry of which I am now able to publish the results, was set on foot in 1886, the subject being the condition and occupations of the inhabitants of London, and my grateful thanks are due to those friends who helped me at the outset in laying down the principles on which the inquiry has been conducted. It was decided to employ a double method, dividing the people by districts and again by trades, so as to show at once the manner of their life and of their work. The particulars given in the present volume are

[1] *Labour and Life of the People of London.* Edited by Charles Booth. 2d Edition. 10 vols. London, Williams & Norgate, 1889, vol. I, pp. 3-4, 5-7.

confined to the East End of London, and deal but imperfectly with that. Most of 1886 was occupied with preliminary work, 1887 sufficed to complete the district inquiry, and 1888 has been spent on the trades and special subjects.

The special subjects connected with East London have started into great prominence during the time I have been at work. On the question of the " Unemployed " we have seen a house-to-house inquiry instituted by Government, which took as one of its selected districts St. George's-in-the-East. On the influx of poor Jews, under the name of " Foreign Immigration," we have had a Committee of the House of Commons; and there has been the Committee of the House of Lords on the " Sweating System," which is still prolonging its labours. In addition, the whole question of Poor Relief has been laid open by another Committee of the House of Commons, and we have seen a succession of Mansion House inquiries on the same subject. To meet this evident demand for information I offer the pages which follow. The facts as given have been gathered and stated with no bias nor distorting aim, and with no foregone conclusions.

For the district inquiry, resulting in the division of the people into 8 classes, I have relied upon information obtained from the School Board visitors, of whom there are 66 in the district. . . .

The School Board visitors perform amongst them a house-to-house visitation; every house in every street is in their books, and details are given of every family with children of school age. They begin their scheduling two or three years before the children attain school age, and a record remains in their books of children who have left school. The occupation of the head of the family is noted down. Most of the visitors have been working in the same district for several years, and thus have an extensive knowledge of the people. It is their business to re-schedule for the Board once a year, but intermediate revisions are made in addition, and it is their duty to make themselves acquainted, so far as possible, with new comers into their districts. They are in daily contact with the people, and have a very considerable knowledge of the parents of the school children, especially of the poorest amongst them, and of the conditions under which they live. No one can go, as I have done, over the description of the inhabitants of street after street in this huge district, taken house by house and family by family — full as it is of picturesque details noted down from the lips of the visitor to whose mind they have been recalled by the open pages of his own schedules — and doubt the genuine character of the information and its truth. Of the wealth of my material I have no doubt. I am indeed embarrassed by its mass, and by my resolution to make use of no fact to which I cannot give a quantitative value. The materials for sensational stories lie plentifully in every book of our notes; but, even if I had the skill to use my material in this way — that gift of the imagination which is called "realistic" — I should not wish to use it here. There is struggling poverty, there is destitution, there is hunger, drunkenness, brutality, and crime; no one doubts that it is so. My object has been to attempt to show the numerical relation which poverty, misery, and depravity bear to regular earnings and comparative comfort, and to describe the general conditions under which each class lives.

For the trade inquiries and special subjects, I have been fortunate in obtaining the aid of others, and their work will speak eloquently for itself.

If the facts thus stated are of use in helping social reformers to find remedies for the evils which exist, or do anything to prevent the adoption of false remedies, my purpose is answered. It was not my intention to bring forward any suggestions of my own, and if I have ventured here and there, and especially in the concluding chapters, to go beyond my programme, it has been with much hesitation.

With regard to the disadvantages under which the poor labour, and the evils of poverty, there is a great sense of helplessness: the wage earners are helpless to regulate their work and cannot obtain a fair equivalent for the labour they are willing to give; the manufacturer or dealer can only work within the limits of competition; the rich are helpless to relieve want without stimulating its sources. To relieve this helplessness a better stating of the problems involved is the first step. "We are a long way towards understanding anything under our consideration when we have properly laid it open, even without comment." In this direction must be sought the utility of my attempt to analyze the population of a part of London. The materials gathered together in this volume seem at first sight hardly sufficient for wide generalization or definite conclusions. But if what is shown to exist here may be taken as the most serious thing of the kind with us — if this district contains, as is supposed, the most destitute population in England — we may assume that to state the problem here is to state it everywhere, and to solve it here would be to solve it everywhere.

A present-day historian reviews below the results, measured in terms of living conditions among the working classes, of the work accomplished by the many different reforming movements of the Victorian period.

74. THE RISE OF THE STANDARD OF LIVING, 1850-1900 [1]

Clearly, we can look for no such sensational and obvious changes as the Industrial Revolution immediately produced in men's ways of living. There was no uprooting of a whole social order on the scale of that which followed

[1] G. D. H. Cole, *Short History of the British Working Class Movement, 1789-1925.* London, George Allen & Unwin and The Labour Publishing Co., 1925-7, vol. II, pp. 187-195 (condensed).

the rise of the modern factory system. The destruction of the peasantry had been thoroughly accomplished well before 1850; and the agricultural labourer had little, though the farmer had much, to lose by the decline of agriculture which set in with the great depression of the later 'seventies. Despite the immense growth of the mining industry, the proportion of the British population living in villages continued to decline, and the proportion of town dwellers to increase. But for the agricultural labourers of 1880, driven to the towns in search of work, there was no such wholesale change in the way of life as for the labourers of the early nineteenth century.

The technical changes in industry were not, indeed, less important or far-reaching than those of earlier times. The new methods of steel manufacture, the vast growth of the railway systems, the extraordinarily rapid expansion of the mining and engineering industries, were constantly revolutionizing the methods of production, rendering old kinds of skilled labour obsolete and creating new, replacing craftsmanship by the skill of the machine-tool, and raising up hosts of semi-skilled machine-minders to aid or supersede the skilled tradesmen. The grades and classes of labour were constantly shifting under stress of these changes, and causing drastic readjustments in wage-rates and in Trade Union rules and organisation. The proportion of workers employed in different callings was steadily changing. Cotton and wool were yielding their leadership of the industrial world, among both employers and workers, to metals and mines. The large part played by coal miners and engineers in the history of Victorian Labour is no accident, but a product of changing economic conditions.

Nevertheless, from the standpoint of the workers, the changes of the second half of the century appear far less drastic than those of the earlier period. For, apart from the steady movement of agricultural workers into the mining industry, the shifting was mainly from one factory process to another. The factory had become the recognised and accepted centre of English life; and the vast mass of the workers knew no other way of living.

Within the limits of the factory system, there is no doubt that, on the whole, working-class conditions were getting better. The factory code was being stiffened up, both by legislation and by better inspection and administration; and the methods of the Factory Acts were being gradually applied to fresh industries, including the mines. The hours of labour, still very long, were being slowly reduced, especially at first for children and women. Factories were becoming rather less vile and insanitary; and very slowly sanitary and housing conditions in the towns were being improved. It is, however, a notable fact that overcrowding remained nearly as bad as ever. In 1801 the average number of persons to a house was 5.67; in 1901 it had fallen to 5.2. Nevertheless, the death-rate in England and Wales had been reduced from 22.7 per thousand in 1851–5 to 16 per thousand in 1901–5, and the birth-rate from 34 to 28. The infant mortality rate, on the other hand, had actually risen, from 14.6 per cent. in 1850 to 15.4 per cent. in 1900.

There had been a great decrease in crime, due in part to the diminished ferocity of the criminal law; and the number of paupers had fallen from over a million in 1850 to under 800,000 in 1900, despite the increase in population. An almost universal system of public elementary education had been built up. In 1851 the State spent only £150,000 on this service. In 1901, it was already spending nearly eleven millions, in addition to the sums expended out of local rates. The services of local government in the sphere of public health were practically created during the second half of the century. The conception that it was the State's business to take at least some precautions to safeguard the health of its citizens found expression in a re-modelled system of Local Government to which large powers were entrusted.

These changes undoubtedly made life more tolerable for the ordinary man, and gave him something to hope for in a world that to the generations before had seemed to offer no hope at all. . . .

Of course, it was not for the workers alone that better times came with the settling down of industrialism in the second half of the century. A huge new middle class came into being; the professions, the managerial grades in industry, the middlemen of every sort increased enormously in numbers. Employers and financiers made fortunes undreamed of by the greatest magnates of the Industrial Revolution. In 1851 the professional classes were 2.2 per cent. of total population, and the commercial classes 4.3 per cent. By 1881 the corresponding figures were 6.2 and 7.8. In 1840 under 2,000 persons died leaving more than £500; by 1877 the number had risen to 4,478, and there were more than 1,100 persons with incomes of over £10,000 a year. There can be no doubt that, up to 1880 at least, profits were rising considerably faster than wages.

Wages, however, were rising, both in money and in purchasing power. In the absence of reliable statistics, it is not easy to present any comprehensive view of the change in the wages of the whole industrial population, and it is necessary to fall back on estimates which are admittedly based on somewhat inadequate data. But, though the precise figures are doubtful, the general tendency admits of no dispute. There were set-backs; but between 1850 and 1900 the average real wage, measured in purchasing power, rose at least by seventy, and perhaps by as much as eighty per cent. . . .

Real wages rose sharply at three points — between 1861 and 1864, between 1868 and 1876, and, apart from two brief set-backs in the early and late 'nineties, through the whole period from 1882 to 1900. But, whereas the two earlier advances were mainly due to the rise in money wages, the long rise after 1882 was still more due to the fall in prices.

It will be noticed at once that the great advances in money wages coincide for the most part with periods of exceptional Trade Union activity. The early 'fifties saw the rise of the " New Model " Trade Unionism; the early 'sixties, the great development of mining Trade Unionism under Alexander Macdonald and the great growth and activity of Unionism in the building trades; the late 'sixties and early 'seventies, the great struggle of the Unions with the law, the Nine Hours' movement of the Engineers, further big developments among the miners, and the first rise of Unions among the less skilled workers; the years from 1888 to 1890, the birth of the Miners' Federation, the Gasworkers' and Dockers' Unions, and a host of other active pioneers of the " New " Unionism. The closing years of the century were not, indeed, marked by great industrial activity; but they saw the formation of the General Federation of Trade Unions and of the Labour Representation Committee.

This coincidence of time does not, of course, settle the question of cause and effect. If Union activity helped to bring about these advances in wages, it is no less true that the favourable opportunities presented by periods of good trade helped to call forth this activity. . . .

The whole period of fifty years . . . really falls into two periods of rapid economic advance, separated by a period of acute depression. From 1850 to the middle 'seventies British Capitalism passed through what we have called its " Golden Age." By the end of this period money wages had risen by more than half over the level of 1850, and real wages by at least a third. Then came the period of the great depression, extending, with only a brief interval of good trade in the early 'eighties, from the late 'seventies to the late 'eighties. Over this period money wages fell by about 10 per cent.; but owing to the rapid fall in prices the decline in real wages, apart from loss of earnings through unemployment, was quite small. Then followed the great revival of 1889, bringing big advances in both money and real wages. The slump of the early 'nineties caused some reduction in both; but then the upward movement was sharply resumed. Between the late 'eighties and the end of the century both real and money wages rose by at least 20 per cent. In all, as we have seen, the rise in real wages during the latter half of the century was, on the average of all trades for which particulars are available, certainly not less than 70 per cent.

This rise was by no means equally distributed among the different groups of workers. The heaviest increases seem to have been secured by the cotton operatives, whose wages were approximately doubled during the half century. These, of course, had been among the most desperately exploited of the wage-workers during the first part of the century. According to Mr. Wood, the average earnings of all classes of cotton operatives in 1850 were about 9s. 4d. a week. By 1880 they had risen to 14s. 10d., and by 1900 to 18s.

3d. The workers in the wool industry, on the other hand, better paid in 1850, got only about 40 per cent. more in 1900 than in 1850. Carpenters' money wages actually advanced by less than 25 per cent. between 1850 and 1900.

In mining and iron and steel work, wages rose rather more than the average, and in the building trades considerably more. In engineering, the rise was about the average; but there was a considerable up-grading of unskilled workers to semi-skilled work. On the whole, the constructional trades, on account of their great expansion, tended to improve their relative position. But they were also subject to abnormally heavy fluctuations in wages, owing to their exceptional liability to booms and slumps. This is most marked of all in the mining industry. In the middle 'seventies mining wages rose to 90 per cent. of the 1900 level. Five years later they had fallen to 70 per cent. This extreme fluctuation, of course, largely explains the prevalence of mining strikes and lock-outs. . . .

Over the same period there was, of course, at least as considerable a growth of organisation among the employers. Employers' Associations sprang up to cope with the rising Trade Unions, and, especially towards the end of the century, there was a marked growth of trusts and combines formed for the purpose of regulating prices and output. The attitude and organisation of the employing class was no less responsive than those of Labour to changes in the economic conditions. *Laissez-faire* was abandoned as a principle by capitalists as much as by workers.

The growth of relatively stable Trade Unions and of a stable Co-operative Movement is but one of the signs of a marked change in the habits and outlook of the British workers during the latter part of the century. Though by 1900 the Trade Unions were gradually discarding their "Lib-Lab" policy and Socialism had become a real and powerful force among them, much that they had learned in the Victorian era remained with them as a lasting acquisition. General elementary education, of course, had made a huge difference to manners, habits and social outlook. The rise in wages had made possible ways of living which were beyond the reach of the workers during the bad times of the Industrial Revolution. The improvement in sanitary conditions had profoundly altered, save for the unfortunate slum-dwellers, the conditions of urban life. The sort of appeals which had roused the workers in the 'thirties and 'forties would have made no impression on their successors in the latter part of the century. Though there were still, even in 1900, many thousands of hopelessly exploited "bottom dogs," such as Charles Booth's famous survey had brought to common knowledge ten years before, these were not typical of the organised or organisable working class. In the great industries, the workers had ceased to be a ragged and starving mob, easily roused, either by a Feargus O'Connor or a James Rayner Stephens, or by some one of the many "Messiahs" who sprang up in the early years of the century. They had acquired a status, and in many cases a little " stake in the country," if only to the extent of a few pounds in the " Co-op."

No longer were mass uprisings, huge sudden revolts bred of despair and spreading like wildfire none knew how, likely or even possible. Strikes had become, for the most part, orderly movements, prepared for in advance and conducted by organised bodies and under duly constituted leadership. . . . Socialist propaganda had become far less an appeal to emotions and instincts, and far more an appeal to reason. O'Connor had been hot as hell; Sidney Webb was always as cool as a cucumber.

This is not said by way of praise or blame, but merely as a true account of what had happened. There were working-class leaders in the first part of the nineteenth century as clever, as well-read, and as educated as any since. But the average level of culture immensely changed. In the early days, there was a small minority that read Owen and Carlyle, and a far wider minority that appreciated Cobbett. In the latter part of the century Darwin and Spencer and Huxley were making their mark on working-class thought to an extent that would have been impossible before the coming of popular education.

In certain respects, the wide differences of education hampered the working-class propagandists. In the early part of the century, the workers were left to provide their own newspapers because it was not worth anyone else's while to provide for them. The work of Brougham and Charles Knight, of the *Penny Magazine,* was the beginning of the change. The Mechanics' Institutes, in the 'twenties, and the Society for the Diffusion of Useful Knowledge, in the 'thirties, set themselves to teach the workers what it was good for them to know. But these were subsidised and propagandist, and not commercial, ventures.

The coming of popular education altered the whole position. It became worth while, commercially, to provide reading matter for the poor as well as the rich. The result was seen in a flood of cheap novels, cheap magazines, cheap newspapers. The commercial classes vied with the working-class propagandists in catering for the workers' reading. With ample resources behind them, they made it far harder for the Socialists to maintain a press of their own, or to get the workers' ear. . . . Only *The Clarion,* through Robert Blatchford's special genius as a popular writer, established itself as a commercial success.

To a great extent, in habits and way of life, the upper strata of the workers became assimilated to the lesser middle class. . . . By the end of the century, Socialism itself had become respectable. And all this had happened precisely because the working-class standard of living had risen to a point which made respectability possible.

SECTION IV. THE SOCIAL LEGISLATION OF THE LIBERAL RÉGIME, 1905-1914

The period from 1885 to 1905 was, with slight exceptions, one of Conservatism in politics. Mr. Balfour's Government fell in 1905, however, and the Liberals, led by Sir Henry Campbell-Bannerman, succeeded to power. Victory in the General Election of 1906 consolidated that power and encouraged the Liberals to undertake extensive reforms. The Trade Disputes Act of 1906 was one. In 1907 Chancellor of the Exchequer Asquith suggested that the nation should take over much of the work hitherto left to haphazard development. Asquith became Prime Minister on Campbell-Bannerman's death in 1908, and one of the first of his proposals concerned the care of the aged. The three following excerpts give a fair reflection of the views of three parties, the Liberal, Conservative, and Labour, in that order.

75. ASQUITH ON OLD AGE PENSIONS [1]

MR. ASQUITH: . . . Last year, in introducing the Budget, I said that this Parliament and this Government had come here pledged to social reform, and I pointed to two figures in our modern society that make an especially strong and, indeed, an irresistible appeal, not only to our sympathy, but to something more practical, a sympathy translated into a concrete and constructive policy of social and financial effort. One is the figure of a child. . . .

The other figure is the figure of old age, still unprovided for except for casual and unorganised effort, or, by what is worse, invidious dependence upon Poor Law relief. I said then that we hoped and intended this year to lay firm the foundations of a wiser and a humaner policy. . . .

I need not remind the Committee that this question in one shape or another has been before the country now for the best part of thirty years. The first schemes that were put forward proceeded on the footing either of compulsory or voluntary insurance, accompanied and fortified by State aid. The Royal Commission on the Aged Poor in 1895 reported adversely to all the proposals which had up to that time been made. There followed a series of inquiries into schemes for granting immediate pensions to the aged and deserving poor. . . . Much valuable information was accumulated and classified in the course of these inquiries, with the result, I think, that all the material facts may now be said to have been ascertained. But up to this moment nothing has been done, nothing at all.

In the meantime other countries have been making experiments. The

[1] *Parliamentary Debates*, May 7, 1908. 4th Series, vol. 188. pp. 463-465 (condensed).

German system, which is one of compulsory State-aided assurance, has been in existence since 1889. Under it pensions averaging a little over £16 13s. a year are paid to insured persons of the age of seventy and upwards. The State contribution amounts to less than 40 per cent. of the whole, and it would seem that in 1907 not more than 126,000 persons out of a population of over 52 millions were in receipt of old age pensions.

More instruction, I think, for our purposes is to be derived from the legislation initiated in Denmark in 1891, in New Zealand in 1898, and subsequently in New South Wales and Victoria. These systems, though differing widely in their details, have several important features in common. In the first place, they do not depend for their application upon either voluntary or compulsory contribution on the part of the pensioner. In the next place, they are limited in all cases to persons whose income or property is below a prescribed figure; and, thirdly, in all cases they impose some test or other, varying in stringency and in complexity, of character and desert in regard to such matters, for instance, as past criminality or pauperism. Although both in Denmark and in New Zealand the expenditure upon the pensions has, in the course of time, exhibited a tendency to increase beyond the original estimate, yet the cost of administration has turned out to be relatively small, amounting in New Zealand in 1907 to not more than 1.67 per cent.; and I think I may say that in none of these communities is there any dissatisfaction either with the principles or with the working of the law, and certainly no disposition to go back to the state of things which prevailed before old age pensions were set up.

76. A BISHOP'S DISTRUST OF GOVERNMENT AID TO THE OLD [1]

THE LORD BISHOP OF RIPON: . . . My Lords, there is something in nations which is of more importance to them than mere financial prosperity. The accumulation of the power of wealth which enables nations to raise a considerable revenue through taxation, gives the stamp, as it were, of prosperity, but the best asset of a nation is a manly, vigorous, and numerous race, and the best asset of the race is that the character of its men and women shall never be impaired. A Frenchman once wrote a book concerning what he called the superiority of the Anglo-Saxon race, and in the course of that book he pointed out what he believed to be the one essential factor which contributed to that superiority. He said that in all the history of English life one spirit had prevailed, and that was the spirit of self-reliance. He turned to his countrymen and said, " The danger which we are in today is that we are not rearing our population to self-reliant habits."

[1] *Parliamentary Debates*, July 20, 1908. 4th Series, vol. 192. pp. 1393–1395 (condensed).

He drew the picture of the little farmer in Normandy who would stint himself and live in an unclean and even unwholesome dwelling in order that he might leave a sufficient sum to his children. He pointed then to the English farmer who, he said, so far from crippling himself in order that his sons may be well started in the world, takes the strong and independent line and says, " I made my way in the world and I expect my sons to do the same." " In other words," said the French writer, " the race across the Channel has educated its children in the habits of self-reliance, and to this habit is largely due the superiority and the strength of that race. . . ."

I speak not of those of seventy years of age who are to receive the benefit of this measure. Their characters are formed, their conditions are settled. We are going forward tonight and saying: " Let us help them, let us give to them something which will ease their later years, and if a few have not deserved, well, we will at any rate with large-heartedness forget those who were weak and deal largely and generously with this matter before us, for all these men or women of seventy naturally appeal to the pity and sympathy of our hearts." But when I look beyond and ask whether it is conceivable that we may begin so to hold out the thought that men may be able to receive from the State that which in olden days they won by their own strong labours, self-denial, and thrift, then I am apprehensive lest we should, in attempting to do a good, do a great and grievous wrong, robbing ourselves and our children of that which is the best inheritance, the inheritance of a sturdy, strong, self-reliant manhood, that will take upon itself the responsibilities of life and be equal, therefore, to the responsibilities of Empire. I think none of us can shut our eyes to the fact that there are among us people who are very ready to shirk responsibility, and I, for one, would feel that the whole system and condition of English life had lost its meaning and value if once we should act in such fashion as to remove responsibility, and the sense of responsibility, from the people of this country. We are in this world for responsibility; through responsibility we grow and rise to the height of character which Divine Providence intended us to reach. Let us not, by any action of ours, weaken that which is the best thing we can preserve, the character of the population, for out of that, and out of that alone, will spring the strength and the stability of the nation.

77. *A LABOUR MEMBER'S VIEW OF OLD AGE PENSIONS* [1]

I once said, and I repeat, that no man should sit in this House without having served first for ten years as a Poor Law guardian. He would then know something about human nature. It is not perfect. There are a good many sides to it, but most people who apply for relief are very human, and

[1] William Crooks, July 9, 1908. *Parliamentary Debates.* 4th Series. vol. 192, pp. 196–197.

I do not think they very much object to these inquisitorial examinations as to their character. We were challenged by the hon. Member for Preston (Mr. Harold Cox), who said, "Would you go on any public platform and declare that you are in favour of giving a pension of 5s. per week to a drunken, thriftless, worthless man or woman?" My reply is very prompt to that. A man of seventy with nothing in the world to help him is going to cut a pretty shine on 5s. per week, whether his character be good or bad. What could he do with it? It is not enough to keep him in decency, and he would be well punished for not taking care when he had the opportunity if he had to live on 5s. per week. Who are you, to be continually finding fault? Who amongst you has such a clear record as to be able to point to the iniquity and wickedness of an old man of seventy? I said before, and I repeat, if a man is foolish enough to get old, and if he has not been artful enough to get rich, you have no right to punish him for it. It is no business of yours. It is sufficient for you to know he has grown old.

After all, who are these old men and women? Let me appeal to the noble Lord the Member for Marylebone (Lord Robert Cecil). They are the veterans of industry, people of almost endless toil, who have fought for and won the industrial and commercial supremacy of Great Britain. Is their lot and end to be the Bastille of the everlasting slur of pauperism? We claim these pensions as a right. Ruskin, I think, read you a little homily on the subject — "Even a labourer serves his country with his spade and shovel as the statesman does with his pen, or the soldier with his sword." He has a right to some consideration from the State. Here in a country rich beyond description there are people poverty-stricken beyond description. There can be no earthly excuse for the condition of things which exists in this country today. If it be necessary to have a strong Army and Navy to protect the wealth of the nation, do not let us forget that it is the veterans of industry who have created that wealth; and let us accept this as an instalment to bring decency and comfort to our aged men and women.

John Burns, a working man himself but a Liberal minister, describes the Government's scheme to regulate housing and the proper planning of towns. A Conservative objection to the scheme is given also. The Government's proposals were modified by the Lords so that back-to-back buildings and cellar dwellings were not done away with.

78. *A PROPOSAL FOR HOUSING AND TOWN PLANNING* [1]

The main and essential feature of the Bill is that Part III of the Housing of the Working Classes Act, 1890, which enables local authorities to provide

[1] John Burns, President of Local Government Board, April 5, 1909. *Parliamentary Debates,* Commons, 5th Series, vol. 3. pp. 734–739 (condensed).

new houses for the working classes, and which is now only adoptive, shall be put in force throughout the country. This is an important, a serious and necessary, and, I believe, a practical step that housing reformers have been asking for some years.

Beyond that the Bill gives increased facilities for the acquisition of land for housing the working classes on small holdings terms. . . .

The third improvement is that the provisions in this Bill enable loans to be obtained through the Public Works Loans Commissioners for periods up to eighty years, with the minimum rate of interest possible, and I think desirable.

The fourth provision is that not only will the new Bill, when it becomes an Act, be better enforced by improved machinery than the existing Acts now are, but existing Acts will be embodied in this Bill; and at the end of the Session the whole of the Housing Acts, consolidated into one intelligible and practical working measure, will, I trust, enable the housing of the working classes to be secured by machinery that will act more easily, more promptly, and more efficiently, and at less cost, than now prevails.

The fifth point is that this Bill strengthens and simplifies the present law as regards closing orders, and the demolition of insanitary property unfit for human habitation.

The sixth point of the Bill is that it extends, in Clauses 14 and 15, to houses of a higher rental value than at present, an implied condition in the contract for letting that the houses are fit for human habitation. . . . What we want is to maintain that house in a condition fit for human habitation so long as human beings reside therein. Small though that point is, if vigorously enforced, which we believe under the machinery of this Bill it will be, that small but necessary point will, I trust, create a revolution in the minor conditions of the house, especially in our large towns and cities. . . .

The next portion of the Bill is that portion which deals with town planning. This is a new department in the legislation of this country. I regret that it has come so late. No one can go through the East End of London, or to places like Liverpool, Leeds, Manchester and Glasgow, and see the effect on the physique, morale, happiness, and comfort of men, women, and children, through lack of some such condition as this one hundred, or at least fifty, years ago, but will come to one definite conclusion, that, late though it is, it is better late than never, and that the House of Commons should not lose this opportunity of giving to communities, especially to growing and industrial communities, the opportunity of consciously shaping their own development in a better way than has occurred in the past. I have lately been spending week ends in visiting thirty or forty unemployed works in the East End of London, particularly in close proximity to open spaces, and if Members who do not know the East End of London had been with me, I could have pointed out in a practical way how, even close to places like West Ham Park, Hainault Forest, the western portion of Epping Forest, and Hackney Marshes, and by the River Lea and other places, if we had had this Bill forty or fifty years ago, the amenities of these parks and open spaces could have been enormously added to by maintaining a balance between them and the houses built in their neighbourhood. It is not fair or just to our poor that in many cases you build, as you do, close by a river or a canal, which might be made a pleasurable and healthy amenity by the adoption of a proper system of laying out roadways; it is not fair, I say, that streets should be put the wrong way on, that roads should be formed at the wrong angle, that they should be placed where the sun rarely reaches, but where the wind does always, or where ventilation is denied them, and where the line of greatest resistance is pursued in neglecting those natural and physical opportunities which, under the Town Planning Bill, could be profitably exploited for the whole community — to the benefit not only of the present generation, but particularly of children who are cursed, many of them, in their habitations and environment. . . .

I now come to the third portion of the Bill. That is the portion which deals with the medical officers of health. It is a very important part of the measure. We have sixty-two county councils in the country, and, up to recently, only half of them have had medical officers. I do not think that this country, which for the last hundred years has led the world in public sanitation, should remain longer under the reproach of not having in every county of England and Wales a whole-time medical officer. And we have decided that every county council shall have a whole-time medical officer, devoting all his abilities and services to public health and sanitation. . . .

There are one or two other things to which I must refer before I sit down. The first is with regard to underground dwellings. We are taking steps to abolish underground and cellar dwellings altogether. Personal and public opinion in the last few years has moved rapidly, and the proposals of the Bill practically terminate underground and cellar dwellings for human habitation for the future. We are also seeking to obtain power to prohibit back-to-back dwellings.

79. A CONSERVATIVE'S DISLIKE OF GOVERNMENT CENTRALIZATION [1]

THE EARL OF ONSLOW: There is a peculiarity of the Bill which runs through it from one end to the other to which I feel bound to draw attention. That is the proposal to put in the hands of a Government Department a number of duties which hitherto have always been left either to the

[1] *Parliamentary Debates,* Lords, Sept. 14, 1909. 5th Series, vol. 2. pp. 1150–1151 (condensed).

local authority or to Parliament. This is a practice which I am afraid under His Majesty's Government has been slowly and steadily growing. It is not a practice which I for one can look upon with satisfaction. . . .

We are told that in this respect we ought to take example by what is done on the Continent. We are told that in Germany, Austria, and Holland the local authorities are all required to make town planning schemes. Most of you who have travelled on the Continent would be somewhat loath to see a town laid out even like Vienna or Berlin, with their rings and their rectangular streets. I think travellers visiting some of those cities may look back with affection to the times when we threaded the tortuous labyrinths of Threadneedle Street. Whether that be so or not, at any rate we in this country are not accustomed to be, and do not wish to be, governed by a bureaucracy. Our principles are totally different from those which govern foreign nations. We have our local authorities and our supreme Parliament. I am told there are no fewer than 26,000 local authorities in this country, and I am always filled with amazement and satisfaction when I reflect upon the enormous amount of unpaid labour which citizens of this country are willingly giving in order to look after the affairs of their neighbours. . . . I venture to think that anything which tends to diminish local patriotism will be a very grievous blow to local institutions generally.

No other budget in British history aroused such excitement as that of 1909. Mr. Lloyd George, President of the Board of Trade from 1905 to 1908, succeeded Asquith as Chancellor of the Exchequer. The budget he brought in was far more than a budget, for it contained a whole social policy which some called socialistic and confiscatory, although Mr. Snowden, a Socialist, denied that it was thorough socialism. The budget was passed only after a General Election brought the Peers to the point of acquiescence. The first excerpt is from Mr. Lloyd George's speech introducing the budget; the second is the concluding sentences of a speech by Lord Rosebery, a former Liberal Prime Minister (1894-5), who was unable to accept much of the new Liberal program.

80. LLOYD GEORGE BRINGS IN THE BUDGET OF 1909[1]

Taxation of Land

The first conviction that is borne in upon the Chancellor of the Exchequer who examines land as a subject for taxation is this: that in order to do justice he must draw a broad distinction between land whose value is purely agricultural in its character and composition, and land which has a special value

[1] *Parliamentary Debates,* Commons, April 29, 1909. 5th Series. vol. 4. pp. 532-540 (condensed).

attached to it, owing either to the fact of its covering marketable mineral deposits or because of its proximity to any concentration of people. Agricultural land has not, during the past twenty or thirty years, appreciated in value in this country. In some parts it has probably gone down. I know parts of the country where the value has gone up.But there has been an enormous increase in the value of urban land and of mineral property. And a still more important and relevant consideration in examining the respective merits of these two or three classes of claimants to taxation is this: the growth in the value, more especially of urban sites, is due to no expenditure of capital or thought on the part of the ground owner, but entirely owing to the energy and the enterprise of the community. . . .

Still worse, the urban landowner is freed in practice from the ordinary social obligations which are acknowledged by every agricultural landowner towards those whose labour makes their wealth. . . . The rural landowner has the obligation to provide buildings and keep them in repair. The urban landowner, as a rule, has neither of these two obligations. There is that essential difference between the two. The urban landlord and the mineral royalty owner are invariably rackrenters. They extort the highest and the heaviest ground rent or royalty they can obtain on the sternest commercial principles. They are never restrained by that sense of personal relationship with their tenants which exercises such a beneficent and moderating influence upon the very same landlord in his dealings with his agricultural tenants. And the distinction is not confined merely to the rent. Take the conditions of the tenancy. I am not here to defend many of the terms which are included in many an agricultural agreement for tenancy. I think many of them are oppressive, irritating, and stupid. But compared with the conditions imposed upon either a colliery owner or upon a town lessee they are the very climax of generosity. Take this case — and it is not by any means irrelevant to the proposals which I shall have to submit to the Committee later on. What agricultural landlord in this country would ever think of letting his farm for a term of years on condition, first of all, that the tenant should pay the most extortionate rent that he could possibly secure in the market, three, or four, or even five times the real value of the soil; that the tenant should then be compelled to build a house of a certain size and at a certain cost, and in a certain way, and that at the end of the term he, or rather his representatives, should hand that house over in good tenantable repair free from encumbrances to the representatives of the ground owner who has not spent a penny upon constructing it, and who has received during the whole term of lease the highest rent which he could possibly screw in respect of the site? Why, there is not a landlord in Great Britain who would ever dream of imposing such outrageous conditions upon his tenant. And yet these are the conditions which are imposed every day in respect of urban sites; imposed upon tradesmen who have no choice in the matter; imposed upon professional men and business men who have got to live somewhere within reasonable distance of their offices; imposed even on workmen building a house for themselves, paying for it by monthly instalments out of their wages for thirty years purely in order to be within reasonable distance of the factory or mine or workshop at which they are earning a living. . . .

My present proposals are proposals both for taxation and for valuation. Although very moderate in character, they will produce an appreciable revenue in the present year and more in future years. The proposals are three in number.

Unearned Increment

First, it is proposed to levy a tax on the increment of value accruing to land from the enterprise of the community or the landowner's neighbours. . . . The valuations upon the difference between which the tax will be chargeable will be valuations of the land itself — apart from buildings and other improvements — and of this difference, the strictly unearned increment, we propose to take one-fifth, or 20 per cent, for the State. . . .

Duty on Undeveloped Land

The second proposal relating to land is the imposition of a tax on the capital value of all land which is not used to the best advantage. The owner of valuable land which is required or likely in the near future to be required for building purposes, who contents himself with an income therefrom wholly incommensurate with the capital value of the land in the hope of recouping himself ultimately in the shape of an increased price, is in a similar position to the investor in securities who re-invests the greater part of his dividends; but while the latter is required to pay income tax both upon the portion of the dividends enjoyed and also upon the portion re-invested, the former escapes taxation upon his accumulating capital altogether, and this, although the latter by his self-denial is increasing the wealth of the community, while the former, by withholding from the market land which is required for housing or industry, is creating a speculative inflation of values which is socially mischievous.

We propose to redress this anomaly by charging an annual duty of 1/2d. in the pound on the capital value of undeveloped land. The same principle applies to ungotten minerals, which we propose similarly to tax at 1/2d. in the pound, calculated upon the price which the mining rights might be expected to realize if sold in open market at the date of valuation. The tax on undeveloped land will be charged upon unbuilt-on land only, and . . . all land having a purely agricultural value will be exempt.

Further exemptions will be made in favour of gardens and pleasure grounds not exceeding an acre in extent, and parks, gardens, and open spaces which are open to the public as of right, or to which reasonable access is granted to the public, where that access is recognised by the Commissioners of Inland Revenue as contributing to the amenity of the locality. Where undeveloped land forms part of a settled estate, provision will be made to enable a limited owner who has not the full enjoyment of the land to charge the duty upon the corpus of the property. The valuation upon which the tax will be charged will be the value of land as a cleared site. . . .

Reversion Duty

My third proposal under the head of land is a 10 per cent reversion duty upon any benefit accruing to a lessor from the determination of a lease, the value of the benefit to be taken to be the amount (if any) by which the total value of the land at the time the lease falls in exceeds the value of the consideration for the grant of the lease, due regard being had, however, for the case of the reversioner whose interest is less than a freehold. . . .

81. OPPOSITION TO THE BUDGET AS A SOCIALIST MEASURE[1]

I cannot help thinking that the Government is dallying with Socialism. . . . Had I any doubt it would be removed by the joyful acceptance with which the proposals of the Government have been received and hailed in Socialist circles, and if you get the votes of Socialists you cannot shake yourself free from their compromising embraces. . . . One or two of the Ministers . . . are proclaiming loudly that we have arrived at the parting of the ways, that they must drum out the half-hearted and cashier the laggards in their party. I am afraid they are right. It is the parting of the ways. Let me read an extract from an article by the eminent French economist, M. Jules Roche. . . . He asks why a deficit suddenly reappeared in this Budget when we have had a yearly surplus since 1904. He answers the question thus: — "That the party which has governed England since the last election has put into practice the method adopted by us (that is, the French) of so-called social laws, voted unexpectedly without investigation and without forethought." To begin with, the Old-Age Pensions have immensely exceeded the credit anticipated. A deficit has been the result. . . . Such is the first result, inevitable in England as in France, as in every country, that the party of social policy promises blessings and produces ruin.

England has begun to enter upon this path. Let her persist in it a few years one will see where it will lead the country which liberty made the

[1] The *Times*. London, September 11, 1909.

richest in the world and the mightiest since the Roman Empire. . . . I wish
to speak with restraint as I speak with regret. . . . I think my friends are
on the path that leads to Socialism . . . but on that path I, at any rate, cannot follow them an inch (loud cheers). Any form of protection is an evil,
but Socialism is the end of all, the negation of faith, of family, of property,
of monarchy, of Empire. . . .

SECTION V. THE IRISH QUESTION

Catholic Emancipation was secured in 1829 and in 1869 the Anglican
Church was disestablished in Ireland, but the agrarian problem was slow in
receiving attention, although O'Connell made every effort to attract the
attention of the Government to it. The fundamental difficulty lay in the
ownership of a large part of Ireland's soil by non-resident, alien landowners.
The tenant asked fair rent, the right not to be evicted at the landlord's will,
the right to transfer his interest in his holding, and just compensation for
improvements he had made. The agrarian movement was carried on parallel
with the political agitation for Home Rule, and it is impossible entirely to
separate the two. Charles Stuart Parnell made himself unquestioned leader
of the Irish Nationalists in the House of Commons and held that place from
the middle 'seventies until he was ruined by his connection with a divorce
scandal in 1890, and the discipline maintained over the Irish by this Anglo-
Irishman and his skill in parliamentary fence remain to this day unexcelled.

82. PARNELL, DAVITT, AND THE LAND LEAGUE[1]

Meanwhile Connaught had given birth to the Land League. Cromwell's
curse had come home to roost. . . .

It was in Mayo the new movement began. A meeting, convened by Davitt
and Joseph Brennan, assembled on Sunday, August 20, 1879, at Irishtown,
a small out-of-the-way place, scarcely worthy of notice on the map, but in
the midst of territory where the full rigours of Irish landlordism had been
endured by successive generations of the peasants. Agrarian serfdom was
their only birthright. . . . What differentiated the gathering at Irishtown
from the many other agrarian meetings held in different parts of the country
was that the people and their spokesmen resolved to follow it up, and to
impart a continuity to their movement which had never resulted from such
efforts elsewhere. Accordingly, no sooner was the first meeting over and
past than arrangements were pushed on for another and a more elaborate

[1] M. M. O'Hara, *Chief and Tribune, Parnell and Davitt.* Dublin, Talbot Press, 1919, pp.
94–97; 100–104; 144–145 (condensed).

demonstration in a more important part of the county. Westport, the chief town of Mayo, was the place selected. . . .

Parnell travelled from London for the meeting. It poured rain, yet crowds came from long distances, and the first great demonstration of the new movement . . . was a success. . . .

He declared land purchase to be the only possible final solution of the Irish agrarian problem; but meanwhile, if the tenant paid a fair rent, he should enjoy the fruits of his industry. " Now, what must we do in order to induce the landlords to see the position? " he asked; and he answered in the memorable and now hackneyed phrase — " You must show the land-lords that you intend to hold a firm grip on your homesteads and lands. You must not allow yourselves to be dispossessed as you were dispossessed in 1847." That was the whole movement in a nutshell. It was amplified and expounded in a thousand variants, but in these few sentences Parnell mapped out the course the peasantry of Ireland were to follow, and did follow, during a whole generation. " I should be deceiving you," he added significantly, " if I told you that there was any use relying upon the exertions of the Irish members of Parliament on your behalf," but " God helps him who helps himself." The peroration was startlingly brief, and in a manner that he very often affected. " You have a great country to struggle for, a great country before you. It is worth a little exertion on your part; it is worth a little time. Do your best, and your country will thank you for it and your children hereafter. . . ."

The Irish National Land League was established at a meeting, which Davitt convened, in the Imperial Hotel, Sackville Street, Dublin, on October 21. Mr. Andrew Kettle presided. The organisation destined to become so famous and formidable was christened by a revolution proposed by Father Behan, a devoted and patriotic priest, and the objects of the League were tersely and moderately stated as the reduction of rack-rents and the creation of a peasant proprietary. . . .

The movement was an instantaneous success, as far as the organisation of the tenantry was concerned. The fact is that Ireland was fully ripe for the effort. The need was violently urgent; the leaders were desperately earnest. . . .

A Land Act had been passed in 1870. It purported to secure for the tenant on eviction compensation for his improvements, and in some cases also for disturbance. Gladstone professed to believe that this Act would be the " final settlement " of the Irish land problem. Final is the most foolish word in the vocabulary of a statesman. The Act made no provision against rack-rent. It did not stay eviction. It failed, as everybody who knew anything at all about the subject knew it must. And now, in 1879, the last state of the Irish farmer was worse than the first. Foreign competition had made an inroad on his prices, and a series of very inclement seasons had shattered his crops. He was fearfully hard hit from every direction. English official opinion made light of his plight. . . . Of course, the whole evil was rooted in alien rule, in confiscation, and the subjugation of the native race. The movement undertaken by Davitt was actually for the reconquest of Ireland from the conqueror. It was in every sense of the word a national question he tackled, though the details were applicable to one section of the community only. The circumstances were favorable for the raising of the whole great issue. Urgent need compelled a piecemeal solution, the tenantry had to be saved immediately from famine and wholesale eviction, and, therefore, attention was concentrated on the sheer necessities of the case, but there could be no mistake about the end in view, which was nothing more nor less than Ireland for the Irish.

The potato — "Raleigh's fatal gift " — failed the peasants once more. Evictions were on the increase. The spectre of famine stared Erin in the two eyes. Davitt at his earlier meetings was careful to advise restraint. Outrage he knew well would hurt the people's cause. But his eloquence was strong and stirring. He minced no words about the landlords. He stripped their rapacity naked to the world. . . . Ominous cries were raised at many of the meetings. Parnell did not tend to soften emotions by his less perfervid oratory. If anything, his speeches were more calculated to inflame the people than were the burning periods of the Fenian. For, in his own stern, calculating way he rubbed hard and goading facts into their heads, and fixed their minds with inexorable deliberation on the relentless features of their case, their bitter need, their appalling outlook, their past sufferings, their patent grievances, the rank injustice which afflicted them. Worse, still, he breathed a confidence into them by the almost audacious faith of his dogmatism. He told them that they had the remedy in their own hands, expatiated on their inherent strength, of which they had seemed unconscious, and, in imperturbable accents which compelled conviction, promised them victory if only they stood manfully together. "Keep a firm grip of your homesteads " became the first article of their creed.

The two men were superb figures for the work. Davitt was fluent and eloquent from his early days. He had a rich, deep voice, resonant and thrilling. He spoke with a fanatic's strength, and he coloured all his words with the glow of a highly emotional nature. His hair was raven black. His eyes had an uncanny sparkle. His ample brow was puckered in a frown that never lifted. Yet over his strikingly luminous face his feelings played constant pranks. He could almost frighten with a glance. His smile was bewitchingly tender. His scorn was inimitable. His pathos was hard, yet homely. He spoke like a great peasant, with a doric grace that fascinated his class, and he appeared before them slashed and furrowed with suffering. Who could resist that tall, young, one-armed man, so evidently sincere, who was marred by the marks of chains and fetters borne for his country's sake! He looked much older than his years, and all his hearers knew that prison had aged him prematurely. Yet the exaltation of his cause lifted him out of his weakness, and as he faced the peasantry of Mayo he exhaled a fire and vehemence which made them absolutely obedient to his sway.

Parnell has been described at this period as bearing all the marks of imperious leadership upon him. He was a tall, .wiry, willowy, handsome man. He was smart and spruce, gay and triumphant. He walked with a light, springy step, held himself straight as an arrow, and his every movement was graceful and energetic. He spoke softly, and with an English accent, but he could send his voice far, and under the influence of strong feeling, make it incisive and penetrating. He usually spoke slowly, as if measuring and weighing his words, but a gust of passion sometimes swept words from him with a swiftness and force which carried audiences off their feet. He had by this time become quite fluent and steady on the platform, but he had the art of compression, and in a brief space covered a great expanse of thought. His sentences were short and crisp, and could be remembered easily. He rarely essayed rhetoric, but there are many eloquent passages in the speeches which he made at the beginning of the Land League. His illustrations were always excellent and apt, and often not without a spice of rich humour. But it was his personality, that almost indefinable thing, which acted like a spell upon all who listened to him. There was no waste in his oratory. His words and phrases were exact, inevitable, appropriate. He was intensely interesting to watch and listen to. There was dignity in his appearance and bearing. He might have stood to a sculptor as a model of self-confidence and command.

Parnell went into the land movement with extraordinary eagerness. He took on the whole program — fair rents, fixity of tenure, free sale, land purchase. Starting from Dublin in August . . . he swept through Leinster and Munster; Tipperary, Tullow, Cork, Navan, Enniscorthy, Limerick and Galway saw him in turn, and everywhere he felt in the enthusiasm of the crowds an unmistakable national endorsement of his leadership. He was beyond all question at the moment the most popular man in Ireland. His name raised cheers everywhere. His presence attracted thousands. His phrases passed from man to man. . . .

"Depend upon it, that the measure of the Land Bill of next session will be the measure of your activity and energy this winter; it will be the measure of your determination not to pay unjust rents; it will be the measure of your determination to keep a firm grip of your homesteads; it will be the measure of your determination not to bid for farms from which others have been evicted, and to use the strong force of public opinion to deter any unjust man amongst yourselves — and there are many such — from bidding for such farms. If you refuse to pay unjust rents, if you refuse to take farms from which others have been evicted, the land question must be settled, and settled in a way that will be satisfactory to you. It depends, therefore, upon yourselves, and not upon any Commission or any Government. When you have made the question ripe for settlement, then, and not till then, will it be settled. Now, what are you to do to a tennant who bids for a farm from which another man has been evicted? (Several Voices — 'Shoot him.') I think I heard somebody say, ' Shoot him.' I wish to point out to you a very much better way — a more Christian and charitable way, which will give the lost man an opportunity of repenting. When a man takes a farm from which another has been unjustly evicted, you must show him on the roadside when you meet him; you must show him in the streets of the town; you must show him in the shop; you must show him in the fair-green and in the market-place, and even in the place of worship, by leaving him alone; by putting him into a moral Coventry; by isolating him from the rest of his country, as if he were the leper of old — you must show him your detestation of the crime he has committed; and you may depend upon it, that there will be no man so full of avarice, so lost to shame, as to dare the public opinion of all right-thinking men and to transgress your unwritten code of laws."

Gladstone, whose first Home Rule for Ireland Bill had been defeated in the Commons in 1886, persisted in his efforts, but a second bill, brought in in 1893, although it passed the Commons, was wrecked in the Lords and caused the old leader's retirement from politics. The Home Rule movement remained alive in Ireland under the leadership of John Redmond and from 1905 on he exerted pressure on the Liberals to pass the measure in exchange for support of the Liberal social policy. In 1912 Asquith acceded to the demand, and, amid a furor of bitter opposition, directed especially from Ulster by Sir Edward Carson, insisted on carrying a bill that would give Home Rule to the whole of Ireland. The four next extracts give something of the temper of the times. In the spring of 1914 civil war seemed close, arms were being smuggled into both parts of Ireland, forces were drilling, and in the British army itself sympathy with Ulster was so keen that many officers were guilty of insubordination in refusing to proceed to the enforcement of the act if it should be passed. The outbreak of the Great War intervened; the bill was passed, but with a proviso that it should not go into effect until the conclusion of the War.

83. *A GREAT HOME RULE DEMONSTRATION* [1]

DUBLIN, March 31.

From the spectacular point of view the Nationalist demonstration in Dublin today was a great success. . . . Immense pains were taken to make the meeting a representative and impressive demonstration of Nationalist Ireland's passionate desire for the Home Rule Bill which it has not yet seen. . . . Sixty-four special trains were run to the capital from all parts of Ireland. Twenty-five of these came from the south and 18 from Ulster.

The area of the meetings made an impressive show when the procession arrived and broke up around the different platforms . . . Mr. Redmond's platform was the chief centre of interest. . . . I calculate the attendance at about 100,000. . . .

Mr. John Redmond, M. P., in the course of his speech said:

This great gathering is worthy of the solemn moment at which we stand in the history of our country. . . . I desire today to say that I entertain a confident belief that the Home Rule Bill will be a great measure. (Cheers.) It will be adequate for the purpose of those who promote it.

Now what are these purposes? First, to put an end, once for all, to the disastrous and ruinous war which has gone on between Ireland and England and the Empire. The Irish people, I believe, have always been willing to make peace with England. To-day they are eager for the war to end. The second purpose is to enable Ireland, with dignity and self-respect, to enter for the first time into co-partnership in the Empire with perfect good faith and with perfect loyalty, on a footing of equality and of liberty. The third purpose is to re-establish national self-government in Ireland by a Parliament fully representative of all creeds and classes, a Parliament with power to govern all purely Irish affairs in accordance with the dictates of Irish public opinion, and a Parliament with adequate financial resources for the development of Ireland, so that they may be able to turn her in the near future into a prosperous land which will be able to support herself, and which in the future will, I believe, be well able to bear her own share of Imperial obligations.

84. *SIR EDWARD CARSON SPEAKS FOR ULSTER* [2]

Sir E. Carson was loudly cheered on rising to address the meeting. He said the demand of Ulster loyalists was plain, honest, and simple. It was that they should be allowed to continue as citizens of the United Kingdom under

---

[1] The *Times*. London, April 5, 1912 (condensed).
[2] The *Times*. London, January 12, 1912.

the same King and under the same Parliament in which they were born. (Cheers) They asked no more, and they would accept no less. They wished for no ascendancy, and they would have none over them. They asked for no separate Parliament for Ulster. They would accept none. They would remain as they were, and if England and Scotland told them that they could not remain as they were they would take the matter into their own hands and they would keep it in their own hands until they were admitted back to what was their birthright. (Cheers.)

85. A PROTESTANT EMPHASIZES THE RELIGIOUS ISSUE [1]

The real evil, as every Irishman knows to his bitter cost, is that religious intolerance is habitually and rigidly exercised against Roman Catholics by the Roman Catholic priesthood. The Irish Roman Catholic is the slave of the priest. That he should be taught this religious dogma or that is another affair with which no one need interfere. But the priest claims all. He claims the body and the soul and the goods of his people, and enforces his claim with threats of grievous physical ill in this world and the fires of purgatory in the next. No man can marry without permission of the priest. If he takes to wife a Protestant, the Church, under the *Ne Temere* decree, declares the marriage null and void, and the children of it are denounced as bastards. No man can buy or sell or hold a farm but by leave of the priest. No man dare vote but as the priest directs. No man san save a penny more than the priest will spare him, unless the poor wretch hoards in secret. There is not an honest man who knows what Ireland is to-day who will not vouch for the absolute truth of every one of these statements.

Now if Ireland were wholly Roman Catholic, to confer Home Rule upon her would be virtually to confer the power of civil governance upon the Roman Catholic priesthood. But, as about one-fourth of the population is Protestant, the effect of granting Home Rule to Ireland would be to place the Protestant minority at the mercy of a Roman Catholic majority. Hence the outbreak of civil war will instantly follow upon the institution of an Irish Government. Amid the shadow-dance of politics, the vacillations, whisperings, intrigues, boasting, complaints, false promises, and confusions that have stupefied the browbeaten British public, there has been at least one real thing, and its name is Ulster. There are (let us say) two hundred thousand or so resolute men in northeast Ulster who have made a last stand against the betrayal by consent which has been so smoothly proceeding during the last five years.

[1] L. Cope Cornford in the *National Review*. London, January, 1912.

86. *A TWENTIETH-CENTURY SOLEMN COVENANT*[1]

The terms of the Solemn Covenant against Home Rule to be signed by the Unionists of Ulster on Ulster Day, September 28, are as follows: —

Being convinced in our consciences that Home Rule would be disastrous to the material well-being of Ulster as well as of the whole of Ireland, subversive of our civil and religious freedom, destructive of our citizenship, and perilous to the unity of the Empire, we, whose names are underwritten, men of Ulster, loyal subjects of his Gracious Majesty, King George V., humbly relying on the God Whom our fathers in days of stress and trial confidently trusted, hereby pledge ourselves in Solemn Covenant throughout this our time of threatened calamity to stand by one another in defending, for ourselves and our children our cherished position of equal citizenship in the United Kingdom, and in using all means which may be found necessary to defeat the present conspiracy to set up a Home Rule Parliament in Ireland; and, in the event of such a Parliament being forced upon us, we further solemnly and mutually pledge ourselves to refuse to recognize its authority. In sure confidence that God will defend the right, we hereto subscribe our names, and, further, we individually declare that we have not already signed this Covenant.

SECTION VI. THE EMPIRE AND BRITISH BUSINESS

The "Little England" point of view, held by many Liberals, that discouraged the imperial policy of the Conservatives, was discredited in the last years of the nineteenth century, and the apostles of "Greater Britain" held sway. Of these none was more persuasive than Professor Seeley, and his share in awakening enthusiasm for world empire was, perhaps, as great as that of Cecil Rhodes, Joseph Chamberlain or Rudyard Kipling, for he influenced a whole new generation of university men.

87. *AN EXPANSIONIST ON "GREATER BRITAIN"*[2]

I endeavoured to judge the Empire by its own intrinsic merits and to see it as it is, not concealing the inconveniences which may attend such a vast expansion or the dangers to which it may expose us, nor finding any compensation for these in the notion that there is something intrinsically

---

[1] The *Times*. London, September 27, 1912.
[2] J. R. Seeley, *The Expansion of England*. London, Macmillan & Co., 1888, pp. 295–301 (condensed).

glorious in an Empire "upon which the sun never sets," or, to use another equally brilliant expression, an Empire "whose morning drum-beat, following the sun and keeping company with the hours, encircles the globe with an unbroken chain of martial airs." But though there is little that is glorious in most of the great Empires mentioned in history, since they have usually been created by force and have remained at a low level of political life, we observed that Greater Britain is not in the ordinary sense an Empire at all. Looking at the colonial part of it alone, we see a natural growth, a mere normal extension of the English race into other lands, which for the most part were so thinly peopled that our settlers took possession of them without conquest. If there is nothing highly glorious in such an expansion, there is at the same time nothing forced or unnatural about it. It creates not properly an Empire, but only a very large state. So far as the expansion itself is concerned, no one does or can regard it but with pleasure. For a nation to have an outlet for its superfluous population is one of the greatest blessings. Population unfortunately does not adapt itself to space: on the contrary the larger it is the larger is its yearly increment. Now that Great Britain is already full it becomes fuller with increased speed; it gains a million every three years. Probably emigration ought to proceed at a far greater rate than it does, and assuredly the greatest evils would arise if it were checked. But should there be an expansion of the State as well as of the nation? "No," say the pessimists, "or only till the colony is grown-up and ready for independence." When a metaphor comes to be regarded as an argument, what an irresistible argument it always seems! I have suggested that in the modern world distance has very much lost its effect, and that there are signs of a time when states will be vaster than they have hitherto been. In ancient times emigrants from Greece to Sicily took up their independence at once, and in those parts there were almost as many states as cities. In the eighteenth century Burke thought a federation quite impossible across the Atlantic Ocean. In such times the metaphor of the grown-up son might well harden into a convincing demonstration. But since Burke's time the Atlantic Ocean has shrunk till it seems scarcely broader than the sea between Greece and Sicily. Why then do we not drop the metaphor? I have urged that we are unconsciously influenced by a historic parallel which when examined turns out to be inapplicable. As indeed it is true generally that one urgent reason why politicians should study history is that they may guard themselves against the false historical analogies which continually mislead those who do not study history! These views are founded on the American Revolution, and yet the American Revolution arose out of circumstances and out of a condition of the world which has long since passed away. England was then an agricultural country by no means thickly peopled; America was full of religious refugees animated by ideas which in England had lately passed out of fashion. . . . At any rate all the conditions of the world are altered now. The great causes of division, oceans and religious disabilities, have ceased to operate. Vast uniting forces have begun to work, trade and emigration. Meanwhile the natural ties which unite Englishmen resume their influence as soon as the counteracting pressure is removed, I mean the ties of nationality, language and religion. The mother-country having once for all ceased to be a step-mother, and to make unjust claims and impose annoying restrictions, and since she wants her colonies as an outlet both for population and trade, and since on the other hand the colonies must feel that there is risk, not to say also intellectual impoverishment, in independence, since finally intercourse is ever increasing and no alienating force is at work to counteract it, but the discords created by the old system pass more and more into oblivion, it seems possible that our colonial Empire so-called may more and more deserve to be called Greater Britain, and that the tie may become stronger and stronger. Then the seas which divide us might be forgotten, and that ancient preconception, which leads us always to think of ourselves as belonging to a single island, might be rooted out of our minds. If in this way we moved sensibly nearer in our thoughts and feelings to the colonies, and accustomed ourselves to think of emigrants as not in any way lost to England by settling in the colonies, the result might be, first that emigration on a vast scale might become our remedy for pauperism, and secondly that some organisation might gradually be arrived at which might make the whole force of the Empire available in time of war. . . .

Perhaps we are hardly alive to the vast results which are flowing in politics from modern mechanism. . . . We now see states with vivid political consciousness on territories of two hundred thousand square miles and in populations of thirty millions. A further advance is now being made. The federal system has been added to the representative system, and at the same time steam and electricity have been introduced. From these improvements has resulted the possibility of highly organised states on a yet larger scale. Thus Russia in Europe has already a population of nearly eighty millions on a territory of more than two millions of square miles, and the United States will have by the end of the century a population as large upon a territory of four millions of square miles. We cannot, it is true, yet speak of Russia as having a high type of organisation; she has her trials and her transformation to come; but the Union has shown herself able to combine free institutions in the fullest degree with boundless expansion. . . .

Lastly let us observe that the question, whether large states or small states are best, is not one which can be answered or ought to be discussed absolutely. We often hear abstract panegyrics upon the happiness of small states. But observe that a small state among small states is one thing and a small state among large states quite another. Nothing is more delightful than to read of the bright days of Athens and Florence, but those bright days lasted only so long as the states with which Athens and Florence had to do were states on a similar scale of magnitude. Both states sank at once as soon as large country-states of consolidated strength grew up in their neighbourhood. The lustre of Athens grew pale as soon as Macedonia rose, and Charles V. speedily brought to an end the great days of Florence. Now if it be true that a larger type of state than any hitherto known is springing up in the world, is not this a serious consideration for those states which rise only to the old level of magnitude? Russia already presses somewhat heavily on Central Europe; what will she do when with her vast territory and population she equals Germany in intelligence and organisation, when all her railways are made, her people educated, and her government settled on a solid basis? — and let us remember that if we allow her half a century to make so much progress her population will at the end of that time be not eighty but nearly a hundred and sixty millions. At that time which many here present may live to see, Russia and the United States will surpass in power the states now called great as much as the great country-states of the sixteenth century surpassed Florence. Is not this a serious consideration, and is it not especially so for a state like England, which has at the present moment the choice in its hands between two courses of action, the one of which may set it in that future age on a level with the greatest of these great states of the future, while the other will reduce it to the level of a purely European Power looking back, as Spain does now, to the great days when she pretended to be a world-state.

Part of the " Greater Britain " policy was a return to protective duties and the granting of preferential rates to the colonies in an effort to tie the whole Empire together as an economic as well as a racial and sentimental unit. To this work the quondam radical mayor of Birmingham, at one time the dangerous radical of Gladstone's ministry, but since 1886 a Unionist, Joseph Chamberlain, devoted the last years of his life. Protection, which had passed out of British political ideas by 1860, again became an issue.

88. PROTECTION AND COLONIAL PREFERENCE [1]

Free imports have destroyed, at all events for the time, and it is not easy to recover an industry when it has once been lost — but they have destroyed sugar-refining for a time as one of the great staple industries of the country, which it ought always to have remained. They have destroyed agriculture. Mr. Cobden said — and again I am sure he spoke the truth as it appeared to him — that he was convinced that, if his views were carried out, not an acre

[1] Speech by Joseph Chamberlain at Greenock, Scotland, October 7, 1903. *Glasgow Herald,* October 8, 1903.

of ground would go out of cultivation in this country, and no tenant farmer would be worse off. I am not here to speak to an agricultural audience; but if I were, what a difference there would be between that expectation and hope of Mr. Cobden's and the actual circumstances of the case! Agriculture, as the greatest of all trades and industries of this country, has been practically destroyed. Sugar has gone. Silk has gone. Iron is threatened. Wool is threatened. Cotton will go! How long are you going to stand it? At the present moment these industries, and the working men who depend upon them, are like sheep in a field. One by one they allow themselves to be led to slaughter, and there is no combination, no apparent prevision of what is in store for the rest of them. Do you think, if you belong at the present time to a prosperous industry, that your prosperity will be allowed to continue? Do you think that the same causes which have destroyed some of our industries, and which are in the course of destroying others, will not be equally applicable to you when your turn comes? This is not a case in which selfishness will pay. This is a case in which you should take warning by the past, in which you can show some foresight as to the future.

What is the remedy? What is it that the Prime Minister proposed at Sheffield? He said (I am not quoting his exact words) : Let us get rid of the chains which we ourselves have forged, which have fettered our action. Let us claim the same freedom as every other civilized nation. Let us say to these foreign countries, " Gentlemen, we desire to be friends with you. We are Free Traders in the best sense of the word. We are ready to exchange freely; but, if you say that it is your settled policy that you will not buy from us, we will tax your exports to us. We will not look farther afield — no, we will look nearer home. We will go to our own friends and kinsmen who are perfectly ready to meet us on equal terms, who ask only for reciprocal preference."

Then we are told that if we do this the foreigners will be angry with us! Has it come to that in Great Britain? It is a craven argument; it is worthy of the little Englander; it is not possible for any man who believes in his own country. . . . I do not believe in a war of tariffs, but if there were to be a war of tariffs, I know we should not come out second best. Why, at the present time ours is the greatest market in the whole world. We are the best customers of all those countries. There are many suitors for our markets. We may reject the addresses of some, but there is no fear that we shall not have other offers. It is absolutely absurd to suppose that all these countries, keenly competitive among themselves, would agree among themselves to fight with us when they might benefit at the expense of their neighbours. Why, at the present time we take from Germany about twice as much as she takes from us. We take from France about three times as much. From the United States of America we take about six times as much as they take from us. Who is it that stands to lose if there is to be a war of tariffs?

And there is something else. We have what none of these countries have. We have something, the importance of which I am trying to impress upon my countrymen, which at present they have not sufficiently appreciated. We have a great reserve in the sons of Britain across the seas. There is nothing we want that they cannot supply; there is nothing we sell that they cannot buy. One great cause for the prosperity of the United States of America, admitted by everyone to be a fact, is that they are a great Empire of over 70,000,000 of people; that the numbers of these people alone, without any assistance from the rest of the world, would ensure a large amount of prosperity. Yes; but the British Empire is even greater than the United States of America. We have a population — it is true, not all a white population — but we have a white population of over 60,000,000 against the 70,000,000 — who are not all white, by the by — of America. We have, in addition, 350,000,000 or more of people in the States under our protectorate, under our civilisation, sympathising with our rule, grateful for the benefits that we accord to them — all of them more or less prospective or actual customers of this country.

In times past we have in some inconceivable way ignored our colonies. We have not appreciated their greatness. We have not had imagination enough to see that, great as they are, there is no limit to what they may become. We have gone through a time — it is a most significant fact — when the men who advocated Free Trade in this country were at the same time absolutely indifferent to all idea of Empire, and considered the Colonies as an encumbrance which we should be glad to get rid of. That lasted for thirty years, and in the course of that time we tried hardly the patience of our sons across the seas. We tried hardly their love of us, their devotion to the Mother Country. They began to think that we had no sympathy with their aspirations; that we only regarded them as troublesome children and wished to get them out of the house, and therefore that it would be their duty to break with the sentiment which would otherwise have held us together; that it would be their duty absolutely to fend for themselves, and leave out of account everything which concerned the Empire of which they form a part.

That was not their fault. That was our fault! and although now we have done our best to correct that impression, although now there is no man living who thinks, or, if there is one who thinks, there is not one who dares to say, that he would wish to get rid of the Colonies, that he does not desire a closer union — yet we have a good deal to make up for. We have to show that, whereas at one time we or our ancestors advocated separation, we are now prepared to do all in reason that is demanded of us in order to create a greater and a closer union.

CHAPTER VII

PROBLEMS OF DEMOCRACY AND
NATIONALISM, (1849-1871)

SECTION I. FRANCE

The constitution of the Republic set up in France as a result of the Revolution of 1848 provided that the President of the Republic should hold office for four years and should not be eligible for re-election until after another four years had passed. But Louis Napoleon, who had been elected President by an overwhelming majority, was too ambitious to yield to this provision of the constitution. So with a little group of fellow conspirators he brought about the coup d'état *of December 2, 1851, overthrowing the Legislative Assembly and setting up his own autocratic power. The* coup d'état *paved the way for the proclamation of the Second Empire a year later.*

The following defense of the coup d'état *by one of the conspirators may be compared with Gambetta's fiery denunciation of it some years later. (See Selection 92.)*

89. A FAVORABLE VIEW OF THE COUP D'ÉTAT OF NAPOLEON III [1]

(Paris) Sunday (December 14)

EVERYTHING is going as well as one could wish except in some Departments of the South, where Socialism (denied by your friends at Panshanger [2]) asserts itself by murder, plunder, fire and cruelties and brutalities which respect neither age nor sex. There is hardly one in this country, except those in whom party spirit extinguishes all other feeling, who does not admit that in 1852, what now takes place in some localities, would have covered the whole country and been too powerful for the army to have suppressed it. From all the Departments come thanksgivings and blessings to those who

[1] A letter of the Comte de Flahault to Madame de Flahault, Paris, December 14, 1851, quoted in *The Secret of the Coup d'État*. Edited with an Introduction by the Earl of Kerry. London, Constable, 1924, pp. 134–136.

[2] We learn from Henry Greville, who was one of the party then staying at Panshanger with Lord and Lady Cowper, that it consisted of the Cannings, Sydneys, Bessboroughs, Shelburnes, De Mauley, Granville, F. Leveson, and Charles Greville — besides Mme. de Flahault and her unmarried daughter Georgine.

have had the courage to save the country from such misfortunes. I could quote to you authorities which are entitled to a little more respect on those matters than those who know nothing of the state of the country and judge of everything on the principle of " King, Lord and Commons." Dumond is arrived from his Department in the South, and though from a feeling of propriety and attachment to his friends he does not adhere to the Government, admits that by his coup d'état the President has saved the country. He says that even in Paris no one can have a notion how low the Assembly had fallen in public opinion. I could quote to you Pasquier, Segur (the father not the son, who cuts me dead), Guizot, most of the Legitimists, the Duc De Noailles, etc., etc., etc., I don't mention Montalembert, Mérode, and all impartial men. The only ones who are violent are the Orleanists, who had hoped to make the coup d'état against the President. Every proof has been found of this in M. Baze's [1] papers, and, if those of the other persons arrested had been seized, it would have shown that they were all in the plot. But that formality was neglected, and even those of M. Baze were only thought of five days after his arrestation. What is very amusing is that there is a great outcry against the Government for having arrested Deputies who were assembled to decree the *déchéance* (fall) of the President, to forbid all authorities civil and military obeying him, who had named a General to take command of the troops, and were actually proclaiming their decree from the window to the people by the mouth of Berryer! In old times of civil war they would have been shot, and they are furious against me because I say that they only showed this Roman dignity and energy because they knew there was no danger.

I was in hopes that I could have voted to-day, in which case I should have set out to-morrow, but I cannot do it till next Sunday. God grant that the President may have 7 millions of votes. If they had any sense at Claremont they would have told all their adherents to vote for him, and it would have done more for their future chances than anything they can do.

In the conversation here quoted between Prosper Mérimée, the well-known writer, and Nassau Senior, Mérimée alleges that three motives, of which hatred of Austria and the Papal Government at Rome was the chief, influenced Napoleon III to aid the kingdom of Piedmont-Sardinia in the war of 1859 against Austria. Just what Napoleon's motives were, no one, of course, can say with certainty; but Mérimée's conjectures are suggestive.

[1] One of the three *questeurs de la chambre* who were arrested in the small hours of December 2.

90. POSSIBLE MOTIVES OF NAPOLEON III IN AIDING THE ITALIANS IN THE WAR OF 1859 [1]

II. Conversation between Mérimée and Senior:

Senior. — What do you suppose to have been his (Napoleon's) motive for the war (of 1859) if it were not the fear of the Carbonari?

Mérimée. — The motives were three. First and foremost was his hatred of Austria and of the Roman government. He hates them both with the intensity of a conspirator. Such feelings must be his earliest recollections. When, after the insurrection in which his brother died, he was carried a prisoner to the Roman frontier, and then pardoned and driven out, he said he would pay another visit to the Cardinals.

Senior. — I can understand his hating the Cardinals; but what quarrel has he with Austria?

Mérimée. — Every Italian, and he is an Italian by education, hates Austria. Then he has to revenge her conduct during the Crimean war.

Senior. — So have we, and yet you see we bear no malice.

Mérimée. — A nation may forget her *rancunes* (grudges); an individual, at least the individual of whom we are speaking, does not.

Senior. — Has he any real sympathy with the Italian people?

Mérimée. — Sympathy with them as the enemies of Austria, but he cares little about their real happiness. After he had written his letter to Ney [2] in 1850 he never thought more about Papal misgovernment. It affects him as the misgovernment of the Bosnians or of the Mongols affects us. We say, ' It is very atrocious,' and forget it. His second motive is the desire of military glory, first for himself, next for us. He hopes to add a brilliant page to French history, with his name at the beginning. His third motive is that he believes that military success will establish his dynasty.

Senior. — In none of these motives is France interested; she does not hate Austria; she has more military glory than she wants; and she would be as happy under an Orleans dynasty as under a Bonaparte one.

Mérimée. — Thence the Emperor's anxiety to make out Austria to be the aggressor, in which, by his own dexterity, by the mismanagement of Austria, and by your (England's) assistance, he has in a great degree succeeded.

Nassau Senior, an eminent economist of the nineteenth century and at one time Professor of Political Economy at Oxford, travelled extensively

---

[1] Nassau Senior, *Conversations with M. Thiers, M. Guizot, and other Distinguished Persons during the Second Empire.* Edited by his daughter M. C. M. Simpson. 2 vols. London, Hurst and Blackett, 1878, vol. II., pp. 244–245. Conversation between Mérimée and Senior.

[2] A private letter approving highly of the Roman expedition.

and delighted in conversing with leading men in the countries he visited. In his record of these conversations he has much to say of opinions prevalent in France in regard to Napoleon III.

The decline of Napoleon's popularity, especially after 1860, is evident from Senior's account which unfortunately ends with the year 1863.

91. CONTEMPORARY OPINIONS OF NAPOLEON III[1]

I. February, 1854.

After Madame de Circourt left us I called on Guizot. We talked of Louis Napoleon. " His two years of absolute power," said Guizot, " have changed him much. His ambition is yielding to his vanity. I will not say that he has altogether thrown away his wild notions of conquest, but he has put them aside. He is now seeking for excitement by the reckless expenditure of boundless wealth. He delights in the improvements which begin by destruction. The *cité* of Paris looks like a town that has been bombarded. Whole acres of buildings are cleared away every day. In vain those who are to be ejected protest. They are told to take their indemnity and be silent. Houses that were built not six months ago according to plans furnished by the Government have been pulled down because they interfere with some new arrangement. But if he destroys like Attila or Genghis Khan, he builds like Aladdin. His furniture too and his equipages are all in the Aladdin style."

II. April, 1854. Statement by M. Grimblot.

Then as to misgovernment. There is occasional tyranny, but it has diminished as the opposition which occasioned it has subsided; and the general administration is good. The country is prosperous; see with how little suffering or even complaint the scarcity has been supported; and, I must own, that I think the control which is exercised by the Government over the press one of the elements of its stability. A press like yours, or like that of America, which would attack it by reasoning, and invective, and ridicule, and would not be answered — for all the writers are hostile to it — which

[1] Nassau Senior, *Conversations with M. Thiers, M. Guizot, and other Distinguished Persons during the Second Empire*. Edited by his daughter M. C. M. Simpson. 2 vols. London, Hurst and Blackett, 1878 and 1880.

I. February, 1854, (vol. I, pp. 218–219).
II. April, 1854, (vol. I, p. 353).
III. April, 1857, (vol. II, pp. 131–132).
IV. March, 1858, (vol. II, pp. 176–177).
V. 1860, (vol. II, p. 328).
VI. March 21, 1862, (vol. II, pp. 55–59).
VII. March 29, 1863, (Lavergne to Senior, vol. II, p. 186).
VIII. April 2, 1863, (Lanjuinais to Senior, vol. II, p. 188).

would expose its bad political economy, its military incompetence, its extravagance, and its corruption, would destroy it in six weeks.

III. April, 1857.

Sunday, April 26th. — Dumon breakfasted with us. We talked of Louis Napoleon's position.

Dumon. — It is certainly stronger than it was last year; every day of continued prosperity strengthens it, and whatever be the partial complaints, the constant improvement in the revenue, in defiance of bad harvests and bad vintages, shows that the general prosperity is great. The expenses of the Court and of the public buildings in Paris alarm a stranger; but they do not seriously affect our finances, and they flatter our imagination and our vanity. So as to the colossal and sudden fortunes which are springing up, they are obtained perhaps scandalously; they represent perhaps almost as much loss as gain; but those who are ruined by the game disappear. Those who succeed in it stimulate the cupidity and raise the courage, and perhaps blunt the consciences and the moral sense, of the standers-by. They are like the gainers of the great prizes in the lottery. The forty per cent. profit of the Crédit Mobilier last year, its twenty-three per cent. this, the doubling and tripling of the value of its shares, have drawn to the Course millions and millions which, in quieter times, would have been spent in buying bits of land at forty years' purchase, or lent to a notaire, or perhaps buried in a garden. I believe that they have contributed more to the sudden development of avarice and vanity in France, than what is called the return of confidence or Californian gold, or what is not without its effect, the closing of all the paths of ambition, except through wealth. A serious check to our prosperity, an unsuccessful war, more inundations, more bad harvests, more bad vintages, might produce a crisis which would sweep away the Empire; but in the absence of such contingencies I think that he has it for his life.

IV. March, 1858.

I spent the evening (of March 8, 1858) at Madame Mohl's. I spoke of the unpopularity, or worse than unpopularity, into which Louis Napoleon seemed to have fallen as far as I could judge from the conversation of the few people whom I had seen.

Mohl. — It is much greater in the class of society which you do not see. The ouvriers (workmen) have been principally struck at. They were already angry at the high price of apartments and of food. Like all uneducated persons, they exaggerate the power of a Government, and think that the Emperor can give them cheap lodgings and bread and wine if he liked. Instead of doing so, he inflicts imprisonment and banishment on persons who, perhaps were '*emeutiers*' (rioters) in 1848, but have been for years well-conducted '*pères de famille*' (fathers of families.) The number so treated is, of course, enormously exaggerated. These arrests, and the law which has sanctioned them, have produced, as it was intended that they should do, much fear; but they have excited more irritation. I do not think that he was ever before so unpopular among the working classes in Paris. The natural effects of that unpopularity will not be prevented by compression. He is compressing an elastic gas. Some day the resisting force will be greater than the compressing force and then woe to those who are near to the explosion.

V. 1860.

Senior. — Is he (Napoleon III) stronger than he was when I was in Paris in May last year?

Thiers. — On the whole he is. The treaty,[1] indeed, has done him great mischief with the trading classes. It has taught them practically that under a despot, who is totally unrestrained by law or principle, who has no settled rule of conduct, and changes the political, the territorial, the manufacturing, and the commercial systems of France according to the whim of the moment — nothing is stable or safe. The quarrel with the Pope too has been mischievous. But these injuries have been more than compensated by his military success, and above all by the acquisition of Savoy. The worst humiliation of 1815 has been wiped out, and a portion at least of our natural frontier has been restored to us. Even I, who am among those who most disapprove his general conduct, feel grateful.

VI. March 21, 1862.

To-day Cornelis De Witt called on us. We asked him whether he thought the position of the Emperor altered since we met this time last year.

De Witt. — Sensibly deteriorated. He has been sinking ever since the *attentat* of 1858. The shock impaired the obstinacy, the self-confidence, and the intrepidity, which were among the causes of his early successes.

Senior. — And yet his Italian campaign — the only great thing that he has done — was done after 1858.

De Witt. — Do you call that a great thing?

Senior. — Certainly. For a man of fifty, who never saw a gun fired, to take command of 250,000 men, opposed to a still greater force of some of the best troops in Europe, and in two months gain two victories, and dictate a peace, is one of the greatest things recorded in history. I do not recollect anything that resembles it.

---

[1] A commercial treaty with England made in 1860. The treaty was a great step in the direction of free trade. (Editor's note.)

De Witt. — That is the outside, but when you look into it, you find that the Austrian army, though good, was wretchedly commanded; that neither Magenta nor Solferino was decisive; that he himself took no part in either; that the peace was not such a one as he wished, or had promised to France and to Italy; that he was not able to enforce its stipulations; that the result has been to give us on our very frontier a neighbour twenty-two millions strong, instead of a dependent ally. And that this has been done in defiance of his wishes, of his entreaties, of his remonstrances, and almost of his commands — that the Pope has refused even to listen to him, that Cavour behaved to him contemptuously, and Garibaldi insolently. The only sovereign who has treated him with deference is Mr. Lincoln.

Then there is no doubt that there is considerable distress. His friends attribute it to the American civil war, his enemies to the enormous unproductive expenditure of the government, and, influenced by the government, and imitating it, of the higher classes. The public at large, to the commercial treaty. I believe that all these three causes have contributed to it, and that the third cause is the least efficient. But the operatives and capitalists put it foremost, and cannot perceive that it must be temporary, and that, as all commerce is barter, there cannot be a permanent increase of imports, without at least an equal increase of exports. Simple as this proposition is, the French cannot understand it, and if you read the debates, you will see that Pouyer Quertier and others do nothing but exaggerate our imports, and that Auguste Chevalier and Baroche waste all their time in showing that they are smaller than they appear to be, and that they will diminish.

Senior. — You believe that there is great distress?

De Witt. — I do.

Senior. — And in Paris?

De Witt. — In Paris, perhaps more than anywhere else. A friend of mine — a very charitable man — told me that in visiting his poor people, *il avait flairé la détresse.* He had found in many of their rooms a smell of spirits. For the workman, when he cannot get sufficient food, often keeps up his courage, and obtains temporary strength, by the use of alcohol.

I attribute much of the distress to a fourth cause, a sense of political insecurity. When the Emperor's letter to Montauban, calling the French a degenerate people, was published, an acquaintance of mine, a great manufacturer, dismissed seven hundred of his workmen.

The general result is, that there is deep and wide discontent. I do not think a 24th of February impossible. A conspiracy to effect one was discovered a couple of months ago. It is said that Persigny wished to allow it to break out, but that all the ministers advised its being stifled, by the arrest of the leaders. We are told that two hundred are in prison. It is difficult to know how to deal with them. To try them will be dangerous; it will put evil thoughts into people's heads. It is dangerous to let them loose, and there are among them men, such as S——, a great manufacturer, who cannot be secretly disposed of.

Senior.— But while he has the army, need he fear an *émeute?*

De Witt.— The army sympathises with the nation. . . .

Fould's exposure of the state of our finances has done Louis Napoleon immense harm. It convicts him not only of waste, but of deception. Year after year he maintained, through his ministers, that the receipts fully equalled the expenditure, and now a deficit of forty millions sterling is shown. Soon after Fould's letter was published, I went to Val Richer. My friends at Lisieux and Pont l'Éveque could talk of nothing else. ' You told us all this,' they said, ' last year and the year before, but we could not believe you. Now it is the minister himself who tells it to us.' If there were a general election, I could come in by acclamation, merely because I should be an opposition candidate.

The deficit requires fresh taxation, unless we are to borrow to pay the principal of our debts, and to borrow more, in order to pay the interest of the new loan.

VII. *March 29, 1863. Lavergne to Senior.*

The Bonaparte prestige is gone. *Celui-ci* [1] remains only because there is no one to take his place, and because we fear that in the gap made by his fall the *Rouges* (Reds) might rush in.

VIII. *April 2, 1863. Lanjuinais to Senior.*

You attribute what you call our silent, abject submission, to our dread of deportation. It is produced by deeper and more generous motives than mere personal alarm. It is founded on the recollections of June, 1848, and on the histories of 1793. It is founded on the fear that, in the attempt to obtain liberty, we may endanger civilisation.

Louis Napoleon and his co-conspirators proclaim that rather than lose the means of gratifying, to its utmost degree, their ambition, their vanity, their luxury, and their hatreds, which their unrestrained power now showers on them, they will call to their aid all the evil passions of the uneducated masses.

The angry discontent with the rule of Napoleon III, which gained ground rapidly during the latter part of his reign, found voice in vehement attacks on the Government, of which the following speech of Leon Gambetta was the most startling.

A subscription had been undertaken to erect a monument to Baudin, a

1 The Emperor Napoleon. (Editor's note.)

republican deputy who had perished in the street-fighting that accompanied the coup d'état *of Louis Napoleon. Outraged by this bold move the Government had ordered the prosecution of those responsible for the subscription. And Gambetta, a young lawyer hitherto but little known, but destined to play a leading part in the early history of the Third Republic, helped conduct the defense. It was in the course of that defense that he stigmatized in scathing language " the men of the second of December."*

His speech may be compared with the Comte de Flahault's defense of the coup d'état. *(See Selection 89.)*

92. *GAMBETTA'S DENUNCIATION OF THE COUP D'ÉTAT OF NAPOLEON III* [1]

Yes! On the second of December there were grouped around a pretender men whom France had not known up to that time, men who had neither talent, nor honor, nor rank nor position, the sort of men who, at all periods, are accomplices of deeds of violence, the sort of men of whom one can say what Sallust said of the rabble that surrounded Catiline, what Caesar himself said in describing his accomplices, the eternal scum of orderly society:

Aere alieno abruti et vitiis onusti

or, as Corneille translates:

Un tas d'hommes perdus de dettes et crimes, [2]

It is with the aid of such men that throughout the ages institutions and laws have been overthrown, and the human conscience has been powerless to prevent it, despite the long, sublime line of thinkers and martyrs, Socrates, Thraseas, Cicero, Cato and the rest, who have protested in the name of desecrated religion, of wounded morality, of righteousness crushed under the soldier's boot.

But here it cannot be like that. When we come before you, magistrates, and say to you these things you should give us aid and protection. These men have claimed to have saved France. There is one decisive means of knowing whether their claim is a fact or an imposture. When a country really passes through a supreme crisis, to which it seems that everything is going to succumb, even the very foundations of society, then do you know what happens? It is at such a time that those whom the nation is accustomed to acclaim as its leaders, because they have been rendered illustrious by their talents and their virtues, come forward to save it. Now if I appraise, if I analyze the worth of the men who have claimed to have saved the country on the second of December, I find among them not one dis-

[1] Reinach, *Discours et plaidoyers politiques de M. Gambetta,* vol. I, Paris, Charpentier, 1881., pp. 12–14; 16–17 (condensed). Translation.

[2] A mass of men engulfed in debts and crimes. (Editor's note.)

tinguished character, while on the opposite side I see coming to their country's aid men like Michel de Bourges, Charras, both now dead, — Ledru
was already exiled, — and many others drawn from the *élite* of the most
widely separated political parties: for example our Berryer, that illustrious
man who now lies dying, and who but yesterday sent us this letter, the
letter of a man of noble heart, the last testament of indignation, a proof
that all parties support the claims of justice.

Where were Cavaignac, Lamoricière, Changarnier, Leflo, Bedeau, and
all the leaders, the honor and pride of our army?

Where were M. Thiers, M. de Remusat, the authorized representatives
of the Orleanist, Legitimist, Republican parties, where were they? At Mazas,
at Vincennes[1] these men who defended law and order! On the way to
Cayenne, to Lambessa,[2] these victims of an ambitious frenzy. That, gentlemen, is the way that France was saved! After that, do you think that they
have any right to claim that they have saved society, when what they really
did was to strike a blow at their country?

$$\cdot \quad \cdot \quad \cdot \quad \cdot \quad \cdot \quad \cdot \quad \cdot \quad \cdot \quad \cdot \quad \cdot \quad \cdot \quad \cdot \quad \cdot$$

Listen, you who for seventeen years have been absolute, "discretionary"
masters of France, — it is your own word; — we say nothing of the use you
have made of her treasures, of her blood, of her honor and of her glory;
we shall not speak of her compromised integrity, nor of what has become of
the fruits of her industry, assuming that no one is ignorant of the financial
catastrophes, which at this very moment undermine our footsteps; but that
which characterizes you best because it is the evidence of your own remorse,
is that you have never dared to say: "We will place among the solemn
festivals of France, we will celebrate as a national holiday, the second of
December!" And yet all the successive forms of government in this country
have been honored by honoring the day of their birth. The 14th of July, the
10th of August are festival days; the days of July were celebrated also, and
even the 24th of February; there are only two anniversaries, the 18th Bru-
maire and the 2nd of December, which have never been raised to the rank of
days of commemoration, because you know that if you should so raise
them, they would be rejected by the conscience of the nation.

Well! this anniversary which you have never adopted, we claim; we
take it for ourselves; we shall celebrate it always, unceasingly; each year
it shall be the anniversary of our dead up to the day when the country, having once more become master of itself, shall impose on you the great national expiation in the name of liberty, equality and fraternity.

---

[1] *i.e.,* in prison. (Editor's note.)   [2] *i.e.,* on the road to exile. (Editor's note.)

SECTION II. GERMANY

Reaction followed hard on the heels of the failure of the German Revolution of 1848. As the following selection shows, the King of Prussia was particularly indignant at the schoolmasters of his kingdom, who had long done much to further the cause of liberalism and who had played an active part in the Revolution. In 1854 regulations were issued, a primary aim of which was to develop docile teachers and pupils, loyal and obedient subjects of the King of Prussia.

The selection illustrates well the use of education as a political instrument. And it must be admitted that the attempt to mold the mind of youth to the purposes of those in power was far more cleverly conceived than the repressive but crude and provocative measures of the Metternich system. It may well be that the loyalty developed in the German schools was the chief factor in preventing the outbreak of another revolution in Germany until desperation precipitated it in 1918.

93. REACTION IN PRUSSIAN EDUCATION AFTER THE REVOLUTION OF 1848 [1]

Frederick William IV on Teachers Seminaries. — How suddenly the wind changed in educational quarters is shown by the proceedings at a conference of teachers in training colleges held in 1849 under the management of Privy-councillor Stiehl after the King had regained control of the government. The representatives of the training colleges had been selected by the Ministry of Education and the matters to be discussed had been drawn up beforehand and submitted for their consideration. Just what the government expected of this packed conference is shown in an address made by the King in person at one of the sessions. The address is frequently quoted in part, but it is so vivid and reveals so much that it seems worth while to give a rather extensive extract from it in this connection.

" All the misery which has come to Prussia during the past year is to be credited to you and only you. You deserve the blame for that godless pseudo-education of the common people which you have been propagating as the only true wisdom and by means of which you have destroyed faith and loyalty in the minds of my subjects and turned their hearts away from me. Even while I was yet Crown Prince I hated in my innermost soul this tricked-out, false education strutting about like a peacock, and while I was

[1] Edward H. Reisner, *Nationalism and Education since 1789.* New York, The Macmillan Company, 1922, pp. 161–170 (condensed).

Regent I made every effort in my power to overthrow it. I will go ahead on this beaten path without allowing myself to deviate from it. First of all, these seminaries every one must be removed from the large cities to small villages, in order that they may be kept away from the unholy influence which is poisoning our times. And then everything that goes on in them must be subjected to the closest supervision. I am not afraid of the populace, but my bureaucratic government in which up to now I have had proud confidence, is being undermined and poisoned by these unholy doctrines of a modern, frivolous, worldly wisdom. But as long as I hold the sword hilt in my hands, I shall know how to deal with such a nuisance."

Official Reorganization of Seminaries and Folkschools: Regulations of 1854. — The Constitution of 1850 promised a comprehensive law governing education in the state of Prussia. The active agitation for school reform through the promulgation of such a general education code kept up until Karl von Raumer became Minister of Education toward the end of the year 1850. He expressed himself as opposed to any immediate attempt to draw up a general law and proceeded to show it to be superfluous through the introduction of his educational policies through official regulations. By means of this weapon he waged war on agitation among schoolmen by forbidding attendance at the meetings of general educational associations. In place of these dangerous meetings he organized conferences at the various normal schools, which could be supervised and controlled. He made it illegal to publish the educational writings of Adolph Diesterweg and Friedrich Froebel, although his opposition to the principles of the kindergarten are said to have arisen from the confusion in his mind of Friedrich with Karl Froebel, who was a political radical of the day. The culmination of this repressive policy and the complete triumph in school affairs of the party conservative in politics and orthodox in religion, occurred with the publication of the Regulations of October 1, 2, and 3, 1854.[1] These orders deal respectively with the organization and the curriculum of the Evangelical normal schools, the schools preparatory to the normal schools, and the one-class elementary schools. The educational organization resulting from these three Regulations is highly instructive as an example of a well-thought-out and carefully planned effort to use a national system of schools for the development of a desired culture among an entire people.

General Principles to Govern Instruction in Teachers Seminaries. — The Regulation of October 1, relating to the Evangelical Seminaries of the Monarchy, states by way of preliminary that the day of freedom for them was at an end. Hitherto they had been allowed great freedom in organizing their

---

[1] These Regulations are given in full in Lewin, *Geschichte der Entwicklung der Preussischen Volksschule*, pp. 258–292.

curricula and in choosing educational ways and means. From now on they were to accept their mission as being the preparation of teachers for the primary schools through the use of definitely assigned materials and methods of instruction. Only when specific permission was given by the government were these limitations to be exceeded.

The purpose of the seminary being to prepare teachers of religion, reading and language, writing, arithmetic, singing, home geography and nature study, national history, and drawing, in the one-class elementary schools, the instruction of the students in the seminary was to be limited to the study of the subjects he was later on going to teach. The Regulations condemned the former tendency to increase as much as possible the sphere of instruction and to give a broad cultural training, and they specifically stated that the subject-matter of the elementary school was to prevail and govern in every particular and to constitute the main province of seminary instruction. The practice-school was declared to be the center about which all the work of the seminary should be organized, particularly in the last two years.

A larger principle of education was introduced when the Regulation stated the ultimate aim of the normal school to be not so much the teaching of facts, but rather the shaping of the mind and conscience of the student so that he might be properly fitted for his work in the primary schools " which are to help train the youth into Christian and patriotic modes of thought and into domestic virtues." Accordingly the student, while in the normal school, must be surrounded by a certain set of conditions that would form him to a particular mould. He must be made sincerely and deeply religious; he must be made patriotic; he must be made thorough master of the modes of schoolroom experience which he would be expected to pass on to his pupils in the primary schools. In order to realize the last point, the prospective teacher's experience was to be very definitely limited. His instruction must take place " according to the same principles and in the fundamentals in the very form which the treatment of the same subjects would require in the elementary school." Within this limited field of subject-matter he was to be trained to quick and clear comprehension, clear and accurate reorganization, and simple and correct reproduction of thoughts read and heard. Wherever possible, printed manuals were to be made the basis of instruction and from the content of these books the teacher of teachers was not to diverge by making it the subject of criticism or the object of supplementation.

* * * * * * * * * * * * * * *

Strong Emphasis on Religious Instruction. — The new subject-matter in religion, in view of the danger of too much, or even of any, freedom in this field, was to be designated as instruction in the catechism. Luther's shorter catechism, or where circumstances called for its use, the Heidelberg catechism, was to be the text studied. What supplementation this work required was to be contained in a syllabus, which was "completely to comprise in definite form all that which prospective schoolmasters need to know."

.   .   .   .

Reading and the German Language. — . . . Control over the student's private reading was to be exercised in connection with language study. A suitable selection of reading material was to be made each year, which was not to include the "so-called classical literature." Only that was to be permitted "which by reason of its content and attitude was likely to lead to orthodox church life, Christian morals, patriotism, and reflective consideration of Nature."

.   .   .   .

History and Geography. — The instruction in history and geography was to center in the Fatherland and both subjects were to be, as far as possible, interdependent. . . . It was declared to be the main business of the seminary teacher to make his pupil familiar, as he studied the story of the past, with memorable events, significant social institutions, and great personages in the history of Prussia and Germany, and thereby to "increase his reverence and love for the Royal House of Hohenzollern." History was to be taught thoroughly and with enthusiasm, and was to be given "fruitful connection with the life and viewpoint of the common people." In connection with the study of history, the great national anniversaries were to be given special prominence and to be used as the means of making the pupil familiar with the best selections of patriotic poetry and popular music.

.   .   .   .

General Principles Underlying the Conduct of the Primary Schools. — The Regulation dated October 3 dealt with the place of the primary or folk school in the national economy and described the ways and means, methods, and subject-matter, whereby it might be made effectively to serve its purpose. . . . The elementary schools had been allowed to follow the general intellectual trend of the new century in which they had been given a new form and a larger development. It was now high time, however, to eliminate unauthorized extravagant and erroneous elements and to install in their place a truly Christian education for the common people. . . . The teacher was enjoined in the words of the official formula to "lead the youth into knowledge of the history of our rulers and our people, as also of the divine guidance which has revealed itself in the same, and to fill the minds and hearts of the pupils with love for their king, and respect for the laws and institutions of the Fatherland."

Influence of the Regulations of 1854.— The Regulations of 1854 have in many ways been definitive of the character of the Prussian and the German folk school since that time. . . . The direction given to the education of the children of the common people in those days when political liberalism met its decisive defeat, held over as a settled national policy until the downfall of the Empire and the declaration of a Republic following the armistice of 1918. . . .

It was in connection with his attempt to persuade the Lower House of the Prussian Parliament to vote credits to pay for the army increases desired by King William I that Bismarck made his famous " blood and iron" speech. In the refusal of the House to grant the credits the mid-century Prussian liberal movement, already greatly discredited by the failure of the Revolution of 1848, made its last stand. Failing to persuade the House, Bismarck, in defiance of the Constitution of 1850, proceeded arbitrarily to levy and collect the taxes necessary to pay for the increases.

94. EXTRACT FROM BISMARCK'S SO-CALLED " BLOOD AND IRON" SPEECH [1]

Not to Prussia's liberalism but to her power is Germany looking; Bavaria, Würtemberg, Baden may indulge in liberalism, but no one will on that account assign to them Prussia's rôle; Prussia must gather up her strength and hold it in readiness for the opportune moment which has already slipped by several times; Prussia's borders, since the Treaty of Vienna, have not been favorable to a healthy state life; not by speeches and majority votes are the great questions of the day decided — that was the great mistake of 1848 and 1849 — but by iron and blood.

Prussia having won a decisive victory over Austria in the battle of Sadowa on July 3, 1866, the temptation was strong to crush the Austrian army and to exact of the defeated state heavy compensation. Bismarck, however, was far-sighted enough to realize the unwisdom of such a course for the future relations of Austria and Prussia.

In his Reflections and Reminiscences *Bismarck tells of the difficulty he had in persuading the King of Prussia not to exact of Austria the pound of flesh.*

---

[1] Delivered in the Budget Commission of the Lower House of the Prussian Parliament, September 30, 1862. Quoted in Hohlfeld, *Deutsche Reichsgeschichte in Dokumenten.* Berlin, Deutsche Verlagsgesellschaft für Politik und Geschichte, 1927, I Halbband, p. 27. Translation.

95. *BISMARCK PERSUADES THE KING OF PRUSSIA TO TREAT AUSTRIA LENIENTLY AFTER DEFEATING HER IN THE WAR OF 1866* [1]

We had to avoid wounding Austria too severely; we had to avoid leaving behind in her any unnecessary bitterness of feeling or desire for revenge; we ought rather to reserve the possibility of becoming friends again with our adversary of the moment, and in any case to regard the Austrian state as a piece on the European chessboard and the renewal of friendly relations with her as a move open to us. If Austria were severely injured, she would become the ally of France and of every other opponent of ours; she would even sacrifice her anti-Russian interests for the sake of revenge on Prussia.

On the other hand, I could see no future acceptable to us for the countries constituting the Austrian monarchy, in case the latter were split up by risings of the Hungarians and Slavs or made permanently dependent on those peoples. What would be put in that portion of Europe which the Austrian state from Tyrol to the Bukowina had hitherto occupied? Fresh formations on this surface could only be of a permanently revolutionary nature. German Austria we could neither wholly nor partly make use of. The acquisition of provinces like Austrian Silesia and portions of Bohemia could not strengthen the Prussian state; it would not lead to an amalgamation of German Austria with Prussia, and Vienna could not be governed from Berlin as a mere dependency.

If the war were continued, the probable theatre would be Hungary. The Austrian army which, if we crossed the Danube at Pressburg, would not be able to hold Vienna, would scarcely retreat southwards, where it would be caught between the Prussian and Italian armies, and, by its approach to Italy, once more revive the military ardour of the Italians which, already depressed, had been restricted by Louis Napoleon; it would retreat towards the east, and continue its defence in Hungary — if only in the expectation of the prospective intervention of France and the weakening of Italy's interest in the matter, through France's agency. Moreover I held, even from a purely military standpoint, and according to my knowledge of Hungarian territory, that a prosecution of the war there would not repay us, and that the successes to be won there would be out of all proportion to the victories we had hitherto gained, and consequently be calculated to diminish our *prestige* — quite apart from the fact that the prolongation of the war would pave the way for a French intervention. We must finish off rapidly; before France won time to bring further diplomatic action to bear upon Austria. To all this the King raised no objection, but declared the actual terms inadequate,

[1] Bismarck, *The Man and the Statesman*. Translated under the supervision of A. J. Butler. 2 vols., London, Smith, Elder & Co., 1898, vol. II, pp. 48–53.

without, however, definitely formulating his own demands. Only so much was clear, that his claims had grown considerably since July 4. He said that the chief culprit could not be allowed to escape unpunished, and that justice once satisfied, we could let the misguided partners off more easily, and he insisted on the cessions of territory from Austria which I have already mentioned. I replied that we were not there to sit in judgment, but to pursue the German policy. Austria's conflict in rivalry with us was no more culpable than ours with her; *our task was the establishment or initiation of German national unity under the leadership of the King of Prussia.*

Passing on to the German states, he spoke of various acquisitions by cutting down the territories of all our opponents. I repeated that we were there not to administer retributive justice, but to pursue a policy; that I wished to avoid, in the German federation of the future, the sight of mutilated territories, whose princes and peoples might very easily (such is human weakness) retain a lively wish to recover their former possessions by means of foreign help; such allies would be very unreliable. The same would be the case if, for the purpose of compensating Saxony, Würzburg or Nuremberg were demanded of Bavaria, a plan, moreover, which would interfere with the dynastic predilection of his Majesty for Anspach. I had also to resist plans which were aimed at an enlargement of the Grand Duchy of Baden, the annexation of the Bavarian Palatinate, and an extension in the region of the lower Main. The Aschaffenburg district of Bavaria was at the same time regarded as a fit compensation to Hesse-Darmstadt for the loss of Upper Hesse, which would result from the projected Main frontier. Later, at Berlin, the only part of this plan still under negotiation was the cession of that portion of Bavarian territory which lay on the right bank of the Main, inclusive of the town of Baireuth, to Prussia; the question then arose whether the boundary should run on the Northern or Red Main or the Southern or White Main. What seemed to me to be paramount with his Majesty was the aversion of the military party to interrupt the victorious course of the army. The resistance which I was obliged, in accordance with my convictions, to offer to the King's views with regard to following up the military successes, and to his inclination to continue the victorious advance, excited him to such a degree that a prolongation of the discussion became impossible; and, under the impression that my opinion was rejected, I left the room with the idea of begging the King to allow me, in my capacity of officer, to join my regiment. On returning to my room I was in the mood that the thought occurred to me whether it would not be better to fall out of the open window, which was four storeys high; and I did not look round when I heard the door open, although I suspected that the person entering was the Crown Prince, whose room in the same corridor I had just passed. I felt his hand on my shoulder, while he said: " You know that I was against this war. You considered it necessary, and the responsibility for it lies on you. If you are now persuaded that our end is attained, and peace must now be concluded, I am ready to support you and defend your opinion with my father." He then repaired to the King, and came back after a short half-hour, in the same calm, friendly mood, but with the words: " It has been a very difficult business, but my father has consented." This consent found expression in a note written with lead pencil on the margin of one of my last memoranda, something to this effect: " Inasmuch as my Minister-President has left me in the lurch in the face of the enemy, and here I am not in a position to supply his place, I have discussed the question with my son; and as he has associated himself with the Minister-President's opinion, I find myself reluctantly compelled, after such brilliant victories on the part of the army, to bite this sour apple and accept so disgraceful a peace." I do not think I am mistaken as to the exact words, although the document is not accessible to me at present. In any case I have given the sense of it; and, despite its bitterness of expression, it was to me a joyful release from a tension that was becoming unbearable. I gladly accepted the royal assent to what I regarded as politically necessary without taking offence at its ungracious form. At this time military impressions were dominant in the King's mind; and the strong need he felt of pursuing the hitherto dazzling course of victory perhaps influenced him more than political and diplomatic considerations.

The only residuum that the above note of the King's, which the Crown Prince brought me, left in my mind was the recollection of the violent agitation into which I had been obliged to put my old master, in order to obtain what I considered essential to the interests of the country if I were to remain responsible. To this day these and similar occurrences have left no other impression upon me than the painful recollection that I had been obliged to vex a master whom personally I loved as I did him.

The question of the origins of the Franco-Prussian War, like that of the origins of the Great War, has been the subject of heated controversy between French and German historians who have all too often allowed nationalistic sympathies to influence their judgment.

Fortunately a distinguished American historical scholar, Dr. R. H. Lord, has entered this field and has given students of this mooted question the best interpretation of it now available. In the following extract from Dr. Lord's book a balance is struck between the French and German views of responsibility.

96. THE QUESTION OF RESPONSIBILITY FOR THE WAR OF 1870[1]

Among all the wars that took place in Europe from the downfall of the first Napoleon to the world conflict of our day, the Franco-German War of 1870 was the most bitterly contested, the most sanguinary, the most dramatically decisive, and the most fateful in its consequences for the peace of the world. To the victorious nation it still represents the most glorious page in their history. In the minds of the vanquished it has rankled as no other disaster that has ever befallen them. Inevitably, the causes of, and still more the responsibilities for, the outbreak of this struggle have ever since been debated with an intensity of interest such as has seldom been aroused by any historical question.

As to the responsibilities of France, opinion is not very deeply divided. France was in the wrong, in the first place, in so far as she had since 1866 attempted to block the unification of Germany. In taking her stand on "the line of the Main" and opposing the union of the South German states with the North German Confederation, she had been denying to the German people the right to settle their own affairs, in a way which, in spite of all extenuating circumstances, cannot be justified. It is true, on the other hand, that in 1870 this opposition was apparently weakening; that the French cabinet then in power seems to have been pledged not to intervene in case the South Germans voluntarily sought union with the North; and that, if peace could have been preserved for a few years longer, the French people would probably have made up their minds to accept the inevitable.

After the crisis provoked by the Hohenzollern Candidacy for the throne of Spain had arisen, an influential and noisy section of the French public and of the Parisian press adopted an attitude of reckless bellicosity and did their utmost to render war inevitable. As for the government, the charges so generally current immediately after the downfall of the Second Empire that Napoleon III and his ministers had deliberately sought for war, are no longer seriously made even in Germany (save for rare exceptions). It is now commonly held that the Emperor, although vacillating and inclined at times to defer too much to the clamors of the war party, would, on the whole, very much have preferred to keep the peace. Much the same may be said of Émile Ollivier, the head of the cabinet, and of the Foreign Minister, the Duc de Gramont. Nevertheless, although the intentions of the French government of that time have been vindicated, the wisdom of their policy has not been. Except for Gramont and Ollivier themselves, in their not too convincing *apologiae,* nearly all French historians have denounced that policy with a

[1] R. H. Lord, *The Origins of the War of 1870.* Cambridge, Harvard University Press, 1924, pp. 3-9. (First paragraph on page 8 omitted.)

vigor that should leave nothing to be desired east of the Rhine. Indeed, it can scarcely be denied that the French ministers, by premature threats of war, notably in their public declaration of July 6, by their unnecessary and imprudent demands on July 12, and in general by their too persistent efforts to achieve a complete and spectacular diplomatic victory, did much to bring on the conflict and to drag their country into "the most imprudent war that ever was."

Much more difficult, and still beset with controversy, is the question of the responsibilities of Germany. Here, after a brief period when Napoleon was made the scapegoat for everything, French historians began an offensive which has ever since been vigorously conducted and which received its strongest expression in Ollivier's dictum: "The real author of the war, he who willed it, sought it, premeditated it, prepared it, rendered it inevitable at the appointed moment, was Bismarck."

Such attacks were for a long time greeted east of the Rhine only with contemptuous or angry denials, based on a deeply rooted conviction of Germany's complete innocence of any responsibility for the war. In the eyes of the German public the *Kriegsschuldfrage* [1] for 1870 was as definitively settled against France as in the mind of the French public to-day the similar question about 1914 is settled against Germany. Hence, for nearly a quarter of a century, German historians confidently took their stand upon the official version of the affair put forth by Bismarck at the time of the war. It was maintained that the policy of the Prussian government before the war had been thoroughly peaceful. The candidacy of Prince Leopold of Hohenzollern for the Spanish throne was no "intrigue of Bismarck against France," but a matter which the German Chancellor had had nothing to do with, and of which he had known very little down to the time of the explosion at Paris. This candidacy had, indeed, been only a private affair of the Hohenzollerns, which did not in the least concern the Prussian government and about which King William had been consulted only as head of the family, not as head of the Prussian state. Similarly, no fault could be found with Bismarck for the fact that, when the King had firmly but courteously rejected an outrageous demand of the French ambassador at Ems, the Chancellor had communicated a telegram on that subject to the newspapers and had sent it around to "a few" of his envoys, purely "for their information." In short, Germany had neither sought, nor given any occasion for, war: the conflict was due solely to the dynastic necessities of Napoleon or to the jealousy, megalomania, and chauvinism of the French people.

Such comfortable theories were then rudely shattered by a series of disclosures that came during the eighteen-nineties. On the one hand, the publication of the diary of King Charles of Roumania for the first time revealed

[1] War Guilt Question. (Editor's note.)

something of the secret history of the Hohenzollern Candidacy, and proved that Bismarck had, indeed, been the chief promoter of that project so loaded with dynamite. On the other hand, the fallen Chancellor himself, by conversations, by communications to the press, and finally by his memoirs, revealed to a somewhat shocked nation how by his crafty reëditing of the "Ems Telegram" and the well-calculated publicity he had given it, he had tried, at the supreme moment of the diplomatic crisis, to goad the French into war. These disclosures, which confirmed a good part of what Heinrich von Sybel, the chief of Bismarck's historical general staff, had been wont to call the "lying fables" and "inventions" of the Duc de Gramont, compelled a rather nervous and even panicky retreat on the part of German historians from the positions once deemed so impregnable. And as nearly all the new material that has come to light since that time has made their case worse (from a patriotic standpoint), this retreat has continued, and there is some reason to doubt whether it is finished even yet. At all events, one may say that in the past twenty-five years the views of French and German historians on this subject have come very much nearer together, and that on certain larger questions a substantial agreement has been reached.

It is now agreed that, from 1866 on, Bismarck, like most of those prominent in Prussian political and military circles, regarded a war with France as inevitable sooner or later, convinced as he was that France would not peaceably permit the union of South Germany with the North, which was at that time the great object of his policy. It is tolerably well agreed that he also regarded such a war as in itself desirable, believing that the South Germans were not likely to seek that union, at least for a long time to come, unless they were shaken out of their selfishness and apathy by a shock from outside, such as could best be furnished by a great common effort for a national cause, and by a great common victory over "that neighboring nation which was our age-long aggressor." It is clear that he shared Moltke's profound conviction that Germany would enter such a war with every chance of success. It is agreed that, wherever the idea of the Hohenzollern Candidacy may have originated, Bismarck took up the project and worked with all his might and main to put it through, as "a political necessity," although to the day of his death he always tried to conceal or to minimize his share in the matter. Finally, scarcely anyone will now deny that at least in the last stage of the crisis of July, 1870, at the time when he reëdited the Ems Telegram, the Chancellor was working to provoke a war.

Was not that his aim throughout? If he regarded a war with France as inevitable, safe, and desirable, may we not assume that from the outset he deliberately planned to bring one about? In hatching in deep secrecy that plot for the Hohenzollern Candidacy, in a manner calculated to wound equally the interests and dignity of France, at a time when, as all the world knew, Franco-Prussian relations were like a powder-mine in which the least spark might produce an explosion, was he not scheming to provoke an explosion? Lothar Bucher, his chief agent in this affair, later declared that the candidacy was "a trap set for Napoleon," and that as such it had been brilliantly successful. Moritz Busch, another confidant, relates how he one day protested to Bismarck against the latter's attempts to deny "the trap set for Napoleon, which he had also baited afresh by condensing the Ems despatch," and urged that by denying it, he was robbing himself of "the finest leaf from his wreath of laurels." Thereupon, Busch affirms, "these details recalled to him all the circumstances and he no longer denied anything. He brought the conversation to a close with the words: 'We will talk it over some other time,'" but no opportunity for such a later talk ever came. The temptation is great, then, to suppose that in this case as in those of both his earlier wars, Bismarck "had the intention of all the things he did." A great many French writers have affirmed it, but very few German historians have yet been willing to accept this view in full. Nearly all German writers and a fair number of French ones still incline toward theories less damaging to Bismarck's moral reputation.

.   .   .   .

The theory still most commonly held in Germany, with manifold variations in detail, is that Bismarck could not possibly have anticipated the extraordinary course of later events or the seldom paralleled blunders which were to be committed by the French government, and that, in working for the Hohenzollern Candidacy, war was not the outcome that he foresaw or the aim that he had in view. That candidacy, if successful, promised very real advantages to Prussia: a great increase in the prestige of the dynasty, commercial benefits, and, above all, the raising up of a new enemy for Napoleon in the rear, just as, four years before, on the eve of his last war, Bismarck had raised up an enemy at Austria's back by planting Charles of Hohenzollern on the throne of Roumania. It meant winning a new ally for Prussia, who might render somewhat the same services in the future Franco-German war that Italy had rendered in 1866. Manifestly, Bismarck was trying to steal a march upon France, to gain an advantage over her. Obviously, she would take offense, in greater or less degree, whenever the plot came to light. But could he, need he, have foreseen that war must be the inevitable result? That is, indeed, the crux of the whole problem. According to one group of writers, Bismarck expected that Napoleon, sick, fundamentally peaceful, and unprepared for war, would give way once more as on so many previous occasions. Others hold that the Chancellor must have reckoned very seriously with the possibility that the candidacy would lead to war, but that he deliberately took the risk of it, convinced that the game was worth the candle: if Napoleon submitted peaceably, Prussia would greatly have improved her international position; and if Napoleon did not submit, the inevitable war might as well come now, when the Emperor would presumably have to fight Prussia and Spain combined. From this latter theory it is no great jump to the view commonly held in France that Bismarck regarded war as the probable and the desirable outcome of the adventure. Still other German historians, while admitting that the Chancellor was playing a dangerous game, refuse to express an opinion as to how far he anticipated a warlike issue or what his ultimate aim was.

At all events, unless one accepts the view that a Franco-Prussian war was under any circumstances inevitable, it is difficult not to accuse both governments in 1870 of criminally playing with fire. Bismarck deliberately embarked on a project which, whatever its primary aim may have been, did involve placing Napoleon in a position where he might either have to fight or to accept another grave defeat that might involve the downfall of his tottering dynasty. And France then tried to turn the tables by forcing Prussia to confront the alternative of war or a humiliating backdown — and with a statesman like Bismarck the choice was quickly made.

In the following selection Hermann Oncken, Professor of History at the University of Berlin, defends the policy of Bismarck on the eve of the Franco-Prussian War. Basing his interpretations on recently discovered material, drawn chiefly from the Austrian archives, he argues that in 1869 Napoleon III was attempting to form a Triple Alliance, composed of France, Austria, and Italy, his main objects being to dismember Prussia, reducing her " to the size and importance of Bavaria and Saxony," and to reduce Germany as a whole to a mere collection of weak states. Bismarck's policy, Professor Oncken contends, was therefore shaped by the necessity of meeting the impending danger of encirclement by the proposed Alliance.

97. BISMARCK'S POLICY ON THE EVE OF THE FRANCO-PRUSSIAN WAR [1]

Only against the background of this encirclement of 1869 with its extreme danger for the German body politic, which was just in a transitional state of development, does the policy of Bismarck appear in its true setting. It has often been characterized as a policy of " blood and iron," although the phrase was intended to apply only to a trial of strength between German powers and never to a trial with foreign states. In other words it applied to a conflict which was as inevitable for the achievement of German unity

---

[1] Hermann Oncken, *Napoleon III and the Rhine. The Origin of the War of 1870–1871.* Translated by Edwin H. Zeydel. New York, Alfred A. Knopf, 1928, pp. 133–137.

as was the similar struggle, simultaneously raging in the United States, for the preservation of American national unity. It has been overlooked by the opponents of Bismarck's policy that after the decision of Königgrätz this policy was inspired by a deep sense of responsibility for the peace of Europe and maintained a predominantly defensive attitude. In fact, from the summer of 1867 on it was more and more forced into the defensive by its opponents. The German historians too have often been guided by the false assumption that because this policy was crowned with success in 1870-1871, it had a definite objective in view from the very start and pursued it with an air of Machiavellian superiority. In contrast to the bright progress towards victory the dangers encountered by Bismarck's policy are left too much in obscurity, whereas they should be recognized as realities and thrown into high relief. For this reason nothing is more absurd than to look upon Bismarck as the new Machiavelli, endowed with diabolical arts and surrounded by innocent, unsuspecting contemporaries who despised "blood and iron," when in reality he had as his opponents a Napoleon, a Beust and a Victor Emmanuel. A policy of might is common to all states. But Napoleon's policy was reprehensible and was prepared at all times to interfere in the sphere of national interest of another state, while Bismarck's policy, without infringing upon the vital national interests of others, constantly restricted itself to the problem of gradually satisfying the urge of the German nation for unification, without seriously endangering peace. If, in the face of a policy of encirclement which threatened some day to stifle Germany's future, he sought counter-weights in Europe and got in touch with Hungarian elements, who were on their own account opposed to an active German policy on the part of the Viennese cabinet, he had a right to do so. And if finally he included in his calculations the efforts of the Spanish to win over the Archduke Leopold of Hohenzollern, he was again merely doing his duty and exercising the right of self-defence. Of course it can not be denied that this candidacy was meant to be a counter-balance. And it is just as certain that in comparison with the weighty, serious reality of the Triple Alliance it was as light and insignificant as a feather; at the decisive moment it proved an illusion, the substance of which was to burst like a bubble. Hence there is no justification for condemning this act of Bismarck (as has frequently been done, most recently by an American) because it was bound to "offend" France. As if the United States had a short time before hesitated to "offend" the daredevil policy of Napoleon in Mexico and inflict upon it a defeat which in world history has the same significance as the thunderclap of Sadowa had in continental Europe! Why should Bismarck have been considerate in view of this conspiracy led by Napoleon, which, had it been successful, would have hurled Germany back into the darkest ages of internal dissolution and external dependence?

Naturally even he could not yet foresee all the dangers, but it was his foremost duty to meet the eventualities which his political instinct sensed. Rifle in hand, he fulfilled his duty without a formal challenge, and without overstepping the line of watchful waiting which he had drawn at the time of the customs parliament in May, 1868. As the dark clouds were already gathering and the rumors of war growing apace, he declared on February 19, 1869, in his instructions to the North German representative in Paris that he did not fear war and that the threatening reports in various forms had come from Paris again and again since the summer of 1866: " In the face of all this we can do naught but trust in our strength and remain calm, so that beyond the Rhine too the impression will gain ground that we can not be intimidated." Toward the end of March he had representations made to the Italian government because it did not officially deny the rumors of a triple alliance. Thereupon the Italian minister read to him a private letter of the Premier General Menabrea, who described France as a fully charged battery which was bound to explode at the slightest contact. He said that it was incumbent upon Prussia carefully to avoid every such contact and circumvent the conflict, and to do its best to satisfy and disinterest France. Bismarck was right in replying to this ambiguous advice that it seemed to him that Paris rather than Berlin was the right address for petitions in the interest of concilation and peace, and that Germany's defensive strength was the only means of disinteresting France. What made Bismarck so sure of himself was not only his realization of the irreconcilability of interests which stood in the way of a final union of his opponents but also his deep conviction that he was representing the cause of the future, the unity of a great nation, transcending all intrigues and contingencies.

In the matter of responsibility for the Franco-Prussian War one of the strongest counts against Bismarck is his condensation of the " Ems Despatch." Leopold of Hohenzollern having refused the crown of Spain, to the relief of the French who had feared that a dangerous combination might result between Hohenzollerns in Spain and Hohenzollerns in Prussia, the French Ministry, still unsatisfied, demanded of the King of Prussia, through the French Ambassador, that the Hohenzollern candidacy should never be renewed. The King of Prussia courteously refused; and his refusal was telegraphed from Ems to Bismarck in Berlin. Whereupon Bismarck condensed the telegram in such a way as to provoke the people in both France and Prussia to fever heat. War followed.

In his Reflections and Reminiscences *Bismarck tells the story of his condensation of the " Ems Despatch."*

98. *BISMARCK'S CONDENSATION OF THE EMS DESPATCH;* I. *BISMARCK'S OWN STORY* [1]

All these considerations, conscious and unconscious, strengthened my opinion that war could be avoided only at the cost of the honour of Prussia and of the national confidence in it. Under this conviction I made use of the royal authorisation communicated to me through Abeken, to publish the contents of the telegram; and in the presence of my two guests I reduced the telegram by striking out words, but without adding or altering, to the following form: " After the news of the renunciation of the hereditary Prince of Hohenzollern had been officially communicated to the imperial government of France by the royal government of Spain, the French ambassador at Ems further demanded of his Majesty the King that he would authorise him to telegraph to Paris that his Majesty the King bound himself for all future time never again to give his consent if the Hohenzollerns should renew their candidature. His Majesty the King thereupon decided not to receive the French ambassador again, and sent to tell him through the aide-de-camp on duty that his Majesty had nothing further to communicate to the ambassador." The difference in the effect of the abbreviated text of the Ems telegram as compared with that produced by the original was not the result of stronger words but of the form, which made this announcement appear decisive, while Abeken's version would only have been regarded as a fragment of a negotiation still pending, and to be continued at Berlin.

After I had read out the concentrated edition to my two guests, Moltke remarked " Now it has a different ring; it sounded before like a parley; now it is like a flourish in answer to a challenge." I went on to explain: " If in execution of his Majesty's order I at once communicate this text, which contains no alteration in or addition to the telegram, not only to the newspapers, but also by telegraph to all our embassies, it will be known in Paris before midnight, and not only on account of its contents, but also on account of the manner of its distribution, will have the effect of a red rag upon the Gallic bull. Fight we must if we do not want to act the part of the vanquished without a battle. Success, however, essentially depends upon the impression which the origination of the war makes upon us and others; it is important that we should be the party attacked, and this Gallic overweening and touchiness will make us if we announce in the face of Europe, so far as we can without the speaking-trumpet of the Reichstag, that we fearlessly meet the public threats of France."

This explanation brought about in the two generals a revulsion to a

[1] Bismarck, *The Man and the Statesman.* Translated under the supervision of A. J. Butler. Vol. II, pp. 99–100.

more joyous mood, the liveliness of which surprised me. They had suddenly recovered their pleasure in eating and drinking and spoke in a more cheerful vein. Roon said: " Our God of old lives still and will not let us perish in disgrace." Moltke so far relinquished his passive equanimity that, glancing up joyously towards the ceiling and abandoning his usual punctiliousness of speech, he smote his hand upon his breast and said: " If I may but live to lead our armies in such a war, then the devil may come directly afterwards and fetch away the ' old carcass.' "

In the following selection Professor Oncken attempts to justify Bismarck's condensation of the Ems Despatch.

99. BISMARCK'S CONDENSATION OF THE EMS DESPATCH; II. PROFESSOR ONCKEN'S VIEW [1]

The historical import of the Ems despatch lies not in the fact that it broke off peaceful negotiations by an offensive act which rendered war inevitable, but rather, as the French foreign minister admitted, in the fact that it disturbed the war-plotting intrigue of the French and their plan of protracting the negotiations for the sake of winning time for further preparations. If this is granted, the despatch must be interpreted as a defensive act on Bismarck's part which with unerring instinct tore the veil from the ambiguities designed to secure for the bellicose French the most favorable moment for action. Was it Bismarck's duty to wait patiently for the moment which suited his opponent best? After the challenges of the past week there could be no doubt what the French wanted, and as for Bismarck's revision of the despatch, it must be judged in the light of the language which the official French governmental organs had been using. If the despatch has been compared with the blare of a trumpet, it was but a fitting answer to the warlike spirit which had long robbed the French statesmen of their senses. For the question of guilt therefore the Ems despatch — the fact that it is hardly mentioned in the Austrian diplomatic correspondence can scarcely be due to chance — must be regarded as of secondary importance, and the French conception, which seizes upon the despatch as the decisive factor — the memoirs of Lord Grey show how the legend continues to live — seeks to make an artificially isolated diplomatic event of a fragmentary nature the key to the catastrophe, instead of looking at it in its larger aspect. The bomb merely exploded too soon, or rather the French felt constrained to light the fuse a little earlier than they had planned.

Professor Oncken's summary of what he holds to be the causes of the Franco-Prussian War, given in the following extract, may be compared with Professor Lord's view of the origins of the conflict. (See Selection 96.)

[1] Hermann Oncken, *Napoleon III and the Rhine. The Origin of the War of 1870–1871.* Translated by Edwin H. Zeydel. New York, Alfred A. Knopf, 1928, pp. 177–178.

100. CAUSES OF THE WAR OF 1870 [1]

With soldierly frankness the French military attaché in Berlin, Colonel Stoffel, discussed the true cause of the war at the time of its outbreak. He said that the war was the result of the preponderance of Prussia since 1866 and that this preponderance required France to secure her boundaries. Such security, she felt, she could attain only by acquiring the German territory west of the Rhine, and French possession of the Rhine alone could guarantee the peace between the two nations. These utterances are in agreement with the facts as we have revealed them according to the documents, except that the documents go even farther and show that already prior to the war of 1866 Napoleon had a Rhine policy and by an unsuccessful intrigue had himself helped to establish the order which later he believed he could subvert only by conquering the Rhine. This is corroborated by the fact that as late as August 6, the day of the battle of Wörth, Prince Metternich, who had a deeper insight than anyone else into the Napoleonic policies of 1863–1870, spoke outright of the Rhine as the chief war aim. This fact, usually kept dark in France nowadays, was emphasized on September 18, 1919, by the French socialist J. Longuet in a parliamentary address, when he said that it should not be forgotten that the yearning for the left bank of the Rhine was responsible for the war of 1870.

SECTION III. ITALY

The Italian Revolution of 1848, begun with high hopes, succumbed in the end to the military power of Austria and other forces of reaction. There followed a period of stern repression throughout most of Italy. The harshness of this repression in Lombardy and Venetia is clearly brought out in the selection that follows, and it is easy to see from it why hatred of Austria long persisted in the peninsula, even after Italy had joined with Austria and Germany in the Triple Alliance.

101. AUSTRIAN REACTION IN ITALY AFTER THE FAILURE OF THE ITALIAN REVOLUTION OF 1848–1849 [2]

The Restoration of the Old Regime was most odious in Lombardy and Venetia, because there it brought back the foreign masters. Austrian influences prevailed again in the Duchies and in Tuscany and in Naples, but the

---

[1] Hermann Oncken, *Napoleon III and the Rhine.* Translated by Edwin H. Zeydel. New York, Alfred A. Knopf, pp. 183–184.

[2] William Roscoe Thayer, *The Life and Times of Cavour.* 2 vols., Houghton Mifflin Company, 1911, vol. I, pp. 153–155.

Lombards and Venetians had to bear in addition the bodily presence of the Austrians themselves. Their provinces were placed under martial law, and Field-Marshal Radetzky, the veteran of four score and three years[1] recently victorious at Custozza and Novara, was appointed governor-general. If ever a soldier deserved the gratitude of his sovereign that man was Radetzky. Though driven from Milan by the surprising insurrection of March, 1848, he lost neither head nor heart. He rallied his fugitive troops in the Quadrilateral, checked the onslaught of the elated Italians, waited, stubbornly waited, for reinforcements which might never reach him; was unmoved by news of the general dissolution of the Government at Vienna and of the Emperor's flight: and when the time came, he turned and crushed his foe. Verona was a mighty fortress and Mantua was well-nigh impregnable, but without the determination in Radetzky's heart, Verona and Mantua and Italy itself would probably have been lost forever to Austria. And not only Italy, the Hapsburg dynasty and the existence of its polyglot Empire, held together by the balancing of mutual antagonisms, depended on Radetzky's rocklike stability. He was not a master of warfare, but he had an iron resolution, which won battles without fighting them, and proved the salvation of his cause.

Until 1852 the Constitution extorted from the Emperor in 1848 was supposed to be in force, but Radetzky paid no attention to it. A soldier, he naturally chose the soldier's way of exacting obedience. Cruel punishments did not move him: indeed, he evidently believed that a display of cruelty would serve as an effective deterrent against further rebellion. It was a time when physicians who did not know what else to do bled their patients. Radetzky favored blood-letting, not only for its wholesome effect on the patient, but for the relief it gave the operator. The Austrian officers and soldiers thirsted to be revenged on the people that had humiliated them in 1848. They had always regarded the Italians as effeminate and servile; yet those creatures whom they despised had chased them from Milan and Venice and almost wrested Northern Italy from them. Radetzky felt no reluctance against allowing his men to let off some of their pent-up wrath. He did not look too closely into the cases of Italians arrested on political or treasonable charges; nor did he reprove his lieutenant, Marshal Haynau, who, having put down the revolt at Brescia, unmoved alike by the magnificent heroism of the vanquished and by the demands of common humanity, took an atrocious vengeance on the Brescians. An affair which passed under Radetzky's own eye illustrated the temper of the Governor-General, the Austrians and the natives. On the Emperor's birthday (Aug. 18, 1849) the Austrians had their appropriate celebration, with Te Deums in the Duomo, and a military parade; but the Milanese held sullenly aloof. A certain Annetta Olivari, a

---

[1] Born in 1766; died in 1858.

glove-dealer by day and a courtesan in the favor of Austrian officers by night, flaunted the Imperial colors from her window. Italian passers-by shook their heads, murmured, and hissed, while Austrians in the Caffé Mazza opposite clapped their hands and laughed derisively. A crowd collected: then suddenly platoons of soldiers, with bayonets fixed, rushed upon the scene. Some of the Italians were jabbed or trampled and several were arrested. After a mock trial, fifteen men and two women were stripped and flogged in public at the Castello. Others went to prison. By Radetzky's command the Olivari woman received from the Municipality of Milan a present of 30,000 lire. Worst of all, the Municipality paid perforce five florins 17½ kreutzers for ice and vinegar, eight florins for the rods used, and four florins for the services of the soldiers detailed to act as nurses to the victims of the flogging. If a victim was on the point of fainting, he was given vinegar to smell, until he regained sufficient strength to bear the rest of the blows allotted to him: to flog an unconscious person would have been, of course, a waste of time and muscle. When the punishment was over, ice was rubbed on the bleeding welts and more vinegar was applied to the nostrils. But there are smarts deeper than the flesh can feel, wounds to pride and decency which will not close, and these were inflicted upon the Milanese by the brutal charges for ice, vinegar and rods.

The failure of the Italian Revolution of 1848 had made it clear to Count Cavour and other keen men in the peninsula that Italy could not hope to free herself from Austrian domination without foreign aid. So it was to attract the attention of Europe and pave the way for this foreign aid that Cavour caused a little Piedmontese army to be sent to participate against Russia in the Crimean War. After the War, in which the Piedmontese troops had won high praise for their valor, Cavour moved heaven and earth to have the Italian question brought before the Congress of Paris which had assembled to settle the terms of peace with Russia.

In his masterly biography of Cavour, William Roscoe Thayer gives a graphic account of what happened at the Congress of Paris when the Italian question was at last brought up.

102. THE ITALIAN QUESTION BROUGHT BEFORE THE CONGRESS OF PARIS, 1856 [1]

To meddle as little as possible in outside discussion . . . was the Emperor's true policy: but Cavour had driven his suggestion in so deep that the Italian problem haunted him, and on March 19, (1856) he consented that

[1] William Roscoe Thayer, *The Life and Times of Cavour.* 2 vols., Houghton Mifflin Company, vol. I, pp. 381–386.

it should be brought before the Congress. He stipulated, however, that the treaty of peace should be signed first, to prevent disputes over side issues from imperiling that. The sum of Cavour's labours therefore was to be only an unofficial airing of Italian grievances before a Congress which had finished its work and was impatient to adjourn!

On Sunday, March 30, the treaty was signed. Not until April 8 was held the session at which Walewski, " with a somewhat solemn air," remarked that although their definite tasks had been achieved, the French government thought it would be well for them to discuss, quite informally, some of the questions which might disturb the peace they had just made. . . .

Walewski then took up these questions, among them the problems of Italy.

Lord Clarendon spoke next. After touching briefly on the Greek troubles and deploring the excesses of the Belgian press, he turned to the affairs of Italy. The foreign occupation, he pointed out, was tending to become permanent. Although it had already lasted eight years the time for its ceasing seemed as far off as ever. It virtually upset the European equilibrium. That was a question which vitally interested all the Powers at the Congress — a problem which they ought to take immediate steps to solve. He recognized that the conditions of the Pope's government were such as to render it unsafe to withdraw foreign support at once. That government, he said emphatically, must be reformed from top to bottom. Clarendon had been growing more and more heated as he drew nearer and nearer to the heart of his subject: now he threw away reserve and gave free rein to his indignation. His was not the flash-in-the-pan fury of a shallow or theatrical nature: but the indignation of a self-controlled English thoroughbred, a statesman and diplomat who was by training not less than by temperament disinclined to rant. He drew up a terrible indictment against Pius the Ninth's government, going into details which he had learned not merely from Italian Liberal sources, but from England's accredited agents in Italy. He described with equal fire the corrupt administration and the misery and degradation of the people who were subjected to it. He declared squarely that the Papal government was the worst in the world — the shame of Europe. No Italian statesman, Cavour wrote the next day, could have drawn up an arraignment more powerful or more true: it sounded like the speech of a member of the Left in the Piedmontese Parliament. Lord Clarendon not merely approved Walewski's tentative criticism of the King of Naples, but asserted that, in spite of his own reluctance to interfere in the affairs of other countries, he believed it to be the duty of the Powers to compel King Ferdinand to listen to the voice of justice and of humanity. They ought, he said, to make their warnings so plain that Bomba [1] would be compelled to heed them.

[1] A nickname for King Ferdinand of Naples. (Editor's note.)

With what feelings Count Buol [1] listened to this onslaught can be imagined. He would have hurled back an angry denunciation, had he not deemed it more prudent to express his astonishment that topics had been introduced into the Congress quite foreign to its purpose. He had neither instructions to negotiate about them, nor even powers to discuss them. When he was told that he might telegraph his Court for advice, he replied peremptorily that he would never do that; and that he would urge his Emperor to refuse the request if it were made. President Walewski proved quite unable to soothe the surly Austrian, who had certainly taken a logical stand. When Russia's turn to speak came, Count Orloff said that, as he too lacked competence, he would say nothing. Baron Manteuffel, although also uninstructed, assured the Congress that Prussia was always ready to consult about questions which affected the peace of Europe: whereupon, he proceeded to complain against the abnormal condition of the Swiss Canton of Neuchâtel.

The word now fell to Cavour. At last, after nine years of tireless energy as publicist and statesman and after a life-time of unquenchable hope, he was to speak in behalf of Italy in a Congress of the European Powers. He had a hundred reasons for allowing passion to prompt his eloquence: the sufferings of his down-trodden countrymen and their needs; the insults, the thwarting, the defeats heaped upon his beloved Piedmont; the dynastic aspirations of the King he served; his own ambition, which had been baffled and might at any moment be ruined by the truculence of Austria in league with the craftiness of Rome; the conviction that the struggle he was waging rose above personal or dynastic or even national interests and involved civilization itself, by substituting for an old world order, grown corrupt and inefficient through age, new ideals, new methods for the uplifting of mankind — any of these considerations might have let loose a volley of invectives. And there nearly opposite, across the green table, as if to tempt him, sat Buol and Hübner, — taunting, defiant, supercilious, implacable, — the visible embodiment of that Austria who had cursed Italy for fifty years, had striven to exclude Piedmont from the Congress, and now waited impatiently for a chance to annihilate her.

Happily, Cavour listened to none of these promptings. Judging wisely that Lord Clarendon's volcanic explosion required no afterclap, he adopted a moderate tone, in which, while protesting formally against the conditions of Italy, he seemed to speak without rancor. Instead of vituperating the Austrian envoys, he began by acknowledging that they had a perfect right to keep out of this discussion, but he urged that it was most important for the welfare of Europe that the opinions of the Powers on the Italian situation should be publicly recorded. " The occupation of the Roman States," he said, confirming Clarendon's charges, " evidently tends to become permanent.

---

[1] Austria's representative at the Congress of Paris. (Editor's note.)

It has lasted for eight years, and there is no indication to lead us to suppose that it will ever end. Indeed, the causes — or the pretexts — which brought it about, subsist with the same force as at the epoch when it was begun. The condition of the Romagna, instead of improving, has grown worse: which is proved by the fact that Austria feels obliged to maintain the state of siege at Bologna and to use the same rigorous measures as when she entered that town. Such a state of things, contrary to the treaties, destroys the political balance in Italy and constitutes a very real danger for Piedmont. In fact, Austria, buttressed by Ferrara and by Piacenza, — whose fortifications she is working to increase, — contrary to the spirit if not to the letter of the treaty of Vienna, dominates the entire right bank of the Po, and, stretching along the Adriatic, she is the actual mistress of the larger part of Italy. The Powers in Congress assembled ought not by their silence to sanction such a state of affairs. Piedmont in particular, being especially menaced, must protest. For this reason I demand that the opinion of the plenipotentiaries of France and of Great Britain, as well as my formal protest, be inserted in the protocol." " Passing to the question of Naples," Cavour writes in his confidential summary of the debate, " I strongly supported what Lord Clarendon had said, adding that the conduct of the King, by discrediting royalty and making regular governments odious, strengthened the forces of the Revolutionary Party and constituted a veritable danger for the other Italian States."

Baron Hübner did not miss the opportunity to retort that Cavour had spoken of the Austrian occupation of the Papal States as if it were unique: why had he neglected to mention the French garrison in Rome? And speaking of occupations, how about the Piedmontese contingent in the Principality of Monaco? Cavour, however, could not be silenced by this apparent homethrust. He desired most heartily, he said, that every foreign soldier should be withdrawn from the Papal States: but he pointed out that there was a radical difference, so far as concerned the political equilibrium of Italy, between an isolated corps of French troops at Rome, and the occupation by the Austrians of provinces contiguous to Lombardy and Venetia. As for the Monaco affair, the Piedmontese " army " to which Hübner alluded consisted of fifty men; these he would willingly recall from Mentone and leave the Prince to the mercy of his subjects, provided " Piedmont is not held responsible for the ducking in the sea which the Prince would probably undergo."

After a few unimportant, scattering remarks from other members of the Congress, and an attempt by Walewski to sweeten its close by a spray of rose-water, the session adjourned. It took nearly a week of wrangling to draft the protocol. The Austrians fought to have every reference to the Italian Question expunged: the English and Cavour insisted that there should be no omission, and Walewski, instructed by the Emperor, sided with them.

Still, as finally made public, the official report of that stormy meeting, from which dates a new era in the affairs of Italy, is colorless and emasculate. But the truth spread through Paris by word of mouth, and by private despatches to all the Cabinets of Europe, and was soon commented upon in the press.

Cavour, who refrained throughout from overestimating the immediate gains to be won at the Congress, wrote: "Nevertheless, two facts will remain, which are not without some importance. First, the stigma branded on the conduct of the King of Naples by France and England in the face of united Europe; and, second, the condemnation aimed by England at the Clerical government in terms as precise and energetic as the most zealous Italian patriot could have desired." Having realized early in the negotiations that he could secure no material benefit, Cavour did not repine that Austria had been too stubborn and France too hesitating to grant some merely palliative measure. He rejoiced that Austria's stubbornness, made more offensive by Buol's personal truculence, must have irritated Napoleon and convinced him, "as I have had the honor to repeat to him several times, that the Italian Question admits of but one real, efficacious solution — the cannon."

Having attracted attention and enlisted sympathies at the Congress of Paris, Cavour proceeded to work on the feelings of Napoleon III to secure the help of France in driving Austria out of Italy. Finally the Emperor was won over. At Plombières in the Vosges Mountains where he and Cavour met on July 21, 1858, Napoleon agreed that France would aid Piedmont in a war against Austria, provided Austria attacked Piedmont.

In his Cavour, *Maurice Paléologue, distinguished French diplomat and man of letters, describes the situation on the eve of the Austro-Sardinian War.*

103. THE STAGE IS SET FOR THE AUSTRO-SARDINIAN WAR OF 1859 [1]

The preliminaries of the drama moved on apace, especially the negotiations for that "treaty of offensive and defensive alliance" for which the basis had been laid at Plombières. Everything was carried out in the most profound secrecy by Victor Emmanuel and Cavour, on the one side, and the Emperor and his cousin on the other; Nigra, by means of constant journeys, made an exchange of views possible.

On 24 December (1858), except for a few details of phraseology, the agreement was complete. The signatures alone were wanting. By the political

---

[1] Maurice Paléologue, *Cavour*. Translated by Ian F. D. Morrow and Muriel M. Morrow. London, Ernest Benn Limited, 1927, pp. 189–192.

treaty, to which were added military and financial conventions, France undertook to support Piedmont if she were attacked by Austria, the essential object of the alliance being to set Italy free from Austrian domination; when that had been done, Piedmont was to annex Lombardy, Venetia, the duchies of Parma and Modena, the Legations and the Marches; an independent kingdom was to be set up in the centre of the Peninsula, the authority of the Pope was to be maintained in the province of Rome, and the duchy of Savoy and county of Nice were to be annexed by France.

When the negotiations were at last completed, Napoleon III decided to reveal their existence to his Foreign Minister. In his consternation Walewski uttered a cry of alarm, " Sire, permit my devotion, which you cannot question, the privilege of telling you that you have committed yourself to a fatal course." He thereupon resigned. But an affectionate letter from his sovereign, and perhaps an even more intimate influence, decided him to recall his resignation. He followed his master on his " fatal course."

On 1 January 1859 the Diplomatic Corps in full uniform assembled at the Tuileries to present their homage to the Emperor Napoleon III. Affecting his most sibylline expression, the Emperor received with ceremonious coldness the compliments of the Papal Nuncio. But when the Austrian ambassador stood before him his eyes suddenly flashed, and in a slow and deliberate voice he uttered these words: " I regret that the relations between our two countries are not as good as formerly. Be good enough, however, to assure the Emperor Francis Joseph that my personal feelings towards him are unchanged." These grave words, uttered under circumstances so solemn on the threshold of the New Year, resounded immediately through the world with a sinister intonation.

It meant war — of course. Public opinion was infatuated with the idea. On the Paris Bourse business ceased. Funds fell, and the most solid securities depreciated.

Scarcely had the public mind become a little calmer when on 11 January a speech from the throne pronounced on the previous day at Turin caused universal consternation. It was still more grave than the words uttered to Hübner. " The year is beginning under a dark sky," said Victor Emmanuel. " Our situation is not without danger, for while we respect the treaties we cannot fail to hear the cry of distress which rises to our ears from so many parts of Italy. Strong in our union, confident in our good faith, we await with caution and resolution the decrees of Providence."

The general disquietude increased throughout Europe, and well-nigh a panic ensued. " They have fired the powder," said Prince Albert, who was awaiting the explosion from one day to the next. With unconcealed joy Cavour wrote to one of his collaborators: " We have at last caught Austria in a trap from which she can never escape without the firing of cannon."

The three great leaders of the Italian unification movement, Mazzini, Garibaldi, and Cavour, were men strikingly different in temperament. Mazzini was a prophet and a dreamer, impractical in action. Garibaldi was a rough, warm-hearted soldier, sensitive and often undiplomatic. Cavour was essentially a statesman and a diplomat, a practical man. Furthermore, Mazzini was an ardent republican, Cavour a convinced Monarchist. It was natural, then, for these men sometimes to work at cross-purposes and for antagonisms to develop.

When Garibaldi undertook his expedition of the Thousand against the Kingdom of Naples, in Sicily and southern Italy, in 1860, Cavour was alarmed lest all that had previously been accomplished toward the aggrandizement of Piedmont and the expulsion of Austria from Italy should be undone. So he refused to give the expedition his open support, thus offending many of Garibaldi's supporters.

In his Memoirs of Francesco Crispi, *who was one of the organizers of the expedition of the Thousand and who later became Prime Minister of Italy, Thomas Palamenghi-Crispi takes a distinctly unfavorable view of Cavour's attitude toward the expedition and severely criticizes his attitude toward Mazzini.*

104. *AN UNFAVORABLE VIEW OF CAVOUR'S ATTITUDE TOWARD GARIBALDI AND MAZZINI* [1]

The news of the departure of the Thousand for Sicily had caused much surprise. The Sardinian government itself was amazed when it became known that a handful of men had set out to conquer a State that was defended by sea by the strongest navy in Italy, and by land by a numerous and well-disciplined army. The thoughts of many flew to the noble folly of the Bandiera brothers and of Pisacane; while others suspected that Cavour had secretly aided Garibaldi in his advance towards what would probably prove total destruction, because the hero had become embarrassing to him. But the country in general, and especially the youth of the nation, in whom ideas of liberty and nationalism were fomenting hotly, saw only the heroic beauty of the action, and knowing little of the true state of Sicilian matters, anticipated not bloody defeat but splendid victory.

When the news of the successful landing became known, and was quickly followed by that of the victory at Calatafimi, where on the open field the Thousand had defeated regular troops three times as numerous as themselves,

[1] *The Memoirs of Francesco Crispi.* Translated by Mary Prichard-Agnetti, from the Documents collected and edited by Thomas Palamenghi-Crispi. 3 vols., London, Hodder and Stoughton, 1912, vol. I, pp. 237–241. (The extract is by Thomas Palamenghi-Crispi.)

a great flame of enthusiasm swept the peninsula. The impulse to hasten thither, to have a part in the glory, to help in some way, seized one and all, for all now knew that the time had come when Italy would indeed be made.

The Sardinian government was also quick to perceive this fact.

Revolution was shaping national destinies, and Count Cavour's chief anxiety was for the security and prestige of the Piedmontese monarchy. Diplomacy could ignore these events, for the "non-intervention policy" had been accepted by the whole of Europe. England would certainly not be opposed to a popular uprising in Italy — she who had encouraged Italy to fight her own battles against her oppressors. Louis Napoleon could not bring back as enemies those very troops whom, but the year before, he had brought as comrades to the Italians on the battlefields of Lombardy. But how about history? History would declare that the domination of the House of Savoy, of that small country at the foot of the Alps, had spread throughout Italy not by virtue of its own policy and prowess, but thanks to the strength of the people, directed by the revolution.

Personally also the haughty minister, conscious of his own worth, and proud of having forced this aged Europe to observe the fluttering in the breast of the sleeping beauty, about to awake — proud of having constrained the powers to accept the liberation of Lombardy, and furthermore of having prevented them from offering any resistance to the annexation by Piedmont of the small states of Central Italy — personally also Count Cavour must have experienced bitter humiliation on seeing the fruit he had believed to be still unripe about to be boldly gathered by the hand of another.

The state of Cavour's mind may therefore be easily imagined when the first fabulous news (the adjective is his own) reached him in Turin very shortly after the occurrence of the great events. He had not prevented the expedition — it would perhaps be more exact to say he had been unable to prevent it — but he had used every means in his power to persuade Garibaldi to relinquish it. For a year the General's friends among the Sicilian emigrants had been urging him to postpone the action in Sicily for an indefinite period, and even as late as the fifth of May (1860) several persons had repaired to Villa Spinola at Quarto to seek to dissuade him. But when he was once on his way, and the probability of success immediately became apparent, could Cavour persist in his disapproval? It would have been impossible indeed. Public sentiment became suddenly so inflamed by this triumphant audacity, and it so thoroughly roused the spirit of chivalry in Victor Emmanuel himself, that had Cavour not consented to support the undertaking he would have been forced to retire from government. He therefore lent it his support by openly tolerating enlistment, removing the ban of confiscation from the supplies of arms, offering no opposition to the sailing of ships from Genoa with volunteers, and granting various other favours. But although forced by the good conduct of the revolution to lend it his support, he had not relinquished any of his early animosity against it. Nevertheless, the moment had arrived when monarchy and revolution must cease to look askance at each other and join hands, for revolution was creating for monarchy what monarchy was incapable of creating for herself — Unity.

Cavour's animosity was indeed unjustifiable.

No one had any right to doubt Garibaldi's sincerity when he landed at Marsala with the Italian flag and in the name of Victor Emmanuel. Better than anyone else Cavour was acquainted with Garibaldi's personal devotion to the King; he knew of the letter the leader of the Thousand had despatched to the sovereign on setting out from Quarto, and was aware of his long-established conviction that the great majority of the people were not in favour of a republic, and his consequent declaration that he would contribute neither morally nor materially towards its establishment. Cavour was, moreover, aware that since 1849 Mazzini and Garibaldi had not been on good terms.

Nor could he doubt the monarchical sentiments of Garibaldi's lieutenants, of such men as Sirtori, Bixio, Türr, and others, no matter what their origin might have been, for he had always reckoned them among his own friends.

Crispi he knew only through police reports, which in all countries reveal only the darkest side. Had he taken the trouble to sift the truth of these reports he would have discovered an ardent patriot and a man of sterling characteristics in this Sicilian exile who was expelled from Piedmont in 1853, and forced to leave Turin — at the beginning of 1860. . . .

Cavour was equally unjust to Mazzini.

As long as the period of dark conspiracy against the existing order lasted, that is, conspiracy against those foreign governments that oppressed and those national governments that from prudence or weakness endured oppression — as long as the persistent propaganda for the principles of nationalism was based upon the republican ideal — the resentment against the formidable conspirator felt by men who judged the Italian problem by other standards, and with different sentiments, may easily be accounted for. But when, moved by the joy of seeing Italy delivered from the foreigner, and united, Mazzini publicly and privately renounced his prejudice, and in no ambiguous language, saying: "I will freely accept unity under the King — The dream of my life has ever been Unity!" — when it became manifest that, if a people in whom consciousness of their rights had been awakened had risen up in their pride of nation to achieve liberty, this praiseworthy action was due precisely to that persistent propaganda, then Cavour's attitude toward Mazzini ought to have become unbiassed and more just. But, on the contrary, he continued to regard Mazzini as the enemy. *Mazzinian* still remained a term of opprobrium, and stamped a man as dangerous, and the anti-Mazzinian phraseology of the conservatives, which had been formed during the long years of preparation, retained all its significance, all its strength. Mazzini therefore had much to suffer during the year 1860. The monarchical party continued to hate him; the ex-republicans who had sacrificed their early principles that Italy might be made were forced to drop him in order to avoid the accusation of insincerity. Had Cavour possessed a more generous spirit, instead of allowing him to be hunted like a beast of prey, he would have recognised the services Mazzini had rendered, the results of which were shining with so pure a light at the very time. He might even have been able, had he seized the solemn moment when Mazzini declared he would create no division by "talking republic," to hold him to these sentiments, and attach him definitely to that Italian monarchy which was being established by the suffrage of the entire nation. Thus the great epic of Italian Unity would have been enacted without the renewal of the story of Saturn in connection with one of its greatest workers.

In contrast with Palamenghi-Crispi's sharp criticism of Cavour stands the following laudatory estimate of the man and his achievements by Maurice Paléologue.

105. PALÉOLOGUE'S ESTIMATE OF CAVOUR AND HIS WORK[1]

Could Italy have been created without Cavour? It is as though one asked if the American Revolution could have been brought about without Washington. It becomes then a question of estimating the value of individual effort in the conduct of human affairs, the value of initiative, will-power, intellect, audacity, of one man's ability, at grips with the infinitely complex nature of the unknown forces that rule the world. It is no more than a paradox for Tolstoy to depict the great figures in history as puppets and tools, "having no influence upon the irresistible progress of events." On the other hand, has not Richelieu greatly exaggerated the efficacy of individual action, and is he not rather too regardless of the natural course of events when he declares in his trenchant way: "If they had imprisoned Luther whenever he began to preach, they would have had no Reformation?"

It would of course be useless to pretend that Cavour was the sole creator of the *Risorgimento*. Preparing through long ages, hidden during centuries in the heart of the people, heralded by all thinkers and poets since Dante and Petrarch, the awakening of Italy was preëminently a manifestation of the national spirit. But in the *Risorgimento,* as it was brought about under Cavour's leadership, there was nothing that was inevitable or pre-ordained,

[1] Maurice Paléologue, *Cavour.* Translated by Ian F. D. Morrow and Muriel M. Morrow. London, Ernest Benn Limited, 1927, pp. 296–298.

either in the method or the time of its accomplishment. Far from it. If the organisation and direction of the *Risorgimento* had remained in the hands of the revolutionaries, the national drama would have degenerated into barren chaos. The end would not have come for twenty or thirty years, and then only after many futile revolts, after many risings and conspiracies had been suppressed with bloodshed. From the day on which Cavour took charge, everything changed both in internal and in external affairs. Italian patriotism was disciplined under the banner of Savoy; a new spirit animated it; dissension, disunion, vain dreaming, gave way to ordered, logical, and practical action. Thenceforward, decisive events followed upon one another in logical sequence as if one gave birth to another. Thus the dispatch of an expeditionary corps to the Crimea led to participation in the Congress of Paris; to the interview at Plombières; to the Franco-Piedmontese Alliance of 28 January 1859; to Magenta and Solferino; to the Treaty of Zurich; to the annexation of the Duchies, of the Romagna, and of Tuscany; to the interview at Chamberg; to Castelfidardo; to Naples; to Palermo; and finally to the proclamation of the Kingdom of Italy. In this linked chain of events can we not see the guiding hand, the controlling mind?

An attempt to account for the special quality that enabled Cavour to obtain such results discloses that it was the union in him of faculties generally incompatible if they are especially keen. Daring with prudence, for example; flexibleness with opinionativeness; impetuous driving power with charming persuasiveness; methodical calculation with intuitive anticipation; keen intellect with potent inspiration; vivid imagination with cold reason; an equal aptitude for comprehending general ideas or positive facts; material interests and the interests of the common weal. The union of these attributes made him at one and the same time the man for national crisis and the man for orderly government. In the supreme hierarchy of statesmen none transcends him.

CHAPTER VIII

RUSSIA (1825–1881)

SECTION I. NIKOLAI I, 1825–1855

The new tsar, Nikolai I, a much younger brother of Alexander I, was born in 1796 and became acquainted with public affairs only after the liberal tide had ebbed at the Russian court. He was primarily a soldier, and he viewed all questions from the point of view of discipline, order, and the preservation of that which was. Alexander Herzen, the son of a wealthy nobleman, became, under French revolutionary and Decembrist influences, one of the chief leaders of a moderate socialist group, at first in Moscow University, later in a larger society. He left Russia in 1847, then thirty-five years old, and spent the rest of his life in Europe, editing the Kolokol, or Bell, a Russian periodical which had immense effect on thought in Russia up to the middle 'sixties. He died in 1870. His autobiography, from which these sketches are taken, is one of the warmest, most intimate, and most revealing personal records in all literature.

106. PICTURES OF THE ARCH-AUTOCRAT [1]

I HAD grown up with a great respect for Alexander, and recalled mournfully how I had seen him not long before in Moscow. When we were out walking, we had met him beyond the Tverskoy Gate; he was quietly riding along with two or three generals, returning from Hodynki, where there had been a review. His face was gracious, his features soft and rounded, his expression tired and melancholy. When he was on a level with us, I raised my hat, he bowed to me, smiling. What a contrast to Nicholas, who always looked like a slightly bald Medusa with cropped hair and moustaches. In the street, at the court, with his children and ministers, with his courtiers and maids of honour, he was incessantly trying whether his eyes had the power of a rattlesnake, of freezing the blood in the veins.

· · · · · · ·

After celebrating the execution [2] Nicholas made his triumphal entry into Moscow. I saw him then for the first time; he was on horseback riding beside

---

[1] Alexander Herzen, *My Past and Thoughts*. Translated from the Russian by Constance Garnett. 6 vols. London, Chatto & Windus, 1924–1927, vol. I, pp. 55, 63–64.

[2] The execution in 1826 of the *Dekabristi* or Decembrists.

a carriage in which the two empresses, his wife and Alexander's widow, were sitting. He was handsome, but there was a coldness about his looks; no face could have more mercilessly betrayed the character of the man than his. The sharply retreating forehead and the lower jaw developed at the expense of the skull were expressive of iron will and feeble intelligence, rather of cruelty than of sensuality; but the chief point in the face was the eyes, which were entirely without warmth, without a trace of mercy, wintry eyes. I do not believe that he ever passionately loved any woman, as Paul loved Anna Lopuhin, and as Alexander loved all women, except his wife; " he was favourably disposed to them," nothing more.

In the Vatican there is a new gallery in which Pius VII., I believe, has placed an immense number of statues, busts and statuettes, dug up in Rome and its environs. The whole history of the decline of Rome is there expressed in eyebrows, lips, foreheads; from the daughters of Augustus down to Poppaea, the matrons have succeeded in transforming themselves into co-cottes, and the type of cocotte is predominant and persists; the masculine type, surpassing itself, so to speak, in Antinous and Hermaphroditus, divides into two. On one hand there is sensual and moral degradation, low brows and features defiled by vice and gluttony, bloodshed and every wickedness in the world, petty as in the hetaira Heliogabalus, or with sunken cheeks like Galba; the last type is wonderfully reproduced in the King of Naples. . . . But there is another — the type of military commander in whom everything social and moral, everything human has died out, and there is left nothing but the passion for domination; the mind is narrow and there is no heart at all; they are the monks of the love of power; force and austere will is manifest in their features. Such were the Emperors of the Praetorian Guard and of the army, whom the turbulent legionaries raised to power for an hour. Among their number I found many heads that recalled Nicholas before he wore a moustache. I understand the necessity for these grim and inflexible guards beside what is dying in frenzy, but what use are they to what is youthful and growing?

The following picture of Nikolai's régime and what it did to Russia is by the famous Czech historian who later became first President of the Czechoslovak Republic.

107. THE PLAGUE ZONE UNDER NIKOLAI I [1] [2]

Strict subordination, unquestioning obedience, were Nicholas' system. In his psychology men were mere machines, or at most, animated slaves. " I

[1] Thomas G. Masaryk, *The Spirit of Russia*. Translated from the German by Eden and Cedar Paul. London, L. George Allen & Unwin, 1919, vol. I, 105–114 (condensed).

[2] The system of transliteration of Russian names used in this excerpt is that employed

regard the whole of human life as service," he said on one occasion. The anti-revolutionary mission of Russia therefore began with the reign of this " supreme lord of the narrow world," as Frederick William IV termed him. Žukovskii the poet, tutor to the next tsar, who was in Paris during the February revolution, in his letters to the heir to the throne eloquently pointed the moral that in the universal deluge Russia was the ark of salvation, not for herself alone, but for the rest of the world. Žukovskii hoped that the reigning tsar would keep his country remote from the European plague, would isolate it from the infection by building a Chinese wall. It was the unmistakable design of Providence that Russia should continue to constitute a separate and entirely independent world.

In European policy, Nicholas, like Alexander, was, therefore, protector of legitimism. He was the declared opponent of Louis Philippe, condemning as unlawful the French monarch's election and investiture of the bourgeoisie. It was in this spirit that in the year 1849 he sent troops to assist in suppressing the revolution in Hungary. In 1853 he ordered Serbia to dismiss the premier Garašanin (senior) because that statesman had been a pupil of Kossuth and Mazzini. Metternich's policy in Austria and Germany was a delight to Nicholas. He was not without objections to Napoleon III, but he accepted the coup d'état. Metternich, in turn, sought and found in Nicholas a protector against the revolution, of which he had himself been regarded as the chief opponent, and the Austrian chancellor came to terms with Russia in order to keep Germany and Italy dependent. In Europe Nicholas was admired by all conservatives and reactionaries, and by some actually worshipped, as for example by his brother-in-law Frederick William IV, who said: " I thank God upon my knees for having vouchsafed to me the profound grief I experience at the death of Tsar Nicholas, for having vouchsafed to me to be the tsar's faithful friend in the best sense of the word." Nicholas, for his part, was devoted to the kings of Prussia, highly esteeming Prussian accuracy and orderliness. He preferred Germans in the army and in the administration.

With Nicholas began the " plague zone which extended from 1825 to 1855 " (Herzen). Reaction became a carefully considered police system, the tsar in person assuming the office of chief superintendent of police, for this was the literal significance of the foundation in 1826 of the famous " third section of the departments under his majesty's immediate supervi-

---

by writers in those Slavic languages that use the Latin alphabet. Wherever they could, the editors have followed approximately the scheme in use at the British Museum, which is designed for readers of English. Except where it would seem pedantic, they have sought to keep the Russian form of names, instead of the English equivalents. In using passages from a variety of authors and translations, however, they have not ventured to alter the system of transliteration employed, hence the variations that may perplex but seem unavoidable.

sion," which down to the year 1880 was devoted to the attempt to gag Russia intellectually. The notorious Benckendorff, who had secured the tsar's favour through his zeal in the suppression of decabrism, was appointed chief of this institution. Later he also became chief of the gendarmerie, consecrating all his energies to the work of repression.

In this sketch it would be difficult to give an adequate idea of the abominable stupidity and provocative brutality that characterised reaction under Nicholas. For the utterance of liberal ideas conflicting with the official program, leading men were simply declared insane. This happened to Čaadaev and to a number of officers inclined towards revolutionary notions. In one case Nicholas had the death announced of a certain Engelhardt whose sentence had in reality been commuted to imprisonment for life; his wife was compelled to wear mourning; and the very number of his grave in the churchyard was entered in the records. When the poet Ševčenko and his associates were sentenced in 1847 as members of the slavophil Cyrillo-Methodian Union, the tsar aggravated the punishment in the case of Ševčenko, to whom the use of writing materials was denied. In his diary the poet complains that while the pagan Augustus permitted Ovid to write, this indulgence was forbidden to himself by the Christian ruler. Not merely was the tsar chief officer of police, but in his own exalted person he revised the sentences of the courts. In the year 1837 two Jews were condemned to death in Odessa because, from fear of the plague, they had attempted to escape across the frontier. Nicholas commuted the death penalty as follows: " The convicts are to run the gauntlet — a thousand men — twelve times. God be thanked, with us the death penalty has been abolished, and I will not reintroduce it." This is but one among numerous instances of the theocratic sovereign's power of self-deception and of his cruelty — for who had proposed that the decabrists should be quartered and who had commuted their punishment to hanging? In the year 1838 a student named Sočinskii gave the director of the surgical academy a box on the ear. He was sentenced to run the gauntlet — five hundred men — three times. Nicholas revised the sentence thus: " To be carried out in the presence of all the students of the academy. Subsequently the offender, instead of being sent to Siberia, is to spend ten years, wearing fetters, in the disciplinary battalion at Kronstadt." It is hardly necessary to add that though there was no capital punishment, the men thus sentenced died under the blows of the soldiers.

The severities of Nicholas were hardly credible. The wives of the decabrists who followed their husbands to Siberia were not permitted to return to Russia after the death of these; those among the decabrists who lived on into the reign of Alexander II received amnesty from that ruler. Only to one like Nicholas was it possible to have sane men declared insane, or to inflict upon Dostoevskii and the Petraševcy the tortures of a death sentence.

Herzen, too, and some of his acquaintances, suspected of Saint-Simonism, were arrested. They were condemned to death in the first instance, but by the tsar's clemency the sentences were commuted, first to imprisonment and subsequently to exile.

Here is an additional contribution to the psychology, perhaps it would be better to say the psychopathology, of Tsar Nicholas. A young man named Poleẑaev wrote a satire upon contemporary student life. The work was circulated in manuscript, and a copy fell into the hands of the emperor, who was especially incensed at the strictures upon the church and political institutions. He sent for the author and compelled him to read the composition aloud to himself and the minister for education. After a severe reprimand, wherein the writing was stigmatised as a product of decabrist sentiment, Nicholas kissed his victim upon the forehead and dismissed him with the sentence that he was to serve at the front, the minister's advocacy averting a worse issue. The tsar granted the offender the privilege of writing to his sovereign in order to recount progress on the right path. Poleẑaev availed himself of this privilege to beg for pardon, or at least for a mitigation of punishment, but his petitions were disregarded, and his biographers tell us how the unhappy man was tantalised, how in his despair he took to drink, and how finally in 1837 he died of consumption, at the age of two and thirty years. We learn from Poleẑaev's verses what the age of Nicholas seemed to reflective minds.

All independent thought was to be inexorably suppressed; higher education was to be reduced to the minimum of essential knowledge; philosophy and literature, attempts at general culture and at the attainment of a philosophic outlook upon the universe, were to be stifled in the germ. Count Uvarov, minister for education from 1833 to 1849, addressing the governing committees of the schools, announced his advent to office in the following terms: " It is our joint task to secure that the culture of the nation shall be carried on in the unified spirit of Orthodoxy, autocracy and patriotism." Yet more thoroughly did Uvarov, in the course of the same year, formulate this trinitarian doctrine as " the main principle of the social system of education," writing as follows: " Amid the rapid decay of religious and civil institutions in Europe, amid the widespread diffusion of revolutionary ideas, it becomes our duty to establish the foundations of the fatherland so firmly that they cannot be shaken. We must find a basis from which right conduct can spring; we must discover energies which will develop the distinctive characteristics of Russia, and will ultimately enable our country to assemble the sacred heritage of nationality into a compact whole, to which we must anchor our salvation. How fortunate is it that Russia has preserved ardent faith in those saving principles in default of which right conduct is impossible, without which an energetic and worthy life is unknown. A Russian devoted to his fatherland is as little willing to permit the subtraction of a single dogma from our Orthodox faith as he would be to allow the theft of a pearl from the crown of Monomachus. Autocracy is the main condition of Russia's political existence. In conformity with these two national bases is the third basis, equally important and equally strong — patriotism."

The official program of reaction — Orthodoxy, autocracy, and patriotism — had thus been formulated. To the present day this program constitutes the alpha and omega of official political wisdom; it is the program of the Russian theocracy, which declares the tsar's will a divine revelation, and deduces bureaucratic politics and administration from God's will thus revealed. In the first section of the fundamental law of 1832 (it became section 4 when the law was re-edited in 1906), autocracy is defined in the following terms: "The tsar of all the Russias is an autocratic and absolute monarch. God himself commands us to obey the tsar's supreme authority, not from fear alone, but as a point of conscience." The theocratic relationship of the tsar to the church is thus defined: "The Russian tsar, as a Christian sovereign, is supreme protector and defender of the dogmas of the Greco-Russian faith and supervisor of Orthodoxy and of good order in general throughout holy church. In this sense he is spoken of as the head of the church." (Fundamental Law of 1906, Section 64.)

Similarly Filaret, authoritative exponent of church doctrine under Alexander II, redefined the divine mission of the tsar in the sense of the *Stoglav,* saying: "God has given us the autocratic tsar after the image of His own universal dominion."

Peter the Great had proposed to establish at the academy a chair of natural law. Under Nicholas, in the year 1849, legal proceedings were taken against Solncev, professor at the university of Kazan, because he had deduced the principles of law from the healthy human reason instead of from the gospels.

To Peter, the church was no more than means to an end, and he was little concerned about his subjects' inner convictions. The same may be said of the empresses who succeeded Peter, for even under Catherine II reaction remained incomplete. In the reign of Alexander I closer supervision of the schools and of literature had begun; and attempts had been made at the radical extirpation of Voltairism. Nicholas, however, was the first tsar to adapt his mentality to religion (though not indeed in every respect!) that he might be enabled to exploit the church effectively for his own ends. At his court there was no place for Krüdener and other prophets; Photius was to rule men's minds. Even Photius was not a persona grata to Nicholas, and no long time elapsed before the tsar dismissed Arakčeev. The autocrat was strong enough to assume for himself the rôles of Photius and Arakčeev. There can be no doubt that his firmness of will contributed to make him appear the born autocrat.

By religion Nicholas chiefly understood fear of the Lord; the Lord was conceived by him as an anthropomorphic being, simultaneously God and tsar. In the training colleges for cadets the priests were to suggest to their pupils that the greatness of Christ had been displayed above all in His submission to the government, in the way in which He had shown Himself to be " an example of obedience and discipline." To the army recruits, who had to look forward to a term of service lasting twenty-five years, the chaplains preached: " God chooses men for all professions as He wills. You are chosen and destined for the military career by the will of God. . . . God wills that you shall serve God and the great tsar as soldiers. . . . Before you were born, it was God's determination that you should become warriors."

Military discipline prevailed in the schools. Count Protasov, a cavalry general, was appointed chief procurator of the synod in 1836 and held office until 1855. Army discipline was introduced into the seminaries. " I know only the tsar," was his favourite saying. Nevertheless he found place in the curriculum for the " revolutionary " natural sciences, since as a soldier he recognised their value.

Nicholas desired in good earnest to realise Uvarov's formula. Russia had the advantage over Europe of possessing the only true faith, and uniformity of religious belief was to prevail. The outcome of this ecclesiastical policy was the adoption of harsh police measures against the raskolniki and other sectaries, such as the dukhobors; and it was the same policy which induced the enforcement of religious uniformity.

Hardly had Nicholas become tsar when he abolished the chair of philosophy at Moscow university. Driving past the university on one occasion, looking very serious, he pointed to the building and said, " There is the wolf's den." The less developed universities were dealt with in accordance with this estimate. A fuller activity had begun at the universities during the liberal epoch of Alexander I, with the issue of the studies' ordinance of 1804, although even then the police outlook towards these institutions was not abandoned. In 1835 Uvarov reorganised the universities in conformity with his general program, making the study of theology and ecclesiastical history obligatory in all faculties. In 1850, owing to the alarm inspired by the revolution of 1848, certain disciplines, and notably the study of European constitutional law, were banished from the university as deleterious; whilst philosophy was reduced to courses upon logic and psychology which had in future to be delivered by theologians, the pretext given for the change being " the blameworthy development of this science by German professors." The historian Granovskii was not permitted to lecture on the reformation. The number of students was restricted to three hundred. The object of universities was announced to be, " the education of loyal sons for the Orthodox church, of loyal subjects for the tsar, and of good and useful citizens for the fatherland."

Reform of the higher schools (1847) was effected in conformity with the restrictions imposed on the universities. The study of classical tongues was discontinued lest youth should be corrupted by the reading of Greek authors who had written in republics.

The history of recent Russian literature is filled with stories of the oppression which great writers had to suffer under Alexander and still more under Nicholas. The work of Griboedov, Puškin, Lermontov, and Gogol was hindered in every possible way. Banishment was a frequent penalty. Books were mutilated by the censorship. Newspapers were suppressed.

The events of 1848 caused intense anxiety to Nicholas, and a regular witches' sabbath of reaction was inaugurated. The members of the Petraševcy group (the two Dostoevskiis, Plesčeev, Durov, etc.) were all prosecuted; measures were taken against Saltykov; Ostrovskii, Turgenev, Kirěevskii, Homjakov, and Herzen, successively fell into disfavour — Turgenev's offence being an obituary notice of Gogol! It was forbidden to mention the very name of Bělinskii, and those who wished to refer to him had to employ circumlocutions!

Censorship was developed to an almost incredible extent. There were twenty-two distinct censorships. Criticism of the government and of official proceedings was absolutely prohibited. Even those who at a later date were considered pillars of reaction, even such men as Bulgarin, were now suspect as revolutionaries; Pogodin suffered the same fate; to the ultra-reactionaries Uvarov actually seemed insufficiently reactionary, and he had to resign his position as minister for education. Upon a ministerial report which concluded with the word "progress," Nicholas wrote the comment, "Progress? What progress? This word must be deleted from official terminology."

Such intensity of reaction was only possible because society ("society" still meaning the aristocracy alone) had completely abandoned the enlightened and humanitarian ideas that culminated in the decabrist revolt. Nicholas I was possible because such men as Prince Vjazamskii and Puškin had become afraid of "jacobinism," and because Gogol had been able to torment and starve himself back into Orthodoxy.

Although Nikolai proclaimed aloud his abhorrence of a secret police, he welcomed the following memorandum, and on it based the organization of the so-called "Third Section."

108. THE THIRD SECTION OF THE IMPERIAL CHANCERY [1]

The events of the 14th of December, and the horrible plots which for more than ten years have led up to this explosion, are sufficient proof of

[1] Memorandum (in French) of Benckendorff to Nicholas I. N. K. Shilder, *Imperator Nikolai Pervyi evo zhizn i tsarstvovanie.* St. Petersburg, 1903, vol. I, pp. 780–781.

the incapacity of the police of the Empire, and also of the urgent need of organizing a system according to a plan well thought out and zealously acted on. A secret police is not always possible; honest men are frightened by it and knaves see through it.

The opening of letters is already a function of the police inspectors and an important one. . . . For that it is necessary to have in certain places heads of postal bureaus who are honest and of proved loyalty. . . .

In order that the police may be effective and cover the entire extent of the Empire, they must have a known headquarters with branches stretching out to all points; they must be feared and they must be respected for the moral qualities of their chief.

He should have the title of Minister of Police and Inspector of Military and Provincial Gendarmes. This title alone will give him the confidence of all honest people who would like to warn the government of plots or give it important information. Scoundrels, conspirators, and dupes who repent of their mistakes or seek to buy their pardon by confession, will know where to go.

With this title he would secure the coöperation of all officers of the police scattered in all the towns of the Empire and all divisions of the army; he could place intelligent men there and employ clean men (*hommes purs*), who often, finding the rôle of a disguised spy repugnant, in uniform will devote themselves to this task, which makes them coöperators with the government.

Promotions, crosses, citations, give more encouragement to the officer than sums of money to secret agents, who frequently play a double game of spying both for and on the government. The Minister of Police should travel every year, visiting from time to time the great fairs and sales where he might easily establish useful contacts with men who are greedy for money, and so tempt them.

If he is wise he will give his confidence to no one. Even the head of the chancery should not know all the agents employed or their connections.

His personal interest, the fear of losing a position that ought to be very lucrative to him, will assure the loyalty of this chief of the chancery as regards those matters that he absolutely must be cognizant of.

Krylov (1768–1844), the great fable writer, never espoused radical ideas and always retained court favor, yet he did express his opinion of the corruption of both the tsar's officials and his courts.

109. THE PEASANTS' CHANCE OF JUSTICE[1]

THE PIKE

Against a pike was lodged the plaint: —
He'd made the pond a home unpleasant;
It was a reason for restraint,
And, that the rogue in person should be present,
He, from the water, in a tub was brought.
The magistrates nearby, collecting,
In a rich meadow pasture sought,
Here is a list of those the captive's case affecting:
Two asses gathered there,
Two ancient, sorry horses and of goats a pair,
While also, as a general inspector,
A fox was of the prosecution the director.
Among the people, rumour said: —
This pike supplied the fox with fish: his table spread.
Nevertheless, the judges were in no way partial;
Letting no wile or trend of vulpine tricks
Obscure their crystal vision, they must fix
Upon a judgment free from politics;
Against the guilty one their forces marshall,
And sinners to deter, suspend him from a beam.
" My lord," pronounced the fox, " I am for death as sentence;
Hanging is over good, despite the rogue's repentance;
The punishment should be remarkable, extreme;
To make a wicked life both dangerous and frightful,
The pike should now be drowned." " A verdict rightful,"
Exclaimed the judges, " surely no way spiteful,"
And threw the pike into a stream.

THE PEASANTS AND THE RIVER

Peasants, who cursed in consternation
　　　　The devastation
Wrought by the rivulets and streams,
At the Spring flooding; not half-hearted
But keen for satisfaction, nursing pleasant dreams,
Unto the River that received such brooks, departed.

[1] Ivan A. Krilov, *Fables*. Translated from Russian by C. F. Coxwell. London, Kegan Paul, Trench, Trubner & Co., n.d. pp. 40–41, 100–101.

Oh! to denounce them there was cause,
For here the crops were scattered;
Too, that the mills were washed away, such mattered;
Counting drowned beasts, one could not pause.
Yet peacefully the River flowed and hastened proudly!
How on its banks men, women sped
        And nothing said
Against it e'er of evil loudly!
Its size the peasants touches, wears
Away their anger, undermines their reason.
When they have nearer come, they gaze, at that sad season,
And surely know the River's treason.
Shamefully half their goods away it bears!
Yet, never troubling it with their affairs,
The simple peasants watched its course with silent glances;
Then at each other gave a look,
Their heads slow shook,
And the road took
Homewards! They deemed, 'mid life's mischances,
To struggle 'gainst oppressors is but useless toil,
If base superiors are sharers in the spoil!

Before his long and final exile in Europe, Herzen was sent away to Eastern Russia, where he saw much of local officials and their ways. The following is typical enough.

110. THE PLUNDERING OFFICIAL[1]

Gogol lifted one corner of the curtain and showed us Russian officialdom in all its ugliness; but Gogol cannot help conciliating by his laughter; his immense comic talent gets the upper hand of his indignation. Moreover, in the fetters of the Russian censorship, he could scarcely touch upon the melancholy side of that foul underworld, in which the destinies of the unhappy Russian people are forged.

There, somewhere in grimy offices, from which we make haste to get away, shabby men write and write on grey paper, and copy on to stamped paper — and persons, families, whole villages are outraged, terrified, ruined. A father is sent into exile, a mother to prison, a son for a soldier, and all this breaks like a thunderclap upon them, unexpected, for the most part undeserved. And for the sake of what? For the sake of money. A tribute must be paid . . . or an inquiry will be held concerning some dead drunkard,

[1] Alexander Herzen, *My Past and Thoughts*. Translated from the Russian by Constance Garnett. 6 vols. London, Chatto & Windus, 1924–1927, vol. I, 295–296, 304–310.

burnt up by spirits and frozen to death. And the head-man collects and the village elder collects, the peasants bring their last kopeck. The police-inspector must live; the police-captain must live and keep his wife too; the councillor must live and educate his children, the councillor is an exemplary father.

.   .   .   .

Among my acquaintances was one venerable old man, a police-captain dismissed from his position by a Committee of Inquiry instituted by the Senators' revision. He spent his time drawing up petitions and getting up cases, which was just what he was forbidden to do. This man, who had been in the service immemorial ages, had stolen, doctored official documents, and collected false evidence in three provinces, twice been tried, and so on. This veteran of the rural police liked to tell amazing anecdotes about himself and his colleagues, not concealing his contempt for the degenerate officials of the younger generation.

" They're giddy-pates," he said; " of course they take what they can get, there is no living without it, but it is no use looking for cleverness or knowledge of the law in them. I'll tell you, for instance, about one friend of mine. He was a judge for twenty years and only died last year. He was a man of brains! And the peasants don't remember evil against him, though he has left his family a bit of bread. He had quite a special way of his own. If a peasant came along with a petition, the judge would admit him at once and be as friendly and pleasant as you please.

" ' What is your name, uncle, and what was your father's? '

" The peasant would bow and say, ' Yermolay, sir, and my father was called Grigory.'

" ' Well, good health to you, Yermolay Grigoryevitch, from what parts is the Lord bringing you here? '

" ' We are from Dubilovo.'

" ' I know, I know. You have a mill, I fancy, on the right from the track.'

" ' Yes, sir, the mill of our commune.'

" ' A well-to-do village; the land is good, black soil.'

" ' We don't complain against God, kind sir.'

" ' Well, that is as it should be. I'll be bound you have a good-sized family, Yermolay Grigoryevitch? '

" ' Three sons and two daughters, and I have married the elder to a young fellow who has been with us five years.'

" ' I daresay you have grandchildren by now? '

" ' Yes, there are little ones, your honour.'

" ' And thank God for it! increase and multiply. Well, Yermolay Grigoryevitch, it is a long way you have come, let us have a glass of birch wine.'

" The peasant makes a show of refusing. The judge fills a glass for him, saying, 'Nonsense, nonsense, my man, the holy Fathers have nothing against wine and oil today.'

" 'It's true there is nothing against it, but wine brings a man to every trouble.' Then he crosses himself, bows, and drinks the birch wine.

" 'With such a family, Grigoryevitch, I'll be bound life is hard? To feed and clothe every one of them you can't manage with one wretched nag or cow; there would not be milk enough.'

" 'Upon my word, sir, what could I do with only one horse? I have three, I did have a fourth, a roan, but it was bewitched about St. Peter's fast; the carpenter in our village, Dorofey, may God be his judge, hates to see another man well off and has an evil eye.'

" 'It does happen, it does happen. And you have big grazing lands, of course; I'll be bound you keep sheep?'

" 'To be sure, we have sheep too.'

" 'Ah, I've been too long talking with you. It's the Tsar's service, Yermolay Grigoryevitch, it is time I was in the Court. Had you come about some little business or what?'

" 'Yes, your honour.'

" 'Well, what is it? some quarrel? Make haste and tell me, old man! it is time I was going.'

" 'Well, kind sir, trouble has come upon me in my old age. Just at Assumption, we were in the tavern and came to high words with a peasant of a neighbouring village, such a mischievous man, he is always stealing our wood. We had hardly said a word before he swung his fist and gave me a punch in the chest. "Keep your blows for your own village," I said to him, and just to make an example, I would have given him a push, but being drunk perhaps, or else it was the devil in it, hit him in the eye — and, well, I spoilt his eye, and he is gone with the church elder straight to the inspector — wants to have me up to be tried in the court.'

" While he tells this story, the judge — our Petersburg actors are nothing to him — grows graver and graver, makes his eyes look dreadful, and does not say a word.

" The peasant sees and turns pale, lays his hat at his feet and takes out a towel to mop his face. The judge still sits silent and turns over the leaves of a book.

" 'So I have come here to you, kind sir,' says the peasant in a changed tone.

" 'What can I do in the matter? What a position! And what did you hit him in the eye for?'

" 'That's true indeed, sir, what for. . . . The evil one confounded me.'

" 'It's a pity! a great pity! to think that a household must be ruined! Why, what will become of the family without you, all young people and little grandchildren, and I am sorry for your old woman, too.'

" The peasant's legs begin to tremble.

" ' Well, kind sir, what have I brought on myself ? '

" ' Look here, Yermolay Grigoryevitch, read for yourself . . . or perhaps you are no great reader ? Well, here is the article on maiming and mutilation . . . to be punished by flogging and exile to Siberia.'

" ' Don't let a man be ruined! Don't destroy a Christian! Cannot something be done ? . . .'

" ' What a fellow! Can we go against the law ? Of course, it is all in human hands. Well, instead of thirty strokes we might give five.'

" ' But about Siberia ? . . .'

" ' That's not in our power to decide, my good man.'

" ' The peasant pulls out of his bosom a little bag, takes out of the bag a bit of paper, out of the paper two and then three gold pieces, and with a low bow lays them on the table.

" ' What's this, Yermolay Grigoryevitch ? '

" ' Save me, kind sir.'

" ' Nonsense, nonsense, what do you mean ? Sinful man that I am, I do sometimes accept a token of gratitude. My salary is small, so one is forced to, but if one accepts it, it must be for something! How can I help you ? It would be a different thing if it were a rib or a tooth, but a blow in the eye! Take your money back.'

" The peasant is crushed.

" ' I'll tell you what; shall I talk to my colleagues and write to the governor's office ? Very likely the case will come into the courts of justice, there I have friends, they can do anything, only they are a different sort of people, you won't get off for three gold pieces there.'

" The peasant begins to recover his faculties.

" ' You needn't give me anything. I am sorry for your family, but it is no use your offering them less than two grey notes.'

" ' But, kind sir, as God is above, I don't know where I am to turn to get such a mint of money — four hundred roubles — these are hard times.'

" ' Yes, I expect it is difficult. We could diminish the punishment in view of your penitence, and taking into consideration that you were not sober . . . and, there, you know people get on all right in Siberia. There is no telling how far you may have to go. . . . Of course, if you were to sell a couple of horses and one of the cows, and the sheep, you might make it up. But it would take you a time to make up that money again! On the other hand, if you do keep the horses, you'll have to go off yourself to the ends of the earth. Think it over, Grigoryevitch; there is no hurry, we can wait till tomorrow, but it is time I was going,' adds the judge, and puts the gold pieces he had refused into his pocket, saying, ' This is quite unnecessary. I only take it not to offend you.'

"Next morning you may be sure the old screw brings three hundred and fifty roubles in all sorts of old-fashioned coins to the judge.

"The judge promises to look after his interests: the peasant is tried and tried and properly scared and then let off with some light punishment, or with a warning to be careful in future, or with a note that he is to be kept under police supervision, and he remembers the judge in his prayers for the rest of his life.

"That's how they used to do in old days," the discharged police-inspector told me; "they did things properly."

The peasants of Vyatka are, generally speaking, not very long-suffering, and for that reason the officials consider them fractious and troublesome. The rural police find their real gold mine in the Votyaks, the Mordvahs, and the Tchuvashes; they are pitiful, timid, dull-witted people. Police-inspectors pay double to the governor for appointments in districts populated by these Finnish tribes.

The police and the officials do incredible things with these poor creatures. If a land-surveyor crosses a Votyak village on some commission, he invariably halts in it, takes an astrolabe out of his cart, sticks a post into the ground and stretches a chain. Within an hour the whole village is in a turmoil. "The surveyors, the surveyors!" the peasants say with the horror with which in 1812 they used to say, "The French, the French!" The village elder comes with the commune to do homage. And the surveyor measures everything and writes it down. The elder entreats him not to measure, not to do them injury. The surveyor demands twenty or thirty roubles. The Votyaks are greatly relieved, they collect the money — and the surveyor goes on to the next Votyak village.

If a dead body comes into the hands of the police, they take it about with them for a fortnight, if it is frosty weather, from one Votyak village to another, and in each one declare that they have just picked it up, and that an inquest and inquiry will be held in their village. The Votyaks buy them off.

SECTION II. ALEXANDER II, 1855–1881

Prince Peter Kropotkin (1842–1920) gives in his Memoirs *a picture of life on a country estate and in a nobleman's town house in the closing days of serfdom. Bondage is shown here, not at its worst, but at its best.*

III. LIFE IN TOWN AND COUNTRY [1]

To maintain such numbers of servants as were kept in our house would have been simply ruinous, if all provisions had to be bought in Moscow;

[1] Peter Kropotkin, *Memoirs of a Revolutionist*. Boston, Houghton Mifflin Company, 1899, pp. 36–51 (much condensed).

but in those times of serfdom things were managed very simply. When winter came, father sat at his table and wrote the following:—

"To the manager of my estate, Nikólskoye, situated in the government of Kalúga, district of Meschóvsk, on the river Siréna, from the Prince Alexéi Petróvich Kropótkin, Colonel and Commander of various orders.

"On receipt of this, and as soon as winter communication is established, thou art ordered to send to my house, situated in the city of Moscow, twenty-five peasant-sledges, drawn by two horses each, one horse from each house, and one sledge and one man from each second house, and to load them with (so many) quarters of oats, (so many) of wheat, and (so many) of rye, as also with all the poultry and geese and ducks, well frozen, which have to be killed this winter, well packed and accompanied by a complete list, under the supervision of a well-chosen man;" and so it went on for a couple of pages, till the next full stop was reached. After this there followed an enumeration of the penalties which would be inflicted in case the provisions should not reach the house situated in such a street, number so and so, in due time and in good condition.

Some time before Christmas the twenty-five peasant sledges really entered our gates, and covered the surface of the wide yard.

"Frol!" shouted my father, as soon as the report of this great event reached him. "Kiryúshka! Yegórka! Where are they? Everything will be stolen! Frol, go and receive the oats! Uliána, go and receive the poultry! Kiryúshka, call the princess!"

All the household was in commotion, the servants running wildly in every direction, from the hall to the yard, and from the yard to the hall, but chiefly to the maid-servants' room, to communicate there the Nikólskoye news: "Pásha is going to marry after Christmas. Aunt Anna has surrendered her soul to God," and so on. . . .

When the sledges had been unloaded, the hall filled with peasants. They had put on their best coats over their sheepskins, and waited until father should call them into his room to have a talk about the snow and the prospects of the next crops. They hardly dared to walk in their heavy boots on the polished floor. A few ventured to sit down on the edge of an oak bench; they emphatically refused to make use of chairs. So they waited for hours, looking with alarm upon every one who entered father's room or issued from it.

.   .   .   .

Our best time, of course was in the country. As soon as Easter and Whitsuntide had passed, all our thoughts were directed toward Nikólskoye. However, time went on,— the lilacs must be past blooming at Nikólskoye,— and father had still thousands of affairs to keep him in town. At last, five or six peasant-carts entered our yard: they came to take all sorts of things which had to be sent to the country-house. The great old coach and the other coaches in which we were going to make the journey were taken out and inspected once more. The boxes began to be packed. Our lessons made slow progress; at every moment we interrupted our teachers, asking whether this or that book should be taken with us, and long before all others we began packing our books, our slates, and the toys that we ourselves had made.

Everything was ready: the peasant-carts stood heavily loaded with furniture for the country-house, boxes containing the kitchen utensils, and almost countless empty glass jars which were to be brought back in the autumn filled with all kinds of preserves. The peasants waited every morning for hours in the hall; but the order for leaving did not come. Father continued to write all the morning in his room, and disappeared at night. Finally, our stepmother interfered, her maid having ventured to report that the peasants were very anxious to return, as haymaking was near.

Next afternoon, Frol, the major-domo, and Mikhael Aléeff, the first violin, were called into father's room. A sack containing the "food money" — that is, a few coppers a day — for each of the forty or fifty souls who were to accompany the household to Nikólskoye, was handed to Frol, with a list. All were enumerated in that list: the band in full; then the cooks and the under-cooks, the laundresses, the under-laundress who was blessed with a family of six mites, " Polka Squinting," " Domna the Big One," " Domna the Small One," and the rest of them.

The first violin received an "order of march." I knew it well, because father, seeing that he never would be ready, had called me to copy it into the book in which he used to copy all " outgoing papers ": —

" To my house servant, Mikhael Aléeff, from Prince Alexéi Petróvich Kropótkin, Colonel and Commander.

" Thou art ordered, on May 29th, at six A.M., to march out with my loads, from the city of Moscow, for my estate, situated in the government of Kalúga, district of Meschóvsk, on the river Siréna, representing a distance of one hundred and sixty miles from this house; to look after the good conduct of the men entrusted to thee, and if any one of them proves to be guilty of misconduct or of drunkenness or of insubordination, to bring the said man before the commander of the garrison detachment of the separate corps of the interior garrisons, with the inclosed circular letter, and to ask that he may be punished by flogging (the first violin knew who was meant), as an example to the others.

" Thou art ordered, moreover, to look especially after the integrity of the goods entrusted to thy care, and to march according to the following order: First day, stop at village So and So, to feed the horses; second day, spend the night at the town of Podólsk;" and so on for all the seven or eight days that the journey would last.

Next day, at ten instead of six, — punctuality is not a Russian virtue

("Thank God, we are not Germans," true Russians used to say),—the carts left the house. The servants had to make the journey on foot; only the children were accommodated with a seat in a bath-tub or basket, on the top of a loaded cart, and some of the women might find an occasional resting-place on the rim of a cart. The others had to walk all the hundred and sixty miles. As long as they were marching through Moscow, discipline was maintained: it was peremptorily forbidden to wear top-boots, or to pass a belt over the coat. But when they were on the road, and we overtook them a couple of days later, and especially when it was known that father would stay a few days longer at Moscow, the men and the women—dressed in all sorts of impossible coats, belted with cotton handkerchiefs, burned by the sun or dripping under the rain, and helping themselves along with sticks cut in the woods—certainly looked more like a wandering band of gypsies than the household of a wealthy landowner. Similar peregrinations were made by every household in those times, and when we saw a file of servants marching along one of our streets, we at once knew that the Apúkhutins or the Pryánishnikoffs were migrating.

The carts were gone, yet the family did not move. All of us were sick of waiting; but father still continued to write interminable orders to the managers of his estates, and I copied them diligently into the big "outgoing book." At last the order to start was given. We were called downstairs. My father read aloud the order of march, addressed to "the Princess Kropótkin, wife of Prince Alexéi Petróvich Kropótkin, Colonel and Commander," in which the halting-places during the five days' journey were duly enumerated. True, the order was written for May 30, and the departure was fixed for nine A.M., though May was gone, and the departure took place in the afternoon: this upset all calculations. But, as is usual in military marching-orders, this circumstance had been foreseen, and was provided for in the following paragraph:—

"If, however, contrary to expectation, the departure of your highness does not take place at the said day and hour, you are requested to act according to the best of your understanding, in order to bring the said journey to its best issue."

Then, all present, the family and the servants, sat down for a moment, signed themselves with the cross, and bade my father good-by. "I entreat you, Alexis, don't go to the club," our stepmother whispered to him. The great coach, drawn by four horses, with a postilion, stood at the door, with its little folding ladder to facilitate climbing in; the other coaches also were there. Our seats were enumerated in the marching-orders, but our step-mother had to exercise "the best of her understanding" even at that early stage of the proceedings, and we started to the great satisfaction of all.

The journey was an inexhaustible source of enjoyment for us children.

The stages were short, and we stopped twice a day to feed the horses. As the ladies screamed at the slightest declivity of the road, it was found more convenient to alight each time the road went up or down hill, which it did continually, and we took advantage of this to have a peep into the woods by the roadside, or a run along some crystal brook. The beautifully kept highroad from Moscow to Warsaw, which we followed for some distance, was covered, moreover, with a variety of interesting objects: files of loaded carts, groups of pilgrims, and all sorts of people. Twice a day we stopped in big, animated villages, and after a good deal of bargaining about the prices to be charged for hay and oats, as well as for the samovars, we dismounted at the gates of an inn. Cook Andréi bought a chicken and made the soup, while we ran in the meantime to the next wood, or examined the yard of the great inn.

. . . .

Beyond Kalúga we had to cross for a stretch of five miles a beautiful pine forest, which remains connected in my memory with some of the happiest reminiscences of my childhood. The sand in that forest was as deep as in an African desert, and we went all the way on foot, while the horses, stopping every moment, slowly dragged the carriages in the sand. When I was in my teens, it was my delight to leave the family behind, and to walk the whole distance by myself. Immense red pines, centuries old, rose on every side, and not a sound reached the ear except the voices of the lofty trees. In a small ravine a fresh crystal spring murmured, and a passer-by had left in it, for the use of those who should come after him, a small funnel-shaped ladle, made of birch bark, with a split stick for a handle. Noiselessly a squirrel ran up a tree and the underwood was as full of mysteries as were the trees. In that forest my first love of nature and my first dim perception of its incessant life were born.

Beyond the forest, and past the ferry which took us over the Ugrá, we left the highroad and entered narrow country lanes, where green ears of rye bent toward the coach, and the horses managed to bite mouthfuls of grass on either side of the way, as they ran, closely pressed to one another in the narrow, trenchlike road. At last we caught sight of the willows which marked the approach to our village, and all of a sudden we saw the elegant pale yellow bell tower of the Nikólskoye church.

For the quiet life of the landlords of those times Nikólskoye was admirably suited. There was nothing in it of the luxury which is seen in richer states; but an artistic hand was visible in the planning of the buildings and gardens, and in the general arrangement of things. Besides the main house, which father had recently built, there were, round a spacious and well-kept yard, several smaller houses, which, while they gave a greater degree of independence to their inhabitants, did not destroy the close intercourse of the family life. An immense "upper garden" was devoted to fruit trees, and through it the church was reached; the southern slope of the land, which led to the river, was entirely given up to a pleasure garden, where flower-beds were intermingled with alleys of lime-trees, lilacs, and acacias. From the balcony of the main house there was a beautiful view of the river, with the ruins of an old earthen fortress where the Russians offered a stubborn resistance during the Mongol invasion, and further on a great area of yellow grain-fields bordered on the horizon by woods. . . .

Large parties were organized, also, in which all the family took part, sometimes picking mushrooms in the woods, and afterward having tea in the midst of the forest, where a man a hundred years old lived alone with his little grandson, taking care of bees. At other times we went to one of father's villages where a big pond had been dug, in which golden carp were caught by the thousand, — part of them being taken for the landlord and the remainder being distributed among all the peasants. My former nurse lived in that village. Her family was one of the poorest; besides her husband, she had only a small boy to help her, and a girl, my foster-sister, who became later on a preacher and a "virgin" in the Nonconformist sect to which they belonged. There was no bound to her joy when I came to see her. Cream, eggs, apples, and honey were all that she could offer; but the way in which she offered them, in bright wooden plates, after having covered the table with a fine snow-white tablecloth of her own make (with the Russian Nonconformists absolute cleanliness is a matter of religion), and the fond words with which she addressed me, treating me as her own son, left the warmest feelings in my heart. I must say the same of the nurses of my elder brothers, Nicholas and Alexander, who belonged to prominent families of two other Nonconformist sects in Nikólskoye. Few know what treasuries of goodness can be found in the hearts of Russian peasants, even after centuries of the most cruel oppression, which might well have embittered them.

• • • • • • • • • • • •

Serfdom was then in the last years of its existence. It is recent history, — it seems to be only of yesterday; and yet, even in Russia, few realize what serfdom was in reality. There is a dim conception that the conditions which it created were very bad; but those conditions, as they affected human beings bodily and mentally, are not generally understood. It is amazing, indeed, to see how quickly an institution and its social consequences are forgotten when the institution has ceased to exist, and with what rapidity men and things change. I will try to recall the conditions of serfdom by telling, not what I heard, but what I saw.

Uliána, the housekeeper, stands in the passage leading to father's room, and crosses herself; she dares neither to advance nor to retreat. At last, after having recited a prayer, she enters the room, and reports, in a hardly audible voice, that the store of tea is nearly at an end, that there are only twenty pounds of sugar left, and that the other provisions will soon be exhausted.

" Thieves, robbers! " shouts my father. " And you, you are in league with them! " His voice thunders throughout the house. Our stepmother leaves Uliána to face the storm. But father cries, " Frol, call the princess! Where is she? " And when she enters, he receives her with the same reproaches.

" You also are in league with this progeny of Ham; you are standing up for them;" and so on, for half an hour or more.

Then he commences to verify the accounts. At the same time, he thinks about the hay. Frol is sent to weigh what is left of that, and our stepmother is sent to be present during the weighing, while father calculates how much of it ought to be in the barn. A considerable quantity of hay appears to be missing, and Uliána cannot account for several pounds of such and such provisions. Father's voice becomes more and more menacing; Uliána is trembling; but it is the coachman who now enters the room, and is stormed at by his master. Father springs at him, strikes him, but he keeps repeating, " Your highness must have made a mistake."

Father repeats his calculations, and this time it appears that there is more hay in the barn than there ought to be. The shouting continues; he now reproaches the coachman with not having given the horses their daily rations in full; but the coachman calls on all the saints to witness that he gave the animals their due, and Frol invokes the Virgin to confirm the coachman's appeal.

But father will not be appeased. He calls in Makár, the piano-tuner and sub-butler, and reminds him of all his recent sins. He was drunk last week, and must have been drunk yesterday, for he broke half a dozen plates. In fact, the breaking of these plates was the real cause of all the disturbance: our stepmother had reported the fact to father in the morning, and that was why Uliána was received with more scolding than was usually the case, why the verification of the hay was undertaken, and why father now continues to shout that " this progeny of Ham " deserve all the punishments on earth.

Of a sudden there is a lull in the storm. My father takes his seat at the table and writes a note. " Take Makár with this note to the police station, and let a hundred lashes with the birch rod be given to him."

Terror and absolute muteness reign in the house.

The clock strikes four, and we all go down to dinner; but no one has any appetite, and the soup remains in the plates untouched. We are ten at table, and behind each of us a violinist or a trombone-player stands, with a clean plate in his left hand; but Makár is not among them.

" Where is Makár? " our stepmother asks. " Call him in."

Makár does not appear, and the order is repeated. He enters at last, pale, with a distorted face, ashamed, his eyes cast down. Father looks into his plate, while our stepmother, seeing that no one has touched the soup, tries to encourage us.

"Don't you find, children," she says, "that the soup is delicious?"

Tears suffocate me, and immediately after dinner is over I run out, catch Makár in a dark passage, and try to kiss his hand; but he tears it away, and says, either as a reproach or as a question, "Let me alone; you, too, when you are grown up, will you not be just the same?"

From the beginning of the century many thoughtful Russians had come to the conclusion that peasant bondage was a thing that must go. Even Nikolai I had appointed committees to investigate the whole problem and, although he was unwilling to press change against the wishes of the nobility, he acknowledged that serfdom was opposed to the wisdom of the age. It was the catastrophe of the Crimean War that opened Russians' eyes to the weakness of the entire structure of government and society itself in their Empire. Criticism, long proscribed, sprang up in abundance, and Alexander II prepared for the essential reform by putting a committee to work on ways and means. Under the chairmanship of Count Rumiantsev a plan was worked out, rather more radical than the nobility relished, but acceptable to the tsar. The proclamation of the Emancipation marks a significant era in Russian history, even though it be acknowledged that the freeing of the serfs juridically did not solve the problem of economic bondage.

112. THE UKAZ THAT ABOLISHED SERFDOM IN RUSSIA [1]

By the grace of God, we, Alexander II., Emperor and Autocrat of all the Russias, King of Poland, Grand Duke of Finland, &c., to all our faithful subjects make known:—

Called by Divine Providence and by the sacred right of inheritance to the throne of our ancestors, we took a vow in our innermost heart so to respond to the mission which is intrusted to us as to surround with our affection and our Imperial solicitude all our faithful subjects of every rank and of every condition, from the warrior who nobly bears arms for the defence of the country to the humble artisan devoted to the works of industry; from the official in the career of the high offices of the State to the labourer whose plough furrows the soil.

In considering the various classes and conditions of which the State is composed we came to the conviction that the legislation of the empire having

[1] *Annual Register for 1861,* pp. 207–212 (condensed).

wisely provided for the organization of the upper and middle classes and having defined with precision their obligations, their rights, and their privileges, has not attained the same degree of efficiency as regards the peasants attached to the soil, thus designated because either from ancient laws or from custom they have been hereditarily subjected to the authority of the proprietors, on whom it was incumbent at the same time to provide for their welfare. The rights of the proprietors have been hitherto very extended and very imperfectly defined by the law, which has been supplied by tradition, custom, and the good pleasure of the proprietors. In the most favourable cases this state of things has established patriarchal relations founded upon a solicitude sincerely equitable and benevolent on the part of the proprietors, and on an affectionate submission on the part of the peasants; but in proportion as the simplicity of morals diminished, as the diversity of the mutual relations became complicated, as the paternal character of the relations between the proprietors and the peasants became weakened, and, moreover, as the seigneurial authority fell sometimes into hands exclusively occupied with their personal interests, those bonds of mutual good-will slackened, and a wide opening was made for an arbitrary sway, which weighed upon the peasants, was unfavourable to their welfare, and made them indifferent to all progress under the conditions of their existence.

These facts had already attracted the notice of our predecessors of glorious memory, and they had taken measures for improving the conditions of the peasants; but among those measures some were not stringent enough, insomuch that they remained subordinate to the spontaneous initiative of such proprietors who showed themselves animated with liberal intentions; and others, called forth by peculiar circumstances, have been restricted to certain localities or simply adopted as an experiment. It was thus that Alexander I. published the regulation for the free cultivators, and that the late Emperor Nicholas, our beloved father, promulgated that one which concerns the peasants bound by contract. In the Western Governments regulations called " inventaires " had fixed the territorial allotments due to the peasants, as well as the amount of their rent dues; but all these reforms have only been applied in a very restricted manner.

We thus came to the conviction that the work of a serious improvement of the condition of the peasants was a sacred inheritance bequeathed to us by our ancestors, a mission which, in the course of events, Divine Providence called upon us to fulfil.

We have commenced this work by an expression of our Imperial confidence towards the nobility of Russia, which has given us so many proofs of its devotion to the Throne, and of its constant readiness to make sacrifices for the welfare of the country.

It is to the nobles themselves, conformable to their own wishes, that we have reserved the task of drawing up the propositions for the new organization of the peasants — propositions which make it incumbent upon them to limit their rights over the peasants, and to accept the onus of a reform which could not be accomplished without some material losses. Our confidence has not been deceived. We have seen the nobles assembled in committees in the districts, through the medium of their confidental agents, making the voluntary sacrifice of their rights as regards the personal servitude of the peasants. These committees, after having collected the necessary data, have formulated their propositions concerning the new organization of the peasants attached to the soil in their relations with the proprietors.

These propositions having been found very diverse, as was to be expected from the nature of the question, they have been compared, collated, and reduced to a regular system, then rectified and completed in the superior committee instituted for that purpose; and these new dispositions thus formulated relative to the peasants and domestics of the proprietors have been examined in the Council of the Empire. . . .

In virtue of the new dispositions above mentioned, the peasants attached to the soil will be invested within a term fixed by the law with all the rights of free cultivators.

The proprietors retaining their rights of property on all the land belonging to them, grant to the peasants for a fixed regulated rental the full enjoyment of their close; and, moreover, to assure their livelihood and to guarantee the fulfilment of their obligations towards the Government, the quantity of arable land is fixed by the said dispositions, as well as other rural appurtenances.

But, in the enjoyment of these territorial allotments, the peasants are obliged, in return, to acquit the rentals fixed by the same dispositions to the profit of the proprietors. In this state, which must be a transitory one, the peasants shall be designated as " temporarily bound."

At the same time, they are granted the right of purchasing their close, and, with the consent of the proprietors, they may acquire in full property the arable lands and other appurtenances which are allotted to them as a permanent holding. By the acquisition in full property of the quantity of land fixed, the peasants are free from their obligations towards the proprietors for land thus purchased, and they enter definitely into the condition of free peasants — landholders.

By a special disposition concerning the domestics, a transitory state is fixed for them, adapted to their occupations and the exigencies of their position. On the expiration of a term of two years, dating from the day of the promulgation of these dispositions, they shall receive their full enfranchisement and some temporary immunities. . . .

Aware of all the difficulties of the reform we have undertaken, we place above all things our confidence in the goodness of Divine Providence, who watches over the destinies of Russia.

We also count upon the generous devotion of our faithful nobility, and we are happy to testify to that body the gratitude it has deserved from us, as well as from the country, for the disinterested support it has given to the accomplishment of our designs. Russia will not forget that the nobility, acting solely upon its respect for the dignity of man and its love for its neighbour, has spontaneously renounced rights given to it by serfdom actually abolished, and laid the foundation of a new future, which is thrown open to the peasants. . . .

To render the transactions between the proprietors and the peasants more easy, in virtue of which the latter may acquire in full property their close (homestead) and the land they occupy, the Government will advance assistance, according to a special regulation, by means of loans or a transfer of debts encumbering an estate. . . .

When the first news of this great reform meditated by the Government became diffused among the rural populations, who were scarcely prepared for it, it gave rise, in some instances, to misunderstandings among individuals more intent upon liberty than mindful of the duties which it imposes. But, generally, the good sense of the country has not been wanting. It has not misunderstood either the inspirations of natural reason, which says that every man who accepts freely the benefits of society owes it in return the fulfilment of certain positive obligations; nor the teachings of the Christian law, which enjoins that " every one be subject unto the higher powers " (St. Paul to the Romans, xiii. 1); and to " render to all their dues," and, above all, to whomsoever it belongs, tribute, custom, respect, and honour (Ibid., xiii. 7). It has understood that the proprietors would not be deprived of rights legally acquired, except for a fit and sufficient indemnity, or by a voluntary concession on their part; that it would be contrary to all equity to accept this enjoyment of the lands conceded by the proprietors without accepting also towards them equivalent charges.

And now we hope with confidence that the freed serfs, in the presence of the new future which is opened before them, will appreciate and recognize the considerable sacrifices which the nobility have made on their behalf. They will understand that the blessing of an existence supported upon the base of guaranteed property, as well as a greater liberty in the administration of their goods, entails upon them, with new duties towards society and themselves, the obligation of justifying the protecting designs of the law by a loyal and judicious use of the rights which are now accorded to them. For if men do not labour themselves to insure their own well-being under the shield of the laws, the best of those laws cannot guarantee it to them.

It is only by assiduous labour, a rational employment of their strength and their resources, a strict economy, and, above all, by an honest life, a life constantly inspired by the fear of the Lord, that they can arrive at prosperity and insure its development.

The authorities intrusted with the duty of preparing by preliminary measures the execution of the new organization, and of presiding at its inauguration, will have to see that this work is accomplished with calmness and regularity, taking into account the requirements of the seasons, in order that the cultivator may not be drawn away from his agricultural labours. Let him apply himself with zeal to those labours, that he may be able to draw from an abundant granary the seed which he has to confide to that land which will be given him for permanent enjoyment, or which he has acquired for himself as his own property.

And now, pious and faithful people, make upon the forehead the sacred sign of the cross, and join thy prayers to ours to call down the blessing of the Most High upon thy first free labours, the sure pledge of thy personal well-being and of the public prosperity.

Given at St. Petersburg, the 19th day of February (March 3), of the year of Grace 1861, and the seventh of our reign.

ALEXANDER

The liberal gentry sought to prove their nobility by service with responsibility. When the law courts were reconstructed in 1864 they worked sympathetically and understandingly as justices of the peace, and in the same year they began to serve as members of district zemstvo, *or boards of local government. A Scottish traveler, who sojourned seven years in Russia in the 'seventies, observed them at their work.*

113. THE ZEMSTVO AT ITS HEIGHT OF EFFECTIVENESS [1]

Not long after my arrival in Novgorod I had the opportunity of being present at a District Assembly. In the ballroom of the " Club de la Noblesse " I found thirty or forty men seated round a long table covered with green cloth. Before each member lay sheets of paper for the purpose of taking notes, and before the president — the Marshal of Noblesse for the district — stood a small hand-bell, which he rang vigorously at the commencement of the proceedings and on all occasions when he wished to obtain silence. To the right and left of the president sat the members of the executive (*upráva*), armed with piles of written and printed documents, from which they read long and tedious extracts, till the majority of the audience took to yawning and one or two of the members positively went to sleep. At the close of each

[1] D. M. Wallace, *Russia*. Revised Edition. London, Cassell & Co., 1912, pp. 560–562, 568, 569–570.

of these reports the president rang his bell — presumably for the purpose of awakening the sleepers — and inquired whether anyone had remarks to make on what had just been read. Generally someone had remarks to make, and not unfrequently a discussion ensued. When any decided difference of opinion appeared, a vote was taken by handing round a sheet of paper, or by the simpler method of requesting the Ayes to stand up and the Noes to sit still.

What surprised me most in this assembly was that it was composed partly of nobles and partly of peasants — the latter being decidedly in the majority — and that no trace of antagonism seemed to exist between the two classes. Landed proprietors and their *ci-devant* serfs, emancipated only ten years before, evidently met for the moment on a footing of equality. The discussions were carried on chiefly by the nobles, but on more than one occasion peasant members rose to speak, and their remarks, always clear, practical, and to the point, were invariably listened to with respectful attention. Instead of that violent antagonism which might have been expected, considering the constitution of the Assembly, there was too much unanimity — a fact indicating plainly that the majority of the members did not take a very deep interest in the matters presented to them.

This assembly for the district was held in the month of September. At the beginning of December the Assembly for the Province met, and during nearly three weeks I was daily present at its deliberations. In general character and mode of procedure it resembled closely the District Assembly. Its chief peculiarities were that its members were chosen, not by the primary electors, but by the assemblies of the ten districts which compose the province, and that it took cognisance merely of those matters which concerned more than one district. Besides this, the peasant deputies were very few in number — a fact which somewhat surprised me, because I was aware that, according to the law, the peasant members of the District Assemblies were eligible, like those of the other classes. The explanation is that the District Assemblies choose their most active members to represent them in the Provincial Assemblies, and consequently the choice generally falls on landed proprietors. To this arrangement the peasants make no objection, for attendance at the Provincial Assemblies demands a considerable pecuniary outlay, and payment of the deputies is expressly prohibited by law.

.   .   .   .

Even within its proper sphere, as defined by law, the Zemstvo has not accomplished what was expected of it. The country has not been covered with a network of macadamised roads, and the bridges are by no means as safe as could be desired. Village schools and infirmaries are still far below the requirements of the population. Little or nothing has been done for the development of trade or manufactures; and the villages remain very much what they were under the old Administration. Meanwhile the local rates have been rising with alarming rapidity; and many people draw from all this the conclusion that the Zemstvo is a worthless institution which has increased the taxation without conferring any corresponding benefit on the country. . . .

The Zemstvo has, however, done much more than the majority of its critics admit. It fulfils tolerably well, without scandalous peculation and jobbery, its commonplace, every-day duties, and it has created a new and more equitable system of rating by which landed proprietors and house-owners are made to bear their share of the public burdens. It has done a very great deal to provide medical aid and primary education for the common people, and it has improved wonderfully the condition of the hospitals, lunatic asylums, and other benevolent institutions committed to its charge. In its efforts to aid the peasantry it has helped to improve the native breeds of horses and cattle, and it has created a system of obligatory fire insurance, together with means for preventing and extinguishing fires in the villages — a most important matter in a country where the peasants live in wooden houses and big fires are fearfully frequent. After neglecting for a good many years the essential question as to how the peasants' means of subsistence can be increased, it has latterly, as I have mentioned in the fore-going chapter, helped them to obtain improved agricultural implements and better seed, encouraged the formation of small credit associations and savings banks, and appointed agricultural inspectors to teach them how they may introduce modest improvements within their limited means. At the same time, in many districts it has endeavoured to assist the home industries which are threatened with annihilation by the big factories, and whenever measures have been proposed for the benefit of the rural population, such as the lower-ing of the land-redemption payments and the creation of the Peasant Land Bank, it has invariably given them its cordial support.

If you ask a zealous member of the Zemstvo why it has not done more he will probably tell you that it is because its activity has been constantly re-stricted and counteracted by the Government. The Assemblies were obliged to accept as presidents the Marshals of Noblesse, many of whom were men of antiquated ideas and retrograde principles. At every turn the more en-lightened, more active members found themselves opposed, thwarted, and finally checkmated, by the Imperial officials.

Kropotkin spent much of his youth as a page at the court of Alexan-der II and saw him change from the Emancipator to the tsar of reaction.

114. A CONTEMPORARY ESTIMATE OF ALEXANDER II [1]

On the day of the emancipation of the serfs, Alexander II. was worshiped at St. Petersburg; but it is most remarkable that, apart from that moment of general enthusiasm, he had not the love of the city. . . . Alexander II. had retained too much of the despotic character of his father, which pierced now and then through his usually good-natured manners. He easily lost his temper, and often treated his courtiers in the most contemptuous way. He was not what one would describe as a truly reliable man, either in his policy or in his personal sympathies, and he was vindictive. . . . From the beginning of 1862 he commenced to show himself capable of reviving the worst practices of his father's reign. It was known that he still wanted to carry through a series of important reforms in the judicial organization and in the army; that the terrible corporal punishments were about to be abolished, and that a sort of local self-government, and perhaps a constitution of some sort, would be granted. But the slightest disturbance was repressed under his orders with a stern severity: he took each movement as a personal offense, so that at any moment one might expect from him the most reactionary measures. The disorders which broke out at the universities of St. Petersburg, Moscow, and Kazán, in October, 1861, were repressed with an ever increasing strictness. The University of St. Petersburg was closed, and although free courses were opened by most of the professors at the Town Hall, they were also soon closed, and some of the best professors left the university. Immediately after the abolition of serfdom, a great movement began for the opening of Sunday-schools; they were opened everywhere by private persons and corporations, — all the teachers being volunteers, — and the peasants and workers, old and young, flocked to these schools. Officers, students, even a few pages, became teachers; and such excellent methods were worked out that (Russian having a phonetic spelling) we succeeded in teaching a peasant to read in nine or ten lessons. But suddenly all Sunday-schools, in which the mass of the peasantry would have learned to read in a few years, without any expenditure by the state, were closed. In Poland, where a series of patriotic manifestations had begun, the Cossacks were sent out to disperse the crowds with their whips, and to arrest hundreds of people in the churches with their usual brutality. Men were shot in the streets of Warsaw by the end of 1861, and for the suppression of the few peasant insurrections which broke out, the horrible flogging through the double line of soldiers — that favorite punishment of Nicholas I. — was applied. The despot that Alexander II. became in the years 1870–81 was foreshadowed in 1862. . . .

[1] Peter Kropotkin, *Memoirs of a Revolutionist*. Boston, Houghton Mifflin Co., 1899, pp. 149–151, 183 (slightly condensed).

It has often been said that Alexander II. committed a great fault, and brought about his own ruin, by raising so many hopes which later on he did not satisfy. . . . It was not merely that he raised hopes. Yielding for a moment to the current of public opinion around him, he induced men all over Russia to set to work, to issue from the domain of mere hopes and dreams, and to touch with the finger the reforms that were required. He made them realize what could be done immediately, and how easy it was to do it; he induced them to sacrifice whatever of their ideals could not be immediately realized, and to demand only what was practically possible at the time. And when they had framed their ideas, and had shaped them into laws which merely required his signature to become realities, then he refused that signature. No reactionist could raise, or ever has raised, his voice to assert that what was left — the unreformed tribunals, the absence of municipal self-government, or the system of exile — was good and was worth maintaining: no one has dared to say that. And yet, owing to the fear of doing anything, all was left as it was; for thirty-five years those who ventured to mention the necessity of a change were treated as " suspects "; and institutions unanimously recognized as bad were permitted to continue in existence only that nothing more might be heard of that abhorred word " reform."

New stirrings reached Russia early in the 'sixties from Western Europe, where Positivist philosophy had a great vogue and where a new gospel of Science was finding zealous adherents. Turgenev presents the impact of these new ideas on the moderate liberalism of the Reform Era and the conflict of two generations that is applicable to all eras. In creating the character of Bazarov, Turgenev also gave common currency to the too often misused term of nihilist.

115. THE DEFINITION OF A NIHILIST [1]

Pavel Patrovitch pulled his moustaches. " Well, and what is Mr. Bazarov himself? " he asked, deliberately.

" What is Bazarov? " Arkady smiled. " Would you like me, uncle, to tell you what he really is? "

" If you will be so good, nephew."

" He's a nihilist."

" Eh? " inquired Nikolai Petrovitch, while Pavel Petrovitch lifted a knife in the air with a small piece of butter on its tip, and remained motionless.

[1] Ivan S. Turgenev, *Fathers and Children.* Translated by Constance Garnett. New York, The Macmillan Co., 1920, pp. 35–37.

"He's a nihilist," repeated Arkady.

"A nihilist," said Nikolai Petrovitch. "That's from the Latin, *nihil, nothing,* as far as I can judge; the word must mean a man who—who accepts nothing?"

"Say, 'Who respects nothing,'" put in Pavel Petrovitch, and he set to work on the butter again.

"Who regards everything from the critical point of view," observed Arkady.

"Isn't that just the same thing?" inquired Pavel Petrovitch.

"No, it's not the same thing. A nihilist is a man who does not bow down before any authority, who does not take any principle on faith, whatever reverence that principle may be enshrined in."

"Well, and is that good?" interrupted Pavel Petrovitch.

"That depends, uncle. Some people it will do good to, but some people will suffer for it."

"Indeed. Well, I see it's not in our line. We are old-fashioned people; we imagine that without principles, taken as you say on faith, there's no taking a step, no breathing. *Vous avez changé tout cela.* God give you good health and the rank of a general, while we will be content to look on and admire, worthy . . . what is it?"

"Nihilists," Arkady said, speaking very distinctly.

"Yes. There used to be Hegelists, and now there are nihilists. We shall see how you will exist in void, in vacuum; and now ring, please, brother Nikolai Petrovitch; it's time I had my cocoa."

Nihilism, a new critical state of mind rather than a program or a political creed, was the young man's preoccupation in the 'sixties, but a decade later his successor was eager to apply himself to the service of the Russian people. This generation's cry was "In among the people" (V'Narod), and essentially the Narodnechestvo, or Populist movement, was a mission of enlightenment. Stepniak, later a Terrorist of the most daring character, was first one of the evangelists of education.

116. THE NARODNECHESTVO[1]

In the winter of 1872, in one of the hovels in the outskirts of St. Petersburg, a number of working men gathered round (Prince) Peter Krapotkine, who expounded to them the principles of Socialism, and of the revolution. The rich Cossack Obuchoff, though consumptive and dying, did the same upon

[1] Serghei Stepniak (S. M. Kravchinskii), *Underground Russia.* London, Smith Elder & Co. (John Murray), 1883, pp. 22–26 (condensed).

the banks of his native Don. An officer, Leonidas Sciscko, became a hand-weaver in one of the St. Petersburg manufactories, in order to carry on the propaganda there. Two other members of the same society . . . went into the province of Tver, for the purpose of carrying on the propaganda there among the peasants. . . .

The men and women who had come back from abroad inflamed the public mind with the recital of the great struggle already undertaken by the proletariat of the West; of the " Internationale " . . . , of the Commune and its martyrs; and prepared to go " among the people " with their new prose-lytes in order to put their ideas in practice, . . . and turned anxiously to those, who were few then, who had come back from the work of propagandism, to ask them what were these powerful and mysterious beings — the people — whom their fathers taught them to fear, and whom, without knowing, they already loved with all the impetuosity of their youthful hearts. And those appealed to . . . said . . . that the terrible people were good, simple, trust-ing as children; that they not only did not mistrust, but welcomed them with open arms and hearts; that they listened to their words with the deepest sympathy, and that old and young after a long day of toil pressed attentively around them in some dark and smoky hovel, in which, by the uncertain light of a chip of resinous wood in place of a candle, they spoke of Socialism. . . ; that the communal assemblies were broken up when they came into the vil-lages, as the peasants abandoned the meetings to come and listen. . . . They told . . . that there were indications and rumours denoting that their pa-tience was coming to an end, and that some great storm was felt to be approaching.

All these numerous and powerful influences, acting upon the impression-able minds, so prone to enthusiasm, of the Russian youth, produced that vast movement of 1873-74 which inaugurated the new Russian revolutionary era.

Nothing similar has been seen before or since. It was a revelation rather than a propaganda. At first the book, or the individual, that had impelled this or that person to join the movement could be traced out; but after a while this became impossible. It was a powerful cry, which arose, no one knew where and whence, and which summoned the zealous to the great work of the redemption of country and humanity. And the zealous, heeding this cry, arose, overwhelmed with sorrow and indignation over their past life, and abandoning home and family, wealth and honors, threw themselves into the movement with a joy, an enthusiasm, a faith, such as are experienced only once in a life-time, and which when lost are never found again.

I will not speak of the many young men and young women of the highest aristocratic families who labored fifteen hours a day in the factories, in the workshops, in the fields. Youth is proverbially generous and ready for sacrifice. The most characteristic feature of the movement was that the contagion spread even to the people, advanced in years, who had already a future clearly worked out and a position won by the sweat of their brows — judges, physicians, officers, officials — and these were not among the least zealous.

Yet it was not a *political* movement. It rather resembled a *religious* movement, and had all the contagious and absorbing elements of such a one. People not only sought to obtain a distinct practical object, but also to satisfy an inward sentiment of duty, an inspiration, so to speak, leading them toward their own moral perfection.

With the spring of 1874 all discussion abruptly ceased among the circles of the revolutionary youth. The time for talking was over: actual "work" was in contemplation. The working-people's gear — boots, shirts, etc. — were hurriedly being prepared. Short greetings and laconic answers were heard: "Whither?" — "To the Urals," "To the Volga," "To the South," "To the river of Don," and so on. . . . There were warm wishes for success, and robust squeezings of hands. . . . "The spring is ending; it is high time. . . ." And so, like an electric spark, that cry "to the people" ran through the youth; sure of themselves, daring and wide-awake, though unarmed and unorganized, they dashed in full sight of the enemy, into the storm.

But this noble movement, in contact with harsh reality, was shattered like a precious Sèvres vase, struck by a heavy and dirty stone.

Shattered in their effort to enlighten the masses, many of the young men and women of the Narodnechestvo *turned to a radically different approach, which they outlined in the first number of a paper called* Narodnaya Volya, *or* The Will of the People, *and which appeared on October 1st, 1879. It was the preface to Terrorism.*

117. THE PROGRAM OF THE NARODNAYA VOLYA[1]

By fundamental conviction we are socialists and democrats. We are satisfied that only through socialistic principles can the human race acquire liberty, equality, and fraternity; secure the full and harmonious development of the individual as well as the material prosperity of all; and thus make progress. We are convinced that all social forms must rest upon the sanction of the people themselves, and that popular development is permanent only when it proceeds freely and independently, and when every idea that is to be embodied in the people's life has first passed through the people's consciousness and has been acted upon by the people's will. The welfare of the people

[1] George Kennan, *Siberia and the Exile System*, 2 vols. London, Century Co., 1891, vol. II, pp. 495–499.

and the will of the people are our two most sacred and most inseparable principles.

A

1. If we look at the environment in which the Russian people are forced to live and act, we see that they are, economically and politically, in a state of absolute slavery. As laborers they work only to feed and support the parasitic classes; and as citizens they are deprived of all rights. Not only does the actual state of things fail to answer to their will, but they dare not even express and formulate their will; they cannot even think what is good and what is bad for them; the very thought that they can have a will is regarded as a crime against the State. Enmeshed on all sides, they are being reduced to a state of physical degeneration, intellectual stolidity, and general inferiority.

2. Around the enchained people we see a class of exploiters whom the state creates and protects. The state itself is the greatest capitalistic power in the land, it constitutes the sole political oppressor of the people, and only through its aid and support can the lesser robbers exist. This bourgeois excrescence in the form of a government sustains itself by mere brute force — by means of its military, police, and bureaucratic organization — in precisely the same way that the Mongols of Genghis Khan sustained themselves in Russia. . . .

B

1. We are of opinion, therefore, that it is our first duty, as socialists and democrats, to free the people from the oppression of the present Government, and bring about a political revolution, in order to transfer the supreme power to the nation. . . .

2. We think that the will of the people would be sufficiently well expressed and executed by a national Organizing Assembly, elected freely by a general vote, and acting under the instructions of the voters. This, of course, would fall far short of an ideal manifestation of the people's will; but it is the only one that is practicable at present, and we therefore think best to adopt it. Our plan is to take away the power from the existing Government, and give it to an Organizing Assembly, elected in the manner above described, whose duty it will be to make an examination of all our social and governmental institutions, and remodel them in accordance with instructions from the electors.

C

Although we are ready to submit wholly to the popular will, we regard it as none the less our duty, as a party, to appear before the people with our program. This program we shall use as a means of propaganda until the revolution comes, we shall advocate it during the election campaign, and we shall support it before the Organizing Assembly. It is as follows:

1. Perpetual popular representation, constituted as above described and having full power to act in all national questions.

2. General local self-government, secured by the election of all officers, and the economic independence of the people.

3. The self-controlled village commune as the economic and administrative unit.

4. Ownership of the land by the people.

5. A system of measures having for their object the turning over to the laborers of all mining works and factories.

6. Complete freedom of conscience, speech, association, public meeting, and electioneering activity.

7. Universal right of franchise, without any class or property limitation.

8. The substitution of a territorial militia for the army. . . .

D

In view of the stated aim of the party its operations may be classified as follows:

1. *Propaganda and agitation.* Our propaganda has for its object the popularization, in all social classes, of the idea of a political and democratic revolution as a means of social reform, as well as popularization of the party's own program. Its essential features are criticism of the existing order of things, and a statement and explanation of revolutionary methods. The aim of agitation should be to incite the people to protest, as generally as possible, against the present state of affairs, to demand such reforms as are in harmony with the party's purposes, and, especially, to demand the summoning of an Organizing Assembly. The popular protest may take the form of meetings, demonstrations, petitions, leading addresses, refusals to pay taxes, etc.

2. *Destructive and terroristic activity.* Terroristic activity consists in the destruction of the most harmful persons in the Government, the protection of the party from spies, and the punishment of official lawlessness and violence in all the more prominent and important cases in which such lawlessness and violence are manifested. The aim of such activity is to break down the prestige of Governmental power, to furnish continuous proof of the possibility of carrying on a contest with the Government, to raise in that way the revolutionary spirit of the people and inspire belief in the practicability of revolution, and, finally, to form a body suited and accustomed to warfare.

3. *The organization of secret societies and the arrangement of them in connected groups around a single center.* The organization of small secret societies with all sorts of revolutionary aims is indispensable, both as a means

of executing the numerous functions of the party and of finishing the political training of its members. . . .

4. *The acquirement of ties, and an influential position in the administration, in the army, in society, and among the people.* The administration and the army are particularly important in connection with a revolution, and serious attention should also be devoted to the people. The principal object of the party, so far as the people are concerned, is to prepare them to coöperate with the revolution, and to carry on a successful electioneering contest after the revolution — a contest that shall have for its object the election of purely democratic delegates to the Organizing Assembly. The party should enlist acknowledged partizans among the more prominent classes of the peasantry, and should prearrange for the active coöperation of the masses at the more important points and among the more sympathetic portions of the population. . . .

5. *The organization and consummation of the revolution.* In view of the oppressed and cowed condition of the people, and of the fact that the Government, by means of partial concessions and pacifications, may retard for a long time a general revolutionary movement, the party should take the initiative, and not wait until the people are able to do the work without its aid.

6. *The electioneering canvass before the summoning of the Organizing Assembly.* However the revolution may be brought about — as the result of an open revolution, or with the aid of a conspiracy — the duty of the party will be to aid in the immediate summoning of an Organizing Assembly, to which shall be transferred the powers of the Provisional Government created by the revolution or the conspiracy. During the election canvass the party should oppose, in every way, the candidacy of *kulaks* of all sorts, and strive to promote the candidacy of purely communal people.

CHAPTER IX

INTERNAL DEVELOPMENTS ON THE CONTINENT

SECTION I. THE THIRD FRENCH REPUBLIC

In the following selection an attempt is made to show that the excesses of the first French Republic at the time of the Reign of Terror in 1793 and 1794 were influential in postponing the definitive establishment of a republican government in France. Oscillating between monarchical rule and ideas of liberty, equality, and fraternity, it took France nearly a century to take her stand firmly on the principles of the Revolution of 1789.

The selection may serve as a convenient summary of French internal political history from 1815 to 1886.

118. THE STRUGGLE TO ESTABLISH A REPUBLIC[1]

IN 1815 Napoleon fell; and it might seem as though it were natural for France to return then to the Republican form of government for which it had been so enthusiastic in 1793. There was, however, no question of doing so. Having at last overthrown Napoleon, the Allies, as well as a large part of the French people themselves, " still shuddered at the memory of the Terror."[2] To the upper classes, especially, the Republic meant Jacobinism, the guillotine, the horrors of 1793.[3] Nor were the liberties which grew naturally from the principles of the Declaration of the Rights of Man restored. The Bourbon king, Louis XVIII, came back, it is true, as a constitutional, rather than as an absolute monarch. The results of the Revolution were by no means entirely undone; the economic results, especially, remained. But the press was shackled, even though a certain freedom had been guaranteed it by the king. The Republicans were not allowed to form associations or to hold open meetings. The suffrage, instead of being made universal, was put in the hands of the wealthy and well-to-do taxpayers. While the reaction from the Terror was not the sole reason for the establishment of these limitations on democracy, it certainly was an important one.

If France at this period had little use for Republicanism, however, neither

---

1 Jonathan F. Scott. From an unpublished paper.
2 Guérard, *French Civilization in the Nineteenth Century*, p. 91.
3 Weill, *Le parti républicain*, p. 1.

did she incline toward absolutism. After Charles X had succeeded to the throne in 1824, boasting that he and Lafayette were the only men who had not changed since 1789, after he had begun to assert his prerogative and to show clearly his determination to be as far as possible an absolute ruler after the fashion of Louis XIV, the country grew uneasy and restless. Only a small, gleeful band of Ultra-Royalists rejoiced. Finally when the king issued the fateful July Ordinances of 1830, arbitrarily dissolving the newly-elected Chamber and wrapping new and heavier chains around the press, the bolder and more discontented elements in Paris took matters into their own hands. The Bourbon Monarchy was overthrown and Charles was forced to abdicate and flee to England.

The success of the Revolution of 1830 was largely due to the Republicans; but they failed to reap the rewards of victory. Under the surface, indeed, the leaven of Republicanism had been working; the idea was more popular than it had been in 1815. But still there remained the old fear that the establishment of this form of government would mean a return to the excesses of 1793. It was of these excesses that the Duke of Orleans spoke to some of the ardent young Republicans who came to talk with him shortly after the abdication of Charles. It was to the effects of these excesses that the Republican journalist August Fabre a little later referred. "The Convention," he wrote in 1831, "by depriving France of her most energetic and purest patriots, victims of her fury, prepared for the fall of the Republic, and has rendered its Renaissance almost impossible by linking to this name so beautiful, memories of ruin and of blood."[1] "The Republicans," says Guérard, "were distrusted by the ruling class; not only were the imperishable memories of the Terror working against them, but, for the last fifteen years they had been unable to assert their existence except through riots and conspiracies."[2] The venerable Lafayette, indeed, might possibly have turned the day for the Republic. He considered it wise, however, to declare himself for monarchy in the person of Louis Philippe, Duke of Orleans. The two men met on a balcony of the hôtel de Ville, embraced, and accepted graciously the plaudits of the populace. France was thus given a new king; and the new monarchy, Lafayette promised, would be "the best of Republics."

Louis Philippe had, indeed, come to the throne on a platform savoring of liberalism, and so for a short time liberalism dared raise its head. The suffrage qualification was reduced slightly, though suffrage was by no means made universal. The press enjoyed a brief period of freedom such as it had not known either under Napoleon or during the reigns of Louis XVIII and Charles X. Then followed riots engineered by disgruntled, discontented Republicans; and Louis Philippe, laying aside the mask of

---

[1] Weill, ibid., p. 35.   [1] Op. cit., p. 101.

engaging *bonhomie* which had done so much to promote his popularity and secure him a throne, revealed the autocratic temper underneath. Laws were passed in restraint of political liberty; Republican newspapers were fined out of existence and Republican leaders were imprisoned. By 1840 quiet had been restored and for the ensuing eight years the Prime Minister, Guizot, was able by questionable but effective means to maintain a Parliamentary majority to support the autocratic, though by no means tyrannous policy of his sovereign.

Then, in 1848, came the explosion. Underneath the calm surface of Guizot's policy of peace, prosperity and political stagnation, discontent had seethed and boiled. Intelligent people had resented being deprived of their political liberties and the Republican idea had spread. Economic grievances had added to the trouble; if employers were growing rich, workingmen were all too frequently living on starvation wages. Hence new scenes of violence on the streets of Paris, riots, cries for the resignation of Guizot, and then for the abdication of Louis Philippe. And so Louis Philippe, frightened perhaps by the defection of the National Guard, followed the example of his predecessor Charles X, abdicated, fled to England, and so passed into obscurity.

This time the Republic was really established, proclaimed on the 24th of February, 1848, and ratified later by the people in national assembly. Again men's souls were filled with the democratic idealism of the dawn of the first Revolution. Trees of Liberty were planted everywhere, and the clergy, the one element heretofore consistently hostile to the Revolution, solemnly yet joyfully blessed them. Had there been no further violence France might possibly have been a Republic from that time on.

Some of those who had brought about the Revolution, however, were still dissatisfied. Industrial discontent had bred socialism. The Socialists had been partly responsible for the overthrow of the Bourgeois Monarchy of Louis Philippe; and now they demanded that certain of their theories be given a trial. Especially they demanded that the Government furnish work for all who asked for it. Hence so-called national workshops were established; and from all quarters of France men flocked to Paris to find labor in the crude tasks set them by the new Government. Badly bungled, the scheme broke down. The workshops were abolished and the workers were offered the choice of enrolment in the army or employment on public works. Fiercely angered, the men turned on the Government, organized, erected barricades, and for four days fought with the courage of despair. Paris had perhaps never known such desperate street-fighting. In the end, at awful cost to both sides, General Cavaignac succeeded in putting down the insurrection.

The effects of these terrible June Days were in certain respects similar to those of the Terror of 1793 and 1794. Dreams of social regeneration had turned into nightmares. Optimism died. Democracy became increasingly unpopular. Men longed above all things for stability, order, even at the price of liberty. "The conservative classes trembled retrospectively," says Guérard, "at the thought of the danger they had gone through. They craved for authorities that would maintain material order, and moral order as one of its conditions. The Church and a strong government! Such was the cry of the frightened bourgeoisie. 'Let us throw ourselves at the feet of the bishops!' said Duvergier de Hauranne, a member of the liberal opposition."[1]

So France threw herself, not only at the feet of the bishops, but at the feet of another Bonaparte, a new autocrat, Louis Napoleon. In the course of the next four years the Second Republic became the Second Empire, with Louis Napoleon, now Napoleon III, as Emperor. The freedom of the press disappeared. Universal suffrage existed in theory but not in fact, for power lay almost entirely in the hands of the Emperor and his coterie. Liberty was stifled. The insurgents of June, 1848, who had fought in the name of liberty, had paved the way for its suffocation. After 1859 the Emperor did, indeed, under pressure, offer gasping France a semblance of liberalism; but not until another decade had passed did the country really begin to breathe the air of freedom. Murmurs against the Emperor now grew louder and louder.

Then, in 1870, the peaceful course of history was again violently deflected, this time by the Franco-Prussian War. The hordes came tumbling into France from the other side of the Rhine, shut up Marshal Bazaine in Metz, defeated MacMahon and his army at Sedan and took prisoner the Emperor. When the news of Napoleon's capture reached Paris a mob rushed to the hôtel de Ville and there proclaimed the Third Republic.

This time the Republic had apparently come to stay. Yet not immediately did democracy come entirely into its own. Universal suffrage was put in force, indeed, but not at once did the Bonapartists, Orleanists, Legitimists, all those who wished to bring back the monarchy, give up the struggle. The Constitutional laws of 1875 provided for a republican form of government, but MacMahon, a monarchist, had been elected President in 1873. The monarchists only awaited the opportunity to place a king on the throne of France. But that opportunity never came. In 1877 MacMahon attempted to assert his personal power by choosing a ministry in sympathy with himself rather than with the majority in the legislative bodies. In the elections that followed he failed to secure the support of the country and in 1879 he resigned. With his resignation came the definitive triumph of the Republic.

Then followed democratic legislation, legislation founded on the principles of the Declaration of the Rights of Man, legislation which the Red Terror had helped to postpone. The right to hold meetings without

[1] Op. cit., pp. 126–127.

preliminary governmental authorization was made legal in 1881, though even in this matter remembrance of the violence of the Jacobins and other clubs caused such associations as theirs to be forbidden. " The Government," says Hanotaux, " obtained a disputed victory on Article VII, by which clubs were interdicted. Memories of the first Revolution, and of 1848 aroused a hesitating support of 257 votes against 180." [1] The same year a law was passed giving the press practically unlimited freedom, a freedom for which it had fought, with varying fortunes, for generations. In 1884 limitations on the right of association were removed in that workingmen were now given the right to form trade unions freely. Finally, between 1880 and 1886, state education was made free, compulsory, and secular. In the founding of the Third Republic and in this subsequent legislation the great Revolution at last came into its own.

The history of France since 1789 seems, from all this, to warn against a resort to violence as a means of altering the social order. In 1814, even after the terribly costly experience with absolutism in the person of Napoleon I, the establishment of a Republic was simply not to be thought of; for it was inextricably associated in the minds of men with the bloody excesses of 1793. In 1830 the situation was not so very different. Republican ideas, it is true, had made progress; but memories of the Terror, coupled with disgust at Republican conspiracies and outbreaks of more recent years, led France to reject the Republic and to compromise on the supposedly liberal Louis Philippe. Louis Philippe, however, soon revealed his autocratic temper and feeling against him grew. In 1848 it seemed as though democracy were at last going to realize itself. For nearly a decade Republicans had discarded violence in favor of quiet propaganda, and the Republic when it was first proclaimed was truly popular. Then came the June Days; and Frenchmen, horrified by this early manifestation of " Bolshevism," threw themselves at the feet of autocracy. Not till 1870 was France ready to give the great experiment another trial. Then in the maelstrom of war Louis Napoleon lost his throne. Then finally the principles of the French Revolution whose realization the Red Terror had so long been instrumental in postponing, began with trembling and hesitation to come into their own. Yet not till after the fall of MacMahon in 1879 did these principles crystallize in Republican legislation providing for freedom of meeting, freedom of the press, and free, compulsory education. The French Revolution had taken nearly a century to fulfill itself.

After legislation from 1880 to 1886 had made education in France free, compulsory, and secular the number of state schools (lay schools, écoles laïques) increased rapidly while the influence of the Church schools declined.

1 *Contemporary France*, vol. IV, p. 516.

Education tended more and more to reflect the ideals and aims of the Third Republic. As the following extract shows, the lay school now emphasized the teaching of loyalty to the Republic and to the principles of the French Revolution of 1789, as well as the development of a spirit of patriotism ready for all the emergencies that might arise in case of a new war with Germany.

119. THE INCULCATION OF NATIONALISM IN FRENCH SCHOOLS AFTER 1870 [1]

As the battle of Jena awoke the slumbering nationalism of Prussia, so Sedan aroused from the comfortable lethargy of the Second Empire the patriotism of France. Like Fichte before him, Gambetta set his hopes for the future of his country on the development of a truly national system of education. The task of France, however, was not entirely similar to that of Prussia. Prussia's object was, first of all, to escape from the domination of the military genius who had conquered, humiliated, and insulted her. Behind this immediate aim lay the dream of a patriotism not narrowly Prussian but broadly German, a patriotism which was to draw together the divided elements of a noble race, and to raise that race to new heights of greatness under the rule of the Hohenzollerns. In the accomplishment of this latter purpose the school played a part not sufficiently recognized by historians.

The work of French patriotism was, first, to develop adequate national defense and rehabilitate national prestige. Secondly, it was to place on a firm foundation the insecure structure of the Republican form of government. The strength and glory associated with the ancient monarchy were to be revived by a democracy imbedded in the hearts of the people. The school was to sustain the state in its efforts to solve the problems which the Franco-German War had ushered in.

The educational renaissance of France may be divided into four periods. During the first of these — lasting more than a decade from the founding of the Third Republic — Republicanism engaged with clericalism in a struggle to control the public school. However lofty the teachings of the Church — and what doctrines could be nobler than the fundamental tenets of Catholicism? — ardent republican patriots did not believe the clerical interpretation of them to be sufficiently adapted to the pressing needs of the time. The Church might indeed teach love of France, but logically this love must be subordinated to devotion to Catholic principles. Patriotism could at best be only the second of virtues; republicans would place it first. Furthermore, the Church was implanting, in the hearts of the young, belief in monarchy,

[1] Jonathan F. Scott, *Patriots in the Making.* D. Appleton and Company, 1916, pp. 244–251.

opposition to the Republic. It was largely because of its power over the rising generations that Gambetta and his followers determined to crush clericalism. They would substitute the religion of *La Patrie* for Christianity itself.

In the early eighties the *école laïque* was established; and the second period of the educational renaissance began. The religion of the Fatherland held the field without a rival. The education of patriotism and loyalty was placed on a sound basis by the government, by devoted textbook writers, by zealous teachers. Children were trained to the belief that love of country was the first of duties, and that the first element of that duty was to defend France from her enemies in time of war. Above all thought of self, the Fatherland must be enshrined in the hearts of her citizens. Hence her future defenders must learn courage, must be ready to endure the rigors of military training, must be prepared to make the pecuniary sacrifices which an adequate national defense would necessarily entail. They must not slumber in the false security of ignorance, but must be ever watchful in the presence of ever-threatening perils.

Nor did the schoolbook writers of this period, or at any rate a goodly proportion of them, hesitate to point out where they conceived the chief source of danger to lie. In their view the foe of 1870 was watching and waiting, preparing to plunge its talons into the heart of France, to tear away flesh and vitals till the very lifeblood flowed out, leaving the country a dead carcass to be devoured by the imperial eagle. These writers taught, too, that Germany had already taken her pound of flesh in the form of Alsace-Lorraine, leaving in the breast of France a gaping wound. That wound must be healed. The younger generations must regain what the men of 1870 had, with all their courage, been unable to hold.

At the same time the school was used to intrench the Republican form of government. Instead of learning to look forward to the re-establishment of monarchy as had the children of the 'seventies, the pupils of the *école laïque* were taught to shun the very thought of a royalist restoration, of imperialism, of dictatorship. Nor was the Church treated with that complete justice which the ideal of toleration demanded and which the government proclaimed would be realized. The religious beliefs of many little hearts were wounded; many were turned against the Church of their forefathers. In partial excuse it may be said that in the angry tempest of the time strict neutrality in matters of religion was practically impossible to many temperaments, however honestly they might strive for its attainment. On the other hand, French youth were taught to distrust the extreme opposite of clericalism; they were warned to avoid the pitfalls of revolutionary socialism. To the principles of the Revolution of 1789, however, they were instructed to give their heartfelt allegiance, for these principles, they were told, constituted the foundations of French liberty. The Third Republic was continuing and developing these principles, as well as restoring the prestige of France and conferring new blessings on those living under her enlightened rule. In fine, to this Republic its future citizens must be prepared to render " the last full measure of devotion "; this was the law and the prophets of the religion of *La Patrie*.

From the time of its establishment the lay school has continuously inculcated patriotism and loyalty. Toward the close of the nineteenth century, however, began a period of reaction against the intense nationalism of earlier years. Disciples of various intellectual, political and social creeds clamored for recognition in the school, and attempted to undermine certain tenets of the religion of *La Patrie*. Thus a group of scientific historians demanded that unswerving devotion to truth alone should characterize the writing and teaching of their subject. They insisted also that the attention given to military campaigns and exploits should be diminished, while the history of civilization should be brought to the foreground. Their efforts were crystallized in the programs of 1902; the glow of patriotic history seemed to pale before the cold, white light of science and the doctrine of evolution.

Furthermore, humanitarian ideals knocked for admission at the door of the *école laïque*. These ideals ranged in scope from a mild opposition to chauvinism, to a belligerent pacifism and a disheveled anarchy. Supporting them were the more or less ill-balanced theories of certain intellectuals, the clamors of syndicalism, and the pecuniary discontent of a teaching proletariat. In the textbooks the doctrines of these people appeared chiefly in protests against war and international hatreds, in assertions of the brotherhood of man. Among certain teachers they sometimes took the form of acceptance of the tenets of international, revolutionary socialism, expressing themselves, perhaps, in insults to the French flag. Nationalists spoke of the crisis of patriotism in the schools.

But the movement lacked depth. It probably weakened but little the carefully fostered psychology of national defense, though it must have curbed chauvinism and modified the teaching of *revanche*. Furthermore, its influence was brief. While the wild cries of anti-patriotism were resounding through the air, alarming those who held their country's good dearer than aught else, suddenly the German menace loomed darkly along the horizon of peace and prosperity.[1] As the cloud grew blacker and blacker, the frightened onlookers ceased their petty squabbles and prepared to face unitedly the coming storm. Thus the years immediately preceding the Great War constituted the fourth and last period of the educational revival. Not that revolutionary socialism died a sudden death; men sang the " Internationale " on the

[1] At the time of the Morocco crisis of 1905.

very eve of the great conflict. But the crisis was passed. New school manuals appeared, intensely patriotic in character. The *jeunesse intellectuelle* showed new vigor, was more athletic, and above all responded more fervently than ever to the loudly voiced appeal for devotion to the Fatherland. France was herself again.

The greatest immediate result of the education of patriotism and loyalty has been to lay a psychological foundation for a determined resistance to attack. In this respect the patriotism taught in the French schools is perhaps superior to that taught in Germany, since it is more discerning, more critical of national errors. In France are inculcated the misfortunes as well as the triumphs of the Fatherland; in Germany it is chiefly the triumphs. In so far, then, as education is a determining factor, the morale of the French soldier should be better in defeat than that of the German. If the tide should turn against the Hohenzollern Empire it will not be well for her sons to have imbibed a fanatical belief in her invincibility.[1]

In 1894 Alfred Dreyfus, a Jewish captain in the French army, was accused of treason. Tried and convicted he was sentenced to imprisonment for life and was transported to Devil's Island where he was kept in solitary confinement.

Later, however, the case was reopened. In certain circles the feelings grew that Dreyfus was innocent and suspicion centered on a certain Major Esterhazy. Accused in his turn, Esterhazy, however, was acquitted after a farcical trial. Immediately afterward Émile Zola, a well-known novelist, wrote a scathing letter, "I Accuse," charging grave injustice in the conduct of Dreyfus's case. Zola was then brought to trial by the Government and condemned to imprisonment. But a higher court reversed the decision. Finally Dreyfus was not only pardoned but retried, acquitted, and reinstated in the army with the rank of major.

Dragging on for more than a decade the Dreyfus case took on an extraordinary political and social significance. Conservatives of various kinds — monarchists, the wealthy classes, the nobility, the Church, the army — were bitterly opposed to Dreyfus. Liberals, in general, took up the cudgels in his behalf. Out of the resultant turmoil developed some of the leading political issues of the early twentieth century.

In the first of the two following selections Dreyfus tells the story of his accusation. The second is a translation from Zola's famous letter.

[1] This was written in 1916.

120. THE DREYFUS AFFAIR, I. CAPTAIN DREYFUS TELLS HOW HE WAS ACCUSED OF TREASON[1]

On Saturday, the 13th of October, 1894, I received an official note requesting me to go on the following Monday morning to the War Department, to be present at the general inspection. . . .

On Monday morning I took leave of those dear to me. My little son Pierre, then three and a half years old, who was accustomed to go with me to the door when I went out, accompanied me that morning as usual. This circumstance became one of my keenest remembrances in my misfortune. Often in my nights of agony and despair I have recalled the moment when I had clasped my child in my arms for the last time, and that recollection seemed to endow me with renewed strength and will.

The morning was fine and cool, the sun had risen above the horizon, dissipating the thin, light fog, and everything indicated a splendid day. As I arrived at the War Office a short time in advance, I strolled for some moments before the building, and then went up to the offices. Upon entering I was received by Commandant Picquart, who seemed to be waiting for me, and who at once took me into his private room. I was surprised to see none of my comrades, as officers are always assembled in groups at the general inspection. After a few minutes of trivial conversation, Commandant Picquart conducted me to the private office of the Chief of the General Staff. My surprise was great upon entering. Instead of meeting the Chief of the General Staff, I was received by Commandant du Paty de Clam, in uniform. Three persons in civilian dress, who were completely unknown to me, were also present. These three men were M. Cochefort, Chief of the Secret Police, his secretary, and M. Gribelin, Keeper of the Records. Commandant du Paty came up to me and said in a trembling voice, " The general is coming; whilst you are waiting, as I have a letter to write and have a sore finger, will you kindly write it for me? " However singular this request, made in such circumstances, I at once assented. I sat down at a little table already prepared, and Commandant du Paty seated himself close to me, following my hand with his eye. After first directing me to fill up an inspection form, he dictated to me a letter in which certain passages recalled the letter of accusation, which I heard of afterwards, and which was known by the name of the " Bordereau." In the course of the dictation the commandant said sharply, " You tremble." I did not tremble. At the court-martial of 1894 he explained this brusque exclamation, saying that he had noticed that I did not tremble during the dictation, and that he had consequently thought I was playing a part, and had therefore endeavoured to shake my

[1] Alfred Dreyfus, *Five Years of My Life*. Translated from the French by James Mortimer. London, George Newnes, 1901, pp. 4–9. By permission of Doubleday, Doran and Company.

self-assurance. This vehement remark surprised me greatly, as well as the hostile attitude of Commandant du Paty. But as there was no suspicion in my mind, I supposed he was finding fault with my handwriting. My fingers were cold, as the temperature outside was chilly, and I had only been for a few moments in a warm room. I therefore replied to him, " My fingers are half frozen."

As I continued to write without emotion, Commandant du Paty tried a fresh manoeuvre, and said to me violently, " Pay attention; it is a serious matter." Though surprised at conduct as rude as it was unexpected, I said nothing, and simply endeavoured to write better. From that moment Commandant du Paty, as he stated before the court-martial of 1894, considered that I had all my presence of mind, and that it was useless to continue the experiment any further. The scene of the dictation had been arranged in advance in every detail, but the result had not answered the expectations of those who had devised it.

As soon as the dictation was finished Commandant du Paty rose, and, placing his hand on my shoulder, exclaimed in a loud voice, " In the name of the law, I arrest you. You are accused of the crime of high treason!" Had a thunderbolt fallen at my feet the effect produced upon me could not have been more violent. I stammered a few disconnected words, protesting against an infamous accusation which nothing in my life could justify.

Then M. Cochefort and his secretary rushed upon me and searched me; I did not offer the slightest resistance, but cried to them, " Take my keys, open everything in my house. I am innocent." Then I added, " Show me at least the proofs of the infamous act which you pretend I have committed." " The charges are overwhelming," they replied, but refused to give me any information concerning their precise nature.

I was then taken to the military prison in the Rue du Cherche-Midi, by Commandant Henry, accompanied by an officer of the Secret Police.

121. THE DREYFUS AFFAIR, II. "I ACCUSE"[1]

I accuse Lieutenant-Colonel du Paty de Clam of having been the diabolical author, unwittingly, I would believe, of a miscarriage of justice, and of having afterwards, for three years, defended his ill-omened work by the most absurd and culpable tricks.

I accuse General Mercier of having made himself an accomplice, at least by weakness of will, in one of the greatest acts of injustice of the century.

[1] Extract from a Letter of Émile Zola to the President of the French Republic, January 13, 1898. *L'Affaire Dreyfus. Le procès Zola. Compte-rendu sténographique.* 2 vols., Paris, Stock, 1898, vol. I, pp. 13–14. (Translation.)

I accuse General Billot of having had in his hands the sure proofs of the innocence of Dreyfus and of having suppressed them, thus rendering himself guilty of the crime of outraging humanity and outraging justice, for a political purpose and to save the face of the General Staff, which had been compromised.

I accuse General Boisdeffre and General Gonse of having made themselves accomplices of the same crime, the first without doubt affected by his passion for the Church, the other affected perhaps by that *esprit de corps* which would transform the War Office into a Holy Place, that must not be attacked.

I accuse General de Pellieux and Commandant Ravary of having carried on a villainous investigation characterized by the most monstrous partiality, of which we have in the report of the second an imperishable monument of naïve audacity.

I accuse the three handwriting experts, Messrs. Belhomme, Varinard and Couard, of having made false and fraudulent reports, unless a medical examination should prove that they are affected with infirmity of eyesight and of judgment.

I accuse the departments of the War Office of having conducted in the Press, particularly in the *Éclair* and in the *Echo de Paris,* an abominable campaign, to mislead public opinion and to cover up their errors.

Finally I accuse the first Council of War of having violated justice in condemning an accused man on the basis of a document which has remained secret and I accuse the second Council of War of having officially concealed this illegality, thus in its turn committing the crime against justice of knowingly acquitting the guilty.

SECTION II. GERMANY

In a diary which he kept during the Franco-Prussian War Frederick, at that time Crown Prince and later for a brief period (March to June, 1888) German Emperor, gives an account of the proclamation of the German Empire in the Hall of Mirrors, in the palace of Versailles, on January 18, 1871. The proud triumph of Germany on that day stands in vivid contrast with the scene in the same Hall of Mirrors on June 28, 1919, when, after the Empire had fallen, the German delegates were forced to sign the humiliating Treaty of Versailles.

The title " Frederick III " is likely to mislead the student unless he remembers that while Frederick was the first of his name to become German Emperor he was the third Frederick to become King of Prussia.

122. PROCLAMATION OF THE GERMAN EMPIRE AT VERSAILLES, JANUARY 18, 1871 [1]

In the salons and the "*Chambre à coucher de la Reine*" was stationed the guard of the King's Staff as Guard of Honour. In the *Salle des Glaces,* to the left if one came in from the *Salon de la Paix,* and with backs to the window, stood the Prussian and Bavarian non-commissioned officers and men appearing as deputations, and over against them the officers — all decorated with the Iron Cross. As, over and above these, all officers and officials who were not on duty and could be got at in cantonments had permission to be here to-day, the gigantic hall was so full that the *Salon de la Paix* had also to be used. The platform was at the opposite end in front of the *Salon de la Guerre.* In the central window stood a field altar, before which the King took his stand, surrounded in a half-circle by all the Princes, and where Chaplain Rogge from Potsdam was to read the abridged liturgy and offer a simple prayer. As the order to the men, "Off helmets for prayer," had been forgotten, I was obliged myself to give it out loud, on which the choir of singers, made up of musicians from the different regiments here, accompanied by the band of military music, struck up the hymn "*Sei Lob und Ehr*" with fine effect in these great rooms. But the "simple prayer" consisted of a criticism of Louis XIV, with a rather tactless and tedious historical-religious dissertation on the significance of the 18th January for Prussia; the conclusion, which dwelt upon the German question and its solution as affected by to-day's event, struck another note by its fervent and effective language. During this part of the ceremony I let my eyes wander over the assembly and turn to the ceiling where Louis XIV's self-glorifications, expressed in allegories and explanatory boastful inscriptions, have for special contrast the disruption of Germany, and asked myself more than once if it was really true that we were at Versailles to witness there the re-establishment of the German Empire — so like a dream did the whole thing seem to me.

Then, after the Te Deum had been sung, the King proceeded, followed by us all, to the platform erected before the *Salon de la Guerre,* on which the non-commissioned officers with the flags and standards were already posted, and summoned the ensign with the shot-riddled colours of the 1st battalion of the Foot Guards regiment, as well as the three of his Grenadier regiment, one of whom carried another no less torn, to come right up to him, so that they stood close behind His Majesty and elbow to elbow with me. To right and left of these specially conspicuous central groups the German Reigning Princes and Hereditary Princes took their place, behind whom again the flags and standards were lined up.

[1] *The War Diary of the Emperor Frederick III. 1870–1871.* Translated and edited by A. R. Allison. London, Stanley Paul and Co., 1927, pp. 271–273.

After His Majesty had read aloud in the familiar fashion a short address to the German sovereigns, Count Bismarck came forward, looking in the grimmest of humours, and read out in an expressionless, business-like way and without any trace of warmth or feeling for the occasion, the address " to the German People." At the words " Enlarger of the Empire," I noticed a quiver stir the whole assemblage, which otherwise stood there without a word.

Then the Grand Duke of Baden came forward with the unaffected, quiet dignity that is so peculiarly his, and, with uplifted right hand, cried in a loud voice: " Long live His Imperial Majesty the Emperor William! " A thundering hurrah, at the least six times repeated, shook the room, while the flags and standards waved above the head of the new Emperor of Germany and *" Heil dir im Siegerkranz,"* rang out. The moment was extraordinarily affecting, indeed overwhelming, and was in every way wonderfully fine. I bent a knee before the Emperor and kissed his hand, whereupon he raised me and embraced me with deep emotion. My feelings I cannot describe, all quite understood them; even among the flagbearers I remarked unmistakable signs of emotion.

Then the Princes, one after the other, offered their congratulations, which the King accepted with a friendly handshake, a sort of defile past being formed, though never really marshalled properly because of the unavoidable crush. Next the King went along the line of flags and their bearers; then he stepped down from the platform and, making his way down the hall, spoke a few words in passing to the officers and men standing on either side. I had sent orders to the band, directly the Emperor was on the point of leaving the hall, to play the Hohenfriedberg march, so that His Majesty parted from the assemblage to the strains of that noble air, and finally left the Palace amid the cheers of the Staff Guard of Honour.

A dinner at the Préfecture, at which His Majesty said to me that from now I ought to be addressed as " Imperial Highness," though indeed my precise title was still unknown to him, concluded this noteworthy day, the evening of which the Princes in a body spent at my quarters.

The Versaillese understand the matter in the sense that our King is being proclaimed as French Emperor, but they cannot comprehend why we did not first consult the French. Some imagined we were capitulating to the victorious Parisians, and that was why we were removing the flags (!)

I have witnessed Coronations, Oaths of Allegiance and many unusual ceremonies, but I have known none either so august or so well contrived and so incomparable in external significance. For one thing, the vast importance of the moment was directly connected with our victories, and further, all witnesses just now gathered in these rooms were not any customary guests, but men who for months past had devoted their lives to the common cause of the Fatherland, which now, before their eyes, was receiving its consecration. Germany had her Emperor again!

Few books of comparatively recent years have aroused greater interest among thinking people than Norman Angell's Great Illusion. *Angell maintains that under modern social and economic conditions war does not pay and his book is primarily an attempt to prove this thesis.*

In the following selection he argues, specifically, that the huge indemnity paid by France to Germany after the Franco-Prussian War was far from being an economic benefit to Germany and that in the years following the war France made sounder financial progress than Germany.

123. EFFECTS OF THE INDEMNITY PAID TO GERMANY BY FRANCE AFTER THE FRANCO-PRUSSIAN WAR [1]

In politics it is unfortunately true that ten dollars which can be seen bulk more largely in the public mind than a million which happen to be out of sight but are none the less real. Thus, however clearly the wastefulness of war and the impossibility of effecting by its means any permanent economic or social advantage for the conqueror may be shown, the fact that Germany was able to exact an indemnity of a billion dollars from France at the close of the war of 1870–71 is taken as conclusive evidence that a nation can "make money by war."

In 1872, Sir Robert (then Mr.) Giffen wrote a notable article summarizing the results of the Franco-German War thus; it meant to France a loss of 3500 million dollars, and to Germany a total net gain of 870 millions, a money difference in favor of Germany exceeding in value the whole amount of the British National Debt!

An arithmetical statement of this kind seems at first sight so conclusive that those who have since discussed the financial outcome of the war of 1870 have quite overlooked the fact that, if such a balance-sheet as that indicated be sound, the whole financial history of Germany and France during the forty years which have followed the war is meaningless.

The truth is, of course, that such a balance-sheet is meaningless — a verdict which does not reflect upon Sir Robert Giffen, because he drew it up in ignorance of the sequel of the war. It does, however, reflect on those who have adopted the result shown on such a balance-sheet. Indeed, Sir Robert Giffen himself made the most important reservations. He had at least an inkling of the practical difficulties of profiting by an idemnity, and indicated plainly that the nominal figures had to be very heavily discounted.

---

[1] Norman Angell, *The Great Illusion*. G. P. Putnam's Sons, New York and London, **Fourth** Edition, 1913, pp. 88–92; 96–97; 99–100. Used by courtesy of the publishers.

A critic [1] of an early edition of this book seems to have adopted most of Sir Robert Giffen's figures, disregarding, however, certain of his reservations, and to this critic I replied as follows:

In arriving at this balance my critic, like the company-promoting genius who promises you 150 per cent for your money, leaves so much out of the account. There are a few items not considered, e.g. the increase in the French army which took place immediately after the war, and as the direct result thereof, compelled Germany to increase her army by at least one hundred thousand men, an increase which has been maintained for forty years. The expenditure throughout this time amounts to at least a billion dollars. We have already wiped out the "profit," and I have only dealt with one item yet — to this we must add, — loss of markets for Germany involved in the destruction of so many French lives and so much French wealth; loss from the general disturbance throughout Europe, and still greater loss from the fact that the unproductive expenditure on armaments throughout the greater part of Europe which has followed the war, the diversion of energies which is the result of it, has directly deprived Germany of large markets and by a general check of development indirectly deprived her of immense ones.

But it is absurd to bring figures to bear on such a system of bookkeeping as that adopted by my critic. Germany had several years' preparation for the war, and has had, as the direct result thereof, and as an integral part of the general war system which her own policy supports, certain obligations during forty years. All this is ignored. Just note how the same principle would work if applied in ordinary commercial matters; because, for instance, on an estate the actual harvest only takes a fortnight, you disregard altogether the working expenses for the remaining fifty weeks of the year, charge only the actual cost of the harvest (and not all of that), deduct this from the gross proceeds of the crops, and call the result "profits"! Such "finance" is really luminous. Applied by the ordinary business man, it would in an incredibly short time put his business in the bankruptcy court and himself in gaol!

But were my critic's figures as complete as they are absurdly incomplete and misleading, I should still be unimpressed, because the facts which stare us in the face would not corroborate his statistical performance. We are examining what is from the money point of view the most successful war ever recorded in history, and if the general proposition that such a war is financially profitable were sound, and if the results of the war were anything like as brilliant as they are represented, money should be cheaper and more plentiful in Germany than in France, and credit, public and private, should be sounder. Well, it is the exact reverse which is the case. As a net result of the whole thing Germany was, ten years after the war, a good deal worse off,

[1] *London Daily Mail,* December 15, 1910.

financially, than her vanquished rival, and was at the date trying, as she is trying today, to borrow money from her victim. Within twenty months of the payment of the last of the indemnity, the bank rate was higher in Berlin than in Paris, and we know that Bismarck's later life was clouded by the spectacle of what he regarded as an absurd miracle; the vanquished recovering more quickly than the victor. We have the testimony of his own speeches to this fact, and to the fact that France weathered the financial storms of 1878–9 a great deal better than did Germany. And today, (1911), when Germany is compelled to pay nearly 4 per cent for money, France can secure it for 3. . . . We are not for the moment considering anything but the money view — the advantages and disadvantages of a certain financial operation — and by any test that you care to apply, France, the vanquished, is better off than Germany, the victor. The French people are as a whole more prosperous, more comfortable, more economically secure, with greater reserve of savings and all the moral and social advantages that go therewith, than are the Germans, a fact expressed briefly by French Rentes standing at 98 and German Consols at 83. There is something wrong with a financial operation that gives these results.

The something wrong, of course, is that in order to arrive at any financial profit at all essential facts have to be disregarded, those facts being what necessarily precedes and what necessarily follows a war of this kind. In the case of highly organized industrial nations like England and Germany, dependent for the very livelihood of great masses of their population upon the fact that neighboring nations furnish a market for their goods, a general policy of " piracy," imposing upon those neighbors an expenditure which limits their purchasing power, creates a burden of which the nation responsible for that policy of piracy pays its part. It is not France alone which has paid the greater part of the real cost of the Franco-German War, it is Europe — and particularly Germany — in the burdensome military system and the general political situation which that war has created or intensified.

. . . .

The decade from 1870–1880 was for France a great recuperative period, although for several other nations in Europe it was one of great depression, notably, after the " boom " of 1872, for Germany. No less an authority than Bismarck himself testifies to the double fact. We know that Bismarck was astonished and dismayed by seeing the regeneration of France after the war taking place more rapidly and more completely than the regeneration of Germany. This weighed so heavily upon his mind that in introducing his Protectionist Bill in 1879 he declared that Germany was " slowly bleeding to death," and that if the present process were continued she would find herself ruined. Speaking in the Reichstag on May 2, 1879, he said:

"We see that France manages to support the present difficult business situation of the civilized world better than we do; that her Budget has increased since 1871 by a milliard and a half, and that thanks not only to loans; we see that she has more resources than Germany, and that, in short, over there they complain less of bad times."

. . . .

Two tendencies plainly show the condition of Germany during the decade which followed the war: the enormous growth of Socialism—relatively much greater than any which we have ever since seen—and the immense stimulus given to emigration.

Perhaps no thesis is commoner with the defender of war than this; that, though one may not be able in a narrow economic sense to justify an enterprise like that of 1870, the moral stimulus which victory gave to the German people is accepted as being of incalculable benefit to the race and the nation. Its alleged effect in bringing about a national solidarity, in stimulating patriotic sentiment and national pride, in the wiping out of internal differences and Heaven knows what, are claims I have dealt with at greater length elsewhere, and I wish only to note here that all this high-falutin does not stand the test of facts. The two phenomena just mentioned—the extraordinary progress of Socialism and the enormous stimulus given to emigration during the years which immediately followed the war—give the lie to all the claims in question. In 1872–73, the very years in which the moral stimulus of victory and the economic stimulus of the indemnity should have kept at home every able-bodied German, emigration was, relatively to the population, greater than it has ever been before or since, the figures for 1872 being 154,000 and for 1873 134,000. And at no period since the fifties was the internal political struggle so bitter—it was a period of repression, of prescription on the one side and class-hatred on the other—"the golden age of the drill-sergeant," some German has called it.

Having reached the conclusion that the repressive measures against socialism which he had sponsored had merely strengthened the socialist vote in Germany, Bismarck, to placate the discontented workingman, turned to social insurance. Under his influence the German Parliament passed laws insuring workers against sickness and accident, old age and incapacity.

These laws, developed further by later legislation, constitute the most significant contribution of the German Empire to the cause of social reform.

In the following selection a keen English observer comments on Bismarck's policy in relation to these laws and makes a brief, interesting comparison between the attitude of the English Government and that of the German Government toward labor law reform.

124. THE GERMAN SOCIAL INSURANCE LAWS[1]

Was Bismarck ever a social reformer by study and reasoned conviction? It is doing him no injustice to answer this question negatively. Upon this, as upon most questions, he was guided by intuition and instinct. He saw that things were wrong, and without troubling about scientific theories and sanctions, he tried, by heroic measures and straight cuts, to make them right. Yet his solicitude for the working classes was an acquired solicitude, and he arrived at it under the pressure of political difficulties. The whole bent of his mind was against any interference with the "natural" relations of capital and labour. When, as late as 1877, the Prussian Minister of Commerce prepared a bill which was intended to afford to the working classes greater protection in matters affecting their physical and moral welfare, Bismarck criticized it so severely that it had to be dropped. He regarded the labour question still as essentially one of more or less wages, of longer or shorter hours of employment, and he was far more concerned that employers should not be unduly crippled in their power to meet labour's just demands than that work should be done under ideal conditions. For traces of any genuine comprehension of social problems, or even of intimate knowledge of the working classes, Bismarck's speeches will be searched in vain. They abound in vivid intuitions of economic truth, in true and sagacious reflections upon social relations, and invaluable dicta of common sense and worldly wisdom, which even the best trained sociologist may still read with profit, but they reflect a mind influenced rather by expediency than deep conviction and impelling enthusiasm. He passed social laws because they were necessary; social reform was never to him a passion, but always a policy.

When, however, Bismarck had once decided to enter this untried path, progress was far easier for him than it was for the early reformers in England, where the prejudices and preconceptions to be overcome were so many and so deeply rooted. Individualism seemed to have conquered in Germany, but the truth was that the victory had merely been that of the handful of men who had for the time controlled fiscal and economic policy in the Ministries, and it lasted only so long as they lasted. Never did individualism obtain a firm hold upon national thought. The theory that the State had an unquestionable right to interfere in any direction in which the common good was endangered, and that it was the special duty of the Crown to hold the balance between conflicting interests, had for generations been a ruling tradition of Prussian statecraft. Now, in the conditions incidental to a time of transition, this tradition proved of immense value. It was not necessary to

---

[1] William H. Dawson, *The German Empire 1867–1914 and the Unity Movement.* New York, The Macmillan Company, 1919, vol. II, pp. 39–42.

create precedents for State action; precedents existed in abundance, and all that was needed was to go back to the forsaken ways.

The student who compares the different lines followed by social movements, particularly as reflected in labour law reforms, in England and Germany will find an invaluable clue in the fact that these movements have relied for their chief impetus in one country upon self-help and in the other upon State initiative and furtherance. In England the tendency was to set labour free from fetters and then leave it to fight its own battles. Hence freedom to organize in trade unions was given to the English working classes as early as 1825. In Germany the tendency was the other way. There labour has never yet been free, and such liberty of action as it enjoys today was gained in England half a century ago. To Governments still steeped in the traditions of absolutism it seemed safer to admit a tacit obligation to do for labour what it was not able or allowed to do for itself. That labour has so seldom given proof of gratitude for the boons conferred upon it is chiefly due to the fact that the State has never seriously tried to view labour questions from the labour standpoint, and that reforms for its benefit have too often been carried out only under pressure. " While we laud and magnify the great deeds of the Imperial Government in social politics," writes a German historian of social movements, Dr. F. Naumann, " it must never be forgotten that many of these great deeds were only necessary because of the gigantic blunders of the same Government, and that all the laws for the protection of skilled workmen are a poor substitute for the free activity of the trade unions."

Inheriting these traditions, Bismarck decided before the Empire was ten years old to embark upon the largest and most original experiment in constructive social reform ever attempted, an experiment which threw into the shade the best that had been done by the heavy-handed but well-meaning patriarchalism of the past. Brushing on one side all questions of wages and hours of labour, as questions which the working classes should be left to settle with their employers, and ignoring all demands for the right of free organization and combination, as opening up a vista of dangerous possibilities at a time when Socialistic doctrines were making ominous headway, he proposed a great scheme of social insurance by which the workers were to be afforded care and provision in all the vicissitudes of industrial life — medical treatment and maintenance in sickness, generous compensation in the event of accident, support during periods of unemployment, and finally pensions in the time of old age and permanent disablement.

SECTION III. ITALY

Whether one takes a favorable or an unfavorable view of the influence of socialism in the kingdom of Italy before the Great War its importance as a factor in Italian history at that time is evident from the extracts here quoted.

125. THE INFLUENCE OF SOCIALISM IN ITALY BETWEEN 1870–1914.

I. An Unfavorable View [1]

Fascism arose and achieved success as a reaction to what we may describe as anti-patriotism. Before the war the political life of Italy had been to a large extent a game not between political parties, but between political leaders, especially since the fall of the Right in 1876. From that time onwards there have not been until quite recent times any definite political parties, but each leader had a small group of followers, which might be enlarged by the accession of seceders from some other group, or by that of some other leader with his own following who was prepared to enter a coalition. There were tendencies, such as that of the so-called Moderates who were mildly Conservative, that of the men of the Left who were vaguely Radical, and the small band of Republicans. But none of these were organized parties in the ordinary acceptance of the term, or had a large following outside Parliament, for the mass of the public took little interest in politics.

In the early 'nineties, a new party arose with a systematic basis of principles and organization, which from small beginnings rapidly developed and became a political force which no Government could afford to disregard — the Socialists. Italian Socialism adopted the international aspect of the creed which Socialism in other countries soon discarded, and, taking advantage of the neglect by other political groups, too absorbed in the Parliamentary game and personal ambitions, of the economic conditions of the masses, raised this problem with great vigour, thereby creating a popular platform for themselves. In this, their action cannot be criticized, but they were decidedly blameworthy in waging war against existing institutions and in depicting them as the cause of the poverty of the working classes; they thus promoted a campaign of class hatred and anti-patriotism among the masses, and a Socialist came to be synonymous with an enemy of his own country. In the period following the formation of united Italy, the conditions of the lower classes were undoubtedly bad. The country was poor, its natural resources, inadequate in themselves, were not properly exploited, agricultural

[1] Luigi Villari, *The Fascist Experiment*. London, Faber and Faber, Ltd., 1926, pp. 1–9 (condensed).

and industrial education, as well as ordinary education, was neglected, and the general economic system of the country antiquated and unable to cope with the competition of more advanced countries. A serious error of the Socialists was that they based their policy on the distribution of the insufficient existing wealth of the country, instead of trying to increase production. There were, it is true, also inequalities of distribution and social injustices to be redressed, but inadequate production was the real weak point of the economic system. The Socialists, however, adopted the attitude of enemies of the State, held up the Monarchy, the army and navy, justice and the civil services, to obloquy, and professed to believe that until these were swept away the people could never come into their own. There was a curious contradiction between their hostility to the State and their advocacy of the nationalization of all wealth and means of production.

.   .   .   .

Other political groups, not being organized and having no definite principles to oppose to Socialism, adopted a merely negative attitude and also denied, or at all events ignored, the social evils which undoubtedly did exist. . . . A purely negative attitude, like that of the Constitutional groups, being always a weak one, the Socialists grew in numbers and influence, and while they never constituted a majority, and their intransigence precluded them from joining any Government, they often dominated the Government in office and blackmailed it into concessions likely to win them the support of the masses. . . .

A general atmosphere of scepticism and disregard of the higher ideals of national life was thus created, and people lived on from day to day, looking after their own small interests and hoping that unpleasant shocks would be avoided. . . .

The political and administrative situation continued to remain unsatisfactory. Intrigue of every kind was rife, fresh scandals were ever bursting on the public, which, as far as politics were concerned, seemed to be interested in little else, while with the growth of Socialism and Anarchism strikes on a large scale broke out, often accompanied by serious riots. There were troubles in Sicily and the Lunigiana in 1893, a state of siege had to be proclaimed at Milan and elsewhere in 1898, and on July 29th, 1900, King Humbert, one of the best and most kind-hearted of men, was murdered by an Anarchist at Monza. The Socialist party grew in numbers and improved its organization, especially in the industrial North and in the rich agricultural areas of the Po valley. The Government was too weak and pusillanimous to cope with the situation, and as no class of citizens could secure improvements in their condition or get real wrongs redressed without promoting agitations or strikes, a premium was put upon disorder, and the extremists took advantage of this stage of things to secure followers for their creed even among people who had no belief in Socialism.

. . . .

In this turmoil of civil strife, partizan intrigue and struggle for private or class interests, the general welfare of the nation as a whole was forgotten, and the politicians failed to realize that Italy was not an isolated unit detached from the rest of the world, but an integral part of the community of nations and that she must assert herself in the international field if she was to exist as a great Power.

. . . .

II. A Favorable View [1]

Yet it was to the growth of this Socialist party that Italy owed her emergence from the state of perpetual disturbance and rioting, culminating in the Milanese massacres of May, 1898, which had marked her history during the 'nineties. Much infected in its earlier stages with the anarchism of Bakounine and the French Communards, Italian Socialism became definitely Marxite and less revolutionary in the early eighties, under the leadership of Andrea Costa and Filippo Turati. As the only living creed that offered hope to the suffering people, it drew to itself the best of the young intellectuals as well as the artisans, and gradually extended its influence over the peasants by accepting the co-operative movement which had already done much to raise the condition of the rural population (1896). Crispi's savage and indiscriminate persecution of Socialists, Republicans and Radicals during his second ministry (1893–96) drew his victims together in the working alliance of the Extreme Left, and it is to the social programme advocated by this party, in season and out of season, that Italy largely owes the saner domestic policy that has followed the opening of the new century.

SECTION IV. AUSTRIA–HUNGARY

Racial and national hatreds became an increasingly grave problem in Austria-Hungary after the suppression of the Revolution of 1848, leading finally to the overthrow of the Dual Monarchy and the substitution of new states based, in part at any rate, on the principle of nationality.

The disorderly scenes in the Austrian Parliament, depicted in the following selection, reflect the divisive influences prevalent before the Great War in the Austrian part of the Dual Monarchy. In the Hungarian Parliament

---

[1] Janet P. Trevelyan, *A Short History of the Italian People.* G. P. Putnam's Sons, 1920, p. 543. Used by courtesy of the publishers.

the dominance of the Magyar race and an iron discipline kept disorder within bounds.

126. PRE–WAR PARLIAMENTARY SESSIONS IN AUSTRIA AND HUNGARY.[1]

In all comment on the political life of the Dual Monarchy the sharp cleavage between the life, aims and methods of the two halves, of Austria and of Hungary, must be kept in view. Nothing, for example, could be more strikingly dissimilar than an average session of the Reichsrat in Vienna and of the Chamber of Deputies in Budapest.

The structures in which the two legislative bodies are housed are both fine and impressive. The one in Budapest, standing close to the banks of the mighty Danube River, is evidently modelled after Westminster in London; it rises in its white beauty and in its graceful spires skyward in variegated splendour. The one in Vienna is as though it had been transplanted from the rocks of Parthenon — classical in outline, covering great surface but of medium height, ornate with bronze sculptures of Athenian grace and suppleness, an ancient temple devoted to the adoration of the gods. But which gods? As a matter of fact, Eris, the goddess of discord, has been worshipped most there.

Vividly I recall the last visit I paid this transcendently stately pile. It was in March, 1914. There was no ceremonial barrier to overcome. The doorkeeper in his mediaeval glory of tinsel and silver-tipped staff willingly let me pass. He may have thought that no stranger could eclipse the noise and confusion prevailing inside. For it was at the height of the obstructionist tactics embraced by the opposition that I sought admission. If Pope's lines: For forms of government let fools contest; What's best administered is best, ever was true, surely it did not apply to Austria and its parliament. For there is a total absence of dignity and efficiency there, and the bulk of the 500 delegates or thereabouts whom I saw on entering the press gallery looked and behaved like a band of madmen. It was a question about the rights and privileges of one of the eight officially recognized " national tongues," I think it was Ruthenian, that had wrought them all to such a fearful pitch. It was, I believe, a question which to an outsider appeared of minor importance. But to these men in the foreground of the immense hall it must have seemed a question of life and death. This is what burst on my astonished view: About a score of men, all decently clad, were seated or standing each at his little desk. Some made an infernal noise violently opening and shutting the lids of these desks. Others emitted a blaring sound from little toy trumpets;

[1] Wolf von Schierbrand, *Austria-Hungary: The Polyglot Empire.* New York, Stokes, 1917, pp. 115–120.

others strummed jew's-harps; still others beat snare drums. And at their head, like a bandmaster, stood a grey-bearded man of about 65, evidently the leader of this wilful faction, directing the whole pandemonium in volume and in tempo. The sum of uproar thus produced was so infernal that it completely drowned the voice of a man who was evidently talking from his seat in another part of the house, for one could see his lips moving and the veins in his temples swelling. Bedlam let loose! That was the impression on the whole. The obstructionist tactics, which I happened to witness at their zenith, were being carried out with the declared intention of overcoming the resistance to the measure advocated by the little minority of Ruthenian delegates. After listening to this infernal concert for a brief spell, in fact until my nerves gave way, I inquired outside and heard the matter stated as I described it. I was told that not only this Ruthenian fraction, but every other in the Reichsrat as well, in its fraction and committee rooms had stowed away, in a locked and safe place, a complete assortment of such instruments of torture — whistles and bell sleighs,[1] mouth harmonicas, cow bells and trombones, specially manufactured noise-producers warranted to overtop everything, etc., etc. Each party, each fraction, each faction, each individual delegate owned an arsenal of these things, merely for the purpose of making all legitimate business in the Reichsrat impossible, at the mere whim of one or a set of those " representatives " of the Austrian people. Strange but true.

It was, I think, Sydney Smith — or some other witty Englishman — who gave it as his opinion that the " solemn ass " was the most unbearable of the human species. If so, Austria is well off in that respect. Asses there are, plenty of them, both bipeds and quadrupeds — but " solemn " asses — no, never. Not one. Such an utter lack of dignity I have not encountered in any other parliament of the world. There is no mace-bearer there. No " naming of names " — that dread threat in the American Congress. No cry of " I spy a stranger! " All this would be of no avail in the Austrian parliament. There they throw inkwells at one another; hold their fists in close proximity to their neighbour's proboscis; call not only names, but very foul names. The " speaker " — here they call him the president — is inured to all this. It leaves him cold. And he has absolutely no authority, no power to control or prevent all this; he cannot stop any of these outrages. When he intends to call any member to order, to rebuke any one, or to deprive him of the word — he is at once outshouted and his plan is frustrated. The only practical remedy he has is to suspend the session, and that, as a rule, is usually precisely the thing that the obstructionist or obstructionists want. It is this utter lack of authority of the presiding officer of the Reichsrat that is responsible for the success of all the innumerable obstructionist campaigns waged there in the

---

[1] Sleigh bells?

past. It is because of this that at the recent reconvening of the Reichsrat (after a lapse of more than three years) one of the chief items in the outlined programme of reform was the thorough alteration in the code of parliamentary rules, rules that have obtained unchanged for more than a generation. It has been anarchy systematised.

Now, in the Hungarian parliament things proceed exactly in the opposite way. Count Stephen Tisza, the " man of iron " as he was called, while majority leader and premier during the most troublous period of the war and some time before, carried on a regimen of Spartan discipline. On one occasion, when the opposition became so boisterous as to make business impossible, he called on the " parliamentary guard," a small but effective military body that had taken the oath of blind obedience to the speaker, and pointed to a small group of inveterate obstructionists. And when these would not yield, Tisza gave another significant nod, and the guards drew their sabres and prepared for slaughter. Then the most obstinate gave way. In the midst of the war I witnessed a stormy session of the Hungarian Chamber. A great onslaught had been made on Tisza by his ablest foe, Count Julius Andrassy, the leader of the great Constitutionalist Party, and that had been followed by further attacks made by Karolyi and Apponyi, who charged the statesmen in power with reactionism in withholding the franchise even from the defenders of the country. The air was at white heat. An electric spark would have set it ablaze. But Tisza faced his foes like a lion. He bore the brunt of the spirited debate that followed. No insulting epithet fell from the lips of any of the speakers. Tisza's henchmen were like a Roman cohort. No break could be made in their ranks. They stood to their doughty leader like good men and true. The magic of numbers was with them, and they knew it. And victory perched on their banners. All done by and within strictly constitutional methods. And throughout one could feel that all these men, determined opponents though they were to the stern premier who was not their choice, remained Hungarian patriots, loyal to the core to the country of their birth, content to accomplish what they could by strictly parliamentary means — all Hungarians in fact. By contrast what a humiliating spectacle did the Reichsrat of Austria offer to view! There the men of each little province, of each section of a province, thought only of that and let the remainder go by the board.

SECTION V. RUSSIA, 1881–1914

The Terrorist campaign of the Narodnaya Volya *brought about on March 1st, 1881, the assassination of Alexander II. A few days later the following open letter was sent to his son and successor.*

127. LETTER SENT TO ALEXANDER III BY THE EXECUTIVE COMMITTEE [1]

March 10, 1881.

YOUR MAJESTY: Although the Executive Committee understands fully the grievous oppression that you must experience at this moment, it believes that it has no right to yield to the feeling of natural delicacy which would perhaps dictate the postponement of the following explanation to another time. There is something higher than the most legitimate human feeling, and that is duty to one's country — the duty for which a citizen must sacrifice himself and his own feelings, and even the feelings of others. In obedience to this all-powerful duty we have decided to address you at once, waiting for nothing, as will wait for nothing the historical process that threatens us with rivers of blood and the most terrible convulsions.

The tragedy enacted on the Ekaterìnski canal was not a mere casualty, nor was it unexpected. After all that had happened in the course of the previous decade it was absolutely inevitable; and in that fact consists its deep significance for a man who has been placed by fate at the head of governmental authority. . . .

You are aware, your Majesty, that the Government of the late Emperor could not be accused of a lack of energy. It hanged the innocent and the guilty, and filled prisons and remote provinces with exiles. Tens of so-called "leaders" were captured and hanged, and died with the courage and tranquillity of martyrs; but the movement did not cease — on the contrary it grew and strengthened. The revolutionary movement, your Majesty, is not dependent upon any particular individuals; it is a process of the social organism; and the scaffolds raised for its more energetic exponents are as powerless to save the out-grown order of things as the cross that was erected for the Redeemer was powerless to save the ancient world from the triumph of Christianity. The Government, of course, may yet capture and hang an immense number of separate individuals, it may break up a great number of separate revolutionary groups, it may even destroy the most important of existing revolutionary organizations; but all this will not change, in the slightest degree, the condition of affairs. Revolutionists are the creation of circumstances; of the general discontent of the people; of the striving of Russia after a new social framework. It is impossible to exterminate the whole people; it is impossible, by means of repression, to stifle its discontent. Discontent only grows the more when it is repressed. . . . This we actually see

[1] George Kennan, *Siberia and the Exile System*. London, The Century Co., 1891, II, pp. 499–503 (condensed).

from the history of the last ten years. Of what use was it to destroy the
Dolgùshintsi, the Chaikòftsi,[1] and the workers of 1874? Their places were
taken by much more resolute democrats. Then the awful repressive measures
of the Government called upon the stage the terrorists of 1878–9. . . . In vain
it destroyed tens of revolutionary circles. From among those incomplete
organizations, by virtue of natural selection, arose only stronger forms, until,
at last, there has appeared an Executive Committee with which the Government has not yet been able successfully to deal.

A dispassionate glance at the grievous decade through which we have
just passed will enable us to forecast accurately the future progress of the
revolutionary movement, provided the policy of the Government does not
change. The movement will continue to grow and extend; deeds of a terroristic nature will increase in frequency and intensity, and the revolutionary
organization will constantly set forth, in the places of destroyed groups,
stronger and more perfect forms. Meanwhile the number of the discontented
in the country will grow larger and larger; confidence in the Government,
on the part of the people, will decline; and the idea of revolution — of its
possibility and inevitability — will establish itself in Russia more and more
firmly. A terrible explosion, a bloody hurly-burly, a revolutionary earthquake
throughout Russia will complete the destruction of the old order of things.
. . . Whence proceeds this lamentable necessity for bloody conflict? It arises,
your Majesty, from the lack in Russia of a real government in the true sense
of that word. A government, in the very nature of things, should only give
outward form to the aspirations of the people and effect to the people's will.
But with us — excuse the expression — the Government has degenerated into
a mere camarilla, and deserves the name of a usurping " gang " much more
than does the Executive Committee.

Whatever may be the *intentions* of the Tsar, the *actions* of the Government have nothing in common with the popular welfare, or popular aspirations. The Imperial Government subjected the people to serfdom, put the
masses into the power of the nobility, and is now openly creating the most
injurious class of speculators and jobbers. All of its reforms result merely in
a more perfect enslavement and a more complete exploitation of the people.
It has brought Russia to such a pass that, at the present time, the masses of
the people are in a state of pauperism and ruin; are subjected to the most
humiliating surveillance, even at their own domestic hearths; and are powerless even to regulate their own communal and social affairs. The protection
of the law and of the Government is enjoyed only by the extortionist and the
exploiter, and the most exasperating robbery goes unpunished. But, on the
other hand, what a terrible fate awaits the man who sincerely considers

---

[1] Revolutionary " circles " of the late 'sixties and early 'seventies. Stepniak and Kropotkin
belonged then to Chaikovskii's circle. (Editor's note.)

the general good! You know very well, your Majesty, that it is not only socialists who are exiled and prosecuted. . . .

These are the reasons why the Russian Government exerts no moral influence, and has no support among the people. These are the reasons why Russia brings forth so many revolutionists. These are the reasons why even such a deed as Tsaricide excites in the minds of a majority of the people only gladness and sympathy. Yes, your Majesty! Do not be deceived by the reports of flatterers and sycophants — Tsaricide, in Russia, is popular.

From such a state of affairs there can be only two exits: either a revolution, absolutely inevitable and not to be averted by any punishments, or a voluntary turning of the Supreme Power to the people. In the interest of our native land, in the hope of preventing the useless waste of energy, in the hope of averting the terrible miseries that always accompany revolution, the Executive Committee approaches your Majesty with the advice to take the second course. Be assured, so soon as the Supreme Power ceases to rule arbitrarily, so soon as it firmly resolves to accede to the demands of the people's conscience and consciousness, you may, without fear, discharge the spies that disgrace the administration, send your guards back to their barracks, and burn the scaffolds that are demoralizing the people. The executive Committee will voluntarily terminate its own existence, and the organizations formed about it will disperse, in order that their members may devote themselves to the work of culture among the people of their native land.

We address your Majesty as those who have discarded all prejudices, and who have suppressed the distrust created by the actions of the Government throughout a century. We forget that you are the representative of the authority that has so often deceived and that has so injured the people. We address you as a citizen and as an honest man. We hope that the feeling of personal exasperation will not extinguish in your mind your consciousness of your duties and your desire to know the truth. *We* also might feel exasperation. You have lost your father. We have lost not only our fathers, but our brothers, our wives, our children and our dearest friends. But we are ready to suppress personal feeling if it be demanded by the welfare of Russia. We expect the same from you.

We set no conditions for you — do not let our proposition irritate you. The conditions that are prerequisite to a change from revolutionary activity to peaceful labor are created, not by us, but by history. These conditions, in our opinion, are two.

1. A general amnesty to cover all past political crimes; for the reason that they were not crimes but fulfilments of civil duty.

2. The summoning of representatives of the whole Russian people to examine the existing framework of social and governmental life, and to remodel it in accordance with the people's wishes.

We regard it as necessary, however, to remind you that the legalization of the Supreme Power, by the representatives of the people, can be valid only in case the elections are perfectly free. . . .

We declare solemnly, before the people of our native land and before the whole world, that our party will submit unconditionally to the decisions of a National Assembly elected in the manner above indicated, and that we will not allow ourselves, in future, to offer violent resistance to any Government that the National Assembly may sanction.

And now, your Majesty, decide! Before you are two courses, and you are to make your choice between them. We can only trust that your intelligence and conscience may suggest to you the only decision that is compatible with the welfare of Russia, with your own dignity, and with your duty to your native land.

THE EXECUTIVE COMMITTEE

Alexander III proved consistently opposed to political reform and his reign (1881–1894) was more reactionary than his father's. An American writer, George Kennan, made an extensive trip through Siberia in the late 'eighties and visited many of the prisons and exile groups. The publication of his book made a great impression on Western Europe and America.

128. ADMINISTRATIVE ARREST IN RUSSIA [1]

Exile by administrative process means the banishment of an obnoxious person from one part of the empire to another without the observance of any of the legal formalities that, in most civilized countries, precede the deprivation of rights and the restriction of personal liberty. The obnoxious person may not be guilty of any crime, and may not have rendered himself amenable in any way to the laws of the state, but if, in the opinion of the local authorities, his presence in a particular place is " prejudicial to public order," or "incompatible with public tranquillity," he may be arrested without a warrant, may be held from two weeks to two years in prison, and may then be removed by force to any other place within the limits of the empire and there be put under police surveillance for a period of from one year to ten years. He may or may not be informed of the reasons for this summary proceeding, but in either case he is perfectly helpless. He cannot examine the witnesses upon whose testimony his presence is declared to be " prejudicial to public order." He cannot summon friends to prove his loyalty and good character, without great risk of bringing upon them the same calamity that

[1] George Kennan, *Siberia and the Exile System.* 2 vols. London, The Century Co., 1891, I, pp. 242–243.

has befallen him. He has no right to demand a trial, or even a hearing. He cannot sue out a writ of habeas corpus. He cannot appeal to his fellow-citizens through the press. His communications with the world are so suddenly severed that sometimes even his own relatives do not know what has happened to him. He is literally and absolutely without any means whatever of self-defense.

After the breakdown of the Narodnaya Volya *and the general failure of all the revolutionary movements that had been organized, a group of Russians gathered in Switzerland and developed, through the study of Marx, the nucleus of the Social Democratic Party of Russia that was later to father the Bolshevik Party. These exiles included Georghi Plekhanov, Boris Axelrod, Vera Zasulich and Lev Deich, or Deutsch. In the course of smuggling propaganda literature through Germany, Deich was arrested by the German Government and eventually extradited to Russia whence he was sent to Siberia. This was in 1886. He escaped in 1902.*

129. THE BEGINNING OF A CONVICT CAREER [1]

A fortnight later I was informed that a party of convicts would start for Moscow that evening. I was to accompany them, and accordingly must assume the convict garb. After eighteen years I think of that day with a shudder.

First of all, I was taken into a room where was stored everything necessary to the equipment of a convict under sentence. On the floor lay piles of chains; and clothes, boots, etc., were heaped on shelves. From among them some were selected that were supposed to fit me; and I was then conducted to a second room. Here the right side of my head was shaved, and the hair on the left side cut short. I had seen people in the prison who had been treated in this fashion, and the sight had always made a painful impression on me, as indeed it does on everyone. But when I saw my own face in the glass a cold shudder ran down my spine, and I experienced a sensation of personal degradation to something less than human. I thought of the days — in Russia not so long ago — when criminals were branded with hot irons.

A convict was waiting ready to fasten on my fetters. I was placed on a stool, and had to put my foot on an anvil. The blacksmith fitted an iron ring round each ankle, and welded it together. Every stroke of the hammer made my heart sink, as I realized that a new existence was beginning for me.

The mental depression into which I now fell was soon accompanied by physical discomfort. The fetters at first caused me intolerable pain in walking,

[1] Leo Deutsch, *Sixteen Years in Siberia*. Translated by Helen Chisholm. London, John Murray, 1903, pp. 95–97 (New York, E. P. Dutton).

and even disturbed my sleep. It also requires considerable practice before one can easily manage to dress and undress. The heavy chains — about 13 lbs. in weight — are not only an encumbrance, but are very painful, as they chafe the skin round the ankles; and the leather lining is but little protection to those unaccustomed to these adornments. Another great torment is the continual clinking of the chains. It is indescribably irritating to the nervous, and reminds the prisoner at every turn that he is a pariah among his kind, " deprived of all rights."

The transformation is completed by the peculiar convict dress, consisting — besides the coarse linen underclothing — of a grey gown made of special material, and a pair of trousers. Prisoners condemned to hard labour wear a square piece of yellow cloth sewn on their gowns. The feet are clad in leathern slippers nicknamed " cats." All these articles of clothing are inconvenient, heavy, and ill-fitting.

I hardly knew myself when I looked in the glass and beheld a fully attired convict. The thought possessed me — " For long years you will have to go about in that hideous disguise." Even the gendarme regarded me with compassion.

" What won't they do to a man? " he said. And I could only try to comfort myself by thinking how many unpleasant things one gets used to, and that time might perhaps accustom one even to this.

My own clothes I gave away to the warders, and any possessions of value — watch, ring, cigarette-case — I sent by post to relations. I kept only my books. I had been given a bag in which to keep a change of linen; and into it I also put a few volumes of Shakespeare, Goethe, Heine, Molière, and Rousseau, thus completing my preparations for travelling.

Evening came. The officer in command of the convoy appeared in the prison courtyard with his men and took the party in charge. I was conducted to the office. A *statyehny spìsok* is prepared for each individual convict, in which his name and place of exile are entered, and also a list of the exciseable things he takes with him. In the *statyehny spìsok* of each political prisoner his photograph is pasted, and in mine there were two.

The officer carefully went through all these *dossiers*. We were then arranged in processional order. The soldiers surrounded us; the officer lifted his cap and crossed himself.

" A pleasant journey! Good-bye! " called out the prison officials.

" Thanks. Good-bye! " cried the officer. He then gave the signal to start, and off we marched at a slow pace to the station.

Turgenev wrote the following in France in the early 'eighties, shortly before he died. It was not published among his works but was much copied and handed about.

130. " THE THRESHOLD " [1]

I see a huge building, in the front wall a narrow door, which is wide open; beyond it stretches a dismal darkness. Before the high threshold stands a girl — a Russian girl.

The impenetrable darkness is breathing frost, and with the icy breeze from the depth of the building a slow, hollow voice is coming.

" O you! waiting to cross this threshold, do you know what awaits you? "

" I know it," answers the girl.

" Cold, hunger, hatred, derision, contempt, insults, prison, suffering, even death? "

" I know it."

" Complete isolation, alienation from all? "

" I know it. I am ready. I will bear all sorrow and miseries."

" Not only if inflicted by enemies, but by kindred and friends? "

" Yes, even by them."

" Well, are you ready for self-sacrifice? "

" Yes."

" For an anonymous self-sacrifice? You shall die, and nobody, nobody shall know even whose memory is to be honoured."

" I want neither gratitude nor pity. I want no name."

" Are you ready — for a crime? "

The girl bent her head.

" I am ready even for a crime."

The voice paused a while before renewing its questioning.

" Do you know," it said, at last, " that you may lose your faith in what you believe now; that you might come to feel that you were mistaken, and have lost in vain your young life? "

" I know that also. And, nevertheless, I will enter."

" Enter, then! "

The girl crossed the threshold, and a heavy curtain fell behind her.

" A fool! " gnashed some one outside.

" A saint! " answered a voice from somewhere.

It was inevitable that the Industrial Revolution should be tardy in reaching so undeveloped a land as Russia. When it did come it created new conditions there as elsewhere, especially the urban proletariat that so many Russians had hoped Russia would never have. Industrialization was to carry with it the germs of the Revolutions of 1905 and 1917. Professor Mavor,

---

[1] Ivan S. Turgenev, a prose poem, printed in Stepniak (Serghei Kravchinskii), *The Russian Storm Cloud*. London, Swan Sonnenschein & Co., 1886, pp. 45–46.

a Canadian scholar, made the most extensive and authoritative study that has yet appeared in English on Russian economic history.

131. THE INDUSTRIAL REVOLUTION IN RUSSIA [1]

There were large industrial establishments in Russia prior to Emancipation in 1861. These establishments belonged in some cases to the State, in other cases to great nobles and smaller gentry, and in others to merchants or even to prosperous peasants. Under pre-emancipation conditions peasants not infrequently left their villages by permission of their owners, and worked in the towns, paying *obròk* to their owners. In addition to such workers, who offered themselves for hire, there were freed peasants and proletarian or impecunious gentry, and other free or quasi-free people. There was thus the nucleus of a free hirable class of artisans, although the existence of such a class was not yet recognized.

But development in any serious sense of industrial enterprise was not compatible with bondage. Capitalistic enterprise could not grow, at least until the concurrent growth of a free and mobile class of artisans. This class begins to appear in considerable numbers only after Emancipation. Even then, however, there were limitations of the supply. The mobility of the peasant was still imperfect, for the system of *mutual guarantee* prevented the peasants from leaving their villages without permission of the *volost* court, and this permission was not always granted. When it was granted, the condition was attached that the payments of taxes and other customary payments by the absentees were to be maintained. One class of peasant was, however, at once set free for industrial employment. This was the class of . . . domestic serfs, who were not allotted any land and for whom there was no provision, restrictive or otherwise, under the Emancipation Act. Unless they desired to remain as domestic servants, and unless their former owners desired them to remain, they were practically obliged to resort to the towns for employment. . . .

Apart from the question of the supply of labour, the general economical conditions in Russia prior to the Emancipation were not favourable to the growth of industry on any extensive scale. The economic life of the country was highly self-contained. Each estate, and sometimes each village, was a little world practically complete within itself. Even the noble landowners, who spent a portion of the year in the capitals, transported to their town houses from their estates almost the whole of the produce necessary for their support and for the support of their numerous retinue of servants. With the exception of iron, tea, cotton, and a few other staple commodities not at that

[1] James Mavor, *Economic History of Russia*. 2d Edition. 2 vols. London, J. M. Dent & Sons, 1925, II, pp. 361, 363–365. By permission of E. P. Dutton & Co., New York.

time produced in Russia in sufficient quantities to satisfy the existing demand, only articles of luxury were imported, or even transferred from place to place. The great commerce which had been characteristic of early Russia, and which had been the basis of its economical and political strength, had disappeared. The " immobilization " of labour had as inevitable concomitant the " immobilization " of goods. There were, moreover, almost no railways. There was no banking system, and as yet there was but a trifling circulation of money in the country. Yet there are those who look back upon the age of bondage as an age of relative abundance — an age in which there was no freedom, but in which there was in general plenty to eat. All the conditions which have been described had to be greatly modified before extensive industry was possible. The changes began immediately after Emancipation. The creation of Land Redemption Banks and the negotiation of foreign loans provided a financial basis; railways were built rapidly in European Russia, and numbers of foreign capitalists — principally English, German, Belgian, and French — established factories for the manufacture of cottons, woolens, &c., in the late 'sixties and in the 'seventies. Some of the ancient towns developed into industrial centres. The regions specially affected by the industrial movement at this time were the Moskovskaya *gub.*, St. Petersburg and its neighbourhood, the Baltic Provinces, and parts of Poland.

The growth of the railway system in the 'seventies and the protective tariff, which reached its fullest development in 1891, stimulated industry enormously. From this time onward the urban proletariat, which, owing to the various causes indicated above, had previously no considerable existence in Russia, began to become numerous and influential. Movement from the villages ceased to be impeded by the Government, and artisans began to crowd into the towns. The excess of labour at once rendered labour cheap, and rendered the employers indifferent to the comfort of the labourers. The beginning of the process of industrial development on an extensive scale was not accompanied by the ameliorative legislation which, initiated in England, had been carried far in Germany and France — in all countries, in fact, in which the concentration of workmen in industrial towns had been taking place. Ere long the rigorous exploitation of labour brought the grievances of the workmen under the notice of the Government. Long hours, inadequate wages, and still more importantly, the knowledge that workmen in other countries were reputed to be better off than those in Russia, led to demands upon the Government to intervene. In countries where a measure of *laisser faire* existed, the natural and obvious method of labour association was productive, to a certain extent, of improved conditions. Even in such countries the power of the State was invoked in restricting the hours of labour, in regulating the system of " truck," and in providing for the protection of the working men against exposed machinery and in inevitably dangerous occupations. But in Russia such steps were taken slowly, and they were regarded by the workmen as inadequate, while labour association was practically prohibited.

Side by side with private enterprises, there were established Government factories for the manufacture of cloth, paper, tinned provisions, &c., together with metal refineries, foundries, porcelain works, &c. &c. These activities of the Government were supplemented by the factories belonging to the Udeli, in which large numbers of men were employed.

The circumstances that many of the private enterprises were brought into existence by the high protective duties, and that these enterprises were encouraged by the Government, as well as the circumstance that the Government in its own factories . . . pursued methods similar to those of the private firms, made it inevitable that the responsibility for the situation should rest upon the shoulders of the Government. The labour question thus from the middle of the 'seventies assumed a definite political aspect.

Count Serghei Witte, one of the " Baltic barons " of German descent who played so energetic a part in Russian history, was Minister of Transportation under Alexander III, and later Minister of Finances, an office which he held for ten years under Nikolai II. In opposition to von Plehve and other ultra-reactionaries who feared most of all the creation of a large urban proletariat, Witte favored industrialization and the adoption of modern western technological methods.

132. *WITTE'S OWN ACCOUNT OF HIS FINANCIAL WORK* [1]

Among my purely financial reforms the first place belongs, no doubt, to the introduction of the gold standard of currency. This measure definitely established Russia's credit and put her financially on an equal footing with the European Powers. It was owing to this reform that we weathered the wretched Japanese War and the subsequent domestic upheaval. Without it, an economic and financial collapse would have occurred at the very beginning of the war, and all the economic achievements of the recent decades would have been annihilated. . . . In the beginning, nearly the whole of thinking Russia was opposed to the reform. Very few of our financial and economic experts had any theoretical or practical knowledge of the matter in its entirety. . . . We had grown accustomed to paper currency as one gets used to chronic disease, in spite of the fact that gradually it ruins the organism. . . . Besides, among the advocates of the metallic standard there was

[1] *The Memoirs of Count Witte.* Translated from the original Russian manuscript and edited by Abraham Yarmolinsky. Garden City, Doubleday, Doran & Co., 1921, pp. 58–62, 72–78 (condensed).

no uniformity of opinion as to whether gold, silver, or both should be made the basis of currency. To the bi-metallists abroad belonged Alphonse Rothschild, head of the Rothschild firm in Paris, and his friend Léon Say, Minister of Finances under Thiers. It is noteworthy that the French Government did not hesitate to carry on an intrigue against my plan to make gold the standard of Russian currency. . . . In interfering with my reform the French were prompted by purely selfish reasons. France had an enormous amount of silver money and she was much interested in raising the price of silver. If Russia had based its currency on both gold and the depreciated silver, the price of the latter metal would have risen and the wealth of France increased by hundreds of millions of francs. Fortunately, however, Russia did not enter the road pointed out by Méline and, in spite of all the obstacles, the great reform, the glory of the present reign, was successfully carried out.

Speaking of my currency reform, it is often asked why I based it on the depreciated ruble and why I did not adopt a smaller unit than the ruble. Nominally the ruble was worth four francs, but on January 3 (15), 1897, when the reform was enacted, the rate of exchange was 2.66 2/3 (about 52 cents) per ruble. To avoid a perturbation in the economic life of the country, I adopted the latter rate. As a result, the transition to the new standard of currency passed practically unnoticed by the population. . . .

The economic wealth and consequently the political strength of a country depend upon three factors: natural resources, capital, and labour, physical and intellectual. With regard to natural resources, Russia is extremely rich, although she is unfavourably situated because of the rigorous climate in many of her sections. In capital, that is, accumulated values, she is poor, for the reason that the history of the country is a continuous chain of wars, not to speak of other reasons. Considering her population, she is rich in physical labour and also in intellectual resources, for the Russians are a gifted, sensible, and God-fearing people. All these factors of production are intimately correlated in the sense that only their concerted and coördinated action can produce wealth. At present, owing to the development of communication, natural resources are easily transported, and owing to the growth of international credit, capital is even more easily shifted. In view of this, labour has acquired an exceptional importance in the creation of wealth. It follows that I had to give especial attention to the development of both capital and labour. In the first place, it was necessary to stabilize the national credit. I hope that financial history will acknowledge the fact that never did Russian credit stand higher in both domestic and international money markets than at the time when I was Minister of Finances. It was not my fault that our military adventures have so thoroughly injured our credit. . . . It is of the utmost importance to both the foreign and domestic investor that we should have a governmental régime under which adventures like the Japanese War would be impossible, and that the nation should cease to become the object of experiments in the hands of a self-seeking and irresponsible court camarilla. Our creditors can have no faith in a régime under which they lost twenty per cent of their investments.

During my administration of the country's finances, I increased the state debt approximately nineteen hundred million rubles, and I spent even more on railroads and amortization of the debts of the Imperial Bank for the purpose of restoring the gold standard of our currency. Thus the money borrowed was expended for productive purposes exclusively. That money has increased the country's capital.

Owing to the confidence of foreign capital in Russia's credit, which I built up, our country obtained several billion rubles of foreign capital. There are people, and their number is not small, who hold this against me. Oh, folly and ignorance! No country has ever developed without foreign capital. . . . In this respect I had to contend with such statesmen as I. N. Durnovo, Plehve, and other members of the Committee of Ministers. Nicholas, as usual, favoured now one, now the other viewpoint. . . . A great many people, including the Emperor, opposed the importation of foreign capital to Russia for purely nationalistic considerations. They argued that Russian natural resources should be exploited by " true " Russians and with the aid of Russian money. They overlooked the fact that the amount of available capital in Russia was very small. As a result, industrial concessions were usually granted to " true " Russians, who subsequently sold them to foreigners and pocketed a round sum of totally unearned money. Thus, for instance, I recall that a certain retired Colonel, by the name of Vonlyarlyarski, obtained a concession for mining gold on the Kamchatka Peninsula. Several months later he sold it to a foreign corporation.

The development of our national labour was another great problem. The productivity of Russian labour is exceedingly low, this being due to the climate, among other reasons. For the latter reason, tens of millions are idle several months during the year. The scarcity of ways of communication is another factor lowering the productivity of labour. After the Turkish War of the '70's railroad construction was suspended, and it fell to my lot to resume the building of railways. In this respect, I have succeeded in achieving a good deal, for during my administration I doubled the railroad mileage. It is noteworthy that the Ministry of War was constantly thwarting my efforts. This Ministry supported me only when I proposed to build railroads of a strategic importance. Often strategic railroads were built counter to my recommendation. Besides, the direction of non-strategic railroads was often distorted to suit the purposes of the War Ministry. In this respect, General Kuropatkin, and especially the former Chief of Staff Obruchev, did a great deal of harm. . . . Thus I strained every effort to develop a railroad net. Military considerations, with which his Majesty often naturally sided, prevented me from building the lines most productive economically. As a result, the system yielded a deficit.

After dealing with the railroads for forty years, I can say that in most cases the strategic considerations of our War Ministry regarding the direction of the road are pure fantasy. . . . For thirty years we were building railroads with a view to a war in the West, and we have wasted no end of energy in that section. In the end the war broke out in the Far East.

To create new sources for the application of labour, it was more than desirable to develop our industry. Alexander the Third, with his characteristic firmness and wisdom, was the first to recognize and carry out this policy. In this respect I was his faithful assistant. It was imperative to develop our industries not only in the interest of the people, but also of the State. A modern body politic cannot be great without a well-developed national industry. As Minister of Finances, I was also in charge of our commerce and industry. As such, I increased our industry threefold. This again is held against me. Fools! It is said that I took artificial measures to develop our industry. What a silly phrase! How else can one develop an industry? Whatever men do is to a certain extent artificial. The measures taken by me were much less artificial and drastic than those practised by many foreign countries. The only thing I did was to support the protectionist tariff introduced by Vyshnegradski under Alexander III. This I did in the face of a strenuous opposition on the part of the large landowners. All my efforts to facilitate the formation of joint-stock companies were systematically thwarted by the Ministry of the Interior and Plehve particularly. I have also been blamed for having issued industrial loans from the Imperial Bank. In reality, these loans amounted only to some 50,000,000 rubles. Besides, a considerable portion of this sum was lent, without my approval, to members of the court camarilla or their friends. . . .

Railroad construction and industrial expansion diverted some four or five million men from agriculture, thus increasing, so to speak, the country's land resources by 20,000,000 to 25,000,000 desiatins. Much more will have to be done in the future to fertilize Russian labour. The very conditions under which the people live and work will have to be changed. At present a Russian works as he drinks. While he drinks less than a member of any other nationality, he gets drunk more frequently. While he works less, he overworks himself more frequently than anyone else. . . .

During my administration of the country's finances, their condition left nothing to be desired. Not only did we have no deficit, but each year there was a considerable excess of State income over State expenditures. This circumstance enabled me to keep in the Treasury large sums of free cash amounting at times to several hundred million rubles. This policy of mine was oftentimes criticized. It was pointed out that neither France, England or Germany kept unemployed cash in their state treasuries and it was argued that it would be much more advisable to invest these funds profitably. My critics merely demonstrated their ignorance of Russia's national economics. Given the Russian Empire's huge foreign debts, by far exceeding the indebtedness of any of the above-cited Western countries, it was necessary to keep a reserve fund in order to check, in a case of emergency, a panicky fall of Russian securities abroad. It must also be taken into consideration that Russia is essentially an agricultural country. The year's crops, its chief wealth, depend on the capricious elements and are an uncertain factor. This again necessitates the keeping of a reserve fund in anticipation of the lean years. I must also say that I was prompted to keep large sums of free cash in the Treasury by the feeling, which never left me after the accession of Emperor Nicholas to the throne, that sooner or later a bloody drama would be staged in this or that part of the country.

When I left the post of Minister of Finances, the free cash funds in the Treasury amounted to 380,000,000 rubles. This sum enabled the Empire to exist without a loan when the Russo-Japanese War broke out soon afterwards. It also enabled us, later, to conclude a loan on terms more favourable than we would have been forced to accept, had we not been in a position, thanks to this cash surplus, to make the world feel that our need was not urgent and immediate.

In 1894 Alexander III died and his son Nikolai II, a weak, ignorant, and sentimental young man, ascended the throne. Hopes for a less repressive reign were forwarded to Nikolai and were met with the short rejoinder that follows. It was an ill omen, but a true one, for the era that preceded Revolution.

133. THE LAST ROMANOV ANNOUNCES HIS POLICY [1]

I am glad to see here the representatives of all the different classes of the country assembled to express to me their submissive and loyal feelings. I believe in the sincerity of those feelings which are inherent in every Russian heart. But it has been brought to My knowledge that during the last months there have been heard in some zemstvos the voices of those who indulged in . . . senseless dreams with respect to the participation of the zemstvos in the general direction of the internal affairs of the State. Let it be known by all that I shall devote my whole power to the best service of the people, but that the principle of autocracy will be maintained by me as firmly and unswervingly as by my lamented father.

[1] Alexander Kornilov, *Modern Russian History*. New York, Alfred A. Knopf, 1919, II, 278.

The mystery of Father Gapon has never been solved. He was active in St. Petersburg in the opening years of the century in the work of building up workers' clubs, at times with the seeming approval of the Government. Reverses in the Japanese War led to discontent in Russia and to industrial strikes. On Sunday, January 9th, 1905, Father Gapon headed an unarmed procession of working men toward the Winter Palace, with the following petition which he meant to present to Nikolai II.

134. FATHER GAPON'S PETITION TO THE TSAR [1]

SIRE, — We, working men and inhabitants of St. Petersburg of various classes, our wives and our children and our helpless old parents, come to Thee, Sire, to seek for truth and defence. We have become beggars; we have been oppressed; we are burdened by toil beyond our powers; we are scoffed at; we are not recognized as human beings; we are treated as slaves who must suffer their bitter fate and who must keep silence. We suffered, but we are pushed farther into the den of beggary, lawlessness, and ignorance. We are choked by despotism and irresponsibility, and we are breathless. We have no more power, Sire, the limit of patience has been reached. There has arrived for us that tremendous moment when death is better than the continuation of intolerable tortures. We have left off working, and we have declared to the masters that we shall not begin to work until they comply with our demands. We beg but little; we desire only that without which life is not life, but hard labour and eternal torture. The first request which we made was that our masters should discuss our needs with us; but this they refused, on the ground that no right to make this request is recognized by law. They also declared to be illegal our requests to diminish the working hours to eight hours daily, to agree with us about the prices for our work, to consider our misunderstandings with the inferior administration of the mills, to increase the wages for the labour of women and of general labourers, so that the minimum daily wage should be one ruble per day, to abolish overtime work, to give us medical attention without insulting us, to arrange the workshops so that it might be possible to work there, and not find in them death from awful draughts and from rain and snow. All these requests appeared to be, in the opinion of our masters and of the factory and mill administrations, illegal. Every one of our requests was a crime, and the desire to improve our condition was regarded by them as impertinence, and as offensive to them.

Sire, here are many thousands of us, and all are human beings only in appearance. In reality in us, as in all Russian people, there is not recognized any human right, not even the right of speaking, thinking, meeting, dis-

1 Printed in James Mavor, *Economic History of Russia.* 2d Edition. 2 vols. London, J. M. Dent & Sons, 1925, II, 469–472 (condensed). By permission of E. P. Dutton & Co., New York.

cussing our needs, taking measures for the improvement of our condition. We have been enslaved, and enslaved under the auspices of Thy officials, with their assistance, and with their co-operation. Every one of us who dares to raise a voice in defence of working-class and popular interests is thrown into jail or is sent into banishment. For the possession of good hearts and sensitive souls we are punished as for crimes. Even to pity a beaten man — a man tortured and without rights — means to commit a heavy crime. All the people — working men as well as peasants — are handed over to the discretion of the officials of the Government, who are thieves of the property of the State — robbers who not only take no care of the interests of the people, but who trample these interests under their feet. The Government officials have brought the country to complete destruction, have involved it in a detestable war, and have further and further led it to ruin. We working men have no voice in the expenditure of the enormous amounts raised from us in taxes. We do not know even where and for what is spent the money collected from a beggared people. The people are deprived of the possibility of expressing their desires, and they now demand that they be allowed to take part in the introduction of taxes and in the expenditure of them.

The working men are deprived of the possibility of organizing themselves in unions for the defence of their interests. . . .

Russia is too great. Its necessities are too various and numerous for officials alone to rule it. National representation is indispensable. It is indispensable that people should assist and should rule themselves. To them only are known their real necessities. Do not reject their assistance, accept it, order immediately the convocation of representatives of the Russian land from all ranks, including representatives from the working men. Let there be capitalists as well as working men — official and priest, doctor and teacher — let all, whatever they may be, elect their representatives. Let everyone be equal and free in the right of election, and for this purpose order that the elections for the Constitutional Assembly be carried on under the condition of universal, equal, and secret voting. This is the most capital of our requests. In it and upon it everything is based. This is the principal and only plaster for our painful wounds, without which our wounds will fester and bring us rapidly near to death. Yet one measure alone cannot heal our wounds. Other measures are also indispensable. Directly and openly as to a Father, we speak to Thee, Sire, about them in person, for all the toiling classes of Russia. The following are indispensable:

I. Measures against the ignorance and rightlessness of the Russian people:

1. The immediate release and return of all who have suffered for political and religious convictions, for strikes, and national peasant disorders.

2. The immediate declaration of freedom and of the inviolability of the person — freedom of speech and press, freedom of meetings, and freedom of conscience in religion.

3. Universal and compulsory elementary education of the people at the charge of the State.

4. Responsibility of the Ministers before the people and guarantee that the Government will be law-abiding.

5. Equality before the law of all without exception.

6. Separation of the Church from the State.

II. Measures against the poverty of the people:

1. Abolition of indirect taxes and the substitution of a progressive income tax.

2. Abolition of the Redemption Instalments, cheap credit, and gradual transference of the land to the people.

3. The orders for the military and naval ministries should be fulfilled in Russia, and not abroad.

4. The cessation of the war by the will of the people.

III. Measures against the oppression of labour:

1. Abolition of the factory inspectorships.

2. Institution at factories and mills of permanent committees of elected workers, which, together with the administration (of the factories) would consider the complaints of individual workers. Discharge of working men should not take place otherwise than by resolution of this committee.

3. Freedom of organization of co-operative societies of consumers and of labour trade unions immediately.

4. Eight-hours working day and regulation of overtime working.

5. Freedom of the struggle of labour against capital immediately.

6. Normal wages immediately.

7. Participation of working-class representatives in the working out of projects of law upon workmen's State insurance immediately.

The reception the demonstrators met with is narrated by three correspondents, the first two English, the last a Frenchman.

135. "*RED SUNDAY*" *IN ST. PETERSBURG* [1]

A

Startling events took place on Sunday in St. Petersburg. On Saturday the strikers continued their agitation with great activity, and compelled the closing of numerous factories. . . . Father Gapon, the priest who has been

[1] *London Weekly Times.* January 27, 1905.

prominent in organizing the movement, on Saturday afternoon sent his secretary to the Minister of the Interior with a letter strongly urging that the Tsar should meet his people in front of the Winter Palace the next day, and stating that his Majesty had nothing to fear. . . . The Metropolitan anathematized Father Gapon for "inciting the people in time of trouble. . . ." On Sunday morning the various approaches to the Winter Palace were strongly guarded by detachments of infantry, Uhlans and Cossacks, and there were also detachments of troops at many of the factories and at the city gates. . . . The strikers and their sympathizers began, towards noon, to move towards the Palace from different quarters, but were everywhere confronted by the troops. Collisions soon took place, and though, in at least one instance, the infantry laid down their rifles and refused to fire, the Cossacks and Uhlans charged the crowds without hesitation. The crowd in several places offered a stubborn resistance, and large numbers, including women and children, were killed and wounded. . . . The Tsar remained throughout the day at Tsarskoe Selo. . . . The strikers and revolutionists are under control. The movement has, however, spread to other centres of population.

B

St. Petersburg awoke this morning to find itself in a state of siege. . . . There were five degrees of frost. The air was crisp and invigorating and the sky almost cloudless. . . .

I noticed a significant change in the bearing of the passers by. Instead of flocking up the steps of St. Isaac's Cathedral, as usual on Sunday morning, they were all silently wending their way, singly or in small groups, in the direction of the Winter Palace. No observer could help being struck by the look of sullen determination on every face. As the people turning the corners came within view of the Winter Palace, they craned their necks and with eager eyes directed on the square attempted to see what was happening.

Already a crowd of many thousands had collected, but was prevented from entering the square by mounted troops. . . . Presently the masses began to press forward threateningly. The cavalry advanced at a walking pace, scattering the people right and left. . . . Down to the last moment no one seemed to believe that anything serious was likely to happen. . . . Within a space of two hours the city has been plunged into a state of open revolution.

[A crowd of workers came from the Putilov Steel Works to the rendezvous.]

The strikers in the front ranks fell on their knees and implored the Cossacks to let them pass, protesting that they had no hostile intentions. They refused, however, to be intimidated by blank cartridges, and orders were given to load with ball.

The passions of the mob broke loose like a bursting dam. The people seeing the dead and dying carried away in all directions, the snow on the street and pavements soaked with blood, cried aloud for vengeance.

Meanwhile the situation at the Palace was becoming momentarily worse. The troops were reported to be unable to control the vast masses which were constantly surging forward. Reinforcements were sent, and at 2 o'clock here also the order was given to fire. Men, women, and children fell at each volley, and were carried away in ambulances, sledges and carts. It was no longer a workman's question. The indignation and fury of every class were aroused.

Father Gapon, marching at the head of a large body of workmen, carrying a cross and other religious emblems, was wounded in the arm and shoulder.

C

I was present to-day at the most horrible spectacle I have ever witnessed. . . . I have seen blood flow in streams on the hardened snow. I have seen police agents, sword in hand, slash blindly about them. I have seen their revolvers used wildly against the crowd. I have seen whole companies of infantry discharging murderous volleys on the shrieking crowd. And on all sides the dead with the wounded falling upon them and the horrible pell-mell, in which women and children covered with blood fall in the snow. It is not a strike. It is a revolution.

Industrial and agrarian agitation grew so menacing in 1905 that, coupled with the increasingly bold criticism of the Constitutional Democrats (Kadets), it drove the Government to issue the October Manifesto. This step was followed in 1906 by the granting of a constitution and the setting up of a parliamentary body called the Imperial Duma, which functioned until 1917 but, after 1907, badly and without genuine power. The first Duma was dominated by the Kadets, who demanded substance as well as show of a constitutional régime, but the Kadets were eliminated from later Dumas and reaction was the order of the day.

136. THE OCTOBER MANIFESTO [1]

The rioting and agitation in the capitals and in many localities of OUR Empire fills OUR heart with great and deep grief. The welfare of the Russian Emperor is bound up with the welfare of the people, and its sorrows are HIS sorrows. The turbulence which has broken out may confound the people and threaten the integrity and unity of OUR Empire.

[1] *Polnoe Sobranie Zakonov Rossiiskoi Imperii*, XXV, 1905, 754. English translation taken from F. A. Golder, *Documents of Russian History*, New York, Century Co., 1927, pp. 627–628.

The great vow of service by the Tsar obligates US to endeavor, with all OUR strength, wisdom, and power, to put an end as quickly as possible to the disturbance so dangerous to the Empire. In commanding the responsible authorities to take measures to stop disorders, lawlessness, and violence, and to protect peaceful citizens in the quiet performance of their duties, WE have found it necessary to unite the activities of the Supreme Government, so as to insure the successful carrying out of the general measures laid down by US for the peaceful life of the state.

We lay upon the Government the execution of OUR unchangeable will:

1. To grant to the population the inviolable right of free citizenship, based on the principles of the freedom of person, conscience, speech, assembly, and union.

2. Without postponing the intended elections for the State Duma and in so far as possible, in view of the short time that remains before the assembling of that body, to include in the participation of the work of the Duma those classes of the population that have been until now entirely deprived of the right to vote, and to extend in the future, by the newly created legislative way, the principles of the general right of election.

3. To establish as an unbreakable rule that no law shall go into force without its confirmation by the State Duma and that the persons elected by the people shall have the opportunity for actual participation in supervising the legality of the acts of authorities appointed by US.

We call on all the true sons of Russia to remember their duties toward their country, to assist in combating these unheard-of disturbances, and to join US with all their might in reëstablishing quiet and peace in the country.

Given in Peterhof, on the seventeenth [thirtieth] day of October in the year of our Lord 1905, and the eleventh year of OUR reign.

NICHOLAS

The one capable minister Nikolai II appointed after Witte's dismissal was Piotr Stolypin, who was premier from 1906 until his assassination in 1911. Stolypin was reactionary in politics, yet in his land policy he furthered the work begun forty-five years earlier in the Emancipation of the serfs.

137. STOLYPIN'S LAND LAW [1]

The law upon which all subsequent projects of land reform in Russia must be based is contained in the ukase of 9th November 1906. This law effected a fundamental change in the relation between the peasant and the

[1] James Mavor, *Economic History of Russia.* 2d Edition, 2 vols. London, J. M. Dent & Sons, 1925, II, pp. 340–341. By permission of E. P. Dutton & Co., New York.

land. Old Russian habits of thought about landownership had attached to the idea of land possession a collective character. The rights of the community in the land were more or less definitely recognized, both before and after the emancipation of the serfs. The proprietor of the land could not do with it precisely what he liked. It was, in early times, when held as a *votchina*,[1] his own heritable property, and in later times the distinction between *votchinal* ownership and other forms being obscured or obliterated, it became also heritable whether it was in *votchinal* ownership, properly speaking, or not. But the later history of landownership is especially characterized by restrictions upon the mobility or free transference of land. Land could not be sold to persons not authorized to possess land, and in this category were large classes of the community; land might not be sold without the peasants who cultivated and lived upon it, etc. The community, as represented by the State, imposed these regulations, and thus confirmed its claim to an interest in the land. Moreover, the taxes upon land being assessed in accordance with the number of peasants living upon it, it was the interest of the community to see that none of its members evaded his just obligations by leaving the community, which was responsible for the payment of his quota of the taxes. In order to make the " mutual guarantee " effective, it was necessary for the community, as represented in the *volost,* to regulate the distribution of the land, and to see that each peasant took enough land to enable him to support his family and to contribute his quota of the taxes. In short, the community appeared everywhere; legislation was directed either towards securing the interest of the State or community as central authority, or of the *volost* or *mir* or community as local authority. The interest of the individual peasant family was secured by the presence of its head in the *volost* assemblies, and by his right to appear in the *volost* court. But the right of the individual peasant was not explicitly recognized, excepting that, with the permission of his family and of the *volost,* he could " separate," and in " separation " could receive a specific share of the land of the family. . . . But the community land and the community interest in it remained. There was practically no land in individual family heritable tenure.

The ukase of 9th November 1906 changed all that. Under it every householder, independently altogether of the will of the community, was endowed with the right to fix in property, personal to himself and heritable, that portion of land which belonged to his family at the last distribution. This right involved the further rights to sell the land, and to distribute it among his descendants at his own discretion, although his powers in this connection were much modified by local customs as well as by general civil law. In order to prevent the accumulation of large blocks of land in few hands, the ukase provided that no single purchaser might purchase more than 25 des-

[1] Mediaeval form of hereditary land tenure. (Editor's note.)

siatines [1] from any individual seller. The ukase of 9th November 1906 may thus be held to have in reality introduced into Russian law the conception of individual ownership of property, and thus to have brought in this respect Russian law into conformity with the law of Western Europe upon the subject.

[1] *Dessiatina* is equivalent to approximately 2.8 acres. (Editor's note.)

CHAPTER X

THE NEAR EASTERN QUESTION (1814–1914)

SECTION I. THE BEGINNINGS OF BALKAN INDEPENDENCE

The victorious sweep of Ottoman power was first checked in 1699 when the Treaty of Karlowitz diminished Turkey's European possessions. As the eighteenth century progressed, it became clearer that the Turks were on the defensive. The Russo-Turkish War of 1768–1774, which Katherine II successfully prosecuted, led, in the midst of an all-European intrigue, to the signing of peace at Kuchuk-Kainardji in 1774. In this treaty might be read for the first time the Eastern Question, which was a question not merely in the general sense but was literally a question the solution of which racked the brains of the statesmen of Europe. It was: When Turkish power declines to the point of extinction, what is to become of the European territories of the Ottoman Empire, and especially Constantinople, coveted of all East-European nations, the cultural centre of the Greeks and the Tsargrad of the Russians? Russia wished to be able to interfere in Ottoman affairs and several articles of this treaty gave her an opportunity.

138. THE ELASTIC PARTS OF THE TREATY OF KAINARDJI [1]

ARTICLE VII. The Sublime Porte promises constantly to protect the Christian Religion in all its Churches, and also agrees that the Ministers of the Imperial Court of Russia may make Representations in favour of the Church to be erected at Constantinople, as well as those officiating therein, and promises to receive these remonstrances as coming from a trustworthy person in the name of a sincerely friendly neighboring Power.

[Article VIII. Permission to Russian subjects to visit Jerusalem and other places.]

Article XIV. Besides the Private Church, the Court of Russia shall have the right, in the same manner as other Powers, to erect a Church at Galata, in the street called Bey-Ugla, which Church shall bear the name of Russo-Greek Church, and shall always be under the protection of the Russian Minister, exempt from all Taxes, and secure from attacks. . . .

[1] Edward Hertslet, *Map of Europe by Treaty.* 4 vols. London, 1875–1891, vol. III, p. 2011 (excerpts).

Article XVI. . . . 2. Not to put, in any manner whatever, any obstacle to the exercise of Divine Worship, free in every respect, or to prevent the building of New Churches, or the repair of the old ones, as they were before. . . .

The Serbs, under Kara George in 1804–1813 and, more successfully in 1815–1817 under Milan Obrenovits, were the first of the Balkan peoples to rise but the Greeks followed in 1821 and proclaimed their independence. The long war that was fought to secure the substance of what the following declaration enunciated was successful only through the aid of Great Britain, Russia, and France, whose intervention in 1827 obliged the Turk finally to yield independence to an abbreviated Greek state, the first of the Balkan nations to acquire its freedom.

139. THE GREEK DECLARATION OF INDEPENDENCE [1]

The National Assembly to the Greeks

The Greek nation, wearied by the dreadful weight of Ottoman oppression, and resolved to break its yoke, though at the price of the greatest sacrifices, proclaims today, before God and men, by the organ of its lawful representatives, met in a national assembly, its independence.

Descendents of a generous and enlightened nation, witnesses of the happiness which the sacred aegis of law secures to the civilized nations of Europe! Ye all know, that the measure of our sufferings was full. It was impossible for us any longer to bear, without being charged with cowardice and stupidity, the cruel scourge of Ottoman rule. Has not the Turk, during four centuries, trampling under foot reason and justice, disposed of us as his caprice prompted? We flew to arms then, in order to avenge the injuries which an insolent tyrant had heaped on our country; injuries utterly unexampled, and which left far behind it all the various shapes of oppression which have ever desolated and dyed the earth with carnage.

Our warfare against the Turks, far from being the effect of a seditious and jacobinical movement, or the pretext of an ambitious faction, is a national war, undertaken for the sole purpose of reconquering our rights, and securing our existence and honour. In vain did injustice, by depriving us of all securities, hope to stifle in our hearts the conviction of their necessity. As if, formed out of the vilest materials, we were condemned by nature to perpetual servitude; doomed to crouch beneath the wild sway of ferocious tyrants, who came from afar to subdue and to crush us! No, a thousand

[1] John L. Comstock, *History of the Greek Revolution, Compiled from Official Documents of the Greek Government*, etc. New York, 1829, pp. 499–500.

ages of proscription would not bar the sacred rights, whose creation was the work of nature herself. They were torn from us by violence; and violence, more righteously directed, may one day win them back, and hold them forth in all their reviving brilliancy to the admiration of the universe. In a word, they are rights which we have never ceased reclaiming in the very heart of our country, by every method which occasional opportunities placed in our power.

Strong in these principles, and wishing to advance as the equals of the Christians of Europe, in the paths of civilization, we combined into one great war all the partial and secret conflicts which we had long waged against the Ottoman empire. We swore to conquer, and to behold our country governed by just laws, or to disappear from the face of the earth. During ten months God has blessed our steps in this glorious but rugged road. Our arms have been often victorious, but often they have experienced resistance. We are struggling to remove the obstacles which retard our triumph. Our political organization was then deferred, and the nation, solely occupied in repelling a lasting danger, foresaw that appearance of disorder which ever follows great convulsions, and which the injudicious alone can make a matter of reproach against us.

As soon as circumstances allowed us to think of a plan of government, we saw the Greek continent of the east and west, the Peloponnesus, and the islands, successively proceed in their organization, and prepare the way for that general constitutional system which was necessary to direct the progress of our revolution. For this purpose, the deputies of the provinces and of the islands, being duly authorized, and having met in a national assembly, and after deliberately considering the state of the country, have decreed the basis and the provisional form of the government which is to preside over the future destinies of your country. This government, founded on justice, instituted by universal consent, is now the only legitimate and national government. The nations of Greece will therefore hasten to recognize it.

Two august bodies, the executive power and the senate, will be at the head of the administration, supported by the judicial power, which will discharge its duties quite independently of the former.

The assembly declares to the nation, that, having completed its task, it this day dissolves itself. It is the duty of the nation to submit to the laws and the authorities which emanate from it. Grecians! but a little while since, ye said, " no more slavery! " and the power of the tyrant has vanished. But it is concord alone which can consolidate your liberty and independence. The assembly offers up its prayers, that the mighty arm of the Most High may raise the nation towards the sanctuary of his eternal wisdom. Thus discerning their true interests, the magistrates, by a vigilant foresight, the people, by a sincere devotion, will succeed in founding the long-desired prosperity of our common country.

EPIDAURUS, the 15th of January, 1822,
and the First Year of Independence.

SECTION II. THE SICK MAN OF EUROPE

It was in St. Petersburg, in a conversation with the British ambassador, that Nikolai I originally applied the phrase, " the Sick Man of Europe," to Turkey, but the idea is expressed clearly enough in conferences that took place on the occasion of the tsar's visit in 1844 to England. At this time Sir Robert Peel was Prime Minister; and the Earl of Aberdeen, Foreign Secretary; while Baron Stockmar, a German, was a confidential adviser at times to Queen Victoria.

140. THE SICK MAN OF EUROPE[1]

The subject which appears to be occupying most of the Emperor's thoughts is the East, and this, very probably, is the main reason of his visit. Perhaps he wished himself to see, and to sound, and to compare what he may see and hear, with the reports of his diplomatic agents.

He said to Aberdeen: " Turkey is a dying man. We may endeavour to keep him alive, but we shall not succeed. He will, he must die. That will be a critical moment. I foresee that I shall have to put my armies in movement, and Austria must do the same. I fear nobody in the matter, but France. What will she require? I fear much: in Africa, in the Mediterranean, in the East itself. Do you remember the expedition to Ancona? Why should she not undertake similar ones to Candia or Smyrna? In such a case, must not England be on the spot with the whole of her maritime forces? Thus a Russian army, an Austrian army, a great English fleet, all congregated together in those parts. So many powder barrels close to the fire, how shall one prevent the sparks from catching? . . ."

On the occasion of the Emperor's conversation with Sir Robert Peel the windows were open. The Emperor spoke so loud that the persons outside could hear all that he said, and the Premier was obliged to ask His Majesty to withdraw to the end of the room. . . .

In this conversation, too, it was apparent that the East was at that time exclusively occupying the Emperor's attention.

" Turkey," he said, " must fall to pieces. Nesselrode denies this, but I

---

[1] *Memoirs of Baron Stockmar*, by his son Baron E. von Stockmar. Translated from the German by G. A. M. 2 vols. London, 1873, II, pp. 106–109 (condensed).

for my part am fully convinced of it. The Sultan is no genius, but he is at least a man. Let some misfortune happen to him, what then? A child with a Regency. I don't claim one inch of Turkish soil, but neither will I allow that any other shall have an inch of it."

The Premier replied, that England, in regard to the East, was in a similar position, except that, on one point, the policy of England was slightly modified, namely in regard to Egypt. Too powerful a Government there — a Government that might close the commercial road across Egypt against England, or refuse the transit of the English overland mails — could not be agreeable to England.

The Emperor went on: "We cannot now stipulate as to what shall be done with Turkey when she is dead. Such stipulations would only hasten her death. I shall therefore do all in my power to maintain the *status quo*. But nevertheless, we should keep the possible and eventual case of her collapse honestly and reasonably before our eyes. We ought to deliberate reasonably, and endeavour to come to a straightforward and honest understanding on the subject."

When Nikolai I returned home in 1844 he was under the impression that the British Government shared his opinion that the demise of " the Sick Man of Europe" was approaching and desirable, and that Russia and Great Britain should act together in dividing the estate. Common action with Russia was, however, the last thing in the minds of most British statesmen, and certainly in that of Palmerston, Foreign Secretary for many years and later Prime Minister. Palmerston, a Liberal in politics and in certain policies, was the precursor of Disraeli in his belief in the importance of upholding British prestige and British influence the world over. When the house of Don Pacifico, a Jew who moved from Gibraltar to Athens, was sacked by a mob, Palmerston at once sent a fleet to coerce the Greek Government. His policy in this act was at variance with Russian ideas and was due to his desire to maintain British authority to offset Russian influence in the Near East. Criticism in the House of Commons led to a famous speech by Palmerston, of which these are the closing sentences.

141. PALMERSTON'S DEFENCE OF AN AGGRESSIVE FOREIGN POLICY [1]

For while we have seen . . . the political earthquake rocking Europe from side to side — while we have seen thrones shaken, shattered, levelled; institutions overthrown and destroyed — while in almost every country of

[1] Hansard's *Parliamentary Debates*. 3rd Series, vol. CXII, pp. 443–444. June 25, 1850.

Europe the conflict of civil war has deluged the land with blood, from the Atlantic to the Black Sea, from the Baltic to the Mediterranean; this country has preserved a spectacle honourable to the people of England, and worthy of the admiration of mankind.

We have shown that liberty is compatible with order; that individual freedom is reconcilable with obedience to the law. We have shown the example of a nation, in which every class of society accepts with cheerfulness the lot which Providence has assigned to it; while at the same time every individual of each class is constantly striving to raise himself in the social scale — not by injustice and wrong, not by violence and illegality — but by preserving good conduct, and by the steady and energetic exertion of the moral and intellectual faculties with which his Creator has endowed him. . . . I contend that we have not in our foreign policy done anything to forfeit the confidence of the country. . . . I maintain that the principles which can be traced through all our foreign transactions, as the guiding rule and directing spirit of our proceedings, are such as deserve approbation. I therefore fearlessly challenge the verdict which this House, as representing a political, a commercial, a constitutional country, is to give on the question now brought before it; whether the principles on which the foreign policy of Her Majesty's Government has been conducted, and the sense of duty which has led us to think ourselves bound to afford protection to our fellow subjects abroad, are proper and fitting guides for those who are charged with the Government of England; and whether, as the Roman, in days of old, held himself free from indignity, when he could say *Civis Romanus sum;* so also a British subject, in whatever land he may be, shall feel confident that the watchful eye and the strong arm of England will protect him against injustice and wrong.

British foreign policy from the fall of Napoleon to the time when German rivalry seemed the greater menace, was based on fear of Russia's dominating the Near East and, consequently, the approach to India. Palmerston was well represented at Constantinople by Stratford Canning, one of the most distinguished of a long line of British diplomats who, far from home, took much of the initiative in determining British policy. In 1854 the Russians, long protectors of Orthodox Christians in Turkey, were negotiating to remedy a grievance they felt in regard to the treatment of Christians at the religious shrines of Jerusalem. The episode described concerns the mission of Prince Menshikov to Constantinople and reveals the way in which the British envoy assisted the Ottoman Government in its resistance to the Russian demands.

142. *ON THE EVE OF THE CRIMEAN WAR*[1]

The real grievances had been repaired; nevertheless Nicholas selected this particular stage of the business to deliver more than usually peremptory orders to his representative, and Prince Menshikov, who must now have perceived clearly his blunder, was forced to send in the Note of 5 May. In this composition he acknowledges the receipt of the firmans[2] granting all the original Russian demands concerning the Holy Places, but " having obtained so far no response to the third and most important point, which requires guarantees for the future, and having received the command to redouble his pressure in order to come to the immediate decision of the question which forms the chief object of the Emperor's solicitude, the ambassador finds himself under compulsion at once to address the Foreign Secretary and formulate his demands in the final limits of his instructions." He gave the Porte five days to decide, and threatened painful consequences in case of further delay. Enclosed with the Note was a *Projet de Convention,* which contained the old demand of Russia on behalf of the Greek Church, with the old effect of giving Russia the right of interference in the internal affairs of the Ottoman Empire. . . .

Lord Stratford's analysis of the Note of 20 May was sent to Reshid in the following memorandum:

The *Projet* of an official Note or Declaration proposed by Pr. Menshikov to Reshid Pasha on 20 May should be examined with an earnest desire to make it an instrument of reconciliation.

We can hardly expect the Porte to give up what the Cabinet, the Council, and the Sultan have determined to be inadmissible. But if the essential objections be withdrawn in the proposed Note, or if the Note admits of such modification as would have the effect of withdrawing them, the Porte should doubtless be encouraged to close with the ambassador's offer, in spite of the rupture which has been declared by him.

Now, the main essential points on which Pr. Menshikov has hitherto insisted and which the Porte has determined to reject are the form of agreement having the force of a treaty, and the reference of the Sultan's confirmation of his Christian subjects' privileges to the requisition and protection of Russia. The first object of inquiry therefore is this; Does the Note in letter or spirit contain those two objections? Take each of them in succession. With respect to the first, we perceive that the phrase of " having the force of a treaty " does not appear in the Note. The words are expunged. Do their meaning and spirit remain? Now can anyone having the Note in his hand

---

[1] Stanley Lane-Poole, *The Life of the Right Honourable Stratford Canning, Viscount Stratford de Redclyffe.* 2 vols. London, Longmans, Green & Co., 1888, II, pp. 263, 270.

[2] A *firman* was an Ottoman decree. (Editor's note.)

answer this question negatively? It has all the characteristics of an engagement binding solemnly the Porte for its strict execution in perpetuity to Russia, and giving that Power a distinct right to call the Porte to account for any remissness in that respect.

As to the second objection, the whole tenor of the preamble goes to make the Sultan's declaration in favour of his Christian subjects an immediate consequence of Prince Menshikov's embassy, and therefore no longer an act of grace on his part binding their affections to him and resting on his honour, as an independent sovereign pledged in the face of Europe, whose goodwill is essential to his safety, but as a deed of compliance with foreign dictation having for its immediate result the introduction of Russian influence, to be exercised with all the force of acknowledged right, into a department of internal administration affecting the religious sentiments and worldly interests of more than ten millions of the Sultan's subjects.

An anonymous writer concludes a volume on Russian aggressiveness in the Near East with the following paragraphs, which are representative of British opinion on the eve of the Crimean War.

143. AN ENGLISH APPREHENSION OF RUSSIAN AIMS [1]

If the object of the Emperor be to obtain spiritual and ecclesiastical dominion over the whole Orthodox Greek Church for himself and his successors — and on no other ground does his recent conduct appear to be explicable — there is no probability that he will relinquish an object of such magnitude while there remains a prospect of success; no present sacrifice would be of much weight in deterring him from the prosecution of that which, if attained, would, with all its almost inevitable consequences, be a greater acquisition than the greatest and most successful of his predecessors have ever made. The problem of the future fate of the Ottoman Empire in Europe would then be solved by the Christian population that inhabits it in concert with their spiritual chief. While Turkey can maintain the independence of the Patriarch and Synod of Constantinople, who is the head of the Greek Church in the Ottoman Empire, the object of the Czar cannot be accomplished; and there are not wanting indications that the spiritual chief of the Greeks in Turkey begins to see the danger to which his authority is exposed. But if we allow the Sultan to be despoiled of his rights, and deprived of the power to protect the independence of the ecclesiastical authorities, preserved and maintained by his predecessors since the conquest of Constantinople by the Ottomans, it will be too late to speak of the integrity

[1] *The Progress and Present Position of Russia in the East.* London, 1854, pp. 168–170 (condensed).

and independence of Turkey or the Sovereign rights of the Sultan; the spiritual dominion of the Czar will be extended over all Turkey in Europe, Greece, and part of Austria, and will assuredly draw temporal dominion after it. Who will venture to maintain that Germany, or Italy, or France could, in such a condition of things, be truly independent? The influence of such a power would predominate in every cabinet, and affect the decision of every question. Her support would everywhere sustain the partisans of her system, and enable them to triumph over their opponents. The unacknowl edged weight of her influence, and dread of her power, would gradually modify the institutions of Europe, and silence every voice that was raised against her. Have we not already had sufficient indication, in Germany and elsewhere on the Continent, of the support she affords to her partisans in foreign states, and the success with which she has thwarted and injured those who were hostile to her views and her system? It is while the resources of the Ottoman Empire are still entire, not after they have been shattered in a single-handed combat with too powerful an antagonist, that the mischief can be prevented. Hitherto the allies of Turkey have given her no material assistance, and Russia, having hurled defiance in the face of Europe, maintains her aggressive position, and treats with arrogant disdain the efforts of the Western Powers to preserve peace. . . .

If Russia is resolved to try her strength, with France and England and Turkey combined against her, she will develop great resources and maintain an obstinate struggle. Let us hope that our tardiness to accept the combat is but an indication that we foresee its magnitude; and that the two great Western Powers, warned as it were by a mighty voice from the tomb against "a little war," are prepared, if negociation has failed, at once to put forth all their strength — to hit hard — and to strike home.

France, Sardinia, and Turkey supported Great Britain in the Crimean War of 1854–1856 and the allies were able to dictate peace at Paris. The war was one of the least significant in European history and the terms of the peace among the least lasting.

144. THE TREATY OF PARIS OF 1856[1]

Art. I. From the day of the exchange of the Ratifications of the present Treaty there shall be Peace and Friendship between Her Majesty the Queen of the United Kingdom of Great Britain and Ireland, His Majesty the Emperor of the French, His Majesty the King of Sardinia, His Imperial Majesty

[1] Edward Hertslet, *Map of Europe by Treaty*. 4 vols. London, 1875–1891, vol. II, pp. 1250 ff. (excerpts).

the Sultan, on the one part, and His Majesty the Emperor of all the Russias, on the other part; as well as between their heirs and successors, their respective dominions and subjects, in perpetuity.

Art. II. Peace being happily re-established between their said Majesties, the Territories conquered or occupied by their armies during the War shall be reciprocally evacuated. . . .

Art. VII. Her Majesty the Queen . . . , His Majesty the Emperor of Austria, His Majesty the Emperor of the French, His Majesty the King of Prussia, His Majesty the Emperor of all the Russias, and His Majesty the King of Sardinia, declare the Sublime Porte admitted to participate in the advantages of the Public Law and System of Europe. Their Majesties engage, each on his part, to respect the Independence and the Territorial Integrity of the Ottoman Empire; Guarantee in common the strict observance of that engagement; and will, in consequence, consider any act tending to its violation as a question of general interest.

Art. VIII. If there should arise between the Sublime Porte and one or more of the other Signing Powers, any misunderstanding which might endanger the maintenance of their relations, the Sublime Porte, and each of such Powers, before having recourse to the use of force, shall afford the other Contracting Parties the opportunity of preventing such an extremity by means of their Mediation.

Art. IX. His Imperial Majesty the Sultan having, in his constant solicitude for the welfare of his subjects, issued a Firman, which, while ameliorating their condition without distinction of Religion or of Race, records his generous intentions towards the Christian population of his Empire, and wishing to give a further proof of his sentiments in that respect, has resolved to communicate to the Contracting Powers the said Firman, emanating spontaneously from his Sovereign will.

Art. X. The Convention of 13th of July, 1841, which maintains the ancient rule of the Ottoman Empire relative to the Closing of the Straits of the Bosphorus and of Dardanelles, has been revised by common consent. . . .

Art. XI. The Black Sea is Neutralized; its Waters and its Ports, thrown open to the Mercantile Marine of every Nation, are formally and in perpetuity interdicted to the Flag of War, either of the Powers possessing its Coasts, or of any other Power. . . .

Art. XIII. The Black Sea being Neutralized according to the terms of Article XI, the maintenance or establishment upon its Coast of Military-Maritime Arsenals becomes alike unnecessary and purposeless; in consequence, His Majesty the Emperor of all the Russias, and His Imperial Majesty the Sultan, engage not to establish or to maintain upon that Coast any Military-Maritime Arsenal.

Art. XV. The Act of the Congress of Vienna, having established the principles intended to regulate the Navigation of Rivers which separate or traverse different States, the Contracting Parties stipulate among themselves that those principles shall in future be equally applied to the Danube and its Mouths. They declare that its arrangement henceforth forms a part of the Public Law of Europe, and take it under their Guarantee. . . .

Art. XVI. With a view to carry out the arrangement of the preceding Article, a Commission, in which Great Britain, Austria, France, Prussia, Russia, Sardinia and Turkey, shall each be represented by one delegate, shall be charged to designate and to cause to be executed the Works necessary below Isatcha, to clear the Mouths of the Danube, as well as the neighbouring parts of the Sea, from the sands and other impediments which obstruct them, in order to put that part of the River and the said parts of the Sea in the best possible state for Navigation. . . .

Art. XXII. The Principalities of Wallachia and Moldavia shall continue to enjoy under the Suzerainty of the Porte, and under the Guarantee of the Contracting Powers, the Privileges and Immunities of which they are in possession. No exclusive Protection shall be exercised over them by any of the guaranteeing Powers.

There shall be no separate right of interference in their Internal Affairs.

Art. XXVIII. The Principality of Servia shall continue to hold of the Sublime Porte, in conformity with the Imperial Hats[1] which fix and determine its Rights and Immunities, placed henceforward under the Collective Guarantee of the Contracting Powers.

In consequence, the said Principality shall preserve its Independence and National Administration, as well as full Liberty of Worship, of Legislation, of Commerce, and of Navigation. . . .

SECTION III. THE EVENTS CULMINATING IN THE TREATY OF BERLIN, 1878

In opposition to Disraeli's policy of maintaining Turkey's existence and authority in the Near East, as a counterpoise to Russia, Gladstone was shocked at Turkish misrule in Christian lands. The massacres of 1876 were, perhaps, the first that deeply stirred Western Europe. In Russia the indignation was so great that Alexander II went to war in 1877 with the Ottoman Empire.

[1] A *hat* was an Ottoman charter or grant. (Editor's note.)

145. GLADSTONE ON THE BULGARIAN MASSACRES[1]

An old servant of the Crown and State, I entreat my countrymen, upon whom far more than perhaps any other people of Europe it depends, to require, and to insist, that our Government, which has been working in one direction, shall work in the other, and shall apply all its vigour to concur with the other States of Europe in obtaining the extinction of the Turkish executive power in Bulgaria. Let the Turks now carry away their abuses in the only possible manner, namely by carrying off themselves. Their Zaptiehs and their Mudirs, their Bimbashis and their Yuzbachis, their Kaimakams and their Pashas, one and all, bag and baggage, shall, I hope, clear out from the province they have desolated and profaned. This thorough riddance, this most blessed deliverance, is the only reparation we can make to the memory of those heaps on heaps of dead; to the violated purity alike of matron, of maiden, and of child; to the civilization which has been affronted and shamed; to the laws of God or, if you like, of Allah; to the moral sense of mankind at large. There is not a criminal in an European gaol, there is not a cannibal in the South Sea Islands, whose indignation would not rise and overboil at the recital of that which has been done, which has too late been examined, but which remains unavenged; which has left behind all the foul and all the fierce passions that produced it, and which may again spring up, in another murderous harvest, from the soil soaked and reeking with blood, and in the air tainted with every imaginable deed of crime and shame. That such things should be done once, is a damning disgrace to the portion of our race which did them; that a door should be left open for their ever-so-barely possible repetition would spread that shame over the whole. . . .

We may ransack the annals of the world, but I know not what research can furnish us with so portentous an example of the fiendish misuse of the powers established by God " for the punishment of evil-doers, and for the encouragement of them that do well." No Government ever has so sinned; none has so proved itself incorrigible in sin, or which is the same, so impotent for reformation. If it be allowable that the Executive power of Turkey should renew at this great crisis, by permission or authority of Europe, the charter of its existence in Bulgaria, then there is not on record, since the beginnings of political society, a protest that man has lodged against intolerable misgovernment, or a stroke he has dealt at loathsome tyranny, that ought not henceforward to be branded as a crime.

[1] William E. Gladstone, *Bulgarian Horrors and the Question of the East.* London, 1876, pp. 61–63.

The Serbs had engaged in 1876 in rebellion against Turkey but had accepted promises which the Turks made to pacify them. These promises had not been kept, and the entrance of Russia in a war on the Turks brought Serbia again into the arena.

146. SERBIA'S PROCLAMATION OF WAR IN 1877 [1]

To my beloved People,

In my Proclamation of 21st February (5th March) of this year, I announced to my beloved people that the defence of the holy cause, for which we were last year obliged to draw the sword, has passed into more powerful hands. But since the time that Servia concluded peace with the Ottoman Porte, the Turkish race has enriched its history with new, unheard-of horrors. Rapine, waste and slaughter to-day fill all the provinces of the Turkish Empire, but more especially do the Turks vent their wrath on all who bear the Servian name. The Mussulman fanaticism, inflamed with vengeance, vents itself especially on those long-suffering brethren of ours who at the time of the war found refuge and protection in Servia, although by Article II of the Treaty we concluded on 16th/28th February, with the Ottoman Porte, a complete amnesty is stipulated for them. Relying on the good faith of the International Convention, we induced the greater part of the marytrs to return to their hearths; but having returned with confidence in our advice they were, alas! under various pretexts, subjected anew to tortures and violence by their Mahommedan oppressors. In vain were the steps my Government took at Constantinople against this flagrant infraction of the Treaty. The Ottoman Porte left the fresh acts of violence unpunished, and trampled on the solemn promise it had made us.

Servians! after such a breach of the Treaty which the Porte concluded with us we are no longer obliged to remain in the trying condition which changed us from champions of freedom to patient spectators of those ruthless endeavours by which the Porte is evidently bent on extirpating the Servian race. . . .

And although the brave Russian army needs not our assistance to crown with success the holy cause which the Emperor Alexander has taken under his mighty protection, nothing in the world can free us from the duty which the Servian nation has to fulfil as a member of the community of Eastern Christian nations, which Servia must fulfil toward herself and her race. Nations cannot attain true freedom until they have purchased it by their own exertions, and, if necessary, by their blood. . . .

Servians! we take up arms to-day in a holy, national and Christian cause.

[1] Edward Hertslet, *Map of Europe by Treaty*. 4 vols. London, 1875–1891, vol. IV, pp. 2648–2650 (condensed).

After the example of my grandfather, behold I place myself again at the head of the armed Servian nation. On the banner which Obrenovits IV unfurls again are written, "Liberty and National Independence." Under this banner you have already given splendid proofs of your patriotism and self-devotion.

We now take a bold step; let us join hands with those of our brethren from whom we have been separated since the day of Kossovo.

To-day or never has struck the hour in which we must, once and for all, complete the great national task which the heroes of Takova so gloriously began, and which we last year recommenced.

And so, heroes, forward, beside the victorious banners of the Tsar liberator, with faith in God Almighty, the Protector of the Right, for the liberation of our oppressed brethren and for the independence of our country Servia!

Forward, heroes, it is the will of God.

MILAN M. OBRENOVITS IV c. p.,

Prince of Servia

Belgrade, 1/13 December, 1877.

Despite the stubborn resistance of the Turkish armies, the tsar's troops forced their way to the very defences of Constantinople and dictated the Peace of San Stefano, which, among other provisions, established a large independent Bulgarian state. The Powers stepped in, largely through the determination of Disraeli to check Russian predominance in the Balkans, and insisted on a general congress. At the Congress of Berlin, over which Bismarck presided, Russia was obliged to concede much that she had gained at San Stefano, including the complete independence and the large dimensions of Bulgaria, but the Treaty of Berlin did mark for several of the Balkan states the beginning of a new era of independent life.

147. THE TREATY OF BERLIN [1]

Art. I. Bulgaria is constituted an autonomous and tributary Principality under the suzerainty of His Imperial Majesty the Sultan; it will have a Christian Government and a national militia.

[Art. II. defines the boundaries of Bulgaria.]

The Prince of Bulgaria shall be freely elected by the population and confirmed by the Sublime Porte, with the assent of the Powers. No member of the reigning dynasties of the Great European Powers may be elected Prince of Bulgaria. . . .

[1] Edward Hertslet, *Map of Europe by Treaty.* 4 vols. London, 1875–1891, vol. IV, pp. 2759 ff. (excerpts).

Art. IV. An Assembly of Notables of Bulgaria, convoked at Tirnovo, shall, before the election of the Prince, draw up the Organic Law of the Principality. In the districts where Bulgarians are intermixed with Turkish, Roumanian, Greek or other Populations, the rights and interests of these populations shall be taken into consideration as regards the elections and the drawing up of the Organic Law.

Art. XIII. A province is formed south of the Balkans which will take the name of " Eastern Roumelia," and will remain under the direct political and military authority of His Imperial Majesty the Sultan, under conditions of administrative autonomy. It shall have a Christian Governor-General.

[Art. XIV. defines the boundaries of Eastern Roumelia.]

Art. XXV. The Provinces of Bosnia and Herzegovina shall be occupied and administered by Austria-Hungary. The Government of Austria-Hungary, not desiring to undertake the administration of the Sandjak of Novi-Bazar, which extends between Servia and Montenegro in a south-easterly direction to the other side of Mitrviotza, the Ottoman Administration will continue to exercise its functions there. Nevertheless, in order to assure the maintenance of the new political state of affairs, as well as freedom and security of communications, Austria-Hungary reserves the right of keeping garrisons and having military and commercial roads in the whole of this part of the ancient Vilayet of Bosnia. . . .

Art. XXVI. The independence of Montenegro is recognized by the Sublime Porte and by all those of the High Contracting Parties who had not hitherto admitted it.

Art. XXXIV. The High Contracting Parties recognize the independence of the Principality of Servia, subject to . . .

[There follow articles stipulating equality of religions, boundaries, etc.]

Art. XLIII. The High Contracting Parties recognize the independence of Roumania, subject to . . . [The conditions much the same as with Servia.]

Art. LII. In order to increase the guarantees which assure the freedom of navigation on the Danube which is recognized as of European interest, the High Contracting Parties determine that all the fortresses and fortifications existing on the course of the river from the Iron Gates to its mouths shall be razed, and no new ones erected. No vessel of war shall navigate the Danube below the Iron Gates with the exception of vessels of light tonnage in the service of the river police and Customs. The " stationnaires " of the Powers at the mouths of the Danube may, however, ascend the river as far as Galatz.

Art. LIII. The European Commission of the Danube on which Roumania shall be represented is maintained in its functions, and shall exercise them henceforth as far as Galatz in complete independence of the territorial authorities. . . .

Art. LXI. The Sublime Porte undertakes to carry out, without further delay, the improvements and reforms demanded by local requirements in the provinces inhabited by the Armenians, and to guarantee their security against the Circassians and Kurds.

It will periodically make known the steps taken to this effect to the Powers, who will superintend their application.

SECTION IV. THE TIMES OF ABDUL HAMID II

No sultan since the sixteenth century has aroused so widespread an interest as Abdul Hamid II, who reigned from just before the War of 1877 until the Young Turks achieved success more than thirty years later. A French publicist seeks to explain this mysterious and much-feared despot.

148. THE SULTAN ABDUL HAMID II [1]

All those who have approached the Sultan Abdul Hamid II agree that he gives the appearance of a very gentle person. Although his polished reserve is at the first meeting disconcertingly cold, he takes pains to make himself affable and to win all his visitors over. He is ever even-tempered and his conversation friendly; he shows decided intelligence and a very lively turn of mind; yet he is not in the least a cultivated man, for his enjoyment of literature is limited to the gross farces of the Turkish theatre and mystery and murder stories of our popular press. . . . Naturally timid, he has a tenacity that can not be worn down and an unlimited wilfulness. His piety, which perhaps is assumed, is narrow and superstitious, and his manner of living is so sober as to approach austerity. . . .

The diplomats who have sojourned in Constantinople have all begun by falling under this man's charm, and many have never escaped from it; a personal charm that is produced by the extreme politeness that this autocrat shows to whomever he is talking to, the attention he pays to their remarks, the authority he pretends to ascribe to their advice, the clear proofs of his application to affairs, the good will and even scrupulousness that are indicated in his questions and answers. He knows how to listen. One never leaves his audience chamber other than content and touched. . . .

Only by a tremendous effort, or because of long experience, is one able to distrust, or free oneself from the spell of, a man who seems so good, so sincere and, at the same time, so unhappy. For everything about him — his speech and his silences, the nervous tightening of the lips, the quick breathing, the terror in the eyes, and even the pallor of the cheeks showing

[1] Victor Bérard, *La politique du Sultan*. Paris, Armand Colin, 1900, pp. 79–83 (condensed). Translation.

through the rouge — everything betrays constantly unreasoning and incurable fear. It took hold of him while he was growing up, even before he entered public life, and day by day and little by little, it made him over and remodeled him. Born September 22d, 1842, he came to the throne on August 31st, 1876 by means of the *coup d' état* that overthrew and put in confinement his brother Murad, three months after the overthrow and suicide of his uncle Abdul Aziz. With nothing of the physical or mental make-up of the Turk about him, in appearance and character rather resembling the Arab or Armenian, dark, small, thin and delicate, nervous and irascible, at once violent and deceitful, he had passed for a confirmed libertine so long that his licentious living had endangered his health. Then, all at once, the fear of death had made an ascetic of him. He who had become sultan through conspiracy and murder soon saw, or thought he saw, the same schemes and the same men that had ruined his uncle and his brother working for his own destruction. . . . Then every day palace intrigues, rivalry of eunuchs or guards, quarrelling ministers, and the battles of the ambitious and the greedy. Everyone around him in a turmoil, twisting about, conspiring. Against whom, if not himself? And so uninterrupted mistrust developed the reign of fear.

This fear dominates and explains the whole man. It has made him cautious and reflective, tricky and cunning. It has killed his pride and arrogance, his passions and his vices, but at the same time it has stifled generosity, frankness, honor, and every emotion, save egotism alone, every ambition and every thought but the care of saving his life.

Sir Charles Eliot spent many years in the Near East and came to know the Turk intimately. What he says is pertinent to the relations of Moslem and Christian throughout the Levant.

149. THE TURK'S WAY OF LOOKING AT THE CHRISTIAN[1]

If we assume that it is desirable to continue the Ottoman Government — an assumption which no one but a Turk need make — we must admit that this implies the superiority of Turks to Christians. It does not mean the equality of Turks and Christians; that is a thing which is talked of but never realised, for the very good reason that it is impossible. As long as force rules, the Turks are superior to the Christians. They are stronger, braver, and more united. But when force does not rule, when progress, commerce, finance, and law give the mixed population of the Empire a chance

[1] *Turkey in Europe.* By Odysseus (Sir Charles Eliot). London, Edward Arnold & Co., 1900, pp. 163–165.

of redistributing themselves according to their wits, the Turk and the Christain are not equal; the Christian is superior. He acquires the money and land of the Turk, and proves in a law-court that he is right in so doing. One may criticise the Turkish character, but given their idiosyncrasies, one must admit that they derive little profit from such blessings of civilisation as are introduced into the country. Foreign syndicates profit most, and after them native Christians, but not the Osmanli, except in so far as he can make them disgorge their gains. Those who have associated with Turks will have discovered a fact which it is difficult for the rest of the world to believe, namely, that they are afraid of Christians. The periodical outbreaks formerly called "atrocities," but now described as "events" (a beautiful euphemism which the Sublime Porte has imposed on the diplomatic language of Europe), appear to us as a cowardly slaughter of unarmed men and helpless women and children. But no doubt the average Turk regards these same events as necessary measures of self-defence. He is always ready to believe that the Armenians and Bulgarians are importing arms or planning to burn down Constantinople, and says with sincere alarm that no Moslim's life is safe. I have met many liberal Turks who talked freely of liberty and equality, but never one who did not approve of the Armenian massacres of 1895–6 and attempt to justify them. The converse of this is, that the Christians in Turkey do not feel any more sympathy for liberal or "Young Turks" than they do for old and bigoted ones; for young or old, radical or conservative, their complaints and hopes are confined to their own race and religion, and take no account of the majority of the population in their dominions.

The Turkish reformer and the Christian have nothing in common, and the mass of Turks mistrust the reformer. Even in such a matter as military reform, where there can be no doubt that improvements are in the interest of the Moslim, and the Moslim only, the Turk will not take the view which his friends think he obviously ought to take. Foreign military instructors have again and again presented recommendations, and again and again they have been rejected, sometimes openly, sometimes with a pretence of acceptance, but always quite firmly. The Turk has a dim perception that even in military matters he cannot understand and practise European methods. If he tries to do so, the control will pass out of his hands into those of people who are cleverer than himself. But though he may think them clever, he does not on that account feel any respect for them. He regards them as conjurors who can perform a variety of tricks, which may be, according to circumstances, useful, amusing, or dangerous; but for all Christendom he has a brutal, unreasoning contempt — the contempt of the sword for everything that can be cut, and today the stupid contempt of a blunt sword.

SECTION V. THE YOUNG TURK REVOLUTION AND ITS CONSEQUENCES

Abdul Hamid in his palace at Yildiz got more and more out of touch with sentiment throughout his Empire, among Moslems as well as among the subject Christians whom he despised. This account is by an English lawyer whose long residence in the capital gave him cognizance of the many intrigues that were on foot and the general dissatisfaction that prevailed, and who watched the Young Turk movement grow and, in 1908, triumph. The sultan's concessions, which included the constitution he had granted in 1876 and then suspended indefinitely, were made insincerely, and in 1909 there was an attempt to restore his power. On its failure the Young Turks deposed Abdul Hamid, although they retained the dynasty. Abdul's brother succeeded him as Mohammed V.

150. THE YOUNG TURK REVOLUTION [1]

I have already mentioned that the misgovernment in Turkey had led to the formation of committees, both in and out of Turkey, with the object of bringing about a change of government. Every foreign power interested in the good government of Turkey, but especially England, France, and Italy, was anxious in its own interest to effect reforms throughout the empire generally. The massacres in Armenia had disgusted not merely the whole of the Christian population of the empire, but thoughtful men among the Turks. In the Public Works Department nothing could be done without bakshish.[2]

. . . .

I remember at the time having a long consultation on legal matters with eight or ten of the leading advocates in Constantinople. One of the oldest and ablest members present declared that the Courts of Law were never so rotten as at that time, that the administration of justice was worse than it had been twenty years earlier. " I quite agree with you," said another old lawyer; " at that time if you wanted to get hold of a judge you found his man and made your bargain with him. Nowadays the judges will come round themselves." All agreed that in cases where the rights were in the slightest degree doubtful a decision had to be paid for. If the man had influence a judgment might be obtained without bribery, but ordinarily not

---

[1] *Forty Years in Constantinople: The Recollections of Sir Edwin Pears. 1873–1915.* London, Herbert Jenkins, 1916, pp. 218–238 (condensed).

[2] Bakshish is a bribe. (Editor's note.)

otherwise. The whole administration of the country was rotten through and through.

There were two grievances in particular that made the Moslems, as distinct from the Christians, opposed to the Government. The first was palace espionage, the second the terrible restriction of travel applied both to Moslems and Christians. The average Moslem has the virtues of a dominant race. He is usually one who tells the truth and has the courage of his opinions. But it was commonly said that neither in the streets nor in their private houses were they free from the espionage of the Sultan's agents.

. . . .

In the country districts the misgovernment was most markedly seen in the want of protection to life and property. A mine-owner would not venture to work the mine without taking the *zaptiehs,* or police, of the neighbourhood into his pay. Many mines were in consequence shut down. Natives and foreigners alike who had acquired tracts of land let them go to rack and ruin rather than pay the sums which the police and local government tried to exact from them.

The condition of the army and navy aroused the indignation of the best among the Moslems. Young officers who had passed through the military schools were sent off to regiments in the provinces and not allowed to return to the Bosporus. I remember a conversation with a captain amongst them whom I knew well. He declared that there was no *camaraderie* in the army, and that he himself did not know who were the other officers in his regiment. The navy, as I have already mentioned, had been allowed to become nearly worthless. Promotion in it was due to palace favouritism. . . .

The Sultan's palace at Yildiz was surrounded by troops commanded by ignorant officers. Amongst these troops in the later years of Abdul's reign the Albanians held so favoured a position as to render plausible the statement made to me by an officer of the Genie, a corps corresponding to our Royal Engineers, that the army would like the chance of attacking the regiments around Yildiz and of killing every man in them. What Abdul Hamid apparently dreaded both in the army and navy was a tendency towards improvement of any kind. In 1908 it was commonly believed that at least 20,000 of the most intelligent officers in the two services had been banished to remote provinces. The story was common that others had entered the palace, but had never been seen alive again.

It was from such causes that when we reached the year 1908 the disaffection towards the Sultan had become general. The chief committees in Paris and Salonica, after a long search for reforms, had arrived at the conclusion that the most practical remedy was the establishment of constitutional government. A fairly well-drawn Constitution, drafted by Midhat Pasha, had been accepted by Abdul Hamid in December, 1876, and promulgated, as already stated, as a counterstroke to the proposals of reforms made by Lord Salisbury, General Ignatief, and the other members of the European Conference. A Turkish parliament had actually met, but Abdul Hamid, finding that it could not be dictated to, had solved the difficulty to his own satisfaction by bundling off the whole of the members in the course of a single night from Constantinople (July, 1877) and decreeing that the portion of the Constitution which related to representative government should remain in abeyance. During these long years of misgovernment the really workable instrument of Midhat had never been forgotten. To have openly advocated its re-establishment would, however, have meant the suppression of any newspaper in the Empire.

. . . .

The Salonica Committee, as nearly as I can fix the date, was established in the autumn of 1905. Of course anyone known to be connected with a revolutionary Committee would have been at once seized, and therefore it had to have recourse to secret methods; and an organisation said to be founded on the lines of freemasonry was established and soon had branches throughout the empire. There was always some display of secrecy in the election of its members and the promulgation of its orders. . . .

In Paris the Young Turks had already taken the title of the Committee of Union and Progress, often indicated in later times by its initials as the C. U. P. It is undoubted that during the two or three years preceding 1908 the movement spread throughout the empire with great rapidity. In presence of the great army of spies people had become desperate, and the old question was constantly asked amongst Europeans, " Were the spies themselves loyal to Abdul Hamid? " *Quis custodiet custodes ipsos?* The answer is that as the movement increased there is good reason to believe that some of the spies themselves played a double game. But the Committee probably got more information about the doings at Yildiz than did Yildiz about the doings of the Committee.

The great feature about the organisation of the Committee was, in my opinion, its secrecy. No ordinary member knew more than two or three persons who were associated with him. He did not know who were the leaders, and influential men amongst them told me that it was very rare that the chairman at one meeting appeared more than once. The Committee was a great power without visible organisation, but which soon made its influence felt throughout the empire. One of the first objects of the Salonica Committee, which soon became much more powerful than that in Paris, was to obtain influence in the Third Army Corps, which was stationed in Macedonia. It was to this province that the undue proportion of young military officers trained in the military schools of the Harbia in Constantinople had been sent by Abdul Hamid. Thus the ground was well prepared for sowing disaffection. It is said that by the end of 1907 practically the whole of the Third Army Corps had sworn fidelity to the Constitution. But other portions of the army, and especially in Asia Minor and Adrianople, had come under the influence of the Committee.

. . . .

In truth the regime of misrule under Abdul Hamid was rapidly drawing to an end. He had begun the system of arbitrary rule by appointing Ministers who, so far as he could accomplish it, were deprived of power. After a while, and sometimes ostentatiously, he named sub-ministers who were chosen for their known hostility to their chiefs. The Ministers often became mere clerks. In a conversation with one of them some years ago, after dwelling upon the universal corruption that prevailed in every department, he remarked that we should never get rid of it until the Sultan was changed. To my reply that the mere change of sovereign would probably not be a remedy, he answered, " We shall at least get back government by Ministers instead of by the palace clique." The Minister was right in the position he took up, because amongst the evils of Abdul's rule was the tacit permission given them to fill their pockets at the expense of the State so long as they were subservient to his wishes.

The results of corruption had steadily increased. Customhouse duties were divided between the Exchequer and the officials. The Valis, or Governors, paid for their appointments and often contributed a portion of their salaries to the palace gang which kept them in place. In return, no inconvenient questions were asked of their extortions in the provinces. Public meetings were everywhere forbidden, and during the last four or five years of Abdul Hamid's reign no wedding festivity or dinner-party could take place among Turkish subjects without the permission of the authorities and a scrutiny of the list of invited guests. An attempt was even made to prevent evening parties and balls at wealthy European houses, and when, with the aid of the Embassies, this demand was resisted, spies were stationed round the houses to forbid the entrance of Turkish subjects.

Not a line was permitted to be printed in any newspaper office until it had passed the censor. If a historian had to depend for his information upon files of Turkish newspapers, Egypt during these years would be considered to be still under the direct rule of the Sultan as it was before 1879. The word Armenia was not permitted to be printed. " There is no such place," said the chief censor. Macedonia was tabooed also, and this to such an extent that it was difficult for the Bible Society to obtain permission to print a translation of the text of St. Paul's message, " Come over into Macedonia and help us."

The censor claimed that the sections of the three provinces into which Macedonia had been divided should be substituted. Theatrical performances were censored with equal severity. " Hamlet " and " Julius Caesar " and a host of French historical plays were forbidden because they spoke of killing a king.

After the massacres in 1895–97 nearly all the Armenians had been expelled from Constantinople, and the result was that the industrious mass of guardians and workmen, who had been in the habit of sending the largest portion of their income to their villages in Armenia, were thrown out of work and their families reduced to starvation. The army of spies was constantly increased. Some of the smaller fry only received a salary of £2 to £3 a month. One man, a foreigner, is known to have obtained £90 a month. One year's Budget of Turkey set the sum of £1,200,000 aside for spies.

Thousands of men belonging to every class of the community, Mahometans as well as Christians, were denounced and taken for secret examination to the palace or other police authorities. Very few were ever sent for trial, but were dealt with arbitrarily. Abdul Hamid made a serious mistake in dealing with suspected Mahometans. They were usually banished from the capital and sent into remote provinces. There they became the centers of revolution. The whole empire was thus prepared for revolution when an organisation should declare for it. Everywhere there were exiles of ability and energy above the average, and full of a sentiment of hostility towards the Sultan. In some of the provinces, as for example in Erzeroum, the exiles were so numerous and so superior in reputation and ability to the Governor and officials, that they practically became the rulers of the provinces, and in one case which I reported in the year 1906, the population, led by the exiles, dictated to and obtained from the Sultan a change of governor.

In the army the system of espionage destroyed its *esprit de corps* and created a strong current of dissatisfaction among the officers, who were thus prepared during the two or three years preceding 1908 to welcome the emissaries of revolution. As the months passed on and the system of espionage failed, Abdul Hamid's only remedy was to make it the stricter. The local post was abolished because it faciliated conspiracy. Letters to and from the provinces in the Turkish post were ostentatiously opened and delivered open.

So long as the Sultan confined his persecution to the Christian communities, the Moslems made no strong objection, though in justice to them I must repeat that there was always a considerable number who condemned the Armenian massacres and other atrocities, sometimes out of sympathy with the innocent victims, but more usually because they recognised the injury that was done to the welfare of the country. When, however, Abdul

Hamid began to make himself objectionable to Moslem and Christian alike, misfortune made the two parties join forces. During the first half of 1908 the Committee of Union and Progress was joined by numbers of Turks, Albanians, Bulgarians, and Greeks.

A curious development of the movement was due to Turkish women. Though there were female spies, yet the manner of life of Turkish ladies was more favourable to the new movement. It offers many facilities for carrying messages which are not at hand for men, for Turkish public opinion would not permit either spies or ordinary police agents to search them. They were much more outspoken than their husbands and brothers. Moreover, a large number of the wealthier class of Turkish women had received education in French and English, and their ideas had been influenced by what they read. They played a large part as emissaries of the revolutionary party. They conveyed letters and verbal messages from one harem to another. They were not less active in Macedonia than were their sisters in the capital. The agents of the Government endeavoured to preserve the loyalty of the troops by representing the revolutionary movement as one favoured by Greeks and Bulgarians and against the Faithful, but Turkish women instinctively knew better.

The Sultan's spies no doubt sent hundreds of reports on the situation to Yildiz. The Sultan became alarmed, and, ever eager to crush disaffection, sent a Commission to Salonica with instructions to stamp out the movement everywhere, but especially in the army. In Constantinople we heard much about this Commission, and for the first time we learned that Yildiz was afraid of an insurrection. The satisfactory feature about it to us foreigners, and to all the Christian population, was that it was confined strictly to Moslems. The Commission was composed of some of the ablest of the adherents of the Sultan. The general belief existed that it would be followed by many executions. Its immediate effect, however, was very different from what Abdul Hamid anticipated. Two officers in the army took to the Resna Mountains and boldly declared themselves in opposition to Abdul Hamid; these two men, whom the Commission had reported to Yildiz as the leaders amongst the disaffected in Salonica, were Niazi Bey and Enver Bey, now Enver Pasha, the Minister of War. Niazi was the first man to raise the flag of revolt. This was on July 5, 1908.

The Turkish general in the northern portion of Macedonia was Shemsi Pasha. Niazi had publicly declared for the Constitution, and the secret Committee had issued manifestoes in favour of it, which were posted in Monastir, the largest town in that district of the country. But the Committee and Niazi had chosen and well prepared their ground. In the country between Monastir and Ochrida the great majority of the soldiers had sworn fidelity to the Constitution. When Shemsi marched against Niazi he was shot ostentatiously in broad daylight in Monastir itself by one of the officers of the army which he commanded, who, when he had killed his man, walked coolly away, not a hand being raised to arrest him. When the news reached Yildiz frantic telegrams were sent to stamp out the movement. Nazim Bey . . . endeavoured to crush out the rebellion. But it soon became evident that the army in Macedonia would not act against the rebels. Forty-eight officers were arrested on the report of Nazim on July 8, and sent off at once to Constantinople, their principal accuser being Hakki Bey. Two days afterwards Hakki was shot in Salonica, and on the following day, July 11, Nazim Bey was wounded in open day in the streets of the same city. His would-be assassin was not even arrested. Nazim immediately returned to Constantinople to report to the Sultan, and a second Commission was sent on a similar mission to its predecessor.

Enver Bey, who had been attached to the staff of Hilmi Pasha, was the first man accused by this second Commission. They, however, acted with more cunning than their predecessors. Enver was invited by Abdul Hamid in flattering terms to proceed at once to Constantinople to inform His Majesty of the position, and at the same time promises of promotion were made to him. Enver, however, was much too suspicious to be caught by this kind of flattery. He therefore, as already mentioned, went to the Resna Hills, and with him there went a considerable number of soldiers. The movement of Niazi had become an insurrection. Two days after Hakki Bey had been shot the C. U. P. publicly associated itself with the insurrection. At the same time the Second Army Corps, which was stationed at Adrianople, supported the demands of the Macedonian troops, and when the Committee cabled direct to the Sultan that unless he granted the Constitution the Third Army Corps would march on Constantinople, the Second Army Corps associated themselves with its comrades.

. . . .

When Shemsi was shot, and when the revolt began rapidly to spread throughout Macedonia in July, Ferid Pasha was ordered by the Sultan to take measures with the heads of the army to put an end to it and to punish the discontented. Ferid pointed out that this was not the business of the Grand Vizier, but of the Minister of War. Let me remark in passing that Turkish Ministers have always been very susceptible to any invasion of the privileges of their ministry. The Sultan however, instead of leaving the matter to his Minister of War, took it into his own hands. He had shown on many previous occasions that he believed he was much more competent than any Minister, and the one institution in which he still had confidence was that of espionage. To set spies to work, and then set others to spy upon them, was his great panacea against political troubles. He at once ordered forty spies to report upon the conduct of the troops in Macedonia, and of course to send the names of those officers whose loyalty to him was doubtful. Unfortunately for Abdul the object of the mission became at once known and was resented by the great mass of army officers to whom espionage of course was peculiarly obnoxious. Shortly after the Revolution General von der Goltz published a letter in the *Neue Freie Presse* in which he expressed the opinion that the system of espionage was the principal grievance of the Turkish soldier. When the mission of the forty spies was known, many men who had hesitated to join the disaffected party now saw their safety lay in throwing in their lot with those who demanded reforms. An influential number of officers telegraphed to the palace their request that the Chamber of Deputies should be assembled. Abdul Hamid soon learned, for the telephone was constantly working between Yildiz and Salonica, that this demand was backed by the whole Third Army Corps, that is, by nearly all the troops in Macedonia.

. . . .

Then came a telegram to Yildiz which sounded the knell of Abdul's rule. It was sent either on July 21 or 22, 1908, and demanded the re-establishment of the Constitution, or abdication, mentioning at the same time that the revolted troops had sworn not to lay down their arms until the Constitution was established.

. . . .

The Sultan even yet hesitated to accept the recommendation, and his telegram to Hilmi, who was in Salonica, urged resistance. But the Committee were determined, and at their request Hilmi sent a telegram to the Sultan stating that he was in the power of the Committee and would be shot if the Constitution were not proclaimed within forty-eight hours. Then, but not until the evening of July 22, Ferid Pasha resigned. He had never declared himself in favour of the Committee of Union and Progress, but he knew the country too well to advise His Majesty to resist a demand which had become almost universal.

Then the Sultan recognised that he must bow to the storm. He sent for the two men whom public opinion generally recognised as the men of the highest reputation in the ministerial class. One was Kutchuk Saïd and the other Kiamil Pasha. Each of these men had at one time believed his life to be in danger from Abdul Hamid's vengeance. . . . They were summoned to the palace because they had the reputation of being favourable to Constitutional Government and to British institutions, and therefore likely to be popular. On the evening of the 22nd the Sultan published an irade declaring that Parliament would be convoked.

All ranks and classes in Constantinople went delirious with joy. The proprietors of the Turkish newspapers met together and agreed to a resolution which they immediately carried into effect to turn out the censors from each of their offices. The decree only spoke of a Representative Chamber. The Turkish papers chose to interpret it as granting all the rights under Midhat's Constitution, a document which during thirty years had been idolised by Turkish reformers as a symbol of liberty. The popular cries became, " Vive la Constitution! " and " Vive le Sultan! " A new cry taken up everywhere at once followed, " Down with the spies! " a cry so dangerous that Abdul Hamid and the creatures around him who were opposed to the popular movement dared not interfere. . . .

The Revolution was an unmistakably popular movement. By this I do not mean that it was without leaders, but that people of all ranks were full of the revolutionary spirit, and, once action had commenced, the leaders would have been incapable of stopping it. Newspaper people, who had felt as acutely as any section of the population the burdens of Abdul Hamid's coercion, were among the first to take steps to support the Revolution. They all denounced the system of espionage. At the last moment Abdul declined to go to St. Sophia. Had he gone he would have been frantically welcomed. As it was, throughout the 24th the mere announcement of the Sultan's intention to cross the Horn and go thither made Abdul for the time popular. An enormous crowd, however, gathered before Yildiz, which is about three miles from Stambul. They clamoured to see the Sultan, and kept up a continual shout for him and the Constitution. When he shewed himself at the window in reply to these cries he was cheered by a mob consisting about equally of Moslems and Christians. From the window he made a short speech, in which he declared that henceforward all his subjects, without reference to race or religion, would be treated alike.

On Sunday, July 26th, a crowd of Mollahs and softas, the latter being students of Moslem law, made another demonstration at Yildiz in which the cry was raised for the first time in the Sultan's presence, " Down with the spies! " The Sheik-ul-Islam was present, and other leading men representing the chief teachers of Islam. The Shiek-ul-Islam swore the Sultan to respect the Constitution of Midhat. This was another distinct step confirming the popular interpretation of the original irade which spoke only of the assembling of Parliament. The Council of Ministers met, and an order was issued abolishing the item in the Budget which provided for the pay of the spies. The Moslem portion of the crowd on this Sunday passed from Yildiz to the residence of the Armenian Patriarch in Pera in order to express their fraternal feelings with his community, and subsequently visited the Orthodox Patriarch and even the Bulgarian Exarch.

Speeches were delivered in many places, in mosque yards, even in the great mosque of Sultan Ahmed itself on the Hippodrome. Everywhere it was proclaimed that the Revolution meant " hurriet," or liberty, equality, and fraternity, above all no distinction of men on account of their creed. In conversation with two of the leading speakers, of whom one was a Jew, they spoke with enthusiasm of the sincere desire which existed among the leaders of the Revolution to have the adherence of all Christian denominations of the empire. The Armenians responded cordially, and on this Sunday and on the following days speeches were delivered by leading Armenians and Greeks declaring that henceforward it would be possible for the Christians of the empire to co-operate cordially with their Moslem brethren for the benefit of the empire.

I had seen something of both these demonstrations. In that of the Monday, which took place before the Town Hall of Pera, immediately opposite to which is my own house, I estimated that there were at least 2,000 Turkish officers and military students in the great crowd. In the processions which went through the streets it seemed to me that every public carriage in the place had been taken possession of. Such carriages in Constantinople are usually open, and an arrangement had been made in which a *saracli,* or mollah, should be seated side by side with a Christian priest. At the principal points passed by this procession, prayers were publicly offered up for the Sultan and for the Constitution.

The sight was a novel one. Hundreds of carriages, nearly all with occupants of two different faiths, thousands of people, about equally divided between Moslems and Christians, prayers clearly and distinctly read either from a carriage or from some point of vantage, and the whole crowd standing in the usual Turkish attitude of devotion, that is, with the hands held up horizontally, the palms skyward. At the end of each prayer there came a great volume of *Amin,* followed usually by cheers for the Constitution. These processions were undoubtedly carefully organised, but none the less the enthusiasm was general and honest.

Three events in the non-Turkish dominions of the Ottoman Empire at once followed the Young Turk Revolution. The first was the proclamation issued on October 5th, 1908, by Prince Ferdinand of Bulgaria.

151. BULGARIA PROCLAIMED INDEPENDENT [1]

By the will of our never-to-be-forgotten liberator and the great kindred Russian nation, aided by our good friends and neighbours, the subjects of the king of Roumania, and by the Bulgarian heroes, on February 18, 1878, the chains were broken which had for so many centuries enslaved Bulgaria, once a great and glorious power.

[1] *London Weekly Times,* October 9, 1908.

From that time until to-day, full thirty years, the Bulgarian nation, still cherishing the memory of those who had laboured for its freedom, and inspired by its traditions, has worked incessantly for the development of its beautiful country; and, under my guidance and that of the late Prince Alexander, it has become a nation fit to take a place as an equal among the civilized States of the world, and has shown itself capable of progress in science, art, and industry. While advancing along this path nothing should arrest the progress of Bulgaria, nothing should hinder her success. Such is the desire of the nation, such is its will. Let that desire be fulfilled. The Bulgarian nation and its chief can have but one sentiment, one desire. Practically independent, the nation was impeded in its normal and peaceful development by certain illusory and formal limitations which resulted in a coldness in the relations of Turkey and Bulgaria. I and the nation desire to rejoice in the political development of Turkey. Turkey and Bulgaria free and entirely independent of each other may exist under conditions which will allow them to strengthen their amicable relations and devote themselves to peaceful internal development.

Inspired by the sacred purpose of satisfying national requirements and fulfilling national desires, I proclaim, with the blessing of the almighty, Bulgaria, united since September 6, 1885, an independent kingdom.

In conjunction with the nation I believe that this act will meet the approbation of the great powers.

The second event brought about by revolution in Turkey was the following proclamation by the aged Austrian emperor. Like the Bulgarian manifesto two days before, it completed a process begun a generation earlier by the Treaty of Berlin. The path from this definite movement of Austria in the direction of the Balkans to the assassination at Sarajevo in 1914 is well marked for, from 1908 on, Serbia regarded her Hapsburg neighbor as her enemy and the oppressor of her compatriots. Further, she now saw in Austrian power the barrier which would seek to keep her from access to the Adriatic.

152. ANNEXATION OF BOSNIA AND HERZEGOVINA[1]

We, Francis Joseph, Emperor of Austria, King of Bohemia, and Apostolic King of Hungary, to the inhabitants of Bosnia and Herzegovina:

When a generation ago our troops crossed the borders of your lands, you were assured that they came not as foes, but as friends, with the firm determination to remedy the evils from which your fatherland had suffered so grievously for many years. This promise given at a serious moment has

[1] *London Weekly Times,* October 9, 1908.

been honestly kept. It has been the constant endeavour of our government to guide the country by patient and systematic activity to a happier future.

To our great joy we can say that the seed then scattered in the furrows of a troubled soil has richly thrived. You yourselves must feel it a boon that order and security have replaced violence and oppression, that trade and traffic are constantly extending, that the elevating influence of education has been brought to bear in your country, and that under the shield of an orderly administration every man may enjoy the fruits of his labours.

It is the duty of us all to advance steadily along this path. With this goal before our eyes, we deem the moment come to give the inhabitants of the two lands a new proof of our trust in their political maturity. In order to raise Bosnia and Herzegovina to a higher level of political life we have resolved to grant both of those lands constitutional governments that are suited to the prevailing conditions and general interests, so as to create a legal basis for the representation of their wishes and needs. You shall henceforth have a voice when decisions are made concerning your domestic affairs, which, as hitherto, will have a separate administration. But the necessary premise for the introduction of this provincial constitution is the creation of a clear and unambiguous legal status for the two lands.

For this reason, and also remembering the ties that existed of yore between our glorious ancestors on the Hungarian throne and these lands, we extend our suzerainty over Bosnia and Herzegovina, and it is our will that the order of succession of our House be extended to these lands also. The inhabitants of the two lands thus share all the benefits which a lasting confirmation of the present relation can offer. The new order of things will be a guarantee that civilization and prosperity will find a sure footing in your home.

SECTION VI. THE BALKAN WARS

A third repercussion followed the Revolution of 1908 and that was the declaration by the Cretans that their island, essentially Greek in character, was part of the Hellenic kingdom. Greece was too fearful of taking action without the Powers' consent to accept the Cretans' advances, and the union of Crete with Greece was postponed until the Balkan Wars. One result of the greater intimacy, however, was the coming of the Cretan, Eleutherios Venezelos, to Athens, where in 1910 he became premier. He it was who brought about the alliance of Balkan states that conquered Turkey in 1912–1913. J. D. Bourchier, a veteran correspondent of the Times, *was in a position to know what happened and M. Venezelos himself has said that these articles of Bourchier's were the best that appeared in the press. The Serbo-Bulgarian and Greco-Bulgarian treaties are given also.*

153. THE INCEPTION OF THE BALKAN LEAGUE OF 1912[1]

. . . .

After the Russo-Turkish War of 1877 a deep feeling of disillusionment prevailed among the Balkan States, and the general dissatisfaction resulting from the provisions of the Berlin Treaty, which ignored the principle of nationalities to suit the interests of certain Great Powers, led to various suggestions for a combination of the young States with a view to the protection of their own interests. The movement was supported by M. Ristitch, the Servian statesman, who believed that a reformed or constitutional Turkey might find a place in the proposed confederation; it was also regarded with favour by King Charles of Rumania and Prince Alexander of Bulgaria, but all hope of its realization was shattered by the revolt of Eastern Rumelia in 1885, which provoked violent agitations in Servia and Greece. Both States demanded "Compensation" for the aggrandisement of Bulgaria; King Milan, instigated by Austria, declared war against the neighbouring State, but was defeated at Slivnitza; in the following year Greece was coerced by a naval demonstration of the Powers, and Prince Alexander, whose patriotic policy rendered him a *persona ingrata* to Russia and Austria alike, fell a victim to a conspiracy organized by the partisans of Russia. After his fall Bulgaria, under the rule of Stamboloff, was for some years wholly engaged in resisting Russian pretensions, while Servia, after the withdrawal of King Milan in 1888, fell under Russian influence. The breach between the two States thus remained open; Austria lent a covert support to Prince Ferdinand, Prince Alexander's successor, and for some years nothing more was heard of a Balkan Alliance. . . .

The institution of foreign "control" in Macedonia under Austro-Russian auspices after the Bulgarian insurrection of 1903 did nothing to mitigate the conflict of races and creeds which was sedulously encouraged by the Sultan Abdul Hamid. . . . Macedonia had now become more than ever the cockpit of the struggle between the rival Christian nations. An attempt, indeed, was made under Russian auspices in 1905 to bring Servia and Bulgaria together by means of a Customs union, which, it was hoped, would form the prelude to an alliance, but Austria found means of strangling the new compact at the birth, and its collapse was followed by mutual recriminations.

Looking back on the bitter animosities of these years we can only marvel at the reconciliation which has enabled the Balkan States to unite their forces against the common foe. Such a miracle could only have been brought about by the appearance of a *deus ex machina* — in this case the divine solution

[1] J. D. Bourchier in the *Times*, London, June 4, 5, 11, 1913.

was provided by the Young Turks. The Young Turk revolution, with its promise of liberty, justice, and equality for all, was welcomed by the Balkan nations with enthusiasm — tempered, perhaps, by the reflection that the regeneration of Turkey would perpetuate the political *status quo,* but nevertheless, on the whole, sincere. When reaction raised its head at Constantinople, large numbers of Christian volunteers marched with the army of Mahmud Shevket to the capital. But the true character of the Turkish revolution was not long in revealing itself; the movement was, in fact, a last effort of the Moslem minority to retain its ascendency in the face of growing resistance on the part of the subject-races and impending European intervention. The revival of the Constitution was little more than an ingenious device for appeasing Liberal sentiment abroad, while furnishing a pretext for the abrogation of the historic rights of the Christian nationalities at home. That the subject-peoples would combine in defence of their rights, and that their reconciliation would react on the kindred States across the frontier, was not foreseen by the inexperienced but self-confident soldiers and politicians who now directed the destinies of the Turkish Empire.

At first, however, the Young Turk movement produced little change in the mutual relations of the Balkan States, and the proclamation of Bulgarian independence which followed in October, 1908 tended to increase the jealousy with which Bulgaria was regarded by her neighbours. . . .

It was not till 1910 that a series of events took place in Macedonia which precipitated the formation of a Balkan Alliance. In the spring of that year, after suppressing an Albanian revolt with merciless rigour, the Turkish military authorities turned their attention to Macedonia. No revolt had taken place in that country, but it was nevertheless decided to carry out a general disarmament of the population. . . . The full history of the horrors which then took place has never been disclosed; the Great Powers which had withdrawn their military officers from the country without obtaining any guarantee for its future good government, refrained from publishing the reports of their Consuls. . . . No hope of redress appeared on any side, and a community of suffering led the Christian races in Macedonia to forget their quarrels. The reconciliation, which began from below — it would hardly be exaggeration to say that Macedonian peasants laid the foundation of the Balkan Alliance — passed upwards and outwards; the clergy, who at first opposed it, and the upper classes yielded to its influence. Eventually amenities were exchanged between the Greek Patriarch and the Bulgarian Exarch; joint representations were addressed to the Porte by the spiritual chiefs and friendly conversations began to take place between Balkan statesmen. . . .

It was clear that a deliberate policy aiming at the complete obliteration of all national sentiment among the subject-populations was being systematically applied, and that, should its enforcement be allowed to continue, the hopes which the Christian races had cherished for generations would be extinguished for ever. The immanence of this danger led to the combination of the two most important Christian elements in Macedonia — an eventuality which the Sultan Abdul Hamid had always dreaded and had always succeeded in preventing. When the dethroned Monarch, in his retirement at Salonika, heard of the reconciliation between Greeks and Bulgarians he could not refrain from an expression of *Schadenfreude;* an irreparable blunder had been committed by the new régime. He may have occasion to rejoice once more should the victors fall out over the partition of the spoil. . . .

The principal trouble with Greece, however, lay in Turkey's aggressive assertion of her shadowy right in Crete; ostensibly to enforce her claims a pitiless boycott of Greek commerce was inaugurated under Kerim Aga, the "boss" of the Salonika quay porters, and great losses were suffered by Greeks of all classes. The protecting Powers of Crete shifted their attitude to please the Young Turks; the humiliations to which Greece was subjected led to the revolt of the Military League; the League, by a strange nemesis, brought to Athens M. Venezelos, the founder of the Balkan Alliance and the principal author of Turkey's misfortunes. . . .

During the spring of 1911 the writer, who had spent the previous winter at Sofia, had many opportunities of discussing the whole Balkan situation with M. Venezelos at Athens. . . . The really urgent feature in the situation was the campaign of repression which was being mercilessly prosecuted in Macedonia with the acquiescence if not the connivance of the Powers. . . . It was in the hope of procuring some respite for the Christian communities, now threatened with denationalization, if not extinction, that M. Venezelos determined to invoke the coöperation of the Bulgarian Government. . . .

Accordingly in April, 1911, a proposal to this effect was transmitted to Sofia through a private channel. The document was a brief one; it proposed (1) an *entente* with a view to common action for the defence of the privileges of the Christians in Turkey; (2) an eventual defensive alliance to provide against a Turkish attack . . . on either of the contracting parties. At the same time long private letters were written to King Ferdinand and M. Gueshoff. . . . With the exception of King George and M. Venezelos, no Greek was aware of what had taken place; the diplomatic world knew nothing; a little later the able and experienced Greek minister at Constantinople, Mr. Gryparis, who for several months acted as Foreign Minister at Athens, was admitted to the secret. The document was sent under seal in the hands of a trustworthy person *via* Corfu to a well-known Englishman in Vienna, who delivered it to the Bulgarian Legation, whence it was transmitted, still under seal, to M. Gueshoff. At Sofia, as at Athens, complete secrecy was maintained with regard to the proposal; even at a later stage, when negotiations were placed on a diplomatic basis, most of the members of the Greek and Bulgarian Governments knew practically nothing of what was passing. The two Prime Ministers ciphered and deciphered their messages themselves and no subordinate was allowed to see them. . . .

The aims of Servia were not altogether the same as those of Greece, but Bulgarian statesmanship contrived to dovetail the proposals on either side and to bring about a combination which effected the overthrow of Turkish rule in Europe.

In the eyes of most Servians, Austria, which holds a large proportion of the Serb race in subjection, has always been the enemy *par excellence*. The Serb element in Turkey was in comparison small, and though national indignation was legitimately aroused by the impunity accorded to Albanian lawlessness in Kossovo and Old Serbia, hostility to Turkey took a second place in the popular mind; even the idea of obtaining Turkish aid against Austria was sometimes entertained. . . . Ever since the reconciliation of Bulgaria with Russia in 1895 the various efforts which have been made to bring about a Serbo-Bulgarian *rapprochement* have in the main been due, as in the present case, to Russian inspiration. The aims of Servia were practically identical with those of Russia; it was hoped to bring about a Slav combination in the Balkans destined to checkmate the policy of Austria, to obstruct her dreaded advance toward Salonika, and eventually to effect the union of the Serb race. The Bulgarian programme, avowed or unavowed, was somewhat different; there was the same dread of Austrian encroachment, but the Turk was the real enemy; the heart of the nation was with its oppressed kindred in Macedonia and its desire was to achieve their liberation.

154. THE SERBO–BULGARIAN ALLIANCE OF 1912 [1]

H. M. Ferdinand I, King of the Bulgarians, and H. M. Peter I, King of Serbia, convinced of the community of the interests and the oneness of the destinies of their States and of the two brother peoples, Bulgarian and Serbian, and determined jointly to defend those interests with their combined forces, and to make every effort successfully to safeguard them, have arrived at the following agreement:

Article I. The kingdom of Bulgaria and the kingdom of Serbia mutually guarantee their political independence and the integrity of their territories, pledging themselves absolutely and without restriction of any sort to give aid each to the other with the full strength of their forces in the event of an attack on either of the two kingdoms by one or several States.

Article II. The two contracting parties further pledge themselves mutually to come to each other's aid, with the full strength of their forces, in case any one of the great powers should attempt to annex, occupy, or take

[1] Quoted from *Le Matin*, November 26, 1913, in *Nouveau recueil général de traités*. 3e Série, Tome VIII. Leipzig, 1915, p. 3. Translation.

possession with its troops, even temporarily, of any part whatsoever of the territories of the Balkan Peninsula at present under Turkish domination, if either of the two contracting parties considers that this is done contrary to its vital interests and constitutes a *casus belli*.

Article III. The two contracting parties pledge themselves not to make peace separately or without a preliminary understanding.

Article IV. A military convention will be concluded in order that the execution of the present treaty may be assured in full and in a way that conforms to the aims that are being pursued. . . .

Secret Codicil

Article II. All territorial gains brought about by common action, as contemplated in the first and second articles of the treaty . . . are to fall under the joint rule (condominium) of the two allied states. The settlement of them will not be delayed beyond three months after the reëstablishment of peace, and will be based on the following principles:

Serbia recognizes Bulgaria's right to the territories east of the Rhodope Mountains and the River Struma; Bulgaria recognizes Serbia's right to those situated to the north and west of the Shar Planina Mountains.

155. THE GRECO–BULGARIAN ALLIANCE OF 1912[1]

Treaty of Defensive Alliance between Bulgaria and Greece

Whereas the two kingdoms firmly desire the maintenance of peace in the Balkan Peninsula, and are better able to preserve it by means of a strong defensive alliance;

Whereas, furthermore, the peaceful coëxistance of the different nationalities in Turkey, on the basis of a real and genuine political equality, and respect for the rights conceded either by treaty or otherwise to the Christian nationalities of the Empire, constitute conditions necessary to the maintenance of things as they are in the East;

Whereas, finally, coöperation between the two kingdoms, in the sense indicated, is by its very nature such as to improve their relations with the Ottoman Empire, and to bring about and assure an understanding between the Greek and Bulgarian elements in Turkey;

The government of H. M. the king of the Bulgarians and the government of H. M. the king of the Hellenes, pledging themselves not to permit any aggressive interpretation of their purely defensive agreement, and resolved to conclude an alliance of peace and mutual protection in the terms stated below, have named for their plenipotentiaries. . . .

[1] Quoted from *Le Matin*, November 26, 1913, in *Nouveau recueil général de traités*. 3e Série, Tome VIII. Leipzig, 1915, p. 12. Translation.

Article I. If, in opposition to the sincere desire of the two high contracting parties, and despite a policy on their part that avoids any act of aggression or provocation towards the Ottoman Empire, either one of the two States should be attacked by Turkey, whether by invasion of her territory, or by a systematic infringement of the rights arising from treaties or of the fundamental principles of international law, the two high contracting parties pledge themselves to lend reciprocal aid with their entire armed forces and thereafter to make no peace unless conjointly and by agreement with each other.

. . . .

[Four articles in all, followed by a Declaration.]

Article I shall not be valid in the event of a war that might arise between Greece and Turkey in consequence of the admission to the Greek Parliament of Cretan deputies contrary to the will of the Ottoman government; in this event Bulgaria is pledged only to maintain towards Greece a benevolent neutrality.

The First Balkan War revealed unexpected qualities in the Balkan peoples. The spirit of nationalism clearly had developed among them and with it was combined the most warlike zeal.

156. BULGARIANS AND SERBS AT WAR WITH THE TURKS[1]

The next thing which strikes you is the manner in which the [Bulgarian] people value the war. To say that they are modest about it would be to understate the case altogether. Their attitude towards their victories is like that of a public school boy who, when in the company of his relations, meets a schoolfellow in the holidays. They seem discreetly to ignore their achievements and their prowess. The Servians talk enthusiastically; so do the Greeks, I am told; the Bulgarians say nothing. Evidently they have known and they know exactly what they want to do and exactly how they mean to do it, and to that great end everything else is subordinate. . . .

There is a toughness of fibre about this people which is remarkable and strikes one at first sight, an absence of slovenliness, and a directness, a unity, and a singleness of purpose. . . .

You have only got to be a day in Servia to realise the spirit of the people. They are full of a concentrated fire of patriotism. The war to them is a question of life and death. And they regard their access to the sea as a question of life and death for their country. They have been the driving power in this war. They have had to make the greater sacrifices; and the part they have played has certainly not yet been fully realised or appreciated. The

[1] Maurice Baring, *Letters from the Near East.* London, Smith Elder & Co. (John Murray), 1913, pp. 114, 116, 138–140 (condensed).

Servians are less reserved than the Bulgarians, but they have the same single-ness of purpose and the same power of cleaving fast to one great idea. Not only has justice not been done to the Servians with regard to the part they have played in the whole campaign, but the actual fighting which they accomplished has been inadequately dealt with in the English Press. . . . There is no doubt that at the battle of Kumanovo and still more at the battle of Perlepe some of the severest fighting of the whole war took place. While I was at Uskub the campaign started in the Press complaining of Ser-vian barbarities, massacres, etc. . . . It is probably true that irregular bands or isolated units of soldiery, *on both sides,* did each other the maximum of harm in the most disagreeable way possible; just as the Catholics and Protestants did to each other in the days of the religious wars. If the Alba-nians complain of being massacred by the Servians, little sympathy can be given them, for massacre has been a constant factor in ordinary and every-day life. Likewise the Bulgarians and the Servians cannot complain of being massacred by the Turks. The extermination of a village by a band which was in a position to exterminate has from time immemorial been a recog-nised move in the code of Balkan warfare.

Each of the Balkan allies accomplished his allotment of the work. The Greek navy swept the Aegean and recovered the islands, while the army occupied the coast that included Salonika. The Bulgars met the chief Turk-ish forces and drove them to the gates of Constantinople. The Serbs and Montenegrans conquered Old Serbia and much of Macedonia, as well as reaching outlets on the Adriatic. Turkey was obliged to cede practically all her European territories.

157. THE TREATY OF LONDON, MAY 30, 1913[1]

Article II. H. M. the Emperor of the Ottomans cedes to Their Majesties the Allied Sovereigns all the territories of his Empire on the European conti-nent west of a line drawn from Enos on the Aegean Sea to Midia on the Black Sea, with the exception of Albania.

Article III. H. M. the Emperor of the Ottomans and Their Majesties, the Allied Sovereigns, resign to H. M. the Emperor of Germany, H. M. the Emperor of Austria . . . , M. the President of the French Republic, H. M. the King of Great Britain and Ireland . . . , H. M. the King of Italy, and H. M. the Emperor of all the Russias, the charge of establishing the fron-tiers of Albania, and all other questions concerning Albania.

Article IV. H. M. the Emperor of the Ottomans cedes to Their Majesties the Allied Sovereigns the island of Crete and renounces in their favor all rights, whether of sovereignty or other, which he possessed on that island.

[1] *Nouveau recueil général de traités.* 3e Série, Tome VIII. Leipzig, 1915, p. 17. Translation.

Article V. H. M. the Emperor of the Ottomans and Their Majesties the Allied Sovereigns commit to [here are written the titles of the heads of the same six Great Powers as above] the task of making decisions as to the fate of all the Ottoman islands in the Aegean Sea, with the exception of the island of Crete, and of the peninsula of Mount Athos.

Agreements between Serbia, Greece, and Bulgaria had been made as to the division of what was to be gained from Turkey. Austria prevented the realization of Serbia's ambitions and the allies fell out soon after their common victory had humbled Turkey. In the Second Balkan War (1913) Serbia, Montenegro and Greece were aided by Rumania, and before long Turkey reëntered the war against Bulgaria, who shortly was defeated and obliged to accept much diminished boundaries in Macedonia, the loss of a bit of Danubian land to Rumania, and the return of most of Thrace to the Turks. Hatreds were kept burning that found an outlet in the Great War a year later.

158. THE VICTORS QUARREL OVER THE SPOILS [1]

A.

Belgrade, June 19

The Bulgarian reply to the Servian Note asking a revision of the Serbo-Bulgarian Treaty of March, 1912, was presented this afternoon at the Foreign Office here. . . . There is little doubt that the Bulgarian Government refuses to agree to the Servian demand. . . . Little is hoped from the meeting of Premiers in St. Petersburg, even if it should take place. . . .

For the first time calm and competent observers in Belgrade talk of war as inevitable, and unless one side suddenly gives way it would seem as if the immediate and authoritative intervention of the European Concert can alone prevent a catastrophe. It was Europe which at the instance of Austria forbade Servia to possess a port of her own on the Adriatic, and so deprived her " of the fruit of her victories." It is for Europe to decide what reparation should or can be made to Servia elsewhere. This country needs and demands easy commercial access to Salonika and such a territorial arrangement as shall give a common frontier with Greece. No mere admonition of the Powers can do any good. . . .

B.

Sofia, June 19

The *Bulgaria* . . . publishes an article today stating that Bulgaria values the advice of those who point out the horrors and dangers of a fratricidal war, but that she cannot bargain for peace at the price of the amputation of

[1] The *Times*, London. June 20, 1913.

a portion of the national body. Such a sacrifice should not be asked of her. Bulgaria shelters within her former frontiers 250,000 to 300,000 Macedonian refugees, and has already made heavy sacrifices in allowing a portion of Bulgarian Macedonia to be regarded . . . as disputable territory, and in submitting its fate to the arbitration of Russia. That is the last sacrifice Bulgaria will make. . . .

The journal *Utro* . . . states that Austria-Hungary is resolved to intervene in the Serbo-Bulgarian dispute, should Russia assign any portion of Western Macedonia beyond the "contested zone" to Servia. Austria-Hungary has great economic interests to guard in Western Macedonia, and cannot allow Servia to appropriate the valley of the Vardar. . . .

SECTION VII. THE BAGDAD RAILWAY

One of the great factors in Near Eastern history in the quarter-century preceding the Great War, the economic exploitation of Asia Minor and Mesopotamia by Germany, is best described by the author of the most authoritative work on that subject.

159. GERMANY'S BAGDADBAHN PROJECT [1]

During the summer of 1888 the Oriental Railways — from the Austrian frontier, across the Balkan Peninsula *via* Belgrade, Nish, Sofia, and Adrianople, to Constantinople — were opened to traffic. Connections with the railways of Austria-Hungary and other European countries placed the Ottoman capital in direct communication with Vienna, Paris, Berlin, and London (*via* Calais). The arrival at the Golden Horn, August 12, 1888, of the first through express from Paris and Vienna was made the occasion of great rejoicing in Constantinople and was generally hailed by the European Press as marking the beginning of a new era in the history of the Ottoman Empire. To thoughtful Turks, however, it was apparent that the opening of satisfactory rail communications in European Turkey but emphasized the inadequacy of such communications in the Asiatic provinces. Anatolia, the homeland of the Turks, possessed only a few hundred kilometres of railways; the vast areas of Syria, Mesopotamia, and the Hedjaz possessed none at all. Almost immediately after the completion of the Oriental Railways, therefore, the Sultan, with the advice and assistance of the Ottoman Public Debt Administration, launched a program for the construction of an elaborate system of railway lines in Asiatic Turkey.

[1] Edward M. Earle, *Turkey, The Great Powers, and the Bagdad Railway*. New York, The Macmillan Co., 1923, pp. 29–33 (condensed), 72–75.

The existing railways in Asia Minor were owned, in 1888, entirely by French and British financiers, with British capital decidedly in the predominance. The oldest and most important railway in Anatolia, the Smyrna-Aidin line — authorized in 1856, opened to traffic in 1866, and extended at various times until in 1888 it was 270 kilometres in length — was owned by an English company. British capitalists also owned the short, but valuable, Mersina-Adana Railway, in Cilicia, and held the lease of the Haidar Pasha-Ismid Railway. French interests were in control of the Smyrna-Cassaba Railway, which operated 168 kilometres of rails extending north and east from the port of Smyrna. It was not until the autumn of 1888 that Germans had any interest whatever in the railways of Asiatic Turkey. . . .

But the great dream of Abdul Hamid was the great dream of Wilhelm von Pressel: the vision of a trunk line from the Bosporus to the Persian Gulf, which, in connection with the existing railways of Anatolia and the new railways of Syria, would link Constantinople with Smyrna, Aleppo, Damascus, Beirut, Mosul, and Bagdad. As early as 1886 the Ottoman Ministry of Public Works had suggested to the lessees of the Haidar Pasha-Ismid Railway that they undertake the extension of that line to Angora with a view to an eventual extension to Bagdad. The proposal was renewed in 1888, with the understanding that the Sultan was prepared to pay a substantial subsidy to assure adequate returns on the capital to be invested. The lessees of the Haidar Pasha-Ismid line, however, were unable to interest investors in the enterprise and were compelled to withdraw altogether from railway projects in Turkey-in-Asia. Thereupon Sir Vincent Caillard, Chairman of the Ottoman Public Debt Administration, endeavored to form an Anglo-American syndicate to undertake the construction of a Constantinople-Bagdad railway, but he met with no success.

The opportunity which British capitalists neglected German financiers seized. Dr. Alfred von Kaulla, of the *Württembergische Vereinsbank* of Stuttgart, who was in Constantinople selling Mauser rifles to the Ottoman Minister of War, became interested in the possibilities of railway development in Turkey. With the coöperation of Dr. George von Siemens, Managing Director of the *Deutsche Bank,* a German syndicate was formed to take over the existing railway from Haidar Pasha to Ismid and to construct an extension thereof to Angora. On October 6, 1888, this syndicate was awarded a concession for the railway to Angora and was given to understand that it was the intention of the Ottoman Government to extend that railway to Bagdad *via* Samsun, Sivas, and Diarbekr. The Sultan guaranteed the Angora line a minimum annual revenue of 15,000 francs per kilometre, for the payment of which he assigned to the Ottoman Public Debt Administration the taxes of certain districts through which the railway was to pass. Thus came into existence the Anatolian Railway Company (*La Société du Chemin de*

Fer Ottomane d'Anatolie), the first of the German railway enterprises in Turkey.

The German concessionaires were not slow to realize the possibilities of their concession. They elected Sir Vincent Caillard to the board of directors of their Company, in order that they might receive the enthusiastic coöperation of the Ottoman Public Debt Administration and in order that they might interest British capitalists in their project. With the assistance of Swiss bankers they incorporated at Zurich the *Bank für orientalischen Eisenbahnen*, which floated in the European securities markets the first Anatolian Railways loan of eighty million francs — more than one fourth of the loan being underwritten in England. Shortly thereafter this same financial group, under the leadership of the *Deutsche Bank*, acquired a controlling interest in more than 1500 kilometres of railways in the Balkan Peninsula, by purchasing the holdings of Baron Hirsch in the Oriental Railways Company. The *Bank für orientalischen Eisenbahnen* became a holding company for all of the *Deutsche Bank's* railway enterprises in the Near East.

Under the direction of German engineers, in the meantime, construction of the Anatolian Railway proceeded at so rapid a rate that the 485 kilometres of rails were laid and trains were in operation to Angora by January, 1893. About the same time a German engineering commission, assisted by two technical experts representing the Ottoman Ministry of Public Works and by two Turkish army officers, submitted a report on their preliminary survey of the proposed railway to Bagdad. This was enthusiastically received by the Sultan, who reiterated his intention of constructing a line into Mesopotamia at the earliest practicable date.

In 1887 there was no German capital represented in the railways of Asiatic Turkey. Five years later the *Deutsche Bank* and its collaborators controlled the railways of Turkey from the Austro-Hungarian border to Constantinople; they had constructed a line from the Asiatic shore of the Straits to Angora; they were projecting a railway from Angora across the hills of Anatolia into the Mesopotamian valley. In coöperation with the Austrian and German state railways they could establish through service from the Baltic to the Bosporus and, by ferry and railway, into hitherto inaccessible parts of Asia Minor. Almost overnight, as history goes, Turkey had become an important sphere of German economic interest. Thus was born the idea of a series of German-controlled railways from Berlin to Bagdad, from Hamburg to the Persian Gulf!

The Ottoman Government apparently was well pleased with the energetic action of the German concessionaires in the promotion of their railway enterprises in Turkey. In any event, a tangible evidence of appreciation was extended the Anatolian Railway Company by an imperial *iradé* of February 15, 1893, which authorized the construction of a branch line of 444 kilometres from Eski Shehr (a town about midway between Ismid and Angora) to Konia. The new line, like its predecessor, was guaranteed a minimum annual return of 15,000 francs per kilometre, payments to be made under the supervision of the Ottoman Public Debt Administration. The obvious advantages of developing the potentially rich regions of southern Anatolia, and of providing improved communication between Constantinople and the interior of Asia Minor, led the Anatolian Company to hasten construction, with the result that service to Konia was inaugurated in 1896.

· · · · · · · · · · · · · · · · · ·

The starting point of the new railway was to be Konia. This town of 44,000 inhabitants, situated high in the Anatolian plateau, was a landmark in the Near East. It was once the capital of the Seljuk Turks and during its heyday had been a crossroads of the caravan routes of Asia Minor. Along one of these old routes to the northwest ran the Anatolian Railway, with which the Bagdad line was to be linked. From Konia the new railway was to cross the Anatolian table-lands, at an average altitude of 3500 feet, passing through the towns of Karaman and Eregli. Just beyond the latter town are the foothills of the Taurus, the first of the mountain barriers between Asia Minor and the Mesopotamian valley. In crossing the Taurus range the railway was to pass through the famous Cilician Gates, down the eastern slope into the fertile Cilician plain. At Adana, center of the trade of this region, a junction was to be effected with the existing railway to Mersina, a small port on the Mediterranean.

Formidable engineering difficulties faced the succeeding stretch of the railway. Beyond Adana stood the second mountain barrier of the Amanus range, through which there was no natural pass, and it was apparent that costly blasting and tunneling would be required before the hills could be pierced. Once beyond the mountains the railway could be carried quickly to Aleppo, a city of 128,000, "the emporium of northern Syria," and a meeting place for the Mesopotamian, Syrian, and Anatolian trade-routes. At this point connections were to be established with the important railways of Syria, providing direct communication with Hama, Homs, Tripoli-in-Syria, Beirut, Damascus, Jaffa, and Jerusalem. In fact, enthusiastic Syrians have prophesied that when all projected transcontinental railways are completed in Europe, Asia, and Africa, Aleppo will become "the crossroads of the world" — a junction point for rail communication between Berlin and Bagdad, Calais and Calcutta, Bordeaux and Bombay, Moscow and Mecca, Constantinople and Cairo and Cape Town. Seventy miles away from Aleppo, along one of the few good wagon roads in Turkey, lay the important Mediterranean port of Alexandretta. Leaving Aleppo, the Bagdad Railway was to turn east, crossing a desert country, to Nisibin and to Mosul, on the Tigris.

From this sector of the railway it was proposed to construct several short spurs into the Armenian foothills, as well as a longer branch from Nisibin to Diarbekr and Kharput.

The city of Mosul is the northern gateway to the Mesopotamian valley, the " Land of the Two Rivers." In medieval times it was a center of caravan routes between Persia, Mesopotamia, Syria, and Anatolia, and once was famed for its textile manufactures, which produced a cloth named after the city, " muslin." It is located on the site of a suburb of the ancient city of Nineveh and guards a high pass leading through the mountains into Armenia. In 1903 it had a population of 61,000 and bade fair, after the completion of the Bagdad Railway, to regain some of its lost lustre. South and southeast of Mosul flows the Tigris River all the way to the Persian Gulf. Along the valley of this river was to run the new railway, through the towns of Tekrit, Samarra, and Sadijeh, to Bagdad.

In 1903 the splendor of the ancient city of Bagdad was very much dimmed. Although it still was the center of an important caravan trade with Persia, Arabia, and Syria, its prosperity was but a name compared with the riches which the city had enjoyed before the commercial revolution of the sixteenth century. The population of 145,000 — in part nomad — was to a large extent dependent upon the important export trade in dates and cereals, amounting, in 1902, to almost £1,000,000. All told, the trade of Bagdad was valued at about £2,500,000 annually. Whether the shadow of the former great Bagdad could be transformed into a living thing was an open question.

Five hundred miles south of Bagdad is the Persian Gulf, the proposed terminus of the Bagdad Railway. About sixty miles north of the Gulf, located on the Shatt-el-Arab — the confluence of the Tigris and Euphrates Rivers — is the port of Basra, the outlet for the trade of Bagdad. Communication between these two Mesopotamian cities was carried on, in 1903, by means of a weekly steamer service operated by the English firm of Lynch Brothers, and under the name " The Euphrates and Tigris Steam Navigation Company, Ltd." The Lynch Brothers — typical British imperial pathfinders — had established themselves at Basra during the decade 1840–1850 and had succeeded during the following half-century in securing a practical monopoly of the river trade from Bagdad to the Persian Gulf. The absence of effective competition and the hesitancy of the Turkish Government to grant permission for the operation of additional steamers were responsible for a totally inadequate service. It was not uncommon for freight to stand on the wharves at Bagdad and Basra for three months or more awaiting transportation. Under these circumstances it was to be expected that freight charges would be exorbitant; it cost more to transfer cargoes from Bagdad to Basra than from Basra to London. The advent of the Bagdad Railway promised great things for the trade of lower Mesopotamia and Persia.

It was the aim of the Turkish Government and the concessionaires not only to compete with the river trade of the Tigris, but to develop the Euphrates valley as well, there being no steamer service on the latter river. With this in mind, it was decided to divert the railway beyond Bagdad from the Tigris to the Euphrates and down the valley to Basra. For a time Basra was to mark the terminus of the railway; the concession made provisions, however, for the eventual construction of a branch " from Zubeir to a point on the Persian Gulf to be agreed upon between the Imperial Ottoman Government and the concessionaires."

Of considerable importance was a proposed branch line from Sadijeh, on the Tigris, to Khanikin, on the Persian frontier. This railway, it was believed, would take the place of the existing caravan route from Bagdad to Khanikin and thence to Teheran. The annual value of British trade alone transported *via* this route was estimated at about three quarters of a million pounds sterling.

The Bagdad Railway, as thus projected, was one of the really great enterprises of an era of dazzling railway construction. Here was a transcontinental line stretching some twenty-five hundred miles from Constantinople, on the Bosporus, to Basra, on the Shatt-el-Arab — a project greater in magnitude than the Santa Fé line from Chicago to Los Angeles or the Union Pacific Railway from Omaha to San Francisco. It was a promise of the rejuvenation of three of the most important parts of the Ottoman Empire — eastern Anatolia, northern Syria, and Mesopotamia. It was to open to twentieth-century steel trains a fifteenth-century caravan route. It was to replace the camel with the locomotive.

CHAPTER XI

SOCIAL FACTORS AND TENDENCIES (1814-1914)

SECTION I. SOCIALISM, COMMUNISM, AND SYNDICALISM

Socialists differ widely among themselves as to the meaning of socialism. Primarily, however, it signifies the control of the means of production and distribution by the State and the operation of these by the State for the benefit of the masses of the people. It does not mean that private property should be confiscated and then divided equally among all.

One of the earliest Socialists was the Count Henri de Saint-Simon, 1760-1825, a Frenchman who, after fighting in the American Revolution, returned to France, amassed a fortune in land speculation, used up this fortune in social experiments and thereafter lived in poverty. This " Utopian Socialist" exercised virtually no direct practical influence on the existing social order. But, as the following extract shows, he left behind him devoted followers. And these followers laid the foundations of modern French socialism.

160. EARLY FRENCH SOCIALISM. THE ST. SIMONIANS IN THE REIGN OF LOUIS PHILIPPE[1]

THE revolution of July had given to St. Simonianism a singularly energetic impulse. That which in the first instance was but a school, was now a family. Combining with the authority of lofty intellect and solid acquirements, the passion for proselytism, the first adepts, men of the world, jealous sectaries, spread themselves about in every direction; holding out to orators the promise of a noble arena, a stirring theme; tempting poets and artists with the bait of reputation easily acquired; proving to the *savants* that the existing science of liberalism was false and hollow, without aim or scope, as without heart or feeling; talking to the women about the fine arts, love, and liberty. The success of these efforts was rapid; they soon made plenty of individual conquests, and they then began to think of collective triumphs. The hierarchy was founded: the college first, then the second degree, then the third degree. The *Globe,* which the retreat of the doctrinaires had left in the hands of M. Pierre Leroux, a powerful thinker and writer, became

[1] Louis Blanc, *The History of Ten Years, 1830-1840.* 2 vols. London, Chapman and Hall, 1844, vol. I, pp. 557-559 (condensed).

the daily journal of the school which was already possessed of the *Organisateur*. It was no sooner hinted that money was wanting than money flowed in. M. d'Eichthal furnished a considerable sum. To a letter from Bazard and Enfantin, M. Henri Fournel, who was then at Creuzot, instantly replied by the offer of his whole fortune, his reply being thus subscribed: " Henry and Cecilia Fournel for their child." In a society overrun with the coarsest and most narrow-minded mercantilism, there was something in a very high degree marvellous and touching in this burst of generous enthusiasm. The far larger portion of the journals of this period were mere trading speculations: the *Globe* was distributed gratuitously.

The zeal of the adepts animated them to the most vigorous exertions. The quiet, modest conferences which, before the revolution of July, were held in the Rue Taranne, were now succeeded by the vehement and noisy harangues of the Rue Taitbout. Here men, full of eloquence, such as Messieurs Barrault, Charlton, Laurent, Abel Transon, repaired to exercise in turns the sovereignty of the mighty harangue. Nothing could be more curious than the spectacle presented by these assemblies. Around a vast hall, beneath a roof of glass, there arose three tiers of boxes. On the stage in front of these, and of an ample pit, the red benches of which as the clock struck twelve were crowded with an eager audience, there arranged themselves every Sunday, seated in three rows, a number of young and serious-looking men habited in blue, among whom might be seen also a few ladies dressed in white, with violet-coloured scarfs. By and bye there appeared, leading forward the preacher of the day, the two supreme fathers of the society, Messieurs Bazard and Enfantin. As they advanced to the front, the disciples rose with looks of tender veneration; while among the spectators there immediately prevailed an intense silence, contemplative or ironical, according to the mood in which they came. After a short pause the preacher began. Many among the audience listened at first with a smile on their lips, and raillery in their eyes; but after the orator had spoken for a while, there would be one feeling amongst his hearers of astonishment mingled with admiration; and the most sceptical found themselves irresistibly impelled into an earnest meditation upon the discourse, if not into a secret emotion, in sympathy with it.

Every thing tended to render this propaganda active, triumphant. The family established in the Rue Monsigny, was like a glowing fire, reflecting brilliant light upon those whom its genial warmth drew around it. The doctrine developed itself here, amid the inspiring bustle and gaiety of elegant soirées, under the powerful influence of fascinating women. Abandoning their occupations, their dreams of fortune, their early associations of the heart, engineers, artists, physicians, advocates, poets, rushed hither to throw into one common association their most exalted hopes; some brought their books, others their furniture; their meals were taken in common, and they assiduously studied this new religion of human brotherhood. The name of father was given to the members of each superior degree by those of the inferior degrees; and the females who had entered themselves of this intellectual colony, were addressed by the gentle names of mother, sister, daughter. Here centered the relations, constantly extending themselves, which established between these Parisian innovators and their provincial allies, an unintermitting correspondence; and this was the point whence there set forth, bent upon sowing the seed of St. Simonianism throughout the length and breadth of France, missionaries who everywhere left traces of their course; who made their way into shops and into drawing rooms, into huts, hôtels, and châteaux; received here with enthusiasm, there with hootings, but everywhere indefatigable in their ardent zeal. Thus MM. Jean Reynaud and Pierre Leroux were sent to Lyons, which they kindled into a flame, and which was destined to retain an imperishable memory of their presence.

.   .   .   .

The march of humanity, according to the St. Simonians, was towards a state of things in which individuals should be classed according to their capacity, and salaried according to their works. Property then, as it now exists, was to be abolished because it furnishes a certain class of men with the means of living by the labour of others, because it gives sanction to the division of society into workers and idlers; because in fine, in contempt of all obvious notion of equity, it places those who produce much and consume little, in the hands of those who consume much, and produce little, or even nothing, to be worked and made use of at their pleasure. But the existing system of inheritance was not only unjust, according to the St. Simonians; it was in the lowering of wages and the rise of rent and interest; and very naturally; but then the workers would demand just the contrary. The gradual development of labour, then, would involve the continual reduction of the rate of interest, and of the rent of land and houses. This being the case, the St. Simonians asked, what would become of the proprietors when the reduction should have become so great, that it would be no longer possible for them to live solely upon the interest of their money, and the rents of their lands and houses? They must perforce work. But the proprietor-worker dying, his son might not have the same tastes, or the same peculiar capacity as his father. For instance, the artist son of a proprietor-cultivator, finding it impossible for him to live on the rents of his patrimonial estate, would be necessarily subjected to the alternative of either altogether pauperizing himself by cultivating, unskilfully and against his inclination, the domains he had succeeded to, or of selling them, in order to obtain the means of devoting himself to the profession more suitable to his turn of mind. And similar social phenomena presenting themselves throughout the whole extent of society, was it not evident, that there would arise a necessity for a general liquidation, which the state alone would be in a position to regulate, and the direction of which, it would be to the clear interest of the proprietors themselves to confide to the state?

The " Communist Manifesto" was issued in 1848 by an organization known as the Communist League. It had been drawn up by Karl Marx and Frederick Engels, two of the founders of modern socialism, as a sort of a party platform for an international gathering of workmen held in London under the auspices of the League.

The words of this bitter denunciation of capitalism have echoed round the world. It should not be assumed, however, that all Socialists and Communists subscribe in full to its revolutionary ideas.

161. EXTRACTS FROM THE COMMUNIST MANIFESTO [1]

A SPECTRE is haunting Europe — the spectre of Communism. All the powers of old Europe have entered into a holy alliance to exorcise this spectre; Pope and Czar, Metternich and Guizot, French Radicals and German police-spies.

Where is the party in opposition that has not been decried as communistic by its opponents in power? Where the Opposition that has not hurled back the branding reproach of Communism, against the more advanced opposition parties, as well as against its reactionary adversaries?

Two things result from this fact.

I. Communism is already acknowledged by all European Powers to be itself a Power.

II. It is high time that Communists should openly, in the face of the whole world, publish their views, their aims, their tendencies, and meet this nursery tale of the Spectre of Communism with a Manifesto of the party itself.

To this end, Communists of various nationalities have assembled in London, and sketched the following manifesto, to be published in the English, French, German, Italian, Flemish and Danish languages.

. . . .

The history of all hitherto existing society is the history of class struggles.

. . . .

The modern bourgeois society that has sprouted from the ruins of feudal society, has not done away with class antagonisms. It has but established new

[1] Karl Marx and Frederick Engels, *Manifesto of the Communist Party*. Authorized English translation. Chicago, Charles H. Kerr and Company.

classes, new conditions of oppression, new forms of struggle in place of the old ones.

Our epoch, the epoch of the bourgeoisie, possesses this distinctive feature; it has simplified the class antagonisms. Society as a whole is more and more splitting up into two great classes directly facing each other: Bourgeoisie and Proletariat.

. . . .

The bourgeoisie, wherever it has got the upper hand, has put an end to all feudal, patriarchal, idyllic relations. It has pitilessly torn asunder the motley feudal ties that bound man to his "natural superiors," and has left remaining no other nexus between man and man than naked self-interest, than callous "cash payment."

. . . .

In proportion as the bourgeoisie, i.e. capital, is developed, in the same proportion is the proletariat, the modern working-class, developed, a class of laborers, who live only so long as they find work, and who find work only so long as their labor increases capital. These laborers, who must sell themselves piecemeal, are a commodity, like every article of commerce, and are consequently exposed to all the vicissitudes of competition, to all the fluctuations of the market.

. . . .

Modern industry has converted the little work-shop of the patriarchal master into the great factory of the industrial capitalist. Masses of laborers, crowded into the factory, are organized like soldiers. As privates of the industrial army they are placed under the command of a perfect hierarchy of officers and sergeants. Not only are they the slaves of the bourgeois class, and of the bourgeois State, they are daily and hourly enslaved by the machine, by the over-looker, and, above all, by the individual bourgeois manufacturer himself.

. . . .

But with the development of industry the proletariat not only increases in number, it becomes concentrated in greater masses, its strength grows, and it feels that strength more. The various interests and conditions of life within the ranks of the proletariat are more and more equalized, in proportion as machinery obliterates all distinctions of labor, and nearly everywhere reduces wages to the same low level. The growing competition among the bourgeois, and the resulting commercial crises, make the wages of the workers ever more fluctuating. The unceasing improvement of machinery, ever more rapidly developing, makes their livelihood more and more precarious; the collisions between individual workmen and individual bourgeois take more and more the character of collisions between two classes. Thereupon the workers begin to form combinations (Trades' Unions) against the bourgeois.

This organization of the proletarians into a class, and consequently into a political party, is continually being upset again by the competition between the workers themselves. But it ever rises up again, stronger, firmer, mightier.

It has become evident that the bourgeoisie is unfit any longer to be the ruling class in society, and to impose its conditions of existence upon society as an over-riding law. It is unfit to rule, because it is incompetent to assure an existence to its slave within his slavery, because it cannot help letting him sink into such a state that it has to feed him, instead of being fed by him. Society can no longer live under this bourgeoisie, in other words, its existence is no longer compatible with society.

The essential condition for the existence, and for the sway of the bourgeois class, is the formation and augmentation of capital; the condition for capital is wage-labor. Wage-labor rests exclusively on competition between the laborers. The advance of industry, whose involuntary promoter is the bourgeoisie, replaces the isolation of the laborers, due to competition, by their involuntary combination, due to association. The development of Modern Industry, therefore, cuts from under its feet the very foundation on which the bourgeoisie produces and appropriates products. What the bourgeoisie therefore produces, above all, are its own grave-diggers. Its fall and the victory of the proletariat are equally inevitable.

The immediate aim of the Communists is the same as that of all the other proletarian parties; formation of the proletariat into a class, overthrow of the bourgeois supremacy, conquest of political power by the proletariat.

The distinguishing feature of Communism is not the abolition of property generally, but the abolition of bourgeois property. But modern bourgeois private property is the final and most complete expression of the system of producing and appropriating products, that is based on class antagonism, on the exploitation of the many by the few.

In this sense, the theory of the Communists may be summed up in the single sentence: Abolition of private property.

The Communists are reproached with desiring to abolish countries and nationalities.

The working men have no country. We cannot take from them what they have not got. Since the proletariat must first of all acquire political supremacy, must rise to be the leading class of the nation, must constitute itself the nation, it is, so far, itself national, though not in the bourgeois sense of the word.

National differences, and antagonisms between peoples, are daily more and more vanishing, owing to the development of the bourgeoisie, to freedom of commerce, to the world-market, to uniformity in the mode of production and in the conditions of life corresponding thereto.

The supremacy of the proletariat will cause them to vanish still faster. United action, of the leading civilized countries at least, is one of the first conditions for the emancipation of the proletariat.

. . . .

The proletariat will use its political supremacy, to wrest, by degrees, all capital from the bourgeoisie, to centralize all instruments of production in the hands of the State, i.e., of the proletariat organized as the ruling class; and to increase the total of productive forces as rapidly as possible.

Of course, in the beginning, this cannot be effected except by means of despotic inroads on the rights of property, and on the conditions of bourgeois production; by means of measures, therefore, which appear economically insufficient and untenable, but which, in the course of the movement, outstrip themselves, necessitate further inroads upon the old social order, and are unavoidable as a means of entirely revolutionizing the mode of production.

These measures will of course be different in different countries.

Nevertheless in the most advanced countries the following will be pretty generally applicable:

1. Abolition of property in land and application of all rents of land to public purposes.

2. A heavy progressive or graduated income tax.

3. Abolition of all right of inheritance.

4. Confiscation of the property of all emigrants and rebels.

5. Centralization of credit in the hands of the State, by means of a national bank with State capital and an exclusive monopoly.

6. Centralization of the means of communication and transport in the hands of the State.

7. Extension of factories and instruments of production owned by the State; the bringing into cultivation of waste lands, and the improvement of the soil generally in accordance with a common plan.

8. Equal liability of all to labor. Establishment of industrial armies, especially for agriculture.

9. Combination of agriculture with manufacturing industries; gradual abolition of the distinction between town and country, by a more equable distribution of population over the country.

10. Free education for all children in public schools. Abolition of children's factory labor in its present form. Combination of education with industrial production, etc., etc.

When, in the course of development, class distinctions have disappeared, and all production has been concentrated in the hands of a vast association of the whole nation, the public power will lose its political character. Political power, properly so called, is merely the organized power of one class for oppressing another. If the proletariat during its contest with the bourgeoisie is compelled, by the force of circumstances, to organize itself as a class, if, by means of a revolution, it makes itself the ruling class, and, as such, sweeps away by force the old conditions of production, then it will, along with these conditions, have swept away the conditions for the existence of class antagonisms, and of classes generally, and will thereby have abolished its own supremacy as a class.

In place of the old bourgeois society, with its classes and class antagonisms, we shall have an association, in which the free development of each is the condition for the free development of all.

. . . .

The Communists disdain to conceal their views and aims. They openly declare that their ends can be attained only by the forcible overthrow of all existing social conditions. Let the ruling classes tremble at a Communistic revolution. The proletarians have nothing to lose but their chains. They have a world to win.

Workingmen of all countries, unite!

Brilliant as Karl Marx's thinking was, time has revealed certain significant errors in his calculations. Bertrand Russell, English mathematician and philosopher, discusses some of these miscalculations in his Proposed Roads to Freedom, *a lucid exposition of the chief advanced social theories of the present time.*

162. FLAWS IN THE THEORIES OF KARL MARX [1]

Two questions are raised by Marx's work (*Das Kapital*): First, Are his laws of historical development true? Second, Is Socialism desirable? The second of these questions is quite independent of the first. Marx professes to prove that Socialism *must* come, but scarcely concerns himself to argue that

[1] Bertrand Russell, *Proposed Roads to Freedom*. New York, Henry Holt and Company, 1919, pp. 25–28.

when it comes it will be a good thing. It may be, however, that if it comes, it will be a good thing, even though all Marx's arguments to prove that it must come should be at fault. In actual fact, time has shown many flaws in Marx's theories. The development of the world has been sufficiently like his prophecy to prove him a man of very unusual penetration, but has not been sufficiently like to make either political or economic history exactly such as he predicted that it would be. Nationalism, so far from diminishing, has increased, and has failed to be conquered by the cosmopolitan tendencies which Marx rightly discerned in finance. Although big businesses have grown bigger and have over a great area reached the stage of monopoly, yet the number of shareholders in such enterprises is so large that the actual number of individuals interested in the capitalist system has continually increased. Moreover, though large firms have grown larger, there has been a simultaneous increase in firms of medium size. Meanwhile the wage-earners, who were, according to Marx, to have remained at the bare level of subsistence at which they were in the England of the first half of the nineteenth century, have instead profited by the general increase of wealth, though in a lesser degree than the capitalists. The supposed iron law of wages has been proved untrue, so far as labor in civilized countries is concerned. If we wish now to find examples of capitalist cruelty analogous to those with which Marx's book is filled, we shall have to go for most of our material to the Tropics, or at any rate to regions where there are men of inferior races to exploit. Again: the skilled worker of the present day is an aristocrat in the world of labor. It is a question with him whether he shall ally himself with the unskilled worker against the capitalist, or with the capitalist against the unskilled worker. Very often he is himself a capitalist in a small way, and if he is not so individually, his trade union or his friendly society is pretty sure to be so. Hence the sharpness of the class war has not been maintained. There are gradations, intermediate ranks between rich and poor, instead of the clear-cut logical antithesis between the workers who have nothing and the capitalists who have all. Even in Germany, which became the home of orthodox Marxianism and developed a powerful Social-Democratic party, nominally accepting the doctrine of *Das Kapital* as all but verbally inspired, even there the enormous increase of wealth in all classes in the years preceding the war led Socialists to revise their beliefs and to adopt an evolutionary rather than a revolutionary attitude. Bernstein, a German Socialist who lived long in England, inaugurated the " Revisionist " movement which at last conquered the bulk of the party. His criticisms of Marxian orthodoxy are set forth in his *Evolutionary Socialism*. Bernstein's work, as is common in Broad Church writers, consists largely in showing that the Founders did not hold their doctrines so rigidly as their followers have done. There is much in the writings of Marx and Engels that cannot be fitted into the rigid orthodoxy which grew up among their disciples. Bernstein's main criticisms of these disciples, apart from such as we have already mentioned, consist in a defense of piecemeal action as against revolution. He protests against the attitude of undue hostility to Liberalism which is common among Socialists, and he blunts the edge of the Internationalism which undoubtedly is part of the teachings of Marx. The workers, he says, have a Fatherland as soon as they become citizens, and on this basis he defends that degree of nationalism which the war has since shown to be prevalent in the ranks of Socialists. He even goes so far as to maintain that European nations have a right to tropical territory owing to their higher civilization. Such doctrines diminish revolutionary ardor and tend to transform Socialists into a left wing of the Liberal Party. But the increasing prosperity of wage-earners before the war made these developments inevitable. Whether the war will have altered conditions in this respect, it is as yet impossible to know. Bernstein concluded with the wise remark that: " We have to take working men as they are. And they are neither so universally paupers as was set out in the Communist Manifesto, nor so free from prejudices and weaknesses as their courtiers wish to make us believe."

Though Karl Marx was undoubtedly one of the intellectual giants of the nineteenth century it is evident from the selection that follows that his overbearing, dogmatic manner weakened his influence over those with whom he came in contact.

163. AN IMPRESSION OF KARL MARX IN 1848 [1]

In the course of the summer [of 1848] Kinkel [2] and I were invited to represent the club [3] at a congress of democratic associations in Cologne. This assembly, in which I remained a shy and silent observer, became remarkable to me in bringing me into personal contact with some of the prominent men of that period, among others, the leader of the communists, Karl Marx. He could not have been much more than thirty years old at that time, but he already was the recognized head of the advanced socialistic school. The somewhat thick-set man, with his broad forehead, his very black hair and beard and his dark sparkling eyes, at once attracted general attention. He enjoyed the reputation of having acquired great learning, and as I knew very little of his discoveries and theories, I was all the more eager to gather words of wisdom from the lips of that famous man. This expectation was disappointed in a peculiar way. Marx's utterances were indeed full of meaning, logical and

[1] *The Reminiscences of Carl Schurz,* 3 vols. New York, The McClure Company, 1907–1908, vol. 1, pp. 139–140. Now published by Doubleday, Doran and Company.

[2] Schurz's friend, Professor Kinkel, of the University of Bonn. (Editor's note.)

[3] A democratic club, growing out of the Revolution of 1848 and composed of citizens, students, and professors. (Editor's note.)

clear, but I have never seen a man whose bearing was so provoking and intolerable. To no opinion, which differed from his, he accorded the honor of even a condescending consideration. Everyone who contradicted him he treated with abject contempt; every argument that he did not like he answered either with biting scorn at the unfathomable ignorance that had prompted it, or with opprobrious aspersions upon the motives of him who advanced it. I remember most distinctly the cutting disdain with which he pronounced the word " bourgeois "; and as a " bourgeois," that is as a detestable example of the deepest mental and moral degeneracy he denounced everyone that dared to oppose his opinion. Of course the propositions advanced or advocated by Marx in that meeting were voted down, because everyone whose feelings had been hurt by his conduct was inclined to support everything that Marx did not favor. It was very evident that not only had he not won any adherents, but had repelled many who otherwise might have become his followers.

From this meeting I took home with me a very important lesson : that he who would be a leader and teacher of men must treat the opinions of his hearers with respect; that even the most superior mind will lose influence upon others if he seeks to humiliate those others by constant demonstrations of his superiority. That public man will be most successful in enlightening and winning the ignorant who puts himself upon their standpoint, not with condescension, but with sympathy.

Syndicalism is at once an offshoot of socialism and a repudiation of it, The Syndicalists, mostly radical workingmen, have lost confidence in the parliamentary State as a means of improving fundamentally the condition of the industrial classes. Even in the accession of the Socialist party to power they see little hope. They claim that Socialists who are elected to office tend to become " bourgeois " and to neglect the interests of the workers. Therefore Syndicalists would substitute " one big union (i.e. a gigantic trade union) for the parliamentary State. In other words, they would replace existing political representative government by an organization primarily economic in character and deriving power from the working-classes.

In the following selection the character and methods of Syndicalism are discussed by Bertrand Russell.

164. SYNDICALISM[1]

The essential doctrine of Syndicalism is the class-war, to be conducted by industrial rather than political methods. The chief industrial methods advocated are the strike, the boycott, the label and sabotage.

[1] Bertrand Russell, *Proposed Roads to Freedom*. New York, Henry Holt and Company, 1919, pp. 65–71.

The boycott, in various forms, and the label, showing that the work has been done under trade-union conditions, have played a considerable part in American labor struggles.

Sabotage is the practice of doing bad work, or spoiling machinery or work which has already been done, as a method of dealing with employers in a dispute when a strike appears for some reason undesirable or impossible. It has many forms, some clearly innocent, some open to grave objections. One form of sabotage which has been adopted by shop assistants is to tell customers the truth about the articles they are buying; this form, however it may damage the shopkeeper's business, is not easy to object to on moral grounds. A form which has been adopted on railways, particularly in Italian strikes, is that of obeying all rules literally and exactly, in such a way as to make the running of trains practically impossible. Another form is to do all the work with minute care, so that in the end it is better done, but the output is small. From these innocent forms there is a continual progression, until we come to such acts as all ordinary morality would consider criminal; for example, causing railway accidents. Advocates of sabotage justify it as part of war, but in its more violent forms (in which it is seldom defended) it is cruel and probably inexpedient, while even in its milder forms it must tend to encourage slovenly habits of work, which might easily persist under the new regime that the Syndicalists wish to introduce. At the same time, when capitalists express a moral horror of this method, it is worth while to observe that they themselves are the first to practice it when the occasion seems to them appropriate. If report speaks truly, an example of this on a very large scale has been seen during the Russian Revolution.

By far the most important of the Syndicalist methods is the strike. Ordinary strikes, for specific objects, are regarded as rehearsals, as a means of perfecting organization and promoting enthusiasm, but even when they are victorious so far as concerns the specific point in dispute, they are not regarded by Syndicalists as affording any ground for industrial peace. Syndicalists aim at using the strike, not to secure such improvements of detail as employers may grant, but to destroy the whole system of employer and employed and win the complete emancipation of the worker. For this purpose what is wanted is the General Strike, the complete cessation of work by a sufficient proportion of the wage-earners to secure the paralysis of capitalism. Sorel, who represents Syndicalism too much in the minds of the reading public, suggests that the General Strike is to be regarded as a myth, like the Second Coming in Christian doctrine. But this view by no means suits the active Syndicalists. If they were brought to believe that the General Strike is a mere myth, their energy would flag, and their whole outlook would become disillusioned. It is the actual, vivid belief in its possibility which inspires them. They are much criticised for this belief by the political

Socialists, who consider that the battle is to be won by obtaining a Parliamentary majority. But Syndicalists have too little faith in the honesty of politicians to place any reliance on such a method or to believe in the value of any revolution which leaves the power of the State intact.

Syndicalist aims are somewhat less definite than Syndicalist methods. The intellectuals who endeavor to interpret them — not always very faithfully — represent them as a party of movement and change, following a Bergsonian *élan vital,* without needing any very clear prevision of the goal to which it is to take them. Nevertheless, the negative part, at any rate, of their objects is sufficiently clear.

They wish to destroy the State, which they regard as a capitalist institution, designed essentially to terrorize the workers. They refuse to believe that it would be any better under State Socialism. They desire to see each industry self-governing, but as to the means of adjusting the relations between different industries, they are not very clear. They are anti-militarist because they are anti-State, and because French troops have often been employed against them in strikes; also because they are internationalists, who believe that the sole interest of the working man everywhere is to free himself from the tyranny of the capitalist. Their outlook on life is the very reverse of pacifist, but they oppose wars between States on the ground that these are not fought for objects that in any way concern the workers. Their anti-militarism, more than anything else, brought them into conflict with the authorities in the years preceding the war. But, as was to be expected, it did not survive the actual invasion of France.

The doctrines of Syndicalism may be illustrated by an article introducing it to English readers in the first number of *The Syndicalist Railwayman,* September, 1911, from which the following is quoted:

"All Syndicalism, Collectivism, Anarchism aims at abolishing the present economic status and existing private ownership of most things; but while Collectivism would substitute ownership by everybody, and Anarchism ownership by nobody, Syndicalism aims at ownership by Organized Labor. It is thus a purely Trade Union reading of the economic doctrine and the class war preached by Socialism. It vehemently repudiates Parliamentary action on which Collectivism relies; and it is, in this respect, much more closely allied to Anarchism, from which, indeed, it differs in practice only in being more limited in range of action." (*Times,* Aug. 25, 1911.)

In truth, so thin is the partition between Syndicalism and Anarchism that the newer and less familiar " ism " has been shrewdly defined as " Organized Anarchy." It has been created by the Trade Unions of France; but it is obviously an international plant, whose roots have already found the soil of Britain most congenial to its growth and fructification.

Collectivist or Marxian Socialism would have us believe that it is distinctly a *Labor* Movement; but it is not so. Neither is Anarchism. The one is substantially *bourgeois;* the other *aristocratic,* plus an abundant output of book-learning, in either case. Syndicalism, on the contrary, is indubitably *laborist* in origin and aim, owing next to nothing to the " Classes," and, indeed, resolute to uproot them. The *Times* (Oct. 13, 1910), which almost single-handed in the British Press has kept creditably abreast of Continental Syndicalism, thus clearly set forth the significance of the General Strike:

' To understand what it means, we must remember that there is in France a powerful Labor Organization, which has for its open and avowed object a Revolution, in which not only the present order of Society, but the State itself, is to be swept away. This movement is called Syndicalism. It is not Socialism, but, on the contrary, radically opposed to Socialism, because the Syndicalists hold that the State is the great enemy and that the Socialists' ideal of State or Collectivist Ownership would make the lot of the Workers much worse than it is now under private employers. The means by which they hope to attain their end is the General Strike, an idea which was invented by a French workman about twenty years ago, and was adopted by the French Labor Congress in 1894, after a furious battle with the Socialists, in which the latter were worsted. Since then the General Strike has been the avowed policy of the Syndicalists, whose organization is the Confédération Générale du Travail.'

Or, to put it otherwise, the intelligent French worker has awakened, as he believes, to the fact that Society (*Societas*) and the State (*Civitas*) connote two separable spheres of human activity, between which there is no connection, necessary or desirable. Without the one, man, being a gregarious animal, cannot subsist; while without the other he would simply be in clover. The ' statesman ' whom office does not render positively nefarious is at best an expensive superfluity."

" L'Internationale" is the most famous of all Socialist songs. Its words were written by Eugene Pottier (1816–1887) who was born and died in Paris. The words were first heard in the Paris Commune of 1871. The tune was composed in 1888 by Alphonse Degeyter, a Belgian blacksmith who lived in the French city of Lille and died there in 1915.

Wherever Socialists or Communists march in procession in any part of the world they are pretty sure to sing the " Internationale" in one of the many languages into which it has been translated.

The first three verses are quoted on page 410.

165. L'INTERNATIONALE [1]

Paroles de
Eugène POTTIER

Musique de
DEGEYTER

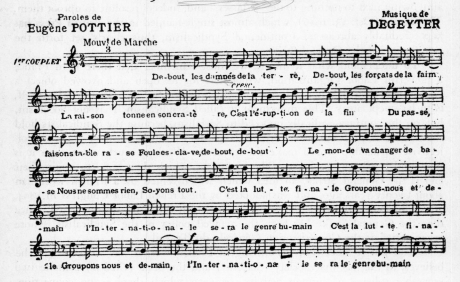

Ils n'est pas de sauveurs suprêmes:
Ni Dieu, ni César, ni tribun;
Producteurs, sauvons-nous nous mêmes!
Décrètons le salut commun!
Pour que le voleur rende gorge,
Pour tirer l'esprit du cachot,
Soufflons nous mêmes notre forge,
Battons le fer quand il est chaud!
C'est la lutte finale, etc.

Hideux dans leur apothéose,
Les Rois de la mine et du rail
Ont-ils jamais fait autre chose
Que dévaliser le travail?
Dans les coffres-forts de la bande
Ce qu'il a créé s'est fondu;
En décrètant qu'on le lui rende
Le peuple ne veut que son dû.
C'est la lutte finale, etc.

[1] Dorey, Editeur. 39 Boulevard de Strasbourg, Paris, A.D. 224.

SECTION II. ANARCHISM

Anarchism is the most extreme of all the leading schemes for revolution-izing the social order. Repudiating all authority in family, church, and state, it would substitute free co-operation among men for the restraints of govern-ment. It is usually associated in the popular mind with shooting and bomb-throwing, but it is only fair to point out that many anarchists are opposed to the employment of such methods to attain their ends.

One of the leading anarchists of recent times was Prince Peter Kropotkin, (1842–1921), from whose writings a brief extract is here quoted. At one time an officer in the tsar's army and a geographical scientist of repute, this Russian nobleman espoused the cause of anarchism and was forced to live most of his life in exile. His writings on scientific subjects and on anarchism are numerous.

166. ANARCHISM [1]

Educated men — " civilized," as Fourier used to say with disdain — tremble at the idea that society might some day be without judges, police, or gaolers.

But, frankly, do you need them as much as you have been told in musty books? Books written, be it noted, by scientists who generally know well what has been written before them, but, for the most part, absolutely ignore the people and their every-day life.

If we can wander, without fear, not only in the streets of Paris, which bristle with police, but especially in rustic walks where you rarely meet passers by, is it to the police that we owe this security? Or rather to the absence of people who care to rob or murder us? I am evidently not speak-ing of the one who carries millions about him. That one — a recent trial tells us — is soon robbed, by preference in places where there are as many policemen as lamp-posts. No, I speak of the man who fears for his life and not for his purse filled with ill-gotten sovereigns. Are his fears real?

Besides, has not experience demonstrated quite recently that Jack the Ripper performed his exploits under the eye of the London police — a most active force — and that he only left off killing when the population of Whitechapel itself began to give chase to him?

And in our every-day relations with our fellow-citizens, do you think that it is really judges, gaolers, and the police that hinder anti-social acts from

[1] Peter Kropotkin, *Anarchism: Its Philosophy and Ideal* (Pamphlet). San Francisco, Free Society, 1898, pp. 15–17.

multiplying? The judge, ever ferocious, because he is a maniac of law, the accuser, the informer, the police spy, all those interlopers that live from hand to mouth around the Law Courts, do they not scatter demoralization far and wide into society? Read the trials, glance behind the scenes, push your analysis further than the exterior façade of law courts, and you will come out sickened.

Have not prisons — which kill all will and force of character in man, which enclose within their walls more vices than are met with on any other spot of the globe — always been universities of crime? Is not the court of a tribunal a school of ferocity? And so on.

When we ask for the abolition of the State and its organs we are always told that we dream of a society composed of men better than they are in reality. But no; a thousand times, no. All we ask is that men should not be made worse than they are, by such institutions!

Once a German jurist of great renown, Ihering, wanted to sum up the scientific work of his life and write a treatise, in which he proposed to analyze the factors that preserve social life in society. *Purpose in Law* (*Der Zweck im Rechte*), such is the title of that book, which enjoys a well-deserved reputation.

He made an elaborate plan of his treatise, and, with much erudition, discussed both coercive factors which are used to maintain society: wagedom and the different forms of coercion which are sanctioned by law. At the end of his work he reserved two paragraphs only to mention the two non-coercive factors — the feeling of duty and the feeling of mutual sympathy — to which he attached little importance, as might be expected from a writer in law.

But what happened? As he went on analyzing the coercive factors he realized their insufficiency. He consecrated a whole volume to their analysis, and the result was to lessen their importance! When he began the last two paragraphs, when he began to reflect upon the non-coercive factors of society, he perceived, on the contrary, their immense, outweighing importance; and instead of two paragraphs, he found himself obliged to write a second volume, twice as large as the first, on these two factors: voluntary restraint and mutual help; and yet, he analyzed but an infinitesimal part of these latter — those which result from personal sympathy — and hardly touched free agreement, which results from social institutions.

Well, then, leave off repeating the formulae which you have learned at school; meditate on this subject; and the same thing that happened to Ihering will happen to you: you will recognize the infinitesimal importance of coercion, as compared to the voluntary assent, in society.

On the other hand, if by following the very old advice given by Bentham you begin to think of the fatal consequences — direct, and especially indirect

— of legal coercion, like Tolstoy, like us, you will begin to hate the use of coercion, and you will begin to say that society possesses a thousand other means for preventing anti-social acts. If it neglects those means to-day, it is because, being educated by Church and State, our cowardice and apathy of spirit hinder us seeing clearly on this point. When a child has committed a fault, it is so easy to hang a man — especially when there is an executioner who is paid so much for each execution — and it dispenses us from thinking of the cause of crimes.

In the following selection Bertrand Russell comments briefly on some of Kropotkin's ideas and on some of the methods and characteristics of anarchists.

167. COMMENTS ON ANARCHISM [1]

The system at which Kropotkin aims, whether or not it be possible, is certainly one which demands a very great improvement in the methods of production above what is common at present. He desires to abolish wholly the system of wages, not only, as most Socialists do, in the sense that a man is to be paid rather for his willingness to work than for the actual work demanded of him, but in a more fundamental sense: there is to be no obligation to work, and all things are to be shared in equal proportions among the whole population. Kropotkin relies upon the possibility of making work pleasant: he holds that, in such a community as he foresees, practically everyone will prefer work to idleness, because work will not involve overwork or slavery, or that excessive specialization that industrialism has brought about, but will be merely a pleasant activity for certain hours of the day, giving a man an outlet for his spontaneous constructive impulses. There is to be no compulsion, no law, no government exercising force; there will still be acts of the community, but these are to spring from universal consent, not from any enforced submission of even the smallest minority. We shall examine in a later chapter how far such an ideal is realizable, but it cannot be denied that Kropotkin presents it with extraordinary persuasiveness and charm.

We should be doing more than justice to Anarchism if we did not say something of its darker side, the side which has brought it into conflict with the police and made it a word of terror to ordinary citizens. In its general doctrines there is nothing essentially involving violent methods or a virulent hatred of the rich, and many who adopt these general doctrines are personally gentle and temperamentally averse from violence. But the general tone of the Anarchist press and public is bitter to a degree that seems scarcely

[1] Bertrand Russell, *Proposed Roads to Freedom.* New York, Henry Holt and Company, 1919, pp. 50–52.

sane, and the appeal, especially in Latin countries, is rather to envy of the fortunate than to pity for the unfortunate. A vivid and readable, though not wholly reliable, account, from a hostile point of view, is given in a book called " *Le Péril Anarchiste,*" by Félix Dubois, which incidentally reproduces a number of cartoons from anarchist journals. The revolt against law naturally leads, except in those who are controlled by a real passion for humanity, to a relaxation of all the usually accepted moral rules, and to a bitter spirit of retaliatory cruelty out of which good can hardly come.

SECTION III. THE NEW SCIENTIFIC SPIRIT

The publication of Darwin's Origin of Species *in 1859 led to furious controversy. The theory of evolution, set forth by Darwin, clashed with popular theological beliefs. Most of the clergy and their followers rallied to the support of these beliefs while evolution found ardent partisans among those who looked to science for light.*

The opposing forces clashed in dramatic combat at the meeting of the British Association for the Advancement of Science at Oxford in 1860. The theologians found their champion in the suave and eloquent Bishop Wilberforce, the evolutionists in the eager young scientist, Thomas Henry Huxley. The story of the encounter follows.

168. THE DEBATE BETWEEN THOMAS HUXLEY AND BISHOP WILBERFORCE [1]

The famous Oxford Meeting of 1860 was of no small importance in Huxley's career. It was not merely that he helped to save a great cause from being stifled under misrepresentation and ridicule — that he helped to extort for it a fair hearing; it was not that he first made himself known in popular estimation as a dangerous adversary in debate — a personal force in the world of science which could not be neglected. From this moment he entered the front fighting line in the most exposed quarter of the field.

Most unluckily, no contemporary account of his own exists of the encounter. Indeed, the same cause which prevented his writing home the story of the day's work nearly led to his absence from the scene. It was known that Bishop Wilberforce, whose first class in mathematics gave him, in popular estimation, a right to treat on scientific matters, intended to " smash Darwin "; and Huxley, expecting that the promised debate would be merely an appeal to prejudice in a mixed audience, before which the scientific arguments of the Bishop's opponents would be at the utmost disadvantage, in-

[1] Leonard Huxley, *Life and Letters of Thomas Henry Huxley,* 2 vols. New York, D. Appleton, 1900, vol. I, pp. 192–199.

tended to leave Oxford that very morning and join his wife at Hardwicke, near Reading, where she was staying with her sister. But in a letter, quoted below, he tells how, on the Friday afternoon, he chanced to meet Robert Chambers, the reputed author of the *Vestiges of Creation,* who begged him "not to desert them." Accordingly he postponed his departure; but seeing his wife next morning, had no occasion to write a letter.

Several accounts of the scene are already in existence: one in the *Life of Darwin* (vol. ii. p. 320), another in the 1892 *Life,* p. 236 *sq.;* a third that of *Lyell* (vol. ii. p. 335), the slight difference between them representing the difference between individual recollections of eye-witnesses. In addition to these I have been fortunate enough to secure further reminiscences from several other eye-witnesses.

Two papers in Section D, of no great importance in themselves, became historical as affording the opponents of Darwin their opportunity of making an attack upon his theory which should tell with the public. The first was on Thursday, June 28. Dr. Daubeny of Oxford made a communication to the Section, "On the final causes of the sexuality of plants, with particular reference to Mr. Darwin's work on the *Origin of Species.*" Huxley was called upon to speak by the President, but tried to avoid a discussion, on the ground " that a general audience, in which sentiment would unduly interfere with intellect, was not the public before which such a discussion should be carried on."

This consideration, however, did not stop the discussion; it was continued by Owen. He said he "wished to approach the subject in the spirit of the philosopher," and declared his "conviction that there were facts by which the public could come to some conclusion with regard to the probabilities of the truth of Mr. Darwin's theory." As one of these facts, he stated that the brain of the gorilla "presented more differences, as compared with the brain of man, than it did when compared with the brains of the very lowest and most problematical of the Quadrumana."

Now this was the very point, as said above, upon which Huxley had made special investigations during the last two years, with precisely opposite results, such as, indeed, had been arrived at by previous investigators. Hereupon he replied, giving these assertions a " direct and unqualified contradiction," and pledging himself to " justify that unusual procedure elsewhere," — a pledge which was amply fulfilled in the pages of the *Natural History Review* for 1861.

Accordingly it was to him, thus marked out as the champion of the most debatable thesis of evolution, that, two days later, the Bishop addressed his sarcasms, only to meet with a withering retort. For on the Friday there was peace; but on the Saturday came a yet fiercer battle over the "Origin," which loomed all the larger in the public eye, because it was not merely the contradiction of one anatomist by another, but the open clash between Science and the Church. It was, moreover, not a contest of bare fact or abstract assertion, but a combat of wit between two individuals, spiced with the personal element which appeals to one of the strongest instincts of every large audience.

It was the merest chance . . . that Huxley attended the meeting of the section that morning. Dr. Draper of New York was to read a paper on the "Intellectual Development of Europe considered with reference to the views of Mr. Darwin." "I can still hear," writes one who was present, "the American accents of Dr. Draper's opening address when he asked 'Air we a fortuitous concourse of atoms?'" However, it was not to hear him, but the eloquence of the Bishop, that the members of the Association crowded in such numbers into the Lecture Room of the Museum, that this, the appointed meeting-place of the section, had to be abandoned for the long west room, since cut in two by a partition for the purposes of the library. It was not term time, nor were the general public admitted; nevertheless the room was crowded to suffocation long before the protagonists appeared on the scene, 700 persons or more managing to find places. The very windows by which the room was lighted down the length of its west side were packed with ladies, whose white handkerchiefs, waving and fluttering in the air at the end of the Bishop's speech, were an unforgettable factor in the acclamation of the crowd.

. . . .

The clergy, who shouted lustily for the Bishop, were massed in the middle of the room; behind them in the north-west corner a knot of undergraduates (one of these was T. H. Green, who listened but took no part in the cheering) had gathered together beside Professor Brodie, ready to lift their voices, poor minority though they were, for the opposite party. Close to them stood one of the few men among the audience already in Holy orders, who joined in — and indeed led — the cheers for the Darwinians.

So "Dr. Draper droned out his paper, turning first to the right hand and then to the left, of course bringing in a reference to the *Origin of Species* which set the ball rolling."

An hour or more that paper lasted, and then discussion began. The President "wisely announced *in limine* that none who had not valid arguments to bring forward on one side or the other would be allowed to address the meeting; a caution that proved necessary, for no fewer than four combatants had their utterances burked by him, because of their indulgence in vague declamation."

First spoke (writes Professor Farrar) a layman from Brompton, who gave his name as being one of the Committee of the (newly formed) Economic section of the Association. He, in a stentorian voice, let off his theological venom. Then jumped up Richard Greswell with a thin voice, saying much the same, but speaking as a scholar; but we did not merely want any theological discussion, so we shouted them down. Then a Mr. Dingle got up and tried to show that Darwin would have done much better if he had taken him into consultation. He used the blackboard and began a mathematical demonstration on the question — " Let this point *A* be man, and let that point *B* be the mawnkey." He got no further; he was shouted down with cries of " mawnkey." None of these had spoken more than three minutes. It was when these were shouted down that Henslow said he must demand that the discussion should rest on *scientific* grounds only.

Then there were calls for the Bishop, but he rose and said he understood his friend Professor Beale had something to say first. Beale, who was an excellent histologist, spoke to the effect that the new theory ought to meet with fair discussion, but added, with great modesty, that he himself had not sufficient knowledge to discuss the subject adequately. Then the Bishop spoke the speech that you know, and the question about his mother being an ape, or his grandmother.

From the scientific point of view, the speech was of small value. It was evident from his mode of handling the subject that he had been " crammed up to the throat," and knew nothing at first hand; he used no argument beyond those to be found in his *Quarterly* article, which appeared a few days later, and is now admitted to have been inspired by Owen. " He ridiculed Darwin badly and Huxley savagely; but," confesses one of his strongest opponents, " all in such dulcet tones, so persuasive a manner, and in such well turned periods, that I who had been inclined to blame the President for allowing a discussion that could serve no scientific purpose, now forgave him from the bottom of my heart."

The Bishop spoke thus " for full half an hour with inimitable spirit, emptiness and unfairness." " In a light, scoffing tone, florid and fluent, he assured us there was nothing in the idea of evolution; rock-pigeons were what rock-pigeons had always been. Then, turning to his antagonist with a smiling insolence, he begged to know, was it through his grandfather or his grandmother that he claimed his descent from a monkey? "

This was the fatal mistake of his speech. Huxley instantly grasped the tactical advantage which the descent to personalities gave him. He turned to Sir Benjamin Brodie, who was sitting beside him, and emphatically striking his hand upon his knee, exclaimed, " The Lord hath delivered him into mine hands." The bearing of the exclamation did not dawn upon Sir Benjamin until after Huxley had completed his " forcible and eloquent " answer to the scientific part of the Bishop's argument, and proceeded to make his famous retort.

On this (continues the writer in *Macmillan's Magazine*) Mr. Huxley slowly and deliberately arose. A slight, tall figure, stern and pale, very quiet and very grave, he stood before us and spoke those tremendous words — words which no one seems sure of now, nor, I think, could remember just after they were spoken, for their meaning took away our breath, though it left us in no doubt as to what it was. He was not ashamed to have a monkey for his ancestor; but he would be ashamed to be connected with a man who used great gifts to obscure the truth. No one doubted his meaning, and the effect was tremendous. One lady fainted and had to be carried out; I, for one, jumped out of my seat.

The fullest and probably most accurate account of these concluding words is the following, from a letter of the late John Richard Green, then an undergraduate, to his friend, afterwards Professor Boyd Dawkins: —

I asserted — and I repeat — that a man has no reason to be ashamed of having an ape for his grandfather. If there were an ancestor whom I should feel shame in recalling it would rather be a man — a man of restless and versatile intellect — who, not content with an equivocal success in his own sphere of activity, plunges into scientific questions with which he has no real acquaintance, only to obscure them by an aimless rhetoric, and distract the attention of his hearers from the real point at issue by eloquent digressions and skilled appeals to religious prejudice.

Fifty-seven years after the debate between Huxley and Wilberforce, at another annual meeting of the British Association for the Advancement of Science, Sir Arthur Keith, President of the Association, summed up the case for the Darwinian theory of man's evolution. Sir Arthur argues in his address, from which an extract is here quoted, that the theory is fundamentally in a far stronger position than it was when Darwin wrote his Descent of Man.

169. WAS DARWIN RIGHT? [1]

Fifty-six years have come and gone since that history [Darwin's *Descent of Man*] was written; an enormous body of new evidence has poured in upon us. We are now able to fill in many pages which Darwin had perforce to leave blank and we have found it necessary to alter details in his narrative, but the fundamentals of Darwin's outline of man's history remain unshaken. Nay, so strong has his position become that I am convinced that it never can be shaken.

Why do I say so confidently that Darwin's position has become impregnable? It is because of what has happened since his death in 1882. Since then we have succeeded in tracing man by means of his fossil remains and by his stone implements backward in time to the very beginning of that period of

[1] Extract from the Presidential Address of Sir Arthur Keith to the British Association for the Advancement of Science, August 31, 1927.

the earth's history to which the name Pleistocene is given. We thus reach a point in history which is distant from us at least 200,000 years, perhaps three times that amount. Nay, we have gone further and traced him into the older and longer period which preceded the Pleistocene — the Pliocene. It was in strata laid down by a stream in Java during the latter part of the Pliocene period that Dr. Eugene Dubois found, ten years after Darwin's death, the fossil remains of that remarkable representative of primitive humanity to which he gave the name Pithecanthropus, or apeman. From Pliocene deposits of East Anglia, Reir Moir has recovered rude stone implements. If Darwin was right, then as we trace man backward in the scale of time he should become more bestial in form — nearer to the ape. That is what we have found. But if we regard Pithecanthropus, with his small and simple yet human brain, as a fair representative of the men of the Pliocene period, then evolution must have proceeded at an unexpectedly rapid rate to culminate today in the higher races of mankind.

The evidence of man's evolution from an ape-like being, obtained from a study of fossil remains, is definite and irrefutable, but the process has been infinitely more complex than was suspected in Darwin's time. Our older and discarded conception of man's transformation was depicted in that well-known diagram which showed a single file of skeletons, the gibbon at one end and man at the other. In our original simplicity we expected, as we traced man backward in time, that we should encounter a graded series of fossil forms — a series which would carry him in a straight line toward an anthropoid ancestor.

We should never have made this initial mistake if we had remembered that the guide to the world of the past is the world of present. In our time man is represented not by one but by many and diverse races — black, brown, yellow and white. Some of these are rapidly expanding, others are as rapidly disappearing. Our searches have shown that in remote times the world was peopled, sparsely it is true, with races showing even a greater diversity than those of today and that already the same process of replacement was at work. We have to thread our way, not along the links of a chain, but through the meshes of a complicated network.

We made another mistake. Seeing that in our search for man's ancestry we expected to reach an age when the beings we should have to deal with would be simian rather than human, we ought to have marked the conditions which prevail among living anthropoid apes. We ought to have been prepared to find, as we approached a distant point in the geological horizon, that the forms encountered would be as widely different as are the gorilla, chimpanzee and orang, and confined, as these great anthropoids now are, to limited parts of the earth's surface.

That is what we are now realizing: As we go backward in times we discover that mankind becomes broken up, not into separate races as in the world of today, but into numerous and separate species. When we go into a still more remote past they become so unlike that we have to regard them not as belonging to separate species but different genera. It is among this welter of extinct fossil forms which strew the ancient world that we have to trace the zigzag line of man's descent. Do you wonder we sometimes falter and follow false clues?

We committed a still further blunder when we set out on the search for man's ancestry: indeed, some of us are still making it. We expected that man's evolution would pursue not only an orderly file of stages but that every part of his body — skull, brain, jaws, teeth, skin, body, arms and legs — would at each stage become a little less ape-like, a little more man-like.

Our searches have shown us that man's evolution has not proceeded in this orderly manner. In some extinct races, while one part of the body has moved forward another part has lagged behind. Let me illustrate this point, because it is important. We now know that, as Darwin sat in his study at Down, there lay hidden at Piltdown, in Sussex, not thirty miles distant from him, sealed up in a bed of gravel, a fossil human skull and jaw. In 1912, thirty years after Darwin's death, Charles Dawson discovered this skull and my friend, Sir Arthur Smith Woodward, described it and rightly recognized that skull and jaw were parts of the same individual, and that this individual had lived, as was determined by geological and other evidence, in the opening phase of the Pleistocene period.

We may confidently presume that this individual was representative of the people who inhabited England at this remote date. The skull, although deeply mineralized and thick-walled, might well have been the rude forerunner of a modern skull, but the lower jaw was so ape-like that some experts denied that it went with the human fossil skull at all and supposed it to be the lower jaw of some extinct kind of chimpanzee. This mistake would never have been made if those concerned had studied the comparative anatomy of anthropoid apes. Such a study would have prepared them to meet with the discordances of evolution.

The same irregularity in the progression of parts is evident in the anatomy of Pithecanthropus, the oldest and most primitive form of humanity so far discovered. The thigh-bone might easily be that of modern man, the skull-cap that of an ape, but the brain within that cap, as we now know, had passed well beyond an anthropoid status. If merely a lower jaw had been found at Piltdown an ancient Englishman would have been wrongly labeled, " Higher anthropoid ape." If only the thigh-bone of Pithecanthropus had come to light in Java, then an ancient Javanese, almost deserving the title of anthropoid, would have passed muster as a man.

Such examples illustrate the difficulties and dangers which beset the task of unraveling man's ancestry. There are other difficulties. There still remain great blanks in the geological record of man's evolution. As our search proceeds these blanks will be filled in, but in the meantime let us note their nature and their extent. By the discovery of fossil remains we have followed man backward to the close of the Pliocene — a period which endured at least for a quarter of a million years, but we have not yet succeeded in tracing him through this period. It is true that we have found fossil teeth in Pliocene deposits which may be those of an ape-like man or of a man-like ape. Until we find other parts of their bodies we cannot decide.

When we pass into the still older Miocene period — one which was certainly twice as long as the Pliocene — we are in the heyday of anthropoid history. Thanks to the labors of Dr. Guy E. Pilgrim of the Indian Geological Survey we know already of a dozen different kinds of great anthropoids which lived in Himalayan jungles during middle and later Miocene times; we know of at least three other kinds of great anthropoids which lived in the contemporary jungles of Europe. Unfortunately we have found as yet only the most resistant parts of their bodies — teeth and fragments of jaw. Do some of these fragments represent a human ancestor? We cannot decide until a lucky chance brings to light a limb-bone or a piece of skull, but no one can compare the teeth of these Miocene anthropoids with those of primitive man, as has been done so thoroughly by Professor William K. Gregory, and escape the conviction that in the dentitions of the extinct anthropoids of the Miocene jungles we have the ancestral forms of human teeth.

It is useless to go to strata still older than the Miocene in search of man's emergence. In such strata we have found only fossil traces of emerging anthropoids. All the evidence now at our disposal supports the conclusion that man has arisen, as Lamarck and Darwin suspected, from an anthropoid ape not higher in the zoölogical scale than a chimpanzee and that the date at which human and anthropoid lines of descent began to diverge lies near the beginning of the Miocene period. On our modest scale of reckoning that gives man the respectable antiquity of about one million years.

Our geological search, which I have summarized all too briefly, has not produced so far the final and conclusive evidence of man's anthropoid origin. We have not found as yet the human imago emerging from its anthropoid encasement. Why, then, do modern anthropologists share the conviction that there has been an anthropoid stage in our ancestry? They are no more blind than you are to the degree of difference which separates man and ape in structure, in appearance and in behavior.

I must touch on the sources of this conviction only in a passing manner. Early in the present century Professor G. H. F. Nuttall of Cambridge University discovered a trustworthy and exact method of determining the affinity of one species of animal to another by comparing the reactions of their blood.

He found that the blood of man and that of the great anthropoid apes gave almost the same reaction. Bacteriologists find that the living anthropoid body possesses almost the same susceptibilities to infections and manifests the same reactions as does the body of man.

So alike are the brains of man and anthropoid in their structural organization that surgeons and physiologists transfer experimental observations from the one to the other. When the human embryo establishes itself in the womb it throws out structures of a most complex nature to effect a connection with the maternal body. We now know that exactly the same elaborate processes occur in the anthropoid womb and in no other. We find the same vestigial structures — the same " evolutionary post-marks " — in the bodies of man and anthropoid. The anthropoid mother fondles, nurses and suckles her young in the human manner. This is but a tithe of the striking and intimate points in which man resembles the anthropoid ape. In what other way can such a myriad of coincidences be explained except by presuming a common ancestry for both?

The crucial chapters in Darwin's " Descent of Man " are those in which he seeks to give a historical account of the rise of man's brain and of the varied functions which that organ subserves. How do these chapters stand today? Darwin was not a professional anatomist, and, therefore, accepted Huxley's statement that there was no structure in the human brain that was not already present in that of the anthropoid. In Huxley's opinion the human brain was but a richly annotated edition of the simpler and older anthropoid book, and that this edition, in turn, was but the expanded issue of the still older original primate publication.

Since this statement was made thousands of anatomists and physiologists have studied and compared the brain of man and ape; only a few months ago Professor G. Elliot Smith summarized the result of this intensive inquiry as follows: " No structure found in the brain of an ape is lacking in the human brain, and, on the other hand, the human brain reveals no formation of any sort that is not present in the brain of the gorilla or chimpanzee. . . . The only distinctive feature of the human brain is a quantitative one."

The difference is only quantitative, but its importance cannot be exaggerated. In the anthropoid brain are to be recognized all those parts which have become so enormous in the human brain. It is just these expansions which have given man his powers of feeling, understanding, acting, speaking and learning.

Darwin himself approached this problem not as an anatomist but as a psychologist, and after many years of painstaking and exact observation succeeded in convincing himself that, immeasurable as are the differences between the mentality of man and ape, they are of degree, not of kind. Prolonged researches made by modern psychologists have but verified and extended Darwin's conclusions.

There is much loose talk of the conflict between science and religion. Conflict between the findings of science and certain outworn religious beliefs there certainly is. But there is no reason why anyone who accepts the teachings of science should abandon all religious faith. Dr. Robert A. Millikan, one of the world's leading scientists, winner of the Nobel prize in physics in 1923, points this out in the following brief statement.

170. SCIENCE AND RELIGION [1]

The best of us are only gropers, and yet one cannot refuse to tell a fellow-groper what he sees or thinks he sees with such light as is available to him.

Physics has compelled us to think of a universe which is changing, living, growing, even in its elements — a dynamic instead of a static universe. Thus science here has made a great contribution to religion. The recent discoveries of physicists have taught us a wholesome lesson of humility, wonder and joy in the face of an as yet incomprehensible universe.

Through the celestial mechanics of Galileo mankind began to know a God not of caprice and whim, such as were all the gods of the ancient world, but a God who works through law.

Religion itself is one of the most striking examples of evolution, as seen in the abolition of human sacrifice, in new conceptions of God, in new ideas of the way God works, in a new conception of progress.

Concerning what ultimately becomes of the individual in the process, science has added nothing and subtracted nothing. So far as science is concerned, religion can treat that problem precisely as it has in the past, or it can treat it in some entirely new way if it wishes. For that problem is entirely outside the field of science now, though it need not necessarily remain so. Science has undoubtedly been responsible for a certain change in religious thinking as to the relative value of individual and race salvation.

The new idea of progress, and our part in it and our responsibility for it is now practically universal. This idea is due directly to science, and it marks the latest stage in the evolution of man's conception about the ultimate of the world and his relation to that world — his conception about God and about duty.

The world is, of course, "incurably religious." Why? Because every one who reflects at all must have conceptions about the world which go

[1] Robert A. Millikan, *New York Times*, April 8, 1928. Section 9, p. 1. The article consists of brief excerpts from Dr. Millikan's *Evolution in Science and Religion*, Yale University Press, 1927.

beyond the field of science; that is, beyond the present range of intellectual knowledge.

There are two sorts of dogmatists in the field of religion. One calls himself a fundamentalist; the other calls himself an atheist. They seem to me to represent about the same kind of thinking. Each asserts a definite knowledge of the ultimate which he does not possess. Each has closed his mind to any future truth. Each has a religion that is fixed. Each is, I think, irrational and unscientific.

Religion will be with us so long as man hopes and aspires and reflects upon the meaning of existence and the responsibilities it entails.

SECTION IV. FEMINISM

The movement for the enfranchisement of women, which won its way to final triumph in England despite the indifference or ridicule of many, the vigorous opposition of others, found an early and ardent advocate in the noted economist, John Stuart Mill. In 1851 Mill championed the cause of Women's Rights in an article published in the Westminster Review, *short extracts from which are quoted here. His classic defence of the cause, his book on* The Subjection of Women, *appeared in 1869.*

171. EXTRACTS FROM AN EARLY ARGUMENT FOR THE ENFRANCHISEMENT OF WOMEN [1]

Most of our readers will probably learn from these pages, for the first time, that there has arisen in the United States, and in the most civilized and enlightened portion of them, an organized agitation on a new question, — new, not to thinkers nor to any one by whom the principles of free and popular government are felt as well as acknowledged, but new, and even unheard of, as a subject for public meetings and practical political action. This question is the enfranchisement of women; their admission, in law and in fact, to equality in all rights, political, civil, and social, with the male citizens of the community.

It will add to the surprise with which many will receive this intelligence, that the agitation which has commenced is not a pleading by male writers and orators *for* women; those who are professedly to be benefited remaining either indifferent or ostensibly hostile. It is a political movement, practical in its objects, carried on in a form which denotes an intention to persevere. And it is a movement not merely *for* women, but *by* them. Its first public manifestation appears to have been a Convention of Women, held in the State of

---

[1] John Stuart Mill, " The Enfranchisement of Women," *Westminster Review,* July, 1851.

Ohio, in the spring of 1850. Of this meeting we have seen no report. On the 23d and 24th of October last, a succession of public meetings was held at Worcester, in Massachusetts, under the name of a " Women's-Rights Convention," of which the president was a woman, and nearly all the chief speakers women; numerously re-enforced, however, by men, among whom were some of the most distinguished leaders in the kindred cause of negro emancipation. A general and four special committees were nominated, for the purpose of carrying on the undertaking until the next annual meeting.

. . . .

That the promoters of this new agitation take their stand on principles, and do not fear to declare these in their widest extent, without time-serving or compromise, will be seen from the resolutions adopted by the Convention, part of which we transcribe: —

"*Resolved,* That every human being of full age, and resident for a proper length of time on the soil of the nation, who is required to obey the law, is entitled to a voice in its enactment; that every such person, whose property or labor is taxed for the support of the government, is entitled to a direct share in such government: therefore —

"*Resolved,* That women are entitled to the right of suffrage, and to be considered eligible to office; . . . and that every party which claims to represent the humanity, the civilization, and the progress of the age, is bound to inscribe on its banners, 'Equality before the Law, without Distinction of Sex or Color.'

. . . .

"*Resolved,* That the laws of property, as affecting married persons, demand a thorough revisal, so that all rights be equal between them; that the wife have, during life, an equal control over the property gained by their mutual toil and sacrifices, and be heir to her husband precisely to that extent that he is heir to her, and entitled at her death to dispose by will of the same share of the joint property as he is."

. . . .

It would be difficult to put so much true, just, and reasonable meaning into a style so little calculated to recommend it as that of some of the resolutions. But, whatever objection may be made to some of the expressions, none, in our opinion, can be made to the demands themselves. As a question of justice, the case seems to us too clear for dispute. As one of expediency, the more thoroughly it is examined, the stronger it will appear.

That women have as good a claim as men have, in point of personal right, to the suffrage, or to a place in the jury-box, it would be difficult for any one to deny. It cannot certainly be denied by the United States of

America, as a people or as a community. Their democratic institutions rest avowedly on the inherent right of every one to a voice in the government.

.   .   .   .

Not only to the democracy of America, the claim of women to civil and political equality makes an irresistible appeal, but also to those Radicals and Chartists in the British islands, and democrats on the Continent, who claim what is called universal suffrage as an inherent right, unjustly and oppressively withheld from them. For with what truth or rationality could the suffrage be termed universal, while half the human species remain excluded from it? To declare that a voice in the government is the right of all, and demand it only for a part, — the part, namely, to which the claimant himself belongs, — is to renounce even the appearance of principle. The Chartist who denies the suffrage to women is a Chartist only because he is not a lord: he is one of those levellers who would level only down to themselves.

Even those who do not look upon a voice in the government as a matter of personal right, nor profess principles which require that it should be extended to all, have usually traditional maxims of political justice with which it is impossible to reconcile the exclusion of all women from the common rights of citizenship. It is an axiom of English freedom, that taxation and representation should be co-extensive. Even under the laws which give the wife's property to the husband, there are many unmarried women who pay taxes. It is one of the fundamental doctrines of the British Constitution, that all persons should be tried by their peers; yet women, whenever tried, are tried by male judges and a male jury. To foreigners, the law accords the privilege of claiming that half the jury should be composed of themselves: not so to women. Apart from maxims of detail, which represent local and national rather than universal ideas, it is an acknowledged dictate of justice to make no degrading distinctions without necessity. In all things, the presumption ought to be on the side of equality. A reason must be given why any thing should be permitted to one person, and interdicted to another. But when that which is interdicted includes nearly every thing which those to whom it is permitted most prize, and to be deprived of which they feel to be most insulting; when not only political liberty, but personal freedom of action, is the prerogative of a caste; when, even in the exercise of industry, almost all employments which task the higher faculties in an important field, which lead to distinction, riches, or even pecuniary independence, are fenced round as the exclusive domain of the predominant section, scarcely any doors being left open to the dependent class, except such as all who can enter elsewhere disdainfully pass by, — the miserable expediences which are advanced as excuses for so grossly partial a dispensation would not be sufficient, even if they were real, to render it other than a flagrant injustice: while, far from being expedient, we are firmly convinced that the division of mankind into two castes, one born to rule over the other, is in this case, as in all cases, an unqualified mischief; a source of perversion and demoralization, both to the favored class and to those at whose expense they are favored; producing none of the good which it is the custom to ascribe to it, and forming a bar, almost insuperable while it lasts, to any really vital improvement, either in the character or in the social condition of the human race.

Having come to believe that peaceful methods advanced their cause but little, some of the English suffragists, not many years before the outbreak of the Great War, resorted to violence.

In the first of the two following selections examples of the methods of the militant suffragists are cited. In the second the dignified Lord Curzon, at one time Viceroy of India, at another British Secretary of State for Foreign Affairs, expresses his unqualified disapproval of the actions of these " wild women."

172. THE MILITANT " SUFFRAGETTES " [1]

I. Examples of Suffragist and Anti-Suffragist Disorders

Militant suffragists yesterday chose the two principal Roman Catholic places of worship for their acts of brawling. Several women were ejected from Brompton Oratory for interruptions at midday Mass. In the evening a woman ascended one of the pulpits at Westminster Cathedral and attempted to address the congregation.

A house at Tyler's-Green, near High Wycombe, was burned early on Saturday morning. The usual evidences of militant agency were found.

·   ·   ·   ·   ·   ·   ·   ·   ·   ·   ·   ·   ·

Disorderly demonstrations against the militants occurred at the usual open-air meetings in London.

A suffragist named Nancy Lightman, who was speaking in Hyde Park, was severely handled by a large and angry crowd. She was rescued by the police and taken along with a male sympathizer to the police station in the Park. Later in the day they were both released. A clergyman who was with her was also hustled by the crowd. Another militant suffragist who afterwards attempted to speak had to be rescued in the same manner.

II. Lord Curzon on the Militant Suffragists

Lord Curzon, speaking at the annual meeting of the National League for Opposing Woman Suffrage yesterday afternoon, entered a strong protest against the criminal conduct of the militant suffragists.

[1] *The Times*: London. June 8, 27, 1914.

He said that there could be no doubt that the anti-suffrage cause stood in a stronger position at present than it had done at any time during the past 20 years. That had been due perhaps in the main to the tactics and the errors of their opponents, but it had also been due in no small measure to their own activities. The phenomenon of the year had been the revival of militancy in its most outrageous and abominable forms. The efforts of these wild women had put back the cause which they advocated for at least a decade, if not longer, and they had shown how easily disturbed the mental balance of some women could be and how a perverted line of reasoning could render some women, at any rate, simultaneously indifferent to a sense both of honour and of shame.

The methods of the wild women suggested an evil possibility in the future, for they must not suppose for a moment that with the grant of the vote to one million or five or six million women militancy would necessarily cease. It would find fresh outlets of activity, perhaps even more sinister and more devastating than those with which they were now familiar. Anti-suffragists might be grateful for that warning of future danger, but there was not a thoughtful citizen in the country who did not deplore the continuance of those outrages. Little by little they were breaking down that sense of chivalry and respect which had hitherto existed like a shield to defend women from outrage and insult in the world.

By the law of February, 1918, which enfranchised virtually all Englishmen over twenty-one years of age, the right to vote was granted to a large proportion of Englishwomen.

Extracts from this law follow.

173. GRANT OF THE FRANCHISE TO WOMEN IN ENGLAND, FEBRUARY 6, 1918 [1]

(1) A woman shall be entitled to be registered as a parliamentary elector for a constituency (other than a university constituency) if she —

(a) has attained the age of thirty years; and

(b) is not subject to any legal incapacity; and

(c) is entitled to be registered as a local government elector in respect of the occupation in that constituency of land or premises (not being a dwelling-house) of a yearly value of not less than five pounds or of a dwelling-house, or is the wife of a husband entitled to be so registered.

(2) A woman shall be entitled to be registered as a parliamentary elector for a university constituency if she has attained the age of thirty years and either would be entitled to be so registered if she were a man, or has been

---

[1] Great Britain, *Statutes.* 7–8 George V, Chapter 64, Section 4.

admitted to and passed the final examination, and kept under the conditions required of women by the university the period of residence, necessary for a man to obtain a degree at any university forming, or forming a part of, a university constituency which did not at the time the examination was passed admit women to degrees.

(3) A woman shall be entitled to be registered as a local government elector for any local government electoral area —

(a) where she would be entitled to be so registered if she were a man; and

(b) where she is the wife of a man who is entitled to be so registered in respect of premises in which they both reside, and she has attained the age of thirty years and is not subject to any legal incapacity.

For the purpose of this provision, a naval or military voter who is registered in respect of a residence qualification which he would have had but for his service, shall be deemed to be resident in accordance with this qualification.

CHAPTER XII

THE NEW IMPERIALISM

SECTION I. THE SPIRIT OF THE NEW IMPERIALISM

In the latter part of the nineteenth century there began among the leading nations of the world a wild scramble for control over territory in the weaker and less civilized portions of the globe. This modern imperialistic movement has had some very good results, some very bad ones. Consequently wherever people engage in discussions of foreign policy they are apt to divide into imperialists and anti-imperialists, the imperialists ardently championing, the anti-imperialists violently opposing, this expansionist movement.

In his Stakes of Diplomacy *Walter Lippman approaches the question of imperialism neither as vigorous advocate nor strong opponent. He simply analyzes the problem and points out that, being with us, it " must be solved, not evaded."*

174. THE SPIRIT AND GENERAL CAUSES OF MODERN IMPERIALISM [1]

How does it happen . . . that the people not concerned in a special interest are so ready to defend it against the world? Plain men who have no financial interest in copper will feel aggrieved if American copper interests in a foreign land are attacked. The German people felt " humiliated " because German trade was thwarted in Morocco.

The most obvious reason for this is that the private citizens are in the main abysmally ignorant of what the real stakes of diplomacy are. They do not think in terms of railroad concessions, mines, banking, and trade. When they envisage Morocco they do not think of the Mannesmann Brothers, but of " German prestige " and " French influence." When the Triple Entente compelled Germany to recede in the Moroccan affair of 1911, the rage of the German people was not due to a counting of their economic losses. They were furious, not that they had lost Morocco, but that they had lost the dispute. There is small doubt that the masses of people in no country would risk war to secure mining concessions in Africa. But the choice is never presented to them that way. Each contest for economic privileges appears

[1] Walter Lippmann, *The Stakes of Diplomacy*. New York, Holt, 1915, pp. 76–80; 87–88; 89–91; 93–97; 98; 105–107. (Published now by The Macmillan Company.)

to the public as a kind of sporting event with loaded weapons. The people wish their team, that is, their country, to win. Just as strong men will weep because the second baseman fumbles at the crucial moment, so they will go into tantrums of rage because corporations of their own nationality are thwarted in a commercial ambition.

They may have nothing tangible to gain or lose by the transaction; certainly they do not know whether they have. But they feel that " our " trade is their own, and though they share few of its profits they watch its career with tender solicitude. Above all, they feel that if " our " German traders are beaten in Morocco, the whole value of being a German has been somewhat lessened. This is where business and national prestige flow together. Business is the chief form which competition between nations can assume. To be worsted in that competition means more than to lose money; it means a loss of social importance as well. Trademarks like " Made in Germany " were a constant humiliation to Englishmen, even though they were glad to buy the goods because they were cheaper and better. But when from all over the world Englishmen came home beaten by a greater vitality and more modern organization, their damaged pocketbooks were only the smallest part of their loss. The real wound was the wound of self-respect, the lurking fear that there has been a depreciation in Englishmen. The fear is emphasized by the public opinion of the world which judges by trade efficiency and asks heartrending questions like: Is England decadent? Friendly critics rub salt into the wound by commenting on the obsolete machinery of British manufacture, the archaic habits of British merchants. Is it any wonder that what starts as a loss of dollars and cents is soon transfigured into a loss of the Englishman's importance in the world? But when you attack that you attack the sources of his patriotism, and when he starts to reassert his importance, the proceeding has ceased to appear as a commercial enterprise. It has become a defense of British civilization.

This is the mood for a strong foreign policy, which means a policy that uses political power to increase national prestige. The way to increase national prestige is to win economic victories by diplomatic methods. British diplomacy has been winning them for fifteen years — in Egypt, Persia, Africa. While Germany was capturing trade, Great Britain was scoring the diplomatic victories — the greatest of them being that in Morocco. From an economic point of view England had more to lose than to gain by a French dominion in Morocco. The real economic interest probably lay in that internationalization of Moroccan opportunity for which Germany contended. But England's interest was not primarily economic. Her interest was the defeat of German aggrandizement. She fought German prestige, and by threatening war in Mr. Lloyd George's Mansion House speech she won. She sent German diplomats home to receive the jeers of the German people.

•   •   •   •   •   •   •   •   •   •   •   •   •   •   •   •

This whole business of jockeying for position is at first glance so incredibly silly that many liberals regard diplomacy as a cross between sinister conspiracy and a meaningless etiquette. It would be all of that if the stakes of diplomacy were not real. Those stakes have to be understood, for without such an understanding diplomacy is incomprehensible and any scheme of world peace an idle fancy.

The chief, the overwhelming problem of diplomacy seems to be the weak state — the Balkans, the African sultanates, Turkey, China, and Latin America, with the possible exception of the Argentine, Chile, and Brazil. These states are " weak " because they are industrially backward and at present politically incompetent. They are rich in resources and cheap labor, poor in capital, poor in political experience, poor in the power of defense. The government of these states is the supreme problem of diplomacy. Just as the chief task of American politics to the Civil War was the organization of the unexploited West, so the chief task of world diplomacy today is the organization of virgin territory and backward peoples. I use backward in the conventional sense to mean a people unaccustomed to modern commerce and modern political administration.

This solicitude about backward people seems to many good democrats a combination of superciliousness and greed. I have heard wise old Hindus grow tense with rage at the thought of some cockney Kiplingesque bureaucrat bringing " civilization " to the saturated civilization of the East. I have walked through Boston slums with an Indian, and it was I who did the apologizing. We laughed together over the white man's burden. " I'd rather be in hell than in the British Empire," said the Hindu. " How about being in the Russian or German Empires? " I inquired. " I've thought of it," he replied; " that's why I am a loyal subject of the British Crown."

.   .   .   .

To the dogmatic anti-imperialist it seems absurd that white people do not stay at home and civilize themselves, leaving the Indians and Moors and Hottentots and Yaquis to work out their own salvation. The whole business of expansion by the western peoples is hateful to these liberals. They remember the caste system, the arrogance, the unspeakable horrors of the Congo and Putomayo, the ravishing and despoiling and debauching of natives by the European. It is a hideous story. And yet the plain fact is that the interrelation of peoples has gone so far that to advocate international laissez-faire now is to speak a counsel of despair. Commercial cunning, lust of conquest, rum, bibles, rifles, missionaries, traders, concessionaires have brought the two civilizations into contact, and the problem created must be solved, not evaded.

The great African empires, for example, were not created deliberately by theoretical imperialists. Explorers, missionaries, and traders penetrated these countries. They found rubber, oil, cocoa, tin; they could sell cotton goods, rifles, liquor. The native rulers bartered away enormous riches at trival pieces. But the trading-posts and the concessions were insecure. There were raids and massacres. No public works existed, no administrative machinery. The Europeans exploited the natives cruelly, and the natives retaliated. Concession hunters and merchants from other nations began to come in. They bribed and bullied the chiefs, and created still greater insecurity. An appeal would be made to the home government for help, which generally meant declaring a protectorate of the country. Armed forces were sent in to pacify, and civil servants to administer the country. These protectorates were generally sanctioned by the other European governments on the proviso that trade should be free to all.

.   .   .   .

It is essential to remember that what turns a territory into a diplomatic " problem " is the combination of natural resources, cheap labor, markets, defenselessness, corrupt and inefficient government. The desert of Sahara is no " problem " except where there are oases and trade routes. Switzerland is no " problem " for Switzerland is a highly organized modern state. But Mexico is a problem, and Haiti, and Turkey, and Persia. They have the pretension of political independence which they do not fulfill. They are seething with corruption, eaten up with " foreign " concessions, and unable to control the adventurers they attract or safeguard the rights which these adventurers claim. More foreign capital is invested in the United States than in Mexico, but the United States is not a " problem " and Mexico is. The difference was hinted at in President Wilson's speech at Mobile. Foreigners invest in the United States, and they are assured that life will be reasonably safe and that titles to property are secured by orderly legal means. But in Mexico they are given " concessions," which means that they secure extra privileges and run greater risks, and they count upon the support of European governments or of the United States to protect them and their property.

The weak states, in other words, are those which lack the political development that modern commerce requires. To take an extreme case which brings out the real nature of the " problem," suppose that the United States was organized politically as England was in the time of William the Conqueror. Would it not be impossible to do business in the United States? There would be an everlasting clash between an impossible legal system and a growing commercial development. And the internal affairs of the United States would constitute a diplomatic " problem."

This, it seems to me, is the reason behind the outburst of modern imperialism among the Great Powers. It is not enough to say that they are "expanding" or "seeking markets" or "grabbing resources." They are doing all these things, of course. But if the world into which they are expanding were not politically archaic, the growth of foreign trade would not be accompanied by political imperialism. Germany has "expanded" wonderfully in the British Empire, in Russia, in the United States, but no German is silly enough to insist on planting his flag wherever he sells his dyestuffs or stoves. It is only when his expansion is into weak states — into China, Morocco, Turkey, or elsewhere that foreign trade is imperialistic. This imperialism is actuated by many motives — by a feeling that political control insures special privileges, by a desire to play a large part in the world, by national vanity, by a passion for "ownership," but none of these motives would come into play if countries like China or Turkey were not politically backward.

Imperialism in our day begins generally as an attempt to police and pacify. This attempt stimulates national pride, it creates bureaucrats with a vested interest in imperialism, it sucks in and receives added strength from concessionaires and traders who are looking for economic privileges. There is no doubt that certain classes in a nation gain by imperialism, though to the people as a whole the adventure may mean nothing more than an increased burden of taxes.

Some pacifists have attempted to deny that a nation could ever gain anything by political control of weak states. They have not defined the "nation." What they overlook is that even the most advanced nations are governed, not by the "people," but by groups with special interests. These groups do gain, just as the railroad men who controlled American legislatures gained. A knot of traders closely in league with the colonial office of a great Power can make a good deal of money out of its friendships. Every government has contracts to be let, franchises to give; it establishes tariffs, fixes railroad rates, apportions taxes, creates public works, builds roads. To be favored by that power is to be favored indeed. The favoritism may cost the motherland and the colony dear, but the colonial merchant is not a philanthropist.

The whole question of imperialism is as complex as the motives of the African trader who subsidizes the African missionary. He does not know where business ends and religion begins; he is able to make no sharp distinction between his humanitarianism and his profits. He feels that business is a good thing, and religion is a good thing. He likes to help himself, and to see others helped. The same complexity of motives appear in imperialist statesmen.

. . . .

The whole situation might be summed up by saying that the commercial development of the world will not wait until each territory has created for itself a stable and fairly modern political system. By some means or other the weak states have to be brought within the framework of commercial administration. Their independence and integrity, so-called, are dependent upon their creating conditions under which world-wide business can be conducted. The pressure to organize the globe is enormous.

. . . .

The formula of modern imperialism seems to be that financial groups enter a weak state and create " national interests," which then evoke national feeling. The corruption and inefficiency of the weak state " endanger " the interests; patriotism rises to defend them, and political control follows. The prestige of a Power in the councils of the world depends upon the weight of " interests " and the patriotic fervor with which they are " protected." I am told that it was the State Department at Washington which, in order to secure a diplomatic " foothold," invited the American financial group to enter China. A government which hesitates very long at intervention, as the United States has done in Mexico, depreciates the value of its diplomatic power everywhere.

Out of this complexity of motive there is created a union of various groups on the imperial programme: the diplomatic group is interested primarily in prestige; the military group in an opportunity to act; the bureaucratic in the creation of new positions; the financial groups in safeguarding investments; traders in securing protection and privileges, religious groups in civilizing the heathen, the " intellectuals," in realizing theories of expansion and carrying out " manifest destinies," the people generally in adventure and glory and the sense of being great. These interested groups severally control public opinion, and under modern methods of publicity public opinion is easily " educated."

Who should intervene in backward states, what the intervention shall mean, how the protectorate shall be conducted — this is the bone and sinew of modern diplomacy.

SECTION II. IMPERIALISM IN ASIA

A study of European imperialism in Asia must concern itself with three theatres of operation. One, the Near East, has been dealt with. The Middle East will be left to the last. Here it is a question of the Far East, where, as in each of the other regions, Russia plays a principal rôle. From early times hordes of Asiatics had swept across the plains of Northern Asia to invade the Near East and Europe. In the thirteenth century the greatest of these hurricane movements had been conducted by Genghis Khan and it had led to the enslavement of the Russians for 250 years. In the sixteenth century the Russians returned the visit and Europe came to dominate the descendants of the Great Khan.

175. RUSSIAN EXPANSION IN SIBERIA [1]

In the middle of the sixteenth century, about the time the Spaniards were beginning to garner the golden harvest of the New World and to send their people out into its wildernesses to establish there the power and the civilization of Spain, there was a similar urge towards riches and territory in the opposite corner of Europe.

The growing power of the rulers of Muscovy had been bruited abroad, and inspired their nearer neighbors and even more distant ones with concern for their safety. Some prepared for war; others sent to Moscow rich gifts, which the Russian rulers considered as tribute.

Even beyond the Urals, the high mountain wall which marks the eastern boundary of Europe, had spread the fame of Russian prowess, and the Tartar prince of this region, Kutshum Khan, sought to secure the friendship of the Tsars by sending to Moscow long trains of the finest furs. Furs in Russia were as good as gold in Spain, and if the Khan's gift excited feelings of gratitude in the palace, it excited cupidity elsewhere. When Yermak, an outlawed bandit chieftain, heard of this princely gift, he determined to cross the Ural wall and try his fortune in the lands beyond. In 1580, with less than two thousand men, he set forth. He soon made himself master of Kutshum's country, including his capital, which was known as Sibir. Yermak called the country Siberia, and offered it to the Tsar in exchange for his pardon.

The bargain was struck, and Russia found herself facing a new world across the Urals, with its lure of conquest, riches, and death, as surely as Spain was facing a new world across the Atlantic. And the Russians were no less eager than the Spaniards to enter and explore. They swarmed across the mountain wall and advanced steadily eastward. Cossacks were in the van; herdsmen and farmers followed.

From river valley to river valley they moved, founding towns as they went. By 1651 they had reached Lake Baikal and founded Irkutsk. Thus far they had met no serious resistance, but east of Baikal they were opposed by the Buriats, a powerful tribe of the Mongol race that had produced a Genghis Khan and a Tamerlane. It took the Cossacks four years of hard fighting to subdue these doughty plainsmen. But in the north the advance had been more rapid, and other Cossack bands had reached the sea of Okhotsk as

---

[1] Henry K. Norton, " The Russians in the Far East." A lecture published in Woodhead, Arnold and Norton, *Occidental Interpretations of the Far Eastern Problem*. (Harris Foundation Lectures.) Chicago, 1926, pp. 201–205. Reprinted by permission of The University of Chicago Press.

early as 1636. The territory along the Amur from Baikal to the Pacific was still unknown.

In 1649 the governor of Yakutsk granted the request of the Cossack chieftain, Habarov, that he be allowed to enter this country in search of a short route to the Amur. Habarov started with about seventy men. Violating the governor's instructions that the natives should be treated with consideration, Habarov left behind him a wide trail of burned villages, murdered men, and tortured women. The outraged natives turned upon him, and he was obliged to return for reinforcements. With a larger force he was able to defeat the natives and established a fortified post at Albazin on the Amur River.

Here the Russians first came into contact with the Chinese. China had never occupied the country north of the Amur, but the governor of Manchuria collected an annual tribute in furs for the emperor of China. Habarov, flushed with success, dispatched an embassy to the governor to demand a tribute " as great as he could give," and at the same time asked his own superiors for an army to conquer, not only the Amur country, but Manchuria as well. His embassy was massacred by the natives, and his request for an army was ignored, so Habarov continued his murderous course down the river to its junction with the Ussuri, where the city of Habarovsk now stands. Here he fought off one Manchu army, and slipping around another, fixed his camp on the site of the modern Blagoveshchensk.

Quarrels with his men and with his superiors resulted in Habarov's recall, and without his grim leadership, the Russians had to resist the determined efforts of the Chinese to rid the country of their presence. They were driven out and Albazin destroyed in 1658. But seven years later it was reestablished, and by 1674 had become a large post. The Chinese emperor, Kang Hsi, renewed the struggle, and in 1685 again destroyed the settlement. No sooner had his troops left, however, than the Russians were back rebuilding the fortifications once more.

While Cossack indomitability was winning over Chinese military effort on the Amur, Russian statecraft was losing to Chinese diplomacy at Nertchinsk. By a treaty signed in 1689, China's first treaty with a Western power, Russia agreed to withdraw from the Amur and recognize the river Gorbitza (Argun?) as the boundary between the two empires.

For over one hundred and fifty years Russia contented herself with what she had gained, and made no effort to extend her possessions in the Far East. In 1846, Tsar Nicholas I, disturbed by the increasing interest of Great Britain in China, sent an expedition to explore the mouth of the Amur. The following year he sent out Nicolai Muraviev as governor-general of Siberia. Muraviev was of the breed of empire-builders. He resolved to control the Amur at all costs. The Tsar supported him, and settlements were made at Nikolaievsk, DeCastries Bay, and Alexandrovsk. This was followed by the occupation of Saghalien. Muraviev not only organized armies and colonizing expeditions, but he won over the natives by fair treatment.

Thus it was that when the Crimean War temporarily wrecked the power of Russia in Europe, the Siberian Governor-General was able to continue with his plans in the Far East. In 1854 he started down the Amur with one steamship and seventy-five barges. This expedition enabled him to hold Nikolaievsk against the French and English so that Russia lost no ground in the Far East in the war. Other expeditions followed. The Chinese protested and Muraviev invited them to a conference, at which he assured them that he wanted nothing but peace, but he was going to establish a string of forts along the left bank of the Amur.

At this conference was signed the Convention that follows. The first step led to others and in 1860 the Russians had a well defined position in the Far East and had founded the city of Vladivostok.

176. THE CONVENTION OF AIGUN [1]

The great Russian Empire, and on its behalf the Governor General of Eastern Siberia, the general aide-de-camp of H. M. the Emperor Alexander Nikolaevich, lieutenant general Nikolai Murevev; and the great Ta-Tsing Empire, and on its behalf the general aide-de-camp, Prince I-Chan, grandee of the court, Commander-in-chief on the Amur; desiring to establish a perpetual and closer friendship between the two empires in the interests of their respective subjects, have agreed to the following:

1. The left bank of the Amur River, from its junction with the Argun River to its mouth, shall belong to the Russian Empire, while its right bank as far down as the junction of the Ussuri River shall belong to the Ta-Tsing Empire. The territory between the Ussuri River and the sea shall be, as up to now, held in common by the Ta-Tsing Empire and the Russian Empire, until the frontier between the two States be determined. The navigation of the Amur, Sungari and Ussuri Rivers shall be permitted only to ships of the Ta-Tsing and Russian Empires, and shall be forbidden to ships of all other States. Manchu subjects living on the left bank of the Amur, from the Zeia River as far south as the village of Hormoldzin, shall retain in perpetuity their former lands and domiciles under the administration of the Manchu Government, and the Russian inhabitants shall not be permitted to offend or vex them in any way.

2. In order to promote a friendly mutual intercourse between their respective subjects, permission is given the riverain inhabitants of the Ussuri,

---

[1] Translation from French text given in " Vladimir," *Russia on the Pacific and the Siberian Railway*. London, Sampson, Low, Marston & Co., 1899, pp. 355–356.

Article III.

The duration of the lease shall be twenty-five years from the day this treaty is signed, but may be extended by mutual agreement between Russia and China.

Article IV.

The control of all military forces in the territory leased by Russia, and of all naval forces in the adjacent seas, as well as of the civil officials in it, shall be vested in one high Russian official, who shall, however, be designated by some title other than Governor-General (Tsung-tu) or Governor (Hsün-fu). All Chinese military forces shall, without exception, be withdrawn from the territory, but it shall remain optional with the ordinary Chinese inhabitants either to remain or to go; and no coercion shall be used towards them in this matter. . . .

Article V.

To the north of the territory leased shall be a zone, the extent of which shall be arranged at St. Petersburg between Hsü Ta-jen and the Russian Foreign Office. Jurisdiction over this zone shall be vested in China, but China may not quarter troops in it except with the previous consent of Russia.

Article VI.

The two nations agree that Port Arthur shall be a naval port for the sole use of Russian and Chinese men-of-war, and be considered as an unopened port so far as the naval and mercantile vessels of other nations are concerned. As regards Ta-lien-wan, one portion of the harbour shall be reserved exclusively for Russian and Chinese men-of-war, just like Port Arthur, but the remainder shall be a commercial port freely open to the merchant vessels of all countries.

Article VII.

Port Arthur and Ta-lien-wan are the points in the territory leased most important for Russian military purposes. Russia shall, therefore, be at liberty to erect, at her own expense, forts, and build barracks and provide defences at such places as she desires.

Article VIII.

China agrees that the procedure sanctioned in 1896 regarding the construction of railroads by the Board of the Eastern China Railway shall, from the date of the signature of this treaty, be extended so as to include the construction of a branch line to Ta-lien-wan, or, if necessary, in view of the interests involved, of a branch line to the most suitable point on the coast between Newchwang and the Yalu river. Further, the agreement entered into in September 1896 between the Chinese Government and the Russo-Chinese Bank shall apply with equal strength to this branch line. The direction of this branch and the places it shall touch shall be arranged between Hsü Ta-jen and the Board of the Eastern Railroads. The construction of this line shall never, however, be made a ground for encroaching on the sovereignty or integrity of China.

The Chinese Eastern Railway was a part of the same scheme as the lease on Port Arthur. In addition to the main line from Chita to Vladivostok, a branch was built south from Harbin to Port Arthur.

178. THE CHINESE EASTERN RAILWAY [1]

The Chinese Eastern Railway was, in its first conception, one of those useful but sinister enterprises that produce industrial development and military struggles. It was planned as an instrument of Imperial expansion. A glance at the map will show how it shortened the distance between two points, both on Russian territory. The railway along the Amur valley to Vladivostok was built later. Here was a Russian railway on Chinese territory, guarded along its whole length by Russian troops, with a branch line extending to the south of the Liaotung Peninsula, of which Russia secured a twenty-five years' lease. It is not surprising that its building is generally considered as one of the most important origins of the Russo-Japanese War.

The prime mover in the building of the railway was Count Witte. A secret treaty was signed in 1896 in Moscow between Russia and China whereby China gave Russia the right to build the railway and assigned an extra-territorial strip of land on either side of the railway. The next step was the giving of a concession by the Chinese Government to the Russo-Chinese (afterwards the Russo-Asiatic) Bank for the building of the railway. Count Witte's memoirs clearly define the rôle of the bank in the matter. The bank was to hide the fact that the railway was actually a Government enterprise. Simultaneously with the signing of the contract with China the bank put the business into the hands of the " Chinese Eastern Railway Company," which was formed by the Russian Government, this arrangement preventing the bank from having any further influence on the scheme while preserving for it in form the appearance of a private enterprise. The actual money was provided by the Russian Ministry of Finance. The concession was limited to a term of 80 years, after which the railway was to become the property of the Chinese Government, which had also a right of buying out the concessionaire after 36 years. The building began in August, 1897, and

[1] Arthur Ransome in *Manchester Guardian Weekly*. April 30, 1926.

was practically finished in 1901. There followed the Russo-Japanese War, at the end of which, by the Treaty of Portsmouth, the southern part of the railway, between Port Arthur and Tchan Tchun, was handed over to Japan. Thenceforward the Chinese Eastern Railway consisted of the main line from Manchouli station on the western frontier of Manchuria to Pogranitchnaya on the eastern frontier and the branch line from Kharbin to Tchan Tchun, 1,618 versts[1] in all. Japan had acquired 715 versts of railway.

Russian demands on China were so unmeasured and Japan's apprehensions of Russian dominance in the Pacific so well founded that the War of 1904-5 was unavoidable. There was an unbroken series of Japanese victories which had a tremendous moral effect on all Asiatics, whose sense of inferiority in material things to the Europeans now began to diminish. Oyama, commander-in-chief of the armies of Japan, made the following brief report to his sovereign.

179. A JAPANESE GENERAL TO HIS MIKADO[2]

Since Your Majesty's humble servant Iwao accepted the Imperial Order to become Commander-in-Chief of the Japanese Manchurian Army, we have captured the Russian strategical base at Liao-yang, frustrated the southern movement of the enemy on the Sha-ho, occupied the strong fortress of Port Arthur, destroyed the great Russian scheme at Heikoutai (San-chia-p'u), and repulsed the enemy's enormous forces at Mukden. Securing, also, victories at a number of other engagements, large and small, we succeeded in effecting the final object of the war. I can but attribute these successes to the luminous virtue of Your Majesty and the extraordinary valour of the officers and men. The patriotic support of the nation has also greatly assisted us, while the naval victories much facilitated our movements along the coast and enabled the marine communications, which were essential to a victorious campaign on land, to be kept open. The great exertions of the Japanese Government Departments and representatives abroad likewise contributed materially to the success of the strategic movements by keeping the Army informed as to home and foreign conditions, maintaining a sufficiency of supplies of all kinds, and making efficient sanitary arrangements. We deeply appreciate all the assistance which we thus received. It is a source of sorrow beyond expression that so many officers and men lost their lives at the front. I am greatly moved at the honour of being received by Your Majesty on the restoration of peace and the conclusion of

---

[1] A Russian verst is approximately two thirds of a mile. (Editor's note.)

[2] Text in Frederick McCormick, *The Tragedy of Russia in Pacific Asia*. 2 vols. New York, Outing Publishing Co., 1907, II, pp. 332-333. By permission of The Macmillan Company.

our duties at home and abroad. I am humbly submitting further reports in regard to the conduct of the troops, the management of the horses, the hygienic regulations, the positions of our forces in Manchuria before the conclusion of the armistice, the transport arrangements, and the telegraphic, and postal services. I will also instruct the Commander of each Army to submit a report to Your Majesty concerning the various battles. I humbly submit the above.

Signed — Marquis Oyama Iwao, Commander-in-Chief of the Japanese Manchurian Army, December 7th, 1905.

President Roosevelt invited Japan and Russia to a conference at Portsmouth, N. H., and there the peace was signed that gave Japan the key position in Manchuria and henceforth limited Russia's imperialistic designs in the Far East.

180. THE PEACE OF PORTSMOUTH [1]

Article II. The Imperial Russian Government, acknowledging that Japan possesses in Korea paramount political, military and economical interests, engage neither to obstruct nor interfere with the measures of guidance, protection and control which the Imperial Government of Japan may find it necessary to take in Korea. . . .

Article III. Japan and Russia mutually engage:

1. To evacuate completely and simultaneously Manchuria except the territory affected by the lease of the Liao-tung Peninsula . . . and

2. To restore entirely and completely to the exclusive administration of China all portions of Manchuria now in the occupation or under the control of the Japanese or Russian troops, with the exception of the territory mentioned.

The Imperial Government of Russia declare that they have not in Manchuria any territorial advantages or preferential or exclusive concessions in impairment of Chinese sovereignty or inconsistent with the principle of equal opportunity.

Article IV. Japan and Russia reciprocally engage not to obstruct any general measures common to all countries, which China may take for the development of the commerce and industry of Manchuria.

Article V. The Imperial Russian Government transfer and assign to the Imperial Government of Japan, with the consent of the Government of China, the lease of Port Arthur, Talien and adjacent territory and territorial waters and all rights, privileges and concessions connected with or forming

[1] Quoted from the *Japan Times,* Oct. 16, 1905, in *Nouveau recueil général de traités.* 2ᵉ Série. Tome XXXIII. Leipzig. 1906, pp. 3–10 (excerpts).

part of such lease, and they also transfer and assign to the Imperial Government of Japan all public works and properties in the territory affected by the above mentioned lease. . . .

Article VI. The Imperial Russian Government engage to transfer and assign to the Imperial Government of Japan, without compensation and with the consent of the Chinese Government, the railway between Changchun (Kuan-cheng-tzu) and Port Arthur and all its branches, together with all rights, privileges and properties appertaining thereto in that region, as well as all coal mines in the said region belonging to or worked for the benefit of the railway. . . .

Article VII. Japan and Russia engage to exploit their respective railways in Manchuria exclusively for commercial and industrial purposes and in no wise for strategic purposes.

It is understood that that restriction does not apply to the railway in the territory affected by the lease of the Liao-tung Peninsula.

Article IX. The Imperial Russian Government cede to the Imperial Government of Japan in perpetuity and full sovereignty, the southern portion of the Island of Saghalien and all islands adjacent thereto, and all public works and properties thereon. The fiftieth degree of north latitude is adopted as the northern boundary of the ceded territory. . . .

[15 articles in all]

(Signed) Jutaro Komura
(Signed) K. Takahira
(Signed) Serge Witte
(Signed) Rosen

*Russia and Great Britain had divided Persia in " spheres of influence."
Any efforts Persia might make to control her own affairs had no place in
this scheme of things.*

181. AN INCIDENT IN IMPERIALISTIC PRACTICE[1]

The financial difficulties of the Persian Government were great and ever increasing. It was therefore decided to apply to America for help, with the result that Mr. W. Morgan Shuster reached Persia, with a staff, in 1911. The financial adviser investigated matters, and speedily came to the conclusion that the Augean stable of corruption could only be cleansed by extraordinary powers. These powers were readily bestowed by the Assembly, and Shuster, realizing that the " Democrats " possessed most of the power, threw in his lot with them. He showed great energy but, unfortunately, an

[1] Brigadier-General Sir Percy Sykes, *Persia*. Oxford, The Clarendon Press, 1922, pp. 150–152. Cf. also Selection 203, pp. 484–5.

almost equally great lack of tact. Russia, on the look out for offence, was a formidable opponent, and Shuster started badly by refusing to pay the usual calls on the Legations. He was strongly advised by the Regent not to interfere with the Customs Department that was well managed by its Belgian officials, but he immediately started his operations with this department.

He engaged a British officer of strong pro-Persian and anti-Russian proclivities to organize a Treasury gendarmerie for service all over Persia. The Russian Legation objected, and the appointment was finally cancelled by the officer in question being ordered to return to India.

The Russian Government was determined to get rid of Shuster, and the opportunity soon presented itself. The Persian Government decided to confiscate the property of Shua-u-Saltana, brother of the ex-Shah, who had joined him in his recent attempt to regain the throne. Shuster directed his Treasury gendarmes to seize Shua's palace, but the Russian Consul-General, under the inadequate pretext that Shua owed money to the Russian Bank, sent two of his secretaries with ten Russian Cossacks to anticipate Shuster's action. This party arrested the Treasury gendarmes upon their arrival on the scene. On the following day Shuster dispatched a much stronger body of Treasury gendarmes to the spot, which evicted a small body of Persian Cossacks which they found in possession. The gendarmes were stated to have pointed their rifles at two Russian officials who passed by, but this charge was denied. It would appear that the Russian authorities were entirely in the wrong in the first instance in taking the matter into their own hands and seizing on Shua's property, more especially as he happened to enjoy Turkish protection. But Shuster's folly in sending a large force to turn out a guard posted by the orders of the Russian Consulate-General spoilt the case of the Persian Government. As was inevitable, the Russian Government presented an ultimatum which had to be accepted and Shuster was dismissed. His failure was most regrettable, and the only consolation is, that had he been tactful and suitable in every way, Russia would, sooner or later, have found means by which to oust him.

The East India Company, not the British Government itself, ruled India up to 1858, yet ever behind the Company the British power was apparent and India was a chief preoccupation of British statesmen from the middle of the eighteenth century. An Act of 1834 made the Company definitely responsible to the Crown and this, in turn, made the Crown actually responsible for the governing of India. Here Great Britain has confronted problems unlike any that have had to be solved in other portions of her Empire.

182. PROBLEMS OF RACE IN INDIA [1]

Entrenched against the West behind its philosophies as well as its superstitions, Hinduism has its most formidable stronghold in the social system which it has evolved with caste as its corner-stone. The Sanskrit word *Varna* means both caste and colour, and it may well be that in remote ages caste was little more than a colour-bar erected by the Aryan newcomers who were then a small minority in India to protect their own race from being swamped by the earlier races already in possession of the country, whilst their superior organization and their higher civilization were reducing them to subjection. The colour of their skins was relatively fair, whereas that of the primitive population of India exhibited much darker shades of brown, approaching even to black. In this respect the Aryans might be termed the first white conquerors of India, and in building up a new social structure, and basing it on caste, which was colour, they may well have been prompted by the same considerations as the Western nations of today, who, in their oversea possessions, erect a colour-bar between the whites and the coloured races, black, brown or yellow, in order to maintain their prestige and preserve the purity of their stock, as well as in some cases to protect their economic interests, in the midst of indigenous populations vastly superior to them in numbers, but on a much lower plane of civilization. Today the tables have after long ages been turned and it is the Indians who complain bitterly of the colour-bar enforced against them by the ruling white race in some of our oversea colonies and dominions; but those who know their own history should ask themselves whether their forbears were not the first to create a precedent which the white man is only too ready to follow all over the world today. . . .

But not until more than a hundred years after British rule had been established, and then not primarily against Indians, did the white man set up the colour of men's skins as the great dividing-line between the peoples of the earth. The colour-feeling is very largely a modern growth and the French and most of the nations of Southern Europe are still on the whole free from it. It is strongest amongst the English-speaking peoples of the Old World and the New. It has grown upon Englishmen with the expansion of an Empire in which the coloured races preponderate over the white race in the proportion of seven to one, and nowhere is it quite so strong as in those parts of our oversea Empire in which the climate allows Englishmen to settle and make permanent homes for themselves, and at the same time to acquire land and create great industrial interests, of which the development largely depends upon the cheap labour of a coloured population.

For climatic, besides other reasons, India is never likely to have any large

[1] Sir Valentine Chirol, *India*. London, Ernest Benn, 1926, pp. 14–15, 77–80.

permanent white population, and until late in the XIXth century there were few signs of any such colour-feeling amongst the English in India or of any deep racial antagonism to the white man, as such, on the part of the Indians. Even mixed marriages from which several well-known families have sprung, and other unions more irregular and temporary, were much less infrequent than they are now. To that period dates back a large proportion of the existing community of mixed descent, which was for a long time called Eurasian, but is now officially designated as Anglo-Indian, though with many other strains of European blood besides English. It numbers only 113,000, and, whilst not a few have striven hard and successfully to live up to the best standards of the European ancestry on which they rather pathetically pride themselves, its position as a community grows increasingly painful and precarious, for, like the proverbial poor relations, it gets little sympathy from the white race to whose coat-tails it makes desperate efforts to cling, and none at all from the Indians who resent its claims to any sort of racial superiority far more than they do those of the pure-blooded Englishman.

British rule, in its beginning, had this in its favour to ease relations with the subject race, that, unlike, for instance, Mohammedan domination, it had not been imposed on India by brutal wars of invasion and sheer lust of conquest. It had sometimes been promoted by methods which we should have to reprobate today, but on the whole it had been established quite as much with Indian consent, and often at Indian solicitation, as by British arms; and in almost every war waged for its consolidation and extension the British had had as many Indians fighting on their side as against them. Nor had the British, when they became the masters of India, behaved as conquerors usually behaved in Asia. They respected the customs of the people, tried to understand their needs and gave the humblest folk a new sense of security from arbitrary oppression and a new conception of justice as a boon that was to be neither bought nor sold. They reassured the well-to-do classes by recognizing established rights of property and especially those of the great native landlords, though they erred sometimes through ignorance, as when Cornwallis made the permanent land settlement of Bengal. The still greater ignorance displayed by Macaulay's scathing gibes, not only at Hindu mythology but at all Oriental literature, must have deeply wounded many grave and reverend pundits; but they could find abundant compensation in the sympathy and understanding of the much larger company of Englishmen, often great administrators or missionaries, who threw themselves heart and soul into the study of Indian languages and ancient learning. It was Englishmen in India, Sir William Jones, the first translator of *The Laws of Manu* as well as of *Sakuntala,* the finest of Indian dramas; Colebrook, who continued his work and wrote the first *Sanskrit Grammar;* Charles Wilkins, who translated the *Baghavatghita;* Carey, who was the first English teacher of Sanskrit at the College of Fort William, though the Bengalee vernacular was, perhaps, nearer his heart; H. H. Wilson, who published the first *Sanskrit Grammar;* Tod, the immortal author of the *Annals of Rajasthen* — it was these and many others who blazed the trail for Max Müller and Monier Williams and Roth and Sassen and Burnouf and the great host of European scholars who have revealed to India herself scarcely less than to the Western world the majesty and wealth of the Sanskrit language and its kinship with the whole group of European languages now designated as Indo-European, and the historical as well as literary value of the great body of Hindu literature which is the key to India's civilization.

Dislike and distrust of Western education were not always easy to overcome, but there often grew up between Indian pupils and European teachers a relationship of respect and affection not unlike that which bound the *chela* to his *guru* under the old Hindu dispensation. The Englishman who went out to India in those earlier days to play his part in ruling the country, usually showed the qualities rather than the defects of a class that, whatever its human weaknesses, had been brought up to believe that *noblesse oblige;* and he sought to act up to the maxim by comporting himself as a Christian and a gentleman towards people of a race less fortunately situated than his own, though very different habits of life discouraged any intimate social intercourse. It was by this type of Englishman that the up-country Indian who, as he seldom if ever travelled and therefore never knew any other, chiefly judged the ruling race.

For eight years prior to 1856 India was governed by the Earl of Dalhousie, a strong ruler and an aggressive soldier, who extended British power but awakened fears among the Indian peoples as to British aims. Viscount Canning succeeded him in 1856 and almost at once was involved in difficulties.

183. THE CAUSES OF THE GREAT MUTINY [1]

Lord Canning resolved that thenceforth he would be the master of his own army, and on the 25th of July issued a General Order which decreed that no recruit should for the future be accepted who would not undertake to march whithersoever his services might be required. "There is no fear," he wrote a few months later, "of feelings of caste being excited by the new enlistment regulations in the Bengal army." He deceived himself; for, while he was writing, recruiting officers were complaining that high-caste men had begun to shrink from entering the service, which their brethren had once needed no persuasion to join; and old sepoys were whispering to each other

[1] T. R. E. Holmes, *A History of the Indian Mutiny.* 3rd Edition, London, W. H. Allen & Co., 1888, pp. 75–79.

their fears that the oaths of the new recruits were binding upon themselves also. About the same time that the General Service Enlistment Act had been passed, an ill-judged parsimony had dictated another measure, namely that sepoys declared unfit for foreign service should no longer be allowed to re-tire on invalid pensions, but be utilised for the performance of cantonment duty; and shortly before, it had been decreed that all sepoys without exception should thenceforth pay the regular postage for their letters instead of sending them under the frank of their commandant. These apparently trifling changes seriously added to the existing irritation. The sepoys were now in a mood to believe any lie that reflected discredit upon the Government. Seeing that the warlike Sikhs were favoured by the recruiting sergeant, they persuaded themselves that an entire Sikh army of thirty thousand men was to be raised to supersede them. They listened to the suggestions of clever agitators, who assured them that the Queen had herself sent out Lord Canning for the express purpose of converting them, and that the General Service Enlistment Act was only the first step in his career of persecution. They saw in the rumoured support of missionary societies by Lord Canning, in the rumoured zeal of Lady Canning for the conversion of native women, evidences of the same spirit of proselytism. As a matter of fact, neither the Governor-General nor his wife had done more than those who had gone before them. But it was not unnatural that they should be suspected of having done so. For, little more than a year before, the missionaries had published a manifesto which went to prove that the railways and steamships of the European, by facilitating the material union of all races of men, were to be the indirect instruments for accomplishing their spiritual union under one faith. Regarded as a plain invitation by Government to join the Christian religion, this paper caused great excitement among the natives of Bengal; and William Taylor, the Commissioner of Patna, reported upon the especially dangerous feelings which it had awakened amongst the bigoted Mahometans of his Division. A reassuring proclamation, which the Lieutenant-Governor of Bengal issued in consequence of this warning, did not lessen the general alarm; for the people believed that a Government which could meditate their conversion would be quite capable of making a false statement to lull their suspicions. Nor were the professed ministers of the Gospel the only missionaries. Certain earnest-minded officers of whom a Colonel Wheler was the most prominent, preached to their men with the enthusiasm of Cromwell's captains, and brought down upon themselves the displeasure of Government by their zeal. And, though Canning was himself guiltless of the proselytism with which he was charged, he innocently incurred obloquy by giving formal sanction to the Bill prepared by Dalhousie for the removal of all legal obstacles to the marriage of Hindoo widows. The excitement and alarm which this combination of causes produced were not confined to the sepoys; for these men had friends or relations in every village, and were especially connected by the ties of kinship with the population of Oude and the North-Western Provinces, where our rule had provoked the most bitter animosities. But why should they think that Government wished to convert them? Their imaginations supplied a plausible answer. The white man was bent upon taking away their caste, and making them Christians, in order that, no longer hesitating to eat his strengthening food, or to embark in his ships, they might be able to go forth at his bidding, as warriors endowed with new vigour, to gratify his insatiable ambition by fresh conquests. This, if they could help it, they were resolved that they would never do. They had served the effete Feringhees for scanty wages long enough. Their own day was coming now. Vague ambitions arose in their hearts. Sooner or later, they would vindicate the honour of religion; they would enrich themselves by plunder; they would collect the revenues; they would drive the white upstarts into the sea. And now, as if to give confidence to the disaffected, and to shake the loyalty of the faithful, an old Hindoo prophecy was raked up, which said that in the year 1857, the hundredth since its foundation by the victory of Plassey, the Company's Raj [1] was to be destroyed.

Infuriated by real grievances, haunted by groundless fears, tossed about by idle rumours, the enemies of British rule were still afraid to strike, when the arch-agitators lighted by an accident upon the spell, the potency of which was to liberate the pent-up passions of their dupes, and nerve them to revolt.

A few idle words betrayed the existence of this engine of rebellion. One day in January, 1857, a Lascar, attached to the magazine at Dum-Dum near Calcutta, asked a sepoy of the garrision to give him a drink of water from his lotah. Nettled by the haughty reply that the vessel would be contaminated by the lips of a low-caste man, the Lascar retorted that the sepoy would soon be deprived of his caste altogether; for the Government was busy manufacturing cartridges greased with the fat of cows or swine, and the sepoys would have to bite the forbidden substance before loading.

It is hard to convey to the mind of an English reader an adequate idea of the force of the shock beneath which the imagination of that Brahmin must have reeled when he heard these words. It was all true, then, he must have felt. The Government were really bent upon ruining him. They had devised an expedient which, under the specious pretext of putting a better weapon into his hands, was to destroy his caste, his honour, his social position, everything that made life worth having, and to pave the way for his perversion to Christianity. It must be remembered that not faith, not righteousness, but ritual was the essence of his religion. For him to be told that he was to touch with his lips the fat of the cow was as appalling as it would have been to a medieval Catholic to listen to the sentence of excommunication.

[1] Sovereignty (Hindu). (Editor's note.)

Yet it was all a delusion. There was some foundation for what the Lascar said; that was all. The manufacture of greased cartridges to be used with the new Enfield rifle, which was superseding the old musket, had long been going on; but none were destined to be issued to the sepoys.

The mutiny was put down, the sepoys reconciled and the country pacified, but it was clear that the Crown must now replace the East India Company. This was done in 1858. Queen Victoria's proclamation, accompanying the new legislation, follows.

184. THE CROWN TAKES OVER THE RULE OF INDIA [1]

We hereby announce to the native princes of India that all treaties and engagements made with them by or under the authority of the Hon. East India Company are by us accepted, and will be scrupulously maintained; and we look for the like observance on their part.

We desire no extension of our present territorial possessions: and while we will permit no aggression upon our dominions or our rights to be attempted with impunity, we shall sanction no encroachment on those of others. We shall respect the rights, dignity, and honour of native princes as our own; and we desire that they, as well as our own subjects, should enjoy that prosperity and that social advancement which can only be secured by internal peace and good government.

We hold ourselves bound to the natives of our Indian territories by the same obligations of duty which bind us to all our other subjects; and those obligations, by the blessing of Almighty God, we shall faithfully and conscientiously fulfil.

Firmly relying ourselves on the truth of Christianity, and acknowledging with gratitude the solace of religion, we disclaim alike the right and the desire to impose our convictions on any of our subjects. We declare it to be our Royal will and pleasure that none be in anywise favoured, none molested or disquieted by reason of their religious faith or observances, but that all shall alike enjoy the equal and impartial protection of the law; and we do strictly charge and enjoin all those who may be in authority under us that they abstain from all interference with the religious belief or worship of any of our subjects, on pain of our highest displeasure.

And it is our further will that, so far as may be, our subjects, of whatever race or creed, be freely and impartially admitted to offices in our service, the duties of which they may be qualified, by their education, ability, and integrity duly to discharge.

We know and respect the feelings of attachment with which the natives

[1] *Annual Register for 1858.*

of India regard the lands inherited by them from their ancestors, and we desire to protect them in all rights connected therewith, subject to the equitable demands of the State; and we will that generally, in framing and administering the law, due regard be paid to the ancient rights, usages, and customs of India.

We deeply lament the evils and misery which have been brought upon India by the acts of ambitious men, who have deceived their countrymen by false reports and led them into open rebellion. Our power having been shown by the suppression of that rebellion in the field, we desire to show our mercy by pardoning the offences of those who have been thus misled, but who desire to return to the path of duty. . . .

Our clemency will be extended to all offenders, save and except those who have been or shall be convicted of having directly taken part in the murder of British subjects. With regard to such the demands of justice forbid the exercise of mercy. . . .

When, by the blessing of Providence, internal tranquillity shall be restored, it is our earnest desire to stimulate the peaceful industry of India, to promote works of public utility and improvement, and to administer its government for the benefit of all our subjects resident therein. In their prosperity will be our strength, in their contentment our security, and in their gratitude our best reward. And may the God of all power grant to us, and to those in authority under us, strength to carry out these our wishes for the good of our people.

That bitter Indian resentment at the conduct of affairs by the British was not felt half a century ago was manifested in the proceedings of the early Indian National Congresses. At one of the earliest, in 1886, perhaps the most influential of Hindu leaders spoke as follows.

185. HOW AN INDIAN LEADER FELT TOWARD BRITAIN IN 1886[1]

I ask whether in the most glorious days of Hindu rule, in the days of Rajahs like the great Vikram, you could imagine the possibility of a meeting of this kind, whether even Hindus of all different provinces of the Kingdom could have collected and spoken as one nation. Coming down to the later Empire of our friends the Mohammedans, who probably ruled over a larger territory at one time than any Hindu monarch, would it have been — even in the days of Akbar himself — possible for a meeting like this to assemble composed of all classes and communities, all speaking one language and all having uniform and high aspirations of their own. . . . It is under the civilizing

---

[1] Extract from Presidential Speech of Dadabhai Naoroji, Indian National Congress, 1886. Sir Valentine Chirol, *India*. London, Ernest Benn, 1926. pp. 89–91.

rule of the Queen and the people of England that we meet here together, hindered by none, and are freely allowed to speak our minds without the least fear and without the least hesitation. Such a thing is possible under British rule and under British rule only. Then I put the question plainly: Is this Congress a nursery for sedition and rebellion against the British Government; or is it another stone in the foundation of the stability of that government? There could be but one answer, and that you have already given, because we are thoroughly sensible of the numberless blessings conferred upon us, of which the very existence of this Congress is a proof in a nutshell. Were it not for these blessings of British rule I could not have come here to-day, as I have done, without the least hesitation and without the least fear that my children might be robbed and killed in my absence; nor could you have come from every corner of the land, having performed, within a few days, journeys which in former days would have occupied months. These simple facts bring home to all of us at once some of the great and numberless blessings which British rule has conferred upon us. But there remain even greater blessings for which we have to be grateful. It is to British rule that we owe the education we possess; the people of England were sincere in the declaration made more than half a century ago that India was a sacred charge entrusted to their care by Providence, and that they were bound to administer it for the good of India, to the glory of their own name, and the satisfaction of God.

India entered the Great War with enthusiasm and gave splendid support to Great Britain, but Indian leaders expected their efforts to be rewarded with some considerable measure of autonomy. A slight participation in the government had been granted Indians in 1909 but much more was desired, and in this hope Hindus and Moslems were united. Lord Hardinge, viceroy from 1910 to 1916, recommended partial Home Rule and in 1917 the Secretary of State for India, Mr. Montagu, made the following announcement in Parliament.

186. ENCOURAGEMENT TO INDIAN ASPIRATIONS [1]

The policy of His Majesty's Government, with which the Government of India are in complete accord, is that of the increasing association of Indians in every branch of the Administration, and the gradual development of self-governing institutions with a view to the progressive realization of responsible government in India as an integral part of the British Empire. They have decided that substantial steps in this direction shall be taken as soon as possible, and that it is of the highest importance as a preliminary to considering what these steps should be that there should be a free and informal

---

[1] *Parliamentary Debates,* August 20, 1917, 5th Series, vol. 97, pp. 1695–1696.

Amur and Sungari, subjects of one Empire or the other, to carry on trade relations with each other, and the respective authorities shall protect reciprocally merchants on both banks.

3. . . .

(Signed)   Nikolai Murevev, aide de camp . . .
Pyotr Perovskii, Councillor of State . . .
I-Chan, Commander-in-Chief . . .
Dziraminga, adjutant.

Aigun, May 16, 1858.

Russia was slow in consolidating her position in the Far East and rail connections were not begun until 1891, when the Trans-Siberian Railway promised to bring St. Petersburg and Vladivostok much closer together and to enable Russia to exploit the vast riches of Eastern Siberia and Manchuria. Russia's fortunes in Siberia were managed by a group of adventurers whose plans were really understood imperfectly at the Russian court but very clearly at Tokyo. Japan, to forestall the European aggressor, realized she must first conquer China and possess herself of Manchuria, and with this design she fought the War of 1895 whereby she extorted from China not only Formosa but a twenty-five-year lease of the Liaotung peninsula. This last provision of the Treaty of Shimonoseki was overturned by the intervention of the Powers, led by Russia, who herself coveted this peninsula, with its access to the Yellow Sea at Port Arthur. The Yellow Sea is warm and navigation there can take place the year round, whereas Vladivostok is ice-bound many months. When in 1897 Germany, followed by Great Britain, demanded territory from impotent China, Russia arranged, partly by bribing the Chinese minister, Li Hung Chang, to obtain as her share the lease on Port Arthur which she had insisted China should not give to Japan because it would destroy the integrity of her dominions.

177. THE RUSSIANS' LEASE OF PORT ARTHUR[1]
Article I.

It being necessary for the due protection of her navy in the waters of North China that Russia should possess a station she can defend, the Emperor of China agrees to lease to Russia Port Arthur and Ta-lien-wan, together with the adjacent seas, but on the understanding that such lease shall not prejudice China's sovereignty over this territory.

---

[1] "*Vladimir,*" *Russia on the Pacific and the Siberian Railway.* London, Sampson, Low, Marston & Co., 1899, pp. 360–362.

exchange of opinion between those in authority at home and in India. His Majesty's Government have accordingly decided, with His Majesty's approval, that I should accept the Viceroy's invitation to proceed to India and to discuss these matters with the Viceroy and the Government of India, to consider with the Viceroy the views of local Governments, and to receive with him the suggestions of representative bodies and others. . . . I would add that progress in this policy can only be achieved by successive stages. The British Government and the Government of India, on whom the responsibility lies for the welfare and advancement of the Indian peoples, must be judges of the time and measure of each advance, and they must be guided by the co-operation received from those upon whom new opportunities of service will thus be conferred, and by the extent to which it is found that confidence can be reposed in their sense of responsibility.

Lord Chelmsford became viceroy of India in 1916 and, together with Mr. Montagu, he produced the Montagu-Chelmsford Report in 1918. Upon this report, which recommended a greater participation of Indians in their government, was based the Government of India Act of 1919 setting up the diarchy, a system of rule which gave the provinces a degree of autonomy and provided for the election of a portion of the members of both provincial and all-Indian legislatures. This might have led peaceably to more autonomy had not a group of laws, known as the Rowland Acts, been passed at the same time. These laws fixed severe penalties on seditious meetings and impressed the Indians as the very negation of Swaraj, or Home Rule, which by now they had come ardently to desire. A hartal, or cessation of work, was proclaimed in 1919 and soon after occurred the turning of machine guns on an unarmed crowd of Indians at Amritzur by British troops under command of General Dyer, who had forbidden an assemblage in the town's principal square, the Jalianwalla Bagh. The worst feeling prevailed all over India as a result of this act. The Indians looked for leadership to Mohandas Karamchand Gandhi, called the Mahatma, *which signifies a Great Soul, at one with the Supreme Being. Gandhi had served the Empire well but had come to have misgivings as to British rule.*

187. A DESCRIPTION OF THE MAHATMA[1]

Soft dark eyes, a small frail man, with a thin face and rather large protruding eyes, his head covered with a little white cap, his body clothed in coarse white cloth, barefooted. He lives on rice and fruit, and drinks only

[1] Romain Rolland, *Mahatma Gandhi.* Translated from the French by Catherine D. Groth. New York, The Century Co., 1924, pp. 3–5.

water. He sleeps on the floor — sleeps very little, and works incessantly. His body does not seem to count at all. There is nothing striking about him — except his whole expression of "infinite patience and infinite love." W. W. Pearson, who met him in South Africa, instinctively thought of St. Francis of Assisi. There is an almost childlike simplicity about him. His manner is gentle and courteous even when dealing with adversaries, and he is of immaculate sincerity. He is modest and unassuming, to the point of sometimes seeming almost timid, hesitant, in making an assertion. Yet you feel his indomitable spirit. He makes no compromises and never tries to hide a mistake. Nor is he afraid to admit having been in the wrong. Diplomacy is unknown to him; he shuns oratorical effect or, rather, never thinks about it; and he shrinks unconsciously from the great popular demonstrations organized in his honor. Literally "ill with the multitude that adores him," he distrusts majorities and fears "mobocracy" and the unbridled passions of the populace. He feels at ease only in a minority, and is happiest when, in meditative solitude, he can listen to the "still small voice" within.

This is the man who has stirred three hundred million people to revolt, who has shaken the foundations of the British Empire, and who has introduced into human politics the strongest religious impetus of the last two thousand years.

On August 1st, 1920, Gandhi returned to the Government all his decorations and proclaimed Non-Co-operation, a status not identical with Civil Disobedience, which he considered reserved for a small élite, and not including the refusal of taxes, but which did imply declining to co-operate with the Government in any policy. The first of the three following extracts reveals Gandhi's spiritual attitude toward the political problem. Of the two others one is the Satyagraha *Pledge.* Satya *means just;* agraha *is an attempt. Gandhi has defined the term as "love force or soul force." He had used it earlier in South Africa where he strove for twenty years to protect the rights of Hindus on an alien soil. It is not, he said, passive resistance but "active resistance — resistance which finds outlet, not in violence, but in the active force of love, faith and sacrifice."* Swadeshi *comes from* swa *(self) and* deshi *(country) and is not unlike Sinn Fein, our country for ourselves. The term has usually been applied to economic independence, the return to the spinning wheel and homespun.*

188. THE LAW OF SUFFERING [1]

No country has ever risen without being purified through the fire of suffering. Mother suffers so that her child may live. The condition of

[1] M. Gandhi, *Young India*. New York, The Viking Press, 1923, pp. 230, 233.

wheat-growing is that the seed grain should perish. Life comes out of Death. Will India rise out of her slavery without fulfilling this eternal law of purification through suffering? . . .

What then is the meaning of Non-co-operation in terms of the Law of Suffering? We must voluntarily put up with the losses and inconveniences that arise from having to withdraw our support from a Government that is ruling against our will. Possession of power and riches is a crime under an unjust government, poverty in that case is a virtue, says Thoreau. It may be that, in the transition state, we may make mistakes; there may be avoidable suffering. These things are preferable to national emasculation.

We must refuse to wait for the wrong to be righted till the wrong-doer has been roused to a sense of his iniquity. We must not, for fear of ourselves or others having to suffer, remain participators in it. But we must combat the wrong by ceasing to assist the wrong-doer directly or indirectly.

189. *THE SATYAGRAHA PLEDGE*[1]

Being conscientiously of opinion that the Bills known as the Indian Criminal Law (Amendment) Bill No. I of 1919, and the Criminal Law (Emergency Powers) Bill No. II of 1919,[2] are unjust, subversive of the principle of liberty and justice, and destructive of the elementary rights of individuals on which the safety of the community as a whole and the State itself is based, we solemnly affirm that in the event of these Bills becoming law until they are withdrawn, we shall refuse civilly to obey these laws and such other laws as a committee to be hereafter appointed may think fit and further affirm that in this struggle we will faithfully follow truth and refrain from violence to life, person or property.

190. *THE SWADESHI VOW*[3]

With God as my witness, I solemnly declare that from today I shall confine myself for my personal requirements, to the use of cloth manufactured in India from Indian cotton, silk and wool; and I shall altogether abstain from using foreign cloth in my possession.

The gentle leadership of Gandhi was weakened by the growth of acrimony, and the more militant C. R. Das from 1922 to his death in 1925 swayed the Indian National Congress. In the late 'twenties the agitation for Swaraj became more coherent, despite occasional Hindu-Moslem riots and suspicion, and again Gandhi's influence waxed. The Indian National Congress in De-

1 M. Gandhi, *Young India.* New York, The Viking Press, 1923, p. 1159.
2 The Rowland Acts. (Editor's note.)
3 M. Gandhi, *Young India.* New York, The Viking Press, 1923, p. 1159.

cember 1928 gave the British Government twelve months to prepare for, and set up, dominion status for India, and the Viceroy, Lord Irwin, declared in 1929 that this was his Government's intention. It would take more time, he intimated, than the Indian leaders, Nehru and Gandhi, wished to allow, and on January 1, 1930 the latter began their campaign of non-co-operation and civil disobedience. As these pages go to press (April, 1930) Gandhi, having made a "march to the sea" has manufactured salt in defiance of the government monopoly and civil disobedience approaches violent rebellion. Much moderate opinion inclines, however, to accept a round-table conference with British representatives in which a solution of the impasse *may be sought.*

191. THE PRINCIPLES AND PROGRAM OF SWARAJ [1]

The conclusion is irresistible that it is not by acquiescence in the doctrine of law and order that the English people have obtained the recognition of their fundamental rights. It follows from the survey that I have made, firstly, that no regulation is law unless it is based on the consent of the people; secondly, where such consent is wanting the people are under no obligation to obey; thirdly, where such laws are not only not based on the consent of the people but profess to attack their fundamental rights, the subjects are entitled to compel their withdrawal by force or insurrections; fourthly, that law and order is, and has always been, a plea for absolutism; and lastly, there can be neither law nor order before the real reign of law begins. . . .

What is the ideal which we must set before us? The first and foremost is the ideal of nationalism. Now what is nationalism? It is, I conceive, a process through which a nation expresses itself and finds itself, not in isolation from other nations, not in opposition to other nations, but as part of a great scheme by which, in seeking its own expression and therefore its own identity, it materially assists the self-expression and self-realization of other nations as well: Diversity is as real as unity. And in order that the unity of the world may be established it is essential that each nationality should proceed on its own line and find fulfilment in self-expression and self-realization. The nationality of which I am speaking must not be confused with the conception of nationality as it exists in Europe today. Nationalism in Europe is an aggressive nationalism, a selfish nationalism, a commercial nationalism of gain and loss. The gain of France is the loss of Germany, and the gain of Germany is the loss of France. Therefore French nationalism is nurtured on the hatred of Germany, and German nationalism is nurtured on the hatred of France. It is not yet realized that you cannot hurt Germany without

[1] Presidential Address of Chitta Ranjan Das, Indian National Congress at Gaya, Dec. 1922. An appendix to P. C. Ray, *Life and Times of C. R. Das.* Oxford, Oxford University Press, 1927, pp. 261–274 (extracts).

hurting Humanity, and in consequence hurting France; and that you cannot hurt France without hurting Humanity, and in consequence hurting Germany. That is European nationalism; that is not the nationalism of which I am speaking to you today. I contend that each nationality constitutes a particular stream of the great unity, but no nation can fulfil itself unless and until it becomes itself and at the same time realizes its identity with Humanity. The whole problem of nationalism is therefore to find that stream and to face that destiny. If you find the current and establish a continuity with the past, then the process of self-expression has begun, and nothing can stop the growth of nationality.

Throughout the pages of Indian history, I find a great purpose unfolding itself. Movement after movement has swept over this vast country, apparently creating hostile forces, but in reality stimulating the vitality and moulding the life of the people into one great nationality. If the Aryans and the non-Aryans met, it was for the purpose of making one people out of them. Brahmanism with its great culture succeeded in binding the whole of India and was indeed a mighty unifying force. Buddhism with its protests against Brahmanism served the same great historical purpose; and from Magadha to Taxila was one great Buddhistic empire which succeeded not only in broadening the basis of Indian unity, but in creating, what is perhaps not less important, the greater India beyond the Himalayas and beyond the seas, so much so that the sacred city where we have met may be regarded as a place of pilgrimage of millions and millions of people of Asiatic races. Then came the Mahomedans of divers races, but with one culture which was their common heritage. For a time it looked as if here was a disintegrating force, an enemy to the growth of Indian nationalism, but the Mahomedans made their home in India, and, while they brought a new outlook and a wonderful vitality to the Indian life, with infinite wisdom, they did as little as possible to disturb the growth of life in the villages where India really lives. This new outlook was necessary for India; and if the two sister streams met, it was only to fulfil themselves and face the destiny of Indian history. Then came the English with their alien culture, their foreign methods, delivering a rude shock to this growing nationality; but the shock has only completed the unifying process so that the purpose of history is practically fulfilled. The great Indian nationality is in sight. It already stretches its hands across the Himalayas not only to Asia but to the whole of the world, not aggressively, but to demand its recognition, and to offer its contribution. . . .

We have, therefore, to foster the spirit of Nationality. True development of the Indian nation must necessarily lie in the path of Swaraj. A question has often been asked as to what is Swaraj. Swaraj is indefinable and is not to be confused with any particular system of Government. . . . Swaraj is the natural expression of the national mind. The full outward expression of that mind covers, and must necessarily cover, the whole life history of a nation. Yet it is true that Swaraj begins when the true development of a nation begins, because, as I have said, Swaraj is the expression of the national mind. The question of nationalism, therefore, looked at from another point of view, is the same question as that of Swaraj. The question of all questions in India today is the attainment of Swaraj.

I now come to the question of method. I have to repeat that it has been proved beyond any doubt that the method of non-violent non-co-operation is the only method which we must follow to secure a system of Government which may in reality be the foundation of Swaraj. It is hardly necessary to discuss the philosophy of non-co-operation. I shall simply state the different viewpoints from which this question may be discussed. From the national point of view the method of non-co-operation means the attempt of the nation to concentrate upon its own energy and to stand on its own strength. From the ethical point of view, non-co-operation means the method of self-purification, the withdrawal from that which is injurious to the development of the nation, and therefore to the good of humanity. From the spiritual point of view, Swaraj means that isolation which in the language of Sadhana is called *protyahar* — that withdrawal from the forces which are foreign to our nature — and isolation and withdrawal which is necessary in order to bring out from our hidden depths the soul of the nation in all her glory. I do not desire to labour the point, but from every conceivable point of view, the method of non-violent non-co-operation must be regarded as the true method of " following in the path of Swaraj." . . .

I believe in revolutions, but I repeat, violence defeats freedom. . . .

Non-violence is not an idle dream. It was not in vain that Mahatma declared " put up thy sword into the sheath." Let those who are " of the truth " hear his voice as those others heard a mightier voice two thousand years ago. . . .

I shall place before you one by one the items of work, which, in my opinion, the Indian National Congress should prescribe for the nation.

It should commence its work for the year by a clearer declaration of the rights of the different communities in India under the Swaraj Government. So far as the Hindus and the Mahomedans are concerned there should be a clearer and emphatic confirmation of what is known as the Lucknow Compact, and along with that there should be an emphatic recognition of each other's rights, and each should be prepared to undergo some kind of sacrifice in favour of the other. Let me give an instance to make my meaning clear. Every devout Musalman objects to any music in front of a mosque, and every devout and orthodox Hindu objects to cows being slaughtered. May not the Hindus and the Musalmans of India enter into a solemn compact so that there may not be any music before any mosque and that no cows may be slaughtered? Other instances may be quoted. There should be a scheme of a series of sacrifices to be suffered by each community so that they may advance shoulder to shoulder in the path of Swaraj. As regards the other communities such as Sikhs, Christians and Parsees, the Hindus and the Mahomedans who constitute the bulk of the people should be prepared to give them even more than their proportional share in the Swaraj administration. I suggest that the Congress should bring about real agreement between all these communities by which the rights of every minority should be clearly recognized in order to remove all doubts which may arise and all apprehensions which probably exist. I need hardly add that I include among Christians not only pure Indians, but also Anglo-Indians and other people who have chosen to make India their home. Such an agreement as I have indicated was always necessary, but such an agreement is specially necessary in view of the work which faces us today.

I further think that the policy of exclusiveness which we have been following during the last two years should now be abandoned. There is in every country a number of people who are selfless followers of liberty and who desire to see every country free. We can no longer afford to lose their sympathy and co-operation. In my opinion, there should be established Congress Agencies in America and in every European country. We must keep ourselves in touch with world movements and be in constant communication with the lovers of freedom all over the world.

Even more important than this is participation of India in the great Asiatic Federation, which I see in the course of formation. I have hardly any doubt that the Pan-Islamic movement, which was started on a somewhat narrow basis, has given way or is about to give way to the great Federation of all Asiatic people. It is the union of the oppressed nationalities of Asia. Is India to remain outside this union? I admit that our freedom must be won by ourselves but such a bond of friendship and love, of sympathy and co-operation, between India and the rest of Asia, nay, between India and all the liberty-loving people of the world, is destined to bring about world peace. World peace to my mind means the freedom of every nationality, and I go further and say that no nation on the face of the earth can be really free when other nations are in bondage. The policy which we have hitherto pursued was absolutely necessary for the concentration of the work which we took upon ourselves to perform, and I agreed to that policy whole-heartedly. The hope of the attainment of Swaraj or a substantial basis of Swaraj in the course of the year made such concentration absolutely necessary. Today that very work demands broader sympathy and a wider outlook.

SECTION III. IMPERIALISM IN AFRICA

The way in which a weak state could get itself into difficulties leading to its subjection by a foreign Power or Powers is well illustrated in the case of Egypt. The ruler of Egypt from 1863 to 1879, the Khedive Ismail, embarked on a course of reckless expenditure, to meet which even the most oppressive taxation of his people could not provide adequate funds. England and France, therefore, fearing the country's bankruptcy, resolved to intervene to protect their investors. The result was the establishment of the Dual Control by England and France. This Control lasted from 1879 to 1883, after which England virtually controlled Egypt alone.

The financial weakness of Egypt and the apparent need for foreign control were made clear to the British Parliament in 1876 in a report made by Mr. Stephen Cave in 1876. Extracts from this report follow.

192. EXTRACTS FROM THE REPORT BY MR. CAVE ON THE FINANCIAL CONDITION OF EGYPT [1]

The critical state of the finances of Egypt is due to the combination of two opposite causes.

Egypt may be said to be in a transition state, and she suffers from the defects of the system out of which she is passing, as well as from those of the system into which she is attempting to enter. She suffers from the ignorance, dishonesty, waste, and extravagances of the East, such as have brought her Suzerain [2] to the verge of ruin, and at the same time from the vast expense caused by hasty and inconsiderate endeavours to adopt the civilization of the West.

Immense sums are expended on unproductive works after the manner of the East, and on productive works carried out in the wrong way, or too soon. This last is a fault which Egypt shares with other new countries (for she may be considered a new country in this respect), a fault which has seriously embarrassed both the United States and Canada; but probably nothing in Egypt has ever approached the profligate expenditure which characterized the commencement of the Railway system in England.

The Khedive has evidently attempted to carry out with a limited revenue in the course of a few years works which ought to be spread over a far longer period, and which would tax the resources of much richer exchequers.

We were informed that one of the causes which operates most against

---

[1] Presented to both Houses of Parliament, 1876.
Great Britain. House of Commons. *Sessional Papers*, 1876, vol. 83.
[2] The Ottoman Empire. (Editor's note.)

the honesty and efficiency of native officers is the precarious tenure of office. From the Pashas downwards every office is a tenancy at will, and experience shows that while dishonesty goes wholly or partially unpunished, independence of thought and action, resolution to do one's duty and to resist the peculation and neglect which pervade every department, give rise to intrigues which, sooner or later, bring about the downfall of honest officials; consequently, those who begin with a desire to do their duty, give way before the obstructiveness which paralyzes every effort.

The public servant of Egypt, like the Roman Proconsul, too often tries to make as much as he can out of his office while it lasts, and the scandal takes place, of the retirement in a few years with a large fortune of men whose salary is perhaps £40 a month, and who have plundered the Treasury on the one hand, and the peasant on the other.

The European employés of the Khedive take care, naturally, that their position should be defined and secured. This gives them freedom of thought, speech and action which has been in many cases most valuable to Egypt. Mr. Acton, sent out from the English Board of Trade, is a most useful member of this class. If men of such character and position were appointed to higher offices in the Civil Service, they would, as we believe, bring about most excellent results. They would be checks upon the adventurers who have preyed upon Egypt; and they would take care that the adviser upon public works should be in every case distinct from the person who benefits by their construction. The actual terms of the contracts require the scrutiny of men of integrity and capacity. It is admitted by contractors themselves that they charge far more than the fair amount for their work because the conditions of the contracts are so unnecessarily and absurdly onerous that they are compelled to make extra charges to protect themselves against possible loss; so that, one way or another, Egypt is the loser. An official of high rank said to us that the great want in Egypt is a body of high-class Europeans, not those who compete with each other to make money, and put pressure upon the Khedive, but men like our Indian officials, who have done so much to raise the tone of the native races.

The principal source of the revenue and of the wealth of Egypt is the land. Agriculture here is almost independent of seasons, but it is dependent upon widely extended, laborious and costly systems of irrigation. Where these are wanting, the land quickly relapses into desert. Where these are supplied, as in Upper Egypt by the Bahr Yussuf and the Bahr Ibrahim, and more to the east by the Sweet-water Canal to Ismailia and Suez, whole tracts of land are brought into cultivation. It is necessary, therefore, that irrigation should be carried on completely and economically, that drainage should accompany it for the purpose of washing the salt out of the subsoil, and that the distribution of water should be carried on justly and regularly. On all these points much improvement is needed. Still the productive power of the land has immensely increased during the administration of the present Ruler.

. . . .

The Daira Samieh, or private estate of the Khedive, consists of some 350,000 feddans of good land, chiefly in Upper Egypt, besides 100,000 feddans [1] of poor land not under cultivation. . . . The most important industry is the cultivation of the sugar-cane and the manufacture of sugar: 40,000 acres are planted with canes, and there are 12 large factories with most elaborate machinery at work.

The fault here, as in so many other instances, has been that this industry has been established without due consideration. Very large factories were built before the land was ready to supply them. They have not been placed in the middle of the estates, but near the main railway; consequently the canes have to be brought many miles by locomotives to the factories, involving a large consumption of coal, and making supervision more difficult. Some factories, full of costly machinery, have been adandoned, others left unfinished with the machinery already on the spot; steam machinery for irrigation has been erected and never used.

. . . .

That the accounts are kept in a slovenly, imperfect manner is evident on the face of them. Take for instance the Budget for 1876, and the " Compte Rendu " for 1875, which contain items jumbled together in a most extraordinary way, such as a railway in Soudan and a canal in Egypt in one sum. If we examine the accounts of the Customs, which are under the Finance Minister, we shall find no complete official table of the imports and exports of each Custom-house in Egypt, specifying the kind, the quantity, the value, and place from whence they came, or their destination. Moreover, the returns of quantity are made on no principle whatever, being sometimes according to weight, sometimes according to number, size of parcel, so many pairs, etc.

. . . .

Statistics show that the country has made great progress in every way under its present ruler, but, notwithstanding that progress, its present financial position is . . . very critical. Still, the expenditure, though very heavy, would not of itself have produced the present crisis, which may be attributed almost entirely to the ruinous conditions of loans raised for pressing requirements, due in some cases to causes over which the Khedive had little control.

. . . .

[1] The feddan nearly corresponds to the English acre.

None of the Egyptian loans costs less than 12 per cent. per annum, while some cost more than 13½ per cent. per annum, and the railways loan even 26.9 per cent. per annum, including sinking funds.

. . . .

As every security of real value is pledged, and as, without the means for meeting the floating debt, a very serious crisis in the financial affairs of Egypt must take place, which would be fatal to the interests of the bondholders under her various loans, it would seem that the most feasible mode of averting the danger would be to buy up, for the purpose of consolidation, the loans of 1860 and 1873, and the bonds of the floating debt. By this means the revenues now pledged would be liberated, and would be available as securities for a new loan, to be issued at a moderate rate of interest.

There is, however, an essential condition on which the success of some scheme of this character depends, namely, that the Khedive should place a person who would command general confidence, such for instance as the financial agent sent out by Her Majesty's Government to take employment under His Highness, at the head of a Control Department which should receive direct from the tax-collector certain branches of revenue to be defined . . . and should have a general supervision of the incidence and levying of the taxes.

. . . .

His Highness should undertake to consider the recommendations made to him by his Control Department, and to remedy any well-substantiated cases of maladministration that might be brought before him. By these means an important element of future wealth and prosperity would be introduced into the country: as the fellaheen thus protected from oppression and able to employ the means now wrung from them by the tax-collectors, in excess of what comes into the State Treasury, would add materially to the present resources of the country.

His Highness should further engage to make no fresh loans without the consent of the Control Department.

. . . .

It would appear from these calculations [1] that the resources of Egypt are sufficient, if properly managed, to meet her liabilities, but that as all her available assets are pledged for the charges of existing loans, some fresh combination is necessary in order to fund at a moderate rate the present onerous floating debt.

The annual charge upon the people of Egypt is heavy and has increased: but the power of meeting it, that is, the wealth of the country as indicated

---

[1] Tables of figures on the finances of Egypt omitted from this extract. (Editor's note.)

by its experts, has increased in a far greater degree. And it must be remembered that this annual charge includes not only a sinking fund for the redemption of debt, but a very large proportion of what we should call local taxation. It also includes the cost of much that is done in this country by private enterprise, such as railways, canals, harbours, docks, etc., besides actual rent of lands belonging to the State, and repayment of advances during periods of scarcity and murrain.

We gather from all the information that we have been able to obtain that Egypt is well able to bear the charge of the whole of her present indebtedness at a reasonable rate of interest; but she cannot go on renewing floating debts at 25 per cent. and raising fresh loans at 12 or 13 per cent. interest to meet these additions to her debt, which do not bring in a single piastre to her Exchequer.

Stephen Cave.

During the Napoleonic Wars Great Britain seized the Dutch Colony on the Cape of Good Hope. Discord speedily arose between the British and the Dutch (Boers) who were unwilling to live under British law and resisted the abolition of slavery. The dissatisfied Boers abandoned the Cape in the Great Trek of 1836–1838 to found new settlements beyond the Orange and Vaal Rivers (the Orange Free State and the South African or Transvaal Republic). British policy toward the Boers alternated between the reannexationist desires of Disraeli and the Conservatives and the " hands off " attitude of the Gladstone Liberals. After several changes of status the Boer republics were recognized in 1884 by the Convention of London as independent states. The discovery of gold in the Transvaal in 1885 caused a rush of British prospectors to Boer territory and the ambitions of Cecil Rhodes, Prime Minister of Cape Colony and diamond mine-owner, were stirred. Beyond wealth he desired a British Dominion in Africa that should stretch unbroken from " Cape to Cairo."

For fourteen years the Uitlanders *(the Boer term for the British adventurers) fretted at the denial to them of political privileges in the Transvaal but, although Dr. Jameson, instigated by Rhodes, made a raid in 1895 with the purpose of annexing the Boer states, the issue came to a head only when in March, 1899, the* Uitlanders' *petition to the British Government came to the sympathetic attention of Joseph Chamberlain in the Colonial Office. Great Britain intervened but met with stubborn insistence on the part of President Kruger of the Transvaal that the Boers must manage their own affairs. The war that followed, from 1899 to 1902, resulted in the reannexation of both Boer states to the British Empire.*

The two extracts that follow are from the more moderate debates of 1899. Sir Henry Campbell-Bannerman, leader of the Liberal Opposition, was against war. The Colonial Secretary, Joseph Chamberlain, was an ardent apologist of Rhodes's Imperialist ideas.

193. SIR HENRY CAMPBELL-BANNERMAN SHOWS AN APPRECIATION OF THE BOER POSITION [1]

For some time past . . . the controversy . . . has been concentrated upon one point; and as the most effective mode of securing some redress for the grievances of the Uitlander, instead of inquiring into and interfering with particular grounds of complaint, which would lead to unpleasant intermeddling, to say no more, in the domestic affairs of another country, it has seemed better rather to enable the Uitlanders to right their position for themselves . . . by becoming citizens of the South African Republic. . . . Now, as to the question of admitting the Uitlanders to the franchise, there has been much expression of surprise and of resentment at the stubborn resistance made to the proposal by the burghers, and especially by President Kruger. . . . I cannot avow myself an admirer of misplaced stubbornness wherever I find it. But, at the same time, there is surely no ground whatever for surprise. . . . It was expressly for the purpose of quietly living by themselves in their own way that they trekked into the north and occupied the country which they now possess. It may not have been a very lofty purpose, but it was a distinct and natural purpose, for it was to preserve their old ways and habits of living undisturbed; and therefore when an invasion of active and restless men of ideas other than their own, and with modern habits, came upon them . . . however much their revenue may be increased by the industry and enterprise of those incomers, still they felt themselves ousted from that life — a narrow life it may be — but still the life that they loved. It is not the case, let us bear in mind, of a few or even of a considerable number of immigrants coming into a great community and demanding municipal or political rights; what the Boers see in it is that they are being swamped and upset in the life which they prefer by this huge invasion. Therefore it is they regard the admission of these newcomers to their privileges with the greatest suspicion.

194. THE COLONIAL SECRETARY SUMS UP THE CASE AGAINST THE BOERS [2]

The Government has made an independent investigation, with the facts at their disposal, of the complaints of the Uitlanders. They have come to the

[1] *Parliamentary Debates.* 4th Series, LXXV, July 28, 1899, pp. 688–689 (condensed).
[2] *Parliamentary Debates.* 4th Series, LXXV, July 28, 1899, pp. 698–702, 715 (condensed).

opinion that they are well founded. . . . I am really happy, on this point, to rest myself on the statement of the right hon. Gentleman opposite [Sir Henry Campbell-Bannerman] made at Ilford the other day. He said: "It can hardly be questioned in any quarter that many of the complaints of the Uitlanders are well founded. They have no municipal government, police protection, organized maintenance of order, or the even-handed administration of justice, which, in all civilised communities, are regarded as the very elements of civil rights and liberty."

In that list, which is ample even if taken by itself, the right hon. Gentleman did not include the absolute loss of any political right whatever, the fact that a community, which is a majority in numbers, which finds at least nine-tenths of the whole taxation of the country, has not even a single seat in, or a single vote for, the governing body of the colony. . . .

I do not want to lay stress on individual grievances. . . . The danger lies in the situation. No doubt, such cases as the murder of the man Edgar, the general misconduct of the police, the subserviency of the courts of justice, the brutal and outrageous treatment of respectable Englishmen and coloured British subjects from the Mauritius and other colonies, are not to be lightly spoken of. They are grievances the continued existence of which would not be tolerated in any other country but the Transvaal, even for the length of time with which we have borne with them patiently. But if these grievances were isolated, and could be considered accidental; if when they are proved we could be sure of prompt and ready redress in answer to friendly remonstrances, I do not say . . . that they themselves would constitute a serious situation. What is serious is that these grievances are the result of a settled policy which has been in existence and pursued with the persistency of the Boer ever since the Convention of 1884 was signed. For fifteen years the Boer oligarchy — it is ridiculous to speak of it as a republic or democratic country — the efforts of that Government have been directed for the past fifteen years, contrary altogether to the spirit of the Convention, and in many cases, I believe, to the letter of the Convention, to place the Uitlanders, who are mainly British subjects, in a position of distinct and definite inferiority to the Boer inhabitants of the Transvaal. . . . In the fifteen years of which I have already spoken we have been five times brought to a crisis under different Governments, and once such a state of things has provoked an insurrection. . . . Just consider the extraordinary position of these people. Here is a country, mainly inhabited by British subjects, surrounded almost for its entire circumference by British colonies, whose foreign relations are under the control of the British Government, and yet where British subjects are placed in a position of humiliating inferiority, where they are subject to injury, and even to outrage, and where the friendly remonstrances of the suzerain Power are treated with contempt. What is the natural and necessary result of this policy? This matter is sometimes discussed as if it were a question of some petty reform — the right hon. Gentleman has tried to represent it as a matter of two years difference in the qualification of the franchise. It is nothing of the kind. It is the power and authority of the British Empire. It is the position of Great Britain in South Africa. It is the question of our predominance and how it is to be interpreted, and it is the question of peace throughout the whole of South Africa. . . .

No one dreams of acquiring the country, which we of our free will retroceded. No one has any wish whatever to interfere with the independence which we have granted; on the contrary, we desire to strengthen this independence. We desire to place it on a firm basis by turning discontented aliens into loyal fellow-citizens of the Dutch. . . . The condition of our non-interference is that the Government of the Transvaal should accept in principle, and make some approach in practice to, that equality of condition between the two white races which was intended to be provided by the Convention, and was certainly promised in the interviews and conferences before the Convention was signed.

CHAPTER XIII

INTERNATIONAL RELATIONS, 1871–1914

SECTION I. GERMAN DIPLOMACY, THE TRIPLE ALLIANCE

After 1871 Bismarck was most anxious to guard against a new war between France and Germany. While he knew that France was not strong enough to undertake alone such a war, he feared that she might secure the aid of other Powers. According to the following selection from his Reflections and Reminiscences *he was also afraid that a great struggle would develop between the principle of monarchy and the forces of radicalism. Fear of international socialism was at that time very strong. With the object of preserving the* status quo, *therefore, he brought about in 1872 an informal union of the rulers of Austria, Russia, and Prussia, known to history as the Dreikaiserbund or League of the Three Emperors. This union was strengthened the following year by a secret military agreement between Russia and Germany, each promising military aid to the other in case of attack by a third European Power, as well as by a written agreement between the three Emperors that they would consult one another on matters where their interests diverged.*

195. THE LEAGUE OF THE THREE EMPERORS (DREIKAISERBUND) [1]

THE triple alliance which I originally sought to conclude after the peace of Frankfort, and about which I had already sounded Vienna and St. Petersburg, from Meaux, in September 1870, was an alliance of the three Emperors with the further idea of bringing into it monarchical Italy. It was designed for the struggle which, as I feared, was before us; between the two European tendencies which Napoleon called Republican and Cossack, and which I, according to our present ideas, should designate on the one side as the system of order on a monarchical basis, and on the other as the social republic to the level of which the anti-monarchical development is wont to sink, either slowly or by leaps and bounds, until the conditions thus created become intolerable, and the disappointed populace are ready for a violent return to monarchical institutions in a Caesarean form. I consider

[1] Bismarck, *The Man and the Statesman.* Translated from the German under the Supervision of A. J. Butler. 2 vols. London, Smith, Elder, and Co., 1898. vol. II, pp. 248–249.

that the task of escaping from this *circulus vitiosus,* or, if possible, of sparing the present generation and their children an entrance into it, ought to be more closely incumbent on the strong existing monarchies, those monarchies which still have a vigorous life, than any rivalry over the fragments of nations which people the Balkan peninsula. If the monarchical governments have no understanding of the necessity for holding together in the interests of political and social order, but to make themselves subservient to the chauvinistic impulses of their subjects, I fear that the international revolutionary and social struggles which will have to be fought out will be all the more dangerous, and take such a form that the victory on the part of monarchical order will be more difficult. Since 1871 I have sought for the most certain assurance against those struggles in the alliance of the three Emperors, and also in the effort to impart to the monarchical principle in Italy a firm support in that alliance. I was not without hope of a lasting success when the meeting of the three Emperors took place at Berlin in September 1872, and this was followed by the visits of my Emperor to St. Petersburg in May, of the King of Italy to Berlin in September, and of the German Emperor to Vienna in the October of the next year. The first clouding over of that hope was caused in 1875 by the provocations of Prince Gortchakoff, who spread the lie that we intended to fall upon France before she had recovered from her wounds.

Russia not having gained all that she had hoped for from the Congress of Berlin in 1878, there was an outburst of indignation in Russia against Bismarck, who was held primarily responsible for this alleged defeat of Russian interests. Continuation of the co-operation between Russia and Germany inaugurated by the Dreikaiserbund *of 1872–1873 therefore became for the time being impossible. So Bismarck turned to Austria and concluded with her in 1879 a defensive alliance, of which the two principal articles are given in the selection that follows. " The Austro-German Alliance," says Professor Fay, " consolidated the Central Empires and became henceforth, until their collapse in November, 1918, the very foundation rock of German policy." (Origins of the World War, vol. I, p. 69.)*

196. EXTRACTS FROM THE AUSTRO–GERMAN TREATY OF 1879 [1]

ARTICLE I.

Should, contrary to their hope, and against the loyal desire of the two High Contracting Parties, one of the two Empires be attacked by Russia,

[1] Pribram, *The Secret Treaties of Austria-Hungary, 1879–1914.* Cambridge, Harvard University Press, 1920, pp. 27, 29.

the High Contracting Parties are bound to come to the assistance one of the other with the whole war strength of their Empires, and accordingly only to conclude peace together and upon mutual agreement.

ARTICLE II.

Should one of the High Contracting Parties be attacked by another Power, the other High Contracting Party binds itself hereby, not only not to support the aggressor against its high Ally, but to observe at least a benevolent neutral attitude towards its fellow Contracting Party.

Should, however, the attacking party in such a case be supported by Russia, either by an active coöperation or by military measures which constitute a menace to the Party attacked, then the obligation stipulated in Article I of this Treaty, for reciprocal assistance with the whole fighting force, becomes equally operative, and the conduct of the war by the two High Contracting Parties shall in this case also be in common until the conclusion of a common peace.

In 1882 Italy sought and obtained an alliance with Austria and Germany. Thus was constituted the famous Triple Alliance which, renewed at intervals, lasted until the outbreak of the World War. In its origins it was essentially defensive in character.

The principal articles of the Treaty of 1882 are given in the following selection.

197. THE TRIPLE ALLIANCE. ARTICLES I TO VII OF THE TREATY OF 1882 BETWEEN AUSTRIA–HUNGARY, GERMANY, AND ITALY, WITH ADDITIONAL MINISTERIAL DECLARATION [1]

ARTICLE I.

The High Contracting Parties mutually promise peace and friendship, and will enter into no alliance or engagement directed against any one of their States.

They engage to proceed to an exchange of ideas on political and economic questions of a general nature which may arise, and they further promise one another mutual support within the limits of their own interests.

ARTICLE II.

In case Italy, without direct provocation on her part, should be attacked by France for any reason whatsoever, the two other Contracting Parties shall

[1] Pribram, op. cit., pp. 65, 67, 69.

be bound to lend help and assistance with all their forces to the Party attacked.

This same obligation shall devolve upon Italy in case of any aggression without direct provocation by France against Germany.

ARTICLE III.

If one, or two, of the High Contracting Parties, without direct provocation on their part, should chance to be attacked and to be engaged in a war with two or more Great Powers nonsignatory to the present Treaty, the *casus foederis* will arise simultaneously for all the High Contracting Parties.

ARTICLE IV.

In case a Great Power nonsignatory to the present Treaty should threaten the security of the states of one of the High Contracting Parties, and the threatened Party should find itself forced on that account to make war against it, the two others bind themselves to observe towards their Ally a benevolent neutrality. Each of them reserves to itself, in this case, the right to take part in the war, if it should see fit, to make common cause with its Ally.

ARTICLE V.

If the peace of any of the High Contracting Parties should chance to be threatened under the circumstances foreseen by the preceding Articles, the High Contracting Parties shall take counsel together in ample time as to the military measures to be taken with a view to eventual coöperation.

They engage henceforward, in all cases of common participation in a war, to conclude neither armistice, nor peace, nor treaty, except by common agreement among themselves.

ARTICLE VI.

The High Contracting Parties mutually promise secrecy as to the contents and existence of the present Treaty.

ARTICLE VII.

The present Treaty shall remain in force during the space of five years, dating from the day of the exchange of ratifications.

MINISTERIAL DECLARATION.

The Royal Italian Government declares that the provisions of the secret Treaty concluded May 20, 1882, between Italy, Austria-Hungary, and Germany, cannot, as has been previously agreed, in any case be regarded as being directed against England.

SECTION II. THE FORMATION OF THE TRIPLE ENTENTE

Toward the end of the second decade after the Franco-Prussian War common fears and suspicion of Germany drew France and Russia closer together. Russian loans, floated in Paris instead of in Berlin, gave thousands of Frenchmen a financial interest in Russia's welfare. Next France began to supply Russia with guns modelled on the Lebel rifle. Then came the French military mission to Russia which paved the way, as is shown in the following selection, for a general understanding between the military authorities of the two countries.

198. FIRST STEPS TOWARD A FRANCO-RUSSIAN ALLIANCE [1]

[Extract from a Letter of M. de Laboulaye, French Ambassador at St. Petersburg, to M. Ribot, Minister of Foreign Affairs.]

St. Petersburg, August 24, 1890.

Private:

After having passed fifteen days at the camp at Krasnoë-Selo and at the Narva manoeuvers, General Boisdeffre is about to return to France. He will convey to Your Excellency his interesting impressions of this useful visit during which he was permitted to be present at the meeting of the two Emperors.[2] But the most important object of his visit, the object for which I had desired to have a French general officer invited to the manoeuvers, is what ought particularly to strike the attention of the Government.

The *rapprochement* between France and Russia which scarcely three years ago seemed to almost everybody an illusion, a mirage with which we allowed ourselves to be deceived, has little by little become so real, so solid, that it is not believed by anyone that an official visit like that of the Emperor William can injure it. It would not have been enough, however, for us merely to state this platonic result; it was necessary to garner the consequences from it. It would have been inexpedient, however, to look for these consequences in the field of politics. Not to speak of the resistance which the independent character of a sovereign who insists on his complete liberty of action would have offered, there were two difficulties on our side which it was important to avoid. The first is that an openly declared *entente* would have immediately consolidated the Triple Alliance which is in a fair way to become enfeebled through want of nourishment; the second, it must be admitted, is that it is to our interest not to reveal a defect of our Constitution, which, for fear of making the executive power too strong, has taken away

---

[1] *Ministère des affaires étrangères. Documents diplomatiques. L'Alliance Franco-Russe.* 1890–1893. Chapter I, No. 1. (Translation.)

[2] The tsar and the German Emperor. (Editor's note.)

from the executive the essential prerogative of concluding treaties and in consequence has deprived our foreign policy of the advantages of secrecy. There remained the field of military affairs. That could be used. After the good proceedings by which we facilitated the arming of the Russian infantry there seemed only one step more to be taken to enter into relations. It was that step which I hoped the special mission of General Boisdeffre could bring about.

Has this hope been realized as fully as was anticipated? From what M. de Boisdeffre has said to me I am inclined to believe so. The intimate conversations which his former position as Military Attaché at St. Petersburg, as well as his present position, enabled him to have almost daily both with the Minister of War and with General Obroutcheff, Chief of the General Staff, make it possible for me to say with authority that a contact has been established, which may be used in their future relations, between the two General Staffs. A first conversation, very vague, has led to others, based on the hypothesis, not to say the principle, that the two armies will have to act simultaneously in case of an attack, in whatever manner it may present itself, of which both would have reason to fear the effects. . . .

Laboulaye.

The general understanding between the military authorities of France and Russia took definite and written form in the Military Convention of August, 1892, the text of which is here quoted in translation. Even this written instrument was signed only by the Russian and French Chiefs of Staff, though it was approved at the time in principle by the tsar. Not until January, 1894, was it given a binding effect by an exchange of diplomatic notes between responsible civil officials of the two countries. This exchange of notes gave the Convention the force of a treaty. But it remained secret until 1918 when it was officially published.

The Franco-Russian Alliance, like the Triple Alliance, was defensive in purpose.

199. THE FRANCO–RUSSIAN ALLIANCE. MILITARY CONVENTION OF AUGUST 18, 1892 [1]

France and Russia, animated by a common desire to preserve peace and having no other purpose than to prepare for the necessities of a defensive war, provoked by an attack of the forces of the Triple Alliance against either of them, have agreed on the following provisions:

1. If France is attacked by Germany, or by Italy supported by Germany, Russia shall employ all her available forces to fight Germany.

[1] *Ministère des affaires étrangères. Documents diplomatiques. L'Alliance Franco-Russe.* Paris, Imprimerie Nationale, 1918, p. 92, No. 71. (Translation.)

If Russia is attacked by Germany, or by Austria supported by Germany, France shall employ all her available forces to fight Germany.

2. In case the forces of the Triple Alliance or of any one of the Powers belonging to it, should be mobilized, France and Russia, at the first word of this event, and without need of a previous agreement, shall mobilize immediately and simultaneously all their forces, and shall transport them as near as possible to their frontiers.

3. The forces available which must be employed against Germany shall be, for France 1,300,000 men, for Russia, 700,000 to 800,000 men.

These forces shall be brought into action so completely and with such speed that Germany will have to fight simultaneously in the East and in the West.

4. The Staffs of the armies of the two countries shall constantly take council together to prepare for and to facilitate the execution of the above-mentioned measures.

They shall communicate to each other, in time of peace, all the information in regard to the armies of the Triple Alliance which is already in their possession or which shall come into their possession.

The ways and means of corresponding in time of war shall be studied and worked out in advance.

5. France and Russia shall not conclude peace separately.

6. The present Agreement shall have the same duration as the Triple Alliance.

7. All the clauses enumerated above shall be kept absolutely secret.

The Fashoda crisis was an outcome of the colonial expansion of England and France in Africa. Both countries were eager to get control of the region of the Upper Nile. In 1898 the French Government sent an expedition under Captain Marchand with orders to take possession of this territory. General Kitchener hurried south from Khartum to prevent the French from achieving their purpose. The two emissaries of imperialism met at Fashoda. The incident led to angry talk of war in both countries.

The story of the Fashoda crisis is told in the recently published British Documents on the Origins of the War.

200. *THE FASHODA CRISIS, 1898* [1]

[Extract from a Telegram sent by Sir Herbert Kitchener (later Earl Kitchener), Sirdar of the Egyptian Army, to Mr. (later Sir) R. Rodd, British Acting Agent at Cairo. Cairo, September 25, 1898.]

[1] *British Documents on the Origins of the War.* G. P. Gooch and Harold Temperley, Editors. Vol. I. *The End of British Isolation*, p. 67, No. 193; p. 171, No. 198; p. 188, No. 227; p. 192, No. 234.

I have just returned here from Fashoda where I found Captain Marchand, accompanied by eight officers and 120 men, located in the old Government buildings, over which they had hoisted the French flag; I had sent a letter announcing my approach the day before my arrival at Fashoda. A small row-boat carrying the French flag brought me a reply from Captain Marchand on the following morning, the 19th September, stating that he had reached Fashoda on the 10th July, his Government having given him instructions to occupy the Bahr-el-Ghazal as far as the confluence of the Bahr-el-Jebel, as well as the Shilluk country on the left bank of the White Nile as far as Fashoda. . . .

When we arrived at Fashoda, Captain Marchand and M. Germain came on board, and I at once stated that the presence of a French force at Fashoda and in the Valley of the Nile was regarded as a direct infringement of the rights of the Egyptian Government and of that of Great Britain, and I protested in the strongest terms against their occupation of Fashoda and their hoisting the French flag in the dominions of His Highness the Khedive. In reply, Captain Marchand stated that he had precise orders to occupy the country and to hoist the French flag over the Government building at Fashoda, and that it was impossible for him to retire without receiving orders from his Government to that effect, but that he did not expect that these orders would be delayed. On my pressing him to say whether, seeing that I had a preponderating force, he was prepared to resist the hoisting of the Egyptian flag at Fashoda, he hesitated and replied that resistance was impossible. I then caused the flag to be hoisted on a ruined bastion of the old Egyptian fortifications about 500 yards south of the French flag, and on the only road which leads to the interior from the French position, which is surrounded by impassable marshes on all sides. Before leaving for the south, I handed to Captain Marchand a formal protest in writing, on behalf of the British and Egyptian Governments, against any occupation by France of any part of the Nile Valley, such occupation being an infringement of the rights of these Governments which I could not recognize.

．　．　．　．　．　．　．　．　．　．　．　．

[Secret Despatch of Sir E. Monson, British Ambassador at Paris, to the Marquess of Salisbury, British Secretary of State for Foreign Affairs. Paris, September 28, 1898.]

Fashoda. Minister of Foreign Affairs (M. Delcassé) initiated to-day a conversation on this burning question by stating that French Minister in London was instructed to speak to your Lordship about it. Much of what passed between us was but a repetition of previous conversations, but his Excellency was just as determined as ever upon the right of France to occupy territory practically abandoned by Egypt, and contested the right of Great

Britain to warn off other Powers which had not recognized her sphere of influence or to assert that France was committing an unfriendly act in advancing on Upper Nile. He at the same time declared his conviction that honest discussion between the two Governments would soon result in an understanding. He reiterated that it is the desire of the present French Government to make a friend of England, adding that between ourselves he would much prefer an Anglo-French to a Franco-Russian Alliance. He again entreated me to take account of existing excitement in France, which is becoming dangerous and might in an instant break out into overt acts, repeating what he had said yesterday: " Do not ask me for the impossible; do not drive me into a corner." He admitted that he knew feeling in England is strong, but he argued that Englishmen are not so excitable as the French, and felt sentimental considerations less deeply. I replied that he could not exaggerate strength of feeling in England on this subject, both on the part of Government and the public, and the knowledge of this caused me great apprehension. He said: " You surely would not break with us over Fashoda? " To which I answered that it was exactly that which I feared. Another observation was: " In such event we shall not stand alone; but I repeat I would rather have England for our ally than that other." Personally, I can see very little hope of their sending M. Marchand an order to leave Fashoda, but at the same time I must state that Minister of Foreign Affairs has several times referred to possibility of " transaction."

· · · · · · · · · · · · ·

[The Marquess of Salisbury to Sir E. Monson. Foreign Office, November 4, 1898.]

The French Ambassador informed me to-day that the decision had been taken by his Government to withdraw M. Marchand's party from Fashoda and to send him back there to carry out that decision, and that orders to that effect had been sent to Cairo.

· · · · · · · · · · · · ·

[Sir E. Monson to the Marquess of Salisbury. Paris, November 11, 1898.]

The language which M. Delcassé held (sic) to me the day before yesterday about Crete, when I asked him his opinion as to Russian and Italian proposals, seemed to be tinctured with a certain bitterness. The gist of what he said was that, in order to maintain the accord between the four Powers, France would agree to anything to which the other three assented.

In fact, his tone seemed to be pitched in the " humiliation " key, and his meaning to be — " What is the use of France having an opinion of her own about anything now-a-days? "

I was the first of his visitors on that reception afternoon, but those of my colleagues whom I have since seen tell me that he was throughout the afternoon profoundly depressed.

Despite the traditional hostility between England and France, bitterly if temporarily intensified by the Fashoda crisis of 1898, certain far-sighted men in both countries toward the end of the nineteenth century began to believe that the two nations should draw closer together. The growing power and assertiveness of Germany gave rise to common fears. In France the moving spirit in the rapprochement *between the two countries was M. Delcassé, who became French Minister of Foreign Affairs in 1898. He found an enthusiastic friend of France across the Channel in the person of King Edward VII, who had spent many of the happiest days of his prolonged youth in Paris or on the Riviera.*

In the spring of 1903, on the occasion of his first formal visit to Paris as King of England, Edward expressed his desire for friendship between the two countries in the following tactful speech.

201. KING EDWARD VII'S PARIS SPEECH OF 1903[1]

It is scarcely necessary to tell you with what sincere pleasure I find myself once more in Paris, to which, as you know, I have paid very frequent visits with ever-increasing pleasure, and for which I feel an attachment fortified by so many happy and ineffaceable memories. The days of hostility between the two countries are, I am certain, happily at an end. I know of no two countries whose prosperity is more interdependent. There may have been misunderstandings and causes of dissension in the past, but that is all happily over and forgotten. The friendship of the two countries is my constant preoccupation, and I count on you all who enjoy French hospitality in their magnificent city to aid me to reach this goal.

Negotiations looking toward an understanding between England and France proceeded rapidly from the summer of 1903 to the spring of 1904. In the following selection are given, first, some of the steps in these negotiations, and second, the terms of the Convention of April 8, 1904, arranged between the two countries on matters relating to Egypt and Morocco. The essential point of this arrangement was that England was to have a free hand in Egypt, France in Morocco. Other less significant Conventions were concluded at the same time, settling long-standing difficulties between the two countries in relation to Madagascar, the New Hebrides, Senegambia, Siam, the New-

---

[1] Quoted in G. P. Gooch, *History of Modern Europe, 1878–1919*, pp. 338–339. New York, Henry Holt and Company, 1923.

foundland fisheries, etc. The net product of all these agreements was the establishment of the famous Anglo-French Entente Cordiale.

202. *THE DEVELOPMENT OF THE ENTENTE CORDIALE BETWEEN ENGLAND AND FRANCE* [1]

[The Marquess of Lansdowne (Secretary of State for Foreign Affairs) to Sir E. Monson (British Ambassador at Paris).]

Foreign Office, July 2, 1903

M. Étienne called upon me at the Foreign Office to-day, and spoke to me at some length and with great freedom in regard to the political relations of France and Great Britain.

He told me that he was paying a short visit to this country in the hopes of promoting a good understanding between the two Governments. There seemed to him to be no really serious points of divergence between them, and the moment appeared to be particularly propitious for such a *rapprochement* as he suggested.

He passed in view the various political questions which have lately occupied the joint attention of the British and French Foreign Offices.

.   .   .   .

At the conclusion of the conversation, M. Étienne expressed his belief that the most serious menace to the peace of Europe lay in Germany, that a good understanding between France and England was the only means of holding German designs in check, and that if such an understanding could be arrived at, England would find that France would be able to exercise a salutary influence over Russia and thereby relieve us from many of our troubles with that country.

.   .   .   .

[The Marquess of Lansdowne to Sir E. Monson.]

Foreign Office, July 7, 1903

The French Ambassador mentioned to me some days before the President's arrival that it would be agreeable to M. Delcassé to meet me during his stay in London, and to discuss with me some of the points with regard to which his Excellency and I had at various times had conversations.

M. Delcassé called upon me this morning, and we exchanged ideas at some length in regard to these questions.

[1] *British Documents on the Origins of the War.* G. P. Gooch and Harold Temperley, Editors. Vol. II, *The Japanese Alliance and the French Entente*, p. 292, No. 256; p. 294, No. 357; p. 298, No. 359; p. 385 ff, No. 416.

After expressing the pleasure which it gave me to have this opportunity of learning his views at first hand, I said that, as he was aware, I had on several occasions discussed with M. Cambon the position of our two countries in Newfoundland, Morocco, Siam, the New Hebrides, and other parts of the world. Those discussions had, up to the present, not led to any definite results. They had, however, I thought, been useful in clearing the ground, and they certainly had led me to the conclusion that the points at issue between the two Governments were few in number, and by no means incapable of adjustment.

M. Delcassé expressed his entire agreement, and added that this view now prevailed in the French Chamber, which was inclined to take a reasonable, not to say friendly, line in regard to all such questions. As for the French Government, they had ceased to desire a wide extension of their Colonial possessions, and were intent, not upon adding to them, but upon consolidating them, and removing all sources of future trouble within them and upon their borders.

I replied that His Majesty's Government were influenced by very similar sentiments, and that I certainly thought the opportunity was in every way propitious for a frank exchange of opinions between the two Governments.

. . . .

[The Earl of Cromer, (British Consul-General and Agent in Egypt), to the Marquess of Lansdowne, Cairo, July 17, 1903.]

. . . .

The main question is manifestly Morocco.

My own opinion, which is one I have entertained for a long time, is distinctly in favour of making concessions in Morocco in return for counter-concessions in Egypt and elsewhere, but if we are to adopt this policy we ought to do so with our eyes open to what it means.

I observe that M. Étienne, in his conversation with you, stated that " the Sultan of Morocco's Government appeared to be on the point of falling to pieces," to which you replied that " these Eastern Monarchies often managed to survive in spite of apparent decay and seemingly unsurmountable difficulties." This is perfectly true, but the reason is also obvious. It is that the agony of these decadent Oriental States, such as Turkey and Persia, is prolonged owing to the dissensions and rivalries amongst the possible heirs to the succession. I think it would be found, in practice, that if once the French succession were secured, the agony of Morocco would not be of long duration. Some opportunity would speedily occur for putting an end to it. Hence, in spite of M. Delcassé's statement, of which I do not doubt the sincerity, that the French Government has no desire to " *brusquer les choses,*" I have very little doubt that, when once the French are assured that they can make good their rights to the succession, without any risk of serious interference on our part, Morocco will, to all intents and purposes, become before long a French province.

The question, therefore, to my mind is this: have we any objection to Morocco becoming a French province? Personally, I see none, provided always (1) that we get an adequate *quid pro quo* in Egypt and elsewhere; and (2) that the French comply with your three conditions as regards Morocco. These, if I understand rightly, are (1) the seaboard is to be neutralised; (2) a proper regard is to be shown to Spanish interests and susceptibilities; and (3) a guarantee is to be obtained that British trade and enterprise will not be placed at any legal disadvantage in Morocco.

. . . .

[Declaration between the United Kingdom and France respecting Egypt and Morocco. Signed at London, April 8, 1904.]

Article I.

His Britannic Majesty's Government declare that they have no intention of altering the political status of Egypt.

The Government of the French Republic, for their part, declare that they will not obstruct the action of Great Britain in that country by asking that a limit of time be fixed for the British occupation or in any other manner, and that they give their assent to the draft Khedivial Decree annexed to the present Arrangement, containing the guarantees considered necessary for the protection of the interests of the Egyptian bondholders, on the condition that, after its promulgation, it cannot be modified in any way without the consent of the Powers Signatory of the Convention of London of 1885.

It is agreed that the post of Director-General of Antiquities in Egypt shall continue, as in the past, to be entrusted to a French *savant*.

The French schools in Egypt shall continue to enjoy the same liberty as in the past.

Article II.

The Government of the French Republic declare that they have no intention of altering the political status of Morocco.

His Britannic Majesty's Government, for their part, recognise that it appertains to France, more particularly as a Power whose dominions are conterminous for a great distance with those of Morocco, to preserve order in that country, and to provide assistance for the purpose of all administrative, economic, financial, and military reforms which it may require.

They declare that they will not obstruct the action taken by France for this purpose, provided that such action shall leave intact the rights which Great Britain, in virtue of Treaties, Conventions, and usage, enjoys in

Morocco, including the right of coasting trade between the ports of Morocco, enjoyed by British vessels since 1901.

Article III.

His Britannic Majesty's Government, for their part, will respect the rights which France, in virtue of Treaties, Conventions, and usage, enjoys in Egypt, including the right of coasting trade between Egyptian ports accorded to French vessels.

Article IV.

The two Governments, being equally attached to the principle of commercial liberty both in Egypt and Morocco, declare that they will not, in those countries, countenance any inequality either in the imposition of customs duties or other taxes, or of railway transport charges.

The trade of both nations with Morocco and with Egypt shall enjoy the same treatment in transit through the French and British possessions in Africa. An Agreement between the two Governments shall settle the conditions of such transit and shall determine the points of entry.

This mutual engagement shall be binding for a period of thirty years. Unless this stipulation is expressly denounced at least one year in advance, the period shall be extended for five years at a time.

Nevertheless, the Government of the French Republic reserve to themselves in Morocco, and His Britannic Majesty's Government reserve to themselves in Egypt, the right to see that the concessions for roads, railways, ports, &c., are only granted on such conditions as will maintain intact the authority of the State over these great undertakings of public interest.

Article V.

His Britannic Majesty's Government declare that they will use their influence in order that the French officials now in the Egyptian service may not be placed under conditions less advantageous than those applying to the British officials in the same service.

The Government of the French Republic, for their part, would make no objection to the application of analogous conditions to British officials now in the Moorish service.

Article VI.

In order to insure the free passage of the Suez Canal, His Britannic Majesty's Government declare that they adhere to the stipulations of the Treaty of the 29th October, 1888, and that they agree to their being put in force. The free passage of the Canal being thus guaranteed, the execution of the last sentence of paragraph 1 as well as of paragraph 2 of Article VIII of that Treaty will remain in abeyance.

Article VII.

In order to secure the free passage of the Straits of Gibraltar, the two Governments agree not to permit the erection of any fortifications or strategic works on that portion of the coast of Morocco comprised between, but not including, Melilla and the heights which command the right bank of the River Sebou.

This condition does not, however, apply to the places at present in the occupation of Spain on the Moorish coast of the Mediterranean.

Article VIII.

The two Governments, inspired by their feeling of sincere friendship for Spain, take into special consideration the interests which that country derives from her geographical position and from her territorial possessions on the Moorish coast of the Mediterranean. In regard to these interests the French Government will come to an understanding with the Spanish Government.

The agreement which may be come to on the subject between France and Spain shall be communicated to His Britannic Majesty's Government.

Article IX.

The two Governments agree to afford to one another their diplomatic support, in order to obtain the execution of the clauses of the present Declaration regarding Egypt and Morocco.

In witness whereof his Excellency the Ambassador of the French Republic at the Court of His Majesty the King of the United Kingdom of Great Britain and Ireland and of the British Dominions beyond the Seas, Emperor of India, and His Majesty's Principal Secretary of State for Foreign Affairs, duly authorized for that purpose, have signed the present Declaration and have affixed thereto their seals.

Done at London, in duplicate, the 8th day of April, 1904.

(Signatures of Lord Lansdowne and M. Paul Cambon follow.)

Secret Article I.

In the event of either Government finding themselves constrained, by the force of circumstances, to modify their policy in respect to Egypt and Morocco, the engagements which they have undertaken towards each other by Articles IV, VI and VII of the Declaration of to-day's date would remain intact.

Secret Article II.

His Britannic Majesty's Government have no present intention of proposing to the Powers any changes in the system of the Capitulations, or in the judicial organisation of Egypt.

In the event of their considering it desirable to introduce in Egypt reforms tending to assimilate the Egyptian legislative system to that in force in other civilised countries, the Government of the French Republic will not refuse to entertain any such proposals, on the understanding that His Britannic Majesty's Government will agree to entertain the suggestions that the Government of the French Republic may have to make to them with a view of introducing similar reforms in Morocco.

Secret Article III.

The two Governments agree that a certain extent of Moorish territory adjacent to Melilla, Ceuta and other *Présides* should, whenever the Sultan ceases to exercise authority over it, come within the sphere of influence of Spain, and that the administration of the coast from Melilla as far as, but not including, the heights on the right bank of the Sebou shall be intrusted to Spain.

Nevertheless, Spain would previously have to give her formal assent to the provisions of Articles IV and VII of the Declaration of to-day's date, and undertake to carry them out.

She would also have to undertake not to alienate the whole or a part of the territories placed under her authority or in her sphere of influence.

Secret Article IV.

If Spain, when invited to assent to the provisions of the preceding article, should think proper to decline, the Arrangement between France and Great Britain, as embodied in the Declaration of today's date, would be none the less applicable.

Secret Article V.

Should the consent of the other Powers to the draft Decree mentioned in Article I of the Declaration of to-day's date not be obtained, the Government of the French Republic will not oppose the repayment at par of the Guaranteed, Privileged and Unified Debts after the 15th July, 1910.

Done at London, in duplicate, the 8th day of April, 1904.

(Signatures of Lord Lansdowne and M. Paul Cambon follow.)

British policy in the Middle East, as in the Near East, was consistently, throughout the period 1815–1907, animated by fear of Russian designs on India. About 1897 fear of Germany began to replace dread of Russia and the next ten years reveal a change in British orientation. France's efforts to reconcile her two great allies met with success when the conflicting ambitions of the British and the Russians in Persia were satisfied by the accord of 1907.

203. *THE TRIPLE ENTENTE. THE ANGLO–RUSSIAN AGREEMENT OF 1907* [1]

This Convention, which aimed at an amicable settlement of all questions likely to disturb the friendly relations of the two countries in Asia generally, and in Persia, Afghanistan and Tibet in particular, was signed on August 31 and officially communicated to the Powers in St. Petersburg on September 24. After reciting the desire of both Governments to maintain the integrity of Persia, and to allow all nations equal facilities for trade in that country, the Convention states that in certain parts, owing to their geographical proximity to their own territories, Great Britain and Russia have special interests. Accordingly (Art. I.); To the north of a line drawn from Kasr-i-Shirin, Ispahan, Yezd and Khakh to the junction of the Persian, Russian and Afghanistan frontiers, Great Britain agrees not to seek for itself or its own subjects or those of any other country any political or commercial concessions, such as railway, banking, telegraph, roads, transport or insurance, or to oppose the acquisition of such concessions by the Russian Government or its subjects. II. Russia gives a similar undertaking concerning the region to the south of a line extending from the Afghan frontier to Gazik, Birjand, Kerman and Bander Abbas. III. Russia and Great Britain agree not to oppose, without previous agreement, the granting of concessions to subjects of either country in the regions situated between the lines above mentioned. All existing concessions in the regions above designated are maintained. IV. The arrangements by which certain Persian revenues were pledged for the payment of the loans contracted by the Shah's Government with the Persian Banque d'Escompte and de Prêts and the Imperial Bank of Persia before the signing of the Convention are maintained. V. In the event of any irregularities in the redemption or service of these loans Russia may institute a control over the revenues situated within the zone defined by Article I. and Great Britain may do the same in the zone defined by Article II. But before instituting such a control the two Governments agree to a friendly exchange of ideas with a view to determining its nature, and avoiding any action in contravention of the principles of the Convention.

With the Convention a letter was published from Sir E. Grey to the British Ambassador at St. Petersburg, announcing that the Persian Gulf lay outside its scope, but that the Russian Government had stated during the negotiations that it did not deny the special interests of Great Britain in the Gulf; and it was intimated that Great Britain reasserted them.

Obviously this Convention is more favourable to Russia than to England in that the northern zone is of far greater commercial value than the southern

[1] Annual Register for 1907.

one. But Russia's influence and commercial position in Northern Persia could hardly have been shaken or checked unless at the risk of war. On the other hand, although the southern zone is of much less commercial value its strategic importance is great, especially as it includes the port of Bander Abbas.

SECTION III. ITALIAN DIPLOMACY

Despite the fact that she was a member of the Triple Alliance, Italy, in the last few years of the nineteenth century, began to drift toward a rapprochement with France. This rapprochement was furthered when Delcassé, in an agreement with England on March 21, 1899, strengthened Italian hope of controlling Tripoli in Northern Africa by indicating that France had no aspirations for territory east of Tunis.

There then followed the secret agreements between responsible officials of France and Italy, from which extracts are here quoted in translation. The net result was that Italy ceased to be a loyal member of the Triple Alliance in spirit though not in letter. In view of this double-dealing Italy's declaration of neutrality at the opening of the Great War is not surprising.

204. THE FRANCO-ITALIAN AGREEMENTS OF 1900-1902. EXTRACTS [1]

[Letter of M. Barrère, French Ambassador at Rome, to the Marquis Visconti Venosta, Italian Minister of Foreign Affairs.]

Rome, 14 December, 1900

Following the conclusion of the Agreement of March 21, 1899, between France and Great Britain, my Government, replying to your honorable predecessor, had occasion to give him, through me, some explanations of a character to dissipate all doubt in regard to the significance of that document.

Since then Your Excellency has expressed the opinion that this assurance, reiterated in a more explicit manner, would help to strengthen the good relations between our two countries.

I have therefore been authorized by the Minister of Foreign Affairs to make known to Your Excellency, because of the friendly relations which have been established between France and Italy, and with the idea that this explanation will lead to their still further improvement, that the Agreement of the 21st of March, 1899, in leaving outside of the division of influence which it sanctions, the vilayet of Tripoli, marks for the French sphere of influence a boundary beyond which the Government of the Republic has no

[1] *Ministère des affaires étrangères. Documents diplomatiques. Les accords Franco-italiens de 1900–1902.* Paris, Imprimerie Nationale, 1920. (Translation.)

intention of going, and that it has no intention of interrupting communication by caravan between Tripoli and the regions specified in the said Agreement.

These explanations, which we have agreed to keep secret, I have no doubt will help to consolidate, in this matter as in others, the friendly relations between our two countries.

[Letter of the Marquis Visconti Venosta, Italian Minister of Foreign Affairs, to M. Barrère, French Ambassador at Rome.]

Rome, 16 December, 1900.

The present situation in the Mediterranean and the eventualities that might come of it have formed between us the subject of a friendly exchange of ideas, our governments being both equally animated by the wish to remove, in this matter also, all that might tend to compromise, in the present and in the future, mutual good-will.

In that which more particularly concerns Morocco, it develops from our conferences that the purpose of the action of France is to exercise and to safeguard the rights which result to her from the proximity of her territory to this Empire.

I have recognized that an action of this sort, thus defined, is not, from our point of view, of a character to injure the interests of Italy as a Mediterranean Power.

It has been made clear, likewise, that if there should develop a modification of the political or territorial status of Morocco, Italy, as a measure of reciprocity, would reserve the right to develop eventually her influence in relation to the Tripoli-Cyrenaica region.

These explanations, which we have agreed to keep secret, will contribute, I am sure, to the consolidation of the friendly relations between our two countries.

[M. Barrère, French Ambassador at Rome, to M. Prinetti, Italian Minister of Foreign Affairs. (Extract)]

Rome, November 1, 1902.

In case Italy should be the object of direct or indirect aggression on the part of one or more Powers, France will maintain a strict neutrality.

The same shall hold good in case Italy, as a result of direct provocation, should be forced, in order to defend her honor or her security, to take the initiative in declaring war. In this eventuality the Royal Government shall communicate previously their intention to the Government of the Republic, which will thus be enabled to determine whether they are clearly acting as a result of direct provocation.

· · · · · · · · · ·

M. Prinetti to M. Barrère. (Extract)

Rome, November 1, 1902.

In case France should be the object of direct or indirect aggression on the part of one or more Powers, Italy will maintain a strict neutrality.

The same shall hold good in case France, as a result of direct provocation, should be forced, in order to defend her honor or her security, to take the initiative in declaring war. In this eventuality the Government of the Republic shall communicate previously their intention to the Royal Government, which will thus be enabled to determine whether they are clearly acting as a result of direct provocation.

SECTON IV. PLAYING WITH THE FIRES OF NATIONALISM

The international friction that developed with the formation of the alliances and the occurrence of international " incidents" was unfortunately stimulated in various countries by unwise books, articles, and speeches. One such article, from which a brief extract is here quoted, appeared in the English periodical, the Saturday Review, *on September 11, 1897. Even today parts of this article are quoted in certain German school-books as evidence that England desired war with Germany. The fallacy of such reasoning is obvious.*

205. " GERMANY MUST BE DESTROYED."[1]

A million petty disputes build up the greatest cause of war the world has ever seen. If Germany were extinguished to-morrow, the day after to-morrow there is not an Englishman in the world who would not be the richer. Nations have fought for years over a city or a right of succession; must they not fight for two hundred and fifty thousand pounds of yearly commerce? . . . To this pass has the muddling of the German Emperor brought Germany, and at a time when England has awakened to what is alike inevitable and her best hope of prosperity. *Germaniam esse delendam.* (Germany must be destroyed.)

The Kaiser William II had an unhappy facility for unintentionally stirring up trouble by his utterances. After the Jameson Raid of 1895, when Dr. Jameson, with 500 followers, went into the Transvaal to overthrow the Boer Government, the Kaiser sent the following telegram to President Kruger of the Transvaal. It naturally aroused great indignation in England.

1 Extract from an article in the *Saturday Review* (London) for September 11, 1897.

206. *THE KAISER'S TELEGRAM TO PRESIDENT KRUGER.* [1]

Berlin, January 3, 1896.

I congratulate you heartily, that you have succeeded, without appealing to the aid of friendly Powers, relying only on your own people and your own energy, against the armed hordes which had broken into your country as destroyers of the peace, in restoring peace and in guarding the independence of the country against attacks from without.

Wilhelm I. R.

German influence in the Near East was viewed with alarm by England, France, and Russia. In 1898 the Kaiser aroused apprehensions in these countries by a trip to the Ottoman Empire, in the course of which he made the following speech at Damascus.

207. *THE KAISER'S SPEECH AT DAMASCUS, NOVEMBER 8, 1898.* [2]

In view of the courtesies which have been extended to us here it behooves me, in the name of her Majesty the Empress as well as in my own behalf, to thank you for the reception, for everything, indeed, which has been done for us in all the cities of this land, above all to thank you for our glorious reception in the city of Damascus. Deeply moved by this overwhelming manifestation, moved, too, by the consciousness of standing on the very spot where one of the most knightly rulers of all time, the great Sultan Saladin, dwelt, a knight without fear and without reproach, who often had to teach his enemies the true way of chivalry, I seize with joy the opportunity, above everything else, to thank His Majesty, the Sultan Abdul Hamid, for his hospitality. May His Majesty the Sultan and the 300 million Mohammedans who, living scattered over the face of the earth, revere him as their Caliph, be assured of this, that at all times the German Emperor will be their friend. I drink to the health of His Majesty the Sultan Abdul Hamid.

In 1908 the Kaiser permitted the publication of an interview which he said — and there is every reason to believe him — was intended to strengthen friendly relations between Germany and England. Instead it had just the opposite effect and anyone who reads the interview can easily see why. There

---

[1] *Die Grosse Politik.* Vol. 11, p. 31. No. 2610. (Translation.)
[2] Quoted in Hohlfeld, *Deutsche Reichsgeschichte in Dokumenten 1849–1926,* Deutsche Verlagsgesellschaft für Politik und Geschichte, Berlin, 1927, Number 113. (Translation.)

was great indignation in Germany as well as in England at this tactless effort of the Emperor. The German Chancellor even went so far as to say that " the knowledge that the publication has not produced the desired result in England, and has aroused excitement and painful regret in Germany, will lead him (i.e. the Kaiser) henceforth to observe even in private conversation the reserve which is essential to the unity of our policy and the authority of the Crown."

The following account of the interview is taken from the London Times.

208. THE KAISER'S "DAILY TELEGRAPH INTERVIEW."[1]

The article referred to appeared yesterday in our contemporary, the *Daily Telegraph*. It is described as being from the pen of a "diplomatist" who has "long passed from public into private life," and is put forward as a "calculated indiscretion" designed to allay the suspicion with which Englishmen sometimes regard the German Emperor. With this object in view, the writer puts on record the substance of "a lengthy conversation" with his Majesty which it was his "recent privilege" to enjoy. We reproduce its leading features in the following summary: —

"The Emperor, who is stated to have spoken with 'impulsive and unusual frankness,' began by declaring that Englishmen, in giving the rein to suspicions 'unworthy of a great nation,' were 'mad as March hares.' 'What more can I do,' he asked, 'than I have done? I declared with all the emphasis at my command, in my speech at Guildhall, that my heart is set upon peace, and that it is one of my dearest wishes to live on the best of terms with England.

"My task is not of the easiest. The prevailing sentiment among large sections of the middle and lower classes of my own people is not friendly to England. I am, therefore, so to speak, in a minority in my own land, but it is a minority of the best elements, just as it is in England with respect to Germany. That is another reason why I resent your refusal to accept my pledged word that I am the friend of England."

The writer reminded his Majesty that "not England alone, but the whole of Europe, had viewed with disapproval the recent action of Germany in allowing the German Consul to return from Tangier to Fez." His Majesty replied, "with a gesture of impatience," that German subjects in Fez were "crying for help and protection."

"And why not send him? Are those who charge Germany with having stolen a march on the other Powers aware that the French Consular representative had already been in Fez for several months when Dr. Vassel set out?"

[1] The *Times*, London, October 29, 1908.

The Emperor then reverted to "the subject uppermost in his mind — his proved friendship for England." It was commonly believed in England, he said, that during the South African war Germany had been consistently hostile to her. German opinion, he admitted, was hostile — "bitterly hostile;" but not so official Germany. In fact, while other European peoples had received and fêted the Boer delegates who came to solicit European intervention, he alone had refused to receive them at Berlin, "where the German people would have crowned them with flowers." His Majesty continued: —

"Again, when the struggle was at its height, the German Government was invited by the Governments of France and Russia to join with them in calling upon England to put an end to the war. The moment had come, they said, not only to save the Boer Republics, but also to humiliate England to the dust. What was my reply? I said that so far from Germany joining in any concerted European action to put pressure upon England and bring about her downfall, Germany would always keep aloof from politics that could bring her into complications with a Sea Power like England. Posterity will one day read the exact terms of the telegram — now in the archives of Windsor Castle — in which I informed the Sovereign of England of the answer I had returned to the Powers which then sought to compass her fall. Englishmen who now insult me by doubting my word should know what were my actions in the hour of their adversity."

These were not the only proofs which his Majesty had given of sympathy with the British cause: —

"Just at the time of your Black Week, in the December of 1899, when disasters followed one another in rapid succession, I received a letter from Queen Victoria, my revered grandmother, written in sorrow and affliction, and bearing manifest traces of the anxieties which were preying upon her mind and health. I at once returned a sympathetic reply. Nay, I did more. I bade one of my officers procure for me as exact an account as he could obtain, of the number of combatants in South Africa on both sides, and of the actual position of the opposing forces. With the figures before me, I worked out what I considered to be the best plan of campaign under the circumstances, and submitted it to my General Staff for their criticism. Then I despatched it to England, and that document, likewise, is among the State papers at Windsor Castle, awaiting the serenely impartial verdict of history. And, as a matter of curious coincidence, let me add that the plan which I formulated ran very much on the same lines as that which was actually adopted by Lord Roberts, and carried by him into successful operation."

In conclusion, his Majesty dwelt upon the importance to Germany of a powerful fleet. Germany must be able to protect her growing commerce and manifold interests "in even the most distant seas." "Germany," he went on, "looks ahead. She must be prepared for any eventualities in the Far East. Who can foresee what may take place in the Pacific in the days to come?" Looking to the accomplished rise of Japan and the possible national awakening of China, he urged that "only those Powers which have great navies will be listened to with respect when the future of the Pacific comes to be solved," and that even England herself may welcome the existence of a German fleet "when they speak together on the same side in the great debates of the future."

SECTION V. INTERNATIONAL CRISES, 1905–1911

The Anglo-French Agreement of 1904 naturally aroused apprehension in Germany. Among other things the German Chancellor, von Bülow, feared that German prestige would suffer from the attempt of France and England to dispose of Morocco without consulting Germany and that France would try to establish an economic monopoly in that country to the injury of German interests. As a protest the Chancellor asked the Kaiser to land at Tangier on his way from Hamburg to Corfu. The Kaiser reluctantly agreed and paid his brief visit on March 31st, 1905.

The incident aroused excitement and indignation in France and there ensued a grave international crisis.

The following account by Baron Schoen, who was with the Kaiser at the time, differs somewhat in detail from certain other narratives of the visit. (See Fay, Origins of the World War, vol. I, p. 184, footnote.)

209. THE MOROCCAN CRISIS OF 1905. THE LANDING OF THE KAISER IN TANGIER.[1]

Gibraltar, 31 March, 1905.

After overcoming no slight technical difficulties in landing in Tangier, a very fitting reception on the quay from Moroccan officials and the German colony. Ride through gaily bedecked streets amid the indescribable jubilation of natives and European population; a magnificent oriental scene, with splendid weather. In the Embassy, reception of Germans, the diplomatic corps, and the envoy of the Sultan, who, on account of his advanced age and a rough sea, had not been able to come on board.

Remarks of His Majesty, all colorless with the exception of what follows. In talking with the French agent, though at first the conversation was

[1] Report of Councillor von Schoen, Envoy in the Imperial Suite, to the Foreign Office. *Die Grosse Politik*, vol. 20, Part I, No. 6589, p. 286 f. (Translation.)

without significance, yet when the latter delivered the respects and greetings of Delcassé, and to a certain extent in his name greeted His Majesty in Morocco, the Emperor replied that his distinguished visit meant that His Majesty desired for Germany free trade and complete equality of rights with other nations. When Count Chérisey was about to acknowledge this very courteously His Majesty remarked that he would like to treat directly with the Sultan as with an equal and the free ruler of an independent country; that he himself would be able to make his just claims valid, and that he expected that these claims would also be respected by France. Count Chérisey grew pale, was about to reply but was prevented by a curt dismissal and withdrew with bent head.

Reception of the honorable great uncle of the Sultan, very formal. Text of the address, which was full of the usual high-sounding phrases but was really rather colorless, together with autograph letter, is to be delivered by the envoy. His Majesty said that he regarded the Sultan as the ruler of a free and independent empire subject to no foreign suzerainty; that he expected for the trade and commerce of Germany advantages equal to those of the other nations engaged in trade; that he himself would always treat directly with the Sultan. He said that reforms which the Sultan might plan to introduce should be executed under honest administration and with a view to maintaining peace and order and always only as they accorded with the customs and views of the people and without doing offence to the teachings of the Koran; that, he said, would make the best impression abroad. European customs and usages could not be introduced precipitately. In this matter the Sultan should listen carefully to advice from the leading men of his country.

At the legation His Majesty also cordially greeted Menebhi in the presence of MacLean. Acceptance of gifts was skilfully avoided. His Majesty communicated, too, to the representatives of the German Press the main reasons for his gracious visit, namely desire for equal rights for all nations and maintenance of the integrity and independence of Morocco.

On the whole the short visit of His Majesty passed off splendidly without any inopportune event and evidently with a great impression made upon Moors and foreigners.

His Majesty was highly satisfied with the visit, especially with the confidential message of the Sultan, conveyed to His Majesty, that he would undertake no reforms without a previous understanding with the Imperial Government.

Our ships were, according to the custom of the country, richly loaded with gifts consisting of natural products of the country.

v. Schoen.

By the Treaty of Berlin in 1878 Austria had been permitted to occupy and administer the provinces of Bosnia and Herzegovina which remained theoretically a part of the Ottoman Empire. She had also been allowed, if for military reasons it seemed necessary, to station troops in the Sanjak of Novibazar, a narrow strip of territory between Serbia and Montenegro; and she used this privilege to keep garrisons in the western portion of this region for a generation.

In 1908, after the Young Turk Revolution, Austria annexed Bosnia and Herzegovina, at the same time withdrawing her troops from the Sanjak. Germany stood firmly by her ally through the grave international crisis that followed.

In the first of the two following letters the Emperor of Austria announces to the German Emperor the annexation. In the second the German Emperor replies.

210. *THE ANNEXATION OF BOSNIA AND HERZEGOVINA BY AUSTRIA–HUNGARY.*[1]

I. Francis Joseph to William II.[2]

Budapest,
September 29, 1908.

My dear Friend,

The most recent events in Turkey, which have led to the establishment of a constitutional state, have not been without a reaction upon the provinces administered by my Government, Bosnia and Herzegovina.

While these provinces, which have developed culturally and materially in so gratifying a manner, have for some time expressed a desire for the establishment of a constitution, these aims have now, in the face of the changed state of affairs in the Ottoman Empire, asserted themselves so vigorously that my Government feels unable longer to oppose them, if the peaceful development of affairs on the southern border of the monarchy is to be secure from disturbance.

As only the sovereign power can undertake to grant a constitution, I shall find myself forced to announce the annexation of Bosnia and Herzegovina.

We shall apprise the Ottoman Empire of this state of affairs and shall notify it at the same time that, as a proof of our eminently peaceful policy and our repudiation of any thought of territorial acquisition in the Balkans,

[1] *Die Grosse Politik,* vol. 26, Part I, p. 97 f., No. 8978; p. 129 f., No. 9006. (Translation.)

[2] Presented by the Austro-Hungarian Ambassador at the German Foreign Office on October 5th, 1908 and despatched to the Emperor at Romington. See also Selection 152. (Editor's note.)

we shall withdraw the troops stationed in the Sanjak and in future shall renounce the exercise of the privileges which the Treaty of Berlin granted us in regard to the Sanjak of Novibazar.

I consider that I owe it to the close relationship which united us as friends and allies to report this matter to you at once. You will, I am sure, judge with friendly good will and will not fail to appreciate the fact that we have acted under pressure of urgent necessity.

Your faithful friend,
Francis Joseph.

II. *William II to Francis Joseph.*

Berlin,
October 14, 1908.

My dear Friend,

I thank you heartily for your friendly letter, in which you have the kindness to inform me of the annexation of Bosnia and Herzegovina. The reasons which have moved you to take this important step I appreciate well. You can in this matter count on my unalterable personal friendship and respect as well as on the close friendship which unites our Empires as Allies. The annexation will surely prove a blessing to the two provinces, which have developed so admirably under your administration.

That you have decided at the same time to withdraw your troops stationed in the Sanjak of Novibazar and in future to renounce the exercise of the privileges which you acquired in the Sanjak through the Treaty of Berlin I consider a wise measure, with which I cannot fail to agree. This step will surely have a good effect, since it bears witness to the peacefulness of your intentions and it will make it easy for Turkey, the kindly treatment and strengthening of which is likewise to the interest of our Allied Empires, to acquiesce in the new state of affairs.

Your faithful friend,
William.

The Kaiser was by no means the only responsible official in any country to indulge in provocative utterances. In 1911 Germany, alarmed at the progress of French influence in Morocco, sent the gunboat Panther *to the port of Agadir. Ostensibly to protect German interests in southern Morocco, the real purpose of this move was to bring pressure to bear on France in order to secure for Germany compensation in the Congo region in case France should establish a protectorate over Morocco.*

Then England intervened. Sir Edward Grey, fearing that Germany was planning to retain Agadir and objecting strongly to that country's acquisition of a port on the Mediterranean, permitted Mr. Lloyd George to voice a warning to Germany at a dinner at the "Mansion House" in London. An extract from Lloyd George's speech follows.

Though Grey and Lloyd George were doubtless convinced that circumstances warranted this warning it naturally aroused a storm of indignation in Germany.

211. THE AGADIR CRISIS OF 1911.[1]

[Extract from Mr. Lloyd George's "Mansion House Speech," July 21, 1911.]

Personally I am a sincere advocate of all means which would lead to the settlement of international disputes by methods such as those which civilization has so successfully set up for the adjustment of differences between individuals, and I rejoice in my heart at the prospect of a happy issue to Sir Edward Grey's negotiations with the United States of America for the settlement of disputes which may occur in future between ourselves and our kinsmen across the Atlantic by some more merciful, more rational, and by a more just arbitrament than that of the sword.

But I am also bound to say this — that I believe it is essential in the highest interests, not merely of this country, but of the world, that Britain should at all hazards maintain her place and her prestige amongst the Great Powers of the world. Her potent influence has many a time been in the past, and may yet be in the future, invaluable to the cause of human liberty. It has more than once in the past redeemed Continental nations, who are sometimes too apt to forget that service, from overwhelming disaster and even from national extinction. I would make great sacrifices to preserve peace. I conceive that nothing would justify a disturbance of international good will except questions of the greatest national moment. But if a situation were to be forced upon us in which peace could only be preserved by the surrender of the great and beneficent position Britain has won by centuries of heroism and achievement, by allowing Britain to be treated where her interests were vitally affected as if she were of no account in the Cabinet of nations, then I say emphatically that peace at that price would be a humiliation intolerable for a great country like ours to endure. National honour is no party question. The security of our great international trade is no party question; the peace of the world is much more likely to be secured if all nations realize fairly what the conditions of peace must be. And it is because I have the conviction that nations are beginning to understand each other better, to appreciate each other's points of view more thoroughly, to be more ready to discuss calmly and dispassionately their differences, that I

[1] The *Times*, London, July 22, 1911.

feel assured that nothing will happen between now and next year which will render it difficult for the Chancellor of the Exchequer in this place to respond to the toast proposed by you, my Lord Mayor, of the continued prosperity of the public purse.

Extract from a LONDON TIMES *Editorial of the same day.*

Mr. Lloyd George's clear, decisive, and statesmanlike reference, at the Bankers' dinner last night, to the European situation, created by the German demands in West Africa will be endorsed without distinction by all his countrymen.

When Bulgaria attacked Serbia at the end of June, 1913, and thus began the second Balkan War, Count Berchtold, Austrian Foreign Minister, became anxious. He told Germany that if Serbia won and a Great Serbia developed through annexations of territory Austria would be obliged to intervene. "The South Slav question," the German Ambassador at Vienna reported him as saying, "that is to say, undisturbed possession of the provinces inhabited by South Slavs, is a vital question for the Monarchy as well as for the Triple Alliance. The Monarchy's South Slav provinces could not be held if Serbia became too powerful." If Russia should intervene, Count Berchtold further asserted, Austria would oppose such action.

The German Government speedily made it clear that it was totally opposed to Austria's embarking on any such dangerous course. Zimmermann, Under-Secretary of State at Berlin, wrote to Vienna a sharp letter in which he quoted the following warning of the German Chancellor, von Bethmann-Hollweg.

The warning was effective. The Austrian Government gave up all thought of intervention against Serbia or Russia in the existing crisis.

212. GERMANY'S WARNING TO AUSTRIA-HUNGARY IN 1913[1]

Austria-Hungary has stated from the beginning that in the present Balkan crisis she is seeking no territorial conquests. She has defined it as her interest in the outcome of the Balkan War that Serbia should not reach the Adriatic and that an Albania capable of living should be constituted. Her first demand has been achieved without difficulty. In regard to the boundary of Albania she has won a victory in the Scutari question and also, in common with Italy, in the question of Albania's southern boundary on the sea coast. The questions

[1] *Die Grosse Politik,* vol. 35, pp. 129–130. (No. 13490. Extract.) (Translation.)

still open — the southern boundary on the mainland, the constitution, and the choice of a ruling prince, etc., will, it is hoped, be satisfactorily settled. In any case the hostilities which have now broken out between Bulgaria, on the one hand, and Serbia and Greece on the other, disturb in no wise the essentials of Austro-Hungarian policy as hitherto marked out. On the contrary these hostilities, apart from the further disturbance brought about to trade and travel, are not undesirable for purely Austro-Hungarian interests. It can only benefit the Dual Monarchy if Bulgaria and Serbia are weak and disunited at the end of the war. Thereby Austria will gain the time which is necessary under all circumstances to restore the modus vivendi with Serbia. How the present hostilities between Bulgaria and Serbia will end no one knows. But this much is certain, that whether Bulgaria or Serbia conquers, both countries will be weakened and filled with hatred for each other! Austria-Hungary should not interfere with this outcome. Even should Serbia be victorious she will still be far from becoming a Great Serbia. For even in that case Serbia will not reach the Adriatic and a few strips of land more or less will not make any difference. Should Austria-Hungary attempt, by diplomatic measures, to chase Serbia out of her newly acquired territories she would have no success but would certainly arouse deadly hatred in Serbia. But should she attempt to accomplish this result by force of arms, such action would mean a European war. Thereby Germany's vital interests would be most seriously affected and I must therefore assume that before Count Berchtold takes any such decisions he will inform us.

I can therefore only express the hope that Vienna will not let herself be disquieted by the nightmare of a Great Serbia but will await further developments in the Bulgarian-Serbian theatre of war. Against the idea of wishing to gobble up Serbia, since it would only lead to the enfeeblement of Austria, I can simply urgently warn.

Zimmerman.

CHAPTER XIV

THE WORLD WAR AND THE PEACE SETTLEMENT

SECTION I. CAUSES OF THE WAR

When the Great War broke out in the summer of 1914 it is safe to say that no one in the world had a clear and comprehensive idea of what it was all about. Attempts to explain its origins began immediately; but these attempts were colored by prejudice and their value weakened because of lack of adequate material from which to draw conclusions.

Since the War, however, a vast mass of valuable material has become available, owing chiefly to the opening of some national archives, the publication of selected documents from others. Competent historians are therefore now in a position to arrive at a fairly adequate understanding of the causes of the conflict, though points of view still differ greatly.

There is no more thorough and impartial student of the subject than Professor Sidney B. Fay of Harvard University, author of " The Origins of the World War." Two selections from Professor Fay's book follow, the first on the underlying, the second on the immediate, causes of the War.

213. THE UNDERLYING CAUSES OF THE WORLD WAR [1]

Obviously, no single volume can hope to deal thoroughly with all these complex and interrelated factors which constitute the underlying causes of the World War. They may be conveniently grouped under five heads: (a) the system of secret alliances; (b) militarism; (c) nationalism; (d) economic imperialism; and (e) the newspaper press.

(a) The System of Secret Alliances

The greatest single underlying cause of the War was the system of secret alliances which developed after the Franco-Prussian War. It gradually divided Europe into two hostile groups of Powers who were increasingly suspicious of one another and who steadily built up greater and greater armies and navies. Though this system of alliances in one sense tended to preserve peace, inasmuch as the members within one group often held their friends

[1] Sidney B. Fay, *The Origins of the World War.* 2 vols., New York, The Macmillan Company, 1928, vol. I, pp. 33–47 (condensed).

or allies in restraint for fear of becoming involved in war themselves, the system also made it inevitable that if war did come, it would involve all the Great Powers of Europe. The members of each group felt bound to support each other, even in matters where they had no direct interest, because failure to give support would have weakened the solidarity of the group. Thus, Germany often felt bound to back up Austria-Hungary in her Balkan policies, because otherwise Germany feared to lose her only thoroughly dependable ally. Similarly, France had no direct political (only financial) interests in the Balkans, but felt bound to back up Russia, because otherwise the existence of the Dual Alliance would have been threatened, the balance of power destroyed, and the best guarantee of French safety from a German attack would have been lost. Likewise, the officials of the British Foreign Office became increasingly convinced that England must support France and Russia in order to preserve the solidarity of the Triple Entente as a check to the Triple Alliance. In the crisis of July, 1914, it was not merely a question of Austria, Serbia and the Balkans; it was a question of the solidarity and prestige of the two groups of Powers into which Europe had become divided.

.   .   .   .

(b) Militarism

A second underlying cause of the War, closely connected with the system of secret alliances, was militarism. The word is often used vaguely. But usually it includes at least two definite conceptions. First, the dangerous and burdensome mechanism of great standing armies and large navies, with the attendant evils of espionage, suspicion, fear, and hatred. Second, the existence of a powerful class of military and naval officers, headed by the General Staff, who tend to dominate, especially at a time of political crisis, over the civilian authorities.

.   .   .   .

From the Franco-Prussian War onwards the military and naval armaments of all the Great Powers tended to grow larger and larger, and the financial burden became heavier and heavier. Armaments were alleged to be for defense and in the interests of peace, according to the fallacious maxim, *si vis pacem, para bellum*.[1] They were intended to produce a sense of security. That was the argument used in getting from legislatures the necessary grants of money. What they really did produce was universal suspicion, fear, and hatred between nations. If one country increased its army, built strategic railways, and constructed new battleships, its fearful neighbors were straightway frightened into doing likewise. So the mad competition in armaments went on in a vicious circle. This was especially the case during and after the

1 If you want peace, prepare for war. (Editor's note.)

Balkan Wars of 1912–1913, when it seemed that the Great Powers might be involved. It was also accentuated by the system of alliances. . . .

Militarism implied also the existence of an influential body of military and naval officers, whose whole psychological outlook was naturally colored by the possibility, if not the " inevitability," of an early war. . . .

In a political crisis the military leaders were always quick to conclude that war was " inevitable," and exerted all their influence to persuade the ruling civilian authorities to consent to an order for general mobilization at the earliest possible moment, in order to gain the advantage of the offensive. But a general mobilization, according to prevailing military opinion, actually did make war inevitable. It was a process virtually impossible to halt when once begun. This was one of the greatest evils of militarism. It is always at a crisis, precisely when it is most difficult for diplomats to keep their heads clear and their hands free, that militarist leaders exert their influence to hasten decisions for war, or get the upper hand altogether.

. . . .

Some militarists believed in " preventive " war — the waging of a war upon a neighbor while he was still weak, in order to prevent him growing stronger later on. So it is often alleged that Germany wanted war in 1914, in order to have a final reckoning with Slavdom before Russia should have completed her " Great Program " of military reorganization in 1916 or 1917. M. Poincaré and his associates are alleged to have wanted war in 1914 before Germany grew any stronger by reason of her rapidly increasing population, wealth, and naval force, and also before French Socialists, revolting against the burden of French military expenditure, should repeal the recently voted three-year term of service. For the same reasons Russian militarists are said to have wanted war sooner rather than later. England even is often said to have been glad of the opportunity to crush the growing German navy before it should become a greater menace to that of England. Though here and there some individual military and naval officers in most countries may have held such views, the present writer does not think that the militarist doctrine of preventive war was a decisive factor in causing the World War. Only in Austria-Hungary did it exercise a strong influence on state policy; here it was generally felt that a conflict with Serbia must come sooner or later, and, as Baron Conrad repeatedly urged, the sooner the better. The murder of the Heir to the Throne was eagerly seized upon as a good excuse for trampling upon the Greater Serbia danger.

. . . .

Generally speaking, it may be said that this aspect of militarism — the influence of the military upon the civilian authorities — was a serious matter in the three eastern monarchies of Germany, Austria, and Russia. It was much less in France, and virtually non-existent in England, where civilian ministers were ordinarily in charge of the army and navy.

. . . .

(c) Nationalism

Nationalism, whose essence and development have recently been so admirably analyzed by a distinguished American historian, must be accounted one of the major underlying causes of the War. In its chronic form of Pan-Germanism, Pan-Slavism, and *revanche,* it nourished hatred between Germany and her two neighbors on the East and West. It worked in curious and devious ways. It had contributed happily to the unification of Germany and Italy. On the other hand, it had disrupted the Ottoman Empire and threatened to disrupt the Hapsburg Monarchy. In its virulent form, it had contributed for a century to a series of wars for national liberation and unity in . the Balkans. It was such an important factor in the Balkan situation and led so directly to the immediate occasion of the World War that some account of it in this corner of Europe will be given below in the chapter on Balkan Problems.

(d) Economic Imperialism

Economic imperialism embraces a series of international rivalries which resulted in large part from the Industrial Revolution in England and its subsequent introduction into the other great countries of the world. It led to quantity production of goods which in turn involved the struggle for new markets and new sources of raw materials. It resulted in a great increase of population, part of which sought to emigrate to the still unoccupied regions of the world, thereby sharpening the colonial rivalry of the Great Powers. It brought about the accumulation of capital which sought investment abroad, thus leading to economic exploitation and political competition. In consequence of these and other factors, the Great Powers began to partition Africa among themselves, to secure territory or exclusive spheres of influence in China, and to build railroads in Turkey and elsewhere. This struggle for markets, raw materials, and colonies became more acute during the last quarter of the nineteenth and the beginning of the twentieth century, owing to the fact that Germany and Italy entered the competition.

. . . .

Generally speaking, however, this economic imperialism is usually exaggerated as one of the underlying causes of the War. It is often said, for instance, that the industrial development of Germany, and the jealousy with which it was regarded by England, made a war between these two countries "inevitable" sooner or later. This, however, is an unsound view. It arises from the fact that economic rivalry tends to become exaggerated in the mind of the public, because it is a subject which touches the pockets of wide classes, and is more generally discussed and perhaps understood than other questions like secret treaties, militarism, or nationalism. It often happens that great merchants or industrialists own or control newspapers which are self-ishly interested in contributing to the exaggeration of these economic questions. But if one reads the diplomatic correspondence of the years before the War, one is struck by the relatively slight importance which is given to these economic rivalries which haunt so largely the mind of the average business man and newspaper editor. It is not so much questions of economic rivalry as those of prestige, boundaries, armies and navies, the Balance of Power, and possible shiftings in the system of alliances, which provoke reams of diplomatic correspondence and raise the temperature in Foreign Offices to the danger point.

(e) The Newspaper Press

Another underlying cause of the War was the poisoning of public opinion by the newspaper press in all of the great countries. This is a subject which is only beginning to receive the careful investigation which it deserves.

214. THE IMMEDIATE CAUSES OF THE WORLD WAR [1]

None of the Powers wanted a European War. Their governing rulers and ministers, with very few exceptions, all foresaw that it must be a frightful struggle, in which the political results were not absolutely certain, but in which the loss of life, suffering, and economic consequences were bound to be terrible. This is true, in a greater or less degree, of Pashitch, Berchtold, Bethmann, Sazonov, Poincaré, San Giuliano and Sir Edward Grey. Yet none of them, not even Sir Edward Grey, could have foreseen that the political results were to be so stupendous, and the other consequences to terrible, as was actually the case.

. . . .

Nevertheless, A European War broke out. Why? Because in each country political and military leaders did certain things, which led to mobilizations and declarations of war, or failed to do certain things which might have prevented them. In this sense, all the European countries, in a greater or less degree, were responsible.

. . . .

One may sum up very briefly the most salient facts in regard to each country.

Serbia felt a natural and justifiable impulse to do what so many other

---

[1] Sidney B. Fay, *The Origins of the World War.* 2 vols., New York, The Macmillan Company, 1928, vol. II, pp. 547–557 (condensed).

countries had done in the nineteenth century — to bring under one national Government all the disconnected Serb people. She had liberated those under Turkish rule; the next step was to liberate those under Hapsburg rule. She looked to Russia for assistance, and had been encouraged to expect that she would receive it. After the assassination, Mr. Pashitch took no steps to discover and bring to justice Serbians in Belgrade who had been implicated in the plot. One of them, Ciganovitch, was even assisted to disappear. Mr. Pashitch waited to see what evidence the Austrian authorities could find. When Austria demanded coöperation of Serbian officials in discovering, though not in trying, implicated Serbians, the Serbian Government made a very conciliatory but negative reply. They expected that the reply would not be regarded as satisfactory, and, even before it was given, ordered the mobilization of the Serbian army. Serbia did not want war, but believed it would be forced upon her. That Mr. Pashitch was aware of the plot three weeks before it was executed, failed to take effective steps to prevent the assassins from crossing over from Serbia to Bosnia, and then failed to give Austria any warning or information which might have averted the fatal crime, were facts unknown to Austria in July, 1914; they cannot therefore be regarded as in any way justifying Austria's conduct; but they are part of Serbia's responsibility, and a very serious part.

Austria was more responsible for the immediate origin of the war than any other Power. Yet from her own point of view she was acting in self-defence — not against an immediate military attack, but against the corroding Greater Serbia and Jugoslav agitation which her leaders believed threatened her very existence. No State can be expected to sit with folded arms and await dismemberment at the hands of its neighbors. Russia was believed to be intriguing with Serbia and Rumania against the Dual Monarchy. The assassination of the heir to the throne, as a result of a plot prepared in Belgrade, demanded severe retribution; otherwise Austria would be regarded as incapable of action, "worm-eaten" as the Serbian Press expressed it, would sink in prestige, and hasten her own downfall. To avert this Berchtold determined to crush Serbia with war. He deliberately framed the ultimatum with the expectation and hope that it would be rejected. He hurriedly declared war against Serbia in order to forestall all efforts at mediation. He refused even to answer his own ally's urgent requests to come to an understanding with Russia, on the basis of a military occupation of Belgrade as a pledge that Serbia would carry out the promises in her reply to the ultimatum. Berchtold gambled on a "local" war with Serbia only, believing that he could rattle the German sword; but rather than abandon his war with Serbia, he was ready to drag the rest of Europe into war.

. . . .

Germany did not plot a European War, did not want one, and made genuine, though too belated efforts, to avert one. She was the victim of her alliance with Austria and of her own folly. Austria was her only dependable ally, Italy and Rumania having become nothing but allies in name. She could not throw her over, as otherwise she would stand isolated between Russia, where Panslavism and armaments were growing stronger every year, and France, where Alsace-Lorraine, Delcassé's fall, and Agadir were not forgotten. Therefore, Bethmann felt bound to accede to Berchtold's request for support and gave him a free hand to deal with Serbia; he also hoped and expected to "localize" the Austro-Serbian conflict. Germany then gave grounds to the Entente for suspecting the sincerity of her peaceful intentions by her denial of any foreknowledge of the ultimatum, by her support and justification of it when it was published, and by her refusal of Sir Edward Grey's conference proposal. However, Germany by no means had Austria so completely under her thumb as the Entente Powers and many writers have assumed. It is true that Berchtold would hardly have embarked on his gambler's policy unless he had been assured that Germany would fulfil the obligations of the alliance, and to this extent Germany must share the great responsibility of Austria. But when Bethmann realized that Russia was likely to intervene, that England might not remain neutral and that there was danger of a world war of which Germany and Austria would appear to be the instigators, he tried to call a halt on Austria, but it was too late. He pressed mediation proposals on Vienna, but Berchtold was insensible to the pressure, and the Entente Powers did not believe in the sincerity of his pressure, especially as they produced no results.

. . . .

General mobilization of the continental armies took place in the following order: Serbia, Russia, Austria, France and Germany. General mobilization by a Great Power was commonly interpreted by military men in every country, though perhaps not by Sir Edward Grey, the Tsar, and some civilian officials, as meaning that the country was on the point of making war, — that the military machine had begun to move and would not be stopped. Hence, when Germany learned of the Russian general mobilization, she sent ultimatums to St. Petersburg and Paris, warning that German mobilization would follow unless Russia suspended hers within twelve hours, and asking what would be the attitude of France. The answers being unsatisfactory, Germany then mobilized and declared war. It was the hasty Russian general mobilization, assented to on July 29 and ordered on July 30, while Germany was still trying to bring Austria to accept mediation proposals, which finally rendered the European War inevitable.

Russia was partly responsible for the Austro-Serbian conflict because of the frequent encouragement which she had given at Belgrade — that Serbian national unity would be ultimately achieved with Russian assistance at Austrian expense. This had led the Belgrade Cabinet to hope for Russian support in case of a war with Austria, and the hope did not prove vain in July, 1914. Before this, to be sure, in the Bosnian Crisis and during the Balkan Wars, Russia had put restraint upon Serbia, because Russia, exhausted by the effects of the Russo-Japanese War, was not yet ready for a European struggle with the Teutonic Powers. But in 1914 her armaments, though not yet completed, had made such progress that the militarists were confident of success, if they had French and British support. In the spring of 1914, the Minister of War, Sukhomlinov, had published an article in a Russian newspaper, though without signing his name, to the effect, " Russia is ready, France must be ready also." Austria was convinced that Russia would ultimately aid Serbia, unless the Serbian danger were dealt with energetically after the Archduke's murder; she knew that Russia was growing stronger every year; but she doubted whether the Tsar's armaments had yet reached the point at which Russia would dare to intervene; she would therefore run less risk of Russian intervention and a European War if she used the Archduke's assassination as an excuse for weakening Serbia, than if she should postpone action until the future.

Russia's responsibility lay also in the secret preparatory military measures which she was making at the same time that she was carrying on diplomatic negotiations. These alarmed Germany and Austria. But it was primarily Russia's general mobilization, made when Germany was trying to bring Austria to a settlement, which precipitated the final catastrophe, causing Germany to mobilize and declare war.

The part of France is less clear than that of the other Great Powers, because she has not yet made a full publication of her documents. To be sure, M. Poincaré, in the fourth volume of his memoirs, has made a skilful and elaborate plea, to prove *" La France innocente."* But he is not convincing. It is quite clear that on his visit to Russia he assured the Tsar's Government that France would support her as an ally in preventing Austria from humiliating or crushing Serbia. Paléologue renewed these assurances in a way to encourage Russia to take a strong hand. He did not attempt to restrain Russia from military measures which he knew would call forth German counter-measures and cause war. Nor did he keep his Government promptly and fully informed of the military steps which were being taken at St. Petersburg. President Poincaré, upon his return to France, made efforts for peace, but his great preoccupation was to minimize French and Russian preparatory measures and emphasize those of Germany, in order to secure the certainty of British support in a struggle which he now regarded as inevitable.

Sir Edward Grey made many sincere proposals for preserving peace; they all failed owing partly, but not exclusively, to Germany's attitude. Sir Edward could probably have prevented war if he had done either of two things. If, early in the crisis, he had acceded to the urging of France and Russia and given a strong warning to Germany that, in a European War, England would take the side of the Franco-Russian Alliance, this would probably have led Bethmann to exert an earlier and more effective pressure on Austria; and it would perhaps thereby have prevented the Austrian declaration of war on Serbia, and brought to a successful issue the " direct conversations " between Vienna and St. Petersburg. Or, if Sir Edward Grey had listened to German urging, and warned France and Russia early in the crisis, that if they became involved in war, England would remain neutral, probably Russia would have hesitated with her mobilizations, and France would probably have exerted a restraining influence at St. Petersburg. But Sir Edward Grey could not say that England would take the side of France and Russia, because he had a Cabinet nearly evenly divided, and he was not sure, early in the crisis, that public opinion in England would back him up in war against Germany. He could resign, and he says in his memoirs that he would have resigned, but that would have been no comfort or aid to France, who had come confidently to count upon British support. He was determined to say and do nothing which might encourage her with a hope which he could not fulfil. Therefore, in spite of the pleadings of the French, he refused to give them definite assurances until the probable German determination to go through Belgium made it clear that the Cabinet, and Parliament, and British public opinion would follow his lead in war on Germany. On the other hand, he was unwilling to heed the German pleadings that he exercise restraint at Paris and St. Petersburg, because he did not wish to endanger the Anglo-Russian Entente and the solidarity of the Triple Entente, because he felt a moral obligation to France, growing out of the Anglo-French military and naval conversations of the past years, and because he suspected that Germany was backing Austria up in an unjustifiable course and that Prussian militarists had taken the direction of affairs at Berlin out of the hands of Herr von Bethmann-Hollweg and the civilian authorities.

The author of the following selection holds that public opinion played a more important part in precipitating the Great War than is generally realized.

In the first section of the selection he contrasts the theory that " men make history " with the theory that the individual leader counts for little in the historical process. He suggests that even " revisionist " historians of the origins of the Great War have leaned too much toward the first theory and have overemphasized the part played by individual leaders in causing the conflict.

In the second section he draws the conclusion, from evidence which cannot be reproduced here in full, that by the time Austria had declared war on Serbia, if not before, public opinion both in Austria and Russia was so worked up that a conflict between these two countries was virtually inevitable.

215. PUBLIC OPINION AS A POSSIBLE CAUSE OF THE GREAT WAR[1]

I.

Two widely divergent theories of history bear vital relationship to the study of the immediate origins of the Great War. The first lays stress on the part played in the historical process by the leaders of men, exalting their achievements, and in consequence, emphasizing their responsibilities. According to this conception it is the titanic few who make or mar human destiny. The other theory minimizes the individual, no matter how great he may be, laying stress instead on social, economic, and political conditions, on an inexorable or almost inexorable march of events, on the reactions of public opinion, as the determining factors in history. According to this theory the leader is hemmed in by influences such as these, and perhaps forced to march in a direction very different from that which he would have chosen had he been completely free. Tolstoi has even gone so far as to say that "all leadership is a kind of flight." The two conceptions are epitomized in the question that has long baffled philosophically-minded historians: Do men make history, or does history make men? Between these two theories the student of the origins of the Great War must, consciously or unconsciously, either choose or compromise.

Sturdy Carlyle is the classic exponent of the idea that men make history. "For as I take it," he says, "Universal History, the history of what man has accomplished in this world, is at bottom the History of the Great Men who have worked here. They were the leaders of men, these great ones, the modellers, patterns, and in a wide sense creators, of whatsoever the general mass of men contrived to do or to attain; all things that we see accomplished in the world are properly the outer material result, the practical realization and embodiment of thoughts that dwelt in the Great Men sent into the world; the soul of the whole world's history, it may justly be considered, was the history of these."

At first sight this theory seems to have the better of it. If one looks only at the surface processes of history, the great individual seems all-important. A king leads forth his hosts to battle and conquers a province; the conquest is glorified and recorded as his personal achievement. He has " made a place

---

1 Jonathan F. Scott, *Five Weeks. The Surge of Public Opinion on the Eve of the Great War.* New York, The John Day Company, 1927, I, pp. 3–14 (slightly condensed); II, pp. 259–264.

for himself in history." Henry the Eighth of England wishes to marry Anne Boleyn, divorces Catherine of Aragon against the will of the Pope, separates himself and his people from the Church of Rome and establishes the Church of England. On the surface the new establishment appears to be, primarily, his personal work. So, too, it is Martin Luther who seems to be chiefly responsible for the Protestant Church in Germany. And it is apparently solely the genius of Napoleon which creates his vast empire; when that genius fails, the whole empire topples and falls to the ground. So a modern social psychologist, rallying to this interpretation or history, asks: " Would Germany now be a nation, but for Frederick the Great and Bismarck? Would America, but for Washington, Hamilton, and Lincoln? Would Italy, but for Garibaldi and Mazzini and Cavour? "

If this popular conception of history has its heroes, it has also its villains. If it attributes to heroes the glorious achievements of the human race, it lays the great calamities at the villains' doors. To many people, perhaps to most people, in England, France, and America, the Kaiser was the villain of the Great War. Such people still believe that he deliberately " willed the war." They look upon him as a man of fiendish character, who brought endless misery and suffering on the world simply in the hope of gratifying his illimitable ambitions. So-called historians have incorporated such stuff in textbooks for children, and it is now being ladled out in school after school. Other persons, a little better-informed, associate von Bethmann-Hollweg and the leaders of the military party in Germany as culprits with the Kaiser. Austria-Hungary is looked upon as the " vassal " of Germany, and the Crime of Sarajevo as the convenient pretext for beginning a war long planned.

The theory of individual responsibility for the immediate origins of the Great War is apparently accepted not only by many ill-informed and misinformed persons in Europe and America, but also, either directly or by implication, by certain diplomats and statesmen who themselves played their parts on the stage or behind the scenes before and during the great struggle. Thus the Italian statesman, Nitti, quotes a leading European statesman as saying to him a few years before the war that, " there was everything to be feared for the future of Europe where the peoples of Russia, Germany and Austria-Hungary, almost two-thirds of the whole continent, were governed in an almost irresponsible manner by men without will or intelligence: the Czar of Russia; the German Kaiser, a madman without a spark of genius, and the Emperor of Austria-Hungary, an obstinate old man, hedged in by ambition." " Not more than thirty persons," he added, " act as a controlling force on these three irresponsible sovereigns, who might assume, on their own initiative, the most terrible responsibilities."

So, too, President Wilson, just before America's entrance into the conflict, differentiated between the German people and the German Government, absolving the people of guilt and accusing the rulers and little groups of ambitious men. Lord Oxford and Asquith holds that the war would probably have been averted in 1914, had it not been for the untimely death of Baron Marschall, who was for a short time German Ambassador at the Court of St. James's. "I am as satisfied as one can be of anything in the domain of conjecture," he says, "that, if he had remained, there would have been no European War in 1914. He was the only German statesman whose personality and authority were such as might have proved adequate not only to dominate the impetuosities and vagaries of the Kaiser, but to override and frustrate the long-laid and short-sighted plans of the military junta in Berlin." Finally Lord Haldane implies the heavy responsibility of a few individual leaders for precipitating the conflict, when he says that "a few unlucky words made all the difference in the concluding days of July, 1914:

"'Ten lines, a statesman's life in each.'"

Even the new and painstaking "revisionist" scholarship, which is doing so much to place the immediate origins of the World War in their true light, has concentrated on the responsibilities of individuals and governments rather than on general influences. In Germany there has been a disposition to place on the shoulders of the Kaiser, von Bethmann-Hollweg and other German leaders, a larger share of responsibility for the outbreak of the titanic struggle than, during the conflict itself, they were supposed by Germans to have borne. Professor Fay, several years ago, emphasized the part played by the Austrian Minister of Foreign Affairs, Count Berchtold, and by certain of the Russian leaders. Professor Barnes later held Berchtold to be but the tool of the Austrian war party, led by Conrad von Hötzendorf, the Chief of Staff. Izvolsky, too, formerly Russian Minister of Foreign Affairs and at the opening of the war Ambassador to France, has figured as a scapegoat. Even Lord Grey has been taken to task. But with certain of the "revisionists" the chief *bête noir* is now M. Poincaré. Indeed, some of them, both in his country and elsewhere, would have him step into the uncomfortable niche so long occupied by the Kaiser, as the arch-conspirator, the Machiavellian plotter of the World War. The reaction against the traditional explanations of the war's origins is a healthy one, and its exponents deserve high praise for the courage they have shown in espousing an unpopular cause for truth's sake; but it is certain that some of them have gone too far in their anxiety to shift the burden of "war guilt" from the shoulders of one individual to those of another, or from one set of individuals to another set.

In contrast with the theory that the individual leader has been of prime importance in the historical process, stand the views of such historical thinkers as Lamprecht and Karl Marx. Lamprecht neglects the element of personality, subordinates the history of politics to that of culture, and puts his emphasis on conditions. " In the reaction against the political school," says Gooch, " he presents Germania without her political backbone." In collective psychology, not in the actions of great men, he thinks to find the true explanation of historical development. Marx teaches that the course of history is determined, not by individuals and institutions, but in the last analysis by economic conditions. From this he evolves his theory of the social revolution. Believing in the materialistic conception of history, holding that the rich are growing richer and the poor growing poorer, he accepts the class-struggle as inevitable. Economic conditions, he maintains, will ultimately force the workers of the world to the wall, and then, having " nothing to lose but their chains," they will in desperation unite and overthrow their masters and oppressors, the capitalists.

In commenting on the immediate origins of the Great War certain statesmen and diplomats seem to lean toward the idea that underlying conditions and the march of events were responsible for the catastrophe, rather than individual leaders. Thus the French Ambassador at the Court of the Tsar wrote in his diary on July 27, 1914: " In relation to the distant and profound causes which have determined the actual crisis, there is no longer individual initiative, there is no longer human will, which can resist the automatic mechanism of unchained forces. We diplomats, we have lost all control over events; we can only attempt to foresee them and to insist that our governments adapt their conduct to them." And the Austro-Hungarian statesman, Andrassy, sets forth his conviction that the World War was rather the result of mistakes, of ill-will, of mistrust and of the instinct of self-preservation than of political calculation. " No Power willed the World War, perhaps not even Russia," he says. " Up to the very last moment attempts were made to find a peaceful way out. The difficulties of the situation, however, were stronger than the will of statesmen."

Statesmen ordinarily as far apart as von Bethmann-Hollweg and Lloyd George testify to the triumph of events over men, in the dark days before the storm broke. In a speech of July 30, 1914, the German Chancellor expressed the belief that " all Governments, including that of Russia, and the great majority of the nations were peaceable themselves, but control had been lost, and the stone had started rolling." Similarly, Lloyd George, in the oft-quoted extract from his speech of December 23, 1920, said that " the more one reads memoirs and books written in the various countries of what happened before the first of August, 1914, the more one realizes that no one at the head of affairs quite meant war at that stage. It was something into which they glided, or rather staggered and stumbled, perhaps through folly, and a discussion, I have no doubt, would have averted it." Clearly the point of view inherent in such statements is that the forces which those in responsible positions attempted to guide, direct and control, finally became too powerful to manage and in the end overwhelmed all in the maelstrom of conflict.

Those who approach the study of war origins from the psychological, rather than from what is commonly known as the "historical" point of view, attempt to indicate and analyze some of these forces. Trotter and MacCurdy, for example, emphasize the importance of the "herd" in relation to war. Man, according to Trotter, is essentially a herd animal, and MacCurdy says that man "is deaf to the voice of one without the herd, but indefinitely suggestible to influences coming from within it."

Now, so far as important wars are concerned, the herd of to-day is the nation. And the people of each nation are continually subject to certain psychological influences which tend to get them into trouble with the people of other nations. Among these psychological influences are national pride, pugnacity, love of power, suspicion and fear. Fear is perhaps the most important influence of all. "The fear motive," says Partridge, "is probably much deeper in human nature, both in the lower and the higher social reactions, than is commonly supposed, the concealment of fear being precisely a part of the strategy of defense. Fear has created more history than it is usually given credit for. The aggressive motive alone, in all probability would never have made history such a story of battles as it has been. Nations usually attribute more aggressive intentions and motives to their neighbours than their neighbours possess, and war is certainly often precipitated by an accumulation of mutual distrust and suspicion."

In the name of patriotism the psychological causes of war have been continually stimulated. The school, the press, in recent times the cinema, and sometimes even the pulpit, have all tended to develop and foster national pride, pugnacity, suspicion of other countries. As a result of such suggestions and of other influences there has grown up in the various nations an atmosphere of distrust, egotism, and irritability which readily develops into a neurosis, such as that described by Mrs. Playne in her *Neuroses of the Nations*.

When a crisis approaches, when war draws near, the coming catastrophe is viewed with horror. But at the same time, along with this horror, "some thoughtful introspectionists admit, can be detected a 'something' which seems to hope that war will come. This 'something,' like the fascination of a horrible spectacle, is, of course, the unconscious wish. When it has come as close to consciousness as this, its shadow, as it were, being seen, war is truly imminent, for now the herd antagonism is mightily augmented by the primitive passion for violence." [1] The last " cause " that serves to precipitate the disaster, and of which historians often make so much, MacCurdy believes to be of little importance; for toward the end people are in a state of such nervous excitement that war has become practically inevitable. The actual declaration of war brings with it a feeling of momentary relief. The suspense is over for the time being, the irrevocable decision taken.

If these psychological interpretations of the causes of war be even approximately correct, public opinion in the various countries must have counted for much in the fateful crisis of the summer of 1914. The acceptance of this point of view does not necessarily imply a mechanistic conception of the historical process. It does not necessarily imply that history makes men rather than that men make history. It does not mean that the leading statesmen in the various governments are relieved of all responsibility for the precipitation of hostilities. It does not mean that they were mere puppets, playing the parts for which fate had cast them. What it does mean is that there was an interaction of influence between leaders and followers, that the leaders were not as free as they appear on the surface to have been, that public opinion, in their own and other countries, had more effect on their actions than is generally supposed.

II.

The chief conclusion resulting from the present investigation is that after the Crime of Sarajevo Austro-German diplomacy created a situation from which public opinion in various countries made a peaceful escape virtually impossible. Should it be clearly proved that the Serbian Government had had foreknowledge of the conspiracy to kill the Archduke and had failed to give the Ballplatz serious and unmistakable warning, then that Government of course would have to bear a grave responsibility for the events that followed. Should it be clearly proved that Russian officials were privy to the plot, their guilt would be double-dyed. To such possibilities as these the historian will naturally keep an open mind; but neither of them has yet been proved. And of course their proof would in no way nullify the responsibilities of Austro-German diplomacy and of public opinion in the five great countries involved in the outbreak of the war.

In defense of the Austrian and German Governments it should be said that the provocation to the Dual Monarchy from Serbia had been protracted and grievous. Furthermore, their object was not to bring on a European conflict, but to abate what seemed to them an intolerable nuisance. When the German Government saw that the danger of a general war was imminent,

[1] MacCurdy, *Psychology of War*, p. 52.

it bitterly regretted its action in giving Austria a free hand with Serbia and made a desperate effort to hold in check its reckless ally.

It can not be said, however, that the Austrian authorities adopted their policy of force at the instance of an overwhelming popular demand. Immediately after the Crime of Sarajevo anger at Serbia was naturally strong and general. But despite anti-Serbian demonstrations and riots, despite the catcalls of some of the more chauvinistic journals, an influential part of the Press at first urged moderation; and the opinion at first prevailed on the Bourse that the Dual Monarchy would continue to pursue a policy of peace. As the days passed, however, resentment against Serbia was fanned by the reckless and provocative language of the Serbian Press as well as by the piecemeal revelations of the results of the investigation into the origins of the Crime of Sarajevo. The conviction grew that the plot was hatched in Belgrade and that King Peter's government was in greater or less degree responsible.

Once the ultimatum had been dispatched, it is hard to see how the Austrian Government could have prevented the war with Serbia, even had it so desired. The Socialists opposed the idea of war vehemently, and continued to oppose it; but with the vast majority of the people the Note was thoroughly popular. Approval of the Austrian Government was expressed widely and emphatically. Its " firmness " in the crisis was contrasted with its former " weakness." Doubts and hesitations were thrown to the winds. According to Dr. Dillon the people were determined on war, not from bellicosity, but from a desire to finish once for all with the Serbian menace. The Serbian reply of July 25th, which many persons in other countries considered entirely too submissive, and which even the Kaiser pronounced a sufficient surrender to the demands of the Dual Monarchy, was held by Austrian opinion to be clearly and thoroughly unsatisfactory. There is perhaps the barest possibility that the Ballplatz, yielding to German pressure, could have accepted the Serbian answer as a basis for negotiations, and by piecing and patching a compromise could have averted the catastrophe of a European conflict. But, in any event, once war had been declared on Serbia on July 28th, control was lost, the situation had gotten completely out of hand. Perhaps Berchtold, after that, would have been glad to retreat. But he was helpless. At that time Austro-Hungarian public opinion, inflexible in its decision to settle its accounts with Serbia at all costs, saw in a localization of the conflict the only hope of keeping the major peace of Europe. Until toward the very last localization seemed to the Austrians quite possible because the danger of Russian intervention was underestimated, and because Austrian opinion counted on a certain sympathy from the Entente Powers, especially from England.

An Austrian attack on Serbia, however, seems to have been one thing that Russian public opinion, in the summer of 1914, would not endure. It is all very well to say that the security of Serbia was not a vital interest to Russia in the sense that relief from the Serbian menace was a vital interest to Austria. The real point to be considered in attempting to relate public opinion to war origins, however, is not that Serbia's territorial integrity was a vital interest to Russia, but that Russian opinion believed it to be so. Racial sentiment, religious sentiment, expansionist sentiment, the Russian interpretation of the theory of the balance of power, fear of Germany and Austria, prejudice against these countries, the burning desire to avenge the annexation of Bosnia and Herzegovina, the belief that "Russia was ready," all united to solidify Russian opinion to defend Serbia. Austrian assurances that the Dual Monarchy would not annex territory were naturally enough brushed aside.

Under these circumstances the severity of Austria's ultimatum to her little Slavic neighbor was enough to arouse the alarmed suspicion that the Dual Monarchy intended to "gobble up Serbia." "*C'est la guerre Européenne*" was the feeling of many. Naturally, then, the Russian authorities began at once (July 24th) to take measures looking toward mobilization. Had Austria yielded on the essential issues, however, orders could have been given to recall these preliminary measures; for they were not such as to render war inevitable. But the Austrian declaration of war on Serbia on July 28th seemed to destroy the last hope of peace. "Up to yesterday," von Chelius telegraphed the German Foreign Office on July 29th, "all in the entourage of the (Russian) Emperor were filled with the hope of a peaceful outcome; to-day, since the declaration of war (Austria's declaration of war on Serbia) they considered a general war almost inevitable. . . . They do not want any war and would like to be able to avoid it, and regret that no Power was successful in restraining Austria from taking the decisive step." And the King of Roumania about this time said that he considered the Russian mobilization against Austria to be "a measure adopted for the purpose of pacifying public opinion." It was well recognized that if Russia and Austria should fight, Germany would undoubtedly participate to sustain Austria. General mobilization of the Russian forces, therefore, was the logical step to take, once the hope of peace with Austria had been given up. In other words, it would seem that if the Russian general mobilization entailed war with Germany, Austria's declaration of war on Serbia had previously entailed the Russian general mobilization. The Russian mobilization is therefore of far less causal significance than many revisionist historians have believed it to be.

On July 23, 1914, the Austrian Note to Serbia, destined to lead to war with Serbia and a little later to the outbreak of the Great War, was presented by Baron Giesl, the Austrian Minister at Belgrade, to the Serbian Government. Serbia was given forty-eight hours in which to reply.

The text of the Note follows.

216. *THE AUSTRIAN ULTIMATUM TO SERBIA*

On the 31st of March, 1909, the Serbian Minister in Vienna, on the instructions of the Serbian Government, made the following declaration to the Imperial and Royal Government:

"Serbia recognizes that the *fait accompli* regarding Bosnia has not affected her rights, and consequently she will conform to the decisions that the Powers may take in conformity with Article 25 of the Treaty of Berlin. In deference to the advice of the Great Powers, Serbia undertakes to renounce from now onwards the attitude of protest and opposition which she has adopted with regard to the annexation since last autumn. She undertakes, moreover, to modify the direction of her policy with regard to Austria-Hungary and to live in future on good neighborly terms with the latter."

The history of recent years, and in particular the painful events of the 28th June last, have shown the existence of a subversive movement with the object of detaching a part of the territories of Austria-Hungary from the Monarchy. The movement which had its birth under the eye of the Serbian Government has gone so far as to make itself manifest on both sides of the Serbian frontier in the shape of acts of terrorism and a series of outrages and murders.

Far from carrying out the formal undertakings contained in the declaration of the 31st March, 1909, the Royal Serbian Government has done nothing to repress these movements. It has permitted the criminal machinations of various societies and associations directed against the Monarchy, and has tolerated unrestrained language on the part of the press, the glorification of the perpetrators of outrages, and the participation of officers and functionaries in subversive agitation. It has permitted an unwholesome propaganda in public instruction, in short, it has permitted all manifestations of a nature to incite the Serbian population to hatred of the Monarchy and contempt of its institutions.

This culpable tolerance of the Royal Serbian Government had not ceased at the moment when the events of the 28th June last proved its fatal consequences to the whole world.

It results from the depositions and confessions of the criminal perpetrators of the outrage of the 28th June that the Serajevo assassinations were planned in Belgrade; that the arms and explosives with which the murderers were provided had been given to them by Serbian officers and functionaries belonging to the Naródna Odbrana; and finally that the passage into Bosnia of the criminals and their arms was organized and effected by the chiefs of the Serbian frontier service.

The above-mentioned results of the magisterial investigation do not permit the Austro-Hungarian Government to pursue any longer the attitude of expectant forbearance which they have maintained for years in the face of the machinations hatched in Belgrade, and thence propagated in the territories of the Monarchy. The results, on the contrary, impose on them the duty of putting an end to the intrigues which form a perpetual menace to the tranquillity of the Monarchy.

To achieve this end the Imperial and Royal Government see themselves compelled to demand from the Royal Serbian Government a formal assurance that they condemn this dangerous propaganda against the Monarchy; in other words, the whole series of tendencies, the ultimate aim of which is to detach from the Monarchy territories belonging to it, and that they undertake to suppress by every means this criminal and terrorist propaganda.

In order to give a formal character to this undertaking the Royal Serbian Government shall publish on the front page of their Official Journal of the 13/26 July the following declaration:

" The Royal Government of Serbia condemn the propaganda directed against Austria-Hungary — *i.e.* the general tendency of which the final aim is to detach from the Austro-Hungarian Monarchy territories belonging to it, and they sincerely deplore the fatal consequences of these criminal proceedings.

" The Royal Government regret that Serbian officers and functionaries participated in the above-mentioned propaganda and thus compromised the good neighborly relations to which the Royal Government were solemnly pledged by their declaration of March 31, 1909.

" The Royal Government, who disapprove and repudiate all idea of interfering or attempting to interfere with the destinies of the inhabitants of any part whatsoever of Austria-Hungary, consider it their duty formally to warn officers and functionaries and the whole population of the kingdom, that henceforward they will proceed with the utmost rigor against persons who may be guilty of such machinations, which they will use all their efforts to anticipate and suppress."

This declaration shall simultaneously be communicated to the Royal Army as an order of the day by His Majesty the King and shall be published in the Official Bulletin of the Army.

The Royal Serbian Government further undertake:

1. To suppress any publication which incites to hatred and contempt of the Austro-Hungarian Monarchy and the general tendency of which is directed against its territorial integrity;

2. To dissolve immediately the society styled " Narodna Odbrana," to confiscate all its means of propaganda, and to proceed in the same manner against other societies and their branches in Serbia which engage in propaganda against the Austro-Hungarian Monarchy. The Royal Government

shall take the necessary measures to prevent the societies dissolved from continuing their activities under another name and form;

3. To eliminate without delay from public instruction in Serbia, both as regards the teaching body and also as regards the methods of instruction, everything that serves, or might serve, to foment the propaganda against Austria-Hungary;

4. To remove from the military service, and from the administration in general, all officers and functionaries guilty of propaganda against the Austro-Hungarian Monarchy whose names and deeds the Austro-Hungarian Government reserve to themselves the right of communicating to the Royal Government;

5. To accept the collaboration in Serbia of representatives of the Austro-Hungarian Government for the suppression of the subversive movement directed against the territorial integrity of the Monarchy;

6. To take judicial proceedings against accessories to the plot of the 28th June who are on Serbian territory; delegates of the Austro-Hungarian Government will take part in the investigation relating thereto;

7. To proceed without delay to the arrest of Major Voija Tankositch and of the individual named Milan Ciganovitch, a Serbian State employee, who have been compromised by the results of the magisterial inquiry at Serajevo;

8. To prevent by effective measures the coöperation of the Serbian authorities in the illicit traffic in arms and explosives across the frontier, to dismiss and punish severely the officials of the frontier service at Schabatz and Loznica guilty of having assisted the perpetrators of the Serajevo crime by facilitating their passage across the frontier;

9. To furnish the Imperial and Royal Government with explanations regarding the unjustifiable utterances of high Serbian officials, both in Serbia and abroad, who, notwithstanding their official position, have not hesitated since the crime of 28th June to express themselves in interviews in terms of hostility to the Austro-Hungarian Government; and, finally,

10. To notify the Imperial and Royal Government without delay of the execution of the measures comprised under the preceding heads.

The Austro-Hungarian Government expect the reply of the Royal Government by 6 o'clock on Saturday evening the 25th July.

SECTION II. TRENCH FIGHTING

In his novel, Men in War, *from which the following selection is taken, Andreas Latzko, a talented Austrian writer who was himself a soldier in the great conflict of 1914–1918, paints a picture of war as he sees it.*

217. REALITIES OF WARFARE [1]

I. Captain Marschner, with his Company, Enters the Front-line Trenches [2]

The trench seemed never to be coming to an end. Marschner felt his strength giving way. He stumbled more frequently and closed his eyes with a shudder at the criss-cross traces of blood that precisely indicated the path of the wounded. Suddenly he raised his head with a jerk. A new smell struck him, a sweetish stench which kept getting stronger and stronger until at a curve of the trench wall, which swung off to the left at this point and receded semicircularly, it burst upon him like a great cloud. He looked about, shaken by nausea, his gorge rising. In a dip in the trench he saw a pile of dirty, tattered uniforms heaped in layers and with strangely rigid outlines. It took him some time to grasp the full horror of that which towered in front of him. Fallen soldiers were lying there like gathered logs, in the contorted shapes of the last death agony. Tent flaps had been spread over them, but had slipped down and revealed the grim, stony grey caricatures, the fallen jaws, the staring eyes. The arms of those in the top tier hung earthward like parts of a trellis, and grasped at the faces of those lying below, and were already sown with the livid splotches of corruption.

Captain Marschner uttered a short, belching cry and reeled forward. His head shook as though loosened from his neck, and his knees gave way so that he already saw the ground rising up toward him, when suddenly an unknown face emerged directly in front of him and attracted his attention, and gave him back his self-control. It was a sergeant, who was staring at him silently with great, fevered, gleaming eyes in a deathly pale face. For a moment the man stood as though paralyzed, then his mouth opened wide, he clapped his hands, and jumped into the air like a dancer, and dashed off, without thinking of a salute.

"Relief!" he shouted while running.

He came to a halt before a black hole in the trench wall, like the entrance to a cave, and bent down and shouted into the opening with a ring of indescribable joy in his voice — with a rejoicing that sounded as if it came through tears:

"Relief! Lieutenant! The relief party is here!"

The captain looked after him and heard his cry. His eyes grew moist, so touching was that childlike cry of joy, that shout from out of a relieved heart. He followed the sergeant slowly, and saw — as though the cry had awakened the dead — pallid faces peering from all corners, wounded men with blood-soaked bandages, tottering figures holding their rifles. Men streamed toward

---

[1] Andreas Latzko, *Men in War*. New York, Boni, and Liveright, 1918, pp. 95–98; 115–120.

[2] This and the following heading are inserted by the Editors. (Editor's note.)

him from every direction, stared at him and with speechless lips formed the word "relief" until at length one of them roared out a piercing "hurrah," which spread like wildfire and found an echo in unseen throats that repeated it enthusiastically. Deeply shaken, Marschner bowed his head and swiftly drew his hand across his eyes when the commandant of the trench rushed toward him from the dugout.

Nothing that betokens life was left about the man. His face was ashen, his eyes like lamps extinguished, glazed and surrounded by broad blue rims. His lids were a vivid red from sleeplessness. His hair, his beard, his clothes were encased in a thick crust of mud, so that he looked as if he had just arisen from the grave. He gave a brief, military salute, then grasped the captain's hand with hysterical joy. His hand was cold as a corpse's and sticky with sweat and dirt. And most uncanny was the contrast between this skeleton hung with clothes, this rigid death-mask of a face, and the twitching, over-excited nervousness with which the lieutenant greeted their liberator.

II. The Italians Attack the Austrian Trenches

Far in the background the sun was sinking. Its great copper disc already cut in half by the horizon seemed to be growing out of the ground. And against that dazzling background black silhouettes were dancing like midges under a microscope, like Indians swinging their tomahawks. They were still mere specks. Sometimes they disappeared entirely and then leaped high, and came nearer, their rifles wriggling in the air like the feet of a polyp. Gradually their cries became audible and swelled louder and louder like the far barking of dogs. When they called "Avanti!" it was a piercing cry, and when the call "Coraggio!" went through their lines, it changed to a dull, thunderous roll.

The entire company now stood close-packed up against the slope of the trench, their faces as of stone, restrained, pale as chalk, with lipless mouths, each man's gun in position — a single beast of prey with a hundred eyes and arms.

"Don't shoot! Don't shoot! Don't shoot!" Lieutenant Weixler's voice yelled without pause through the trench. His command seemed to lay its grasp on every throat and to hold the fingers moveless that greedily clasped the triggers. The first hand grenade flew into the trench. The captain saw it coming, then saw a man loosen from the mass, reel toward the dugout with outstretched arms, bending over, a veil of blood covering his face. Then — at last! — it was a relief — came the beating of the machine guns, and at once the rifles went off, too, like the raging of an angry pack. A cold, repulsive greed lay on all faces. Some of the men cried out aloud in their hate and rage when new groups emerged out there behind the thinning rows. The barrels of the rifles glowed with heat — and still the rumbling cries of " Coraggio! " came nearer and nearer.

As though in a frenzy of insanity, the silhouettes hopped about out there, sprang into the air, fell, and rolled over each other, as though the war dance had only just reached the climax of its paroxysm.

Then Captain Marschner observed the man next to him let his rifle sink for a moment and with hasty, shaking hands insert the bayonet into the smoking barrel. The captain felt as though he were going to vomit. He closed his eyes in dizziness and leaned against the trench wall, and let himself glide to the earth. Was he to — to see — that? Was he to see men being murdered right alongside of him? He tore his revolver from his pocket, emptied it, and threw it away. Now he was defenseless. And suddenly he grew calm and rose to his feet, elevated by a wonderful composure, ready to let himself be butchered by one of these panting beasts who were storming on, chased by the blind fear of death. He wanted to die like a man, without hatred, without rage, with clean hands.

A hoarse roar, a frightful, dehumanized cry almost beside him wrenched his thoughts back into the trench. A broad stream of light and fire, travelling in a steep curve, flowed blindingly down beside him, and sprayed over the shoulder of the tall pock-marked tailor of the first line. In the twinkling of an eye the man's entire left side flared up in flames. With a howl of agony he threw himself to the ground, writhed and screamed and leaped to his feet again, and ran moaning up and down like a living torch, until he broke down, half-charred, and twitched, and then lay rigid. Captain Marschner saw him lying there and smelt the odor of burned flesh, and his eyes involuntarily strayed to his own hand on which a tiny, white spot just under his thumb reminded him of the torments he had suffered in his boyhood from a bad burn.

At that moment a jubilant hurrah roared through the trench, rising from a hundred relieved throats. The attack had been repulsed! Lieutenant Weixler had carefully taken aim at the thrower of the liquid fire and hit at the first shot. The liquid fire had risen up like a fountain from the falling man's stiffening hand and rained down on his own comrades. Their decimated lines shrank back suddenly before the unexpected danger and they fled pell-mell, followed by the furious shots from all the rifles.

The men fell down as if lifeless, with slack faces and lusterless eyes, as though some one had turned off the current that had fed those dead creatures with strength from some unknown source. Some of them leaned against the trench wall white as cheese, and held their heads over, and vomited from exhaustion. Marschner also felt his gorge rising and groped his way toward the dugout. He wanted to go into his own place now and be alone and somehow relieve himself of the despair that held him in its grip.

SECTION III. THE UNITED STATES AND THE WAR

No single act of Germany aroused stronger indignation in the United States than the sinking of the Lusitania *on May 7, 1915. Of the 1200 lives lost 124 were American. Hot-heads in this country demanded an immediate declaration of war on Germany; but President Wilson was not ready to support such drastic action. He did, however, send the following note of warning (signed by Mr. Bryan as Secretary of State) to Germany. Protracted negotiations ensued and finally, in May, 1916, the German Government promised that, until notice was given to the contrary, no merchant vessel, unless it attempted to flee or to resist, would be sunk without due warning and without proper provision for the safety of the lives of passengers.*

218. PRESIDENT WILSON'S FIRST NOTE TO GERMANY ON THE SINKING OF THE LUSITANIA [1]

Department of State,
Washington, May 13, 1915.

To Ambassador Gerard:

Please call on the Minister of Foreign Affairs and after reading to him this communication leave with him a copy.

In view of recent acts of the German authorities in violation of American rights on the high seas which culminated in the torpedoing and sinking of the British steamship *Lusitania* on May 7, 1915, by which over 100 American citizens lost their lives, it is clearly wise and desirable that the Government of the United States and the Imperial German Government should come to a clear and full understanding as to the grave situation which has resulted.

The sinking of the British passenger steamer *Falaba* by a German submarine on March 28, through which Leon C. Thrasher, an American citizen, was drowned; the attack on April 28 on the American vessel *Cushing* by a German aeroplane; the torpedoing on May 1 of the American vessel *Gulflight* by a German submarine, as a result of which two or more American citizens met their death; and, finally, the torpedoing and sinking of the steamship *Lusitania,* constitute a series of events which the Government of the United States has observed with growing concern, distress, and amazement.

Recalling the humane and enlightened attitude hitherto assumed by the Imperial German Government in matters of international right, and par-

---

[1] Albert Shaw, Editor, *The Messages and Papers of Woodrow Wilson.* 2 vols., New York, George H. Doran Company, 1924, vol. I, pp. 239–243 (condensed).

ticularly with regard to the freedom of the seas; having learned to recognize the German views and the German influence in the field of international obligation as always engaged upon the side of justice and humanity; and having understood the instructions of the Imperial German Government to its naval commanders to be upon the same plane of human action prescribed by the naval codes of other nations, the Government of the United States was loath to believe — it cannot now bring itself to believe — that these acts, so absolutely contrary to the rules, the practices, and the spirit of modern warfare, could have the countenance or sanction of that great Government. It feels it to be its duty, therefore, to address the Imperial German Government concerning them with the utmost frankness and in the earnest hope that it is not mistaken in expecting action on the part of the Imperial German Government which will correct the unfortunate impressions which have been created and vindicate once more the position of that Government with regard to the sacred freedom of the seas.

The Government of the United States has been apprised that the Imperial German Government considered themselves to be obliged by the extraordinary circumstances of the present war and the measures adopted by their adversaries in seeking to cut Germany off from all commerce, to adopt methods of retaliation which go much beyond the ordinary methods of warfare at sea, in the proclamation of a war zone from which they have warned neutral ships to keep away. This Government has already taken occasion to inform the Imperial German Government that it cannot admit the adoption of such measures or such a warning of danger to operate as in any degree an abbreviation of the rights of American shipmasters or of American citizens bound on lawful errands as passengers on merchant ships of belligerent nationality; and that it must hold the Imperial German Government to a strict accountability for any infringement of those rights, intentional or incidental. It does not understand the Imperial German Government to question those rights. It assumes, on the contrary, that the Imperial Government accept, as of course, the rule that the lives of noncombatants, whether they be of neutral citizenship or citizens of one of the nations at war, cannot lawfully or rightfully be put in jeopardy by the capture or destruction of an unarmed merchantman, and recognize also, as all other nations do, the obligation to take the usual precaution of visit and search to ascertain whether a suspected merchantman is in fact of belligerent nationality or is in fact carrying contraband of war under a neutral flag.

The Government of the United States, therefore, desires to call the attention of the Imperial German Government with the utmost earnestness to the fact that the objection to their present method of attack against the trade of their enemies lies in the practical impossibility of employing submarines in the destruction of commerce without disregarding those rules of fairness, reason, justice, and humanity, which all modern opinion regards as imperative. It is practically impossible for the officers of a submarine to visit a merchantman at sea and examine her papers and cargo. It is practically impossible for them to make a prize of her; and, if they cannot put a prize crew on board of her, they cannot sink her without leaving her crew and all on board of her to the mercy of the sea in her small boats. These facts it is understood the Imperial German Government frankly admit. We are informed that in the instances of which we have spoken time enough for even that poor measure of safety was not given, and in at least two of the cases cited not so much as a warning was received. Manifestly submarines cannot be used against merchantmen, as the last few weeks have shown, without an inevitable violation of many sacred principles of justice and humanity.

American citizens act within their indisputable rights in taking their ships and in traveling wherever their legitimate business calls them upon the high seas, and exercise those rights in what should be the well-justified confidence that their lives will not be endangered by acts done in clear violation of universally acknowledged international obligations, and certainly in the confidence that their own Government will sustain them in the exercise of their rights.

. . . .

Long acquainted as this Government has been with the character of the Imperial German Government and with the high principles of equity by which they have in the past been actuated and guided, the Government of the United States cannot believe that the commanders of the vessels which committed these acts of lawlessness did so except under a misapprehension of the orders issued by the Imperial German naval authorities. It takes it for granted that, at least within the practical possibilities of every such case, the commanders even of submarines were expected to do nothing that would involve the lives of noncombatants or the safety of neutral ships, even at the cost of failing of their object of capture or destruction. It confidently expects, therefore, that the Imperial German Government will disavow the acts of which the Government of the United States complains, that they will make reparation so far as reparation is possible for injuries which are without measure, and that they will take immediate steps to prevent the recurrence of anything so obviously subversive of the principle of warfare for which the Imperial German Government have in the past so wisely and so firmly contended.

The Government and the people of the United States look to the Imperial German Government for just, prompt, and enlightened action in this vital matter with the greater confidence because the United States and Germany are bound together not only by special ties of friendship but also by the explicit stipulations of the treaty of 1828 between the United States and the Kingdom of Prussia.

Expressions of regret and offers of reparation in case of the destruction of neutral ships sunk by mistake, while they may satisfy international obligations, if no loss of life results, cannot justify or excuse a practice, the natural and necessary effect of which is to subject neutral nations and neutral persons to new and immeasurable risks.

The Imperial German Government will not expect the Government of the United States to omit any word or any act necessary to the performance of its sacred duty of maintaining the rights of the United States and its citizens and of safeguarding their free exercise and enjoyment.

Bryan.

On January 31, 1917, Germany gave notice of her withdrawal of her agreement of May, 1916, with the United States and virtually announced that unrestricted submarine warfare would be renewed. The American Government immediately broke off diplomatic relations with Germany; and on April 2 President Wilson, in a speech, parts of which are here quoted, recommended American participation in the War. On April 6 war was declared by Congress.

219. PRESIDENT WILSON'S ADDRESS TO CONGRESS, RECOMMENDING PARTICIPATION IN THE WAR AGAINST GERMANY [1]

Gentlemen of the Congress:

I have called the Congress into extraordinary session because there are serious, very serious, choices of policy to be made, and made immediately, which it was neither right nor constitutionally permissible that I should assume the responsibility of making.

On the third of February last I officially laid before you the extraordinary announcement of the Imperial German Government that on and after the first day of February it was its purpose to put aside all restraints of law or of humanity and use its submarines to sink every vessel that sought to approach either the ports of Great Britain and Ireland or the western coasts of Europe or any of the ports controlled by the enemies of Germany within the Mediterranean. That had seemed to be the object of the German submarine warfare earlier in the war, but since April of last year the Imperial Government had somewhat restrained the commanders of its undersea craft in conformity with its promise then given to us that passenger boats should

[1] Albert Shaw, Editor, *The Messages and Papers of Woodrow Wilson*. 2 vols., New York, George H. Doran Company, 1924, vol. I, pp. 372–383 (condensed).

not be sunk and that due warning would be given to all other vessels which its submarines might seek to destroy, when no resistance was offered or escape attempted, and care taken that their crews were given at least a fair chance to save their lives in their open boats. The precautions taken were meagre and haphazard enough, as was proved in distressing instance after instance in the progress of the cruel and unmanly business, but a certain degree of restraint was observed. The new policy has swept every restriction aside. Vessels of every kind, whatever their flag, their character, their cargo, their destination, their errand, have been ruthlessly sent to the bottom without warning and without thought of help or mercy of those on board, the vessels of friendly neutrals along with those of belligerents. Even hospital ships and ships carrying relief to the sorely bereaved and stricken people of Belgium, though the latter were provided with safe conduct through the proscribed areas by the German Government itself and were distinguished by unmistakable marks of identity, have been sunk with the same reckless lack of compassion or of principle.

I was for a little while unable to believe that such things would in fact be done by any government that had hitherto subscribed to the humane practices of civilized nations. International law had its origin in the attempt to set up some law which would be respected and observed upon the seas, where no nation had right of dominion and where lay the free highways of the world. By painful stage after stage has that law been built up, with meagre enough results, indeed, after all was accomplished that could be accomplished, but always with a clear view, at least, of what the heart and conscience of mankind demanded. This minimum of right the German Government has swept aside under the plea of retaliation and necessity and because it had no weapons which it could use at sea except these which it is impossible to employ as it is employing them without throwing to the winds all scruples of humanity or of respect for the understandings that were supposed to underlie the intercourse of the world. I am not now thinking of the loss of property involved, immense and serious as that is, but only of the wanton and wholesale destruction of the lives of non-combatants, men, women, and children engaged in pursuits which have always, even in the darkest periods of modern history, been deemed innocent and legitimate. Property can be paid for; the lives of peaceful and innocent people cannot be. The present German submarine warfare against commerce is a warfare against mankind.

It is a war against all nations. American ships have been sunk, American lives taken, in ways which it has stirred us very deeply to learn of, but the ships and people of other neutral and friendly nations have been sunk and overwhelmed in the waters in the same way. There has been no discrimination. The challenge is to all mankind. Each nation must decide for itself how it will meet it. The choice we make for ourselves must be made with a moderation of counsel and a temperateness of judgment befitting our character and our motives as a nation. We must put excited feeling away. Our motive will not be revenge or the victorious assertion of the physical might of the nation, but only the vindication of right, of human right, of which we are only a single champion.

When I addressed the Congress on the twenty-sixth of February last I thought that it would suffice to assert our netural rights with arms, our right to use the seas against unlawful interference, our right to keep our people safe against unlawful violence. But armed neutrality, it now appears, is impracticable. Because submarines are in effect outlaws when used as the German submarines have been used against merchant shipping, it is impossible to defend ships against their attacks as the law of nations has assumed that merchantmen would defend themselves against privateers or cruisers, visible craft giving chase upon the open sea. It is common prudence in such circumstances, grim necessity indeed, to endeavour to destroy them before they have shown their own intention. They must be dealt with upon sight, if dealt with at all. The German Government denies the right of neutrals to use arms to all within the areas of the sea which it has proscribed, even in the defense of rights which no modern publicist has ever before questioned their right to defend. The intimation is conveyed that the armed guards which we have placed in our merchant ships will be treated as beyond the pale of law and subject to be dealt with as pirates would be. Armed neutrality is ineffectual enough at best; in such circumstances and in the face of such pretensions it is worse than ineffectual; it is likely only to produce what it was meant to prevent; it is practically certain to draw us into the war without either the rights or the effectiveness of belligerents. There is one choice we cannot make, we are incapable of making: we will not choose the path of submission and suffer the most sacred rights of our nation and our people to be ignored or violated. The wrongs against which we now array ourselves are no common wrongs: they cut to the very roots of human life.

With a profound sense of the solemn and even tragical character of the step I am taking and of the grave responsibilities which it involves, but in unhesitating obedience to what I deem my constitutional duty, I advise that the Congress declare the recent course of the Imperial German Government to be in fact nothing less than war against the government and people of the United States; that it formally accept the status of belligerent which has thus been thrust upon it; and that it take immediate steps not only to put the country in a more thorough state of defense but also to exert all its power and employ all its resources to bring the Government of the German Empire to terms and end the war.

. . . .

My own thought has not been driven from its habitual and normal course by the unhappy events of the last two months, and I do not believe that the thought of the nation has been altered or clouded by them. I have exactly the same things in mind now that I had in mind when I addressed the Senate on the twenty-second of January last; the same that I had in mind when I addressed the Congress on the third of February and on the twenty-sixth of February. Our object now, as then, is to vindicate the principles of peace and justice in the life of the world as against selfish and autocratic power and to set up amongst the really free and self-governed peoples of the world such a concert of purpose and of action as will henceforth ensure the observance of those principles. Neutrality is no longer feasible or desirable where the peace of the world is involved and the freedom of its peoples, and the menace to that peace and freedom lies in the existence of autocratic governments backed by organized force which is controlled wholly by their will, not by the will of their people. We have seen the last of neutrality in such circumstances. We are at the beginning of an age in which it will be insisted that the same standards of conduct and responsibility for wrong done shall be observed among nations and their governments that are observed among the individual citizens of civilized states.

We have no quarrel with the German people. We have no feeling towards them but one of sympathy and friendship. It was not upon their impulse that their government acted in entering this war. It was not with their previous knowledge or approval. It was a war determined upon as wars used to be determined upon in the old, unhappy days when peoples were nowhere consulted by their rulers and wars were provoked and waged in the interest of dynasties or of little groups of ambitious men who were accustomed to use their fellow men as pawns and tools. Self-governed nations do not fill their neighbour states with spies or set the course of intrigue to bring about some critical posture of affairs which will give them an opportunity to strike and make conquest. Such designs can be successfully worked out only under cover and where no one has the right to ask questions. Cunningly contrived plans of deception or aggression, carried, it may be, from generation to generation, can be worked out and kept from the light only within the privacy of courts or behind the carefully guarded confidences of a narrow and privileged class. They are happily impossible where public opinion commands and insists upon full information concerning all the nation's affairs.

A steadfast concert for peace can never be maintained except by a partnership of democratic nations. No autocratic government could be trusted to keep faith within it or observe its covenants. It must be a league of honour, a partnership of opinion. Intrigue would eat its vitals away; the plottings of inner circles who could plan what they would and render account to no one would be a corruption seated at its very heart. Only free peoples can hold their purpose and their honour steady to a common end and prefer the interests of mankind to any narrow interest of their own.

. . . .

We are now about to accept gauge of battle with this natural foe to liberty and shall, if necessary, spend the whole force of the nation to check and nullify its pretensions and its power. We are glad, now that we see the facts with no veil of false pretence about them, to fight thus for the ultimate peace of the world and for the liberation of its peoples, the German peoples included: for the rights of nations great and small and the privilege of men everywhere to choose their way of life and of obedience. The world must be made safe for democracy. Its peace must be planted upon the tested foundations of political liberty. We have no selfish ends to serve. We desire no conquest, no dominion. We seek no indemnities for ourselves, no material compensation for the sacrifices we shall freely make. We are but one of the champions of the rights of mankind. We shall be satisfied when those rights have been made as secure as the faith and the freedom of nations can make them.

Just because we fight without rancour and without selfish object, seeking nothing for ourselves but what we shall wish to share with all free peoples, we shall, I feel confident, conduct our operations as belligerents without passion and ourselves observe with proud punctilio the principles of right and of fair play we profess to be fighting for.

. . . .

It will be all the easier for us to conduct ourselves as belligerents in a high spirit of right and fairness because we act without animus, not in enmity towards a people or with the desire to bring any injury or disadvantage upon them, but only in armed opposition to an irresponsible government which has thrown aside all considerations of humanity and of right and is running amuck. We are, let me say again, the sincere friends of the German people and shall desire nothing so much as the early reëstablishment of intimate relations of mutual advantage between us, — however hard it may be for them, for the time being, to believe that this is spoken from our hearts. We have borne with their present government through all these bitter months because of that friendship, — exercising a patience and forbearance which would otherwise have been impossible. We shall, happily, still have an opportunity to prove that friendship in our daily attitude and actions towards the millions of men and women of German birth and native sympathy who live amongst us and share our life, and we shall be proud to prove it towards all who are in fact loyal to their neighbours and to the Government in the hour of test. They are, most of them, as true and loyal Americans as if they had never known any other fealty or allegiance. They will be prompt to stand with us in rebuking and restraining the few who may be of a different mind and purpose. If there should be disloyalty, it will be dealt with with a firm hand of stern repression; but, if it lifts its head at all, it will lift it only here and there and without countenance except from a lawless and malignant few.

It is a distressing and oppressive duty, Gentlemen of the Congress, which I have performed in thus addressing you. There are, it may be, many months of fiery trial and sacrifice ahead of us. It is a fearful thing to lead this great peaceful people into war, into the most terrible and disastrous of all wars, civilization itself seeming to be in the balance. But the right is more precious than peace, and we shall fight for the things which we have always carried nearest our hearts, for democracy, for the right of those who submit to authority to have a voice in their own governments, for the rights and liberties of small nations, for a universal dominion of right by such a concert of free peoples as shall bring peace and safety to all nations and make the world itself at last free. To such a task we can dedicate our lives and our fortunes, everything that we are and everything that we have, with the pride of those who know that the day has come when America is privileged to spend her blood and her might for the principles that gave her birth and happiness and the peace which she has treasured. God helping her, she can do no other.

Early in 1918 President Wilson laid down a platform of possible peace on the basis of the " Fourteen Points" which are given in the following selection.

Germany, however, was not ready at the time for peace on these terms. But after suffering decisive military defeat in the summer of 1918 she announced to President Wilson her readiness to make peace on the basis of the " Fourteen Points." President Wilson, replying for the Allies and the United States, agreed to an armistice on these terms, with, however, certain reservations in regard to the freedom of the seas (Point 2), the status of Austria-Hungary (Point 10), and the question of compensation for damage done by Germany to civilians and their property in the Allied Countries. Germany agreed and the cessation of hostilities followed.

Whether or not the subsequent Peace of Versailles was based essentially on the " Fourteen Points" has been a matter of heated controversy.

220. PRESIDENT WILSON'S " FOURTEEN POINTS"[1]

The program of the world's peace, . . . is our program; and that program, the only possible program, as we see it, is this:

[1] Albert Shaw, Editor, *The Messages and Papers of Woodrow Wilson.* 2 vols., New York, George H. Doran Company, 1924, vol. I, pp. 468–470.

1. Open covenants of peace, openly arrived at, after which there shall be no private international understandings of any kind but diplomacy shall proceed always frankly and in the public view.

2. Absolute freedom of navigation upon the seas, outside territorial waters, alike in peace and in war, except as the seas may be closed in whole or in part by international action for the enforcement of international covenants.

3. The removal, so far as possible, of all economic barriers and the establishment of an equality of trade conditions among all the nations consenting to the peace and associating themselves for its maintenance.

4. Adequate guarantees given and taken that national armaments will be reduced to the lowest points consistent with domestic safety.

5. A free, open-minded, and absolutely impartial adjustment of all colonial claims, based upon a strict observance of the principle that in determining all such questions of sovereignty the interests of the populations concerned must have equal weight with the equitable claims of the government whose title is to be determined.

6. The evacuation of all Russian territory and such a settlement of all questions affecting Russia as will secure the best and freest coöperation of the other nations of the world in obtaining for her an unhampered and unembarrassed opportunity for the independent determination of her own political development and national policy and assure her of a sincere welcome into the society of free nations under institutions of her own choosing; and, more than a welcome, assistance also of every kind that she may need and may herself desire. The treatment accorded Russia by her sister nations in the months to come will be the acid test of their good will, of their comprehension of her needs as distinguished from their own interests, and of their intelligent and unselfish sympathy.

7. Belgium, the whole world will agree, must be evacuated and restored, without any attempt to limit the sovereignty which she enjoys in common with all other free nations. No other single act will serve as this will serve to restore confidence among the nations in the laws which they have themselves set and determined for the government of their relations with one another. Without this healing act the whole structure and validity of international law is forever impaired.

8. All French territory should be freed and the invaded portions restored, and the wrong done to France by Prussia in 1871 in the matter of Alsace-Lorraine, which has unsettled the peace of the world for nearly fifty years, should be righted, in order that peace may once more be made secure in the interest of all.

9. A readjustment of the frontiers of Italy should be effected along clearly recognizable lines of nationality.

10. The peoples of Austria-Hungary, whose place among the nations we wish to see safeguarded and assured, should be accorded the freest opportunity of autonomous development.

11. Rumania, Serbia, and Montenegro should be evacuated; occupied territories restored; Serbia accorded free and secure access to the sea; and the relations of the several Balkan states to one another determined by friendly counsel along historically established lines of allegiance and nationality; and international guarantees of the political and economic independence and territorial integrity of the several Balkan states should be entered into.

12. The Turkish portions of the present Ottoman Empire should be assured a secure sovereignty, but the other nationalities which are now under Turkish rule should be assured an undoubted security of life and an absolutely unmolested opportunity of autonomous development, and the Dardanelles should be permanently opened as a free passage to the ships and commerce of all nations under international guarantees.

13. An independent Polish state should be erected which should include the territories inhabited by indisputably Polish populations, which should be assured a free and secure access to the sea, and whose political and economic independence and territorial integrity should be guaranteed by international covenant.

14. A general association of nations must be formed under specific covenants for the purpose of affording mutual guarantees of political independence and territorial integrity to great and small states alike.

SECTION IV. THE BREAKDOWN OF GERMANY

As it became increasingly clear in the early autumn of 1918 that Germany had lost the War loud cries arose within the Empire against the Imperial Government. Minorities boldly and angrily voiced their aspirations. In a tumultous session of the Reichstag on October 23rd Haase, of the Independent Socialist party, called for the overthrow of the Imperial Government and the building of a socialist state. Stychel, representing the Polish party, demanded a free, independent Poland. Ricklin, for the inhabitants of Alsace-Lorraine, Hanssen, for those of Schleswig and Holstein, asserted the right of the minorities they represented to determine their own political fate in accordance with the principle of self-determination.

221. INTERNAL DISSENSION IN GERMANY ON THE EVE OF THE COLLAPSE OF THE EMPIRE [1]

Haase (Koenigsberg)

Gentlemen: Since the last session of the Diet, in July of the present year, a total *change in the political and military situation* has taken place. The world revolution, which this war called forth, has recently developed swiftly. Ancient realms have tumbled into ruins; the Austrian-Hungarian Empire, united by blood and iron, is already dissolved. Turkey does not exist any longer in its old form; Egypt has been linked more firmly to England; Great Britain's influence penetrates Mesopotamia and Palestine; France has made solid her position in Syria; Bulgaria has dissolved her alliance with us and closes a separate peace with the Entente; Austria-Hungary is forced by international events to follow suit; German Imperialism, too, has lost everything in this carnage.

. . . .

We do not find satisfaction in a peace that hinders German capitalism from extension and at the same time strengthens the capitalism of the Entente, delivering other countries over for spoliation. We are and remain disinclined to capitalism in any form. We repudiate the spoliation of mankind by mankind wheresoever it may happen.

The German people feel that they have been deceived by lies and delusions during these past years. The German people are unable to understand how it could be possible — after they had been told daily by officials and newspapers, newspapers even of members of the socialistic party in the government, that we were stepping from victory to victory, — that all of a sudden the German Government was forced to succumb to an armistice and a peace offer.

. . . .

In this embarrassment you (of the parties of the bourgeoisie) have not objected to representatives of working-men, followers of the social-democratic faction, joining the Government side by side with you, in order to save as much of the system as can be saved. Mr. Stresemann was so frank yesterday as to give clear expression of his pleasure in regard to this.

Gentlemen: *Crowns roll down to the pavement,* the crown of the King of the Bulgars, Ferdinand; the crown of the Tsar Nicholas, the crown of the

[1] Extracts from the Speeches of Four Deputies in the Reichstag, at the Session of October 23, 1918. *Verhandlungen des Reichstags.* XIII Legislaturperiode. II Session. Band 314. Stenographische Berichte von der 192. Sitzung am 5. Oktober 1918 bis zur 197. Sitzung am 26. Oktober 1918 und Sachregister. Berlin, 1919. Druck und Verlag der Norddeutschen Buchdruckerei und Verlags-Anstalt. (Translation.)

Austrian-Hungarian Emperor. The crowns which some thought to see come into being, the crowns of Finland, Courland and Lithuania, have melted away like ghosts. Everywhere around us republics are looming into existence, and can you now imagine that Germany alone, surrounded by republics, is to retain the bearer of a crown, the bearer of many crowns and crownlets?

.   .   .   .

Gentlemen: We look into the future with troubled eyes, not only viewing all the hard calamities which press heavily on the people and which in their complete tragedy will appear only after the war, but weighing also the exorbitant burdens which drag the people down and which are becoming heavier from day to day.

.   .   .   .

The German people will not be extinguished, will not be appeased, whatever appearance this peace treaty may have when completed. The salvation from their misery, from their suffering, from their intolerable burdens cannot come to the German people as long as the existing social order remains.

The productivity of agriculture and industry can be increased to the utmost if in place of the present economic order, the only goal of which is profit, the *socialistic economic order* is introduced. To combine the agencies of production is a necessity.

.   .   .   .

Stychel, deputy:

Gentlemen: Before I start with my explanation I should like to say a few words in reference to the remarks made by Count Westarp. Count Westarp demanded categorically, in opposition to the contents of the speech of the Imperial Chancellor, the integrity of the borders of the Empire and declared then, that not the breadth of one foot of German soil in the East must be ceded. Gentlemen: Justice and the Poles do not demand German soil. But it is clear that the chauvinistic principle: "Wherever the German has once put his foot, that is and remains German soil " — has lost its significance.

Count Westarp is of the opinion that the claims of the Poles for restitution were unattainable claims; but in the international peace conference it will be shown, how that matter is there understood.

Between two extremes a peculiar harmony can be noticed here to-day, between Count Westarp and Mr. Deputy Haase. Deputy Haase has also violently opposed a *cession of those Polish parts* of Prussian territory, that would cause a separation from Eastern Prussia. That is significant; but I believe that such opposition will not prove profitable to the endeavor to procure a speedy peace, not profitable to the endeavor of the Government to secure the necessary support of public opinion.

Gentlemen: Mr. Deputy Naumann has urged us to avoid duplicities. That corresponds with our desire. Therefore we speak; for that reason we, the Poles step out from our reserve, which we have guarded so far. Once for all the question must be made clear.

Gentlemen: What we have heard from the side of Count Westarp, was a provocation! (Outcry) — Certainly! And we have the right and the duty to give energetic expression here to our point of view.

. . . .

Gentlemen: The Polish people have never renounced their right to liberty; divided among three foreign powers they have always felt as an entirety, as a unity, longing for freedom. Of the many declarations of the Poles and Polish representatives, I shall mention here only those of 1867 and 1871, which *official declarations* on the part of the *representative of the Polish people* were given here in Berlin. Is there one to be found among German men of honor and intelligence who has no understanding of the elementary call for liberty among the Polish people wherever they are? Can a sincere and sensible man be surprised, especially within the present borders of the German Empire, that the Poles wish to live free in their proper country? Have there been any desire and attempt to arrange anything for the Poles so that they could feel comfortable here? (Acclamations by the Independent Social Democrats.) By exceptional laws and exceptional treatment, by harsh words from the Government and the German press, through chicanery by officials, the Poles were steadily made aware that they, upon the soil of their ancestors, were not justly valued, justly esteemed citizens of the country by which they were forcibly annexed.

Gentlemen: To give a typical instance of the *attitude of the Government towards the Poles* I should like to mention what Minister von Hammerstein said on the 25th of January, 1904 in the Prussian House of Deputies. There he compared the Poles with the Germans and said: " These are not adversaries of equal rank: we are the commanders and the Poles must obey! " (Outcry) That [statement] serves to characterize the attitude of a government hostile to the Poles! (Renewed outcries).

. . . .

Gentlemen: When affairs are set in motion, when the German Government of its own accord has acclaimed the principles of Wilson, including point XIII which reads: " An independent Polish state should be erected which should include the territories inhabited by indisputably Polish populations, which should be assured a free and secure access to the sea and whose political integrity should be guaranteed by international covenant — "

When another condition of Wilson demands that the aspirations of the peoples should be clearly set forth — what argument is there for suppressing in the Polish press every endeavor to make things clear, while the German press from its point of view can do so without any hindrance?

Gentlemen: From the generally sketched principles of Wilson which are expressly approved by the German Government as the basis of the peace, with consideration of the historical rights and ethnographical facts and with no necessity of further comment, there clearly results:

1.) The formation of a sovereign, independent state, composed of all parts of Polish regions, with full possibilities of development, with its own sea coast and seaport, whose political and economic independence and territorial integrity must be guaranteed by international treaty.

As an addition we demand:

2.) The rebuilding and restitution of everything in Polish territory that during the period of the war has been destroyed or taken away.

3.) The coöperation of representatives of all parts of Polish territory at the international peace conference.

. . . .

Ricklin, Deputy:

Gentlemen: In the name of the members of the Alsace-Lorraine group here present I am enjoined to make the following declaration:

The Imperial Chancellor announced in his speech of October the 5th, that *Alsace-Lorraine* shall be autonomous within the Empire. In yesterday's speech he made known to us that an Alsatian has been appointed governor and an Alsatian state secretary. He made the additional remark that he assumed that the new governor would construct and make public, in accord with the party-leaders, a program for the administration of Alsace-Lorraine. The Imperial Chancellor has failed to point out even by a single word, what the German Government expects from the introduction of these reforms in Alsace-Lorraine and what is intended by the Government. But the presumption seems to be justified that by that action it is expected that an influence will be exerted upon the sentiment of the people of Alsace-Lorraine in a sense friendly to Germany. We consider it a duty of conscience to tell the full truth to the German people, lest a fallacious expectation should arise in this matter.

The truth is: Everything that may be undertaken here in Berlin or by the new administration in Strassburg in that direction will not, in the state to which the Alsace-Lorraine question has now come, be able to exert any essential influence upon the *feeling* in Alsace-Lorraine, because of the way that that feeling has changed during the course of the war.

By the German Government's acceptance of the 14 points of Wilson's peace program, especially the 8th point which refers to Alsace-Lorraine, the Alsace-Lorraine question has become international and its solution has been transferred, if not to President Wilson, at any rate to the peace conference.

. . . .

Since we certainly expect that, in discussing the Alsace-Lorraine question, the right of determining their political fate themselves, as claimed by a very large part of the population of Alsace-Lorraine, will be respected, we must now avoid anything that would prejudice the free expression of the will of the Alsace-Lorrainers. The intrinsic change in the constitution which is intended for us, shows (in the opinion of many circles of persons) such a prejudice against the free expression of the will of the people of Alsace-Lorraine that, to say the least, it is likely to irritate public opinion in that area.

Since the Alsace-Lorraine question has taken this form and has become an international problem, we believe the mandate which we have received from our constituents, to obtain for this region autonomy within the Empire, is nullified by the particular circumstances that have developed.

With thanks to those deputies who have supported us all these years in the just desire for maintaining our just demand for autonomy within the Empire we add the declaration, that had this action granting autonomy been carried out earlier in the thorough fashion now planned, it could not only have spared us much misery and reconciled the people of Alsace-Lorraine with their situation, but would also have been of distinct value in helping to prevent this terrible disaster, which the war has brought to the world.

. . . .

Hanssen, Deputy:

The first essential in the program of President Wilson is the execution of the right of self-determination of peoples which Germany has acknowledged, as the Imperial Chancellor a few days ago stated in his speech to the presiding officers of the Lithuanian Taryba. And in point 4 in his speech laying down his program of February 12th the President declared that " all clearly expressed national claims shall find the widest satisfaction."

Gentlemen: All duplicity in international questions must at present be avoided as our colleague Naumann explained yesterday. The seriousness of the hour demands language clear and open. Keeping in mind the above-mentioned view of the Imperial Chancellor, as well as that of President Wilson, I demand as representative of the Danish population of North-Schleswig in the name of right and justice the execution of #5 of the peace treaty of Prague and therewith at the pending meeting of the peace conference the conclusive solution of the *North-Schleswig question,* based upon the right of the peoples to self-determination.

Gentlemen: First, a very short historical retrospect. In the year 1864 the

Danish population of North-Schleswig was torn away forcibly, against their wish and in spite of their solemn protest, by the two great powers, Prussia and Austria, from their old mother country, from their ancestral people to whom they belonged through language, customs, memories and a glorious history of more than a thousand years. Two years later the conquered Austria ceded her rights in the common loot of the war of 1864 to Prussia. The cession was defined in #5 of *the peace treaty of Prague* as follows: " His Majesty the Emperor and King cedes to His Majesty the King of Prussia all his rights to the duchies of Holstein and Schleswig, obtained by the peace of Vienna, October 30th, 1864, with the modification that if the population of the Northern districts of Schleswig make known by a vote their wish to be united to Denmark, their territory shall be ceded to Denmark."

The peace treaty of Prague was laid before the Prussian diet the 20th of September, 1866. On that occasion the cession of North-Schleswig was criticized by several speakers. Against them Bismarck specified exactly his position in regard to the self-determination of peoples by declaring, as per stenographic report:

" I have always been of the opinion, that a population, which persistently and by clearly manifested will makes known that it does not want to be Prussian and German, which by clearly manifested will desires to belong to a directly neighboring country, does not strengthen the Power from which it anxiously desires to be separated. We have accepted the decision and Prussia must observe it; but we shall carry it out in such a manner, that no doubt shall remain from the votes (according to which we shall act), of the free and independent choice, the definite decision, which is thereby manifested."

An excellent principle, a binding word! The Danish population of North-Schleswig has given in succeeding periods again and again clear expression to its wishes and will. But, gentlemen, years have passed, a vote by the people in North-Schleswig, as promised by treaty and accepted by Prussia, has never been executed.

. . . .

All Scandinavia follows with the warmest sympathies the fate of the small brave race of South Jutland. From Henrik Ibsen and Björnstjörne Björnson in Norway to Selma Lagerlöf and Ellen Key in Sweden, from the great Danish poets of the past century to Harald Höffding and George Brandes and beyond these to the younger generation, almost every prominent representative of intellectual life in the North again and again has demanded a just *solution of the North-Schleswig question.* . . .

SECTION V. THE PEACE SETTLEMENT

The three great leaders in the peace-making at Paris in 1919 were Woodrow Wilson, David Lloyd George, and Georges Clemenceau. From some of the criticisms made of these men it might be supposed that the Carthaginian peace imposed on Germany was almost entirely their personal work. It is therefore well to remember, as Mr. Frank Simonds reminds us in the two following selections, that public opinion in the victorious countries played an important rôle at the Peace Conference.

In the first of these selections Mr. Simonds contrasts the situation in 1814–1815 with the situation in 1919, showing how much greater the influence of public opinion was on the peace-making after the Great War than it had been at the Congress of Vienna. In the second he illustrates concretely the effect of public opinion on the proceedings of the Paris Conference.

222. PUBLIC OPINION AND THE PEACE CONFERENCE OF 1919 [1]

The men who made the settlement of Paris in 1814, as they also made the decisions of the Congress of Vienna and the later peace after Waterloo, were men for whom the business in hand had been a life work, and . . . their knowledge, experience, and ability, subject to royal pleasure, which did often hamper and harass them, had full scope. And never under any circumstance had they to consider the question of public opinion as we know it, or submit to the immediate restrictions of parliamentary supervision.

．　．　．　．　．　．　．　．　．　．　．　．　．　．

When one turns to the consideration of the situation which existed a century after the Paris Peace of 1814, on the eve of still another Paris conference, the contrast with the circumstances of the earlier day is impressive.

The kings had gone. Parliaments, beginning with the British, had become representative. The men who were to act for the great European states, and in reality they were Clemenceau and Lloyd George, were not diplomats. Neither had any claim to expert knowledge of foreign affairs. Neither had ever manifested any particular interest in this field. And this was also true of Woodrow Wilson, who acted with them to make the decisions of the "Big Three" and thus to make the settlement of Versailles.

Both the European premiers were lifelong parliamentarians. Both had come to power in the dark days of the war because of their unique power to

[1] Frank H. Simonds, *How Europe Made Peace without America*. New York, Doubleday, Page and Company, 1927, pp. 10–19 (condensed).

give impulsion to legislative bodies and stimulus to democratic peoples facing the tremendous strain incident to the great struggle.

Clemenceau had once been president of the Council and thus measurably conversant with foreign affairs for a brief moment before the war, but both he and Lloyd George had been distinguished throughout their long careers almost exclusively because of their mastery of that peculiar technique which permits contemporary politicians to control majorities, sway public opinion, make or break ministries.

They were, themselves, moreover, in the last analysis, entirely at the command of their respective parliaments which could dismiss them within the hour. For them, as for all premiers, the conditions of continued power were found always in the necessity to maintain control of parliament by that highly difficult device of retaining popular approval, for parliaments are jealous bodies and are ever ready to lay hold upon public opinion as a stick with which to assail the Minister of the moment.

In the field of domestic affairs, moreover, the people have with the passing decades acquired undeniable capacity. Although they may be frequently misled, sometimes deceived, often frankly mistaken, within the limits of their own national existence and experience the people have acquired a grasp of the fundamentals. They know here what they want and why. They are acquiring and they continue to acquire the discipline and self-restraint which are necessary. They have learned to compromise, and rarely, except in transitory bursts of passion, demand the absolute.

But in the nature of things they can, as yet, bring nothing like the same knowledge or the same experience to foreign affairs. The complex problems of international relations and the baffling mysteries of other national existences lived under different conditions of geography, dominated by other traditions and illuminated by other histories are to them unintelligible. They must measure the policies and purposes of every other people by the yardstick of their own experience.

Thus, they will bring to foreign questions the same standards, express the same will, insist upon the same tests which they employ in domestic affairs. They will never question their own knowledge or competence. And, in the last analysis, the choice of any Prime Minister must often be between openly flouting national will, and throwing this national will into violent collision with the similar will of another people.

Thus the absolute break between the conditions of 1814 and 1919 is established. The men who made the older settlement knew the material with which they had to work. They knew it because it was their trade to know it, and their presence at Paris and Vienna was the ultimate proof of their mastery of that trade. Finally, together with knowledge, they had power.

On the contrary, the men who held power in 1919 had come to office by reason of their capacity to deal with an utterly dissimilar set of problems from those presented at the Paris Conference. They had learned a totally different art from that of negotiating abroad, they were masters of the art of dealing with a modern parliamentary democracy. They knew all about this business that a lifelong training could teach them, and they were at Paris precisely because, in the terrible hours of the World War, they had displayed the supreme mastery of this art of leading the peoples.

There is a further circumstance to be noted in presenting the contrast between 1814 and 1919. In its long struggle with monarchy and autocracy, democracy had not only wrested control of domestic affairs from the enemy and thus automatically succeeded to the direction of foreign affairs, it had in the progress of the battle also acquired an instinctive and dominating distrust for methods of the older order, for what it described as " old-fashioned diplomacy " and the men who plied that trade.

As a consequence, although diplomacy had on sufferance continued to play a part, its influence in foreign affairs had steadily diminished in all the years from the Congress of Berlin to the World War. Moreover, after 1914, democracy tended to arrive at the conclusion that this world-wide catastrophe was itself in some mysterious fashion to be charged to diplomacy.

Accordingly, when Clemenceau, Lloyd George, and Woodrow Wilson undertook to make peace at Paris, none of them even thought of employing importantly the machinery of the Foreign Office, the Quai d'Orsay, or the State Department. Diplomatic opinion was rarely asked, diplomatic experience and knowledge were seldom appealed to. On the contrary, all three manifested the same impatience and contempt for the representatives of the profession to which Talleyrand and Metternich had belonged a century before.

* * * * * * * *

Such, then, was the revolution which had taken place in the control of foreign policy in the European world. But the Conference of Paris in 1919 was precisely the first occasion when and where the consequences of the revolution were to be disclosed. If the Congress of Vienna had been the culminating point of the old order, Paris was just as clearly the first authentic revelation of the arrival of a new system and another age.

But if the Paris Conference was the first disclosure of this great transformation, what occurred there was steadily repeated in all the succeeding years. All prime ministers and foreign ministers in Europe, from Versailles to Locarno, were equally helpless in the face of their own public opinions. Each was compelled to adopt policies and resort to measures in which he did not believe, either to avoid disaster at home or save a foreign associate, equally handicapped by a similar national state of mind.

Peace after the first fall of Napoleon, and again after Waterloo, was restored in a few weeks because those who had power were aware of the realities of the international situation. Peace after 1918 was postponed for seven years, because the peoples which had all power at home were uninformed as to the limits of their own power abroad and unaware of the necessity for compromises without which settlement was impossible.

What the monarchs and diplomats had learned before the settlement of 1814, the sovereign peoples learned only after the making of the Treaty of Versailles in 1919.

223. *PUBLIC OPINION AND THE TREATY OF VERSAILLES* [1]

Viewed in retrospect . . . each European people is conscious of the fact that, in January, 1919, its consuming and dominating desire was for peace. How could it be otherwise? Tortured and afflicted by four years of continuous and incredible agonies, exhausted by efforts which have been unequalled in any other age, the longing of all European peoples for peace at the moment of the Armistice cannot be denied.

But what kind of peace did the several peoples desire? To what extent did any desire peace at any price? What were the demands made by the peoples upon their Ministers at the moment when the military decision had placed it within their power to write the terms of a settlement? Here and perhaps only here it may be possible to discover the origin of the causes of the later failures.

The case of the British people is perhaps most illuminating, and it relates to the reparations clauses, which were the cause of so much disaster. In December, 1918, before the Paris Conference had assembled, Lloyd George went before the people of Britain in the notorious " Khaki election." Rightly he judged that this was the moment most propitious for the man who had " won the war " to win another mandate.

Trustworthy contemporary report records the fact that at the outset of this campaign Lloyd George was in a moderate and reasonable mood. But no sooner had his foot touched the platform than with that incredible flair for popular opinion which has made him the greatest politician of modern times, he sensed the temper of the British electorate.

Under the lash of press propaganda, under the stimulus of popular emotion still reacting to the war, responding to continuous heckling of press and audiences alike, Lloyd George promised the British people that, if they would give him a majority, he would go to Paris and " hang the Kaiser " and make the Germans " pay the last farthing," that he would squeeze the

[1] Frank H. Simonds, *How Europe Made Peace without America*, New York, Doubleday, Page and Company, 1927, pp. 50–57 (condensed).

Germans " until the pips squeaked." And on this understanding the British public gave him an enormous majority.

In this episode it would be difficult to discover anything of that secrecy later alleged against the treaty-makers. No open covenant was ever more openly arrived at than this between Prime Minister and people. No detail in proposed foreign policy was ever more frankly and freely submitted to that solemn referendum which is that of the ballot box. Patently the reparations clauses were not inspired in the dark corridors of Paris, but in the great open spaces of the British electoral arena.

It might, perhaps, be conjectured, however, that, since this popular decision was unmistakably based upon transitory war passion and the British public was at the moment incapable of knowing its own mind, it would later and relatively promptly adopt more generous and reasonable conceptions. But, in point of fact, it was the other way — it was Lloyd George who saw the truth first.

In contact with the American financial commission, which could and did view the question objectively, since the United States was not making a reparations claim, Lloyd George was convinced that excessive reparations could not be collected, that the " last farthing " was not available. In conference with the younger economists of his own delegation, he was brought to see that, for a trading and commercial people, reparations even to the extent of the possible might be of doubtful advantage.

But, although he began to see the truth, Lloyd George was daily faced by the contract, and with each edition the London press spread the disquieting rumour that " L. G. Sells Pass " that the Prime Minister, " Wants to Let the Hun Off." The members of Parliament who were chosen with Lloyd George in the recent election became disturbed by the unrest at home, and their protests crowded the wires to Paris.

The British people had sent Lloyd George to Paris to impose a hard peace on the German people; were they going to permit him to impose a soft peace upon themselves? Hardly; if anyone believes that they were prepared for this, let him study the British press of March and April, 1919.

In the end, then, Lloyd George, although he knew better and told the American financial delegates that he knew better, sent General Smuts to President Wilson and obtained the President's consent to include pensions and war allowances in the bill against the German. By this method only could the British share in reparations be more than trifling, because all the devastation was on Continental soil. But by this device the sum total was trebled. There was the origin of the reparations folly, but the choice of the British Prime Minister was between the course he took and an adverse vote in the House of Commons.

The French case is equally illuminating although a trifle less obvious.

Clemenceau and all the French people knew what they needed, as Lloyd George and the British people did not perceive in their own case at the outset. Security was for France the primary objective in the peace-making.

But the French people saw security only in terms of traditional and military solutions. Permanent occupation of the left bank of the Rhine by Allied armies, definite separation of the populations of the left bank from Germany, these were the French demands, and Clemenceau presented them to the Peace Conference.

Instantly, these demands encountered British and American opposition. They were contrary to all Mr. Wilson's conceptions based upon the Fourteen Points; they were utterly inconsistent with all British foreign policy for centuries. Neither the British nor the American people were willing to keep armies perpetually on the Rhine or permanently to support what was in reality an eternal state of war with the German people.

Unable to establish these demands, which were the demands of the French people at the moment, furiously pressed by the Paris newspapers, Clemenceau accepted, instead, an Anglo-American promise to guarantee French security against any new German aggression.

This was not only the maximum to be obtained, but it was the true line of French policy, for it was the single possible line which promised any security. Clemenceau's course was amply vindicated later when the Locarno pacts did give France the British guarantee which was the objective of all his Paris effort.

In the face of all popular opposition, Clemenceau forced the ratification of the Treaty when made. He bullied a hostile Chamber of Deputies which was at the moment more fearful of a " Tiger " in front of it than a people somewhat in the background. To achieve the ratification, Clemenceau had to treat Poincaré, the President of the Republic, like an impertinent butler, and Foch, the marshal of victory, like an insubordinate corporal.

But although the Chamber ratified the Treaty, the French people refused to accept it. They rallied against Clemenceau, now come to private life, and under their stimulus Parliament denied him the Presidency of the Republic which had fallen vacant. The " Father of Victory " became for his people the man who had lost the peace.

Lloyd George bowed to the mistaken will of the people, and he lasted for nearly four years after the Paris Conference. Clemenceau imposed the wise policy upon the French people, and they punished him and continue to reproach him, even when they have accepted what he sought to obtain for them.

This present volume is limited to the discussion of the events which directly concern Germany and her British, French, and American opponents, but there is, perhaps, warrant for appealing to an Italian example, since it is illuminating and apposite. When the question of Fiume arose at the Peace Conference, it precipitated a dispute which threatened to wreck the whole negotiation. It produced a deadlock at a moment when Europe was patently disintegrating.

In this situation, President Wilson, who steadily adhered to the belief that the people, as contrasted with their leaders, were always generous and enlightened, put his doctrine to the test. He had been in Italy during his grand tour before the Conference met. Nowhere had he been welcomed so warmly, cheered so enthusiastically, acclaimed so deliriously. Perhaps there came back to him the memory of the night when he leaned from a Roman balcony and threw kisses to the mad throngs below.

At all events, he suddenly issued an appeal to the Italian people over the head of Orlando, their representative at Paris, who was holding out for Fiume. This appeal was based upon an eloquent and moving statement of the perils to the world of continued delay. It was a request of the Italian people to disown the unregenerate and selfish nationalism of their Paris representative and by an act of national self-abnegation remove the stumbling block to the restoration of peace in the world.

What happened? From the Alps to Sicily there burst forth a unanimous, passionate, violent denunciation of Woodrow Wilson. After years, the embers of this nation-wide conflagration are discoverable in Italy, and they are not yet cold. Obedient to this will thus expressed, D'Annunzio later went to Fiume, following the example of Garibaldi and his Thousand, and took the city by force against the will of Europe.

When one turns to the question of the guilt clause, the reef on which the whole settlement was ultimately wrecked, the fact is beyond discussion that this indictment of sixty millions of Germans proceeded directly from the peoples of the Allied democracies.

No people, no considerable minority within any nation, no popular voice audible to the sentient ear of any politician ever raised a protest against an indictment which was impossible in fact and unwise in policy. For all peoples equally and for all elements within national frontiers, the German people were the people who had invaded Belgium, sunk the Lusitania, devastated northern France. They were by virtue of these facts, which were incontrovertible, a criminal people.

. . . .

No portion of the whole tremendous and ponderous volume, which is the Treaty of Versailles, came so directly and unmistakably from the people, and no representative of any country, not Lloyd George, not Clemenceau, not even Woodrow Wilson, would have dared to face his own people having opposed this judgment at Paris. And, of course, none ever thought of doing that.

The Treaty of Versailles was signed by representatives of Germany and of the countries with which she had been at war, June 28, 1919, in the Hall of Mirrors in Louis XIV's magnificent old palace. The treaty is far too long to quote in full but what seem to be some of its most significant provisions are here given.

224. EXTRACTS FROM THE TREATY OF VERSAILLES

Article 42

Germany is forbidden to maintain or construct any fortifications either on the left bank of the Rhine or on the right bank to the west of a line drawn 50 kilometres to the East of the Rhine.

Article 45

As compensation for the destruction of the coal mines in the north of France and as part payment towards the total reparation due from Germany for the damage resulting from the war, Germany cedes to France in full and absolute possession, with exclusive rights of exploitation, unencumbered and free from all debts and charges of any kind, the coal mines situated in the Saar Basin as defined in Article 48. [Article 48 outlines boundaries. Editor's note.]

Article 49

Germany renounces in favour of the League of Nations, in the capacity of trustee, the government of the territory defined above.

At the end of fifteen years from the coming into force of the present Treaty the inhabitants of the said territory shall be called upon to indicate the sovereignty under which they desire to be placed.

Article 50, Annex, Chapter II

16

The Government of the territory of the Saar Basin shall be entrusted to a Commission representing the League of Nations. The Commission shall sit in the territory of the Saar Basin.

17

The Governing Commission provided for by paragraph 16 shall consist of five members chosen by the Council of the League of Nations, and will include one citizen of France, one native inhabitant of the Saar Basin, not a citizen of France, and three members belonging to three countries other than France or Germany.

The members of the Governing Commission shall be appointed for one year and may be re-appointed. They can be removed by the Council of the League of Nations, which will provide for their replacement.

The members of the Governing Commission will be entitled to a salary which will be fixed by the Council of the League of Nations, and charged on the local revenues.

18

The Chairman of the Governing Commission shall be appointed for one year from among the members of the Commission by the Council of the League of Nations and may be re-appointed.

The Chairman will act as the executive of the Commission. . . .

Section V

Alsace-Lorraine

The High Contracting Parties, recognising the moral obligation to redress the wrong done by Germany in 1871 both to the rights of France and to the wishes of the population of Alsace and Lorraine, which were separated from their country in spite of the solemn protest of their representatives at the Assembly of Bordeaux,

Agree upon the following Articles:

Article 51

The territories which were ceded to Germany in accordance with the Preliminaries of Peace signed at Versailles on February 26, 1871, and the Treaty of Frankfort of May 10, 1871, are restored to French sovereignty as from the date of the Armistice of November 11, 1918.

The provisions of the Treaties establishing the delimitation of the frontiers before 1871 shall be restored.

Article 80

Germany acknowledges and will respect strictly the independence of Austria, within the frontiers which may be fixed in a Treaty between that State and the Principal Allied and Associated Powers; she agrees that this independence shall be inalienable, except with the consent of the Council of the League of Nations.

Article 81

Germany, in conformity with the action already taken by the Allied and Associated Powers, recognises the complete independence of the Czecho-Slovak State which will include the autonomous territory of the Ruthenians to the south of the Carpathians. Germany hereby recognises the frontiers of this State as determined by the Principal Allied and Associated Powers and the other interested States.

Article 87

Germany, in conformity with the action already taken by the Allied and Associated Powers, recognises the complete independence of Poland. . . .

Article 89

Poland undertakes to accord freedom of transit to persons, goods, vessels, carriages, wagons and mails in transit between East Prussia and the rest of Germany over Polish territory, including territorial waters, and to treat them at least as favourably as the persons, goods, vessels, carriages, wagons and mails respectively of Polish or of any other more favoured nationality, origin, importation, starting-point, or ownership as regards facilities, restrictions and all other matters. . . .

Article 102

The Principal Allied and Associated Powers undertake to establish the town of Danzig, together with the rest of the territory described in Article 100, as a Free City. It will be placed under the protection of the League of Nations.

Article 116

Germany acknowledges and agrees to respect as permanent and inalienable the independence of all the territories which were part of the former Russian Empire on August 1, 1914.

In accordance with the provisions of Article 259 of Part IX (Financial Clauses) and Article 292 of Part X (Economic Clauses) Germany accepts definitely the abrogation of the Brest-Litovsk Treaties and of all other treaties, conventions and agreements entered into by her with the Maximalist Government in Russia.

The Allied and Associated Powers formally reserve the rights of Russia to obtain from Germany restitution and reparation based on the principles of the present Treaty.

Article 119

Germany renounces in favour of the Principal Allied and Associated Powers all her rights and titles over her oversea possessions.

Article 159

The German military forces shall be demobilised and reduced as prescribed hereinafter.

Article 160

(1) By a date which must not be later than March 31, 1920, the German Army must not comprise more than seven divisions of infantry and three divisions of cavalry.

After that date the total number of effectives in the Army of the States constituting Germany must not exceed one hundred thousand men, including officers and establishments of depots. The Army shall be devoted exclusively to the maintenance of order within the territory and to the control of the frontiers.

The total effective strength of officers, including the personnel of staffs, whatever their composition, must not exceed four thousand. . . .

Article 181

After the expiration of a period of two months from the coming into force of the present Treaty the German naval forces in commission must not exceed:

6 battleships of the *Deutschland* or *Lothringen* type,
6 light cruisers,
12 destroyers,
12 torpedo boats,

or an equal number of ships constructed to replace them as provided in Article 190.

No submarines are to be included.

All other warships, except where there is provision to the contrary in the present Treaty, must be placed in reserve or devoted to commercial purposes.

Article 198

The armed forces of Germany must not include any military or naval air forces. . . .

Article 231

The Allied and Associated Governments affirm and Germany accepts the responsibility of Germany and her allies for causing all the loss and damage to which the Allied and Associated Governments and their nationals have been subjected as a consequence of the war imposed upon them by the aggression of Germany and her allies.

Article 232

The Allied and Associated Governments recognise that the resources of Germany are not adequate, after taking into account permanent diminutions of such resources which will result from other provisions of the present Treaty, to make complete reparation for all such loss and damage.

The Allied and Associated Governments, however, require, and Germany undertakes, that she will make compensation for all damage done to the civilian population of the Allied and Associated Powers and to their property during the period of the belligerency of each as an Allied or Associated

Power against Germany by such aggression by land, by sea and from the air, and in general all damage as defined in Annex *I* hereto. . . .

Article 233

The amount of the above damage for which compensation is to be made by Germany shall be determined by an Inter-Allied Commission, to be called the *Reparation Commission* and constituted in the form and with the powers set forth hereunder and in Annexes II to VII inclusive hereto.

This Commission shall consider the claims and give to the German Government a just opportunity to be heard.

The findings of the Commission as to the amount of damage defined as above shall be concluded and notified to the German Government on or before May 1, 1921, as representing the extent of that Government's obligations. . . .

Article 234

The Reparation Commission shall after May 1, 1921, from time to time, consider the resources and capacity of Germany, and, after giving her representatives a just opportunity to be heard, shall have discretion to extend the date, and to modify the form of payments, such as are to be provided for in accordance with Article 233; but not to cancel any part, except with the specific authority of the several Governments represented upon the Commission.

Part XIII

Section I

Organisation of Labour

Whereas the League of Nations has for its object the establishment of universal peace, and such a peace can be established only if it is based upon social justice;

And whereas conditions of labour exist involving such injustice, hardship and privation to large numbers of people as to produce unrest so great that the peace and harmony of the world are imperilled; and an improvement of those conditions is urgently required: as, for example, by the regulation of the hours of work, including the establishment of a maximum working day and week, the regulation of the labour supply, the prevention of unemployment, the provision of an adequate living wage, the protection of the worker against sickness, disease and injury arising out of his employment, the protection of children, young persons and women, provision for old age and injury, protection of the interests of workers when employed in countries other than their own, recognition of the principle of freedom of association, the organisation of vocational and technical education and other measures;

Whereas also the failure of any nation to adopt humane conditions of labour is an obstacle in the way of other nations which desire to improve the conditions in their own countries;

The High Contracting Parties, moved by sentiments of justice and humanity, as well as by the desire to secure the permanent peace of the world, agree to the following:

Chapter I. Organisation.

Article 387.

A permanent organisation is hereby established for the promotion of the objects set forth in the Preamble.

The original Members of the League of Nations shall be the original Members of this organisation, and hereafter membership of the League of Nations shall carry with it membership of the said organisation.

Article 388.

The permanent organisation shall consist of:

(1) a General Conference of Representatives of the Members, and

(2) an International Labour Office controlled by the Governing Body described in Article 393.

Section II.
General Principles.

Article 427.

The High Contracting Parties, recognizing that the well-being, physical, moral and intellectual, of industrial wage earners is of supreme international importance, have framed, in order to further this great end, the permanent machinery provided for in Section I and associated with that of the League of Nations.

They recognise that differences of climate, habits and customs, of economic opportunity and industrial tradition, make strict uniformity in the conditions of labour difficult of immediate attainment. But, holding as they do, that labour should not be regarded merely as an article of commerce, they think that there are methods and principles for regulating labour conditions which all industrial communities should endeavour to apply, so far as their special circumstances will permit.

Among these methods and principles, the following seem to the High Contracting Parties to be of special and urgent importance:

First. — The guiding principle above enunciated that labour should not be regarded merely as a commodity or article of commerce.

Second. — The right of association for all lawful purposes by the employed as well as by the employers.

Third. — The payment to the employed of a wage adequate to maintain a reasonable standard of life as this is understood in their time and country.

Fourth. — The adoption of an eight hours day or a forty-eight hours week as the standard to be aimed at where it has not already been attained.

Fifth. — The adoption of a weekly rest of at least twenty-four hours, which should include Sunday wherever practicable.

Sixth. — The abolition of child labour and the imposition of such limitations on the labour of young persons as shall permit the continuation of their education and assure their proper physical development.

Seventh. — The principle that men and women should receive equal remuneration for work of equal value.

Eighth. — The standard set by law in each country with respect to the conditions of labour should have due regard to the equitable economic treatment of all workers lawfully resident therein.

Ninth. — Each State should make provision for a system of inspection in which women should take part, in order to ensure the enforcement of the laws and regulations for the protection of the employed.

Without claiming that these methods and principles are either complete or final, the High Contracting Parties are of opinion that they are well fitted to guide the policy of the League of Nations; and that, if adopted by the industrial communities who are members of the League, and safeguarded in practice by an adequate system of such inspection, they will confer lasting benefits upon the wage-earners of the world.

Part XIV.
Guarantees.

Section I.
Western Europe.

Article 428.

As a guarantee for the execution of the present Treaty by Germany, the German territory situated to the west of the Rhine, together with the bridgeheads, will be occupied by Allied and Associated troops for a period of fifteen years from the coming into force of the present Treaty.

Article 431.

If before the expiration of the period of fifteen years Germany complies with all the undertakings resulting from the present Treaty, the occupying forces will be withdrawn immediately.

The Covenant of the League of Nations, the text of which is here given in full, was incorporated in all the treaties concluded after the Paris Conference with enemy countries. President Wilson and its other protagonists believed that in this Covenant lay the surest guarantee of a new and more peaceful world order.

Amendments which have been incorporated in the Covenant since it was first drawn up are given here in italics.

225. *THE COVENANT OF THE LEAGUE OF NATIONS* [1]

The High Contracting Parties,

In order to promote international co-operation and to achieve international peace and security

by the acceptance of obligations not to resort to war,

by the prescription of open, just and honourable relations between nations,

by the firm establishment of the understandings of international law as the actual rule of conduct among Governments, and

by the maintenance of justice and a scrupulous respect for all treaty obligations in the dealings of organised peoples with one another,

Agree to this Covenant of the League of Nations.

Article 1.

The original Members of the League of Nations shall be those of the Signatories which are named in the Annex to this Covenant and also such of those other States named in the Annex as shall accede without reservation to this Covenant. Such accession shall be effected by a declaration deposited with the Secretariat within two months of the coming into force of the Covenant. Notice thereof shall be sent to all other Members of the League.

Any fully self-governing State, Dominion or Colony not named in the Annex may become a Member of the League if its admission is agreed to by two-thirds of the Assembly, provided that it shall give effective guarantees of its sincere intention to observe its international obligations, and shall accept such regulations as may be prescribed by the League in regard to its military, naval and air forces and armaments.

Any Member of the League may, after two years' notice of its intention so to do, withdraw from the League, provided that all its international obligations and all its obligations under this Covenant shall have been fulfilled at the time of its withdrawal.

Article 2.

The action of the League under this Covenant shall be effected through the instrumentality of an Assembly and of a Council, with a permanent Secretariat.

[1] Being Part I (Articles No. 1 to No. 26 inclusive) of the Treaty of Versailles, 1919.

Article 3.

The Assembly shall consist of Representatives of the Members of the League.

The Assembly shall meet at stated intervals and from time to time as occasion may require at the Seat of the League or at such other place as may be decided upon.

The Assembly may deal at its meetings with any matter within the sphere of action of the League or affecting the peace of the world.

At meetings of the Assembly each Member of the League shall have one vote, and may have not more than three Representatives.

Article 4.

The Council shall consist of Representatives of the Principal Allied and Associated Powers, together with Representatives of four other Members of the League. These four Members of the League shall be selected by the Assembly from time to time in its discretion. Until the appointment of the Representatives of the four Members of the League first selected by the Assembly, Representatives of Belgium, Brazil, Spain and Greece shall be members of the Council.

With the approval of the majority of the Assembly, the Council may name additional Members of the League whose Representatives shall always be members of the Council; the Council with like approval may increase the number of Members of the League to be selected by the Assembly for representation on the Council.[1]

The Assembly shall fix by a two-thirds majority the rules dealing with the election of the non-permanent members of the Council, and particularly such regulations as relate to their term of office and the conditions of re-eligibility.

The Council shall meet from time to time as occasion may require, and at least once a year, at the Seat of the League, or at such other place as may be decided upon.

The Council may deal at its meetings with any matter within the sphere of action of the League or affecting the peace of the world.

Any Member of the League not represented on the Council shall be invited to send a Representative to sit as a member at any meeting of the Council during the consideration of matters specially affecting the interests of that Member of the League.

At meetings of the Council, each Member of the League represented in the Council shall have one vote, and may have not more than one Representative.

[1] The Council now consists of five permanent members, of whom Germany is one, and nine non-permanent members. (Editor's note.)

Article 5.

Except where otherwise expressly provided in this Covenant or by terms of the present Treaty, decisions at any meeting of the Assembly or of the Council shall require the agreement of all the Members of the League represented at the meeting.

All matters of procedure at meetings of the Assembly or of the Council, including the appointment of Committees to investigate particular matters, shall be regulated by the Assembly or by the Council and may be decided by a majority of the Members of the League represented at the meeting.

The first meeting of the Assembly and the first meeting of the Council shall be summoned by the President of the United States of America.

Article 6.

The permanent Secretariat shall be established at the Seat of the League. The Secretariat shall comprise a Secretary General and such secretaries and staff as may be required.

The first Secretary General shall be the person named in the Annex; thereafter the Secretary General shall be appointed by the Council with the approval of the majority of the Assembly.

The secretaries and staff of the Secretariat shall be appointed by the Secretary General with the approval of the Council.

The Secretary General shall act in that capacity at all meetings of the Assembly and of the Council.

The expenses of the League shall be borne by the Members of the League in the proportion decided by the Assembly.

Article 7.

The Seat of the League is established at Geneva.

The Council may at any time decide that the Seat of the League shall be established elsewhere.

All positions under or in connection with the League, including the Secretariat, shall be open equally to men and women.

Representatives of the Members of the League and officials of the League when engaged on the business of the League shall enjoy diplomatic privileges and immunities.

The buildings and other property occupied by the League or its officials or by Representatives attending its meetings shall be inviolable.

Article 8.

The Members of the League recognise that the maintenance of peace requires the reduction of national armaments to the lowest point consistent with national safety and the enforcement by common action of international obligations.

The Council, taking account of the geographical situation and circumstances of each State, shall formulate plans for such reduction for the consideration and action of the several Governments.

Such plans shall be subject to reconsideration and revision at least every ten years.

After these plans shall have been adopted by the several Governments, the limits of armaments therein fixed shall not be exceeded without the concurrence of the Council.

The Members of the League agree that the manufacture by private enterprise of munitions and implements of war is open to grave objections. The Council shall advise how the evil effects attendant upon such manifacture can be prevented, due regard being had to the necessities of those Members of the League which are not able to manufacture the munitions and implements of war necessary for their safety.

The Members of the League undertake to interchange full and frank information as to the scale of their armaments, their military, naval and air programmes and the condition of such of their industries as are adaptable to warlike purposes.

Article 9.

A permanent Commission shall be constituted to advise the Council on the execution of the provisions of Articles 1 and 8, and on military, naval and air questions generally.

Article 10.

The Members of the League undertake to respect and preserve as against external aggression the territorial integrity and existing political independence of all Members of the League. In case of any such aggression or in case of any threat or danger of such aggression the Council shall advise upon the means by which this obligation shall be fulfilled.

Article 11.

Any war or threat of war, whether immediately affecting any of the Members of the League or not, is hereby declared a matter of concern to the whole League, and the League shall take any action that may be deemed wise and effectual to safeguard the peace of nations. In case any such emergency should arise the Secretary General shall on the request of any Member of the League forthwith summon a meeting of the Council.

It is also declared to be the friendly right of each Member of the League to bring to the attention of the Assembly or of the Council any circumstance whatever affecting international relations which threatens to disturb international peace or the good understanding between nations upon which peace depends.

Article 12.

The Members of the League agree that if there should arise between them any dispute likely to lead to a rupture, they will submit the matter either to arbitration *or judicial settlement* or to inquiry by the Council, and they agree in no case to resort to war until three months after the award by the arbitrators *or the judicial decision* or the report by the Council.

In any case under this Article the award of the arbitrators *or the judicial decision* shall be made within a reasonable time, and the report of the Council shall be made within six months after the submission of the dispute.

Article 13.

The Members of the League agree that whenever any dispute shall arise between them which they recognize to be suitable for submission to arbitration *or judicial settlement* and which cannot be satisfactorily settled by diplomacy, they will submit the whole subject-matter to arbitration *or judicial settlement*.

Disputes as to the interpretation of a treaty, as to any question of international law, as to the existence of any fact which if established would constitute a breach of any international obligation, or as to the extent and nature of the reparation to be made for any such breach, are declared to be among those which are generally suitable for submission to arbitration *or judicial settlement*.

For the consideration of any such dispute the court *to which the case is referred shall be the Permanent Court of International Justice, or any tribunal agreed on by the parties to the dispute or stipulated in any convention existing between them.*

The Members of the League agree that they will carry out in full good faith any award *or decision* that may be rendered, and that they will not resort to war against a Member of the League which complies therewith. In the event of any failure to carry out such an award *or decision,* the Council shall propose what steps should be taken to give effect thereto.

Article 14.

The Council shall formulate and submit to the Members of the League for adoption plans for the establishment of a Permanent Court of International Justice. The Court shall be competent to hear and determine any dispute of an international character which the parties thereto submit to it. The Court may also give an advisory opinion upon any dispute or question referred to it by the Council or by the Assembly.

Article 15.

If there should arise between Members of the League any dispute likely to lead to a rupture, which is not submitted to arbitration *or judicial settlement* in accordance with Article 13, the Members of the League agree that they will submit the matter to the Council. Any party to the dispute may effect such submission by giving notice of the existence of the dispute to the Secretary General, who will make all necessary arrangements for a full investigation and consideration thereof.

For this purpose the parties to the dispute will communicate to the Secretary General, as promptly as possible, statements of their case, with all the relevant facts and papers, and the Council may forthwith direct the publication thereof.

The Council shall endeavor to effect a settlement of the dispute, and if such efforts are successful, a statement shall be made public giving such facts and explanations regarding the dispute and the terms of settlement thereof as the Council may deem appropriate.

If the dispute is not thus settled, the Council either unanimously or by a majority vote shall make and publish a report containing a statement of the facts of the dispute and the recommendations which are deemed just and proper in regard thereto.

Any Member of the League represented on the Council may make public a statement of the facts of the dispute and of its conclusions regarding the same.

If a report by the Council is unanimously agreed to by the members thereof other than the Representatives of one or more of the parties to the dispute, the Members of the League agree that they will not go to war with any party to the dispute which complies with the recommendations of the report.

If the Council fails to reach a report which is unanimously agreed to by the members thereof, other than the Representatives of one or more of the parties to the dispute, the Members of the League reserve to themselves the right to take such action as they shall consider necessary for the maintenance of right and justice.

If the dispute between the parties is claimed by one of them, and is found by the Council, to arise out of a matter which by international law is solely within the domestic jurisdiction of that party, the Council shall so report, and shall make no recommendation as to its settlement.

The Council may in any case under this Article refer the dispute to the Assembly. The dispute shall be so referred at the request of either party to the dispute, provided that such request be made within fourteen days after the submission of the dispute to the Council.

In any case referred to the Assembly, all the provisions of this Article and of Article 12 relating to the action and powers of the Council shall apply to the action and powers of the Assembly, provided that a report made by the Assembly, if concurred in by the Representatives of those Members of the League represented on the Council and of a majority of the other Members of the League, exclusive in each case of the Representatives of the parties to the dispute, shall have the same force as a report by the Council concurred in by all the members thereof other than the Representatives of one or more of the parties to the dispute.

Article 16.

Should any Member of the League resort to war in disregard of its covenants under Articles 12, 13 or 15, it shall *ipso facto* be deemed to have committed an act of war against all other Members of the League, which hereby undertake immediately to subject it to the severance of all trade or financial relations, the prohibition of all intercourse between their nationals and the nationals of the covenant-breaking State, and the prevention of all financial, commercial or personal intercourse between the nationals of the covenant-breaking State and the nationals of any other State, whether a Member of the League or not.

It shall be the duty of the Council in such case to recommend to the several Governments concerned what effective military, naval or air force the Members of the League shall severally contribute to the armed forces to be used to protect the covenants of the League.

The Members of the League agree, further, that they will mutually support one another in the financial and economic measures which are taken under this Article, in order to minimise the loss and inconvenience resulting from the above measures, and that they will mutually support one another in resisting any special measures aimed at one of their number by the covenant-breaking State, and that they will take the necessary steps to afford passage through their territory to the forces of any of the Members of the League which are co-operating to protect the covenants of the League.

Any Member of the League which has violated any covenant of the League may be declared to be no longer a Member of the League by a vote of the Council concurred in by Representatives of all the other Members of the League represented thereon.

Article 17.

In the event of a dispute between a Member of the League and a State which is not a Member of the League, or between States not Members of the League, the State or States not Members of the League shall be invited to accept the obligations of membership in the League for the purposes of such dispute, upon such conditions as the Council may deem just. If such invitation is accepted, the provisions of Articles 12 to 16 inclusive shall be applied with such modifications as may be deemed necessary by the Council.

Upon such invitation being given the Council shall immediately institute an inquiry into the circumstances of the dispute and recommend such action as may seem best and most effectual in the circumstances.

If a State so invited shall refuse to accept the obligations of membership in the League for the purposes of such dispute, and shall resort to war against a Member of the League, the provisions of Article 16 shall be applicable as against the State taking such action.

If both parties to the dispute when so invited refuse to accept the obligations of membership in the League for the purpose of such dispute, the Council may take such measures and make such recommendations as will prevent hostilities and will result in the settlement of the dispute.

Article 18.

Every treaty or international engagement entered into hereafter by any Member of the League shall be forthwith registered with the Secretariat and shall as soon as possible be published by it. No such treaty or international engagement shall be binding until so registered.

Article 19.

The Assembly may from time to time advise the reconsideration by Members of the League of treaties which have become inapplicable and the consideration of international conditions whose continuance might endanger the peace of the world.

Article 20.

The Members of the League severally agree that this Covenant is accepted as abrogating all obligations or understandings *inter se* which are inconsistent with the terms thereof, and solemnly undertake that they will not hereafter enter into any engagements inconsistent with the terms thereof.

In case any Member of the League shall, before becoming a Member of the League, have undertaken any obligations inconsistent with the terms of this Covenant, it shall be the duty of such Member to take immediate steps to procure its release from such obligations.

Article 21

Nothing in this Covenant shall be deemed to affect the validity of international engagements, such as treaties of arbitration or regional understandings like the Monroe doctrine, for securing the maintenance of peace.

Article 22.

To those colonies and territories which as a consequence of the late war have ceased to be under the sovereignty of the States which formerly governed them and which are inhabited by peoples not yet able to stand by themselves under the strenuous conditions of the modern world, there should be applied the principle that the well-being and development of such peoples form a sacred trust of civilisation and that securities for the performance of this trust should be embodied in this Covenant.

The best method of giving practical effect to this principle is that the tutelage of such peoples should be entrusted to advanced nations who by reason of their resources, their experience or their geographical position can best undertake this responsibility, and who are willing to accept it, and that this tutelage should be exercised by them as Mandatories on behalf of the League.

The character of the mandate must differ according to the stage of the development of the people, the geographical situation of the territory, its economic conditions and other similar circumstances.

Certain communities formerly belonging to the Turkish Empire have reached a stage of development where their existence as independent nations can be provisionally recognised subject to the rendering of administrative advice and assistance by a Mandatory until such time as they are able to stand alone. The wishes of these communities must be a principal consideration in the selection of the Mandatory.

Other peoples, especially those of Central Africa, are at such a stage that the Mandatory must be responsible for the administration of the territory under conditions which will guarantee freedom of conscience and religion, subject only to the maintenance of public order and morals, the prohibition of abuses such as the slave trade, the arms traffic and the liquor traffic, and the prevention of the establishment of fortifications or military and naval bases and of military training of the natives for other than police purposes and the defence of territory, and will also secure equal opportunities for the trade and commerce of other Members of the League.

There are territories, such as South-West Africa and certain of the South Pacific Islands, which, owing to the sparseness of their population, or their small size, or their remoteness from the centres of civilisation, or their geographical contiguity to the territory of the Mandatory, and other circumstances, can be best administered under the laws of the Mandatory as integral portions of its territory, subject to the safeguards above mentioned in the interests of the indigenous population.

In every case of mandate, the Mandatory shall render to the Council an annual report in reference to the territory committed to its charge.

The degree of authority, control, or administration to be exercised by the Mandatory shall, if not previously agreed upon by the Members of the League, be explicitly defined in each case by the Council.

A permanent Commission shall be constituted to receive and examine the annual reports of the Mandatories and to advise the Council on all matters relating to the observance of the mandates.

Article 23.

Subject to and in accordance with the provision of international conventions existing or hereafter to be agreed upon, the Members of the League:

(a) will endeavour to secure and maintain fair and humane conditions of labour for men, women, and children, both in their own countries and in all countries to which their commercial and industrial relations extend, and for that purpose will establish and maintain the necessary international organisations;

(b) undertake to secure just treatment of the native inhabitants or territories under their control;

(c) will entrust the League with the general supervision over the execution of agreements with regard to the traffic in women and children, and the traffic in opium and other dangerous drugs;

(d) will entrust the League with the general supervision of the trade in arms and ammunition with the countries in which the control of this traffic is necessary in the common interest;

(e) will make provision to secure and maintain freedom of communications and of transit and equitable treatment for the commerce of all Members of the League. In this connection, the special necessities of the regions devastated during the war of 1914–1918 shall be borne in mind;

(f) will endeavour to take steps in matters of international concern for the prevention and control of disease.

Article 24.

There shall be placed under the direction of the League all international bureaux already established by general treaties if the parties to such treaties consent. All such international bureaux and all commissions for the regulation of matters of international interest hereafter constituted shall be placed under the direction of the League.

In all matters of international interest which are regulated by general conventions but which are not placed under the control of international bureaux or commissions, the Secretariat of the League shall, subject to the consent of the Council and if desired by the parties, collect and distribute all relevant information and shall render any other assistance which may be necessary or desirable.

The Council may include as part of the expenses of the Secretariat the expenses of any bureau or commission which is placed under the direction of the League.

Article 25.

The Members of the League agree to encourage and promote the establishment and co-operation of duly authorised voluntary national Red Cross organisations having as purposes the improvement of health, the prevention of disease and the mitigation of suffering throughout the world.

Article 26.

Amendments to this Covenant will take effect when ratified by the Members of the League whose Representatives compose the Council and by a majority of the Members of the League whose Representatives compose the Assembly.

No such amendment shall bind any Member of the League which signifies its dissent therefrom, but in that case it shall cease to be a Member of the League.

CHAPTER XV

REVOLUTIONS AND NEW STATES SINCE 1914

SECTION I. THE RUSSIAN REVOLUTION

The apparent enthusiasm with which Russia entered the Great War could hardly be maintained amid the inefficiency, indifference, and corruption, even treachery, of the Government and high officials, civil and military alike. Late in 1916 the army was demoralized and the country angered to the point of revolt. Spontaneous risings occurred in Petrograd in March, 1917 and, almost without realizing what had happened, the Imperial Duma found itself in a position of power. Nikolai II's removal seemed to all the first step that must be taken. The Duma and his generals advised the action that the tsar took in his train on a siding near Pskov. The Grand Duke Mikhail declined the impossible task resigned to him.

226. THE ABDICATION OF THE LAST ROMANOV [1]

We, Nicholas II, by the Grace of God, Emperor of all the Russias, Czar of Poland, Grand Duke of Finland, etc., to all our faithful subjects be it known:

In the days of a great struggle against a foreign enemy who has been endeavoring for three years to enslave our country, it pleased God to send Russia a further painful trial.

Internal troubles threatened to have a fatal effect on the further progress of this obstinate war. The destinies of Russia, the honor of her heroic Army, the happiness of the people and the whole future of our beloved country demand that the war should be conducted at all costs to a victorious end.

The cruel enemy is making his last efforts and the moment is near when our valiant Army, in concert with our glorious Allies, will finally overthrow the enemy.

In these decisive days in the life of Russia we have thought that we owed to our people the close union and organization of all its forces for the realization of a rapid victory; for which reason, in agreement with the Imperial Duma, we have recognized that it is for the good of the country that we should abdicate the Crown of the Russian State and lay down the Supreme Power.

[1] The *Times*, London, March 19, 1917.

Not wishing to separate ourself from our beloved son, we bequeath our heritage to our brother, the Grand Duke Michael Alexandrovitch, with our blessing for the future of the Throne of the Russian State.

We bequeath it to our brother to govern in full union with the national representatives sitting in the Legislative Institutions, and to take his inviolable oath to them in the name of our well-beloved country.

We call upon all faithful sons of our native land to fulfil their sacred and patriotic duty obeying the Czar at the painful moment of national trials and to aid him, together with the representatives of the nation, to conduct the Russian State in the way of prosperity and glory.

May God help Russia.

A Provisional Government, predominantly bourgeois and made up of Kadets, or members of the Constitutional Democratic Party, but containing Kerenskii, a Socialist Revolutionary, was set up to carry on the administration until a permanent form could be agreed on. The first of the two following documents announces this régime; the second elaborates its policies.

227. THE FORMATION OF A PROVISIONAL GOVERNMENT [1]
FORMATION AND PROGRAM OF PROVISIONAL GOVERNMENT

Citizens, the Provisional Executive Committee of the members of the Duma, with the aid and support of the garrison of the capital and its inhabitants, has triumphed over the dark forces of the Old Régime to such an extent as to enable it to organize a more stable executive power. With this idea in mind, the Provisional Committee has appointed as ministers of the first Cabinet representing the public, men whose past political and public life assures them the confidence of the country.

PRINCE GEORGE E. LVOV, *Prime Minister and Minister of the Interior.*

P. N. MILIUKOV, *Minister of Foreign Affairs*
A. I. GUCHKOV, *Minister of War and Marine*
M. I. TERESCHENKO, *Minister of Finance*
A. A. MANUILOV, *Minister of Education*
A. I. SHINGAREV, *Minister of Agriculture*
N. V. NEKRASOV, *Minister of Transportation*
A. I. KONOVALOV, *Minister of Commerce and Industry*
A. F. KERENSKI, *Minister of Justice*
VL. LVOV, *Holy Synod*

[1] Translation from *Izviestia*, March 16, 1917, published in F. A. Golder, *Documents of Russian History, 1914–1917.* New York, The Century Co., 1927, pp. 308–309.

The Cabinet will be guided in its actions by the following principles:

1. An immediate general amnesty for all political and religious offenses, including terriorist acts, military revolts, agrarian offenses, etc.

2. Freedom of speech and press; freedom to form labor unions and to strike. These political liberties should be extended to the army in so far as war conditions permit.

3. The abolition of all social, religious and national restrictions.

4. Immediate preparation for the calling of a Constituent Assembly, elected by universal and secret vote, which shall determine the form of government and draw up the Constitution for the country.

5. In place of the police, to organize a national militia with elective officers, and subject to the local self-governing body.

6. Elections to be carried out on the basis of universal, direct, equal, and secret suffrage.

7. The troops that have taken part in the revolutionary movement shall not be disarmed or removed from Petrograd.

8. On duty and in war service, strict military discipline should be maintained, but when off duty, soldiers should have the same public rights as are enjoyed by other citizens.

The Provisional Government wishes to add that it has no intention of taking advantage of the existence of war conditions to delay the realization of the above-mentioned measures of reform.

President of the Duma, M. RODZIANKO
President of the Council of Ministers, PRINCE LVOV
Ministers MILIUKOV, NEKRASOV, MANUILOV,
KONOVALOV, TERESCHENKO, VL. LVOV,
SHINGAREV, KERENSKI.

228. *AN EARLY PROCLAMATION OF THE PROVISIONAL GOVERNMENT* [1]

Citizens of Russia:

A great event has taken place. By the mighty assault of the Russian people, the old order has been overthrown. A new, free Russia is born. The great revolution crowns long years of struggle. By the act of October 17, (30) 1905, under the pressure of the awakened popular forces, Russia was promised constitutional liberties. Those promises, however, were not kept. The First State Duma, interpreter of the nation's hopes, was dissolved. The Second Duma suffered the same fate, and the Government, powerless to crush the national

[1] Translation from *Vestnik Vremennago Pravitelstva,* March 20, 1917, published in F. A. Golder, *Documents of Russian History, 1914–1917.* New York, The Century Co., 1927, pp. 311–313.

will, decided, by the act of June 3, (16) 1907, to deprive the people of a part of those rights of participation in legislative work which had been granted.

In the course of nine long years, there were taken from the people, step by step, all the rights that they had won. Once more the country was plunged into an abyss of arbitrariness and despotism. All attempts to bring the Government to its senses proved futile, and the titanic world struggle, into which the country was dragged by the enemy, found the Government in a state of moral decay, alienated from the people, indifferent to the fate of our native land, and steeped in the infamy of corruption. Neither the heroic efforts of the army, staggering under the crushing burdens of internal chaos, nor the appeals of the popular representatives, who had united in the face of the national peril, were able to lead the former Emperor and his Government into the path of unity with the people. And when Russia, owing to the illegal and fatal actions of her rulers, was confronted with gravest disasters, the nation was obliged to take the power into its own hands.

The unanimous revolutionary enthusiasm of the people, fully conscious of the gravity of the moment, and the determination of the State Duma, have created the Provisional Government, which considers it to be its sacred and responsible duty to fulfil the hopes of the nation, and lead the country out onto the bright path of free civic organization.

The Government trusts that the spirit of lofty patriotism, manifested during the struggle of the people against the old régime, will also inspire our valiant soldiers on the field of battle. For its own part, the Government will make every effort to provide our army with everything necessary to bring the war to a victorious end.

The Government will sacredly observe the alliances which bind us to other powers, and will unswervingly carry out the agreements entered into by the Allies. While taking measures to defend the country against the foreign enemy, the Government will, at the same time, consider it to be its primary duty to make possible the expression of the popular will as regards the form of government, and will convoke the Constituent Assembly within the shortest time possible, on the basis of universal, direct, equal, and secret suffrage, also guaranteeing participation in the elections to the gallant defenders of our native land, who are now shedding their blood on the fields of battle.

The Constituent Assembly will issue the fundamental laws, guaranteeing to the country the inalienable rights of justice, equality, and liberty. Conscious of the heavy burden which the country suffers because of the lack of civic rights, which lack stands in the way of its free, creative power at this time of violent national commotion, the Provisional Government deems it necessary, at once, before the convocation of the Constituent Assembly, to provide the country with laws for the safeguarding of civil liberty and equality, in order to enable all citizens freely to apply their spiritual forces to creative work for the benefit of the country. The Government will also undertake the enactment of legal provisions to assure to all citizens, on the basis of universal suffrage, an equal share in the election of local governments.

At this moment of national liberation, the whole country remembers with reverent gratitude those who, in the struggle for their political and religious convictions, fell victims to the vindictive old régime, and the Provisional Government will regard it as its joyful duty to bring back from their exile, with full honors, all those who have suffered for the good of the country.

In fulfilling these tasks, the Provisional Government is animated by the belief that it will thus execute the will of the people, and that the whole nation will support it in its honest efforts to insure the happiness of Russia. This belief inspires it with courage. Only in the common effort of the entire nation and the Provisional Government can it see a pledge of triumph of the new order.

March 19, 1917.

In 1905 the first Soviet of Workers' Deputies was organized and, despite the reaction that then followed, it never ceased to exist as an instrument of the socialist groups. As soon as the Revolution upset the old order the Petrograd Soviet set itself up as an organization parallel to the Provisional Government, and showed a tendency to interfere with the administration. Through Izviestia it announced to the people its purpose of watching the Government closely and of forcing it to interpret correctly the will of all Russia. It was in almost constant session and steadily grew in prestige.

229. TWO PARALLEL GOVERNMENTS [1]

The Provisional Government has two tasks: (1) to prepare for the Constituent Assembly; (2) to govern the country until the Assembly meets. The first task requires no discussion, but the second needs some explanation. The point is that the Government has in its hands a tremendous financial and administrative power and it can, if it so desires, exert great influence on the elections for the Constituent Assembly. It can do even more. It can bring about a state of affairs which the Constituent Assembly, when it meets, must face as accomplished facts, such, for example, as the conclusion of peace, declaration of war, cancellation of commercial agreements, etc. This tremendous power in the hands of the Provisional Government raises the questions (1) whence comes so much power, and (2) how to prevent its use for evil purposes.

[1] Translation of editorial in *Izviestia*, April 7, 1917, published in F. A. Golder, *Documents of Russian History, 1914–1917.* New York, The Century Co., 1927, pp. 315–317.

First of all, it is important to state most emphatically (and it is for the Provisional Government to say it) that it was not the abdication of Nicholas, and after him Michael Romanov, that called to power the Council of Ministers with Prince Lvov at its head. The Provisional Government was called to power by the will of His Majesty, the Revolutionary People, and no one else. Its power and composition were agreed to by the Committee of the State Duma and the Soviet of Workers' and Soldiers' Deputies. The last named, the real incarnation of the revolution, did not, for weighty reasons, take upon itself the executive power, but handed it to the Council of Ministers, with the understanding that it would carry out immediately certain named reforms.

In addition to these reforms, the Soviet reserved to itself the right of active control over the carrying out of the said reforms.

Does the Provisional Government have executive power over the country? Yes, it has. Does it have full and unlimited power? No, it has not. We have not overthrown one autocrat in order to have twelve. What then limits the power of the Provisional Government?

In the first place the vigilant and ever wakeful control of the whole nation, organized and meeting freely. It can always stop, instantly, those measures of the Provisional Government which threaten popular liberty. In the second place, the actual control by the organs of the Petrograd Soviet of Workers' and Soldiers' Deputies.

Now let us examine the forms of control over the actions of the Government. We would say here that first in order comes the unlimited right of free discussion, which we now enjoy and which far exceeds the freedom of speech in England and France. The Government hears all opinions and the voice of the people on all matters, such, for example, as the aims and problems of the war. *This should continue in the future.* The history of English public meetings teaches us that this is a very effective means (of control).

But we live at a time when everything is done at once. Under certain conditions, when the interests of liberty require it, the revolutionary people through its organ, the Soviet of Workers' and Soldiers' Deputies, may and should have a say in the affairs of the Provisional Government. For example, it could not allow Nicholas Romanov to be taken out of the country, and the Executive Committee of the Soviet was right when it took steps to keep the ex-autocrat at Tsarskoe Selo. Such measures should, of course, be taken only after mature deliberation and tactfully, for it is not our purpose to shake the power of the Provisional Government.

How to avoid similar conflicts in the future? It is essential that there should be some kind of tie between the Provisional Government and the Soviet of Deputies, that the Soviet should be kept informed, in good time, of the more important steps of the Provisional Government, and that it should,

570 READINGS IN EUROPEAN HISTORY SINCE 1814 [Chap. XV

in turn, report to the Government its more important activities. There are bound to be clashes, but with mutual good-will and understanding of the State problems of the moment, they are not very dangerous. On some questions, an agreement has already been reached; on others, the Constituent Assembly will act. Until the meeting of that body, the Provisional Government will have to adjust itself as best it can to a certain amount of inconvenient revolutionary control.

Exiles returned to Russia in the months that followed the Revolution and among them were Lenin and Trotskii. A confusion of parties ensued. The Mensheviki, more moderate Social Democrats, and the Socialist Revolutionaries, pressed on their left by the Bolsheviki, the branch of the Social Democrats who favored non-co-operation with all bourgeois groups, forced Lvov and Milyukov out of office in May, 1917 and put Kerenskii at the head of the reorganized Provisional Government. Kerenskii earnestly continued the war, at the same time manifesting his intention of establishing a real democracy in Russia. Throughout the summer the Bolshevik propaganda for peace and a more radical revolution gained ground, until in late October Kerenskii's position was precarious. Nothing in the latter's story of what happened is more interesting than the way in which he was crushed between the Bolshevik Left and the Monarchistic Right, whose abortive attempt, under General Kornilov, he had put down.

230. ON THE EVE OF THE OCTOBER REVOLUTION [1]

After the abortive attempt of the conspirators behind General Koriloff — so fatal in its consequences for the entire country — to overthrow the Provisional Government, the social groups supporting the " dictator " decided to give no aid to the government in the event of its collision with the Bolsheviki. Their strategic plan was not to hinder in any way the success of an armed Bolshevist uprising and, then, after the fall of the Provisional Government they so hated, quickly to suppress the Bolshevist " mutiny." In this way were to be realized finally the aims set for the Koriloff rebellion.

The military and civil strategists who were the authors of this plan were thoroughly convinced that the Bolshevist triumph would entail no serious danger and that within three or four weeks the " sound elements " of the Russian people would make short shrift of the mutinous mass and establish a " strong government " in Russia. Alas, having successfully carried out the first, so-called passive part of this plan, having " overthrown " the Provisional Government with the hands of the Bolsheviki, the " patriots " found them-

[1] Alexander F. Kerensky, *The Catastrophe.* New York, D. Appleton & Co., 1927, pp. 324–334 (condensed).

selves absolutely unable to execute the second, activist part of their program. They failed to defeat the Bolsheviki not only in three weeks but in ten years!

On November sixth it had become quite evident that the uprising was inevitable, that it had already begun. At about eleven o'clock in the morning I appeared before the Council of the Republic and requested from N. D. Avksentieff, the President, permission to make an urgent statement. On taking the floor I informed the council that I had in my possession unmistakable evidence of the organization by Lenin and his lieutenants of an uprising against the Provisional Government. I declared that all possible measures were being taken by the Provisional Government for the suppression of the uprising and that the government would fight to the end against the betrayers of the motherland and of the Revolution. I declared that the government would resort without qualms to the use of force, but that to insure the government's success the immediate coöperation of all parties and groups, and of the entire people, was necessary. I demanded from the Council of the Republic full confidence and coöperation. . . .

Convinced that the representatives of the nation were fully conscious of the seriousness of the situation and of their own responsibility, I returned, without awaiting the actual vote, to Staff Headquarters to resume important unfinished business, confident that within an hour or two I would be informed of the decisions and active preparations of the Council of the Republic in support of the government.

Nothing of the sort happened. The council, torn by inner discords and irreconcilable differences of opinion, could not come to a decision until late into the night. Instead of organizing all their forces for the difficult struggle against the traitors, the leaders of all the anti-Bolshevist and democratic parties wasted the entire day and evening in useless quarrels and disputes. . . .

One must admit that the Bolsheviki were acting with great energy and no less great skill.

While the uprising was in full swing and "Red" troops were in action all over the city, some Bolshevist leaders especially assigned to the task tried, not without success, to make the representatives of the "Soviet democracy" blind to what was actually taking place. The entire night was spent by these acrobats in endless disputes on various formulae supposed to serve as conditions of peace and liquidation of the uprising. By this method of "negotiation" the Bolsheviki gained a great deal of valuable time. The fighting forces of the Socialists-Revolutionists and Mensheviki were not mobilized in time. . . .

Meanwhile, the uprising in the city was developing with tremendous speed. Armed detachments of Bolsheviki were closing in upon the Winter Palace and the Military District Staff Headquarters. Some soldiers of the

Pavlovsk Guards Regiment set up a real ambush in their barracks at the end of Millionnaya street, near the Field of Mars, arresting all "suspicious" persons coming from the direction of the palace. The palace was guarded only by military cadets and a small squadron of armored motor cars.

Immediately upon adjournment of the cabinet meeting, the commander of the garrison and his chief-of-staff appeared before me. They offered to organize an expedition of all the forces loyal to the government, including the Cossacks, for the capture of Smolny Institute, the Staff Headquarters of the Bolsheviki. During this conversation I followed with more and more interest the ambiguous behavior of Colonel Polkovnikoff, being increasingly impressed by the crying contradiction between his all too optimistic and reassuring reports and the sad reality of the situation as I already knew it. It became more than evident that all his reports of the past ten or twelve days concerning the attitude of the troops and the preparedness of his own staff for a decisive struggle with the Bolsheviki had no basis in fact.

The government's commissar attached to the municipal administration, Rogovsky, appeared during my conference with the commander of the troops. He brought alarming news, contradicting in every way the reports just presented by Colonel Polkovnikoff. We learned from Rogovsky, among other things, that a considerable number of warships from the Baltic Fleet had entered the Neva in battle formation, that some of these ships had moved as far as the Nicholayevsky Bridge, and that this bridge had been, in turn, occupied by detachments of mutineers, who were already advancing farther toward the palace bridge. Rogovsky drew our attention especially to the fact that the Bolsheviki were carrying out their plan without any trouble, meeting no resistance on the part of the government troops. To me personally Rogovsky reported his observation that the staff of the Petrograd military district was watching the developments with utter indifference, showing no inclination for activity on its part.

The contradiction between the report presented by Rogovsky and that of Colonel Polkovnikoff was shockingly obvious. There was not a minute more to lose. . . .

I decided to bring into action the volunteer military organizations of the parties, particularly the considerably numerous organization of the Party of the Socialists-Revolutionists.

The hours of the night dragged on painfully. From everywhere we expected reënforcements, but none appeared. There were endless telephone negotiations with the Cossack regiments. Under various excuses the Cossacks stubbornly stuck to their barracks, asserting all the time that "everything would be cleared up" within fifteen or twenty minutes and that they would then "begin to saddle their horses."

On the other hand, the volunteer military forces at the disposal of the party organizations likewise evinced no activity. This rather puzzling circumstance was to be explained by the fact that the party centers, engrossed in endless negotiations with Smolny, and relying more on the force of " resolutions " than on the power of bayonets, had failed to issue the necessary orders in time.

Meanwhile the night hours passed. And the closer morning approached, the tenser grew the atmosphere at the Staff Headquarters. One honest and devoted officer, summoned to duty, came to me and after observing what was going on in the staff building and following closely the actions of Colonel Polkovnikoff declared that he could not term the things he had seen otherwise than betrayal. The many officers assembled in the staff building conducted themselves in their attitude towards the government, and particularly towards me personally, in an increasingly defiant manner. As I learned afterwards they were engaged, on the initiative of Colonel Polkovnikoff, in an agitation for my arrest. At first they did this quietly, in whispers, but towards morning they began to talk quite loudly, almost without embarrassment and without regard to the presence of " strangers." A mad idea had struck the minds of many of them in those moments: without Kerensky it would be easier to " finish " the Bolsheviki and establish finally that so-called " strong government." And there is no doubt that throughout that night Colonel Polkovnikoff and certain other officers of the district staff were in constant contact with conservative anti-government organizations, such as the Council of Cossack Troops, the Union of the Knights of St. George, the Petrograd branch of the Union of Officers and other similar military and civil organizations.

Kerenskii fled on Nov. 7th and that same day, despite the protests of the less radical Socialist parties, the Bolsheviki, headed by Lenin, Trotskii, Kameniev, Lunatcharskii, etc. wrested the power in the Soviets away from the moderates, captured the Winter Palace and took the reins in their own hands. The Smolny Institute was Bolshevik headquarters. John Reed, a twentieth-century Berseker, was an American newspaper correspondent who had become a Communist and was thoroughly in sympathy with the Bolshevik program. The Bolshevik Revolution is known as the October Revolution because the Russian calendar was changed to agree with the Gregorian only after these events had taken place.

231. THE BOLSHEVIKS' SEIZURE OF POWER [1]

Wednesday evening, Oct. 25/Nov. 7

The massive façade of Smolny blazed with lights as we drove up, and from every street converged upon it streams of hurrying shapes dim in the

[1] John Reed, *Ten Days that Shook the World.* New York, Boni & Liveright, 1919, pp. 84–94, 123–139 (condensed).

gloom. Automobiles and motorcycles came and went; an enormous elephant-coloured armoured automobile, with two red flags flying from the turret, lumbered out with screaming siren. It was cold, and at the outer gate the Red Guards had built themselves a bonfire. At the inner gate, too, there was a blaze, by the light of which the sentries slowly spelled out our passes and looked us up and down. The canvas covers had been taken off the four rapid-fire guns on each side of the doorway, and the ammunition-belts hung snake-like from their breeches. A dun herd of armoured cars stood under the trees in the court-yard, engines going. The long, bare, dimly-illuminated halls roared with the thunder of feet, calling, shouting. . . . There was an atmosphere of recklessness. A crowd came pouring down the staircase, workers in black blouses and round black fur hats, many of them with guns slung over their shoulders, soldiers in rough dirt-coloured coats and grey fur *shapki* pinched flat, a leader or so — Lunatcharsky, Kameniev — hurrying along in the centre of a group all talking at once, with harassed anxious faces, and bulging portfolios under their arms. The extraordinary meeting of the Petrograd Soviet was over. I stopped Kameniev — a quick-moving little man, with a wide, vivacious face set close to his shoulders. Without preface he read in rapid French a copy of the resolution just passed. . . .

On the landing I met Riazanov, vice-president of the Trade Unions, looking black and biting his grey beard. " It's insane! Insane! " he shouted. " The European working-class won't move! All Russia — " He waved his hand distractedly and ran off. Riazanov and Kameniev had both opposed the insurrection, and felt the lash of Lenin's terrible tongue. . . .

It had been a momentous session. In the name of the Military Revolutionary Committee Trotzky had declared that the Provisional Government no longed existed.

" The characteristic of bourgeois governments," he said, " is to deceive the people. We, the Soviets of Workers', Soldiers' and Peasants' Deputies, are going to try an experiment unique in history; we are going to found a power which will have no other aim but to satisfy the needs of the soldiers, workers, and peasants."

Lenin had appeared, welcomed with a mighty ovation, prophesying world-wide Social Revolution. . . . And Zinoviev, crying, " This day we have paid our debt to the international proletariat, and struck a terrible blow at the war, a terrible body-blow at all the imperialists and particularly at Wilhelm the Executioner. . . ."

Then Trotzky, that telegrams had been sent to the front announcing the victorious insurrection, but no reply had come. Troops were said to be marching against Petrograd — a delegation must be sent to tell them the truth.

Cries, "You are anticipating the will of the All-Russian Congress of Soviets!"

Trotzky, coldly, "The will of the All-Russian Congress of Soviets has been anticipated by the rising of the Petrograd workers and soldiers!"

So we came into the great meeting-hall, pushing through the clamorous mob at the door. In the rows of seats, under the white chandeliers, packed immovably in the aisles and on the sides, perched on every window-sill, and even the edge of the platform, the representatives of the workers and soldiers of all Russia waited in anxious silence or wild exultation the ringing of the chairman's bell. There was no heat in the hall but the stifling heat of un-washed human bodies. A foul blue cloud of cigarette smoke rose from the mass and hung in the thick air. Occasionally some one in authority mounted the tribune and asked the comrades not to smoke; then everybody, smokers and all, took up the cry "Don't smoke, comrades!" and went on smoking. Petrovsky, Anarchist delegate from the Obukhov factory, made a seat for me beside him. Unshaven and filthy, he was reeling from three nights' sleepless work on the Military Revolutionary Committee.

On the platform sat the leaders of the old *Tsay-ee-kah* [1] — for the last time dominating the turbulent Soviets, which they had ruled from the first days, and which were now risen against them. It was the end of the first period of the Russian revolution, which these men had attempted to guide in careful ways. . . . The three greatest of them were not there: Kerensky, flying to the front through country towns all doubtfully heaving up; Tcheidze, the old eagle, who had contemptuously retired to his own Georgian mountains, there to sicken with consumption; and the high-souled Tseretelli, also mor-tally stricken, who, nevertheless, would return and pour out his beautiful eloquence for a lost cause. Gotz sat there, Dan, Lieber, Bogdanov, Broido, Fillipovsky, — white-faced, hollow-eyed and indignant. Below them the sec-ond *siezd* [2] of the All-Russian Soviets boiled and swirled, and over their heads the Military Revolutionary Committee functioned white-hot, holding in its hands the threads of insurrection and striking with a long arm. . . . It was 10:40 P.M.

Dan, a mild-faced, baldish figure in a shapeless military surgeon's uni-form, was ringing the bell. Silence fell sharply, intense, broken by the scuffling and disputing of the people at the door. . . .

"We have the power in our hands," he began sadly, stopped for a mo-ment, and then went on in a low voice. "Comrades! The Congress of Soviets is meeting in such unusual circumstances and in such an extraordinary mo-ment that you will understand why the *Tsay-ee-kah* considers it unnecessary

---

[1] The initial letters of *Tsentralny Ispolnitelny Komitet* or Central Executive Committee. (Editor's note.)

[2] Session. (Editor's note.)

to address you with a political speech. This will become much clearer to you if you will recollect that I am a member of the *Tsay-ee-kah,* and that at this very moment our party comrades are in the Winter Palace under bombardment, sacrificing themselves to execute the duty put on them by the *Tsay-ee-kah"* (Confused uproar.)

" I declare the first session of the Second Congress of Soviets of Workers' and Soldiers' Deputies open! "

The election of the presidium took place amid stir and moving about. Avanessov announced that by agreement of the Bolsheviki, Left Socialist Revolutionaries and Mensheviki Internationalists, it was decided to base the presidium upon proportionality. Several Mensheviki leaped to their feet protesting. A bearded soldier shouted at them, " Remember what you did to us Bolsheviki when *we* were in the minority! " Result — 14 Bolsheviki, 7 Socialist Revolutionaries, 3 Mensheviki and 1 Internationalist (Gorky's group). Hendelmann, for the right and centre Socialist Revolutionaries, said that they refused to take part in the presidium; the same from Kintchuk, for the Mensheviki; and from the Mensheviki Internationalists, that until the verification of certain circumstances, they too could not enter the presidium. Scattering applause and hoots. One voice, " Renegades, you call yourselves Socialists! " A representative of the Ukrainean delegates demanded, and received, a place. Then the old *Tsay-ee-kah* stepped down, and in their places appeared Trotzky, Kameniev, Lunatcharsky, Madame Kollontai, Nogin. . . . The hall rose, thundering. How far they had soared, these Bolsheviki, from a despised and hunted sect less than four months ago, to this supreme place, the helm of great Russia in full tide of insurrection!

The order of the day, said Kameniev, was first, Organisation of Power; second, War and Peace; and third, the Constituent Assembly. . . .

But suddenly a new sound made itself heard, deeper than the tumult of the crowd, persistent, disquieting, — the dull shock of guns. People looked anxiously toward the clouded windows, and a sort of fever came over them. Martov, demanding the floor, croaked hoarsely, " The civil war is beginning, comrades! The first question must be a peaceful settlement of the crisis. On principle and from a political standpoint we must urgently discuss a means of averting civil war. Our brothers are being shot down in the streets! . . .

Always the methodical muffled boom of cannon through the windows, and the delegates, screaming at each other. . . .

Then came Abramovitch, for the *Bund,* the organ of the Jewish Social Democrats — his eyes snapping behind thick glasses, trembling with rage.

" What is taking place now in Petrograd is a monstrous calamity! The *Bund* group joins with the declaration of the Mensheviki and Socialist Revolutionaries and will leave the Congress! " He raised his voice and hand. " Our duty to the Russian proletariat doesn't permit us to remain here and be responsible for these crimes. Because the firing on the Winter Palace doesn't cease, the Municipal Duma together with the Mensheviki and Socialist Revolutionaries, and the Executive Committee of the Peasants' Soviet, has decided to perish with the Provisional Government, and we are going with them! Unarmed we will expose our breasts to the machine guns of the Terrorists. . . . We invite all delegates to this Congress—" The rest was lost in a storm of hoots, menaces and curses which rose to a hellish pitch as fifty delegates got up and pushed their way out. . . .

Kameniev jangled the bell, shouting, "Keep your seats and we'll go on with our business!" And Trotzky, standing up with a pale, cruel face, letting out his rich voice and cool contempt, " All these so-called Socialist compromisers, these frightened Mensheviki, Socialist Revolutionaries, *Bund* — let them go! They are just so much refuse which will be swept into the garbage-heap of history!" . . .

Thursday, Oct. 26/Nov. 8

The Congress was to meet at one o'clock, and long since the great meeting-hall had filled, but by seven there was yet no sign of the presidium. . . . The Bolshevik and Left Social Revolutionary factions were in session in their own rooms. All the livelong afternoon Lenin and Trotzky had fought against compromise. A considerable part of the Bolsheviki were in favour of giving way so far as to create a joint all-Socialist government. " We can't hold on!" they cried. " Too much is against us. We haven't got the men. We will be isolated, and the whole thing will fall." So Kameniev, Riazanov and others.

But Lenin, with Trotzky beside him, stood firm as a rock. "Let the compromisers accept our programme and they can come in! We won't give way an inch. If there are comrades here who haven't the courage and the will to dare what we dare, let them leave with the rest of the cowards and conciliators! Backed by the workers and soldiers we shall go on."

At five minutes past seven came word from the left Socialist Revolutionaries to say that they would remain in the Military Revolutionary Committee. " See!" said Lenin, " They are following." . . .

It was just 8:40 when a thundering wave of cheers announced the entrance of the presidium with Lenin — great Lenin — among them. A short, stocky figure, with a big head set down in his shoulders, bald and bulging. Little eyes, a snubbish nose, wide, generous mouth, and heavy chin; clean-shaven now, but already beginning to bristle with the well-known beard of his past and future. Dressed in shabby clothes, his trousers much too long for him. Unimpressive, to be the idol of a mob, loved and revered as perhaps few leaders in history have been. A strange popular leader — a leader

purely by virtue of intellect; colourless, humourless, uncompromising
and detached, without picturesque idiosyncrasies — but with the power
of explaining profound ideas in simple terms, of analysing a concrete situation. And combined with shrewdness, the greatest intellectual
audacity.

Kameniev was reading the report of the actions of the Military Revolutionary committee; abolition of capital punishment in the Army, restoration
of the free right of propaganda, release of officers and soldiers arrested for
political crimes, orders to arrest Kerensky and confiscation of food supplies
in private store-houses. . . . Tremendous applause.

Again the representative of the *Bund*. The uncompromising attitude of
the Bolsheviki would mean the crushing of the Revolution; therefore, the
Bund delegates must refuse any longer to sit in the Congress. Cries from the
audience, " We thought you walked out last night! How many more times
are you going to walk out? "

Then the representative of the Mensheviki Internationalists. Shouts,
" What! You here still? " The speaker explained that only part of the Mensheviki Internationalists left the Congress; the rest were going to stay —

" We consider it dangerous and perhaps even mortal for the Revolution
to transfer the power to the Soviets " — Interruptions — " but we feel it our
duty to remain in the Congress and vote against the transfer here!"

Other speakers followed, apparently without any order. A delegate of the
coal-miners of the Don Basin called upon the Congress to take measures
against Kaledin, who might cut off coal and food from the capital. Several
soldiers just arrived from the Front brought the enthusiastic greetings of
their regiments. . . . Now Lenin, gripping the edge of the reading stand,
letting his little winking eyes travel over the crowd as he stood there waiting,
apparently oblivious to the long-rolling ovation, which lasted several minutes.
When it finished, he said simply, " We shall now proceed to construct the
Socialist order! " Again that overwhelming human roar.

" The first thing is the adoption of practical measures to realise peace. . . .
We shall offer peace to the peoples of all the belligerent countries upon the
basis of the Soviet terms — no annexations, no indemnities, and the right of
self-determination of peoples. At the same time, according to our promise,
we shall publish and repudiate the secret treaties. . . . The question of War
and Peace is so clear that I think that I may, without preamble, read the
project of a Proclamation to the Peoples of All the Belligerent Countries. . . ."

His great mouth, seeming to smile, opened wide as he spoke; his voice
was hoarse — not unpleasantly so, but as if it had hardened that way after
years and years of speaking — and went on monotonously, with the effect of
being able to go on forever. . . . For emphasis he bent forward slightly. No

gestures. And before him, a thousand simple faces looking up in intent adoration. . . .

It was exactly 10:35 when Kameniev asked all in favour of the proclamation to hold up their cards. One delegate dared to raise his hand against, but the sudden sharp outburst around him brought it swiftly down. . . . Unanimous.

Suddenly, by common impulse, we found ourselves on our feet, mumbling together into the smooth lifting unison of the *Internationale*. A grizzled old soldier was sobbing like a child. Alexandra Kollontai rapidly winked the tears back. The immense sound rolled through the hall, burst windows and doors and soared into the quiet sky. "The war is ended! The war is ended!" said a young workman near me, his face shining. And when it was over, as we stood there in a kind of awkward hush, some one in the back of the room shouted, "Comrades! Let us remember those who have died for liberty!" So we began to sing the Funeral March, that slow, melancholy and yet triumphant chant, so Russian and so moving. The *Internationale* is an alien air, after all. The Funeral March seemed the very soul of those dark masses whose delegates sat in this hall, building from their obscure visions a new Russia — and perhaps more.

> You fell in the fatal fight
> For liberty of the people, for the honour of the people . . .
> You gave up your lives and everything dear to you,
> You suffered in horrible prisons,
> You went to exile in chains. . . .
>
> Without a word you carried your chains because you could not ignore your suffering brothers,
> Because you believed that justice is stronger than the sword . . .
> The time will come when your surrendered life will count.
> That time is near; when tyranny falls the people will rise, great and free!
> Farewell, brothers, you chose a noble path,
> You are followed by the new and fresh army ready to die and to suffer . . .
>
> Farewell, brothers, you chose a noble path,
> At your grave we swear to fight, to work for freedom and the people's happiness. . . .

At two o'clock the Land Decree was put to vote, with only one against and the peasant delegates wild with joy. . . . So plunged the Bolsheviki ahead, irresistible, over-riding hesitation and opposition — the only people in

Russia who had a definite programme of action while the others talked for eight long months. . . .

At 2:30 A.M. fell a tense hush. Kameniev was reading the decree of the Constitution of Power. . . .

Still silence; as he read the list of Commissars, bursts of applause after each name, Lenin's and Trotzky's especially.

President of the Council: Vladimir Ulianov (*Lenin*)
Interior: A. E. Rykov
Agriculture: V. P. Miliutin
Labour: A. G. Shliapnikov
Military and Naval Affairs — a committee composed of V. A. Avseenko (*Antonov*), N. V. Krylenko, and F. M. Dybenko.
Commerce and Industry: V. P. Nogin
Popular Education: A. V. Lunatcharsky
Finance: E. E. Skvortsov (*Stepanov*)
Foreign Affairs: L. D. Bronstein (*Trotzky*)
Justice: G. E. Oppokov (*Lomov*)
Supplies: E. A. Teodorovitch
Post and Telegraph: N. P. Avilov (*Gliebov*)
Chairman for Nationalities: I. V. Djougashvili (*Stalin*)
Railroads: To be filled later.

232. *THE POSTER THAT ANNOUNCED THE REVOLUTION* [1] TO THE CITIZENS OF RUSSIA!

The Provisional Government is deposed. The State Power has passed into the hands of the organ of the Petrograd Soviet of Workers' and Soldiers' Deputies, the Military Revolutionary Committee, which stands at the head of the Petrograd proletariat and garrison.

The cause for which the people were fighting: immediate proposal of a democratic peace, abolition of landlord property-rights over the land, labor control over production, creation of a Soviet Government — that cause is securely achieved.

LONG LIVE THE REVOLUTION OF WORKMEN, SOLDIERS AND PEASANTS!

Military Revolutionary Committee
Petrograd Soviet of Workers' and Soldiers' Deputies.
25 October, 1917. 10 A.M.

Three important decrees, embodying the promises of the Bolsheviki, follow. Nationalization of industries was left to a later date.

[1] John Reed, *Ten Days that Shook the World.* New York, Boni & Liveright, 1919, p. 95.

233. *DECREE ON THE SOCIALIZATION OF LAND* [1]

(1.) All private ownership of land is abolished immediately without compensation.

(2.) All land-owners' estates, and all lands belonging to the Crown, to monasteries, church lands with all their live stock and inventoried property, buildings and all appurtenances, are transferred to the disposition of the township Land Committees and the district Soviets of Peasants' Deputies until the Constituent Assembly meets.

(3.) Any damage whatever done to the confiscated property which from now on belongs to the whole People, is regarded as a serious crime, punishable by the revolutionary tribunals. The district Soviets of Peasants' Deputies shall take all necessary measures for the observance of the strictest order during the taking over of the land-owners' estates, for the determination of the dimensions of the plots of land and which of them are subject to confiscation, for the drawing up of an inventory of the entire confiscated property, and for the strictest revolutionary protection of all the farming property on the land, with all buildings, implements, cattle, supplies of products, etc., passing into the hands of the People.

(4.) For guidance during the realisation of the great land reforms until their final resolution by the Constituent Assembly, shall serve the following peasant *nakaz* (instructions), drawn up on the basis of 242 local peasant *nakazi* by the editorial board of the "*Izviestia* of the All-Russian Soviet of Peasants' Deputies," and published in No. 88 of said "*Izviestia*" (Petrograd, No. 88, August 19th, 1917).

The lands of peasants and of Cossacks serving in the Army shall not be confiscated.

234. *DECLARATION OF THE RIGHTS OF THE RUSSIAN PEOPLES* [2]

The October Revolution of the workers and peasants has begun under the common banner of deliverance.

The peasants have been freed from the yoke of the great landed proprietors, for there is no more private property in land — it is abolished.

The soldiers and sailors have been freed from the power of autocratic generals; the generals henceforth will be elected and removable at pleasure.

[1] Adopted, Oct. 26/Nov. 8, 1917, by the Congress of Workers', Soldiers' and Peasants' Deputies. Reed, op. cit., pp. 133–134; M. W. Graham, *New Governments of Eastern Europe,* p. 592; R. Labry, *Une Législation Communiste,* pp. 35–36.

[2] Nov. 15, 1917. Translation from *Pravda,* November 16, 1917, published in M. W. Graham, *New Governments of Eastern Europe.* New York, Henry Holt & Co., 1927, pp. 594–595.

The workers have been freed from the caprices and the arbitrariness of the capitalists, for starting from today control will be established by the workers over the workshops and the factories.

There remain but the peoples of Russia, who have been forbearing and have bided their time under the yoke and the arbitrariness, and whom it is necessary immediately to enfranchise and liberate.

In the epoch of Czarism, the peoples of Russia were aroused against each other. The results of this policy are known: massacres and pogroms on one side, enslaving of peoples on the other.

There can be no return to this shameful policy. Today it must be replaced by a voluntary and honest policy of union of the peoples of Russia.

In the epoch of imperialism, after the February revolution, when power passed into the hands of the Cadet bourgeoisie, the policy of incitation was replaced by a dastardly policy of distrust of the peoples of Russia, a policy of chicanery and provocation covering itself by the words of "liberty" and of "equality" of peoples. The results of this policy are known: increase of the antagonism between nationalities, lack of mutual confidence.

This unworthy policy of lies and mistrust, of chicanery and provocation must be definitely ended. It must be replaced today by an open and honest policy, leading to a complete mutual confidence of the peoples of Russia.

It is only thanks to such a confidence that the honest and solid union of all the peoples of Russia can be formed.

It is only thanks to such a union that the workers and peasants of Russia can be welded into a revolutionary force capable of defending itself against every attack on the part of the imperialist and annexationist bourgeoisie.

Starting on this principle, the first congress of soviets, in the month of June of this year, proclaimed the right of the peoples of Russia to self-determination.

The second congress of soviets in the month of October last confirmed this right in a more decisive and more precise fashion.

Executing the will of these soviets, the council of the people's commissaries has resolved to be guided in the question of nationalities by the following principles:

1. The equality and sovereignty of the peoples of Russia.

2. The right of the peoples of Russia to dispose of their own fate, even to separation and the establishment of an independent state.

3. Abolition of all privileges and limitations, national or religious.

4. Free development of national minorities and ethnographic groups inhabiting Russian territory.

Decrees will be prepared immediately after the creation of a commission on nationalities.

In the name of the Russian Republic,
The People's Commissary for Nationalities,

IOUSSIF DJOUGACHVILI STALIN.

The President of the Council of the People's Commissaries,

V. ULIANOV.

235. THE ABOLITION OF CLASSES, November 23, 1917 [1]

Article 1. All classes and divisions into classes, all privileges and delimitations of classes, the organizations, the institutions of classes and all civil grades are abolished.

Article 2. All classes (nobles, merchants, lesser bourgeois, peasants, etc.) and titles (of prince, count and others) and the denomination of civil rank (privy councillor of state, and others) are abolished and there is established the one general designation of citizen of the Republic of Russia.

Article 3. The properties of the class institutions and of the nobility are to pass immediately to the corresponding institutions of the zemstvos.

Article 4. The properties of merchant and bourgeois societies are to pass immediately to the corresponding authorities of the cities.

Article 5. All the institutions of classes, all their business, procedure and archives are to pass to the administration of the corresponding institutions of the cities and the zemstvos.

Article 6. All existing laws on the foregoing subjects are abolished.

Article 7. The present decree enters into force starting from the day when it shall be published and will be applied by the Soviets of Workers', Soldiers' and Peasants' Deputies.

The present decree has been confirmed by the Central Executive Committee of the Soviets of Workers', Soldiers' and Peasants' Deputies, in the session of November 10, 1917, and has been signed by

The President of the Central Committee, SVERDLOV.
The President of the Council of the People's Commissaries, ULIANOV.
The Director of the Affairs of the Council of the People's Commissaries.
BONTCH-BROUEVITCH.
The Secretary of the Council, N. GORBOUNOV.

Vladimir Ilich Ulianov, whose nom de guerre *was Lenin, was born at Simbirsk in 1870. His whole life had been given to revolutionary activity, some of it in Russia, some in exile in Siberia, and much in exile in Switzerland whence he came to Russia in April, 1917. He was recognized as the undis-*

[1] Translation from *Pravda*, November 25, 1917, published in M. W. Graham, *New Governments of Eastern Europe*. New York, Henry Holt & Co., 1927, p. 596.

puted leader of Bolshevism from that time until his final illness overcame him in 1922. He died in 1924.

236. *WHAT LENIN WAS LIKE* [1]

Even in the external image of this modern hero, in Lenin's whole attitude and form, the conventional gesture of the great man is lacking. His exterior was completely that of any everyday man of the mass, and clashed with all the pictures of a hero which the imagination is used to make. On the thousands of Soviet flags, propaganda pictures, emblems and badges, Lenin is now portrayed as an orator, standing on the globe, or set amid the rays of the rising sun; the man himself, however, beneath whose feet the terrestrial sphere rests as a footstool, whose face emerges from the brightness of the sunlight, is in no way distinguished from thousands and tens of thousands of his fellow citizens. He stands before us, his head covered with an ordinary cloth cap, his right hand in his trousers pocket, and we search his countenance in vain for any trace which might betray the important man. Lenin had the face of an average Russian, and all his friends and disciples who had opportunity to observe him at close quarters, and all the painters and sculptors who fixed his features, are unanimous in stating that his face was entirely lacking in anything remarkable; only the little black eyes made a certain impression. The things that might strike a stranger as characteristic, the high, somewhat conical shape of the skull, the Asiatic cheek-bones, and the Mongolian eyebrows, are all quite ordinary in Russia; Lenin's physiognomy has the features which one may meet at every turn in Moscow among the many Russians from the Eastern provinces. Lunacharski, Lenin's friend, disciple, and biographer, himself confesses that the dictator had the commonplace face of a merchant of peasant stock from, say, Iaroslav.

But not only was there nothing remarkable in Lenin's appearance, even the first impression made by his whole manner was in no way remarkable. And yet he was a popular orator, who carried his audiences on to the most violent upheaval in history, although his speech was entirely lacking in the fiery impetus which is, as a rule, absolutely necessary to capture the masses and bend them to your will. His voice was almost always dimmed with huskiness, it generally sounded flat and colourless and his turns of speech lacked all appeal, all oratorical adornment. The style of this man, whose words put a whole continent out of joint, both in writing and speech, was entirely insignificant. Trotski, the second great leader of Russia, was master of the practice of the persuasive orator; his speech had rhythm, dramatic power, and artistic structure; Lenin's oratory had none of these talents at its command. . . .

[1] Rene Fülöp-Miller, *The Mind and Face of Bolshevism.* Translated from the German by F. S. Flint and D. F. Tait. New York, Alfred A. Knopf, 1928, pp. 44–53 (condensed).

He passionately condemned all "fine rhetoric," and regarded it as a sign of intellectual weakness and moral emptiness. The fight against the revolutionary phrase runs through all his works and appeals; he rejected everything which smacked of meaningless rhetoric and literature. Any high-flown sentences in his comrades called forth his angry rejection, a grand gesture roused the sharpest criticism and biting scorn; anything " poetic " or " sublime " incited him to furious outbursts of contempt.

Only language taken from simple talk had value for him, and he himself used to introduce into his style ordinary, easily understood words and phrases which often had even a touch of the coarseness of popular speech. . . .

In his polemics . . . he relied chiefly on emphasis, and when he attacked his enemies, he built up a whole system of angrily ironic interjections by which he exposed his foe to general scorn and turned the whole dispute into a kind of satiric dialogue. . . .

His images and comparisons were always entirely sober and simple; on the whole, he used them only to make the concrete and visible even clearer; he liked to use proverbs and easy images, especially from the Gospels and Krylov's fables; but he never quoted present-day writers.

Not only was Lenin's terse and homely language entirely lacking in all pathos, and his writings free from captivating phrases; even the content of his utterances was always directed entirely to the practical and necessary. He, who had prophesied the victory of Bolshevism twenty years before, never made great promises. His friends can point out now how, even in his book on the future state of society free from class distinctions, no trace of " exuberance " is to be found, although the theme demanded and would have excused a certain passionate exaltation. In all Lenin's utterances, sober and clearly felt practical considerations alone prevail; all his writings are dry discussions of practical politics or utilitarian instructions.

The result was that with Lenin, who had striven for the Utopian kingdom of the future, Utopia was always adjusted exclusively to the nearest momentary interests of the masses; although he had evolved the most violent programme for the overthrow of the whole world and all its century-old conditions, yet in practice he concerned himself only with the next steps which seemed to him necessary to attain his end. . . .

Since he was a fanatical believer in the rightness of his ideas, he was troubled by no doubts, no attacks of despondency, or spiritual conflicts; he was exclusively occupied with realizing his projects. Therefore, even the superhuman labour, the enormous task, which he performed in order to work out and prepare his ideas and translate them into reality, was not an overstrain which could be said to have in any way twisted and distorted his compact nature, but rather the natural expansion of the immense powers possessed by this inimitable and unique being.

Lenin's whole activity had the charm of harmonious freshness and ease. Lunacharski states that Lenin was by no means a friend of toil, and was but rarely seen with a book, or at a desk. He wrote infinitely fast in large writing, and threw his articles on to paper without the least exertion, at any odd time, whenever opportunity offered. He read only in a piecemeal fashion, and never kept long to one book, but he had a sure eye for the significant, and especially for passages which he could use in fighting speeches. It was not so much ideas akin to his own, as ideas opposed to his that set him on fire, for the fighter was always alive in him, and his mind was mainly kindled in criticism. Not only did Lenin write occasional pamphlets with this calmness, speed, and objectivity, but also all those decrees which plunged half a continent into upheaval; for his measures as dictator were to him nothing but the natural expression of what he had recognized to be right, and, for this reason, had resolved to realize. . . .

His friends tell us that he knew, to a degree found in perhaps few other men, the secret of complete relaxation, of the "breathing space," and could procure for himself hours of absolute peace and gaiety, even in the midst of the most stirring events and the most strenuous work. This may explain his playing for hours with children and kittens as his family and friends describe.

From the unanimous descriptions of all his friends, we see that Lenin was anything but a gloomy, reserved man. Nay, we are always hearing of his childish gaiety, his care-free, jolly laugh, which seems to have been particularly characteristic. "Lenin is genuine right through, filled up to the brim with the sap of life" Vorovski wrote of him. "He tries in vain to control his laughter, which, when he puts his hand over his mouth, bursts out at the side."

Lunacharski also testifies to Lenin's cheerfulness in private life: "In the unhappiest moments of his existence, he was serene and always prone to gay laughter; even his anger, terrible though it could be in its effects, had something extraordinarily lovable, almost jovial, about it."

This even temperament made it possible for Lenin to preserve his calm and his prudent glance even in the most difficult and catastrophic moments of the political struggle. He was never nervous, impatient, or excited, but always uniformly attentive, interested, and objective. He was always ready to listen attentively to the most trifling communications of the soldiers, workers, or peasants who came from the most remote villages to lay their grievances before him. In this way, just from the simple reports of these people, he was able to understand the real cares of the masses, to know their needs and wants and think out new ways to help them. He was entirely merged in the mass of his partisans, Klara Zetkin reports; he became homogeneous with them, and never by gesture or attitude tried to obtrude his personality. Klara Zetkin also speaks of his comradely way with young people, and of the fatherly note he knew how to strike in his intercourse with the younger Party members.

There is no doubt that a large part of his success with the Russian masses may be traced to the simplicity of his character; he laid all who came to him under a spell, and he was obeyed as one obeys a trusted and experienced adviser, who is distinguished from those about him merely by greater shrewdness. Even the simplest peasant faced Lenin with a feeling that he was meeting a friend on an equal footing.

Lenin had much of the peasant in him, his simple reliable character, his prudent eye for practical advantage, are all characteristic features of the Russian peasant. "This undoubtedly great proletarian leader," wrote Trotski once, "not only has the appearance of a peasant, but his rugged bearing as well. When he shuts his left eye in deciphering a radio-telegram or an important document, he is the very image of a shrewd peasant who is not to be got round by empty words. His shrewdness is exactly a peasant's shrewdness, but raised to the highest power and equipped with the keenest scientific methods of thought."

Lenin had in common with the peasants not only their shrewdness, but also their tendency to violence: he was intimately one with all the primitive forces of the people, and it was through this that he was able to bring about such a colossal upheaval.

SECTION II. THE GERMAN REVOLUTION

Although the Emperor William II agreed to abdicate as German Kaiser on November 9, 1918, the day of his flight to Holland, he refused at that time to abdicate as King of Prussia. It was not until later in the month that he made a full renunciation of his sovereign rights.

237. ABDICATION PROCLAMATION OF THE EMPEROR WILLIAM II [1]

I herewith renounce for all time claims to the throne of Prussia and to the German Imperial throne connected therewith. At the same time I release all officials of the German Empire and of Prussia, as well as all officers, non-commissioned officers and men of the navy and of the Prussian army, as well as the troops of the federated states of Germany, from the oath of fidelity which they tendered to me as their Emperor, King and Commander-in-chief. I expect of them that until the re-establishment of order in the German Empire they shall render assistance to those in actual power in Germany,

---

[1] Purlitz, *Die Deutsche Revolution*, vol. I, p. 32 (Special Edition for the German Historical Almanac). (Translation.)

in protecting the German people from the threatening dangers of anarchy, famine and foreign rule.

Proclaimed under our own hand and with the Imperial seal attached.

Amerongen, 28 November, 1918.

(signed) Wilhelm.

The German Imperial Government having been overthrown, a National Assembly was elected in January, 1919, by all Germans over nineteen years of age. Meeting later at Weimar this Assembly adopted a new constitution, establishing a federal, republican German Commonwealth (Reich) of eighteen states. Significant provisions of this constitution follow.

238. THE CONSTITUTION OF THE GERMAN REPUBLIC, AUGUST 11, 1919. EXTRACTS [1]

Article 1.

The German Federation is a republic.
Supreme power emanates from the people.

Article 13.

Federal law overrides state law.

If there is a doubt or a difference of opinion as to whether a provision of a state law is consistent with federal law, the competent supreme authorities of the federation or of the state may appeal for a decision to a supreme federal court, in accordance with the more detailed provisions of a federal law.

Article 17.

Every state must have a republican constitution. . . .

Article 20.

The Reichstag is composed of the representatives of the German people. . . .

Article 22.

The representatives are elected by the universal, equal, direct, and secret suffrage of all men and women over twenty years of age in accordance with the principle of proportional representation. Election day must be a Sunday or a public holiday.

Article 23.

The Reichstag is elected for four years. . . .

[1] Heinrich Oppenheimer, *The Constitution of the German Republic*. London, Stevens and Sons, 1923, pp. 219–260. (Appendix.)

Article 33.

The Reichstag and its committees may require the presence of the Federal Chancellor and of every Federal Minister. . . .

Article 41.

The President of the Federation is elected by the whole German people. Every German who has completed his thirty-fifth year is eligible. . . .

Article 43.

The President of the Federation remains in office for seven years. Re-election is permitted.

Before the expiration of that term the President of the Federation may be removed from office, upon the motion of the Reichstag, by a vote of the people. The resolution must be carried in the Reichstag by a two-thirds majority. By such a resolution the President of the Federation is at once suspended from the further exercise of his office. The refusal of the people to sanction his removal from office is equivalent to re-election and carries with it the dissolution of the Reichstag.

Criminal proceedings may not be instituted against the President of the Federation without the consent of the Reichstag.

Article 48.

If a state fails to perform the duties imposed upon it by the federal constitution or by federal law, the President of the Federation may enforce performance with the aid of armed forces. . . .

Article 50.

All orders and decrees of the President of the Federation, including those relating to the defence force, in order to be valid, must be countersigned by the Federal Chancellor or by the competent Federal Minister. Such countersignature implies assumption of responsibility.

Article 52.

The Federal Government consists of the Federal Chancellor and the Federal Ministers.

Article 53.

The President of the Federation appoints and dismisses the Federal Chancellor and, on the latter's recommendation, the Federal Ministers.

Article 54.

The Federal Chancellor and the Federal Ministers require the confidence of the Reichstag for the exercise of their offices. Any one of them must resign if the Reichstag withdraws its confidence from him by an express resolution.

Article 56.

The Federal Chancellor settles the political programme, for which he is responsible to the Reichstag. Within the main lines of this programme each Federal Minister administers independently the department entrusted to him, for which he is personally responsible to the Reichstag.

Article 60.

A Reichsrat will be formed for the representation of the German states in federal legislation and administration.

Article 61.

(As amended by law of March 24th, 1921.)

In the Reichsrat each state has at least one vote. In the case of the larger states one vote will be assigned for every 700,000 inhabitants. A surplus of not less than 350,000 inhabitants is reckoned as 700,000. No single state may be represented by more than two-fifths of the total number of votes.

After joining the German Federation, Austria will be entitled to be represented in the Reichsrat by a number of votes proportional to her population. Meanwhile the Austrian representatives may take part in the deliberations, but may not vote.

The number of votes is settled afresh by the Reichsrat after each general census.

Article 68.

Bills may be introduced by the Federal Government or may originate in the midst of the Reichstag itself.

Federal laws are enacted by the Reichstag.

Article 69.

Before introducing a bill, the Federal Government must obtain the consent of the Reichsrat. If the Federal Government and the Reichsrat cannot agree, the former may introduce the bill all the same, but, in doing so, must explain the divergent views of the Reichsrat.

If the Reichsrat adopts a bill to which the Federal Government does not agree, the latter must introduce the bill, at the same time explaining its own point of view.

Article 73.

A law passed by the Reichstag shall, before its promulgation, be submitted to the popular vote if the President of the Federation so decides within one month.

A law the promulgation of which has been postponed at the instance of one-third of the members of the Reichstag is to be submitted to the popular vote upon the demand of one-twentieth of those entitled to vote.

Again, there may be an appeal to the decision of the people if one-tenth of the voters petition that a draft-law be submitted to the popular vote. Such petition must be based on a complete draft-bill. The Federal Government must submit it to the Reichstag, at the same time explaining its attitude towards it. There will be no appeal to the decision of the people if the desired bill is passed, unamended by the Reichstag.

The budget, laws dealing with taxation or scales of pay can be submitted to the popular vote only at the instance of the President of the Federation.

The mode of procedure in connection with the appeal of the people and the initiative by petition will be regulated by a federal statute.

Article 74.

The Reichsrat may protest against laws passed by the Reichstag. . . .

In case of such protest the law is referred back to the Reichstag for further consideration. If then the Reichstag and the Reichsrat cannot agree, the President of the Federation may, within three months, cause the matter in dispute to be submitted to the popular vote. If the President of the Federation does not exercise this right, the law will not come into force. But if the Reichstag has passed it by a two-thirds' majority as against the protest of the Reichsrat, the President must either promulgate the law within three months or order it to be submitted to the popular vote.

Article 103.

The ordinary jurisdiction is exercised by the Supreme Federal Court of Judicature and by the courts of the states.

Article 143.

The education of the young is to be provided for by means of public institutions. In their organisation the Federation, the states and the local communities co-operate. . . .

Article 145.

School attendance is compulsory — in principle at a public elementary school for eight years and thereafter at a continuation school up to the completion of the eighteenth year. Instruction and the accessories thereto are gratuitous in elementary and continuation schools.

Article 146.

The system of public education is to be developed as an organic whole. A first elementary school common to all is to serve as the foundation of secondary and higher education. The determining factor in this organisation is the variety of occupations, whilst for the admission of a child to a certain type of school its own gifts and inclinations, and not the economic and social position nor the religion of its parents, are decisive. . . .

Article 147.

Private schools which are to serve as substitutes for public schools require a state license and are subject to the state laws. . . .

Private elementary schools are to be licensed only if in a local community there is no public elementary school according with the religious faith or the world philosophy of a minority of those responsible for the education of the young. . . .

Private preparatory schools are to be abolished.

Article 148.

In every school the educational aims must be moral training, public spirit, personal and vocational fitness, and, above all, the cultivation of German national character and of the spirit of international reconciliation. . . .

Article 155.

The distribution and the use of land are under state supervision with a view to the prevention of abuses and in order to secure for every German a healthy dwelling and for all German families, especially large ones, according to their needs suitable homesteads and small holdings. In the law to be enacted concerning homesteads the claims of those who have taken part in the late war will receive special consideration.

Land may be expropriated, if required for houses, for settlements, for bringing it under cultivation, or for the encouragement of agriculture. Entails are to be broken off.

The cultivation and utilisation of the soil is a duty which the landowner owes to the community. The unearned increment in the value of land is to be utilised for the benefit of the community.

All subsoil resources and all natural sources of power, as far as capable of being put to economic uses, are under the supervision of the state. Private royalties are, by law, to be transferred to the state.

Article 156.

The Federation may by law — without prejudice to claims to compensation and with due observance of the rules governing expropriations — convert into social property such private economic undertakings as are suitable for socialisation. . . .

Article 165.

Workmen and employees are called upon to co-operate, on an equal footing, with employers in the regulation of wages and of the conditions of labour, as well as in the general development of the productive forces. The organisations of the two groups of interests and the agreements entered into by them are recognised.

Statutory bodies representative of workmen and employees are to be created for the protection of their social and economic interests, viz., Works' Councils, District Workmen's Councils organised so as to correspond with industrial areas, and a Federal Workmen's Council.

District Workmen's Councils and the Federal Workmen's Council join with representatives of employers and of other interested sections of the community to form District Economic Councils and a Federal Economic Council for the accomplishment of the economic tasks in general and to collaborate in the execution of the socialisation laws in particular. The District Economic Councils and the Federal Economic Council are to be so constituted that all important occupational groups are represented thereon in accordance with their respective economic and social importance.

Bills of fundamental importance in relation to matters of social and economic policy, before being introduced in the Reichstag, shall be submitted by the Federal Government to the Federal Economic Council for an expression of its opinion. The Federal Economic Council itself has the right to initiate such bills. If the Federal Government does not agree with any such bill it is nevertheless bound to introduce it in the Reichstag, with an explanation of its own standpoint. The Federal Economic Council may delegate one of its members to appear before the Reichstag in support of the bill.

Workmen's and Economic Councils may be entrusted with powers of control and of administration within the spheres of activities assigned to them respectively.

The Federation alone has power to regulate the composition and the tasks of the Workmen's and Economic Councils respectively, as well as their relations to other self-governing social bodies.

SECTION III. THE DOWNFALL OF AUSTRIA–HUNGARY

The dissolution of Austria-Hungary illustrates the power of the principle of nationality, against which Metternich, in the first half of the nineteenth century, had battled in vain. The various nationalities in the Empire could not or would not get along together. Hence under the strain of war Austria-Hungary collapsed.

The Paris Conference, then, as Professor Seymour shows in the following selection, was not responsible for the break-up of Austria-Hungary. In the main it simply recognized an accomplished fact. It may be added, however, that the Conference has been severely and deservedly criticized for the way in which certain of the new boundary lines were drawn.

239. THE BREAK-UP OF AUSTRIA-HUNGARY [1]

" If Austria did not exist, it would be necessary to create her." This diplomatic aphorism, coined by a member of one of the very nationalities oppressed by the Hapsburgs, had rung in the ears of European statesmen for many decades. It had become almost axiomatic that the union of Danubian territories was essential to the economic welfare and political tranquillity of southeastern Europe. There were few who did not recognize the service performed for Europe by the Hapsburgs in holding together regions naturally interdependent, and in obstructing the advance up the Danube of that internecine strife which has characterized the political habits of the Balkans. The disruption of the Hapsburg empire would threaten economic dislocation at the same time that it would inflame the nationalistic jealousy and ambition of the peoples that had been crushed under the Hapsburg yoke. The prospect was regarded with a doubt that bordered upon dismay even by the nations that were fighting Austria in the Great War.

But the statesmen of the Peace Conference were confronted by a condition and not a theory. However clearly they recognized the dangers coincident with the disintegration of Austria-Hungary, it was not for them to decide. The question had already been settled by the nationalities of the dying empire, which in the last weeks of the war had set up their own governments, contemptuously brushing away the traditions of centuries. Austria-Hungary as a political entity had crumbled like the one-hoss shay, and the most solemn peace conference imaginable could not put her together again.

Such a disintegration had long been foreshadowed and discussed. The empire had never been a nation, and factors of union and disunion had always engaged in fierce struggles. Ties of language and blood kinship, which form the strongest elements of political integration, were lacking, and neither the political skill nor the good fortune of the Hapsburgs succeeded in welding into a single whole the myriad of peoples who had come to sojourn in the regions that make up the modern Austria-Hungary. The

[1] Charles Seymour, "The End of an Empire: Remnants of Austria-Hungary," in House and Seymour, *What Really Happened at Paris.* New York, Charles Scribner's Sons, 1921, pp. 87–95 (condensed).

development of revolutionary organization during the war was slow. It came first and most effectively among the Czechs, who organized wholesale desertion of Czech battalions from the Hapsburg armies and the betrayal to the Allies of Austrian military secrets. The Jugo-Slavs were more cautious. Especially after the entrance of Italy into the war they showed themselves suspicious of Allied propaganda, for they feared lest emancipation from the Hapsburg yoke might become simply the first step toward enslavement by Italy. Nor were the Allies anxious, at first, to foster revolution, since the disruption of Austria did not enter completely into their diplomatic plans. But the growing conviction that Austria had become the cat's-paw of Germany, combined with the disgust of the subject nationalities, resulted in the encouragement and the success of the revolution. In 1918 Czecho-Slovakia was recognized as an independent Allied state. The newly formulated aims of the Jugo-Slavs for independence and union with Serbia were generally approved, and a cordial, though informal and temporary, understanding with Italy was established.

With the surrender of Bulgaria, the rolling back of the German tide in France, and the defeat of Austrian armies on the Piave the revolution was inaugurated. Irresistibly and with extraordinary quiet it gathered headway. Hapsburg officials and organs of government were not assailed, but simply passed over, and in their place arose the provisional councils representing the nationalities. Within the space of a month the artificial cement that held the empire together had crumbled, loyalty to the emperor had evaporated, and the overlordship of Germans and Magyars had been cast aside. The Tyrol and Trieste were occupied by Italians; at Prague the new Czecho-Slovak Government was solidified; in Croatia the Jugo-Slavs seized the reins of power and prepared for the union with Serbia, while on the coast they took over the Austrian fleet; in Galicia the Poles negotiated with the new national government of Warsaw; in Transylvania the Rumanians were greeted as liberators.

When the peace conference opened, therefore, the empire of Austria-Hungary was a thing of the past. One journalistic critic complains that the conference angrily broke up Austria into jigsaw bits; but the accusation betrays a wealth of ignorance and shows how much easier it is to be critical than correct. The United States and Great Britain would have been glad to create a federation of the Danubian nationalities which, without the vices that had led to the fall of the Hapsburgs, might have accomplished the economic integration and preserved the political order so essential to the tranquillity and prosperity of southeastern Europe. The suggestion would have been no more effective than a tenor solo in a boiler-shop. The nationalities would have none of it. They had freed themselves, they were instinct with the sense of their own capacity, bursting with nationalistic ambitions, suspicious of any federation as likely to revive the tyranny under which they had so long suffered. The Conference lacked the right, as well as the power, to impose union upon them. By virtue of the principle of self-determination it was for the nationalities to determine their own destiny, and if they preferred disunion no one could deny them. The Independent sovereignty of the Czechs had been recognized; the union of the Poles of Galicia with the mass of the nationality in Russia and Germany was generally admitted; the right of Rumania to Transylvania had been acknowledged; and there were few inclined to dispute the union of the Serbs, Croats, and Slovenes of southern Hungary, Austria, and Bosnia, with their kinsmen in Serbia and Montenegro, although the prospect was not hailed with enthusiasm by Italy.

.   .   .   .

The Peace Conference was, accordingly, placed in the position of executor of the Hapsburg estate. The heirs were generally recognized — Czecho-Slovakia, Poland, Rumania, Jugo-Slavia, the new lesser Austria, lesser Hungary, and Italy. The duty of the Conference was to determine the character of the division.

.   .   .   .

The hearings took place in Secretary Pichon's study in the Quai d'Orsay, with its old pearly gray carpet marked with red roses, its rich Gobelin tapestries, and high French windows opening on to the perfect lawns of the foreign office gardens. In the centre, behind the empire desk, sat Clemenceau, squat, stolid, gray of face, his hands clasped quietly, covered by the eternal gray gloves, on his countenance an expression of bored tolerance. In his cynical wisdom he had never believed that the end of the war would bring the millennium; these nationalistic quarrels seemed to him entirely natural, even though inconvenient. His arid humor, his biting sarcasm displayed in an infrequent question, contrasted with the patient earnestness of President Wilson, who sat upon his right, and to whom, it is not uninteresting to note, the claimants appealed by their manner, if not in form, as the man of justice upon whom their hopes rested. Next to the Americans sat Lloyd George and Balfour, perfect contrast. The British prime minister, consumed with an electric energy, always on the edge of his chair, questioning and interrupting; Balfour, with his long legs outstretched, his head on the back of his chair, eyes not infrequently closed, philosophic in his attitude, completely proof against those sudden gusts of enthusiasm which sometimes assailed his chief. Next, on the right were the Japanese, with features immobile as the Sphinx, enigmatic as the Mona Lisa. Facing Clemenceau sat the Italians: Orlando, florid in manner, eloquent in speech; Sonnino, with eagle features, powerful nose, and jaw set like a vise. In the corners were the secretaries. Behind the principals sat the attachés and experts, with their maps and tables of statistics, whispering corrections of the *ex parte* statements which the delegates of the nationalities presented.

The latter stood or sat before Clemenceau's desk, presenting the particular claims of their newly founded or expanding states. There was the black-bearded Bratiano of Rumania, rather moody, fighting for the treaty of 1916, resentful of opposition. Or, contrasting type, the young and smiling foreign minister of the Czecho-Slovak Republic, Edward Benes, magnetic in manner, frank in negotiation. He had done much to organize the revolution that swept aside the Hapsburgs and to build up the Czecho-Slovak army in Siberia; his diplomatic skill had combined with the solid honesty of President Masaryk to win the recognition of the Allies for the infant state. Then again the claimant would be the Pole, Dmowski, with furrowed visage, clear logic, and power of satire that wounded as effectively, though less ostentatiously, as the scalding invective of Bratiano. Paderewski came to Paris only late in the history of the Conference. There also were the Serbs, the patriarchal Pachitch, with white flowing beard, veteran of many a diplomatic battle in the Balkans, and the smooth-spoken Vesnitch, both representing the Serbia of old, together with Trumbitch and Zholger, representatives of the newly freed Austrian Jugo-Slavs.

*In the following selection Dr. Herbert Kraus, Professor of International
Law and Public Law and Political Science at the University of Königsberg,
shows how serious the problem of racial minorities is in Europe at the
present time. The Peace Conference of 1919 did, it is true, make some attempt
to draw the new boundaries of the countries of Europe in accord with the
principle of nationality. But economic considerations and the alleged need
of establishing "strategic frontiers" often intervened; and whenever the
interests of the Central Powers were involved there was a strong tendency
to decide against these interests if there was any doubt as to where to place
a boundary-line. Nevertheless, with the best will in the world, the Peace
Conference could never have redrawn the map of Europe in such a way
as to satisfy all national groups. A serious post-war problem of racial minorities was unavoidable.*

240. *THE PROBLEM OF RACIAL MINORITIES IN EUROPE* [1]

THE multi-nationality state, Austria-Hungary, is dead, but its remains constitute in their turn, with the exception of the national state, German-
Austria, new multi-nationality states and bodies strongly interspersed with
minorities.

In Czecho-Slovakia, for instance, the Czechs are in the absolute majority
only when the Slovakians are included. There are 46 per cent Czechs and
13 per cent Slovakians living there. The fusion of these two groups is of
course quite as much a fiction as is the proclamation of the Czecho-Slovakian
language as the state language of Czecho-Slovakia. By according two
different languages legal equality, one can as little make the same language
of them as black and white can be created the same color by law. Opposite
this 46 per cent plus 13 per cent stand 28 per cent Germans, 8 per cent
Magyars, 3 per cent Ruthenians, and the rest Poles and Jews.

The case of Poland is similar. According to the official Polish census of

[1] Herbert Kraus, *Germany in Transition.* Lectures on the Harris Foundation, 1924. Reprinted by permission of The University of Chicago Press, Chicago. 1924, pp. 115–119, 121–124.

September 30, 1921, among the 25,372,427 inhabitants there are 68 per cent Poles and 32 per cent foreign nationalities. These are the official statistics which are generally disputed by the minorities, however. It is supposed by them that at least 40 per cent minorities lived in Poland, among whom are 1.1 million Germans and 5.7 million Russians, White Russians, Ruthenians, etc. The number of the minorities there, however, especially of the Germans, decreases steadily as a result of Poland's policy of evacuation.

The kingdom of the Serbians, Croatians, and Slovenians is built upon the idea of a Serbian-Croatian-Slovenian nation. The so-called Declaration of Corfu of July 7, 1920, refers to it specifically. In fact, however, there seems to be something out of joint in this composite nation. Before me lies a note dated February, 1922, from the sixty-three Croatian delegates of Croatia, Slovenia, Dalmatia, and Bosnia-Herzegovina united in the Croatian *bloc,* addressed, " To All Free Civilized Peoples and Delegates of the Genoa Conference," which describes this state body as in reality a centralized great Serbian state, and which complains bitterly over the suppression of the Croatian nation. We also read lately among other items of disturbing news from Jugo-Slavia that Stephen Raditch, leader of the Croat nationalists, has been imprisoned. Besides these, this state with over 12,000,000 inhabitants, contains considerable German, Magyar, Bulgarian, Roumanian, Italian, Albanian, Turkish, and Gypsy minorities, among whom are at least 500,000 Germans. On the other hand, at least 2,000,000 of the South Slavs are living under Italian and Grecian sovereignty.

The condition of the territories of the vanquished Central Powers gives us the exact anti-type. They have been thoroughly purged of the people of foreign nationalities, and in the process a great deal was also eliminated which according to the principle of nationality should not have been taken away.

According to the carefully collected statistics of the Austrian scientist, Winkler, the following German minorities living in *compact masses directly adjoining the mother-country* were brought under alien dominion *without a plebiscite:*

Czecho-Slovakia	3,123,000
France	1,614,000
Poland	587,000
Italy	228,000
Lithuania	71,000
Hungary	54,000
Belgium	50,000
Jugo-Slavia	50,000
Denmark	18,000
	5,795,000

In these figures Danzig, with a population of 364,380, is not considered. Nor furthermore are the 6.4 million inhabitants of German-Austria who wish to be united with the German Empire; to say nothing of the 653,000 inhabitants of the Saar, and the 6.5 million inhabitants of the occupied territory, not including the Ruhr district.

With the exception of the small minorities of Danish nationality scattered throughout the part of North Schleswig which remained with Germany, a number of Poles in the districts bordering on Poland, and the Wendish enclave sprinkled through the Saxon Lausitz, there are now no foreign minorities to speak of in Germany. This is especially true in regard to the Protestant Masurians in East Prussia, who feel themselves German, as has been demonstrated by the plebiscite, and by the last Reichstag elections, even though they are supposed to be by extraction a German-Polish mixed race.

. . . .

The treatment of the question of German-Austrian union with the German Empire is . . . most striking. The German-Austrians, as well as the Sudete Germans and all Germans under the sovereignty of the border states surrounding Germany, wish to join the German Empire, and feel themselves a strongly united nation with her inhabitants.

" The Germans cannot renounce uniting the whole German nation in the confines of one Empire," was said in a meeting of the National Assembly, February 6, 1919, by Ebert, the present President of the German Empire,[1] then people's commissioner. Numerous manifestations bear witness to the prevalence of this will on both sides. The Austrian *Staatsgesetzblatt,* for instance, contained a clause in the law published March 12, 1919, on the form of constitution: " German-Austria is a component part of the German Empire." The execution of this clause as well as the introduction of the word " German " in the name of this new state was denied the Austrians by the Treaty of St. Germain. This Treaty contains in Article 88 a direct prohibition of the union of German-Austria with the German Empire without the permission of the Council of the League of Nations, for which decision unanimity is necessary. This finds its counterpart and completion in Article 80 of the Treaty of Versailles. By these prescriptions the active negotiations of union between the German and Austrian governments were terminated. It has become especially quiet in regard to this subject since the Allied and Associated Powers by note of September 2, 1919, extracted a protocol of September 22, 1919, ratified by the Reichstag, from the German government to the effect that Article 61, sentence ii, of the German constitution should be declared invalid, an article which provides that German-

[1] He has since died. (Editor's note.)

Austria after its union with the German Empire should be invested with the right of participation in the Council of the Empire, according to the number of votes of its inhabitants, and until then German-Austria should have an advisory vote in the Council of the Empire.

But the desire for union is not dead. In a voluntary plebiscite held April 24, 1921, 85 per cent of the 98.8 per cent Tyrolese who voted expressed their will to unite with Germany. And on May 29, 99 per cent of the Salzburgers also voted in this sense. The will to union was given a strong expression also in the official speeches which were given March 20 and 21, 1924, on the occasion of the visit of Chancellor Marx and Foreign Minister Stresemann in Vienna.

With my reference to these statistics and facts I have at the same time begun the general characterization of the problem which occupies us. It is, briefly expressed, besides the reparation question, Europe's most complex current political problem, which constitutes a continuous explosive danger for the maintenance of peace.

The dissolution of Austria-Hungary resulted from the idea of the national state; the idea of the national state has become the greatest problem in the fate of the British Empire. The new grouping of the heritage of czaristic Russia with its hundred national groups is to a great extent the result of this principle. The Flemish question in Belgium constantly assumes more actual forms. Unnumbered enmities in the world are based on this idea.

To quote the best German authority on the principle of nationalities, Professor Laun, of Hamburg:

Wherever one looks in Central and Eastern Europe one sees unsolved national enmity. Poles and Lithuanians, Poles and Ukrainians, Czechs and Magyars, Magyars and Roumanians, Magyars and South-Slavonians, South-Slavonians and Albanians, South-Slavonians and Bulgarians, Albanians and Greeks, Bulgarians and Greeks, Greeks and Turks, etc., have become involved in disputes on frontiers under the idea of the Principle of Nationality or " Self-Determination," and although the boundaries established by the peace treaties are on the whole outwardly respected today, none of the temporarily curtailed elements have the least intention of finally relinquishing their co-nationals.

Thus Laun writes, and the worst of it is that Laun's list is not even complete.

SECTION II. FASCISM

Immediately after the end of the Great War Italy became the scene of serious disorders. The Socialists sought to bring about a social revolution such as had occurred in Russia. Workingmen began to turn the owners out of factories and attempted to run these factories themselves. In opposition to the Socialists and the incipient revolution there developed a party whose members, drawn largely from the middle classes, called themselves Fascisti. Conflicts, often violent, occurred between the two parties. Finally, in 1922, the Fascisti, marching on Rome, took the reins of government into their own hands and with the acquiescence of the king set up a virtual dictatorship under Benito Mussolini.

In the first of the two following selections Count Antonio Cippico, who has been a Senator of the Kingdom of Italy since 1923, defends the Fascist Régime. In the second, Francesco Nitti, formerly Italian Prime Minister, now an exile from his native land, severely criticizes the rule of the Facisti.

241. A DEFENSE OF FASCISM [1]

In the last months of 1919 and the early ones of 1920, a good third of Italy was red. Over two thousand of the most flourishing communes were in the hands of the Communists. Their administration was characterized by violence and waste of public money. The government was incapable of protecting the public against the outrages of the reds, who imposed themselves more and more on the life of the people by means of assaults, strikes, blackmail, usurpation and occupation of factories and land. It was, therefore, necessary for those who still kept their belief in the nation, in order and in the sanctity of civil rights, to protect themselves by force of arms, i.e., by answering destructive violence with reconstructive violence.

At the beginning the number of these brave defenders of the nation and of order was small. At the end of March, 1919, about forty spirited young men of the proletariat and middle classes gathered in Milan — in red Milan — around Mussolini, and founded the famous original new Fascismo. This rapidly found adherents, apostles, and willing fighters, from all classes of the nation, in every city and every village, especially in the populous industrial districts of northern and central Italy, where the tyranny was strongest of the Socialist Syndicates and of the Red Councils of workmen founded on the example of Moscow. There was scarcely a factory or a municipality of the rich industrial towns that did not fly a red or black flag, symbol of social war and destruction.

We then witnessed a whole series of just reprisals, which silently and systematically organized the defense of the nation. Here a Communist Coöperative, there a Socialist Chamber of Labor, in another place the offices and printing works of a Bolshevik newspaper, supported by rubles from Moscow, were attacked, besieged, and burnt. Workmen and peasants, who were inscribed in the red leagues and who lorded it over the country, were,

[1] Count Antonio Cippico, *Italy, the Central Problem of the Mediterranean*. New Haven. Published for the Institute of Politics by the Yale University Press, 1926, pp. 73–76; 87–89.

rightly, put *hors de combat* by just measures of reprisals. The authors of these assaults were, in turn, attacked and stabbed, often treacherously, by means of ambuscades and mass attacks. War was declared. But it was not civil war in the real meaning of the word: it was the necessary and legitimate individual defense of the trampled-on rights of all the citizens, above all in defense of the vital interests of the country.

It thus comes about that in Romagna, Tuscany, Lombardy, and Piedmont, risings and encounters between armed bands, looting, and killing increase enormously. The struggle seems unequal — as the Chambers of Labor and the Red Syndicates, in addition to a vast organization and the authority which has accrued to them from the powerlessness of the liberal organs of the state against their criminal arrogance, and their systematic coercion and intimidation both of the working and middle classes, seem determined to undermine the state itself and make themselves masters of it.

The attacks and counter-attacks became every day more frequent and violent. The Fascisti were determined to give no quarter. The mass of the workers, misled by their leaders and organizers, who had promised them shortly the earthly paradise of a communist revolution, rapidly realized the emptiness of such promises, and realized that their leaders were the false and timid prophets of an Asiatic social religion, foreign to Italian civilization and temperament. The workers at last perceived that the Second and Third International were merely organs of disruption, incapable of reconstruction; that internationalism was a lie; that their own interests were identical with those of the nation, till then forgotten and combated.

Incidents of brutal violence occurred, such as the murder at a meeting of the Communal Council of a member of the red municipality of Bologna, Dr. Giordani, who had fought bravely in the Great War; such as the bomb thrown in the Diana Theatre at Milan, which killed at least forty harmless work-people; such as the man-hunts carried out by the reds of Empoli against sailors of the Royal Navy; like the sentence executed on the workmen Scimula and Sonzini, who, because they did not agree with their companions, were condemned by the latter to be thrown alive into the blast furnaces of the factory where they worked at Turin. Such incidents necessarily brought the Italian people, so essentially just and moral, to a rebellion against the tyranny of these brutal social-communist organizers.

In the end, the Fascisti got the upper hand in the bloody fight. They were by now an admirably organized and disciplined army composed of ex-soldiers, well-educated youths, peasants, and workmen, representatives of the best classes of the Italian people, who had seen through the communist propaganda, who had given everything to their country during the war, and who expected no recompense except the prosperity and moral greatness of their nation. They were men of thought and action who were determined to mould by their sacrifices a new Italy, no longer to be a museum of dead things, a vast and useless political and literary academy, nor a dreamy scientific Arcadia, dealing more in words than in deeds.

. . . .

Italy, even in her periods of blindest anarchy, desired vaguely to be a state, led and governed by a firm hand, an economic structure worthy of the capacity of industrial initiative and work. This aspiration, at present incarnated in Fascism, has become her will. In order to reach this goal over three thousand Fascisti, generous, disinterested youths, from all classes of the nation, have laid down their lives.

The Fascist program of national reconstruction was synthetized by Mussolini in June, 1921, when he proposed in Parliament to "define some historical and political positions." He then asked that the functions of the state should be limited to the creation of conditions suitable for individual activity, and of advantage to the consumer, in science, art, economic life, agriculture, industry, and commerce. The state must not confer privileges on one class to the detriment of others. It must resign monopolies: it must be neither banker, manufacturer, dealer, co-operative society, nor newspaper owner. It must not encourage unemployment by the palliative of "doles," nor enrich a favored few and impoverish the rest of the people by means of state contracts granted because of political protection or as gifts disguised under the name of co-operation. It is the state's business to do away with all that is superfluous and useless in the great bureaucratic machine. Only thus can true liberty — not license — and the equality of the citizens before the state be assured; only thus can the state be in condition to assure rapid justice and protection for life and property, and to safeguard the dignity and interests of its subjects in foreign countries.

In those years the prestige of Italy had dwindled miserably. There was no faith in the public finances. It will be opportune to compare some figures of today with those of yesterday. The consolidated war funds in October, 1922, had fallen to 81.08; later on in January, 1924, they were again at par. During 1920 there took place in Italy 1,881 industrial strikes and 189 agricultural strikes, which cost over 30,000,000 working days to the country. During 1923, the first year of the Fascist régime, industrial strikes were reduced to 200 and there was only one agricultural strike, involving the country in a loss of little more than 265,000 working days. In December, 1921, there were 541,000 unemployed; in October, 1924, they had fallen to 117,000, which number is today sensibly decreased. In those troubled years almost all the industries dragged out a precarious existence. Today the activity of the then existing and since established industries has multiplied enormously; the workers work feverishly, forgetful of the unhealthy laziness of that time; they earn good wages; orders for goods are constantly increasing. In 1921 goods were exported to the value of 8,275,000,000 lire. For the first four months alone of this year exports have reached 5,350,000,000; for the corresponding period of 1923 the figures were 800,000,000. Importations of foreign goods amounted in 1921 to 17,266,000,000; in 1924 to 19,387,000,000. In 1921 the railways carried 20,181,000 tons of goods; in 1924, 31,689,000. In 1921 the consumption of electric energy amounted to 4,300,000,000 kilowatts; in 1924 to 6,500,000,000.

242. *AN ARRAIGNMENT OF FASCISM* [1]

Bolshevism and Fascism are the two menaces to the future prosperity of Europe. Both are similar phenomena in that they deny human liberty and involve the exercise of power on the part of an armed minority. Bolshevism sets about establishing the dictatorship of the proletariat — in other words, putting all resources in the hands of the workers and peasants. It attains this end by force. Fascism suppresses all political liberty and all free manifestations, saying that this is necessary to make Italy a great nation and to found an empire. Mussolini has made numerous speeches insulting the decaying corpse of democracy and asserting that liberty is a prejudice of the past. He has announced that Fascism will found an Italian Empire. To found an empire would mean taking some piece of foreign territory — which in this case would be either a French or a British possession, since it would be out of the question to despoil Switzerland, Austria, or Jugoslavia, which lie along the Italian frontiers.

Italy lacks economic resources, and Italian finance is so wretched that public credit has been profoundly shaken. Italy lacks the prime necessities for war — coal, steel, and oil. She also lacks food and cotton. In her present situation, she could not wage war without the support of Great Britain or the United States. Is it possible that these two countries would encourage such absurd, such grotesque, proposals?

Bolshevism has cut down Russia's productive capacity; and her foreign business, which the Government controls, has been utterly disastrous. The truth is that Russia is producing much less than she did before the war — in other words, much less than she did under the deplorable Tsarist régime. Economic production demands above all else order, liberty, and individual initiative — three things that no dictatorship can bring about.

Fascism has seriously weakened Italian production. In spite of appearances Italy has fallen into a state of the greatest economic disorder in the

[1] Nitti, "Probabilities of War in Europe," *Atlantic Monthly*, September, 1928, pp. 419–421.

course of the last six years. Fascism has not bent its efforts to obtaining results, but to producing manifestations. All over the country there are celebrations, parades, and processions of Black Shirts. Wheat and rice production has declined; yet great festivals are held in honor of wheat and rice, and there is a special celebration in behalf of bread. Expressed in gold pounds, — in other words, without statistical manipulation, — the deficit of Italian business has risen from 643 million gold pounds in 1924 to 1259 million gold pounds in 1927. In short, it has almost doubled. Mr. MacLean, the American commercial attaché at Rome, has calculated that domestic business has dropped 40 per cent in the last two years. This is a terrible figure. Nevertheless, Mr. MacLean is a little too optimistic, for the real decline is nearly 50 per cent. The loans negotiated in America have been used to maintain the lira, though no one knows how long this will last, and to stabilize it at its present level.

This extravagant stabilization, however, has ruined all industrial exporters. Italy now suffers more bankruptcies than any other country in Europe. In actual figures she has suffered twice as many as any other country, and, relatively to her industrial power, nine or ten times as many as any other country. Because of this absurd lira stabilization at a false level, undertaken not as a part of any economic programme, but merely as a piece of political bluff, the Italians are obliged to pay almost the same taxes as the French, whose country is at least three times as rich. In short, Italian taxes are heavier than those of any other country.

Since the Government bases itself on violence, it needs an even greater number of special militia to maintain it than Bolshevism does. These groups include militia to maintain general order, the voluntary Fascist militia, the railway militia, the post and telegraph militia, the harbor militia, the forest militia, and, most recently of all, the highway militia. About 200,000 people thus make their living off the Fascist Government, and it is like maintaining an army to support them. The industrialists and farmers have to pay for these militias. Besides this, all producers, both employers and employees, are grouped into corporations which involve still another enormous expense. There are fourteen ministries, but Mussolini scoffs at the rest of the world and occupies seven of them, comprising the office of Prime Minister, of Minister of the Interior, of Foreign Affairs, War, Marine, Aviation, and Corporations — in other words, Minister of Labor. Under these conditions, he is able to involve the country in a war before anyone knows what is happening and before the people can manifest their desires in any way.

All free journals in Italy have been suppressed, and the press is suffering. The amount of paper used for the various daily journals has fallen off about one half or three fifths during the last two years. The ablest Italians are in exile, having either been deported or retired from public life. Poverty is increasing, and the Government has refused to meet its obligations on the Treasury and has forced them to be transformed into a consolidated debt. No criticism is allowed, even the most cordial. The press cannot discuss the economic crisis except to say that everything is going smoothly. Elections have disappeared. Even the Chamber of Deputies is going to be transformed into an assembly named by the Government. The administrators of local government and even the representatives of the chambers of commerce are no longer elected. They are appointed by the Government.

The economic situation is bad, but the financial situation is worse. On the day when Fascism feels itself lost, will it not attempt to distract attention by some international adventure? Is not this what all dictatorships have done in the past?

Fascism and Bolshevism, although apparently direct opposites, act in the same manner. Several centuries before Jesus, Plato, the greatest of Greek philosophers, wrote that dictatorship always ended in war, saying that when the dictator felt himself lost he made war. There is no example in modern history of a dictatorship that has not ended in war, revolution, or both.

" Giovinezza" was originally a war song, published about 1916. It was sung especially by the arditi, *crack troops in the Italian infantry, who wore black shirts. At the Fascist Congress of 1919 at Milan it was adopted, with some slight changes in phraseology, as the official song of the Fascisti.*

Two verses of the song are here given.

243. GIOVINEZZA [1]

1.

Su, compagni in forti schiere,
marciam verso l'avvenire
Siam falangi audaci e fiere,
pronte a osare, pronte a ardire,
Trionfi alfine l'ideale
per cui tanto combattemmo:
Fratellanza nazionale
d'Italiana civilta'
   Giovinezza, giovinezza
   primavera di bellezza,
   nel " fascismo " e' la salvezza
   della nostra liberta'.

2.

Non piu ignava ne' avvilita
resti ancor la nostra gente,
si ridesti a nuova vita
di splendore piu' possente.
Su, leviamo alta la face
che c'illumini il cammino,
nel lavoro e nella pace
sia la vera liberta'.
   Giovinezza, giovinezza
   primavera di bellezza,
   nel " fascismo " e' la salvezza
   della nostra liberta'.

[1] Copyright MCMXXIII by Mauro V. Cardilli, New York.

Giovinezza

Inno dei Fascisti

Versi di
M. MANNI.

Musica di
G. BLANC.
Arr. by M. V. C.

Marziale

M 682 C

SECTION III. TURKEY SINCE THE GREAT WAR

The Ottoman Empire, defeated in the Great War, through its plenipotentiaries, signed the Treaty of Sèvres in 1920. Mustapha Kemal Pasha and a number of Turkish patriots, resigned to the disruption of the Empire but unwilling to accept any such complete annihilation as this treaty contemplates, and especially revolting at the loss of Constantinople and the Greek occupation of Smyrna and its hinterland, met at Angora in the interior and rejected the treaty. In its place they adopted the following pact and agreed to fight until Turkey, with all that was Turkish retained within its borders, could take its proper place among the nations.

244. THE TURKISH NATIONAL PACT OF 1920 [1]

The Deputies of the Ottoman Parliament, having approved and signed the National Pact, of which we give below the copy, declare the principles therein announced to be the limit of sacrifice to which the Ottoman Parliament can consent to go in order to assure itself a just and lasting peace:

ARTICLE 1 — Those territories of the Ottoman Empire populated by an Arab majority and being at the time of the armistice (Oct. 31, 1918) occupied by the enemy armies, shall be ruled according to the will of the local populations. [These territories are Mesopotamia, Syria, Palestine, Arabia and Egypt.]

Those parts of the empire situated on the armistice line inhabited by a Moslem majority, united by religious and cultural ties and animated by a similar desire for the establishment of their ethnical rights, form a complete whole with us which shall suffer under no pretext whatsoever any dissociation. [The territories here referred to are those of Cilicia, which was recovered by the Franco-Turkish agreement of Oct. 20, 1921, and the Mosul province of Mesopotamia, which the British hold.]

ARTICLE 2 — In the case of the three sanjaks which united themselves to us by vote when they were first free, we accept a second plebiscite if necessary. [These are the sanjaks of Kars, Ardahan and Batum in the Caucasus; the Turkish frontiers here are mapped in annexes to the Russo-Turkish Treaty and the Treaty of Kars, drawn between the Angora Government on the one hand and the Caucasian Republics of Georgia, Armenia and Azerbaijan on the other.]

ARTICLE 3 — The juridical status of Western Thrace, which has been

---

[1] Translation of French text. *Current History*, vol. 17, pp. 280–281. November, 1922. Reprinted by special permission of the *Current History Magazine*, a monthly periodical published by the New York Times Co.

made dependent on the Turkish peace, shall be effected in accordance with a free plebiscite.

ARTICLE 4 — The security of the City of Constantinople, which is the seat of the Caliphate of Islam, the capital of the Sultanate and the headquarters of the Ottoman Government, and the security of the Sea of Marmora must be effected. This necessity once admitted, the Ottoman Deputies are ready to subscribe to any decision which may be taken by the Imperial Government, on the one hand, and the interested powers, on the other, with a view to assuring the opening of the Straits to world commerce and international communication.

ARTICLE 5 — The rights of minorities will be confirmed by us on the same basis as is established in other countries by conventions hitherto concluded between the powers of the Entente, their adversaries and certain of their associates — in reliance on the belief that the Moslem minorities of other countries will benefit from similar guarantees.

ARTICLE 6 — With a view to assuring our national and economic development, and giving the country a more regular and more modern administration, the signatories of the present pact consider the possession of complete independence and liberty as the *sine qua non* of our national existence. In consequence, we oppose all juridical or financial restrictions of any nature which would arrest our national development. [This refers to the capitulations, which gave foreigners in Turkey something like a diplomatic status.]

The conditions of settlement of our proved debts shall likewise not be contrary to these principles.

Two analogies to Kemal's program of Westernizing and modernizing the new Turkish Republic, of which he was now dictator, are Peter the Great's titanic attempt in Russia and the later more successful transformation of Japan. The process is still going on after seven years of peace, and since the writers from whom we quote published their work, the Latin alphabet has replaced by decree the Arabic formerly in use. (1928)

245. *THE WESTERNIZATION OF TURKEY* [1]

The increasing momentum of reform under the enlightened despotism of Mustafā Kemāl Pasha has many characteristics of a Renaissance. Seldom has a more rapid transformation been wrought upon the face of a nation than in the new Turkey. A revolutionary zeal descended upon the President as he took the reins of power, and he drove like the wind. Sultan and Sultanate

[1] Arnold J. Toynbee and Kenneth P. Kirkwood, *Turkey.* London, Ernest Benn, Ltd., 1926, pp. 243–244; 253–255 (condensed).

were already gone, swept away by the decision of the Great National Assembly. Caliph and Caliphate next fell before the blast, and were driven forth to find lodgement outside Turkey, if anywhere. The Medresehs or ecclesiastical seminaries were confiscated for State purposes, and their vast properties and endowments made over to the national treasury. Later, the Dervish orders and all similar religious corporations were abolished in the campaign against reaction. Their *tekkehs* and monasteries, like the schools, were appropriated for government purposes and converted into secular educational institutions. Missionary activity was suppressed and Christian Millets abolished. The Capitulations had been repudiated in 1914 and a second time at the Conference of Lausanne, and the economic privileges of foreigners were reduced to unimportance. The women were unveiled, and the women's screen in trams and theatres and public places was done away with. For the men the fez, which had been as distinctive a national headress as the women's veil, was abolished, and with it all the ancient fashions of salutation and salaam. Persian and Arabic words and phrases were being banished from Turkish literature, and even the name of " Ottoman " was discarded in the general holocaust of ancient social possessions. The fires of iconoclasm burnt hot, destroying the harem, the eunuch system, polygamy, as well as certain more genuinely Islamic institutions. The Prophet's mantle and sword were relegated to the museum of antiquities, and the palaces of the Sultans were nationalized. Even the Muslim Friday has been discarded in favour of the Christian Sunday as the weekly day of rest, the calendar and the religious holidays have been revised and Westernized, and the old festivals are vanishing. So this destructive policy of the Angora Government goes on under the iconoclastic influence of Mustafā Kemāl Pasha. Everything reminiscent of the *ancien régime* must go; everything that outwardly connects the new Republic by the most tenuous thread with the traditions of the Ottoman Empire is being swept away, with as clean-sweeping a broom as the Bolsheviks have used in obliterating all outward traces of the Russian Czardom.

Yet a nation cannot live on a purely negative and destructive policy. Mustafā Kemāl is not unaware of this, and accordingly he turns his attention to introducing new measures and new manners and customs of a positive character. The emancipation of women came first, and perhaps too rapidly. The prohibition of alcoholic liquor was tried for a year, but proved an impracticable experiment and was abolished. State monopolies and nationalized industries are taking the place of private enterprise; foreign financial and commercial aid is being rejected in favour of native Turkish effort, though the latter is still notoriously lacking in skill or ability. Most important of all, education is being reformed and promoted with a genuine eagerness. . . .

Under the pressure of war . . . social services of all kinds were newly undertaken by the new type of Turkish women. In consequence the relationship between the sexes began to change rapidly, and the capacities of women were demonstrated by the testing experiences which they underwent. Under these war-conditions, the life of seclusion and subordination, at least in the middle and upper classes, has vanished; among the peasantry, where women had always been co-workers on the land and in the rough life of the farm, the conditions remain the same.

Education became increasingly popular for girls, and the foreign schools and colleges came to be always full. The University of Constantinople opened its doors to women, and for the first time admitted the principle of co-education. Women entered the professions of teaching, of medicine, and of law. They began to work for the further enfranchisement and education of their own sex by writing, lecturing and political agitation. Khālideh Khānum, who was the first Turkish woman to take a University degree, has distinguished herself as a writer in many veins, has served as aide-de-camp to Field-Marshal Mustafā Kemāl Pasha, and by her eloquence, her literary work, and her social activities has made her influence profoundly felt throughout Turkey. Largely through her example, women all over the country were inspired to a vigorous interest in their own progress and opportunities, and were awakened to the realization of their own influence and power.

Socially, they have advanced along Western paths. The old restraints were thrown off; the veil was lifted, and the charshaf or cape, which concealed the hair and descended to the shoulders, will probably share the fate of the fez. Appearance in mixed company at theatres and entertainments has become permissible. Even dancing in public with Turkish men, though not with Christian foreigners, has been countenanced. The women's gallery in theatres and concert halls has been deserted for the main auditorium, where the women now sit beside their male friends and relatives. The curtain separating the women's compartment from the men's in trams and trains has been abolished. Women have even been allowed to take part in theatrical productions on the stage. In every way the manners and customs of the West have gradually permeated Turkish society, and have liberated women from the restrictions and confinement of centuries.

In the matter of marriage, the same process has been at work. Women have grown to realize the degradation and injustice of subjection, and have claimed the rights of companionship on equal terms in the home. . . .

Under the present *régime,* polygamy is not legally proscribed, for the principle rests upon too weighty a text in Islamic law, but plural marriages are distinctly disfavoured and are made subject to such legal formalities and preliminary authorizations as will render them very difficult in practice.

This, it may be, is the Turkish women's greatest triumph, for it represents a complete break not only with the Islamic tradition, but also with the status of inferiority to which the system of polygamy consigned women in the past.

For centuries the Sultan had been also the Caliph, or head of Islam, and Turkish law was no other than the Islamic law. This identity of Church and State no longer exists, for in 1922 Mohammed V was deposed from both functions and in 1924 Abdul Medjid, who had succeeded to the Caliphate, now divorced from the civil authority, which was vested in republican institutions, was also deposed. There is no longer a Caliph and the Moslem world is confused and hesitant.

246. A REVOLUTION IN ISLAM [1]

"Islam reformed," said Lord Cromer, in that imperial epic, *Modern Egypt*, "is Islam no longer. It has yet to be proved that Islam can assimilate civilization without succumbing in the process. It is, indeed, not improbable that in its passage through the European crucible many of the distinctive features of Islam, the good alike with the bad, will be volatilized and that it will eventually issue forth in a form scarcely capable of recognition." That was published eighteen years ago. Since then, the process which he saw beginning has moved toward a catastrophic climax. The full weight of the West has fallen on the Near East, with consequences full of both hope and menace. The House of Islam is divided against itself, and across a great block that lies along a line drawn southwest from Kashgar to the Niger Delta the issues of civilization are in the balance.

Recently Mustapha Kemal sanctioned the execution of several Turks for refusing to comply with the "hats" order. This absurd incident was duly ridiculed, but the press on the whole did not see its real significance. It is an event very much the same in kind as Julian's reopening of the temples, or the Reformers' onslaughts on the "images." It is a war on Islam as an established faith; New Rome shall be no Moslem capital, the tarboosh shall no more be seen in the streets thereof. Here we have, in symbol and in emblem, an epitome of the Islamic situation, and one of the choicer ironies of history. The fear of affronting Moslem opinion in India, the delicacy of the Caliphate question, have for years been dominant factors in our policy. They have won for Turkey a consideration, a forbearance in face of slaughter and misgovernment, which necessity (it was argued) imposed upon us. Young Turkey has deposed and deported the Caliph, dissolved the monasteries, disestablished Islam! She has abdicated her Moslem suzerainty and under the brilliant leadership of Kemal set herself to deliberate

[1] The *Saturday Review*. London. May 29, 1926.

Westernization. Angora, indeed, appears to take the view that the Turks took a fatally wrong turning when they embraced Islam in Turkestan before they descended upon Europe. The Koran has been the cause of their backwardness, the blight on their progress and administration. Islam has been the "dope of the people," and the New Turkey must be liberated. . . . Although its recent dealings with the Kurds, Armenians, or the Phanar [1] disclose no leanings toward Christianity, Angora sees no necessity for the Prophet.

But elsewhere, too, though in less sensational ways, the solidity of Islam has been undermined. The war, with its consequent nationalist passions, has fatally smashed the Pan-Islamic movement. Arabs and Turks were fighting one another; whatever they fought for, it was not a holy war. The result of those years has left Syria, Irak, Palestine, and Egypt under the control of Western Powers, and the holy places at first under British protection and now in the hands of the fanatical Wahabis.[2] Nationalism, as once before in Europe, has come into conflict with "Catholicism," and nationalism certainly looks like winning. In Egypt, Copts and Moslems worked together, cross and crescent on the same banner, during the anti-British risings. In Palestine, Moslem and Christian were united in opposition to Lord Balfour's Zionism. There are similar situations in India. The old religious exclusiveness is breaking; the law of apostasy is invoked no longer, and over the more exposed Moslem areas there is a new widening of mental horizons. It looks as though Pan-Islamism is dead. It remains to be seen whether Islam itself can inspire and direct the new national cultures.

Or rather, to go back to Lord Cromer's dictum, it remains to be seen whether Islam can survive the terrific impact of the West upon it. The war brought numbers of Moslem troops and bearers into close association with Western life and thought; and the post-war desert railways and motor routes have opened a new world to Western travelers, and opened the Western world, in turn, to it. From Bagdad to Damascus, from the Hejaz to Amman, from any of these places to Cairo, Brindisi, Paris, London, has ceased to be a very adventurous journey. It is calculated that more Moslems come to Europe now each year than make the Pilgrimage. The Moslem world is learning to read and write. The chain of French schools across North Africa, British schools in Egypt and Central Africa, in Palestine, Persia, and Northern India, the American University in Cairo — all these are undermining the old faith. Education and the Koran cannot co-exist. . . . The son of the sheik brought up in the Al Azhar graduates in physics at the university. The student class demand emancipation for the women who are to be their

[1] The Greek quarter of Constantinople. (Editor's note.)

[2] A Puritanical Moslem sect of the Arabian desert whose leader, Ibn Saud, made himself ruler of most of Arabia by 1925. (Editor's note.)

companions. Moslem women are leading Feminist movements. The harem and the veil are going out of use; monogamy is becoming normal. This vast central wedge of territory, for centuries impervious and impregnable, is being penetrated by Western thought, and the old faith is inevitably decaying. It is true that the Modernist movement in Islam, centred in Aligarh and Woking, seems to be coming to terms with Western knowledge. It is true that the old orthodox are stimulated to impassioned attempts to recover their weakened hold. But the end of the process seems inevitable. These tendencies are the birth pangs of an Islamic revolution. One of the great religions of the world, with over two hundred and thirty million believers, is beginning to lose the allegiance of the faithful. The vital question is: What will succeed it?

SECTION IV. THE BRITISH ISLES SINCE THE WAR

While the Home Rule Act of 1914 was held suspended during the Great War, the Irish watched the struggle very much as outsiders. Enlistment went on, but not enthusiastically, and Great Britain was slow to enforce conscription in the western island. The more revolutionary Irish, holding in leash an armed body, the Irish Volunteers, and cementing their alliance with the radical labor Citizens Army, which James Connolly and James Larkin had raised, decided in April, 1916, that their time had come. They anticipated the levying of conscription and their own arrest, with the break-up of their forces. On Easter Sunday the seven leaders whose names were signed to the following proclamation took the irrevocable step. They seized the Dublin Post Office, the Four Courts, Dublin Castle, and other strategic positions and published their proclamation.

247. THE PROCLAMATION OF THE "IRISH REPUBLIC"[1]

POBLACHT NA H EIREANN

THE PROVISIONAL GOVERNMENT

of the

IRISH REPUBLIC

To the People of Ireland.

IRISHMEN AND IRISHWOMEN: In the name of God and of the dead generations from which she receives her old tradition of nationhood, Ireland, through us, summons her children to her flag and strikes for her freedom.

[1] Promulgated on Easter Sunday, April 23, 1916, at Liberty Hall, Dublin. From facsimile in Francis P. Jones, *History of the Sinn Fein Movement and the Irish Rebellion of 1916*. New York, P. J. Kenedy & Sons, 1917, p. 284.

Having organised and trained her manhood through her secret revolutionary organisation, the Irish Republican Brotherhood, and through her open military organisations, the Irish Volunteers and the Irish Citizen Army, having patiently perfected her discipline, having resolutely waited for the right moment to reveal itself, she now seizes that moment, and, supported by her exiled children in America and by gallant allies in Europe, but relying in the first on her own strength, she strikes in full confidence of victory.

We declare the right of the people of Ireland to the ownership of Ireland, and to the unfettered control of Irish destinies, to be sovereign and indefeasible. The long usurpation of that right by a foreign people and government has not extinguished the right, nor can it ever be extinguished except by the destruction of the Irish people. In every generation the Irish people have asserted their right to national freedom and sovereignty; six times during the past three hundred years they have asserted it in arms. Standing on that fundamental right and again asserting it in arms in the face of the world, we hereby proclaim the Irish Republic as a Sovereign Independent State, and we pledge our lives and the lives of our comrades-in-arms to the cause of its freedom, of its welfare, and of its exaltation among the nations.

The Irish Republic is entitled to, and hereby claims, the allegiance of every Irishman and Irishwoman. The Republic guarantees religious and civil liberty, equal rights and equal opportunities to all its citizens, and declares its resolve to pursue the happiness and prosperity of the whole nation and of all its parts, cherishing all the children of the nation equally, and oblivious of the differences carefully fostered by an alien government, which have divided a minority from the majority in the past.

Until our arms have brought the opportune moment for the establishment of a permanent National Government, representative of the whole people of Ireland and elected by the suffrages of all her men and women, the Provisional Government, hereby constituted, will administer the civil and military affairs of the Republic in trust for the people.

We place the cause of the Irish Republic under the protection of the Most High God, whose blessing we invoke upon our arms, and we pray that no one who serves that cause will dishonour it by cowardice, inhumanity, or rapine. In this supreme hour the Irish nation must, by its valour and discipline and by the readiness of its children to sacrifice themselves for the common good, prove itself worthy of the august destiny to which it is called.

Signed on Behalf of the Provisional Government
THOMAS J. CLARKE,

SEAN Mac DIARMADA,	THOMAS MacDONAGH,
P. H. PEARSE,	EAMONN CEANNT,
JAMES CONNOLLY,	JOSEPH PLUNKETT.

Easter Week saw the rise and fall of the Irish Republic. Following the first easy successes of the Irish, the British brought up vast forces that finally numbered well over 50,000, with naval guns to shell Dublin. Steadily the Irish were driven closer in and the city was soon in flames. Some of the scenes near the close of the fighting are described below. The seven leaders finally surrendered to save their men's lives. They themselves were all executed at once. A large body of Irish, as well as English, opinion blamed the revolters as suicidal, if not as traitors, but the result of the following six years seems to justify their hope that their revolution, doomed before it began, would force the granting of some sort of autonomy to Ireland.

248. EASTER WEEK IN DUBLIN [1]

At the Post Office there were three lines of barricades, and every effort had been made to make the place impossible of assault. For some hours on Thursday night the building had been under artillery fire, and this bombardment was kept up on Friday morning. Sean MacDermott was in charge of lines of hose, with which one fire after another that was started by the incendiary shells was extinguished, before it was able to secure a hold. One part of the building after another was flooded with water, but the shells fell so fast and so thick that even these efforts were vain to prevent a conflagration.

It was shortly after noon that the fire got beyond control. Men were called from the firing lines to extinguish the blaze, but it foiled all their efforts. Shell after shell fell in the same place, the gunners evidently having discovered that their efforts were meeting with success. Guns were firing from the other side of the Liffey, from the gunboat on the Liffey, from Talbot Street, and from Parnell Street. With the heavy artillery were combined machine guns, that kept up a continuous rain of bullets on the building and on every inch of O'Connell and Henry Streets. . . .

When it was seen that it was impossible to remain in the Post Office, the men were lined up in the yard at the back, and told that an attempt would be made to break through. Even at this time the spirits and the enthusiasm of the men and of their leaders were undiminished. The men cheered when told that they were going to have a hand-to-hand engagement. . . .

The men then began to collect all the foodstuffs that could be obtained. The building was thoroughly searched, in spite of the flames that were now raging and the shells that were dropping into the ruins every minute. The hand grenades had been brought down to the cellar as soon as the bombard-

[1] Francis P. Jones, *History of the Sinn Fein Movement and the Irish Rebellion of 1916.* New York, P. J. Kenedy & Sons, 1917, pp. 383–387 (condensed).

ment had started, and these were now portioned among the men. When all the preparations had been completed, the little band left the building by the side door in Henry Street.

A dash was made across this bullet-swept thoroughfare into Moore Street on the other side. In that dash more than one of these brave men died, riddled with bullets. But his comrades pressed on, led by the intrepid O'Rahilly and safely gained Moore Street, where a barricade had been erected. Here, however, they were exposed to the fire of the military from Parnell Street. The Republicans entrenched themselves in the best manner possible, and began to return the fire of the military.

The deaths in the dash across Henry Street were the first that had taken place among the actual garrison in the Post Office, although men in the Post Office area had been wounded or killed. In spite of all the expenditure of ammunition on the part of the British for days past none of the men in the Post Office with the exception of Connolly had even been scratched.

With the men who made the sortie were President Pearse, Sean MacDermott, James Connolly, who had to be carried, Tom Clarke, and Joseph Plunkett.

The British were not slow to take advantage of the fact that the Irish had evacuated the Post Office. A machine-gun squad that had been operating in Talbot Street moved up to the corner of North Earl Street, so as to be in a position to fire across the side of Moore Street. As this meant that the Republicans would be hemmed in in this narrow street with a cross fire at both sides, it was determined to make an effort to force the retreat of the British in North Earl Street. The O'Rahilly undertook the leadership of the charge, and himself led his men into Henry Street. A heavy volley was directed against the British at the same time, and the rebels charged into O'Connell Street over a ground swept by a deadly cross fire, and forced the British to retire. Having accomplished all they could hope to do at this point, the Republicans also fell back.

A murderous interchange of bullets was now taking place. The British had recovered from their set-back, and, smarting under a sense of defeat, they sent a hurricane of bullets into Henry Street. To this the Republicans replied in kind, and, although they lacked machine guns, their aim was so cool and so deadly that the British in Talbot Street were falling in scores. The first gun crew had been almost wiped out, the officer in charge was a corpse, and the other detachments that were running to the relief were also suffering heavily. One shell and then another burst over Henry Street, and showers of shrapnel followed. It was in the midst of this, one of the bloodiest fights that took place during the Rebellion, that The O'Rahilly fell, mortally shot, and died practically instantaneously.

While the loss of their leader was a sore blow to his men, they continued to fight on and were able to hold the end of Moore Street leading into Henry Street. This was really the rear of the position occupied by this force of the Republicans, as they held the end facing Parnell Street as their main line. But it was obvious that they would be able to hold out here only for a few hours at the most, as the shrapnel was beginning to burst over them, and one after another of the houses and stores along the street blazed up as a result of the bombardment.

It was during the Friday that the British were at last able to complete their cordon around the Four Courts, and this was a serious blow to the men in Moore Street, as it cut off their last line of retreat. . . . When Friday night closed down, it was evident that there was no hope from the country . . . and that the men of Dublin were doomed.

In 1918, at the so-called Khaki Election, the radical Irish Nationalists dominated the polls in Ireland and elected most of their candidates, but those elected refused to sit at Westminster. Instead, they constituted the Dail *Eireann, or Irish Diet, and coercive efforts were ineffective against them. An era of guerilla warfare of the bitterest character lasted until 1921 when Mr. Lloyd George, British Prime Minister, called a conference at 10 Downing Street to try to reach an agreement that would give Ireland Home Rule but not the complete independence which was claimed. The treaty follows. It was signed by Griffith, the intellectual leader, and by Collins, the military chief, of the Irish, but Eamon De Valera, whom they called their president, refused ratification. In spite of him, it was accepted by the majority of Irishmen and went into effect in December, 1922.*

249. *THE AGREEMENT THAT GAVE IRELAND HOME-RULE*[1]

1. Ireland shall have the same constitutional status in the Community of Nations known as the British Empire as the Dominion of Canada, the Commonwealth of Australia . . . with a Parliament having powers to make laws for the peace, order, and good government of Ireland, and an Executive responsible to that Parliament, and shall be styled and known as the Irish Free State. . . .

4. The oath to be taken by Members of the Parliament of the Irish Free State shall be in the following form: — I . . . do solemnly swear true faith and allegiance to the Constitution of the Irish Free State as by law established and that I will be faithful to H. M. King George V., his heirs and successors by law, in virtue of the common citizenship of Ireland with Great Britain

[1] The *Times*, London. December 7, 1921.

and her adherence to and membership of the group of nations forming the British Commonwealth of Nations. . . .

7. The Government of the Irish Free State shall afford to His Majesty's Imperial Forces: —

(a) In time of peace. . . .

(b) In time of war or of strained relations with a Foreign Power such harbour and other facilities as the British Government may require for the purposes of such defence. . . .

8. . . . if the Government of the Irish Free State establishes and maintains a military defence force, the establishments thereof shall not exceed in size such proportion of the military establishments maintained in Great Britain as that which the population of Ireland bears to the population of Great Britain. [Art. 10. Compensation to discharged officials. Arts. 11–15 relate to the possible adherence of Northern Ireland to this Agreement.]

16. Neither the Parliament of the Irish Free State nor the Parliament of Northern Ireland shall make any law so as either directly or indirectly to endow any religion or prohibit or restrict the free exercise thereof or give any preference or impose any disability on account of religious belief or religious status or affect prejudicially the right of any child to attend a school receiving public money without attending the religious instruction at the school or make any discrimination as respects State aid between schools under the management of different religious denominations or divert from any religious denomination or any educational institution any of its property except for public utility purposes and on payment of compensation.

[Arts. 17–18 refer to ratification.]

Decr. 6th 1921

On behalf of the British Delegation	On behalf of the Irish Delegation
D. Lloyd George	Arthur Griffith
Austen Chamberlain	Michael Collins
Birkenhead	Robert Barton
Winston S. Churchill	E. J. Duggan
L. Worthington-Evans	Gavan Duffy
Hamar Greenwood	
Gordon Hewart	

The Irish Free State entered the British Commonwealth of Nations in 1922 as an equal. Northern Ireland refused to abandon its connection with Great Britain and remains partly autonomous, yet with a handful of representatives in the British Parliament. When William T. Cosgrave, President of the Council of the Irish Free State, was in England to attend the Imperial

Conference of 1926 he spoke the following short epilogue to 750 years of hate-filled conflict.

250. THE END OF A LONG CHAPTER[1]

Your country and mine, separated for centuries by a tragic series of events which have now, happily, come to an end, give an example to the world of what can be achieved by free association between nations. My colleagues and myself have the most profound conviction that the relations between us will ripen into a bond of sincere and lasting friendship, and that the people of these two islands, placed by God so close together on the surface of the ocean, while differing by race and characteristics, will henceforth devote themselves rather to discovering grounds for common endeavour and common achievement than to seeking in the pages of history for memories of bitter things which must be buried forever. Let us, then, obtain that lasting peace and friendship which God has surely destined for us.

There has been much post-war discussion of the economic need of a United States of Europe. The peculiar position of Great Britain in the economic groupings of the future is discussed by an eminent economist.

251. WORLD TRADE OR EMPIRE TRADE?[2]

During the coming winter an Imperial Conference will meet in London. It is probable that the League of Nations Economic Conference, for which preparations are now being made, will also meet at about the same time. At the second of these far-reaching suggestions will be discussed for modifying the tariff arrangements of Europe, together with other plans of economic co-operation. Whether these suggestions produce any concrete result or not in the near future, the meeting of the two conferences will compel the British public to ask itself how far our economic future is to be bound up with that of the Empire and how far with that of Europe. . . .

Since the war the political and currency conditions in the various parts of the Empire have been much sounder than those in Europe, the Far East, or even South America, and Imperial trade might therefore have been expected to draw well ahead of British trade with other countries. This has happened to some extent, but the comparative progress has been surprisingly moderate. Thus imports from the Empire have risen from 25 per cent of our total imports in 1913 to nearly 30 per cent in 1925, but the exports of British goods to the Empire have risen from 37¼ per cent of the total in

[1] *Manchester Guardian Weekly*, November 12, 1926.
[2] Walter T. Layton in *Manchester Guardian Weekly*, April 30, 1926.

1913 to only 39⅛ per cent of the total last year, while the re-exports to the Empire of overseas produce has fallen from 12½ per cent to 10½ per cent. The comparatively small progress in British exports is disappointing in view of the fact that there are two abnormal influences which have greatly reduced our exports to other markets. These are, on the one hand, the practical disappearance of Russian trade, and, on the other, the falling off of British exports of coal, which go mainly to Europe. If these two elements are left out the figures show that British exports to the Empire and to the rest of the world have approximately kept pace with one another.

Closer examination shows that such progress as was made in the Empire was very unevenly distributed. In spite of difficulties the value of British exports to Europe (excluding Russia) in 1925 was 40 per cent higher than in 1913. In the same year British exports to New Zealand were 113 per cent up, to the Crown Colonies 110 per cent up, and Australia 75 per cent up. But exports to South Africa were only 38 per cent, to India 21 per cent, and to Canada 11 per cent above the corresponding figures for 1913.

The explanation is partly that the Dominions and India have steadily become more protectionist, and though in most cases we still enjoy a preference, the tariff wall which British goods have to overcome has been stationary or rising except in the case of Canada, while that of the chief European countries has tended to be lower than before the war. . . .

Are we most likely to find the much-needed expansion of our foreign trade in the markets of Europe or of the Empire? It must be admitted that the prospect of attaining free trade within the Empire or of making it self-sufficient is not very promising. India, which is much the largest of the Imperial markets, is evidently determined to maintain some measure of protection against British manufactures. Canada, whatever may happen in the political field, is destined to come increasingly within the economic sphere of influence of the United States — a significant sign of which is the fact that Canadian enterprise is no longer financed mainly from London, but from New York. Even Australia is determined to foster her iron and steel, textile, and other industries and to keep out British goods as fast as she can replace them at home. The ties of Empire are very real and lasting ones, but no one can look at the map of the world and truthfully say that the British Empire is a natural economic unit or that Great Britain can find a complete outlet for her economic activities in the Empire.

On the other hand, Great Britain has close at hand a continent of 300 million people (excluding Russia), enjoying a relatively high standard of living and providing a market with which only the United States can compare. Its purchasing power has been depressed by the world war, and its potential recovery is correspondingly large. To it we are bound, not only by political but by financial ties which are much closer than before the war, and there is some hope that its fiscal policy may move in a liberal direction. It would be folly of Great Britain not to encourage any such tendencies to the utmost.

The moral is obvious. In economics no less than in politics Great Britain is at once both European and Imperial. It is against our interest to be drawn into any external tariff system at all, but our great aim must be low tariffs everywhere.

The Imperial Conference even before the Great War had come to be an important body, but the War, by revealing the peculiar nature of the ties that bind the Empire together, enhanced its importance immensely. At the 1926 Conference the Earl of Balfour headed a committee whose function it was to draw up a formal definition of the relationship that was understood to exist among the members of the British Commonwealth of Nations.

252. *A DEFINITION OF INTER-IMPERIAL RELATIONS* [1]

II. Status of Great Britain and the Dominions

The Committee are of opinion that nothing would be gained by attempting to lay down a Constitution for the British Empire. Its widely scattered parts have very different characteristics, very different histories, and are at very different stages of evolution; while, considered as a whole, it defies classification and bears no real resemblance to any other political organization which now exists or has ever yet been tried.

There is, however, one most important element in it which, from a strictly constitutional point of view, has now, as regards all vital matters, reached its full development — we refer to the group of self governing communities composed of Great Britain and the Dominions. Their position and mutual relation may be readily defined. *They are autonomous Communities within the British Empire, equal in status, in no way subordinate one to another in any aspect of their domestic or external affairs, though united by a common allegiance to the Crown, and freely associated as members of the British Commonwealth of Nations.*

A foreigner endeavouring to understand the true character of the British Empire by the aid of this formula alone would be tempted to think that it was devised rather to make mutual interference impossible than to make mutual co-operation easy.

Such a criticism, however, completely ignores the historic situation. The rapid evolution of the Oversea Dominions during the last fifty years has involved many complicated adjustments of old political machinery to changing conditions. The tendency towards equality of status was both

[1] Report of Committee on Inter-Imperial Relations to Imperial Conference, by them adopted, November 19, 1926. The *Times*. London, November 22, 1926 (excerpts).

right and inevitable. Geographical and other conditions made this impossible of attainment by the way of federation. The only alternative was by the way of autonomy; and along this road it has been steadily sought. Every self-governing member of the Empire is now the master of its destiny. In fact, if not always in form, it is subject to no compulsion whatever.

. . . .

IV. Relations Between the Various Parts of the British Empire

. . . The title of His Majesty the King is of special importance. . . . Twice within the last 50 years has the Royal Title been altered to suit changed conditions and constitutional developments.

The present title . . . is as follows:

"George V, by the Grace of God, of the United Kingdom of Great Britain and Ireland and of the British Dominions beyond the Seas King, Defender of the Faith, Emperor of India."

Some time before the Conference met, it had been recognized that this form of title hardly accorded with the altered state of affairs arising from the establishment of the Irish Free State as a Dominion. . . . We recommend that, subject to His Majesty's approval, the necessary legislative action should be taken to secure that His Majesty's title should henceforward read:

"George V, by the Grace of God, of Great Britain, Ireland, and the British Dominions beyond the Seas King, Defender of the Faith, Emperor of India."

. . . .

A prolonged coal strike, beginning in 1925, was turned in the following year into a General Strike which for a few days crippled Great Britain's business. The strike was then called off by the Trade Union Congress. Three views of the undertaking are given below, the first by a member of the Labour Ministries of 1924 and 1929, the second by a Conservative peer, and the third by an economist of Liberal tendencies.

253. A LABOR LEADER'S VIEW OF THE GENERAL STRIKE [1]

Mr. J. R. Clynes, in his presidential address to the annual conference of the National Union of General and Municipal Workers, said he opposed the idea of a general strike as soon as he heard it was proposed, on the ground that it was futile and wasteful and because it could not succeed and has never succeeded elsewhere.

He said it raises false issues, and the proper industrial purpose is represented as some nefarious political design. Instead of a struggle with the

---

[1] J. R. Clynes, reported in *Manchester Guardian Weekly*, May 28, 1926.

employers it becomes a struggle with the Government, which is backed by unlimited resources.

A national strike would starve the poorest first, and an appeal to force would be answered by superior force. Groups of workers would soon be detached from the main body, and the worst of all forms of a class war would speedily develop — namely, war between sections of the workers. Manifestations of solidarity are admirable, but solidarity without wisdom becomes worthless.

254. LABOR ACCUSED OF GOING TOO FAR[1]

He did not propose to analyse some of the provisions of the Trades Dispute Act of 1906. They were remarkable. However, they would undoubtedly require and receive examination hereafter. (Cheers.) The principle of our law, paradoxical as it might seem, had always been that a man who did wrong should, if he could afford it, pay for the consequences of his wrong. (Laughter.) But for the first time, in the Trades Dispute Act, Parliament laid down the doctrine that a man, however well he could afford to pay for the consequences of his admitted wrong, should be immune from that obligation. How far we had travelled since that decision was taken was indicated in the fact that some twenty gentlemen meeting in a room in London could issue orders to three and a half millions of the population that were to paralyse the life of forty millions. Such a claim in the whole history of democracy had never been put forward before.

255. THE FAILURE OF THE GENERAL STRIKE[2]

The General Strike is over. It has failed because the attempt of a disciplined minority to impose its will by force has run up against the equally disciplined resistance of a nation which realised that the Constitution would be endangered if the attempt succeeded; it has failed because the Trade Unions Council itself never believed it could succeed, and knew that the miners were standing out for impossible terms; it has failed because the essentially orderly and constitutional Labour movement of Great Britain found itself in a false position as soon as it adopted revolutionary methods.

The demonstration that the general strike is for Great Britain a useless and unsuitable weapon will compel the trade union world to reconsider its attitude towards our economic difficulties, and if employers are wise enough to refrain from the temptation to try and smash the workers' organisation the result may be to turn their efforts in the direction of trying to secure

---

[1] Lord Birkenhead, reported in *Manchester Guardian Weekly*, May 28, 1926.
[2] Walter T. Layton in *Manchester Guardian Weekly*, May 28, 1926.

higher wages by increasing production and efficiency instead of disputing about the division of the proceeds of industry.

The rejoinder of Mr. Baldwin's Conservative Government to the General Strike was brought before Parliament in the following April. Its original form was more drastic than the bill as passed in that lockouts were not mentioned and such elastic terms as "bringing ridicule" were used in describing picketers' actions that might be penalized. The act was passed against the angry opposition of both Labour and most of the Liberals.

256. *THE TRADE UNION ACT OF 1927*[1]

An act to declare and amend the law relating to trade disputes and trade unions, to regulate the position of civil servants and persons employed by public authorities in respect of membership in trade unions and similar organizations, to extend section five of the Conspiracy, and Protection of Property Act, 1875, and for other purposes connected with the purposes aforesaid.

[29th July 1927]

Be it enacted . . .

　1. (1) It is hereby declared —

　　(a) that any strike is illegal if it —

　　　(i) has any object other than or in addition to the furtherance of a trade dispute within the trade or industry in which the strikers are engaged; and

　　　(ii) is a strike designed or calculated to coerce the Government either directly or by inflicting hardship upon the community; and

　　(b) that any lock-out is illegal if it — [same phraseology follows as in (a)]

and it is further declared that it is illegal to commence, or continue, or to apply any sums in furtherance or support of, any such illegal strike or lock-out.

　For the purposes of the foregoing provisions —

　　(a) a trade dispute shall not be deemed to be within a trade or industry unless it is a dispute between employers and workmen, or between workmen and workmen, in that trade or industry, which is connected with the employment or non-employment or the terms of the employment, or with the conditions of labour, of persons in that trade or industry; and

　　(b) without prejudice to the generality of the expression "trade or

[1] *Statutes of the Realm*, 17–18 Geo. 5. Chapter 22.

industry " workmen shall be deemed to be within the same trade or industry if their wages or conditions of employment are determined in accordance with the conclusions of the same joint industrial council, conciliation board or other similar body, or in accordance with agreements made with the same employer or group of employers.

. . . .

2. (1) No person refusing to take part or to continue to take part in any strike or lock-out which is by this Act declared to be illegal, shall be, by reason of such refusal or by reason of any action taken by him under this section, subject to expulsion from any trade union or society, or to any fine or penalty, or to deprivation of any right or benefit to which he or his legal personal representatives would otherwise be entitled, or liable to be placed in any respect either directly or indirectly under any disability or at any disadvantage as compared with other members of the union or society, anything to the contrary in the rules of a trade union or society notwithstanding. . . .

(3) As respects any strike or lock-out before the passing of this Act but since the first day of May, nineteen hundred and twenty-six, which, according to the law as declared by this Act, was illegal, this section shall have effect as if it had been in operation when the strike or lock-out took place.

3. (1) It is hereby declared that it is unlawful for one or more persons (whether acting on their own behalf or on behalf of a trade union or of an individual employer or firm, and notwithstanding that they may be acting in contemplation or furtherance of a trade dispute) to attend at or near a house or place where a person resides or works or carries on business or happens to be, for the purpose of obtaining or communicating information or of persuading or inducing any person to work or to abstain from working, if they so attend in such numbers or otherwise in such manner as to be calculated to intimidate any person in that house or place, or to obstruct the approach thereto or egress therefrom, or to lead to a breach of the peace; and attending at or near any house or place in such numbers or in such manner as is by this subsection declared to be unlawful shall be deemed to be a watching or besetting of that house or place within the meaning of section seven of the Conspiracy, and Protection of Property Act, 1875.

(2) In this section the expression " to intimidate " means to cause in the mind of a person a reasonable apprehension of injury to him or

to any member of his family or to any of his dependants or of violence or damage to any person or property, and the expression "injury" includes injury to a person in respect of his business, occupation, employment or other source of income, and includes any actionable wrong. . . .

4. (1) It shall not be lawful to require any member of a trade union to make any contribution to the political fund of a trade union unless he has at some time after the commencement of this Act and before he is first after the thirty first day of December, nineteen hundred and twenty-seven, required to make such a contribution delivered at the head office or some branch office of the trade union, notice in writing . . . of his willingness to contribute to that fund and has not withdrawn the notice . . .; and every member of a trade union who has not delivered such a notice as aforesaid, or who . . . has withdrawn it . . . shall be deemed for the purposes of the Trade Union Act, 1913, to be a member who is exempt from the obligation to contribute to the political fund of the union. . . .

5. (1) Amongst the regulations as to the conditions of service in His Majesty's civil establishments there shall be included regulations prohibiting established civil servants from being members, delegates or representatives of any organization of which the primary object is to influence or affect the remuneration and conditions of employment of its members, unless the organization is an organization of which the membership is confined to persons employed by or under the Crown and is an organization . . . independent of, and not affiliated to any such organization as aforesaid the membership of which is not confined to persons employed by or under the Crown . . ., that its objects do not include political objects, and that it is not associated directly or indirectly with any political party or organization. . . .

6. (4) There shall be added to section five of the Conspiracy, and Protection of Property Act, 1875, the following provision, that is to say:
" If any person employed by a local or other public authority wilfully breaks a contract of service with that authority, knowing or having reasonable cause to believe that the probable consequence of his so doing, either alone or in combination with others, will be to cause injury or danger or grave inconvenience to the community, he shall be liable, on summary conviction, to a fine not exceeding ten pounds or to imprisonment for a term not exceeding three months."

. . . .

A leading economic historian calls attention to the reasons why coal owners and miners failed to agree. Essentially the point is that both can not be satisfied because of the condition of the mines. Back of this looms the question whether Great Britain, no longer enjoying the subsoil advantage she possessed over her rivals of 1750–1900, can expect to retain her leadership among the nations — can even stand out as a first-class Power.

257. *A NEEDED REORGANIZATION OF MINES* [1].

The chapter in which the Commission on the coal industry summarised its recommendations contained in its opening paragraphs the following statement:

" We cannot agree with the view presented to us by the mineowners that little can be done to improve the organisation of the industry, and that the only practicable course is to lengthen hours and to lower wages. In our view large changes are necessary in other directions, and large progress is possible."

What are the defects which the Commission's inquiries revealed? What are the grounds on which, if its recommendations are carried out, progress will take place?

The first point is a simple one, but it is crucial. I refer to the necessity of facing, at least temporarily, some contraction in the scale of the industry. The present position is partly the result of a maladjustment between the world's demand for coal and the world's mining population. In view of the history of the coal industry before the war, such a maladjustment is not at all surprising. Between 1900 and 1913 the world's consumption of coal grew with astonishing rapidity. In the earlier period the industry had not only absorbed the rising generation of mineworkers' families, but had drawn adult recruits from other occupations. When the slump came it was overmanned. The estimated number of British mineworkers was actually higher in 1925, when the output of coal was 248,000,000 tons, than in 1913, when the output was over 280,000,000 tons.

The policy which would meet this situation by keeping as many collieries as possible at work through a drastic reduction of wages and lengthening of hours offers temptations which should be resisted. Pushed to any length it runs the risk of serving as a bounty upon inefficiency. What the public interest requires is not that obsolete or hopelessly uneconomic collieries should be kept in existence, but that they should be closed as speedily as possible, that those which only require more capital in order to pay their way should be aided to reconstruct themselves, and that the development of the more prosperous districts should be accelerated. At the same time the entry of new

[1] R. H. Tawney in *Manchester Guardian Weekly*, June 11, 1926.

recruits into the industry should be strictly regulated; migration should be assisted; and provision should be made for workers who are displaced. . . .

But the Commission did not endorse the tragic view that the days of the British coal industry are numbered and that the present depression is merely the opening phase of a long decline. The real problem, a study of the Report suggests, lies on a different plane. What has happened, it would seem, is that the old days of easy-going affluence, when the British coal industry, the spoiled favourite of fortune, found wealth washed to its shores by the mere tide of economic expansion, have come to an end. It still possesses extraordinary advantages, in the situation and equality of British coal, in the experience and skill of British mine-managers and mineworkers. But the impetus derived from priority of development has been spent. The new economic environment imposes a new economic strategy. What is needed now is science and organisation. The main question which confronted the Commission was how far the coal industry, as hitherto conducted, satisfies that requirement.

To that question the Commission returns what it is difficult to describe as other than a hanging verdict, pronounced in tones of dulcet sweetness. It is complimentary (and rightly complimentary) to the attainments of individuals. But it is critical of the system within which the individuals work, and which, as individuals, they can do little to alter. In the first place, the private ownership of coal is pronounced contrary to the public interest, and it is proposed that the mineral owners shall be compulsorily bought out, the ownership and administration of the property thus acquired by the State being vested in a body of Coal Commissioners to be appointed by the Secretary for Mines.

During the Industrial Revolution English population shifted rapidly from the South to the North of England. Since the Great War unemployment has faced one Government after another and the necessity of transferring thousands of workers from one region and industry to another region and a different industry has been realized. This time the movement is from the North to the South and the result may be again the changing of the face of rural England.

258. AN INDUSTRIAL AND GEOGRAPHICAL SHIFT [1]

The " Ministry of Labour Gazette " for November presents an extremely interesting analysis of the changes in the industrial population of the country during the last four years. From it the progress of what has been called the " new industrial revolution " can be measured. The analysis brings out the

[1] *Manchester Guardian Weekly,* November 25, 1927.

gradual shift of industrial population to the southern half of the country, where the increasing industries are to be found. It can be seen how the old staples, mostly those overstocked during the war, are shedding their surplus. It also shows how one of the worst of these, coal mining, has only just begun to lose in numbers. Thus shipbuilding has lost one in five of its workpeople since 1923; coal mining has lost only one in thirty.

The expanding industries are to a large extent those enjoyed in the home trade, in building, motor construction, artificial silk, the electrical industries, and, above all, the distribution trades.

First, to take the geographical changes. There was an increase in Great Britain and Northern Ireland between July, 1923, and July, 1927, in the total insured population of 601,200 — from 11,402,800 to 12,000,000. Of this increase 433,180, or more than two-thirds, was in the Midlands and southern half of England. The increase for the whole of Great Britain and Northern Ireland in the four years is 5.27 per cent of the numbers of July, 1923. In what may be called the Southern Section (London, South-eastern, South-western, and Midland divisions) the increase is 8.32 per cent. In the Northern Section (North-eastern, North-western, Wales, Scotland, and Northern Ireland divisions) it is only 2.71 per cent.

London and the South-eastern division, which covers roughly the area to the east of a line drawn from the west to Portsmouth, now include 25.2 per cent of the insured population of the country, as compared with 24.2 per cent in 1923. The Southern Section as a whole has 47 per cent of the total in 1927, as against 45.7 per cent in 1923.

Silk, electrical engineering, motor building, brick and tile making, and the distributive trades here expanded more rapidly in the south than in the north. In another group of minor industries the south has expanded while the north has declined. In boot and shoe making, tobacco, and general engineering the south has suffered a less heavy decline than the north.

In the four years, 1923 and 1927, industries containing, in 1923, 5,033,000 workers, increased their numbers by 874,000 to 5,908,000 in 1927. Industries containing, in 1923, 4,158,000 workers, suffered a decline in numbers of 304,000 to 3,854,000.

The changes in so short a period as four years are most striking. In 1923 coal mining included 10.83 per cent of the insured population; in 1927 it included only 9.88. The other old staple manufacturing industries have failed to hold their places in the industrial complexion of the country. The share of shipbuilding has fallen from 2.35 per cent to 1.78 per cent; marine engineering from 0.57 per cent to 0.47 per cent; iron and steel manufacture from 2.09 per cent to 1.81 per cent; general engineering from 5.81 per cent to 4.95 per cent; the woollen and worsted textile industry from 2.35 per cent to 2.05 per cent. In all these actual decreases in the numbers insured have occurred. Cotton, curiously enough, has an increase in the number of its insured persons during the four years of 0.4 per cent, but its share of the national total has declined from 4.94 per cent in 1923 to 4.70 per cent in 1927.

SECTION V. RUSSIA SINCE 1917

The system of government that has been adopted in Russia since 1917 is commonly known as the soviet *system, that is, a system of councils.*

259. *THE GOVERNMENT OF SOVIET RUSSIA* [1]

The Communist Party with its powerful organization and its carefully selected membership is the dominant force in the Soviet Government and indirectly controls the mechanism of Soviet trade, industry and finance. Moreover, the party is the chief force in the Third International, an organization created for the purpose of carrying revolutionary propaganda to foreign countries and preparing for the world revolution.

With few exceptions, the same group which took control of the Russian state in 1917 directs the party today. While in a distinct minority in the party, this group maintains its authority by its prestige, its experience in revolutionary government, and its unflinching will to lead.

The present organization is an elaboration of the structure perfected prior to the revolution. At the head is the plenum of the Central Committee, composed of two bureaus — the Political Bureau, and the Administrative Bureau. The highest party position is occupied by Joseph Stalin, who as General Secretary has inherited much of the authority exercised by Lenin.

The plenum, consisting of some twenty regular members and alternates, is elected by the Central Committee, which, like the Party Central Committee before the revolution, is elected by the Party Congress. The Party Congress meeting once a year discusses the general policy of the party and theoretically enjoys supreme authority in all party matters.

At the foot of the party organization are the Communist " cells," or political clubs, composed of all loyal party members in factories, villages and military units. The duties of the cells consist in propagandizing the masses, admitting new members and in general controlling the political activities of non-Communists around them.

The membership of the party has grown from approximately 100,000 in 1917 to about 1,000,000 at the present time, of whom roughly 50 per cent are workmen, 25 per cent peasants and 25 per cent employees and officials.

[1] *Foreign Policy Association Information Service*, vol. III, No. 15. September 18, 1927, pp. 214–218 (condensed).

The party has two important auxiliaries — the Komsomol (Communist Youth Organization) with a membership of almost two million, and the Pioneers (Communist Children's Organization) with a membership equal to that of the Komsomol. Young people under twenty are admitted to the party only through these organizations.

The strength of the Communist Party rests on the following facts:

1. The direct relationship between the Communist Party and the Soviet Government is perhaps the greatest secret of the party's strength. At the party congress of 1919, it was resolved that:

" The Communist Party makes it its object to win a decisive influence and complete leadership in all the organizations of the workers. . . . In all Soviets it is absolutely necessary to organize the Communist Party groups subject to party discipline. These groups (or ' cells ') must comprise all the members of the Communist Party in a given organization. The Communist Party must win for itself domination over the Soviets and actual control over their leaders through a persistent advancement of its own most dependable members to all high positions in the Soviets."

This resolution has been carried out, and at the present time the leading members of the Communist Party reserve for themselves all the important positions in the government.

The interlocking directorates of the Soviet Government, the Communist Party and the Third International may be illustrated by listing the several positions held by the following important party leaders: Bukharin, Voroshilov, Zinovieff, Kalinin, Mikoyan, Ordjonikidze, Rakovsky, Rudsutak, Rykoff, Stalin, Tomsky, Trotsky, Tzurupa, Chicherin.[1]

All of these members of the Central Committee of the Party are also members of the Central Executive Committee of the Soviet Government; eight of them are members of the Political Bureau of the Party, a committee of nine which determines party policy; four of them form the Russian Delegation of the Central Committee of the Third International; and seven are Commissars of the Union. Bukharin, Rykoff and Stalin hold high positions in the Party, the Government and the Third International.

2. Since the exclusion of the Socialists and Mensheviks from the Central Executive Committee by the decree of July, 1918, the Communist Party has been the only organized political group in Russia. During the critical years of the civil war no political opposition from any source was tolerated; all secret organizations of Mensheviks, Social Democrats and Monarchists were abolished as counter-revolutionary organizations threatening the " dictatorship of the proletariat." At the present time delegates to Soviet congresses designate themselves as Communist or " non-party " representatives.

---

[1] Although since this was written there has been a great change in personnel, the system remains unaltered. (Editor's note.)

3. The institution of a strict censorship over all spoken and printed matter. The distribution of news in Russia is controlled by the Government, which suppresses all attacks on itself or the Communist Party. The dispatches of foreign correspondents are censored, and news of outside events is frequently distorted to serve the political purposes of the government. Private conversations and correspondence are likewise subject to espionage on the part of the secret police and offenders are subject to extreme punishment. The system of espionage reached its highest development during the civil war but continues in a less pronounced form to the present day.

4. The institution of terror against the class enemies of the proletariat was a recognized principle of party policy from 1918 until 1921. During this period many opponents of the Bolshevik régime were killed or exiled. With the establishment of the New Economic Policy in 1921, the activities of the Extraordinary Commission for the suppression of counter revolution gradually subsided, but there is reason to believe that the number of political prisoners confined in Russia is still large and executions for political offenses are not infrequent.

5. The Communist Party maintains strict discipline among its members. Refusal to obey orders of the authorities is punishable by censure or exclusion from the party. The latter punishment is particularly effective since it deprives the culprit of the opportunity of political advancement and degrades him from a higher to a lower social stratum. . . .

The Soviet, or council, is the organ of authority typical of the whole system of government developed by the Bolsheviks. Village and city Soviets exercise local authority, while county, district and provincial congresses composed of delegates from the local Soviets enjoy legislative and executive powers in their respective spheres. At the head of the government are the Soviet congresses of the autonomous republics and the Union Soviet Congresses. . . .

The Constitution of 1923 established a central authority over the existing Soviet Congresses in the autonomous republics, and created a Union Congress, composed of 1517 delegates apportioned among the republics as follows:

Russian Socialist Federal Soviet Republic 1,032
Ukraine 312
White Russia 55
Trans-Caucasian Soviet Federation 63
Uzbek Republic 46
Turcomen Republic 9

One distinguishing characteristic of the Soviet system of government is the absence of any separation between legislative, executive and administrative functions. All three are vested in the Union Congress, which is convened for a short session once in two years. When the Congress is not in session these functions are vested in the Central Executive Committee of 450 members elected by the Congress, which meets three times a year. When neither the Union Congress nor the Central Executive Committee are in session the supreme legislative, executive and administrative organ of authority is the Praesidium, composed of 27 members, which controls the activities of the Council of Commissars, the Soviet Ministry, and names seven of the eleven judges of the Supreme Court. . . .

Representation in all the higher organs of Soviet authority is indirect. The individual voter merely elects members of his local city or village Soviet. Delegates are sent by these local bodies, . . . — to regional congresses, and by a complicated system of further elections to the Union Congress.

The Union Congress elects a Central Executive Committee which in turn elects a Praesidium. The city voter is thus three steps removed from selecting the members of the Praesidium. The village voter is five steps removed.

The franchise in local elections has been strictly limited by the Constitution. Only soldiers and those who earn a living by productive work have the franchise. The following groups are excluded both from voting and holding office:

1. Those who employ others for the sake of profit.
2. Those who live on income not arising from their own labor, interest on capital, industrial enterprise, landed property, etc.
3. Private business men, middle-men, salesmen.
4. Monks and priests of all religious denominations.
5. Criminals, lunatics and members of the former-ruling dynasty.

The procedure of local elections regulated by decrees is as follows: Electoral committees of three members are appointed by the local Soviets and trade unions under a chairman appointed by the Superior Electoral Committee. These committees are in charge of elections and draw up a register of those disfranchised, which is published a week before the elections. The election is carried out at a meeting conducted by the committee for each factory group, village or trade union branch. A representative of the committee announces the name of a candidate and voting then takes place by a show of hands. There is no organized opposition to the candidates proposed. The whole process of election is dominated by the local Communist cells.

In order to insure a preponderance of workmen over peasants in the higher Soviets, it is provided that the City Soviets send one delegate for each 25,000 electors to the Union Congress, while the village Soviets send one for each 125,000 residents.

The representation of village Soviets, moreover, is indirect. . . . The city voters elect their Soviets which send representatives directly to the Union Congress. The village Soviets, however, send representatives only to a district Soviet which in turn sends delegates to a provincial Soviet, and the latter sends the final delegates to the Union Congress.

Closely allied both to the Communist Party and to the Soviet Government is the Third International, — official organ for spreading Communist propaganda abroad. This body was created in 1919 by the Russian Communist Party, at a period when the guiding thought of the Bolshevik leaders was the necessity of a world revolution, without which the prolonged existence of Communism even in Russia was deemed impossible. In an early proclamation signed by Zinovieff, the work of the Communist International was defined as follows:

" The task of the Communist (Third) International is not only to prepare for the victory and to lead the working classes during the period of the seizure of power — it is also its task to direct the entire activity of the working classes after the conquest of power."

The first congress of the Third International was called by the Central Committee of the Communist Party. Lenin, Trotsky, Zinovieff, Stalin, Bukharin, Chicherin and others were present as delegates. Gregory Zinovieff was made head of the organization and held the post until the end of 1926, when he was succeeded by Bukharin, another prominent Russian communist.

Some controversy has arisen from time to time as to whether the responsibility for the activities of the Third International can be attributed directly to the Soviet Government. The Communist Party and the Russian Soviets are closely interrelated with the International through interlocking memberships and an interlocking directorate between the two. As recently as August, 1927, M. Rakovsky, Soviet Ambassador to France and a Soviet official of high importance, signed a manifesto of the Third International, which provoked widespread indignation in France. . . .

While it is now recognized by the Stalin Government that foreign capitalism has become more stable and that there is little probability of an immediate world revolution, the ultimate aim of creating a world dictatorship of the proletariat has never been abandoned.

With the downfall of the tsarist régime many non-Russian parts of the Empire started to break away, a movement made final by the Bolshevik Revolution. Poland, Finland, Esthonia, Latvia and Lithuania thus became independent. For several years after 1917 it appeared that the Ukraina, sections of the Caucasus and the Far Eastern Republic beyond Lake Baikal would maintain themselves as separate nations. In 1922, however, these states, partly through inclination and partly because Russia was too strong for them, were

joined with Russia in the Union of Socialist Soviet Republics (U.S.S.R.).
The declaration of this union and the text of the treaty concluding it follow.

260. DECLARATION OF THE NEW CONSTITUTION [1]

Since the formation of the Soviet Republics, all the countries in the world have been divided into two camps: the camp of capitalism and the camp of socialism.

In the camp of capitalism there reigns national hostility, inequality, colonial slavery and chauvinism, the oppression of nationalities, pogroms and imperialist atrocities.

On the contrary, in the socialist camp there is mutual confidence and peace, national liberty and equality, the coexistence and fraternal collaboration of peoples. The attempts made by the capitalist world through long decades to solve the problem of nationalities by making the free development of peoples coincide with the exploitation of man by man have been fruitless. On the contrary, the skein of nationalist contradictions is becoming more and more tangled, thus menacing the existence of capitalism. The bourgeoisie have shown themselves incapable of harmonizing the collaboration of peoples. It is only in the camp of the soviets, only thanks to the dictatorship of the proletariat, which has grouped about itself the majority of the population, that it has been possible to destroy to its foundations national oppression, to create an atmosphere of reciprocal confidence and to establish the bases of a fraternal collaboration of peoples. It is only thanks to these circumstances that the soviet republics have succeeded in repulsing the attacks of the imperialists of the entire world both from within and from without. It is only thanks to these circumstances that the said soviet republics have been able to put an end to the civil war, assure their existence, and to consecrate themselves to the work of peaceful economic construction.

But the years of war have not passed without leaving their tracks. The devastated countryside, the closed factories, the destruction of productive forces and the exhaustion of economic resources are equally ruins left as a heritage of the war. These devastations render insufficient the isolated efforts of the separate republics towards economic reconstruction. On the other hand, the instability of the international situation and the danger of new attacks render inevitable the creation of a common front by the soviet republics against capitalist encirclement.

Finally, the very structure of soviet power, which is international in its class character, urges the laboring masses of the soviet republic to unite into

---

[1] Dec. 30, 1922. French translation in *Bulletin périodique de la presse russe*, Feb. 12, 1923. English in Malbone W. Graham, *New Governments of Eastern Europe*. New York, Henry Holt & Co., 1927, pp. 606–608.

one socialist family. All these considerations imperiously demand the union of the soviet republics into one confederated state capable of parrying foreign dangers and of assuring at the same time the internal economic prosperity and the free national development of the peoples.

The will of the peoples of the soviet republics expressed in the recent congresses of their soviets which unanimously adopted the decision to form a Union of Socialist Soviet Republics is a certain guarantee that this union is indeed a free union of peoples equal in rights; that each republic has the right freely to leave the union; that entry into the union is open to all soviet republics, both those now in existence and those which may be formed in the future; that the new United-State will be the fitting consummation of the bases of peaceful coexistence and fraternal collaboration of peoples which were laid down in October, 1917; that it will be a sure barrier against world capitalism at the same time that it will constitute a new step in advance, a decisive step by way of uniting the workers of all countries into one World Socialist Soviet Republic.

In making this declaration in the face of the whole world and proclaiming solemnly the solidity of the principles of soviet power which have found their expression in the constitutions of the Socialist Soviet Republics in whose name we are empowered to act, we have resolved to sign the treaty for the formation of the Union of Socialist Soviet Republics.

261. THE CONSTITUTION OF THE U.S.S.R.[1]

The Russian Socialist Federal Soviet Republic (R.S.F.S.R.), the Ukrainian Socialist Soviet Republic (U.S.S.R.), the White Russian Socialist Soviet Republic (B.S.S.R.), and the Trans-Caucasian Socialist Federal Soviet Republic (Georgia, Azerbaijan and Armenia), conclude the present Treaty of Union into one single federal state — the Union of Socialist Soviet Republics — on the following bases:

Competence of the Union

1. The competence of the Union of Socialist Soviet Republics, exercised by its supreme organs, shall include:
   (a) Representation of the Union in international relations;
   (b) Modification of external frontiers of the Union;
   (c) Conclusion of treaties relative to the admission into the Union of new republics;
   (d) Declaration of war and conclusion of peace;

---

[1] Dec. 30, 1922. French translation in *Bulletin périodique de la presse russe*, February 12, 1923. English in Malbone W. Graham, *New Governments of Eastern Europe*. New York, Henry Holt & Co., 1927, pp. 608–614. The Uzbek and Turkoman republics adhered to this Constitution in 1924; the Tajikistan S.S.R., in 1929. (Editor's note.)

(e) Negotiation of foreign state loans;

(f) Ratification of international treaties;

(g) Establishment of regulations for internal and external trade;

(h) Establishment of the general plan and regulation of the national economy of the Union, and the conclusion of concessionary agreements;

(i) Regulation of transport and of posts and telegraphs;

(j) The establishment of the fundamental rules of organization of the armed forces of the Union of Socialist Soviet Republics;

(k) Approval of a single state budget of the Union of Socialist Soviet Republics, the establishment of a monetary, fiduciary and credit system, as well as a system of general taxation and of taxes appropriate for each of the republics and local taxes;

(l) Establishment of general principles of agrarian organization and use of the lands as well as of development of the subsoil, forests and waters throughout the extent of the territory of the Union;

(m) Union legislation on emigration;

(n) The establishment of principles of organization of the courts and of judicial procedure, and also civil and criminal legislation for the Union;

(o) Establishment of fundamental labor legislation;

(p) Establishment of general principles of public instruction;

(q) Establishment of general measures regarding public health;

(r) Establishment of a system of weights and measures;

(s) Organization of a statistical service for the Union;

(t) Fundamental legislation concerning the rights of foreigners within the civil community of the Union;

(u) The right of general amnesty;

(v) The abrogation of decisions of the Congresses of Soviets, of Central Executive Committees and of Councils of the People's Commissaries in the allied republics, which infringe the Treaty of Union.

The Union Congress of Soviets

2. The supreme organ of authority of the U.S.S.R. is the Congress of Soviets of the U.S.S.R. and, in the interval between Congresses, the Central Executive Committee of the U.S.S.R.

3. The Congress of Soviets of the U.S.S.R. shall be composed of representatives of the town soviets in the proportion of one delegate for every 25,000 electors, and of representatives of the provincial Congresses of Soviets on the basis of one delegate for every 125,000 inhabitants.

4. The delegates to the Congress of Soviets of the U.S.S.R. shall be elected at the provincial Congresses of Soviets.

5. Ordinary Congresses of Soviets of the U.S.S.R. shall be convoked by the Central Executive Committee of the U.S.S.R. once a year, extraordinary Congresses shall be convoked by the Central Executive Committee of the U.S.S.R. either on its own initiative or on the demand of at least two of the constituent republics.

The Union Central Executive Committee

6. The Congress of Soviets of the U.S.S.R. elects members of the Central Executive Committee from among the representatives of the Republics of the Union, proportionately to the population of each, to the total number of 371.

7. Ordinary sessions of the C.E.C. of the U.S.S.R. shall be held three times a year. Extraordinary sessions are convoked either following a decision of the presidium of the C.E.C. of the U.S.S.R. or on the demand of the Council of the People's Commissaries of the U.S.S.R. or of the C.E.C. of one of the constituent republics.

8. The Congresses of Soviets and the sessions of the C.E.C. of the U.S.S.R. shall be convoked in the capitals of the Republics of the Union in the order established by the Presidium of the C.E.C. of the U.S.S.R.

9. The C.E.C. of the U.S.S.R. shall elect a Presidium which shall be the supreme organ of power in the Union in the intervals between the sessions of the Central Executive Committee of the Union.

10. The Presidium of the C.E.C. of the U.S.S.R. shall consist of 19 elected members from among which the C.E.C. of the Union shall choose four presidents of the C.E.C. of the Union, according to the number of the Republics in the Union.

The Union Council of People's Commissaries

11. The executive organ of the C.E.C. of the Union shall be the Council of the Commissaries of the People of the U.S.S.R. (the Sovnarkom of the Union) elected by the C.E.C. of the Union for the duration of its powers and consisting of:

The President of the Council of the People's Commissaries of the U.S.S.R.
Vice-Presidents.
The People's Commissary of Foreign Affairs.
The People's Commissary for War and Marine.
The People's Commissary for Foreign Trade.
The People's Commissary for Ways and Communications.
The People's Commissary for Posts and Telegraphs.

The People's Commissary for Workers' and Peasants' Inspection.
The People's Commissary for Labor.
The People's Commissary for Food.
The People's Commissary for Finance.
The President of the Supreme Economic Council.

General Provisions

12. With a view to consolidating revolutionary legality in the territory of the U.S.S.R. and coördinating the efforts of the federated republics in the struggle against counter-revolution, a supreme court, exercising final judicial control, shall be created in the C.E.C. of the U.S.S.R. There shall likewise be created in the Council of People's Commissaries a unified organ of the State Political Department whose president shall form part of the Council of People's Commissaries in a consultative capacity.

13. The decrees and ordinances of the Council of People's Commissaries of the U.S.S.R. shall be binding upon all the Republics of the Union and shall be carried out forthwith throughout the territory of the Union.

14. The decrees and ordinances of the C.E.C. and of the Council of People's Commissaries of the Union shall be published in the languages of current use in the Republics of the Union (Russian, Ukrainian, White Russian, Georgian, Armenian and East Turkish).

15. The Central Executive Committees of the Republics of the Union may have recourse against the decrees and ordinances of the Council of People's Commissaries of the Union in the Presidium of the C.E.C. of the U.S.S.R. without thereby suspending their execution.

16. The ordinances and prescriptions of the Council of People's Commissaries of the U.S.S.R. may be annulled only by the C.E.C. of the U.S.S.R. and its Presidium. The decisions of the individual People's Commissaries of the U.S.S.R. may be annulled only by the C.E.C. of the U.S.S.R., its Presidium, or the Council of the People's Commissaries of the Union.

17. The execution of prescriptions of the People's Commissaries of the U.S.S.R. may not be suspended by the C.E.C. or the Presidia of the Central Executive Committees of the Republics of the Union save in exceptional cases when there is a manifest discrepancy between the orders in question and the ordinances of the Council of People's Commissaries or of the C.E.C. of the U.S.S.R. The suspension of such orders shall be immediately brought to the attention of the Council of People's Commissaries of the U.S.S.R. and of the People's Commissary most directly concerned by the C.E.C. or the Presidium of the Republic of the Union involved.

18. The Council of People's Commissaries of each of the Republics of the Union shall be made up as follows:

The President of the Council of People's Commissaries.

Vice-Presidents.

President of the Supreme Council of National Economy.

People's Commissary for Agriculture.

People's Commissary for Food.

People's Commissary for Finance.

People's Commissary for Labor.

People's Commissary for Interior.

People's Commissary for Justice.

People's Commissary for Workers' and Peasants' Inspection.

People's Commissary for Public Instruction.

People's Commissary for Public Health.

People's Commissary for Social Welfare.

People's Commissary for Nationalities.

Fully empowered representatives of the People's Commissaries of the Union for Foreign Affairs, Foreign Commerce, Ways and Communications, and Posts and Telegraphs also participate in a consultative capacity.

19. The Supreme Council of National Economy and the People's Commissaries for Food, Finances, Labor, and Workers' and Peasants' Inspection of the Republics of the Union, while being immediately subordinated to the Central Executive Committees and to the Councils of People's Commissaries of the Republics of the Union, must conform in their activity to the prescriptions of the respective People's Commissaries of the U.S.S.R.

20. The Republics forming part of the Union have their own individual budgets, which form an integral part of the budget of the Union approved by the C.E.C. of the Union. The budgets of the Republics, as regards the revenues and expenditures, are drawn up by the C.E.C. of the Union. The list of revenues and the amount of each, forming part of the budgets of the Republics of the Union, shall be determined by the C.E.C. of the U.S.S.R.

21. A single nationality of the Union shall apply to all the citizens of the Republics of the Union.

22. The U.S.S.R. has its flag, its coat of arms, and its State seal.

23. The capital of the U.S.S.R. is the city of Moscow.

24. The Republics of the Union shall modify their constitutions conformably to the present Treaty.

25. Ratification, modifications and additions to the present treaty are within the exclusive jurisdiction of the Congress of Soviets of the U.S.S.R.

26. Each Republic of the Union retains the right freely to leave the Union. The present treaty has been signed by the members of the plenipotentiary delegations, to wit:

For the R.S.F.S.R. (signatures)

For the U.S.S.R. (Ukraine) (signatures)

For the Z.S.F.S.R. (Transcaucasian Republics) (signatures)
For the B.S.S.R. (White Russia) (signatures)
The President of the First Congress of the Union of Socialist Soviet Republics,

KALENIN.

The Secretary of the First Congress,

A. ENOUKIDZE.

Moscow, December 30, 1922.

An account of the new régime, as it actually works in a rural locality, is given by a sympathetic English publicist.

262. *A RUSSIAN VILLAGE AND ITS SOVIET* [1]

Year after year, before the Revolution, statistics showed the gradual decline of the Central Russian village. It was rack-rented; it was savagely taxed. The money-lender preyed on it, and every year it raised fewer cattle and more meagre crops. This region could not supply itself with grain. It must import from the rich Volga or the happier South.

The village contrived to live by sending its men to Moscow or its women to the textile factories, which are encountered in the most amazing places in the forest. Why were they there? The coal must travel hundreds, the cotton thousands, of miles. They were there because the soil was hungry and the peasants hungrier still; they were there because labor was cheap.

As I sat among the peasants in the little village of Bogomolova, five versts from Vladimir, and plied them with questions, I realized that the tide had turned. They have begun to think that farming is worth-while.

Before the Revolution each family, on an average, raised grain enough to keep itself in bread for five or six months. Now, among its 140 families, there are only ten which fail to grow sufficient grain for the whole year, and some have a surplus.

Before the Revolution the village had 96 cows; now it has 158. Its horses also show a big increase (40 per cent), and it has begun to market butter, eggs, and wool through its Coöperative Society. What is even more noteworthy, it eats its butter — a new social fact in peasant Russia. But, indeed, the peasant's table is now the destiny of much of the food, especially the grain, which used to be exported — an awkward development for the Russian balance of trade. The village now cleans and selects its seed, and maintains a little communal plant for the purpose. It has also its communal water mill, and a communal smithy. It is proud, moreover, that it is beginning to grow clover — a new crop in Russia.

[1] H. N. Brailsford, *How the Soviets Work*. New York, The Vanguard Press, 1927, pp. 44–51 (condensed).

The foundation of this new prosperity was visible enough when the chairman of the village Soviet brought out the plan of its land. Before the Revolution the soil was divided into the usual long, narrow strips. One strip in three lay fallow every year, which meant that it grew a rich crop of thistles. Year after year the same two or three crops grew in rotation on the same soil. To plough was to scratch the surface, and even farmyard manure was rarely used.

The yield of old-world agriculture in Roman times used to be, we are told, five times the seed sown. In this village their fathers used to reap four-fold. Before the Revolution the average yield had fallen to three-fold. No wonder the conviction grew that farming does not pay. The yield to-day is nine- or ten-fold.

Does Revolution, then, put new heart into the soil? In a sense it does. The soil, to begin with, ceased to pay rent and was at the disposal of the village. At first the old strip system and the three-year rotation survived. Czars might go, and commissars might come, but a peasant does not lightly change his ways.

The Communist Party, however, knows all the devices of propaganda. It issued its newspapers for peasants, teaching them meanwhile to read. It placarded the club and the reading-room, which it had provided for the village, with pictorial posters. It staged an instructive play in the room that serves for theatre. It used the children in the school (wonderful to relate, every child in this village is now at school) to teach their parents. This village, as it happened, had as yet no radio installation, but I saw these incredible innovations in many another village whose aspect had changed in no other respect for countless centuries. Needless to say, the educational possibilities of this invention are fully used. And finally, the Party organized excursions to model farms and pioneering villages which had already adopted the new methods of cultivation.

And so at last conviction came. These may be godless, new-fangled methods — priests and greybeards might shake their heads — but they triple the yield of the soil. And so, with much effort, the consent of the two-thirds majority, which the revolutionary land code requires, was duly obtained. The strips vanished. Four immense fields took their place. By this innovation alone one-third was added to the land in active service.

Each field grows one crop, and the crops follow each other in a seven-years rotation. Nature has proved herself no counter-revolutionary. The nine-fold yield is a fact, and henceforth only a very lazy or a very unlucky family need buy bread. Not content with intensifying its agriculture, Bogomolova had also added nearly one-fifth to its cultivated estate by bringing waste land, which had once been forest, under the plough. What has happened in this village has happened already over one-third of the area of the province, and the pace of innovation quickens. . . .

The central fact is the disappearance of the superior class, whose pretensions degraded, as their claims impoverished the village. The landlord is gone, which means not merely that the payments of land-purchase installments on rent have ceased, but also that the peasants' self-respect is no longer depressed by the arrogant manners of "their betters." Those who have read Tolstoy's terrible description of the descent of a body of troops upon a village to assist in collecting arrears of taxes, will realize that the peasants, also, had felt the whips of the autocracy on their bare backs. The peasant, moreover, has been relieved of all the terror and of most of the burden of military service. In the old days (one recalls the poignant verses of Nekrasof) the village wailed over the departure of a conscript almost as it might lament a death. It dreaded not merely the long absence of its sons; it shrank from the degradations and the savage punishments of the old army. The Red Army, on the contrary, is popular — to enter it means opportunity, promotion, and education. Its term of service, moreover, has been reduced to two years, and its numbers cut down by two-thirds. . . .

To-day the village manages its own affairs through its elected Soviet. There are nine persons in this Soviet, of whom four are women, one for every hundred inhabitants. The village reckons 140 families (737 persons) and with it is grouped a hamlet containing 44 families (229 persons). As in the factory, there are preliminary meetings of unofficial groups to discuss the nomination of candidates, and thereafter their records and opinions are publicly debated at meetings of the whole village, before it finally assembles to vote.

I was too late to witness any village elections, but I gathered that the contest is hotter than in the towns. There is here a real struggle, not, indeed, between organized parties, but between clashing interests and sections of the peasant class. In many villages a sharp line divides the richer peasants, who possess some capital in live-stock, machinery, and hoarded money, from the poorer peasants, who live from hand to mouth. The public debates at the election meeting are often heated, and racy with rustic humor. The Communist Party, of course, does its utmost by preliminary propaganda to influence the elections, but it cannot be accused of pressing the claims of its own members unduly. It had nineteen full members in this village and thirteen members of its League of Youth. But none of the former and only two of the latter sat on the soviet. Even the Chairman, a man of notable energy and ability, who had been the leader in agricultural progress in the village, was not a Communist member, though he obviously was in general sympathy with the Party.

The Chairman of the village soviet is its Executive Officer, and he receives a salary for filling this responsible post. The weak point in the political education of this, and, indeed, of most villages, is that the women are only slowly gaining an interest in public affairs. While 76 per cent of all the electors voted, only 40 per cent of the women did so. The persons disfranchised in this village under the Soviet constitution numbered only nine out of the 966 inhabitants, and included a former Czarist policeman, the local priests, and some persons who offend against Socialist morality by dealing in horses.

The Soviet, in a small compact village like this, has two chief functions. It elects the members (in this case three) who sit on the more important soviet of the parish (*volost*). It also administers the social institutions of the village, the school, the club, and the rest. But all important matters are in practice referred by the Soviet to the village Meeting, which every elector may attend. A new bridge had to be built, when I visited Bogomolova, and a meeting was about to be held to decide whether the men should go with their horses to the forest to fell the necessary timber in the traditional way, or accept the offers of a coöperative group (*artel*) which was willing to do the work under contract. I gathered that the decision was likely to be in favor of employing the expert *artel,* a notable step in economic progress.

Anatol Lunacharskii, the Commissar of Education, is one of the remaining " Old Guard" Bolsheviki.[1] He stepped at once into his present position and issued, within a week of the Revolution, his first pronouncement on education. In no other aspect of the new era in Russia has so great or so unbiased an interest been manifested outside Russia as in its educational theory. It does not follow that all comment is favorable. Professor Karlgren, a Swedish authority, denounces the new schooling vigorously.

263. THE FIRST BOLSHEVIK DECREE ON EDUCATION[2]

The General Line of Educational Activity: Every genuinely democratic power must, in the domain of education, in a country where illiteracy and ignorance reign supreme, make its first aim the struggle against this darkness. It must acquire in the shortest time *universal literacy,* by organising a network of schools answering to the demands of modern pedagogics; it must introduce universal, obligatory and free tuition for all, and establish at the same time a series of such teachers' institutes and seminaries as will in the shortest time furnish a powerful army of people's teachers so necessary for the universal instruction of the population of our boundless Russia.

Decentralisation: The State Commission on People's Education is by no

---

[1] Since this was written Lunacharskii has been retired from the Council of Commissars. For several years the real power in the Commissariat of Education has rested in the hands of Professor Pokrovskii, the historian. (Editor's note.)

[2] Oct. 29/Nov. 11, 1917. Reed, op. cit., pp. 346, 347–348 (condensed).

means a central power governing the institutions of instruction and education. On the contrary, the entire school work ought to be transferred to the organs of local self-government. The independent work of the workers, soldiers and peasants, establishing on their own initiative cultural educational organisations, must be given full autonomy, both by the State centre and the Municipal centres.

The work of the State Commission serves as a link and helpmate to organise resources of material and moral support to the Municipal and private institutions, particularly to those with a class-character established by the workers. . . .

But a real democracy cannot stop at mere literacy, at universal elementary instruction. It must endeavour to organise a uniform secular school of several grades. The ideal is, equal and if possible higher education for all the citizens. So long as this idea has not been realised for all, the natural transition through all the schooling grades up to the university — a transition to a higher stage — must depend entirely upon the pupil's aptitude, and not upon the resources of his family.

The problem of a genuinely democratic organisation of instruction is particularly difficult in a country impoverished by a long, criminal, imperialistic war; but the workers who have taken the power must remember that education will serve them as the greatest instrument in their struggle for a better lot and for a spiritual growth. However needful it may be to curtail other articles of the people's budget, the expenses on education must stand high. A large educational budget is the pride and glory of a nation. The free and enfranchised peoples of Russia will not forget this.

The fight against illiteracy and ignorance cannot be confined to a thorough establishment of school education for children and youths. Adults, too, will be anxious to save themselves from the debasing position of a man who cannot read and write. The school for adults must occupy a conspicuous place in the general plan of popular instruction.

Instruction and Education: One must emphasise the difference between instruction and education.

Instruction is the transmission of ready knowledge by the teacher to his pupil. Education is a creative process. The personality of the individual is being " educated " throughout life, is being formed, grows richer in content, stronger and more perfect.

The toiling masses of the people — the workmen, the peasants, the soldiers — are thirsting for elementary and advanced instruction. But they are also thirsting for education. Neither the government nor the intellectuals nor any other power outside of themselves can give it to them. The school, the book, the theatre, the museum, etc., may here be only aids. They have their own ideas, formed by their social position, so different from the position of those ruling classes and intellectuals who have hitherto created culture. They have their own ideas, their own emotions, their own ways of approaching the problems of personality and society. The city labourer, according to his own fashion, the rural toiler according to his, will each build his clear world-conception permeated with the class-idea of the workers. There is no more superb or beautiful phenomenon than the one of which our nearest descendants will be both witnesses and participants: The building by collective Labour of its own general, rich and free soul.

People's Commissar on Education

A. V. Lunacharsky

264. *A CRITICISM OF BOLSHEVIK EDUCATION* [1]

Now it certainly must not be denied that there are schools where the teachers have succeeded in getting good results from the new methods. The very fact that the educational programme is so indefinite and incompletely thought out as to the standards it sets, enables capable teachers to get a certain freedom of action in carrying it out. Where such do exist — and Soviet-land can show quite a number — the majority, vexatiously enough, an inheritance from the discredited tsaristic schools — they have sometimes succeeded in breathing the spirit of life into the letter of the ostentatious programme and have created a kind of working-school that is both effective and interesting. Such are a number of the educational establishments in and round Moscow and other of the larger cities that are shown to foreign visitors. I can very easily understand that Western educationists, who have seen only these, may return full of ecstasy over the new Russian educational science; I imagine, too, that the Soviet, with material taken from such schools, is able to give such demonstrations in Western Europe of Russian education as grip the imagination of all interested in pedagogics. . . .

When we leave the palace of the People's Commissariat for Education in Moscow and the model schools of the capital and, arriving in the rural districts, are brought face to face with the educational establishments there, we are struck with amazement. The schools that are still working, as a rule, present a perfectly incredible picture. "We soon learnt," Jakovlev reports, "to distinguish the school from other houses in the village. If a house had no window-panes nor doors — then that was a school." All attempts at the maintenance or repair of the rural school-buildings — in a fairly deplorable condition even before — seem, since 1917, to have come to a full stop. With their broken windows, sagging roofs, slanting walls, they give the impression of hopeless decay. There are schools in want of everything. "In winter the

[1] Anton Karlgren, *Bolshevist Russia*. Translated from the Swedish by Anna Barwell. New York, The Macmillan Co., 1927, pp. 268–276, 281–289 (condensed).

schools are not heated and the children sit in their sheepskins," is a statement made by Lunatyarsky a year ago (1925); that the poor teachers have to sit in the unheated schoolrooms without sheepskins he forgot to explain. "There is one lesson-book for four children, and that an old one," Lunatyarsky goes on to say of the schools in a district of Russia. " I came to schools whose whole provision for all their pupils were one or two old worn-out lesson-books. In a little village the master complained of the difficulty he had in teaching geography. The school had, it is true, a couple of old, imperfect lesson-books, published respectively in 1903 and 1910, but had nothing at all in the way of a map. Even paper and pen are lacking in some places. A teacher showed the children's copies. They had been fortunate enough to come upon a few old account-books from some local tsaristic institution, and the pupils now wrote their letters amongst the fading figures. When the paper was all used up in this way, they turned it again and wrote the other way of the paper. Paper of the same kind was used for the drawing-lessons, in which the scanty supply of pencils possessed by the school were used by the pupils, turn and turn about."

This is the picture — if not of all, at any rate of many — of the schools that are still working; in many places the whole movement has been stopped. I visited various villages where the school lay desolate or had been adapted to another purpose; in one village the Soviet's chief representative there had installed his horse in it. Such a use of the school premises does not seem to be uncommon, either. . . . Before the war there were in Russia 62,000 primary schools; during the first revolutionary enthusiasm, when it was a question of striking the whole world with amazement at the Russian proletarian education, their number increased to 67,000, although, as he owns, a number of those newly instituted were certainly only " paper-schools." In 1924 the number was 49,000. A fifth of Russia's pre-revolution schools had gone the way of all flesh. A little later, in the end of last year, it is true that Lunatyarsky found himself in a position to state that the closing of the schools — " that wretched state of affairs " — had been stopped, but any question of the extension of school activity, as he explained, could not be entertained. On the contrary, they must concentrate their efforts on an attempt to maintain the *status quo*. Now a plan has been devised to introduce school-attendance for all in the course of ten years, but the future of this proposal is more than doubtful. Lunatyarsky acknowledges that the cost reaches a figure which has terrified the Council of the People's Commissaries.

The disorganization of the school-teaching brought about by the new pedagogy and the decay of schools as a whole, in consequence of the reduction of the money spent upon them, have together produced a result that still further contributes to reduce the importance of the school in Russian national education. It is, of course, well known that the peasants have always regarded the school with suspicion and have been most unwilling to send their children there. But the school being what it is under Bolshevism, this tendency has become more widespread than ever before. The peasants have lost all confidence in the school, to begin with, on account of its material decay. What sort of learning can it be in a school that is in want of everything, and what sort of teaching from a master in rags? " The schools," says Lunatyarsky, " are so badly equipped that the people do not believe the instruction can be effective." But, to a still greater extent, their animosity to the Bolshevist school is due to their dissatisfaction with the new school methods. " I have seen," says Lunatyarsky, " many schools and talked a great deal with the peasants about the new school. In the great majority of cases the peasants are dissatisfied with it. . . ."

Thus, thanks to the peasants' boycott of the Soviet school, school instruction only reaches a minority of the growing generation. An inquiry by the People's Commissariat for Education, of which Lunatyarsky gave a report in the autumn of 1924, showed that, in certain parts of the country, only 20 per cent. of the children got any teaching at all, and that schools intended for 30 to 40 pupils were attended by 10 or 12. " There are," states a report to the Party's Central Committee in the autumn of 1925, " seldom more than 40 per cent. of the children who are taught in the schools." This phenomenon is stigmatized by Lunatyarsky as " a shame and a disgrace, for, in this respect, we are not up to the bourgeois States."

．　．　．　．　．　．　．　．　．　．　．　．　．

The higher school is to be, first and foremost, a school of Bolshevism; with that end in view they make, to begin with, a thorough cramming of communistic principles the most important branch of study in the school. In this regard the modern Russian school, without one backward glance, passes to a stage which in Western Europe we congratulate ourselves on having passed, viz., the stage when all other subjects have to yield to one only — the catechism. The only difference is that the catechism here is called *politgramota,* the political A B C. Otherwise the cases are perfectly parallel; in its arid dogmatism, in its arrangement of question and answer, the Russian catechism is an exact copy of our childhood's scourge; no doubt it is also, like that, to a great degree beyond the child's comprehension and the object of his detestation. This catechism, then, occupies the place of honour; the new educational rule that youth is not to be worried with knowledge that does not interest him is suspended in this particular without the least hesitation. In this grind, no excuse is accepted. No other knowledge whatever can weigh down the scale against poor achievement in *politgramota.* . . .

University education was to be accessible to all. There could be no question of requiring a certain amount of knowledge in a proletarian society, since that would, of course, mean excluding the proletariate who did not possess such knowledge. The Soviet decree stated clearly and concisely that every sixteen-year-old boy or girl had a right to be entered as a student.

For a time there was a veritable invasion by new academic citizens bursting upon the universities, the majority being people who were not so far above illiteracy. The higher centres of education that already existed proved now totally insufficient, and therefore great numbers of new universities were created. Whether means were forthcoming to maintain them, or teachers to carry them on, was a mere trifle; the proletariate were asking for a share in higher education and had an unqualified right to get their petition granted. One little out-of-the-way corner after another made a demand for its own university and got it. . . . The university conditions soon, however, became such a caricature that a retreat had to be sounded. "As might be expected, the decree had to be limited," Lunatyarsky declares quite frankly. That decrees are issued which, from the very beginning, may be expected to prove impossible evidently appears to him a most normal occurrence. And thus followed stage number two in this strange university policy: the hospitable host, who just before had invited all and sundry to come up and sit down to the higher educational banquet, now, without more ado, took the guests by the collar and bundled them out-of-doors. . . .

This demolishing of the higher education centres has, in certain directions, assumed the character of a perfect pogrom. . . . Amongst the towns I visited was Kasan. In former times it had been the chief centre of education in rural Russia; its university, dating back more than one hundred years, was, next to the university in the capital, the most important in the land and had numbered amongst its alumni a number of Russia's most prominent men, Leo Tolstoy being one. I went to the venerable old university building to get from the secretary's office the address of a professor, one of Russia's leading scholars in the humanistic faculty. But the young man, in sporting costume, at the head of the office coldly informed me that I had made a mistake. No professor of that name was known there, nor was there any faculty of philology — the very way in which he pronounced the word betrayed his unbounded contempt for the idea — here they had the workers' faculty. Now, since Russian workers' faculties . . . in spite of their name, are by no means centres of higher education, that simply meant that the university had been done away with; as a matter of fact, the real faculties had been brought to an end, abolished as superfluous. Some of the humanistic professors — but some only — had found a place of retreat as teachers of elementary subjects in the Government so-called pedagogic institute, a teachers' seminary without the least touch of culture about it.

Lenin was slow to order the nationalization of industries, preferring to take over only such plants as the Government definitely had need of. His scheme, which he called State Capitalism, contemplated the coexistence of state and private industry, at least for some years, with the State in control of the key positions. It was the combination of various factors — sabotage on the part of owners, seizure of factories by workers, and the pressure of external relations — that obliged him to issue the nationalization decree.

265. DECREE NATIONALIZING INDUSTRIES, JUNE 20, 1918 [1]

In order to contend more effectively against economic disorganization and the disorder of provisioning, and to facilitate the dictatorship of the poor, working class, the Council of People's Commissaries decrees as follows:

Article 1. All industrial and commercial establishments hereinafter listed, with their capital and assets of any kind or description, are declared the property of the Russian Federated Socialist Republic.

[Here follows a list that includes these industries: mineral, metallurgical, textile, electrical, lumber, tobacco, rubber, glassware, ceramics, leather, cement, steamships, public utilities, railroads, paper, candles, soap, etc.]

Article 2. The appropriate sections of the Supreme Council of National Economy [Vesenkha] are instructed to elaborate, organize and set up as quickly as possible the administration of the nationalized establishments, in conformity with the decrees already promulgated on this subject, and under the general direction of the Praesidium of the S. C. N. E. . . .

Article 3. Pending the issuance of separate, special instructions from the S. C. N. E. concerning each establishment, the establishments hereby declared the property of the R. S. F. S. R. are to be considered as leased without rent to whomsoever was the proprietor before nationalization; the former management and the proprietors are to finance the said establishments as before and to enjoy the profits therefrom.

Article 4. From the time of publication of this decree the directors and other responsible administrators of the nationalized establishments are responsible to the Soviet Republic for the safekeeping and preservation, as well as the regular functioning, of these enterprises. Persons who abandon their positions without first obtaining the consent of the Council of National Economy, or who neglect their duties in the functioning of the establishments, will not only be held accountable to the R. S. F. S. R. to the amount of their property, but will incur a criminal responsibility in the courts.

Article 5. Without exception, all the technical personnel, the personnel of the workers, administrators, directors, etc., are declared to be in the service of the R. S. F. S. R., and are to receive from the profits, and on the schedules,

[1] *Izviestia.* Moscow. June 30, 1918.

of the establishment the compensation which they received before the present decree nationalizing the industries was issued. Any person belonging to the technical or administrative personnel of a nationalized establishment who abandons his place shall answer for it before the revolutionary tribunal and shall be judged with all the severity of the law.

Article 6. All personal payments and accounts of administrators . . . and proprietors of nationalized establishments will be stopped pending the publication of reports making known the state of the balance sheets and the assets of each establishment.

Article 7. The administrations of all nationalized establishments are required to prepare as quickly as possible their balance sheets for July 1st, 1918.

Article 8. The S. C. N. E. is instructed to elaborate as quickly as possible, and to make known to the respective establishments, detailed instructions for the organization of their administration and for the programs of workers' organizations in connection with the putting in effect of this decree.

Article 9. Establishments belonging to consumers' coöperatives, to such associations and their branches, shall not become the property of the Republic.

Article 10. The present decree shall go into effect as soon as it is signed.

The President of the Council of Commissars:

V. Ulianov

Business Director of the Council of People's Commissars:

V. Bonch-Bruyevich

People's Commissars:

Tsiriup

Nagin

Rykov

Secretary of the Council:

N. Gorbunov

From 1918 to March, 1921 the period of War Communism continued. Its essentials were (1) highly centralized authority, (2) nationalization of industries, (3) requisitioning of grain and other commodities, (4) state organized barter. What to Lenin was a deviation from his policy, caused by civil war, the unfriendliness of foreign nations, and temporary conditions in industry itself, was in the eyes of many Communists the realization of an ideal, a world from which " the root of all evil " had been eradicated. The economic breakdown that was apparent by the end of 1920, when the civil war ceased for the time being, was not due wholly, or even principally, to War Communism; the Great War had brought it about before. However, requisitioning led the peasants to put less land under the plough and a food shortage resulted. Early in 1921 the intolerable nature of conditions was impressed on the Government by a revolt of the Kronstadt sailors. Lenin's associates were now convinced that he was right and the N. E. P. was adopted.

266. *ADOPTION OF THE NEW ECONOMIC POLICY* [1]

Most serious of all was the almost complete neglect of the problem of the peasantry. Trotsky, although in February 1920 he had already pointed out the harmful results of requisitioning, gave no indication in general that he regarded the peasants as anything but " backward " elements to be organised into Socialism. Kollontai lumped them together with the many hostile influences which were " perverting " the Soviet State. In general the disputants tended to regard the problem of the towns as the primary consideration, the solution of which by increasing the output of industry would *ipso facto* solve the difficulties with the village. Actually, however, the towns were at the moment paralysed by the crisis of supplies, and the problem of supplies depended on the peasants. Moreover, any discontent in the countryside soon spread its infection to the town workers and the army, who were frequently separated by no more than a year or two from the village, and sometimes by less — a connection which was very evident in the case of Kronstadt; and the relations of the State with the urban masses could hardly be settled apart from the *smytchka* [2] between village and town.

Almost alone, Lenin, with his quite extraordinary capacity for grasping the essentials of a situation, saw the one course that it was possible at the moment to steer. And here again, as in 1917, it was not merely a case of different reading of the facts or different emphasis on different elements in the situation. Nor is it adequate to say, as Western writers are wont to say for lack of better understanding, that he was a clever opportunist who, seeing that one plan would not work, quickly dropped it and tried another. The significant difference was that he held an entirely new conception of the character of the problem and of the road to be travelled; and this conception many of his colleagues had not yet learned to understand. To him Socialism or Communism was not merely a formal structure, with its plan woven of one's subjective desires and then given shape in the human materials which were to hand. Communism was not a poem born of the cool night wind, nor was it a quest of the mythical land of Cathay. It was a realistic problem of the search for a new social equilibrium; and this, according to the Marxian analysis, consisted in the abolition of the conditions which produced a division into classes. The starting point — the *sine qua non* itself — was the seizure of power by the Party of the workers, and the dealing of a blow at class monopoly by the nationalisation of the banks and large industry. So long as

---

[1] Taken by permission from Maurice Dobb, *Russian Economic Development Since the Revolution,* published and copyrighted by E. P. Dutton & Co., Inc., New York, pp. 159–165 (condensed).

[2] Cf. introduction to Selection 267.

the Party held these " key positions," it would in this degree have effected an " encirclement " of capital, and by having its hands on the main institutional factors could shape the course of social development in the direction of the classless state: with the new pilot at the helm the ship could start its career on the new course. But this did not mean that any ready-made Utopian plan of social organisation could be imposed at will. It did not absolve the Party from the need to manoeuvre appropriately within its given social environment; and the particular forms of organisation which were adopted were not to be devised *a priori* from first principles, but were to be built consistently and in harmony with the basic relationship between the Party and its environment at the existing time. But this basic relationship would alter as the Party managed to modify the environment in the desired direction; and as it altered, the form of the society in adaptation to it would change too, until final equilibrium was reached in the classless society.

The environment within which the Communist Party at this time manoeuvred was a predominantly peasant country, backward industrially and culturally, with the towns essentially dependent on the countryside. Hence an appropriate relationship had to be found with this environment, and the forms of economic organisation of the transitional stage had to be such as harmonised with this foundation. Later, when the Party by its hold on the reins of social development had modified this environment, the foundation and the superstructure would be altered as well. But to design the superstructure without regard to the foundation, or to deal with the problem of either in isolation, was a dangerous waste of time. The basic relationship at present which alone furnished temporary equilibrium was the *smytchka* between worker and peasant; and the form of organisation alone consistent with this foundation was what Lenin called State Capitalism — a system centring round a process of market exchange between Socialist industry in the towns and the backward individualist peasant economy of the countryside, the former necessarily having largely to adapt its own character to the requirements of the latter. As a means of modifying this environment progressively, Lenin relied on two things: electrification and co-operation. The first of these would change the economic face of the country, village and town alike; while the second would tend to draw the peasant into closer community of interest with the workers of the town, and by bringing an ever wider range of the peasants' activities within the sphere of collective administration would gradually transform rural individualism into rural collectivism. Further, to achieve such a transformation of the economic basis of society, the economic problem — the problem of industrial production and organisation — had first of all to be solved. In view of the technical and cultural backwardness of Russia, this solution of the economic problem could not be reached without " learning from the capitalists " and also using them — using them as advisers, as experts and managers, even as independent *entrepreneurs* — anything so long as they were sufficiently harnessed to ensure that they should be used as servants, and had not opportunity to take the bit between their teeth and drive their own course! . . .

The syndicalist proposals, whether of the " workers' opposition " or of Bukharin, he [Lenin] attacked with special severity; since these would lead back to the disintegrating " elemental " tendencies which held sway in the early months of 1918, and were so detrimental to production; since they would elevate the influence of the more backward sections of the workers, who did not see the way clearly and could not see the whole for the part, over the more advanced; since they would tend to create in the workers of each factory a sectional, proprietorial sense, which harmonised ill with the social interest as a whole. Trotsky's proposals, on the other hand, underestimated the importance of contact with, and democratic self-activity of, the rank and file. They would serve to separate the trade unions entirely from the masses and merge them in the State machine, and so to widen the gulf which was beginning to yawn dangerously between the masses and the State.

Lenin's own cure went direct to what he conceived to be the fundament of the problem: it aimed to re-establish the proper relationship between the State and its environment which had been rudely broken in June 1918 by the needs of civil war. This consisted in the re-establishment of the *smytchka* between peasant and worker, without which any progress at all in the towns was impossible. The method of " permanent revolution," or " kindling the class war " in the villages by military means would not achieve this — it would widen the breach and starve the towns. What was necessary was to restore and develop market exchange between the town and the village; and this involved the abolition of the State grain monopoly and the substitution for requisitioning of an ordinary tax — a tax in kind. . . .

Lenin's proposals were adopted unanimously by the 10th Party Congress, despite the grumblings of the Workers' Opposition: in face of Kronstadt and the catastrophic shrinkage of peasant sowings, no less drastic change seemed adequate; and the two cornerstones of the New Economic Policy — the replacing of requisitioning by a tax in kind, and the legalising of the free market for peasant produce — were forthwith laid. Perhaps if the full implications of this change of policy — changes in the organisation of industry to the system of financially independent organs operating freely on the market, the growth of private trade, the restoration of a stable monetary unit and credit system — had been fully realised at the time, concurrence in the change might have been less ready, and fondness for the methods of " war communism " might have stayed the innovator's hand.

Nevertheless, the New Economic Policy was only new in so far as it represented a return to peace after three years of war. It was a return to the path which was being trodden in the spring of 1918. But the return to the path had a surer tread and less encumbrances. The chaotic, disintegrating elements of the "localism" of the early months were gone. A State machinery of administration was no longer entirely lacking. The bourgeois experts had for the most part ceased to "sabotage," and the personnel had improved. Much of the flexibility of decentralisation under the new trust system could, therefore, be achieved, while retaining the necessary cohesion, the necessary harmony between the parts in a designed policy by a centralization of appointment and of general direction. The task of rebuilding still remained a gigantic one; but some of the litter and refuse left by the war period had been cleared away.

A fundamental difference of opinion as to the conduct of the Revolutionary Government has existed, at least since 1924, among the leaders. Trotskii, believing in the imminence of the world revolution, wishes to keep power entirely in the hands of the urban proletariat and to promote their interests almost solely. Joseph Stalin, Secretary of the Communist Party, considers the world revolution a thing indefinitely postponed and is working for the permanence, in a Russia that is 80 per cent peasant, of a revolutionary régime that is essentially proletarian but that maintains the smytchka (a leash with two cords, used for holding a pair of dogs, applied to the interdependence of town and village) by satisfying the peasants and gradually developing a classless society such as Lenin planned. A criticism by Trotskii of Stalin's régime (for Trotskii was exiled in 1927 and in 1929 was sent to Turkey) is followed by a brief defence by Stalin. The controversy, in one form or another, is the essence of Russian political, social, and economic discussion today.[1]

267. THE CASE OF THE BOLSHEVIK OPPOSITION[2]

Lenin . . . called our attention to two facts of supreme importance. First, that there exist in our society these forces hostile to our cause — the Kulak, the Nepman, the bureaucrat — availing themselves of our backwardness and our political mistakes, and relying upon the support of international capitalism. Second, the fact that these forces are so strong that they can push our

[1] It is still too early to include a competent discussion of the Five Year Plan, a huge project devised by *Gosplan*, the State Planning Commission, to achieve between October 1, 1928 and October 1, 1933 an increase in agricultural production of 55 per cent and in industrial production of 133 per cent. The *Turk-Sib* Railway, connecting Siberian grain with the cotton and oil fields of Turkestan, has been completed already, one year ahead of schedule (April 28, 1930). (Editor's note.)

[2] Leon Trotsky, *The Real Situation in Russia*. Translated by Max Eastman. New York, Harcourt, Brace & Co., 1928, pp. 24–38 (condensed).

governmental and economic machine in the wrong direction, and ultimately even attempt — at first in a concealed manner — to seize the wheel of the machine. . . .

Since Lenin uttered his warning, many things have improved with us, but many also have grown worse. The influence of the state apparatus is growing, but with it also the bureaucratic distortion of the workers' state. The absolute and relative growth of capitalism in the country and its absolute growth in the cities are beginning to produce a political self-consciousness in the bourgeois elements of our country. These elements are trying to demoralize — not always unsuccessfully — that part of the Communists with whom they come in contact at work and in social intercourse. The slogan given by Stalin at the fourteenth party congress, "Fire to the left!" cannot but promote this union of the right elements in the party with the bourgeois-Ustrialov [1] elements in the country. . . .

Up to now, the general consumer has received more than 50 per cent of the products he needs from the hands of the private capitalists. For the private capitalist this is the fundamental source of profit and accumulation. The disparity between agricultural and industrial prices, between wholesale and retail prices, the difference between prices in the different branches of rural economy in the different regions and seasons, and finally the difference between domestic and world prices (contraband), are a constant source of private gain.

Private capital is collecting usurious interest on loans and is making money on government bonds.

The rôle of the private capitalist in industry is also very considerable. . . .

The rôle of the indirect taxes in our budget is growing alarmingly at the expense of the direct. By that alone the tax-burden automatically moves from the wealthier to the poorer levels. The taxation of the workers in 1925–1926 was twice as high as in the preceding year, while the taxation of the rest of the city population diminished by 6 per cent. The liquor tax falls, with more and more unbearable heaviness, exactly upon the industrial sections. The growth of income per person for 1926 as compared with 1925 — according to certain approximate calculations — constituted, for the peasants, 19 per cent; for the workers, 26 per cent; for the merchant and industrialist, 46 per cent. If you divide the "peasants" into three fundamental groups, it will appear beyond a doubt that the income of the Kulak increased incomparably more than that of the worker. The income of the merchants and industrialists, calculated on the basis of the tax data, is undoubtedly represented as less than it is. However, even these somewhat colored figures clearly testify to a growth of class differences.

The "scissors," representing the disparity of agricultural and industrial

---

[1] A prominent Nepman, or capitalist operating under the N. E. P. (Editor's note.)

prices, have drawn still farther apart during the last year and a half. The peasant received for his product not more than one and a quarter times the pre-war price, and he paid for industrial products not less than two and two-tenths times as much as before the war. This over-payment by the peasants, and again *predominantly* by the lower level of the peasants, constituting in the past year a sum of about a billion rubles, not only increases the conflict between agriculture and industry, but greatly sharpens the class-differentiation in the country.

On the disparity between wholesale and retail prices, the state industry loses, and also the consumer, which means that there is a third party who gains. It is the private capitalist who gains, and consequently capitalism.

Real wages in 1927 stood, at the best, on the same level as in the autumn of 1925. Yet it is indubitable that during the two years intervening the country grew richer, the general national income increased, the Kulak levels in the country enlarged their stores with enormous rapidity, and the accumulations of the private capitalist, the merchant, the speculator grew by leaps and bounds. It is clear that the share of the working-class in the general income of the country has fallen, at the same time that the share of other classes has grown. . . .

In the recent period there has been a decisive departure on the part of leaders from . . . Leninist ways. The Stalin group is leading the party blindfold. Concealing the forces of the enemy, creating everywhere and in everything an *official appearance* of success, this group gives the proletariat no perspective — or, what is worse, a wrong perspective. It moves in zig-zags, accommodating itself to, and ingratiating itself with, hostile elements. It weakens and confuses the forces of the proletarian army. It promotes the growth of passivity, distrust of leadership and lack of confidence in the power of the revolution. It disguises, with references to Leninist maneuvering, an unprincipled jumping from one side to the other, always unexpected by the party, incomprehensible to it, weakening its strength. The only result is that the enemy, having gained time, moves forward. The " classical " examples of this kind of maneuver on the part of Stalin, Bukharin, Rykov, is their Chinese policy and their policy with the Anglo-Russian committee, on the international field, and within the country, their policy toward the Kulak. . . .

There exist in this country two mutually exclusive fundamental positions. One, the position of the proletariat building socialism, the other, the position of the bourgeoisie aspiring to switch our development to the capitalist rails.

The camp of the bourgeoisie and those layers of the petty bourgeoisie who trail after it are placing all their hopes upon private initiative and the personal interest of the manufacturer. This camp is staking its play on the " strong peasant," aiming to make the coöperatives, the industries, and our foreign trade serve this peasant's interest. This camp believes that the socialist industry ought not to count upon a state budget, that its development ought not to be rapid enough to injure the interest of the farmer capitalist. The struggle for an increased productivity of labor means to the strengthening petty bourgeois a pressure on the muscles and nerves of the workers. The struggle for lower prices means to him a cutting down of the accumulation of the socialist industries in the interest of commercial capital. The struggle with bureaucratism means to him a disorganization of industry, a weakening of the planning centers. It means a pushing into the background of the heavy industries — that is, again, an adjustment in favor of the strong peasant, with the near prospect of an abandonment of the monopoly of foreign trade. That is the course of the Ustrialovs. The name of that course is *capitalism on the installment plan.* . . .

The proletarian course was described by Lenin in the following words: " We can consider the victory of socialism over capitalism and its permanence guaranteed, only when the proletarian state power, having conclusively suppressed the resistance of the exploiters and assured itself of their complete subjection and its complete solidity, reorganizes the whole industry on the basis of large-scale collective production and the newest technique (based on electrification of the entire economy). Only this will make possible such a radical, technical, and social assistance rendered by the cities to the backward and undifferentiated country, as will create the material basis for an immense increase of the productiveness of agricultural and rural labor, impelling the small land proprietors, by the strength of example and their own interest, to pass over to a large-scale collective, machine agriculture."

The whole policy of our party ought to be built up upon this principle — budget, taxes, industry, agriculture, domestic and foreign trade, everything. That is the fundamental stand of the Opposition. *That is the road to socialism.*

Between these two positions — every day drawing nearer to the first — the Stalinists are tracing a line consisting of short zig-zags to the left and deep ones to the right. . . . The Stalin course is the more dangerous and ruinous, in that it conceals a real departure from socialism under the mask of familiar socialist words and phrases.

268. *STALIN IN DEFENCE OF HIS POLICY* [1]

Comrade Kameneff . . . says that by adopting the resolutions of the Fourteenth Party Congress . . . we have made concessions, not merely to the peasantry at large, but to the Kulaks, to the capitalist elements. Is that

---

[1] Joseph Stalin, *Leninism.* Translated from the Russian by Eden and Cedar Paul. London, George Allen & Unwin, 1928, pp. 428–429 (condensed).

true? I maintain that it is false, that to say so is to calumniate the Party. I maintain that no Marxist would say anything of the kind, that only a liberal can do so.

What is the nature of the concessions we made. . . .? Are these concessions within the confines of the New Economic Policy or not? Certainly they are within the confines of that policy. . . . What has happened is that Comrade Kameneff is in a state of mental confusion; that the New Economic Policy permits of a free market, of capitalism, and of wage labour; and that the resolutions passed at the Fourteenth Conference are an expression of the New Economic Policy which was introduced under Lenin. Did Lenin know that the New Economic Policy would, to begin with, be turned to account mainly by the capitalists — by traders and by Kulaks? Of course he knew. But did Lenin, when we introduced the New Economic Policy, maintain that thereby we were making concessions to speculators and to the capitalist elements, and not to the peasantry? No . . . on the contrary, he always maintained that by permitting a free market, by tolerating capitalism, by introducing the New Economic Policy, we were making concessions to the peasantry in the interest of the maintenance and consolidation of our alliance with the peasantry — for the peasantry, under existing conditions, could not continue to exist without a free market, without a certain reinvigoration of capitalism. . . . That is the way in which Lenin treated the problem of concessions. In the same way must we treat the problem of the concessions made in April 1925.

SECTION VI. POLAND AND THE BALTIC

Poland, partitioned in 1772, 1793 and 1795, came to life again in 1918. At present she is one of the larger nations of Europe, but it is thought by many that her inclusion of non-Polish groups is unwise. Her foreign policy is aggressive, anti-Russian, anti-German, anti-Lithuanian. It rests partly on French support, which has been consistent.

269. THE RENASCENCE OF POLAND [1]

Despite the extinction of the Polish State, Poland's spirit and culture survived, stimulated as it was by the Roman Catholic church, which maintained a powerful hold on the people. The attempts of Russia to stamp out Polish traits, the attempts of Bismarck to settle German colonists among the Poles of West Prussia, merely aggravated Poland's desire to regain its lost freedom. The opportunity finally came when the World War broke out. Then came

[1] Raymond L. Buell, *Europe, a History of Ten Years.* New York, The Macmillan Co., 1928, pp. 196–200, 212 (condensed).

into prominence the George Washington of Poland — Marshal Joseph Pilsudski. For many years before the war this fiery soldier had plotted to overthrow Russian rule in Warsaw, and had paid for his efforts by penal servitude in Siberia. Upon the outbreak of the war, he cast in his lot with Austria, which had treated the Poles better than had Russia or Prussia. Thus it was that he found himself in charge of a brigade assigned to service in the Russian campaign.

When Russia collapsed, Pilsudski turned against the other oppressors of Poland — Germany and Austria. For a time he was held captive in a German prison, but following the outbreak of the German revolution was released. He then returned to Warsaw and proclaimed himself head of the first Polish Government.

In this movement for the restoration of Polish independence Pilsudski had the active support of the Allies, especially of France. To France a new Poland meant not only the restoration of an ancient nation, but the creation of a buffer state between Germany and Russia. In the new balance of power, Poland would take the place of Tsarist Russia in France's alliances. . . .

While it was a foregone conclusion that the Peace Conference would recognize the existence of a new Poland, many serious problems arose in delimiting the actual boundaries of this new state. Within the three essentially Polish areas of Russia, Austria, and Prussia, there were about 20,000,000 Poles. According to the Wilsonian principles, this territory — and only this indisputably Polish territory — should be given to the new state. But the Polish leaders, fired with ambitions for new power, and visions of Poland's pristine aristocratic grandeur, were as anxious to violate the principle of nationality as had been the despoilers of Poland more than a hundred years before. At the Paris Peace Conference these leaders demanded the restoration of the frontiers of 1772 so as to give Poland an area of 282,000 square miles, stretching from the Baltic nearly to the Black Sea. Even in 1772 the Poles had formed scarcely half of the population of this region, and in 1918 they had certainly no stronger ethnic claim to the territory. These demands were put forward not only on the basis of history, but in the name of military necessity. Poland had no natural frontiers, and she was open to invasion either by Russia or by Germany. . . .

The Polish Commission of the Paris Peace Conference recommended a provisional frontier between Poland and Russia, which was subsequently known as the Curzon line. . . . But the same intoxicating spirit which led the Poles to seize Vilna and Eastern Galicia, led them to disregard the Curzon line and to embark in 1919–20 upon a war against Russia. . . .

Despite the advice of the Allies and proffers of peace from M. Chicherin, the Poles marched an army into Russia, and joining hands with General Petlura of the feeble Ukrainian Republic, which had declared itself independent of Russia, entered the city of Kiev. Removed several thousand miles from their base at Warsaw, the Poles finally became exhausted and were obliged to retreat. The Allies advised the Poles to retire behind the Curzon line, and urged a conference to negotiate peace between the two warring powers. But the Bolshevik armies pursued the Poles almost to the gates of Warsaw. Aided by Allied munitions, however, and the advice of a French military mission, headed by the brilliant General Weygand, General Pilsudski finally held the Russians at bay. Recovering their strength, the Poles now drove the Bolsheviks eastward, passing Grodno, Brest-Litovsk and Luck. By this campaign Poland practically doubled the territory proposed by the Curzon line, increasing her population to 27,000,000. In October 1920, Russia and Poland signed a peace treaty at Riga in which Russia and Poland recognized boundaries as defined in this campaign. In this treaty each party promised " to respect the national sovereignty of the other and to abstain from any intervention in the internal affairs of the other," and promised not to support communist organizations in the other's territory. . . .

Despite its inauspicious birth, the nation of Poland is coming into its own. Originally regarded as a " puppet " state, or satellite of France, created as an artificial buffer which could not long endure unsupported, Europe has come to look upon Poland as a permanent unit which must be reckoned with in the future. A state of 27,000,000 inhabitants, Poland has territory larger than that of Italy, and in population ranks fourth among the states of continental Europe. The Germans no longer regard the Poles as inferior beings, and although some still use the term *Polnische Wirtschaft* to indicate work carelessly done, Germany is now treating Poland as an equal.

The shiftings of politicians so dissatisfied Marshal Pilsudski that in 1926 he effected a coup d'état and set himself in actual power, although with the title of Minister of War. Since then his dictatorship has grown more irascible and less veiled. Some of the economic problems Poland has to face are discussed in the following article.

270. PROBLEMS OF A REESTABLISHED POLAND [1]

Pilsudski has spent his best years as a revolutionary, who called himself a Socialist, fighting in constant danger of life for his ideal, the resurrection of Poland. But when the new Poland had arisen, it was vastly different in character from that of his dreams. In disgust he withdrew into private life, and watched developments with ever-growing bitterness. He is tired of the political muddles which have marked the seven and a half years of Poland's existence, of the incompetence of the Polish Diet, of the inefficiency shown

[1] The *New Statesman*. London. May 22, 1926.

by the fourteen successive Cabinets, of the corruption prevalent in the Polish civil service and army administration which has found public expression in a series of financial scandals in the law courts. But how does Pilsudski propose to cure the inefficiency of the Polish Diet by constitutional methods, or to form an efficient Cabinet where the men and means are obviously lacking? As to the civil service, before one can enforce decency one has to pay a living wage. . . .

There are two hopeless elements in Poland's situation. The first is that she has excessively extended her frontiers, so as to include over ten and a half million non-Poles in a population of twenty-seven millions. To maintain her dominion over the vast stretch of ethnic Russian lands in the East, and over the Corridor and Upper Silesia in the West, she has to keep up an army far in excess of her financial capacities. Her own army will peacefully ruin her before her opponents move a single battalion. Still, Pilsudski, its creator and an out-and-out militarist, is the last man to reduce it.

But even without this excessive expenditure, Poland's economic and financial position would be very serious indeed. The industry of the late "Russian" Poland grew up within the tariff barriers of the old Russian Empire and worked for its wide and rich markets, in which it enjoyed a preferential position such as it can never obtain in the future. With the loss of these markets it has lost its natural basis. The Upper Silesian industry, on the other hand, has grown up in the very closest union with Germany, and the partition of the country meant a severe blow to both. But while the Germans, with their superior efficiency, and better position with regard to world trade, are managing to readjust themselves to the new situation, the Polish part of Upper Silesia is doomed. Nor is the position of Poland's agriculture better than that of its industry. "German" Poland has lost its preferential position in the adjacent Berlin market, Galicia has lost it in Vienna and Bohemia; and at present Polish agriculture, as a commercial enterprise, has ceased to pay. Moreover, the threat of "agrarian reform" hangs over the heads of the big landowners who in the past were the chief producers for export. An atmosphere of uncertainty pervades the economic life of the Polish countryside.

Last but not least comes the problem of emigration. Before the war from the territories now included in Poland at least sixty thousand Jews and a hundred thousand peasants emigrated to America every year, which, besides easing the position at home, produced a continuous inflow of money remitted by the emigrants to their families or brought back by peasants returning to their native villages. Twelve years have passed since this mass emigration came to an abrupt end, and the inflow of American and Canadian money, which formed a most important item in Polish finance, is ebbing. Moreover, before the war, every summer many hundred thousand Polish peasants used to go as season laborers to Germany; now Germany does not require them to the same extent, and anyhow prefers to do without them. It was possible to establish wide frontiers for Poland with the help of French bayonets, but economically Poland cannot exist without the good-will of Germany and Russia, which she is not likely to obtain with her present frontiers. Emigration to France, which at one time absorbed some of Poland's surplus in men, has practically ceased, and anyhow was never a sufficient substitute for that to America and Germany. In the absence of a demand for laborers from abroad, passports are rightly refused by the Polish Government. As a result the absurd but sinister rumor has gone about villages that it is the landlords who are trying forcibly to keep the peasants at home for their own profit; and it is whispered that " blood will flow."

If the agrarian reform hangs like a menace over the heads of the big landowners, it dangles as an irritating, unfulfilled promise before the eyes of the peasants. For more than seven years it has been " legislated " about; still, so far very little indeed has been done. But how is it to be done? If the peasants had money with which to pay for the land, the big landowners, in their present truly distressed economic position, would be only too glad to sell it at even much less than reasonable prices. But the peasants have not got the money, least of all those who need the land most. If, therefore, confiscation on a practically Bolshevist basis is to be avoided, the land has to be bought for the peasants by the State. Where is the Polish State to find the means for a transaction of such magnitude?

The Lithuania that broke away from the Russian Empire in 1918 was by no means the whole of the historic Grand Duchy of Lithuania that was joined to Poland by the personal union of 1386 and the completer union of Lublin in 1569. A small state, it was diminished further by the loss of Wilno (or Vilnius), its capital city. Since 1920 Kovno has served as its capital. The other Baltic states have been more fortunate and, so far, nothing has seriously threatened the security of Finland, Esthonia or Latvia.

271. LITHUANIA IN CONTACT WITH RUSSIA AND POLAND [1]

Possessed of a responsible constituent authority, it was possible for Lithuania to make her peace with Russia. The soviet government had made overtures repeatedly to the Baltic countries, and when Esthonia and Latvia had started to negotiate, Lithuania . . . found it advantageous to follow. Furthermore, it was recognized that vacillation and hesitation in accepting the prof-

---

[1] Malbone W. Graham, *New Governments of Eastern Europe*. New York, Henry Holt & Co., 1927, pp. 378–382 (condensed).

fers of Russia would only tend, from the Russian standpoint, to make Lithuania an open accomplice of Poland in her schemes for aggrandizement. Accordingly, the Lithuanian delegates made their way to Moscow in the spring of 1920 and on July 12 signed the Treaty of Moscow, by which the state of war between Russia and Lithuania was terminated and peaceful relations were resumed.

The Treaty of Moscow is closely akin to the other settlements, following largely the pattern of the Treaty of Tartu, signed by Esthonia, and even more closely paralleling the settlement reached shortly thereafter between Latvia and Russia at Riga. That the signature took place in Moscow is no indication of abject capitulation to the demands of the soviet; rather is it an evidence of the sincerity of soviet diplomacy, as neither the fact of the soviet victories in the west at the moment of signature, nor the possibility of easy conquest of Lithuania dissuaded the Russian delegation from seeking peace. Furthermore, the identity of treatment, for general purposes, meted out to the three Baltic republics reveals that the soviet plan was based on fixed principles, not subject to revision by reason of a change in military fortunes during negotiations. . . . Thus while an insane peace was being meted out to Turkey at Sèvres under the older pattern of the allies, Russia completed her second settlement on an equitable and sane basis. . . .

It reaffirmed " the right . . . of all nations to free self-determination up to their complete separation from the state into the composition of which they enter," Russia recognizing on this basis, and without reservation, " the sovereign rights and independence of the Lithuanian state, with all the juridical consequences arising from such recognition." Thereby the soviet government abandoned forever, and voluntarily, " all the sovereign rights of Russia over the Lithuanian people and their territory. . . ."

An immediately necessary step for Lithuania after her peace with Russia was to come to an understanding with Poland, thereby to complete the definition of her eastern and southern frontiers. Despite the Polish occupation of Vilnius and despite successive violations of armistice lines imposed by the interallied military commissions, the Lithuanian government, after the reoccupation of Vilnius by the soviet armies and the signature of the Treaty of Moscow, answered the overture of Prince Sapieha on behalf of Poland and opened direct negotiations as proposed by the Treaty of Moscow itself. These led to the now famous Agreement of Suvalkai of October 7, 1920, whereby the line of demarcation between Polish and Lithuanian areas was drawn. The subsequent violation of this agreement by the Poles through the raid of General Zeligowski and his seizure of Vilnius led, as is generally known, to the intervention of the League of Nations in an unsuccessful endeavor to settle the dispute. The unwillingness of Poland to evacuate the region, her collusion with the pseudo-rebel troops of Zeligowski, the continued flouting of the authority of the League, and the final sham plebiscite whereby Poland " acquired " the " Wilno " region need not concern us here. They illustrate with cruel clearness the impossibility of coming to terms with Polish imperialism except by the virtual sacrifice of Lithuanian independence.

In consequence of the failure of the mediatory action of the League and of the turning over of the question to the Conference of Ambassadors, that body, through its confirmation of the frontiers of Poland early in 1923, sanctified the *coup d'état* of Zeligowski and endeavored to extinguish every possibility of appeal from its decision. . . . Only a reopening of the entire question by an impartial international tribunal, as often suggested by Lithuania, can hope to bring the two contesting parties together and to produce a permanent, equitable settlement.

SECTION VII. THE REPARATIONS PROBLEM

In a Note sent to Germany November 5, 1918 the Allies demanded " that compensation will be made by Germany for all damages done to the civilian population of the Allies and to their property by the aggression of Germans by land, by sea and from the air." Article 232 of the Treaty of Versailles comprises the same stipulation in slightly different words.

At the Paris Conference it was decided that such damage should include war-pensions and separation allowances as well as the war losses of Belgium up to the signing of the Armistice.

In the following selection Dr. William MacDonald ably summarizes the history of the Reparations question, a question which has proved one of the thorniest problems of the post-war period.

272. THE REPARATIONS PROBLEM [1]

The controversy which has developed in the international conference at The Hague over the so-called Young plan of reparations settlement makes opportune a summary review of the reparations issue, and in particular a comparison of the provisions of the Young plan and those of the Dawes plan which it would supersede.

Until the Young plan was drawn up, no agreement had been reached by representatives of the Allied Powers and Germany regarding the total amount of reparations which Germany should pay. The treaty of Versailles directed the Reparations Commission to accept from Germany, in acknowledgment of Germany's obligations and as security for their discharge, three

[1] William MacDonald, " Reparations: The Young and Dawes Plans," *The Nation*, August 21, 1929.

issues of bonds: one of 20,000,000,000 gold marks, payable without interest not later than May, 1921; a second of 40,000,000,000 gold marks, bearing interest at 2½ per cent from 1921 to 1926, and thereafter at 5 per cent, and a third of 40,000,000,000 gold marks to be issued whenever the Commission was satisfied that the interest and sinking-fund payments could be met. Further issues might also be provided for, in the discretion of the Commission, in accordance with the amount of damages to be made good and the ability of Germany to pay.

In April, 1921, the Commission made public what is known as the London schedule, providing for the issuance, subject to interest and sinking-fund requirements, of 12,000,000,000 gold marks of " A " bonds, 38,000,000,000 gold marks of " B " bonds, and 82,000,000,000 gold marks of " C " bonds; the " C " bonds, however, to be issued only when the Commission should be satisfied that the interest and sinking-fund requirements could be met. Annual payments of 2,000,000,000 gold marks, together with 26 per cent of the value of German exports, were required. It was not the intention of the Commission that the three bond issues should represent the total of reparations to be exacted from Germany, but there is still a general impression that the total had been fixed at 132,000,000,000 gold marks.

In the meantime the Allies, at the Spa conference in July, 1920, had agreed that France should receive 52 per cent of the receipts from reparations, Great Britain 22 per cent, Italy 10 per cent, Belgium 8 per cent, Greece, Yugoslavia, and Rumania together 6½ per cent, and Portugal and Japan each ¾ of one per cent. The total of 132,000,000,000 gold marks set out in the London schedule was promptly rejected by Germany as impossible, and was generally so regarded elsewhere, but a voluminous exchange of notes among the governments concerned failed to bring agreement upon any other figure.

On November 30, 1923, the Reparations Commission decided to appoint two commissions of experts, one to consider the means of balancing the German budget and stabilizing the currency, the other to consider "the means of estimating the amount of exported capital and of bringing it back to Germany." The underlying purpose of the inquiries was to enable the Commission to gauge the resources of Germany and its capacity to pay. The outcome of the deliberations of these commissions was the Dawes report, submitted to the Reparations Commission on April 9, 1924, accepted by all the interested governments at the London Conference on August 16, and put into effect on September 1.

The Dawes plan did not undertake to determine the total of reparations that Germany should pay, and expressly avoided any consideration of political interest or factors. Instead, the Commission confined itself to estimating, on the basis of a detailed study of the German economic situation, the maximum annuities that Germany could fairly be expected to pay over a series of years, indicating the sources of revenue from which the annuities should be drawn, drafting plans for stabilizing the currency and balancing the budget, and providing an organization for the administration of the plan.

Under the Dawes plan, three sources of revenue were levied upon for the payment of reparations. The ordinary budget, supplied from the usual sources of taxation, was to furnish after the first year (1924–25) various sums, the contribution from this source in the fifth or normal year (1928–29) being fixed at 1,250,000,000 gold marks. This amount was regarded as a " standard payment," to be increased in subsequent years in accordance with an " index of prosperity " which the plan provided. The German railways were to be reorganized and 11,000,000,000 gold marks of first-mortgage railway bonds were to be issued for reparations purposes, the interest, which was fixed at 5 per cent with one per cent for amortization, rising from 330,000,000 gold marks in 1924–25 to 660,000,000 gold marks in 1927–28 and thereafter. A transport tax of 290,000,000 gold marks, partly for reparations and partly for the German government, was to be paid after 1925–26. The third source of revenue was industrial debentures, to be issued to the amount of 5,000,000,000 gold marks, and bearing interest in the fourth and subsequent years to the amount of 300,000,000 gold marks. To aid in stabilizing the currency and balancing the budget, a foreign loan of $200,000,000, to become available in the first year of the plan, was also provided.

The total annual payments under the Dawes plan began with 1,000,000,000 gold marks in the first year, rose to 2,500,000,000 gold marks in the fifth or normal year, and were to continue at that figure, plus a supplement computed on the index of prosperity, indefinitely thereafter. A transfer committee to supervise the transfer of payments from Germany to the creditor countries, a trustee for railway and industrial bonds, commissioners for the railways, for the reorganized bank, and for the " controlled revenues " specially pledged as collateral security for budget contributions and other payments, and an agent for reparation payments in general charge of the operation of the plan, were also created.

The fifth or normal year of the Dawes plan will end next September.[1] In the five years that have elapsed since the plan was put into operation, the payments called for have been fully and punctually met by Germany, and the machinery of the plan has, in general, worked smoothly. On the other hand, the insistence of the German Government that the maximum annuity of 2,500,000,000 gold marks was greater than Germany could continue to pay, together with resentment at the prospect of paying that sum or any other for an indefinite number of years while the aggregate amount of the annuities remained undetermined, turned the attention of the creditor governments in-

[1] 1929. (Editor's note.)

creasingly towards the necessity of re-examining the Dawes plan and agreeing with Germany upon a reparations total.

On September 16, 1928, accordingly, the British, French, Belgian, Italian, German, and Japanese Governments agreed at Geneva to intrust to "a committee of independent financial experts" the "task of drawing up proposals for complete and final settlement of the reparation problem," the proposals to include "settlement of the obligations resulting from existing treaties and agreements between Germany and the creditor Powers." The committee as finally constituted consisted of fourteen members (a delegate and an alternate from each country), the representatives of Great Britain, France, Belgium, Italy, and Japan being appointed by the Reparations Commission on the nomination of their respective governments, those of Germany by the German Government, and those of the United States by the Reparations Commission and the German Government jointly. The committee met at Paris on February 11, 1929, and chose the American delegate, Owen D. Young, a member of the former Dawes committee, as chairman. The committee completed its labors on June 7.

The Young plan bears something of the same resemblance to the Dawes plan that the Constitution of the United States bears to the older Articles of Confederation. The Dawes plan has been, in a sense, revised, but the revision embodies new principles and important changes in details. The cardinal feature of the Young plan is the replacement of the administrative and controlling machinery of the Dawes plan by a Bank for International Settlements, with powers so comprehensive as to make it not merely an elaborately organized agency for handling reparations, but also, in its potential operations at least, a super-bank. In addition to the usual banking functions (except, apparently, that of doing business with private depositors), and those connected with the receipt, accounting, and transfer of reparation payments, the management of bond issues for the commercialization of a part of the payments, and similar matters, the expectation of the experts' committee is that " in the natural course of development " the bank " will, in time, become an organization not simply or even predominantly concerned with the handling of reparations, but also with furnishing to the world of international commerce and finance important facilities hitherto lacking." To this end the bank, whose directors are to be designated by the central banks of issue of the countries represented on the committee, or by other banks if the central banks cannot or do not act, is authorized to buy and sell gold, conduct intermediate credit operations " in the interest of world trade to the extent that the directors of the bank approve," and be prepared, in so far as the transfer of reparation payments into foreign currencies involves either a restriction of imports or an extension of the German export trade, " to promote the increase of world trade by financing projects, particularly in undeveloped countries, which might otherwise not be attempted through the ordinary existing channels."

The Young plan calls for the payment by Germany, for the thirty-seven years ending March 31, 1966, of annuities aggregating 79,483,300,000 marks. The lowest annuity after March 31, 1930, is 1,685,000,000 marks; the highest and last is 2,428,800,000 marks; the average, inclusive of the service of the Dawes loan, is 2,050,800,000 marks, or 449,200,000 marks less than the present "normal" annuity under the Dawes plan. After 1966, and for the twenty-two years ending March 31, 1988, the annuities correspond to the Allied out-payments on their war debts to the United States, the aggregate of these annuities being 34,422,100,000 marks. The grand total of the annuities is 113,905,400,000 marks, representing an estimated "present value," computing interest at $5\frac{1}{2}$ per cent, of 36,996,000,000 marks.

Of the annuities for the first thirty-seven years, 660,000,000 marks are to be paid unconditionally, without the privilege of postponement, and of this amount 500,000,000 marks is allocated, under certain conditions, to France. The unconditional payments, accordingly, represent the part of the annuities that may be "mobilized" or commercialized by the issuance of bonds. The unconditional part of the annuities is to be secured by a tax on the German railways of 660,000,000 marks, the balance of payments being derived from the German budget. With the approval of an advisory committee of the Bank for International Settlements, payment of the conditional annuities may be postponed for not exceeding two years. The annuities of the last twenty-two years are to be met from a sinking fund created by allocating to the fund 80 per cent of the profits of the bank. In a special memorandum attached to the report, but not forming a part of it, the experts of "the four chief creditor countries and of Germany" recommend an agreement by which, in case the war-debt requirements[1] are reduced, two-thirds of the relief shall be credited to Germany and one-third to the creditor countries.

Deliveries in kind are to continue for ten years, but with a progressive reduction from 750,000,000 marks in the first year to 300,000,000 marks in the tenth, the committee having recognized "the necessity for maintaining a transitional period so that all shock to existing economic conditions in Germany should be avoided." The proceeds of reparation recovery acts, under which special duties have been imposed upon imports from Germany, or of any systems that have been substituted for the acts by agreement with Germany, are to be reckoned as deliveries in kind.

Upon the approval and inauguration of the Young plan the machinery of the Dawes plan will cease to operate. The "index of prosperity" will disappear, the duties of the Reparations Commission, the Agent for Reparation

---

[1] The reference is to the foreign war debts of Germany's former enemies. (Editor's note.)

Payments, and all other foreign officials engaged in administering the Dawes plan will end, and all foreign control of the economic life of Germany will be withdrawn. The committee recommend that a general liquidation of all financial questions raised by the war be undertaken by the creditor governments and Germany " in a broad spirit of mutual concession," that no further seizure, retention, or liquidation of German property be made, and that the creditor Powers "abstain from recovering the credits of Germany against her former allies referred to in Article 261 of the Treaty of Versailles, Germany for her part renouncing any net balance which might be due to her as a result of these credits."

SECTION VIII. A SEQUENCE ON DEMOCRACY

The nineteenth century accepted with few misgivings the ideas expressed by the three words: progress, education, democracy. It was agreed that the world was steadily progressing from lower to higher forms, that education applied on a large scale would solve all mysteries, and that democracy could be set up everywhere, and shortly would be, with success. Toward the end of the century it began to occur to a few individuals that it was by no means certain that change was always progressive, that no scheme of education on a large scale had yet given satisfaction, and that democracy had never genuinely been tried. But Mr. Shaw was ready to utter a heresy and Pobyedonostsev dwelt in a land where such remarks were not heresies. That the two men intended their criticism of democracy to suggest diametrically opposite notions does not alter the fact that they were both forerunners of an epoch when the democratic idea was seriously to be challenged. Nor was their difference more startling than that between Lenin and Trostkii, on the one hand, and, on the other, Benito Mussolini, all of whom said that the efficacy of democratic medicine was spent and themselves offered new remedies. Democratic government is not thrown by the board universally, nor is it at all certain that it will be, but nothing in post-war Europe catches the eye so sharply as the silhouettes of Kemal in Turkey, Mussolini in Italy, Primo de Rivera[1] in Spain, Bethlen in Hungary, Pilsudski in Poland, King Alexander in his Yugoslav realm, and Stalin in Russia. In 1929 one can only say that the days of dictators are not passed.

The Fabian memorandum belongs to the middle period of the Fabian society's activity. Konstantin Pobyedonostsev was tutor to Tsar Alexander III of Russia, became Procurator of the Holy Synod, and served Alexander and

---

[1] Since these lines were written Primo de Rivera left office and died, yet the régime that replaced his differs little from it. (Editor's note.)

Nikolai II as chief apologist for reaction until his death in 1907. The Lenin and Trotskii passages were written at the beginning of their agitation against the Provisional Government in 1917, while the article by Mussolini appeared in a periodical which he controlled a few months after the March on Rome of November, 1922.

273. *A SHAVIAN COMMENT ON DEMOCRACY* [1]

No experienced Fabian believes that society can be reconstructed (or rather constructed; for the difficulty is that society is as yet only half rescued from chaos) by men of the type produced by popular election under existing circumstances, or indeed under any circumstances likely to be achieved before the reconstruction. The fact that a hawker cannot ply his trade without a licence whilst a man may sit in Parliament without any relevant qualifications is a typical and significant anomaly which will certainly not be removed by allowing everybody to be a hawker at will. Sooner or later, unless democracy is to be discarded in a reaction of disgust such as killed it in ancient Athens, democracy itself will demand that only such men should be presented to its choice as have proved themselves qualified for more serious and disinterested work than " stoking up " election meetings to momentary and foolish excitement. Without qualified rulers a Socialist State is impossible; and it must not be forgotten (though the reminder is as old as Plato) that the qualified men may be very reluctant men instead of very ambitious ones.

274. *" THE GREAT FALSEHOOD OF OUR TIMES "* [2]

The philosophy of the school of Rousseau has done much evil to humanity. This philosophy took possession of many minds; but at the same time it was all based on one false idea of human perfectibility, and on the assumption in every individual of capacity to comprehend and appreciate those principles of social organisation which it proclaimed.

The prevalent doctrine of the perfection of Democracy and of democratic government, stands on the same delusive foundation. This doctrine presupposes the capacity of the people to understand subtleties of political science which have a clear and substantial existence in the minds of its apostles only. Precision of knowledge is attainable only by the few minds which constitute the aristocracy of intellect; the mass, always and everywhere, is *vulgus,* and its conceptions of necessity are vulgar.

---

[1] From " Memoranda," by G. B. Shaw, printed as Appendix I to Edward R. Pease, *History of the Fabian Society.* London, 1916, pp. 267–268.

[2] K. P. Pobyedonostsev, *Reflections of a Russian Statesman.* Translated by R. C. Long. London, Grant Richards & Humphrey Toulmin, 1898, pp. 44–49.

Democracy is the most complicated and the most burdensome system of government recorded in the history of humanity. For this reason it has never appeared save as a transitory manifestation, with few exceptions giving place before long to other systems. It is in no way surprising. The duty of the State is to act and to ordain: its dispositions are manifestations of a single will; without this government is inconceivable. But how can a multitude of men, or a popular assembly act with a single will? The upholder of Democracy takes little trouble over the decision of this question, but evades it by means of those favourite phrases and formulas: — " The will of the people," " public opinion," " the supreme decision of the nation," " the voice of the people is the voice of God," and others of a like nature. All these phrases signify that a multitude of men on a multitude of questions may form a common conclusion, and, conformably with their conclusion, arrive at a common decision. This may be possible sometimes, but only on the simplest questions. Where questions present the slightest complexity their decision by a numerous assembly is possible only through the medium of men capable of judging them in all their details, and of persuading the people to accept their judgment. In the number of complex questions may be counted all political questions requiring great concentration of the intellectual forces of the most capable and experienced statesmen; on such questions it would be absurd to rely upon unanimity of thought and will in a numerous assembly; the decision of the people could only be ruinous to the State. The enthusiasts of Democracy contend that the people may manifest its will in affairs of State: this is a shallow theory. In reality, we find that popular assemblies are capable only of accepting — through enthusiasm — the opinion expressed by individuals or by a small minority — the opinion, for instance, of the recognised leader of their party, of some local worker of repute, of some organised association, or the impersonal opinion of an influential journal. Thus the discussions which precede decisions become an absurd comedy played on a vast stage by a multitude of heads and voices, the greater the multitude the more unintelligible is the comedy, and the more the *dénouement* depends upon fortuitous and disorderly impulses.

To evade all these difficulties, the system of government by representation has been devised, a system first established, and first justified by success, in England. Thence, through the influence of fashion, it spread to other European countries, but proved successful only in the United States of America, and there by tradition and by right. Yet even in England, the land of their origin, representative institutions are in a critical epoch of their history. The very essence of the idea of representation has submitted already to modifications which have changed its primitive significance. In the beginning, the assemblies of electors, on a strictly limited franchise, sent to Parliament a certain number of persons whose duty it was to represent the opinions of the country, but who were not bound by any definite instructions from the mass of their constituents. It was assumed that these elected representatives were men who understood the real needs of their country, and who were capable of justly controlling the politics of the State. The problem was resolved simply and plainly: it was required to lessen, as far as possible, the difficulties of government by the people, by limiting in number the members of the assemblies summoned for the decision of questions of State. These men appeared in the capacity of free representatives of the people, and not as instruments of the opinions of factions; they were bound by no instructions. But in the course of time this system changed under the influence of that fatal delusion about the great value of public opinion, as enlightened by the periodical Press which gave to the people the capacity to participate directly in the decision of political questions. The idea of representation altogether lost its form, and reappeared as the idea of a *mandate;* or of specific commission. From this point of view each representative is accounted a representative of the dominant opinions of his constituency, or of the party under the banner of which his victory was gained. Thus he is no longer a representative of the country or of the people, but a delegate bound by the instructions of his party. This change in the very essence of the idea of representation was the germ of the disease which has since devoured the whole system of representative government. With the disintegration of parties, elections have taken the character of personal struggle restricted by local interests and opinions, but independent of their primary purpose of subserving the advantage of the State. With the great increase of the numbers in Parliament, most of the members, apart from the interests of party strife, are characterised by indifference to public affairs; they neglect their duty of attendance at all sessions, and of direct participation in the consideration of business. Thus the work of legislation, and the direction of the gravest political affairs, become a play composed of formality, compromise, and fiction. The system of representation has falsified itself in practice.

These deplorable results are all the more manifest where the population of a country is of heterogeneous composition, comprising nationalities of many different races. The principle of nationality may be considered the touchstone which reveals the falseness and impracticability of parliamentary government. It is worthy of note that nationality first appeared as an active and irritant force in the government of the world when it came into contact with the new forms of Democracy. It is not easy to apprehend the nature of this new force, and the ends which it pursues; but it is unquestionable that it contains the source of a grave and complex struggle, impending in the history of humanity, and it is vain to predict to what issues this struggle will lead. Today we see the various races of composite States animated by passionate feelings of intolerance to the political institution which unites them in a single body, and by an equally passionate aspiration to independent government with their generally fictitious culture. We see this not only among those races which have had a history and a separate political life and culture, but, to an equal extent, among races which have never known independence. Autocracy succeeded in evading or conciliating such demands and outbreaks, not alone by means of force, but by the equalisation of rights and relations under the unifying power. But Democracy has failed to settle these questions, and the instinct of nationality serves as a disintegrating element. To the supreme Parliament each race sends representatives, not of common political interests, but of racial instincts, of racial exasperation, and of racial hatred, both to the dominant race, to the sister races, and to the political institution which unites them all. Such is the unharmonious consequence of parliamentary government in composite States, as Austria, in our day, so vividly illustrates. Providence has preserved our Russia, with its heterogeneous racial composition, from like misfortunes. It is terrible to think of our condition if destiny had sent us the fatal gift — an All-Russian Parliament! But that will never be.

275. COMMUNIST CRITICISMS OF "BOURGEOIS" DEMOCRACY [1]

A

Lenin, from "The General Program of the Bolsheviki," written in 1917:
To this day, the most perfect type of bourgeois government has been the parliamentary democratic republic: power vested in a parliament, with the usual machinery of government, the usual system and organs of administration, — a standing army, a police and a bureaucracy, practically unchangeable, privileged, and standing above the nation.

But the new revolutionary epoch, beginning with the end of the nineteenth century and determined objectively by Imperialism, has been pushing to the fore a new type of democratic government which in certain respects ceases to be a government, or, to quote Engels' words, " does not seem to be, properly speaking, a government." This is a government on the model of the Paris Commune, replacing the army and the police by an armed citizenry. . . .

This is the new type of government which the Russian Revolution began to organize between 1905 and 1917. The Republic of the Councils of Workers, Soldiers and Peasants, united in an All-Russian Council of Councils, — this is what is already coming into being in our midst, upon the initiative

---

[1] N. Lenin and Leon Trotzky, *The Proletarian Revolution in Russia.* A collection edited by Louis C. Fraina. New York, The Communist Press, 1918, pp. 82–83, 154–155, 193–196.

of millions of people. This is the government of a democracy which is taking the law into its own hands, which relies on itself alone and will not wait while certain gentlemen, Cadets and professors, elaborate nice little laws for a bourgeois republic of the parliamentary type. . . .

Authority in the usual sense of the word is the power exercised over the masses by a group of armed men distinct from the nation. The new authority, which is now in process of being born, is also a real authority, because we, too, need groups of armed men necessary to preserve order, necessary to crush out ruthlessly all attempts at a counter-revolution, all attempts at keeping in power a Czarist, bourgeois government. But our newly-born authority isn't authority in the proper sense of the word, because those groups of armed men found in many parts of Russia are the masses themselves, the whole nation, not simply groups allowed to rule above the nation, not groups distinct from the nation, privileged individuals practically immovable.

Let us look forward, not backward; let us look away from the democracy of the usual bourgeois type, which enforces the domination of the bourgeoisie by means of an antiquated, monarchistic machinery of government, the police, the army and the bureaucracy. Let us look forward to the advent of the newly-born democracy, which has already ceased to be a democracy, for democracy means the people's authority and the armed masses of the nation could not exercise an authority over themselves.

The word democracy cannot be scientifically applied to the Communist Party. Since March, 1917, the word democracy is simply a shackle fastened upon the revolutionary nation and preventing it from establishing boldly, freely and regardless of all obstacles a new form of power: the Councils of Workers', Soldiers' and Peasants' Delegates, harbinger of the abolition of every form of authority.

B

Trotzkii, from " The Struggle for State Power " by Lenin and Trotzkii, written in 1917:

There have never been so many pacifists as at this moment, when people are slaying each other on all the great highways of our planet. Each epoch has not only its own technology and political forms, but also its own style of hypocrisy. Time was when the nations destroyed each other for the glory of Christ's teachings and the love of one's neighbor. Now Christ is invoked only by backward governments. The advanced nations cut each other's throats under the banners of pacifism . . . a league of nations and a durable peace. Kerensky and Tseretelli shout for an offensive in the name of an " early conclusion of peace."

*   *   *   *   *   *   *   *   *   *   *   *   *

Pacifism springs from the same historical roots as democracy. The bourgeoisie made a gigantic effort to rationalize human relations, that is, to supplant a blind and stupid tradition by a system of critical reason. The guild restrictions on industry, class privileges, monarchic autocracy — these were the traditional heritage of the Middle Ages. Bourgeois democracy demanded legal equality, free competition and parliamentary methods in the conduct of public affairs. Naturally, its rationalistic criteria were applied also in the field of international relations. Here it hit upon war, which appeared to it as a method of solving questions that was a complete denial of all " reason." So bourgeois democracy began to point out to the nations — with the tongues of poesy, moral philosophy and certified accounting — that they would profit more by the establishment of a condition of eternal peace. Such were the logical roots of bourgeois pacifism.

From the time of its birth pacifism was afflicted, however, with a fundamental defect, one which is characteristic of bourgeois democracy; its pointed criticisms addressed themselves to the surface of political phenomena, not daring to penetrate to their economic causes. At the hands of capitalist reality, the idea of eternal peace, on the basis of a " reasonable " agreement, has fared even more badly than the ideas of liberty, equality and fraternity. For Capitalism, when it rationalized industrial conditions, did not rationalize the social organization of ownership, and thus prepared instruments of destruction such as even the " barbarous " Middle Ages never dreamed of. . . .

The source of the ideology of democracy, with all its traditions and illusions, is the *petite bourgeoisie*. In the second half of the nineteenth century, it suffered a complete internal transformation, but was by no means eliminated from political life. At the very moment that the development of capitalist technology was inexorably undermining its economic function, the general suffrage right and universal military service were still giving to the *petite bourgeoisie,* thanks to its numerical strength, an appearance of political importance. Big capital, in so far as it did not wipe out this class, subordinated it to its own ends by means of the applications of the credit system. All that remained for the political representatives of big capital to do was to subjugate the *petite bourgeoisie,* in the political arena, to their purposes, by opening a fictitious credit to the declared theories and prejudices of this class. It is for this reason that, in the decade preceding the war, we witnessed, side by side with the gigantic efforts of a reactionary-imperialistic policy, a deceptive flowering of *bourgeois democracy* with its accompanying reformism and pacifism. Capital was making use of the *petite bourgeoisie* for the prosecution of capital's imperialistic purposes of exploiting the ideologic prejudices of the *petite bourgeoisie*.

Probably there is no other country in which this double process was so unmistakably accomplishing itself as in France. France is the classic land of financial capital, which leans for its support on the *petite bourgeoisie* of the cities and the towns, the most conservative class of the kind in the world, and numerically very strong. Thanks to foreign loans, to the colonies, to the alliance of France with Russia and England, the financial upper crust of the Third Republic found itself involved in all the interests and conflicts of world politics. And yet, the French *petit bourgeois* is an out-and-out provincial. He has always shown an instinctive aversion to geography and all his life has feared war as the very devil — if only for the reason that he has, in most cases, but one son, who is to inherit his business, together with his chattels. This *petit bourgeois* sends to Parliament a radical who has promised him to preserve peace — on the one hand, by means of a league of nations and compulsory international arbitration, and, on the other, with the co-operation of the Russian Cossacks, who are to hold the German Kaiser in check. This radical *député,* drawn from the provincial lawyer class, goes to Paris not only with the best intentions, but also without the slightest conception of the location of the Persian Gulf, and what is the use, and to whom, of the Bagdad Railway. This radical-" pacifistic " *bloc* of deputies gives birth to a radical ministry, which at once finds itself bound hand and foot by all the diplomatic and military obligations and financial interests of the French bourse in Russia, Africa and Asia. Never ceasing to pronounce the proper pacifistic sentences, the ministry and the parliament automatically continue to carry on a world policy which involves France in war. . . .

" We have always been opposed to war: our representatives, our ministry have been opposed to war," says the French *citoyen,* " therefore the war must have been forced upon us, and in the name of our pacifist ideals we must fight it to the finish."

276. FORCE AND CONSENT [1]

Truly, Italian Liberalism, which holds itself to be the sole depository of authentic, immortal principles, bears an extraordinary resemblance to half defunct Socialism, since it too, like the latter, believes that it possesses " scientifically " an indisputable truth, good for all times, places and situations. This is an absurdity. Liberalism is not the last word, nor does it represent the definitive formula on the subject of the art of government. In this art of politics, a most difficult and delicate art, working as it does with the most refractory of materials and in a constant state of movement, since it works with the living and not with lifeless matter, there is not to be found the Aristotelian unity of time, place and action. Men have been governed more or less successfully in a thousand different ways. Liberalism is the product and the technique of the 19th Century, which is not, as Daudet would have

[1] Benito Mussolini, " *Forza e consenso.*" *Gerarchia.* Milan. March, 1923. (Translation.)

it, stupid, since there are not stupid or intelligent centuries but rather an alternation, in greater or less proportions, of intelligence and stupidity in every century. It does not follow that the Liberal scheme of government, good for the 19th century, for a century, that is, dominated by two such phenomena as the growth of capitalism and the strengthening of the sentiment of nationalism, should be adapted to the 20th Century, which announces itself already with characteristics sufficiently different from those that marked the preceding century. The fact means more than the book, experience than doctrine. Now the unmistakable experiences of the post-war period, history in a state of motion before our very eyes, seal the discomfiture of Liberalism. In Russia and in Italy it is being demonstrated that government can be conducted entirely outside, above and opposed to the whole Liberal ideology. Communism and Fascism are alike outside the scope of Liberalism.

But, after all, just what is this Liberalism for which — today — all the enemies of Fascism are more or less disingenuously enthusiastic? Does Liberalism mean universal suffrage and all that goes with it? Does it mean to keep the Chamber in permanent session that it may present the indecent spectacle which has aroused a general loathing? Does it mean, in the name of liberty, to allow the few liberty to destroy the liberty of all? Does it mean giving a free hand to those who declare their hostility to the State and actively labor to demolish it? Is this Liberalism? Very well, if this is Liberalism, it is a theory and a practice of abjection and of ruin. Liberty is not an end but a means. As a means it must be controlled and dominated. And this is where one must speak of " force."

I challenge Liberal gentlemen to tell me if ever in history there has been a government that was based solely on popular consent and that renounced all use of force whatsoever. A government so constructed there has never been and never will be. Consent is an ever-changing thing like the shifting sand on the sea coast. It can never be permanent. It can never be complete. There has never existed a government that has rendered all those governed happy. Whatever solution you should happen to apply to any problem, no matter what — even though you partook of the divine wisdom itself — you would create a category of discontented. If, in all this time, geometry has not succeeded in squaring the circle, politics has had even less success. If it be accepted as an axiom that any system of government whatever creates malcontents, how are you going to prevent this discontent from overflowing and constituting a menace to the stability of the State? You will prevent it by force. By the assembling of the greatest force possible. By the inexorable use of this force whenever it is necessary. Take away from any government whatsoever force — and by force is meant physical, armed force — and leave it only its immortal principles, and that government will be at the mercy of the first organized group that decides to overthrow it. Fascism now throws these lifeless theories out to rot. When a group or a party is in power it is under an obligation to fortify itself and defend itself against all comers. The truth evident now to all who are not warped by dogmatism is that men have tired of liberty. They have made an orgy of it. Liberty is today no longer the chaste and austere virgin for whom the generations of the first half of the last century fought and died. For the gallant, restless and bitter youth who face the dawn of a new history there are other words that exercise a far greater fascination, and those words are: order, hierarchy, discipline. This poor Italian Liberalism that goes sighing and battling for a greater liberty is singularly behind the times. It is completely beyond all comprehension and outside the realm of possibility. Silly notions! There are seeds that die beneath the coverlet of winter, but Fascism, which did not fear to call itself reactionary when many of the liberals of today were flat on their faces before the triumphal beast, need not feel ashamed today to call itself illiberal and anti-Liberal. Fascism will not fall a victim to any cheap magician's tricks.

Know then, once and for all, that Fascism knows no idols and worships no fetishes. It has already stepped over, and if it be necessary it will turn tranquilly and step again over, the more or less putrescent corpse of the Goddess of Liberty.

SECTION IX. TOWARD PERMANENT PEACE

In the hope of strengthening European peace through the solution or adjustment of certain outstanding international problems, representatives of the leading European Powers, including Germany, met in conference in 1925 at Locarno, at the Swiss end of Lake Maggiore. As a result of the discussions there held, certain agreements were reached which were incorporated in a final Protocol and six annexes. Taken as a whole these agreements constitute the Pact of Locarno.

The first of these annexes, the text of which is here given, guarantees the inviolability of existing frontiers between Germany and Belgium and between Germany and France. Germany agrees not to go to war with either of the other two countries, and they agree not to go to war with her, save under certain specified circumstances. Four other annexes provide for peaceful settlement, through arbitration or other specified means between Germany and Belgium, Germany and France, Germany and Poland, and Germany and Czechoslovakia. The final annex takes the form of a Collective Note addressed by the other Powers to Germany, assuring her that her disarmed condition would not exceptionally endanger her if she joined the League of Nations.

The Locarno Conference was probably more significant for the friendly feeling there engendered than for specific agreements reached. So many exceptions were provided for in the treaties that in time of serious international strain it is possible that these treaties would have little real value. But the Conference itself eased that strain; and the " spirit of Locarno " was held to mark the beginning of a new era of international good-will.

277. THE LOCARNO CONFERENCE, 1925[1]

Article 1.

The high contracting parties collectively and severally guarantee, in the manner provided in the following articles, the maintenance of the territorial *status quo* resulting from the frontiers between Germany and Belgium and between Germany and France and the inviolability of the said frontiers as fixed by or in pursuance of the Treaty of Peace signed at Versailles on the 28th June, 1919, and also the observance of the stipulations of articles 42 and 43 of the said treaty concerning the demilitarised zone.

Article 2.

Germany and Belgium, and also Germany and France, mutually undertake that they will in no case attack or invade each other or resort to war against each other.

This stipulation shall not, however, apply in the case of —

1. The exercise of the right of legitimate defence, that is to say, resistance to a violation of the undertaking contained in the previous paragraph or to a flagrant breach of articles 42 or 43 of the said Treaty of Versailles, if such breach constitutes an unprovoked act of aggression and by reason of the assembly of armed forces in the demilitarised zone immediate action is necessary.

2. Action in pursuance of article 16 of the Covenant of the League of Nations.

3. Action as the result of a decision taken by the Assembly or by the Council of the League of Nations or in pursuance of article 15, paragraph 7, of the Covenant of the League of Nations, provided that in this last event the action is directed against a State which was the first to attack.

Article 3.

In view of the undertakings entered into in article 2 of the present treaty, Germany and Belgium and Germany and France undertake to settle by

---

[1] Extracts from the Treaty of Mutual Guarantee between Germany, France, Great Britain and Italy. Initialled, October 16, 1925. Great Britain, Foreign Office, Final Protocol of the Locarno Conference, etc. London, His Majesty's Stationery Office, 1925, pp. 9–13.

peaceful means and in the manner laid down herein all questions of every kind which may arise between them and which it may not be possible to settle by the normal methods of diplomacy:

Any question with regard to which the parties are in conflict as to their respective rights shall be submitted to judicial decision, and the parties undertake to comply with such decision.

All other questions shall be submitted to a conciliation commission. If the proposals of this commission are not accepted by the two parties, the question shall be brought before the Council of the League of Nations, which will deal with it in accordance with article 15 of the Covenant of the League.

The detailed arrangements for effecting such peaceful settlement are the subject of special arrangements signed this day.

Article 4.

1. If one of the high contracting parties alleges that a violation of article 2 of the present treaty or a breach of articles 42 or 43 of the Treaty of Versailles has been or is being committed, it shall bring the question at once before the Council of the League of Nations.

2. As soon as the Council of the League of Nations is satisfied that such violation or breach has been committed, it will notify its finding without delay to the Powers signatory of the present treaty, who severally agree that in such case they will each of them come immediately to the assistance of the Power against whom the act complained of is directed.

3. In case of a flagrant violation of article 2 of the present treaty or of a flagrant breach of articles 42 or 43 of the Treaty of Versailles by one of the high contracting parties, each of the other contracting parties hereby undertakes immediately to come to the help of the party against whom such a violation or breach has been directed as soon as the said Power has been able to satisfy itself that this violation constitutes an unprovoked act of aggression and that by reason either of the crossing of the frontier or of the outbreak of hostilities or of the assembly of armed forces in the demilitarised zone immediate action is necessary. Nevertheless, the Council of the League of Nations, which will be seized of the question in accordance with the first paragraph of this article, will issue its findings, and the high contracting parties undertake to act in accordance with the recommendations of the Council provided that they are concurred in by all the members other than the representatives of the parties which have engaged in hostilities.

Article 5.

The provisions of article 3 of the present treaty are placed under the guarantee of the high contracting parties as provided by the following stipulations: —

If one of the Powers referred to in article 3 refuses to submit a dispute to peaceful settlement or to comply with an arbitral or judicial decision and commits a violation of article 2 of the present treaty or a breach of articles 42 or 43 of the Treaty of Versailles, the provisions of article 4 shall apply.

Where one of the Powers referred to in article 3 without committing a violation of article 2 of the present treaty or a breach of articles 42 or 43 of the Treaty of Versailles, refuses to submit a dispute to peaceful settlement or to comply with an arbitral or judicial decision, the other party shall bring the matter before the Council of the League of Nations, and the Council shall propose what steps shall be taken; the high contracting parties shall comply with these proposals.

Article 7.

The present treaty, which is designed to ensure the maintenance of peace, and is in conformity with the Covenant of the League of Nations, shall not be interpreted as restricting the duty of the League to take whatever action may be deemed wise and effectual to safeguard the peace of the world.

Article 9.

The present treaty shall impose no obligations upon the British dominions, or upon India, unless the Government of such dominion, or of India, signifies its acceptance thereof.

The era of international good feeling inaugurated at Locarno in 1925 bore new fruit the following year in the admission of Germany into the League of Nations. The Seventh Assembly of the League, meeting on September 8th, 1926, unanimously elected Germany to a permanent seat in the Council and the Assembly. Two days later Germany was formally welcomed to membership in the League by M. Nintchich of Jugoslavia, President of the Seventh Assembly. Dr. Stresemann replied for Germany in a speech parts of which are here quoted.

In the course of this speech Dr. Stresemann said that " in many respects the League is the heir and executor of the Treaties of 1919." It has been said that by this Dr. Stresemann meant that Germany looked to the League to remedy what she believes to be the injustices done her and the countries associated with her in the Great War by the treaties concluded at the Paris Conference.

278. GERMANY JOINS THE LEAGUE[1]

Translation: Mr. President, ladies and gentlemen — The President of this High Assembly and the President of the Council of the League of Nations

[1] Address of Dr. Stresemann, September 10, 1926, before the Assembly of the League of Nations, on the Occasion of Germany's Entrance into the League (condensed).
The League of Nations Official Journal. Special Supplement No. 44. Records of the Seventh Ordinary Session of the Assembly. Plenary Meetings. Text of the Debates (p. 51. No. 22).

have been good enough to accord Germany a joyful welcome on her entry into the League. In addressing you from this platform I feel it my first duty to express Germany's thanks to these two gentlemen and to the Assembly. Allow me at the same time to express our gratitude to the Swiss Government, which is now extending its traditional and generous hospitality to Germany as a member of the League of Nations.

More than six years have passed since the League was founded. A long period of development was thus necessary before the general political situation rendered it possible for Germany to enter the League, and even in the present year great difficulties have had to be overcome before Germany's decision could be supplemented by the unanimous decision of the League. Far be it from me to revive matters which belong to the past. It is rather the task of the present generation to look to the present and to the future. I would only say this, that, although an event such as Germany's entry into the League is the outcome of a long preliminary process of development, yet that very fact constitutes perhaps a surer guarantee of its permanence and of its fruitful results.

. . . .

The co-operation of the peoples in the League of Nations must and will lead to just solutions for the moral questions which arise in the conscience of the peoples. The most durable foundation of peace is a policy inspired by mutual understanding and mutual respect between nation and nation.

Even before her entry into the League, Germany endeavoured to promote this friendly co-operation. The action which she took and which led to the Pact of Locarno is a proof of this, and as further evidence there are the arbitration treaties which she has concluded with almost all her neighbours. The German Government is resolved to persevere unswervingly in this line of policy and is glad to see that these ideas, which at first met with lively opposition in Germany, are now becoming more and more deeply rooted in the conscience of the German people. Thus the German Government may well speak for the great majority of the German race when it declares that it will wholeheartedly devote itself to the duties devolving upon the League of Nations.

During the past six years the League has already taken in hand a substantial portion of these tasks, and has done most valuable work. The German delegation does not possess the experience which the members here assembled have acquired. We believe, however, that, as regards the new work which lies before us, the subjects dealt with first should be those in which the individual nations can do most by combining in joint institutions. Among other institutions which the League has created, we have in mind the World

Court, which is the outcome of efforts made to establish an international legal order.

Furthermore, the efforts made towards disarmament are of particular importance for the consolidation of organised international peace. The complete disarmament of Germany was stipulated by the Treaty of Versailles as a preliminary to general disarmament. It is to be hoped that practical steps will be taken to further this general disarmament, and thereby furnish evidence that the lofty ideals of the League of Nations contain within them the seeds of a great positive force.

Germany's relations to the League are not, however, confined exclusively to the possibilities of co-operation in general aims and issues. In many respects the League is the heir and executor of the Treaties of 1919. Out of these Treaties there have arisen in the past, I may say frankly, many differences between the League and Germany. I hope that our co-operation within the League will make it easier in future to discuss these questions. In this respect mutual confidence will, from a political point of view, be found a greater creative force than anything else. It would, indeed, be incompatible with the ideals of the League to group its members according to whether they are viewed with sympathy or with antipathy by other Members.

In this connection I reject most emphatically the idea that the attitude hitherto adopted by Germany in matters concerning the League of Nations has been dictated by such sympathies or antipathies.

Germany desires to co-operate on the basis of mutual confidence with all nations represented in the League or upon the Council.

.　　.　　.　　.　　.　　.　　.　　.　　.　　.

Universality alone can protect the League against the danger of using its political forces for other purposes than in the service of peace. Only on the basis of a community of all nations, without distinction and on a footing of perfect equality, can mutual assistance and justice become the true guiding stars of the destiny of mankind. Upon this foundation alone can that principle of freedom be set for which nations and individuals alike are constantly striving. Germany is fully resolved to found her policy upon these lofty ideals. To all the nations assembled here we can apply the words of that great thinker who said that we belong to a generation which strives from darkness towards the light. It is our fervent hope that the tasks of the League may be fulfilled on the basis of the noble conceptions of peace, freedom and unity. So shall we draw nearer the ideals to which we aspire and it is the firm resolve of Germany to assist whole-heartedly in that task.

Influenced thereto by a conversation with Professor James T. Shotwell of Columbia University, M. Aristide Briand, Minister of Foreign Affairs of the French Republic, addressed a message to the American people early in April, 1927, in which he stated that " France would be willing to enter into an engagement with America mutually outlawing war." After some discussion of the idea in the American press it was taken up by the two Governments and it was finally arranged that instead of an agreement confined to France and the United States a general treaty should be drawn up.

The so-called Briand-Kellogg Treaty, of which the text is here given, was the result. It is not a binding agreement that the signatory Powers will under no circumstances resort to war but rather a declaration of principles, a condemnation of recourse to war as a means of settling international difficulties.

279. THE BRIAND–KELLOGG MULTILATERAL TREATY FOR THE RENUNCIATION OF WAR [1]

THE PRESIDENT OF THE GERMAN REICH, THE PRESIDENT OF THE UNITED STATES OF AMERICA, HIS MAJESTY THE KING OF THE BELGIANS, THE PRESIDENT OF THE FRENCH REPUBLIC, HIS MAJESTY THE KING OF GREAT BRITAIN, IRELAND AND THE BRITISH DOMINIONS BEYOND THE SEAS, EMPEROR OF INDIA, HIS MAJESTY THE KING OF ITALY, HIS MAJESTY THE EMPEROR OF JAPAN, THE PRESIDENT OF THE REPUBLIC OF POLAND, THE PRESIDENT OF THE CZECHO-SLOVAK REPUBLIC,

Deeply sensible of their solemn duty to promote the welfare of mankind;

Persuaded that the time has come when a frank renunciation of war as an instrument of national policy should be made to the end that the peaceful and friendly relations now existing between their peoples may be perpetuated;

Convinced that all changes in their relations with one another should be sought only by pacific means and be the result of a peaceful and orderly process, and that any signatory Power which shall hereafter seek to promote its national interests by resort to war should be denied the benefits furnished by this Treaty;

Hopeful that, encouraged by their example, all the other nations of the world will join in this humane endeavor and by adhering to the present Treaty as soon as it comes into force bring their peoples within the scope of its beneficent provisions, thus uniting the civilized nations of the world in a common renunciation of war as an instrument of their national policy:

Have decided to conclude a Treaty and for that purpose have appointed as their respective Plenipotentiaries:

[1] Signed at Paris, August 27, 1928 by representatives of fifteen countries.

[Here follow the names and titles of the *plenipotentiaries* of the signatory countries]

who, having communicated to one another their full powers found in good and due form have agreed upon the following articles:

Article I

The High Contracting Parties solemnly declare in the names of their respective peoples that they condemn recourse to war for the solution of international controversies, and renounce it as an instrument of national policy in their relations with one another.

Article II

The High Contracting Parties agree that the settlement or solution of all disputes or conflicts of whatever nature or of whatever origin they may be, which may arise among them, shall never be sought except by pacific means.

Article III

The present Treaty shall be ratified by the High Contracting Parties named in the Preamble in accordance with their respective constitutional requirements, and shall take effect as between them as soon as all their several instruments of ratification shall have been deposited at Washington.

This Treaty shall, when it has come into effect as prescribed in the preceding paragraph, remain open as long as may be necessary for adherence by all the other Powers of the world. Every instrument evidencing the adherence of a Power shall be deposited at Washington and the Treaty shall immediately upon such deposit become effective as between the Power thus adhering and the other Powers parties hereto.

It shall be the duty of the Government of the United States to furnish each Government named in the Preamble and every Government subsequently adhering to this Treaty with a certified copy of the Treaty and of every instrument of ratification or adherence. It shall also be the duty of the Government of the United States telegraphically to notify such Governments immediately upon the deposit with it of each instrument of ratification or adherence.